S0-AWF-231

Soaring Praise for
NANCY FRIDAY
and
WOMEN ON TOP

"The musings on the eternally intriguing man-woman thing are often provocative."

—*New Woman*

"Nancy Friday's work . . . demonstrate[s] beyond doubt that the emancipation of women's bodies begins with the emancipation of our minds."

—Faye Wattleton, former president, Planned Parenthood Federation of America

"Nancy Friday must be the most understanding sexologist in the country."

—*San Francisco Chronicle*

"[P]rovocative. . . . Nancy Friday has again compiled a fascinating—some might say titillating—assortment of sexual fantasies."

—*People*

"Enlightening and provocative—*WOMEN ON TOP* provides fascinating insights into what women today think and feel about sex. With a rare blend of frankness and empathy, Friday gives us a clear picture into the complexity and richness of women's lives. Another classic."

—Carol Cassell, Ph.D., author of *Swept Away* and former president of the American Association of Sex Educators, Counselors, and Therapists

"The ultimate guide to safe sex."

—*Vanity Fair*

"[This] collection of unrestrained sexual fantasies . . . could help women shed some inhibitions."

—*Newsweek*

"Nancy Friday makes important points about the changing nature of female sexuality. She's astute in her analysis and unflinching in her detail."

—*Detroit News-Free Press*

"This absorbing, titillating, and empowering feminist book is also a ribald bedside companion."

—*Publishers Weekly*

"Nancy Friday, still the pioneer. The impact of the past generation's revolutionary change in sexuality is revealed in its essence—the hidden recesses of women's erotic fantasy."

—Richard Green, Professor of Psychiatry, University of California

"[A] new world of erotic imagining that has a casual relationship to very real events. . . . Once again, Friday works with sensational material, but also produces a serious book."

—*Sunday Star Ledger* (Newark)

"*WOMEN ON TOP* provides much-needed support in the quest for self-understanding, acceptance, and growth."

—*Bookpage*

Books by Nancy Friday

The Power of Beauty
Women on Top*
Jealousy
Men in Love
My Mother/My Self
Forbidden Flowers*
My Secret Garden*

*Published by POCKET BOOKS

NANCY FRIDAY

Women
on Top

WITHDRAWN

GALLERY BOOKS

New York   London   Toronto   Sydney   New Delhi

G

Gallery Books
A Division of Simon & Schuster, Inc.
1230 Avenue of the Americas
New York, NY 10020

Copyright © 1991 by Nancy Friday

All rights reserved, including the right to reproduce this book
or portions thereof in any form whatsoever. For information address
Gallery Books Subsidiary Rights Department,
1230 Avenue of the Americas, New York, NY 10020

First Gallery Books trade paperback edition December 2012

GALLERY BOOKS and colophon are registered trademarks
of Simon & Schuster, Inc.

For information about special discounts for bulk purchases,
please contact Simon & Schuster Special Sales at 1-866-506-1949
or business@simonandschuster.com.

The Simon & Schuster Speakers Bureau can bring authors to your live
event. For more information or to book an event contact the
Simon & Schuster Speakers Bureau at 1-866-248-3049
or visit our website at www.simonspeakers.com.

Manufactured in the United States of America

10   9   8   7   6   5   4   3   2   1

ISBN 978-1-4767-1560-5
ISBN: 978-1-4391-4074-1 (ebook)

*For Mary of Lexington, Kentucky,
and for my darling Norman*

CONTENTS

CONTENTS

Without this playing with fantasy no creative work has ever yet come to birth. The debt we owe to the play of imagination is incalculable.

Carl Gustav Jung
Psychological Types, 1923

PART I

Report from the Erotic Interior

It's an odd time to be writing about sex. Not at all like the late 1960s and 1970s, when the air was charged with sexual curiosity, women's lives were changing at a rate of geometric progression, and the exploration of women's sexuality—well, it ranked right up there with the struggle for economic equality.

Today's sexual climate is somber. Gone are the lively debates and writings about sex as part of our humanity. The toll of AIDS, reports from the abortion battlefield, and the alarming rise of unintended pregnancies make sex seem more risky than joyful.

By their sheer numbers young men and women twenty years ago made sex a burning issue; later when the time came to go on to more "serious" business, they put the sexual revolution to bed. Implicit in the prim set of their lips today is that they overdid it twenty years ago; like good Calvinist children the Establishment now punishes itself for its former naughty excesses and righteously turns its back on sex. Because they are still the majority who make the rules and write the headlines, they assume they speak for everyone.

They know little of the women in this book.

These women are for the most part in their twenties, the generation that followed the sexual revolution and the initial momentum of the women's movement. Their voices sound like a new race of women compared to those in *My Secret Garden,* my first book on women's sexual fantasies, which was published in 1973 and is now in its twenty-ninth printing. While they have all read that earlier book and taken heart from it, these young women accept their sexual fantasies as a natural extension of their lives. Given the unique period in women's history in which they grew up, how could it be otherwise?

For them the explosive emotions we unleashed in the 1970s are still very much alive. There has never been a sexual hiatus, a cooling-off period. Sex is a given, an energy not to be deferred for "more important things." Their sexual fantasies are startling reflections of their determination to abandon nothing.

Here is a collective imagination that could not have existed twenty years ago, when women had no vocabulary, no permission, and no shared identity in which to describe their sexual feelings. Those first voices were tentative and filled with guilt, not for having done anything but simply for daring to admit the inadmissible: that they had erotic thoughts that sexually aroused them.

More than any other emotion, guilt determined the story lines of the fantasies in *My Secret Garden.* Here were hundreds of women inventing ploys to get past their fear that wanting to reach orgasm made them Bad Girls. All in the privacy of their own minds, where no one would know. But in the mind of the symbiotic child, mother did know. The daughter could be grown and with children of her own, but if she had never emotionally separated from that first person who controlled her totally, how was she to know what was mother's opinion, what was her own? It was as if mother continued to sit in judgment throughout the daughter's life, wagging her finger at the daughter's every sexual move and thought.

The most popular guilt-avoiding device was the so-called

rape fantasy—"so-called" because no rape, bodily harm, or humiliation took place in the fantasy. It simply had to be understood that what went on was against the woman's will. Saying she was "raped" was the most expedient way of getting past the big No to sex that had been imprinted on her mind since early childhood. (Let me add that the women were emphatic that these were not suppressed wishes; I never encountered a woman who said she really wanted to be raped.)

Anonymity also helped. The men in these fantasies were faceless strangers invented to further insure the women against involvement, responsibility, the possibility of a relationship. These males did their job and left. Being fucked by the faceless stranger made it doubly clear: "This pleasure is not my fault! I'm still a Nice Girl, Mom."

Certainly sexual guilt hasn't disappeared, nor has the rape fantasy. There is something very workmanlike and reliable about the traditional bullies and bad people whose intractable presence allows the woman to reach her goal, orgasm. But most of the women in this book take guilt as a given, like the danger of speeding cars. Guilt, they've learned, comes from without, from mother, from church. Sex comes from within and is their entitlement. Guilt, therefore, must be controlled, mastered, and used to heighten excitement. If there is a rape fantasy, today's woman is just as likely to flip the scenario into one in which she overpowers and rapes the man. This sort of thing just didn't happen in *My Secret Garden.*

Fantasy is where the sexual drive does battle with opposing emotions, the selection of which comes out of our individual lives, our earliest sexual histories. What were the forbidden feelings we took in as we grew? In these new fantasies, the emotions that most often dictate the story lines are anger, the desire for control, and the determination to experience the fullest sexual release.

Admitting to anger is new for women. In the days of *My Secret Garden,* nice women didn't express anger. They choked on it and turned whatever rage they felt against themselves.

5

Anger is still a difficult emotion for women to voice in reality, primarily because we get no practice expressing it in that first, most important relationship, opposite mother. But women today at least know they are entitled to anger, and fantasy is a safe playground where they can show rage at all the obstacles that stand in their way, beginning with rage at the enormous difficulty in being sexual plus all the other things a woman today must be. These new women have no models, no blueprints. They have to make themselves up. One of the ways they try out new roles is in their erotic dreams.

Don't misunderstand me; this is not just a book about angry women. These are women's voices finally dealing with the full lexicon of human emotion, sexual imagery and language. Anger is inextricably involved with lust in reality as well as in the erotic imagination. Men's sexual fantasies are also filled with rage at war with eroticism. They take a different story line from women's largely because of men's earliest experiences with woman/mother. But rage is a human emotion, and though history until recently tells us otherwise, it is not exclusive to one sex.

I will never forget these women, for they have swept me up in their enthusiasm and taught me too. "Take that!" they say, using their erotic muscle to seduce or subdue anyone or anything that stands in the way of orgasm. They take the knowledge won by an earlier generation of women who couldn't use it themselves, still being too close to the taboos against which they rebelled. These women look mother square in the face and have their orgasm too.

I have always believed that our erotic daydreams are the true X rays of our sexual souls, and like our dreams at night they change as new people and situations enter our lives to be played out against the primitive backdrop of our childhood. An analyst collects his patients' dreams like gold coins. We should value our erotic reveries no less seriously, because they are the complex expressions of what we consciously desire and unconsciously fear. To know them is to know ourselves better.

Like the X ray of a broken bone held up to the light, a

fantasy reveals the healthy line of human sexual desire and shows where this conscious wish to feel sexual has been shattered by a fear so old and threatening as to be unconscious pressure. As children we feared that the sexual feeling would lose us the love of someone upon whom we depended for life itself; the guilt, planted early and deep, arose because we didn't want the forbidden sexual feeling to go away. Now it is fantasy's job to get us past the fear/guilt/anxiety. The characters and story lines we conjure up take what was most forbidden, and with the omnipotent power of the mind, make the forbidden work for us so that now, just for a moment, we may rise to orgasm and release.

Here, for the first time, these women's voices make it undeniably clear that our erotic fantasies have changed in juxtaposition to what has happened in the past years; they are not simply masturbatory diversions, derivatives of *Playboy* cartoons, but brilliant insights into what motivates real life—clues to our identity as valuable as the dreams we dream at night.

This is not a scientific report. I am by choice not a Ph.D., having decided long ago to retain the writer's freedom. Also, it has always been my belief that women tell me things they say they've never told a living soul because I am Nancy to them and not Dr. Friday. This book, along with *My Secret Garden* and *Forbidden Flowers,* its sequel, represent a unique chronicle of women's sexual fantasies. Before *My Secret Garden* was published, there was nothing on the subject. The assumption was that women did not have sexual fantasies.

The sexual fantasies in *Women on Top* cover the years from 1980 to the present. They were selected from interviews and letters written to me in answer to an invitation to women who wished to contribute to a future book on women's sexual fantasies. The request was printed in the back of *My Secret Garden* and *Forbidden Flowers.* I gave a P.O. Box number and promised anonymity.

My contributors and I may form a special population: I am sufficiently fascinated by sexuality to write about it, and they to read my books and then write to me for reasons ranging from the desire for validation of their sexuality—"I am signing my real name because I want you to know I exist!"—to the exhibitionistic pleasure of seeing their words in print. But there can be no doubt that those who have written speak for a far larger population.

I have chosen to arrange the fantasies in three chapters which denote the themes that most frequently turned up in the thousands of letters and interviews I collected since my earlier books: women in control, women with women, and sexually insatiable women. I've arranged them in chronological order so that we could see how changes in the real world influence the erotic imagination.

Let me tell you how I came to this subject. In the late 1960s I chose to write about women's sexual fantasies because the subject was unbroken ground, a missing piece in the puzzle, and I loved original research. I had sexual fantasies and I assumed other women did too. But when I spoke to friends and people in the publishing world, they said they'd never heard of a woman's sexual fantasy. Nor was there a single reference to women's sexual fantasies in the card catalogues at the New York Public Library, the Yale University library, or the British Museum library, which carry millions upon millions of books—not a word on the sexual imagery in the minds of half the world.

Publishers were intrigued, however, for it was a time in history when the world was suddenly curious about sex and women's sexuality in particular. Editors were frantically signing up any writer who could help flesh out this undiscovered continent called Woman.

I remember vividly the first publisher who rejected *My Secret Garden.* When I mentioned the outline I had drawn up along with a sampling of fantasies, he salivated. "Women's sexual fantasies!" he juicily exclaimed, and then pleaded for me to send them to his office soon, soonest! Before the day was over, they'd been returned, double-sealed, to my apartment. What had he expected? I'll never know, but the ritual was to be repeated by almost every publisher in New York. Let me quickly add that women editors as well as men hated the evidence of what women's sexual fantasies actually were.

This was not innocence on their part, merely their wish not to be told something they had silently always known: We women fantasize just like men, and the images are not always pretty. We know everything long before we are ready to know it, and so we cling to our denials.

As for the behavioral world, the dozens of psychologists and psychiatrists I interviewed informed me that I was on a dead-end street. "Only men have sexual fantasies," they told me. As late as June 1973, the same month *My Secret Garden* was published, permissive *Cosmopolitan* magazine printed a cover story by the eminent and equally permissive Dr. Allan Fromme, stating, "Women do not have sexual fantasies. . . . The reason for this is obvious: Women haven't been brought up to enjoy sex . . . women are by and large destitute of sexual fantasy."

Initially the women I interviewed bore out Fromme's prophecy. "What's a sexual fantasy?" they would ask, or, "What do you mean by suggesting I have sexual fantasies? I love my husband!" or, "Who needs fantasy? My real sex life is great." Even the most sexually active women I knew, who wanted to be part of the research, would strain to understand and then shake their heads.

Then I learned the power of permission that comes from other women's voices. Only when I told them my own fantasies did recognition dawn. No man, certainly not Dr. Fromme, could have persuaded these women to drop the veil from the preconscious—that level of consciousness between the unconscious and full awareness—and reveal the fantasy they had repeatedly enjoyed and then denied. Only women can liberate other women; only women's voices grant permission to be sexual, to be free to be anything we want, when enough of us tell one another it is okay.

Finally after three years of slow-going research—one-on-one interviews, magazine articles inviting women to contribute, advertisements in everything from the *Village Voice* to the London *Times (New York* magazine was too virginal to run the ad)—*My Secret Garden* was published in 1973. After publication there was a final salvo from the media accusing me of inventing the entire book, having made up all the fantasies. (The Cleveland *Plain Dealer* reviewed the book on its sports page, a last defensive hee-haw.)

But within months it seemed that women's erotic reveries had been with us always, so much so that advertisers were using fantasy as a selling tool before the year was over. Today women's magazines, films, books, television, automatically employ fantasy to explain and make real a woman's character. It is astonishing, when you think about it, how quickly women's fantasies have been incorporated into our universal understanding of woman.

Timing is everything. When there is an absolute need to know something, when an intellectual void must be filled, we will accept what only moments earlier we'd rejected for centuries. In 1973 a number of social and economic currents came together, forcing women to understand themselves and change their lives. Sexual identity was a vital missing link. The time was right to take the lid of repression off women's sexual fantasies.

Four years later it would be the identical story with *My Mother/My Self,* the book that grew immediately out of *My Secret Garden*'s questioning of the source of women's terrible guilt about sex. Initially this later book was violently rejected by both publishers and readers. "I threw your book across the room!" "I wanted to kill you!" were typical reader's comments. But what followed was a snowballing acceptance as one woman told another to read this book that talked about the unmentionable: the mother/daughter relationship (another subject about which there was not a word in any of the libraries). If we were to change the repetitious pattern of women's lives, we had to honestly accept what we had with her/mother. Timing.

What then was so threatening to our understanding of human psychology that we had denied the possibility that women have a powerful sexual identity, a private erotic memory?

The answer is as old as ancient mythology: fear that

women's sexual appetite may be equal to—perhaps even greater than—men's. In Greek myth, Zeus and Hera debate the issue and Zeus, postulating that women's sexuality outstrips men's, wins by bringing forward an ancient seer who had been in former lives both male and female.

In the real world, we are equally reluctant to debate too closely man's sexual potency, power, and supremacy. Men "need" sex, we say, in a way women do not. This is, of course, absurd. It was patriarchal society that needed, for its establishment and survival, to believe in male sexual supremacy, or more exactly, women's asexuality. How could man wage his wars, put his shoulder to the industrial wheel if half his brain feared that he was being cuckolded, that the little woman was at home—or worse, not at home—satisfying her insatiable lust? Even her hand on her own body nagged at his suspicion as it awakened the fire he feared he could never quench.

If man did not fear women's sexuality so much, why would he have smothered it, damning himself to a life with a sexually inert, boring wife, forcing him to go to prostitutes for sex? To combine sex and familial love in one woman made her too powerful, him too little.

Women so totally absorbed man's evaluation of our sexuality that we came to judge ourselves by his needs: the less sexual the woman, the Nicer. We took on his police work, becoming one another's jailers.

How ironic that we ourselves made it possible for society to imagine us the sleeping beauties who could only be sexually awakened by a man's kiss. A fairy tale on which we are raised, a myth thought up to assuage the terrible fear that we are not sleeping at all but are wide awake, hot, hungry for sex, our appetites so insatiable we would undermine the economic system, the Protestant work ethic, the social fiber, ultimately rendering men limp, spent, simply put in our power.

And so women were safely divided into madonnas and whores, the one to marry and become a mother, the other to fuck. Men may fantasize sexually voracious women (it is their favorite), but when the dream comes true—as it did

11

briefly in the 1970s—and she stands there, hands on hips, thrusting her cunt in his face, his worst fears are aroused: Can he satisfy her, or will he end up as small and powerless as he once was opposite his first great love, mother, the Giantess of the Nursery?

Women lived in the Good Girl/Bad Girl split until economic forces in the 1960s built to a pitch that exploded into the women's movement and the sexual revolution. So immediate were these two social phenomena that it seemed as if women had been waiting in the wings for centuries, pent up, frustrated, with all of our enormous energies just barely under control.

In that brief time in the 1970s and the early 1980s, many women seemed to enjoy both sex and work. I wish I could re-create for those of you who are too young to have known those years—or for those who have forgotten—how genuinely exciting they were. It was called a sexual revolution, and we who took part in it were convinced that what we said and what we did were acts of sexual freedom that obliterated forever the guilt-ridden standards of our parents on which we'd been raised.

Little did we know how brief that time would be, how very long it takes to change sexual taboos as deeply embedded as those our parents had learned from theirs, or how soon so many of our revolutionary band would retreat, recant, forget.

We look at faded pictures of ourselves dancing on the stage at *Hair,* marching six abreast For Love or Against War, our nipples high and defiant, and we laugh at our twenty-year-old images. Some of us blush as our children ask, "Is that really you, Mom?"

Why do we rush to deny those years, treating them as aberration, a wild, prolonged house party where we drank too much, or surely we wouldn't have stayed so long, done what we did? "See, Mom," our actions say. "The bad booze, bad drugs made me do it. I'm still a Nice Girl."

The fact is, we have become our parents. Not the parents we loved but those parts of our parents we hated: nay-saying, guilty, and asexual.

And so women have become more serious about their work, mothering is once again in vogue, and the nervous issue of sexuality is not discussed. Now when couples mate, they fantasize about remodeling the house, buying cars, acquiring material goods. Even on college campuses, the surveys show that a partner's career potential far outweighs sexual compatibility. On some surveys, sex doesn't even make the charts.

Once, it seemed as if the women's movement for economic and political equality and the sexual revolution were one campaign. But they were merely simultaneous. Society adapted more readily to women's entry into the workplace than to their growing into full sexuality. It is seldom discussed but nonetheless true that economic parity is less threatening to the system than sexual equality.

Nor can we discount the issue of reward, applause, acceptance: Persevering to become an economic success doesn't make a woman a Bad Girl. Our starchy puritanical backbone, which cannot come to terms with the humanity of sexuality, staunchly applauds hard work, even women's work in what was once called "a man's world." In contrast, working hard on one's sexuality, once the party is over, marks a woman, if not Bad, as someone out of step—a retarded hippie, an object of resentment and envy by other women.

There is still, of course, an unjust economic disparity between what men and women are paid for the same work. And more often than not, when women compete with men, they lose. Moreover, there are still splits among women. We are now hearing some of the alienation traditional women felt during the years when the media and world attention were focused on women in the workplace. As more and more working women try to integrate family and home into an already crowded life, there is understandably little sympathy from their sisters who never abandoned the old values. But no matter what else happens, the option to work outside the home has been truly won.

The same cannot be said for the sexual revolution. Slowly and inexorably the social/legal current is sucking women back into a form of sexual slavery, depriving us of the right to control our bodies. Even as we march slowly toward economic parity, it is the loss of our sexuality that will be the means by which society keeps us "in our place." It comes down to what society is most comfortable with, and ours prefers the missionary position.

Revolutions by nature lose ground once the initial momentum wanes. This is especially true of a struggle for women's sexual parity, which we fear. Child care and economic pressures are the givens for working women and those at home. There is only one other demand on time and energy, and it was never reconciled in the first place. Sex. Maybe there are just not enough hours in the day. Supporting oneself economically demands a lot of energy. So does a continued effort to retain a sexuality won late in life. And our thirties, twenties, even adolescence, is late. If something must be abandoned, it will be sexual freedom, with which we never felt comfortable (or we would have used the contraceptives that made our revolution possible).

Let me emphasize that it requires the support of both sexes for the patriarchal system to hold; it tottered in the 1970s only because enough women banded together and loudly demanded change. But that alliance didn't last. We lost much of the potential we might have had as a cohesive unit. The angry feminists, having little sympathy for men or the women who loved men, turned up their noses at the sexual revolution. And both camps alienated traditional women, who had stayed within the family unit and whose values, needs, and very existence were ignored.

If so many schisms hadn't developed among us, we would probably have equal pay by now and whatever else we want too. We blame men for all the injustices against us because it is easier than acknowledging our fear and anger at women/mother. It is the new War Between the Women that has shored up the fortifications of the old system.

What I wish for is more time and a chance for men and women to find an equitable distribution of power, a better sexual deal between us than the one our parents had, which, with all its many faults, at least worked for a long time. Men were the problem solvers, the good providers, the sexual ones, and women—well, we know what women were supposed to be and do. At least The Rules applied to everyone. There was an odd comfort in that. Onerous as the double standard was, the deep conviction that it existed is what made it hold. What society said was what society meant, consciously as well as on the deepest unconscious level.

While that bargain no longer works, the new options and definitions are not as deeply accepted. That requires generations. And without deep societal acceptance, how can mothers—even those who fought for sexual freedom themselves—pass on to their daughters these new ideas of what a woman may do and be? Mothers are the custodians of what is right and wrong; if society doesn't yet believe in sexual parity, how can mother be expected to put her daughter in jeopardy?

Not enough time has gone by in our recent struggles for us to want to abandon the myth of male supremacy. (How can I tell you how long it has taken me to abandon my own need to believe that men would take care of me, even as I grew to be a woman who was perfectly able to take care of herself economically and a man, too?)

In contrast to these dire predictions comes a new and even younger generation whose fantasies fill this book. Among their icons are the exhibitionistic singers/performers on MTV. There stands Madonna, hand on crotch, preaching to her sisters: Masturbate. Madonna is no male masturbatory fantasy. She is a sex symbol/model for other women. Nor is she just a lesbian fantasy—though she is that, too—but rather she embodies sexual woman/working woman, and I think you could put mother in there too. I can see Madonna with a baby in her arms, and yes, the hand still on her crotch.

I doubt that men dream of Madonna when they masturbate unless it is to control her, overpower her, pin her down and show her "what a real man is." No, she is too much woman for most men. Ten years ago when *Men in Love,* my book on men's sexual fantasies, was published, one of their favorite fantasies was the image of a woman bringing herself

15

to orgasm. These were men raised in the 1950s and 1960s, men who longed—at least in the safety of fantasy—for women less sexually bludgeoned than Doris Day. Back then it was exhilarating to think of a woman who had a secret sexual life of her own, a woman who might share half of the responsibility for sex. It was thrilling to men because it went so totally against reality.

Today many young men tell me that the new woman is too frightening, demanding; she wants it all, indeed she may have it all. The poor boy, the beleaguered man—I do not mean for a moment to minimize his ancient fear of women's unleashed sexual appetite. Its deepest roots lie in his female-dominated childhood, just as they did for his father and his father before him, a time when a woman had all the power in the world over his life and which he never forgets. The irony is that men feel it necessary to keep us "in our place" because they believe more in our power than we do.

If I were to pick a time when the sexual current was cut, it would not be the terrible onset of AIDS. That grim epidemic has become the saddest scapegoat for the sexual regression and bigotry that was already under way. No, while AIDS certainly accelerated the demise of healthy sexual curiosity, it was the greed of the 1980s that dealt the death blow.

Sex is antithetical to material greed. By definition greed is an insatiable appetite which is never sated and thus requires constant feeding. Even when they have more than they need, more than they can consume in a lifetime, the greedy cannot relax their iron determination to own, possess even more. Rigidity, the vigilant, ever acquiring eye—these are greed's henchmen, the enemy of sex, which cries out for openness, ease, surrender. For the mating game to even begin, the animal must abandon at least momentarily the search for nuts and berries to pick up the erotic scent. In the very simplest terms, there is no time for sex in a materially greedy world.

That is why it is such an odd time to be writing about sex. Sitting here after a night out with the opinion makers, the moguls of industry (who would blush if I reminded some of them that they once danced half naked on the stage at *Hair*), I feel like one of those soldiers lost in the jungle, still fighting a war that has been over for years.

Don't think that I expect this book to go unobserved. I know who my audience is. Although you and I may not be in the majority, we are numerous. Given the ages of the women in this book, I would imagine that most of you are under forty. While my youngest contributor is fourteen and my oldest sixty-two, the majority of you who talk and write to me about your sexual fantasies are in your twenties. Whether age, marriage, motherhood, career—the usual doors that shut on sex—will inhibit your sexuality, only time will tell. But I believe your sexual lives will run a different course from that of earlier generations of women.

You are the first people to grow up in a world wallpapered with sex. Billboards, books, films, videos, TV, advertising, unrelentingly drill home that sex is a given, therefore good. How can you not be easier with sex? You've spent your lives in a culture that invented sex as a selling tool in the heyday of the sexual revolution. While the inventors themselves may have personally retreated to the asexual rules of their parents against which they once rebelled, we are the world's greatest consumer society and thus reluctant to abandon anything that sells.

What will decide success in maintaining your present sexual ease, your determination to integrate your sexuality more fully into your life, is a very conscious awareness that society lies. We couldn't possibly have changed our deepest, most meaningful beliefs about sex in one generation. Behind the obvious erotic media blitz you've consciously taken in is another message, which says that sex for the sake of pleasure is wrong, immoral, bad. Keep yourself aware of this unconscious siren song wooing you back into being mama's good little girl, and just maybe you will pass on to your children a less muddled message. If you believe in nothing else, believe that sexual repression never sleeps, especially the sexual repression of women.

I got caught up in it myself for a while. I'd intended to resume this research on sexual fantasies five years ago, once

I finished my last book, *Jealousy.* But when I walked out of my writing room after years of grappling with envy, resentment, fear of abandonment, rage, and greed—all relatives of jealousy—it was the late 1980s, and I got sidetracked by its values.

I remember sitting next to a TV anchorman at dinner one night here in Key West, where I'm writing now. He was bone fishing in the Keys and mentioned he had read *My Secret Garden.* Before I could comment, he rushed to explain that he'd come across the book in a summer house he and his wife had rented on Martha's Vineyard. "You see, it was there, in the house, *their* book . . ." Was he afraid that I might think he'd purchased my book and then gone home to masturbate, he, an opinion maker who appeared nightly on millions of TV screens?

I began to assume that people weren't interested in sex anymore. No, that's not true; what honestly happened was that I wanted the anchorman to take me seriously, to admire my work. It wasn't a conscious decision, my temporary devaluation of sex. I just mindlessly fell in with the enemies of sex and for a few years regressed. I wanted to be accepted not by you, the people who love my work, but by them.

At this moment we are closer in spirit than I am to my compatriots of twenty years ago. For the most part they do not read my books. Two of my closest women friends tell me they don't have sexual fantasies—which tells you what an odd duck I am, or they are, depending on where you sit. They cannot understand my desire to write what one of them calls "another one of your masturbatory books, Nancy."

That is not a kind thing to say, but where is it written that friends are always kind, especially women friends when it comes to matters sexual? How many of you have told me that your friends would not condone the knowledge that you masturbate, God forbid have sexual fantasies. It is simply how some women are: It is all right if all the girls are sexual, or if all are not, but it is unacceptable if one enjoys sex while the rest do without. Remember The Rules when we were little girls? No one spoke them out loud, but every girl knew what the others would tolerate and what would get us ostracized.

The Rules still exist. Girls today don't banish the girl who has sex, but they do if she has sex with two men when they have only one. They may accept sex but still police one another to be sure no one gets more than her share. Nowhere do we women act more like little girls than in our refusal to protect ourselves contraceptively. How do you tell women that if we lose the power of our sexuality, if we fail to instill it in our daughters, we will have won the battle but lost the revolution?

It is called envy, this mean resentful eye that cannot bear seeing pleasure, especially sexual pleasure, in another. This is how I've come to understand and be able to live with my friend's derogatory comments about my "masturbatory books." She envies my writing about sex—though she would adamantly deny it—and so she denigrates my work. It is acceptable for me to write about mothers and daughters, jealousy and envy, a new novel perhaps, but not sexuality.

Is that because sex is a waste of time, purposeless and without any redeeming value?

A few years ago I was in Lexington, Kentucky, standing on the country club lawn at a cocktail party, when I was approached by a young woman who was not part of our group. She shyly introduced herself and asked if I was working on a new book on women's sexual fantasies. Had they changed? she asked. Were there new ideas and images that went through women's minds, scenarios that hadn't turned up in my earlier books?

Oh yes, I told her, there was a whole new world of women's erotica that had opened up in answer to and because of the very real changes in women's lives.

As I explained the new ideas, I could see how eager she was, the relief she felt at not being "the only one" to have fantasies not mentioned in *My Secret Garden.* At some point I turned and realized the entire party had closed in around us and was listening avidly.

"In my world we're always confronted by people eager for

19

information," said a newspaper editor standing nearby, "but I've never seen that kind of urgency."

Her name was Mary, the young woman in Lexington, and I have dedicated this book to her because she reminded me that I must not let the opinion makers judge the importance of sexuality. Most of the people I know have been far less able than Mary to integrate sexual acceptance into their lives—maybe because they are older, more successful, more entrenched in their parents' standards, which they'd always kept in their back pockets should the revolution not work out.

When we deny our fantasies, we no longer have access to that wonderful interior world that is the essence of our unique sexuality. Which is, of course, the intent of the sex haters, who will stop at nothing, quoting scripture and verse to locate that sensitive area in each of us. Beware of them, my friends, for they are skilled in the selling of guilt. Your mind belongs to you alone. Your fantasies, like the dreams you dream at night, are born out of your own private history, your first years of life as well as what happened yesterday. If they can damn us for our fantasies, they can jail us for the acts we commit in our dreams.

The intent of my friend's rude remarks about my books on sexuality is that I should stop writing them out of shame. In your life, not everyone will embrace your sexuality. Remember envy, especially between women over matters sexual; do not buy their shame and give up your sexuality so that they can rest more easily.

PART II

Separating Sex and Love: In Praise of Masturbation

It's taken me half a lifetime and the writing of six books, all of which deal at least in part with sexuality, to appreciate the role masturbation plays in our lives, or might play if we weren't so troubled about this simple, private act.

Here is the most natural thing in the world—our own hand on our own genitals, doing something that gives us pleasure and harms no one, practicing the safest sex in the world—yet we feel guilty as thieves, our sense of self lessened when it should be heightened by mastery and self-love.

Masturbation is not, after all, a difficult skill, like learning to play the violin. The hand automatically moves between our legs in the first year of life. Something, someone gets between it and our genitals so early that most of us cannot remember. A message is imprinted on the brain, a warning so fraught with fear that long after we are grown, even after we have allowed a man to put his penis inside us, to touch our genitals, we are ambivalent about touching ourselves. We may do it, but it is a physical act against a mental pressure—this delicate movement of our fingers that is only effective when the mind releases us. Sweet as orgasm feels, we are not left with an enhanced sense of womanliness; we have won the battle but lost our status as Nice Girls.

Masturbation used to be called the great taboo for women because it was sexual satisfaction outside of a relationship. Masturbation meant a measure of autonomy, and nobody wanted women to have that much control over themselves.

Most of the women in this book say they don't feel these negative emotions. They have an ease with the subject of masturbation that is a pleasure to hear, a vocabulary so rich in description of when and how they masturbate that I am dazzled; their sexual fantasies soar into a realm of adventure that makes most of the reveries in *My Secret Garden* read like tentative stuff.

And they were, those early expressions of women's inner erotic world. How can women today know how hard it was for those first women to speak, having no familiar words, no ease with masturbation or in expressing something no other women had yet given them permission to say?

Had I understood then the close kinship between masturbation and fantasy, I might have more easily uncovered the suppressed world of women's erotic reveries while researching that first book. I would have begun my interviews with what was at least known—over half of Kinsey's women surveyed admitted to having masturbated—and then asked my interviewees what was on their minds while they touched themselves. But I hadn't yet learned that for women masturbation without fantasy is rare. It simply hadn't occurred to me that women could be more guilty about what they were thinking than what they were doing.

The hand on the genitals isn't the culprit. The hand may be doing something forbidden, but the hand is obvious, external. It is the mind that carries the genesis of sexual life, inhibits us from orgasm or releases us. Masturbation gets its fire, its life from what is sparked in the mind. The fingers might move across the clitoris indefinitely without orgasm; only when the mind structures the correct image, a scenario meaningful and powerful to us alone because it carries us up and past all fears of reprisals and into that forbidden, interior world that is our own sexual psyche—only then do we come.

After *My Secret Garden* was published, there was one response I would hear from women that became a chorus: "Thank God you wrote the book, I thought I was the only one . . . a freak of nature . . . a pervert . . ." to have erotic dreams, to imagine sex in forbidden places with forbidden people. How dirty, vile I must be, not like Nice Girls who never touch themselves. Toward the end of the 1970s, this guilty sigh of relief lessened as more and more women began to take in the sexual freedoms being offered. Certainly the rape/force fantasy didn't go away, nor will it ever, given the various convoluted sources of pleasure it provides.

But by the early 1980s there was a new breed of woman who didn't identify with the guilty women in *My Secret Garden.* "Where did those women come from?" these new women would exclaim. "I don't feel guilty. I love my body. I masturbate when I feel like it. I lie in the tub under a running faucet, or use my wonderful vibrator or my hand, and this is what I imagine as I get closer and closer to orgasm." Even men's voices pale in comparison to the bravado of some of these women.

Most of the women are in their mid-twenties. They grew up in a climate in which women were talking and writing with exuberance and excitement about sexuality. Whether mother punished them verbally for touching themselves, held their hand over an open flame, or said nothing—often the most damaging—these women continued to act on the premise that their sexuality belonged to them alone. They may have taken in some of mother's guilt, but the voices they listened to most keenly were the voices of their time, and the voices said that mother was old-fashioned, outdated.

This sense of rightness is their legacy from the 1970s, when masturbation came out of the closet. In 1972 the American Medical Association declared masturbation to be "normal." Masters and Johnson extolled it as a treatment for sexual dysfunction. For the first time, popular books were being published telling women it was good to masturbate and how to do it. New studies claimed that women who masturbated at an early age not only had an easier time reaching orgasm in later sexual intercourse, they also had stronger orgasms.

I remember a woman who painted huge canvases of vaginas and conducted classes in masturbation. While women sitting in a group discovering their clitorises may sound as far out and remote as naked hippies dancing in the rain at Woodstock, from this extremism came the small piece of ground that supports the women in this book. It was a different time—a lifetime ago, it seems to me now.

What a cramped, guilt-ridden world we once lived in. And it wasn't all that long ago, not so distant that we can't return, indeed haven't already started slipping back. There is a longing in human nature to go back to what was most known and familiar, even if what was known was cruel and hard. Just as battered children, offered loving new parents, choose to return to their abusive parents, so will adult partners in a devastating marriage often remain with one another because anger and resentment are what is comfortable, familiar.

It is an open question how many of their sexual freedoms the young women in this book will retain, how deeply they have incorporated them. I would like to think we can no more return to that stunted, antisexual world in which women once lived than we can order women out of the workplace and back into the home. But the latter is an economic issue, a necessity for most women, and so it will hold.

The rules against women's sexual freedom have roots that go back to the most primitive society, when men feared the mysteries of female sexuality and reproductive power. To ensure sexual supremacy in the Middle Ages, man invented the chastity belt. In order to control women's prodigious sexual appetite—feared to be insatiable—it became custom in some cultures to remove a woman's clitoris, thus killing the source of sexual pleasure and making her man's property. The operation was called clitoridectomy. When it was deemed necessary to further limit women (reassure men), the labia were also removed. The operation continues to this day in some parts of Africa and the Middle East, where many women do not consider themselves marriageable until they have been mutilated—though it is called circumcision —in this fashion.

To the contemporary Western mind it sounds mad, a sadistic piece of science fiction. But clitoridectomies were performed in this country in the early part of the century. That was your grandmother's or great-grandmother's time, when some of the most eminent, celebrated surgeons in the land routinely took knife in hand and skillfully removed various parts of a woman's genitalia for reasons of insanity, hysteria, and oh yes, hygiene.

Masturbation was considered to be at the core of these female disorders; the removal of the clitoris got to the heart of the problem. Records show that clitoridectomies were still being performed in certain mental hospitals as late as the 1930s.

In time, clitoridectomies were no longer necessary in this country. Men found they didn't have to do anything. Women had so totally taken in men's attitudes toward female sexuality that we had come to judge ourselves by their needs. No Nice Woman would think of touching herself, exploring her sexuality. The less sexual the woman, the nicer. Mothers raised their daughters dutifully in the art of sexual avoidance. Women learned to loathe their genitals. Sex was not a pleasure but a duty. That was in your mother's or grandmother's time. Not long ago. Not long ago at all.

It would seem impossible to unlearn, to forget something as absolutely as the young women in this book know that their bodies belong to them. The litmus test will be when they marry and have to make up rules for their own children. Marriage has a way of regressing us, confronting us with images of how our parents were as husband and wife. Consciously we enjoy imitating those characteristics of theirs we loved most; unconsciously we often become what we liked least in our parents, rigid, obsessed with what the neighbors think, asexual. When we have children of our own, all of this escalates.

When this new generation becomes mothers, will they remember the exhilaration of controlling their own sexual destiny? Will they teach their daughters to love their bodies, allow them to masturbate, to discover their own unique sexuality? Or will they regress, telling themselves what generations of well-intentioned mothers have believed, that in limiting their little girls' sexuality they are protecting them for their own good?

When we lose interest in sex and will not tolerate in others what we once enjoyed ourselves, we are reacting to more than the cautionary voices of our parents; there is a cultural voice, our heritage that has never been comfortable with sex and has abhorred masturbation in particular. Whatever popular support for sexual freedom the women in this book knew growing up, the very real, deep-down "feel" of this country, the fiber and character of the people, is modeled on a Calvinist work ethic and an inherent puritanical attitude toward sex. It would be foolish to think that a few decades of sexual celebration and tolerance could significantly alter our antisexual nature.

It's important to know this, to remind ourselves of it constantly if there is to be any hope that these young women will bring their daughters into a more enlightened age. Knowledge is power. Therefore, we might ask, why has this simple act of masturbation been so singled out for fear and punishment?

Could the answer be that it is not a simple act at all? An ancient Egyptian god, so the myth goes, masturbates into his hand, puts his semen in his mouth, and spews it forth, creating a new race of people. An ordinary human brings him- or herself to orgasm and in a solitary act experiences a resurgence of self, the exhilaration of power. Masturbation, mythic or real, is sexual freedom.

It seems we can live with the knowledge that others are economically better off more easily than we can tolerate the idea that they are freer sexually. Money is power and engenders envy; but sexual freedom must be even greater power, since the envious person cannot rest until he or she has pried into the most private areas of the envied one's life, stripping away everything that causes the intolerable resentment until finally the enviable one is as depleted and asexual as the envious person.

It is understandable that masturbation and sexual fantasy were accredited as "normal" at almost the same moment in history. They go hand in hand, these two good friends, which is why I have chosen to write about masturbation at length. The one reveals the other. Masturbation without fantasy would simply be too lonely.

A LITTLE HISTORY

Historians are always looking for a new lens through which to view and understand the past. The modern history of popular sentiment toward masturbation offers a fascinating perspective on our culture. Having an idea of the depth of feeling against masturbation in general and female masturbation in particular, we may better understand why women have been so late in accepting their sexual fantasies. So long as they were cut off from masturbation, they were cut off from their inner erotic lives.

At times the historic carryings-on over masturbation sound crazed, more theater-of-the-absurd than the real thinking and behavior of our ancestors. Simultaneously there is an eerie ring of recognition.

Take for instance the popular theory that held that a man's semen was limited and represented his entire storehouse of energy. Every time he ejaculated, he lost some of his virility, manhood. A wise man spent his semen as frugally as the money in his bank. Doctors once advised patients to avoid all sex prior to such major events as military engagements, sports competitions, and important business powwows. (When I tell my husband this, he insists many men still believe and act on the myth.) In the latter part of the nineteenth century, nocturnal emissions were thought to be such a terrible waste that doctors recommended nightly cold water enemas before bed.

As for women, we have been seen as bloodsuckers who, given half a chance, would drain a man dry of his precious bodily fluids. (Conversely, simultaneously, and in keeping with the whore/madonna mentality, women have also been seen as hating sex, merely going through the motions to arrive at the far more satisfying maternal emotion.)

For much of the century the only acceptable sexual activity that warranted spending precious semen was procreation, and nothing, nothing was more deplorable, more wasteful and dangerous than masturbation, which purportedly led to epilepsy, blindness, vertigo, deafness, headache, impotency, loss of memory, rickets, and a diminution in the size of the penis, to mention only a few afflictions.

No one in this country typified this kind of maniacal thinking better than two all-American heroes of the nineteenth century, Sylvester Graham and John Harvey Kellogg. The latter hated sex so deeply that he never consummated his long marriage. But like many antipornographers, he was obsessed with the subject of sex in general and determined to eliminate it in the lives of other individuals.

As a highly respected, licensed physician, Kellogg attracted a wide readership for his views on masturbation; circumcision was his remedy for the chronic masturbator, circumcision "without an anaesthetic, as the brief pain attending the operation will have a salutary effect upon the mind, especially if it be connected with the idea of punishment."

Graham and Kellogg shared an aversion to masturbation, and both believed in a mysterious connection between food and sex. Applying a certain Yankee ingenuity to their fanaticism, each in his turn came up with a best-selling, antimasturbation food: Graham invented the graham cracker and Kellogg his famous cornflakes, snacks guaranteed to stave off the longing for the "secret sin" of self-abuse.

Nor did this kind of deluded thinking disappear as we entered the enlightened twentieth century. Here is a description of someone who masturbates taken from a small book published in eighteen editions by the YMCA and recommended reading for Boy Scouts up to 1927:

"As this act is repeated from week to week, or in some extreme cases, every day or two, the youth feels the foundations of his manhood undermined. He notes that his muscles are becoming more and more flabby; that his back is weak, his eyes after a time become sunken and 'fishy,' his hands clammy; he is unable to look anybody straight in the eye. As the youth becomes conscious of his weakness, he loses confidence, refuses to take part in athletic sports; avoids the company of his young women friends; and becomes a non-entity in the athletic and social life of the community. So far as his school record is concerned, he may succeed very well in his studies for a number of years but eventually his memory begins to fail, and just at the time when he is trying to prepare for some useful life work, he wakes up to the realization that his mind is as flabby as his muscles, lacking in force, originality and power to think things out."

It wasn't until the 1959 edition of the *Boy Scout Handbook* that the attitude toward masturbation was softened: "Any real boy knows that anything that arouses him to worry should be avoided. It will help you to throw yourself into a vigorous game, work at an absorbing hobby, strive to live up to your own high ideals. Here, Scouting is your ally, as you live up to the tenth point of the Scout law—'A Scout is Clean.'"

Once the American Medical Association put its "normal" label on masturbation in 1972, the handbook withdrew from the fray, never again to mention masturbation, simply advising Scouts to seek advice and counseling from parents and religious leaders should they have "strong feelings" about what is happening to their bodies. Nor is there any explanation or elaboration as to what these feelings might be.

I've not mentioned the *Girl Scout Handbook* because there is nothing in it on masturbation. Not a word, not ever. Are we to assume that patriarchal society didn't/doesn't care about female masturbation? Omission speaks louder than words.

Early twentieth-century man lived with a dizzying, swivel-headed attitude toward women's sexuality. He needed to see woman as chaste, passive, spiritual, she who was so close to heaven she could save his very soul after a murderous day of competition in the new industrial society. This was known as "the cult of the household nun."

Meanwhile the opposite hemisphere of man's brain was besotted with images of women who were carnivorous in bacchanalian hunger for his body. An eminent doctor warned that female masturbation led to nymphomania, "occurring more commonly in blondes than in brunettes."

There was a popular school of painting early in this century that catered especially to man's split vision of woman. These large oil canvases depicted naked women lying about, usually in pastoral scenes, and allowed a man to gaze for hours, satisfying his voyeuristic fantasies without fear. The women, you see, always had their eyes closed and looked near death, or so obviously exhausted that they were in no position to make demands on the man's precious bodily fluids. And it was understood why they were so worn out; their carefully painted snakelike hands lay suspiciously close to that forbidden area between their legs. Often they were shown in groups, intertwined, their heads on one another's breasts. A man could well imagine what they'd been up to—that left to themselves, we women would soon be encouraging one another in the "criminal" practice of masturbation. Doctors warned that girls' boarding schools were literal hotbeds of young female proselytizers, eager to vamp one another into the practice of masturbation.

Imagine these two warring halves of women long enough and we arrive at the 1950s, when Hollywood created Doris Day and Marilyn Monroe, who satisfied both extremes of men's appetite. You would never imagine Doris's hands between her legs; and Marilyn, poor victim of her own sexual appetite, died young.

WHAT WE WIN FROM MASTURBATION

Could the full-voiced women in this book give up the joy of masturbation? There is always some risk. Could men? Never. The fact that men masturbate is a given, as obvious as the penis between their legs. Mother may not like it when her little boy touches his penis; she tsktsks and takes his hand away, but ultimately she doesn't want to interfere in her son becoming a man. What does she know about men? If anatomy is destiny, then man is destined to masturbate. He may do it with guilt and the torments of hell pounding in his ears, but he does it anyway. That is how men are, we shrug, animals, driven by their testosterone.

Society says it is not how women are. Since time began, a "good mother" takes her daughter's hand away from her vagina with far more determination than she applies to her son and his penis. Mothers know everything there is to know about being a woman: Nice Women don't masturbate.

That is why the women in this book are so significant historically. They are the first generation to grow up with a semblance of sexual acceptance, an ease with masturbation. Will they give their daughters a middle ground between madonna and whore? Will they change the course of women's sexual history? It is by no means certain they will.

Sex and economics are inextricably linked. Today man's economic supremacy is endangered. There is one known, tested solution that could return us to the good old days, for which some part of our unconscious still hankers because it was how our parents grew up and their parents before them: Cut a woman off from her sex. Return women to our traditional asexual role, deprive us of the right to our own body, deprive us of contraceptive rights and the right to abortion, make sex the unenjoyable chore it once was. We will be on the fast track with our feet bound. We will be good wage earners, but remain chattel.

Does that sound extreme? I believe it is reality. Nor do I

blame men alone for this growing tidal wave that may ultimately wash women back into some new form of sexual slavery; there are just as many women as men who would like to return us to that time when all women were equal in asexuality.

When I began this essay, I didn't see female masturbation as the powerful symbol I now believe it to be. Until I saw a grotesque drawing of a woman's genitals before and after a clitoridectomy, I had no image of the lengths to which people will go to keep women "in their place." Surgically remove all traces of sex from between a woman's legs, wipe it clean so that nothing remains but a wound, a scarred slit, and wonder of wonders, the world can rest.

Today, as we are a more "enlightened" people, a mental clitoridectomy will suffice. Projected early enough onto a young female mind, the "ugly" slit between our legs is as untouchable as one of the vaginas butchered by the high-minded doctors of earlier times.

Because the taboo against female masturbation is so deeply embedded, let us think of ways of not losing the ground we've so recently won as expressed by the young women in this book. Our best defense is to make ourselves so consciously aware of what masturbation wins for women that we can't, won't unconsciously slip back:

1. Masturbation teaches us that we are sexual all by ourselves, separate from anyone, including mother.
2. Masturbation is an excellent exercise in learning to separate love and sex, a lesson especially important for women who confuse the two.
3. By teaching ourselves what excites us, we become more orgasmic and better sexual partners, responsible for our share, capable of giving pleasure, better able to give direction in what it is that excites us.
4. If we are loathe to touch what lies between our legs, our revulsion spreads, leaving us eternally dissatisfied with the acceptability of the rest of our bodies.
5. Masturbation teaches us the difference between our clitoris, labia, urethra, and vagina.

6. Masturbation makes us far better candidates for contraceptive responsibility as well as for the sexual education of our children.

7. Last and most obvious, masturbation is one of life's greatest sources of sexual pleasure, thrilling in itself, a release from tension, a sweet sedative before sleep, a beauty treatment that leaves us glowing, our countenance more tranquil, our smile more mysterious. As one of the women in this book puts it, "Masturbation and fantasy is when I am most honest about myself."

THE MOTHER/DAUGHTER DEAL

Masturbation is a great teacher.

Alas, it's one I did not have growing up. No one I knew admitted to masturbation or discussed it. Confused and often incorrect as our ideas on sex with boys were, the language and vocabulary of sex all by ourselves didn't exist. Nor do I remember any punishment or words spoken against masturbation. Giving up the right to touch myself was a sacrifice I made as unquestioningly as I'm sure my mother had made it with her mother. Like many well-educated young women today, I didn't use any contraception when I first had sex. I haven't a doubt in the world that the two are related.

As leader of my group, the intrepid one who would take any dare, I climbed the highest walls, rode on the back of Charleston's horse-drawn ice wagons, explored the abandoned, shuttered house across the street, even stole from Belk's department store.

Since I broke all these other rules in what I now understand was my youthful determination to learn bravery, to never be anxious and frightened as I perceived my mother to be, why didn't I explore and master my own body?

Certainly a map would have helped, given that Houdini

himself designed women's genitals. Here is a mental picture, my earliest unconsummated masturbatory memory: I am lying on my bed and it is summer. My mind is on baseball, my hand aimlessly lying, moving between my legs. I am maybe ten or eleven, no more, because I remember the house we were living in, the wisteria outside the window. Where was it, the source of this tingling pleasure I was feeling, and why did I not continue until I found my clitoris, hidden yes, but not that hidden?

My answer would be that I had already made a bargain with my mother. Made it so long ago and at a time when I was most vulnerable—probably the first year of life—that it had been carved into my very soul, much as a deep cut in a young tree is incised forever. The bargain was never verbalized, never even made conscious to me until I became a writer and began to look for answers to the riddles in my life.

At some point very early in my life I had unconsciously promised my mother never to masturbate if she would love me in the way I had always wanted her to love me. How did I grasp the seriousness of what it meant to her, this business of touching myself? Was it the pained look on her face, the grimace, the turning away, the sharp intake of breath that I would come to associate with her anxiety? I easily gave it up. After all, I was dependent on her for everything, for life itself.

The fact that she never held to her side of the bargain, never loved me in the way I wanted her to, didn't mean I broke my end of the deal; children have a self-protective way of blaming themselves for mothers' failures and inadequacies. Clearly the fault lay in me, and if I'd been a better child, she would have loved me more.

I buried my anger at her. And I didn't masturbate—even though I could have done it in the privacy of my own room; even though she wouldn't have to know. But you see, in the mind of the symbiotic child, still meshed with mother out of anger and love, she would have known. There is a fuzziness where we leave off and she begins, and in that gray area, she lives on in our mind, knowing what we think, what we do, judging us, threatening us with abandonment.

Some children, grown and with children of their own, still hold out for the acceptance and love they wanted when they were little, because the unresolved issues with mother remain just that: untested beneath protective layers of buried anger. It doesn't matter that we wouldn't die if she abandoned us today; to the still unseparated person the taboo against masturbation remains loaded with dire consequences.

Let me add that on her side, mother experiences this same oneness with her daughter. The biological definition of symbiosis is of two organisms living profitably off each other. They would never think of separating.

When I was writing *My Mother/My Self,* I referred to the look-alike clothes in which mothers used to dress themselves and their little girls as a small but significant example of how symbiosis blurs the line between mother and daughter. You didn't see much of those clothes in the late 1970s and the 1980s. They are back. Does that mean mothers are also reading their daughters' diaries, listening in on their phone calls, and in other ways violating the laws of privacy because there is no privacy, no life separate from mother?

When we grow up and fall in love, we make bargains with men based on the one we made with mother. Our adult expectations of the loved one grow out of and are in reaction to that first, most important love experience. We don't like to think our mature, sexual lives have anything to do with the nursery, but there is no other way to explain or understand the deals men and women make.

Lovers' contracts, like the one with her, are too crucial to the love experience to speak out loud. The terms in the small print below the beautifully spoken vows of love aren't even conscious: "Promise that you will take care of me, love me unconditionally, and never arouse in me any fear of abandonment, jealousy, loss of face, or suspicion that any of the many sacrifices I've made for you have been in vain. In return, I am giving myself to you. We will be as one. If you break this deal, I'll die (or I will kill you)."

How can you say something like that? The meanness of the spoken bargain would break the romantic bubble.

37

Besides, the words show our dependency, infantile omnipotence, lack of trust, the hint of reprisals we would extract if our beloved broke the deal. Better never to say the terms, never even make them conscious to ourselves.

Until he looks at another woman in that special way reserved for us alone. Then our reaction is out of all proportion, our anger has a suicidal/killing edge, not just because of the other woman—indeed she is inconsequential —but because of what has been rearoused, a tidal wave of old anger and disappointment that began in that first deal with mother, which he has inherited.

Men don't command women to fall in love in that peculiarly female I'll-die-if-you-leave-me way which is antithetical to sex, being how a baby experiences neediness and not how a grown person experiences love. No, we give up sex and lose ourselves in dependency because that is the love experience we know best, what we were raised on and for. The kind of love we had with mother abhors sex. But we could never be angry at her, in fact don't even know the real source of our rage. We can however be angry at men. Oh my, do they ever get the rage we dare never express at mother/ women.

Men make their deals too, which are also rooted in childhood, but they don't hand over their independence, their identity as part of the adult love exchange. They don't abandon their sexuality in an effort to recapture the asexual deal they once had with mommy. They may lose sexual interest in us, seeing us now as mother/wife, but they still retain their sexual core to either invest in themselves— masturbation—or spend on another woman.

Let me tell you a grown-up story about masturbation, love, and rage, how the unresolved sexual issues between mother and daughter get played out between woman and man. It is my own story.

Did I mention that I didn't masturbate until I was twenty-two? It was also the time of my first conscious sexual fantasy. At that age I was involved with an extraordinary man, whom I've come to appreciate as my sexual emancipator. It was because of him that I threw away my circle pin, my little white gloves, and my bra. You see, he had the comfort level of a great teacher, a sureness of himself and a wisdom that resonated back to the earliest stages of my life: he spoke with the tongue of angels and emanated a quality of sexual leadership that said, "Trust me." I did. Willingly, eagerly, I followed him on the sexual adventure in which he was immersed when we met.

One night early in our relationship we were at his beach house (which he had built himself) and I awoke to find he had left the bed. I walked into the living room and saw him in the early dawn light lying on the sofa masturbating. I was furious. I cried. I said it was because I saw his masturbating, while I was present and available, as rejection. I would say today, however, that my rage had far more to do with my abrupt realization, on seeing him about to bring himself to orgasm, that he had a life separate from me, was not tied to me in that inextricable way that I was enmeshed with him. I was jealous of his hand.

It was the only way I knew to fall in love, symbiotically, the giving over of the self to the beloved. (Let me add that this was not how I presented myself, how the world saw me. I made a flashy external show of sexual assertiveness and economic independence. Even I believed in it—until I fell in love.) Ah, love, the oneness of it all! The bliss of feeling taken care of, weightless, dependent as only a child can and should be dependent on a mother. How dare he break our union, reminding me that I would die—or so I felt—if he should leave me, if only in the throes of his own orgasm!

Don't assume that he masturbated without guilt, or to state it more clearly, that masturbating ever lost its exciting edge of defiance. The lover of my twenty-second summer, like other men, began life with a mother who took his hand away from his penis. What he was up to in the mid-sixties when we met was an all-out determination to separate himself forever from women's sexual rules.

He had assumed, poor soul, that he had a partner on his sexual adventure, when in truth he had a responsibility: me.

Nothing said it more clearly—that we were not alike in how we experienced love and sex—than the difference in our attitudes about masturbation.

HOW MASTURBATION HELPS MEN SEPARATE LOVE AND SEX

Men's deals with mother influence and distort their sexual lives too, but they don't demand the sacrifice of masturbation, of the freedom to choose whether to touch themselves or not. Indeed, masturbation was one of the best tools the man had as a boy in learning emotional separation from mother.

He may begin life in love with mother, seeing himself mirrored in her eyes, even wanting to be like her, softness, empathy, and gentleness being what he loves most about her. But early on he learns he must be different, must go away from her, deny those feminine parts in himself that are like her. He must be "a little man." The first and most obvious way he knows he is different from her and like a man is his penis. It is a visible sign, a familiar part of himself that he is used to touching, if only to urinate throughout the day.

By the time he is twelve or thirteen, he has learned that his penis has a life of its own. Without even being touched, his penis swells and ejaculates. It can be a frightening experience but a valuable lesson, too: his body is telling him that he is a sexual person unto himself. Before he even comprehends the meaning of sex, his body is teaching him. With his own hand he gives himself an erection.

He may be filled with enormous guilt when he touches himself, but defying mother's rules, risking the loss of her love, wins him something too: he now feels different from her, less feminine, more masculine. And besides, he soon finds that he has not lost her love at all. She does not abandon him! That was a baby boy's fear, a bargain he made when he couldn't live without mommy. Well, life has taught him he can be sexual, different, and separate from her and be loved by her too. It is the learning process working at its best, practicing something again and again until finally it is believed. Masturbation becomes part of growing up into his own male identity. It is the reality principle that most little girls dare not test.

Soon, in the company of other little boys, he reinforces what he has been learning on his own. Masturbating together, competing with one another over who can shoot the farthest, being bad, being dirty—and no girls allowed!—becomes a preadolescent rite of passage away from women and into manhood.

In an interview, one man tells me that when he was twelve, he used to masturbate in the powder room, just a few feet away from where the family was having dinner. He could have gone upstairs, where he couldn't hear them, where they couldn't overhear him. But terrifying as it was, he needed to challenge his mother's asexual rules, to have his orgasm on her territory, her pretty powder room.

Yes, he would have aroused the wrath of his father, too, if he had been discovered. But his father's rules had only recently entered his near-adolescent life. It was not his father who had bathed, fed, and loved him in the first years of life. It wasn't father who had lovingly kissed his little penis after a sweet warm bath and then moments later taken the boy's hand away from it. Mothers think these acts are innocent; but on such "innocence" (for which a father bathing his daughter would be jailed) is built a man's lifelong confusion of women's adoration and disapproval of his genitals. Whose penis is it anyway? In his defiant masturbation, he makes his ownership absolutely clear.

Tough, macho slang for masturbation further enhances separation. "Jerking off," "beating my meat," "choking the chicken"—any words that are dirty and different from "girl talk" are practiced again and again.

The boy's vocabulary may not be on target, but he wants the dirty word for the dirty act. Another man tells me that when he was eight or nine, he and his pals would stop in a hidden vacant lot on the way to school and have a group bowel movement. They called what they were doing the Fucking Club. All they knew was that it was bad. If the story offends your Nice Girl sensibility, that is exactly what the Fucking Club intended.

Am I making a romantic idyll out of boyish masturbation, halcyon days of bonding in circle jerks? When I read these pages to my husband, he reminds me that not all boys have happy memories of either solitary or group masturbation. But how can a man understand what it's like for us women? Surely it is relative. Only recently have I begun to encounter women who enjoyed the sexually freeing experience of sitting in a group with other little girls and masturbating. Yes, I understand the guilt the boy/man feels; I've read thousands of masturbatory fantasies that reflect the guilt, but they do it, they masturbate anyway and in spite of the guilt. And each time they do it, they learn once again the electric shock of orgasm, that they are sexually alive, all by themselves.

When young girls do come along, entering the boy's life as abruptly as a devastatingly beautiful early spring day, he is overwhelmed with a mix of emotion. His desire for the girl has an intensity that pulls him away from the camaraderie of boys upon which he had come to depend; former comrades now become rivals. He wants the girl but doesn't want to lose his still-fresh independence.

Part of what he feels when he walks in the moonlight with the girl is a romantic rush, a human desire that is linked exclusively to neither male nor female. But for the boy romance threatens to pull him back into the female-dominated oneness from which he so recently escaped. Romance is a mystery.

The sexual feeling, however, is not. When he puts his arm around the girl and kisses her, the other rush he feels is known, no mystery at all. It is a feeling that he recognizes because his penis is erect. Terrified as he may be of sexual intercourse, not yet even ready for it, he knows nonetheless that what he is feeling is exactly what he feels when he masturbates.

42

THE NICE GIRL RULES

As for the girl being held and kissed in the moonlight, how is she to know that part of what she is feeling is sexual? Nothing has ever happened to her to help her single out, isolate the sexual feeling from all the other emotions and sensations racing through her adolescent mind and body. She has never had an erection. Her body has never signaled to her that this is sex and has nothing to do with the other emotion, romantic oneness.

Perhaps when she was little, nine or ten years old, she felt something wonderful when she put her pillow between her legs and rocked back and forth. Women often trace their first fantasies back to this time, fantasies of being captured by bad pirates, fantasies invariably rooted in ideas of wicked people making them feel the already known forbidden feelings. But no one called these feelings sexual. No one wants to think that a nine-year-old is sexual, God forbid a four-year-old, the other age to which women trace their first sexual stirrings.

The girl has no words for what she is feeling, indeed doesn't want to know the "dirty" words since by now she has been rewarded for being the custodian of goodness, wagging her little finger at her naughty brother. By adolescence the girl is convinced that all the sensations "down there" have to do with love.

Now when the boy kisses her, he awakens these feelings she has grown to associate with soft music, passages in romantic novels, love scenes in films. For years she and the other girls have been sitting in dark cinemas sharing a group feeling closer to a communal swoon than to sex. While the boy has been learning to be brave and independent outdoors, the girl has been inside practicing togetherness, learning to dance with other girls, rolling up one another's hair, exploring the warm closeness of sleepovers. In these tight friendships, girls retain the symbiotic oneness they had

43

with mother, keeping it warm, rehearsing it over and over again until boys are ready for them. And should one of these best friendships flounder, the pain of betrayal is not unlike what a child feels when abandoned by its mother.

Betrayal doesn't teach a much needed lesson in independence, that it is good to have a self to fall back on. What does the girl know of a separate self? All her life she has been rewarded for staying in, preserving relationships.

So there they are in the moonlight, the boy and the girl. He assumes, poor innocent, that she feels what he does, that she has been touching herself as he has. What do young boys know of girls? With one arm around her, his other hand tentatively reaches between her legs. She recoils. She tells him he is vile. She weeps. How could he take her for that kind of girl? After all she's sacrificed to abide by the Nice Girl Rules, doesn't he respect her? He is supposed to be her reward, not her persecutor. Furthermore, he has broken the romantic bubble, the lovely sense of oneness she was feeling in his arms.

He will have to pay for what he has done. If he is ever to get his arm around her again, it will be on her terms. It is the girl's first lesson in deal making, the first inkling that the withholding of sex may be her greatest power.

On his side, the boy acknowledges that she will now decide whether or not there will be any sex. It is an abrupt reminder of the total power a woman once had over him, and while he still wants the girl, he resents the bargain bitterly. And so the groundwork is laid for the unspoken deal. Thus begins the War Between the Men and the Women.

Would any of this change if a woman grew up learning from her own body that she is a sexual person unto herself? Masturbation may not solve everything, but what better way to learn the all-important lesson in the separation and equal importance of love and sex?

Unless she was allowed to pursue the sense of ownership of her body when she was little, by the time the girl reaches adolescence she may no longer want to explore the solitary pleasure of masturbation. She is by now besotted with love/yearning/dying/sighing feelings which encompass the sexual but to her are one indistinguishable high. The idea of having sex all by herself goes against her whole life as a partner in a relationship, a role she identifies with mother, who would never masturbate. Be sexual all by herself? She'd rather die! No, it's the boy's role to make her sexual, bring her to life. But first, first he must make her feel loved, in love, as one with him. She wants to be Swept Away.

THE SWEPT AWAY PHENOMENON

This is what the sex education textbooks call it. "I wanted to be swept away," a sentence heard so often from women with unintended pregnancies that it has become the name of the malady.

The women whose fantasies fill this book sound like a new generation, one that is immune to the Swept Away Phenomenon. Many of them have had varied and exciting real sexual lives, and the language in which they describe what they've done, how they masturbate, and the extraordinary images that run through their minds suggests an equally new level of sexual independence and responsibility.

The latest statistics on unintended pregnancies would suggest, however, that the Swept Away Phenomenon is alive and well. They do not reflect just poor girls in the ghetto but also educated, middle- and upper-middle-class women. The statistics are alarming. They say louder than words how sexually ambivalent the new generation is. For instance: Some 70 percent of all abortion patients are white, according to the National Abortion Federation, although black and Hispanic women have higher rates of abortion. After eighteen years of a declining birth rate in teenagers, there has been an abrupt reversal in the late 1980s—a startling increase of 10 percent in the years 1986–1988 alone. And according to statistics from the early 1990s, more than half of all pregnancies result from unintended conception.

The apparent contradiction between the women in this

book and these statistics is not a contradiction at all. It is possible to be sexually knowing, sexually active and still be controlled by an even more powerful, though unconscious, need to be taken care of. While these women speak and act like a brave new breed, their unconscious feelings about sex are what interest me more because these deep feelings of right and wrong, which we get from our parents, motivate us more powerfully and are the slowest to change.

It would be absurd to suggest that masturbation alone would have taught these young women to take better care of themselves contraceptively, to know the difference between sex and love. Many pressures are working on a young woman who allows herself to become pregnant. But I do not know a better lesson than that which masturbation teaches, or one that lasts a whole lifetime.

To put it another way, if women are guilty about masturbation, they are reluctant to use any form of contraception that involves touching their genitals. As stated in a paper published in the *Journal of Sex Research* in 1985, "Masturbation guilt appeared to account specifically for reluctance to use the diaphragm as a contraceptive device."

I have no way of knowing whether the women in this book are sexually responsible. Most remember a harsh critical attitude toward masturbation when they were young. Or they remember silence, which in its open-endedness allows for an eternity of recriminations. But they masturbate today in spite of what mother said or felt.

"When I was a young girl (about six or seven), I had my first orgasm through masturbation," wrote one twenty-six-year-old woman. "My mother always hid her sexuality and would beat me whenever she caught me masturbating. Nevertheless, I continued to masturbate in secret." In her fantasy, this woman poses nude for a handsome young photographer, who not only approves of her genitals but also adores it when she masturbates. In sexual fantasy, she rewrites history.

The new woman has more in common with her older, traditional sister than she probably realizes; not enough time has gone by to know whether the freedoms expressed by the women in this book will hold. We don't know what effect the increasingly restrictive times in which we live will have on the avowed sexual acceptance these women feel.

We meet in adolescence like people from two different planets. We make unspoken bargains within these young relationships based on a common need but diametrically opposite past sexual experiences and expectations. Years later we may lie down together with the same conscious objective—sexual pleasure—but the union reawakens old needs: When sex is done, he rolls over, satisfied; she lies there, desperately wanting to continue the bond. She thinks he is cold; he fears she wants to own him.

When she becomes pregnant, her doctor asks, "Why didn't you use a contraceptive?"

"I just couldn't. I didn't want to get up and go into that cold bathroom and spoil the moment. I wanted to be swept away."

What does it mean, "swept away"? This is not an adolescent talking now but a grown woman, someone who pays her own rent, is responsible at work, takes care of herself. In all matters but sexual. When it comes to being kissed and held and having a man enter her body, the giving over of herself becomes just that, not a mutual exchange but a deal—a hard word perhaps, but we are not talking about love here, we are talking about sex.

The man may also want to lose himself in the sexual experience, but it is a temporary giving up of the control he must otherwise exert in the daily business of being, proving himself male. Once he has reached orgasm, he knows from past sexual experiences in masturbation and intercourse, he will subside, return to that known level on which he lives.

I've never heard a man explain sex as a desire to be Swept Away. For openers, there are too many jobs a man must perform during sex with a woman that automatically eliminate any idea of his losing consciousness: he must orchestrate the seduction, arouse the woman, and keep himself from coming long enough for her to get close to orgasm. Not all men are this considerate, but even if reaching his own orgasm is the goal of the exercise, he is not going to get there by lying back and waiting for the woman to sweep him away.

No, the Swept Away Phenomenon is indeed peculiar to women raised to think that sex is not their responsibility, not something they want to have a hand in. Be party to our own seduction? Tell the man what it is we want, give him some guidance about what we desire, what turns us on, speak the words out loud? Absolutely not!

Being contraceptively prepared goes against a lifelong addiction to love, a state of mind that includes sexual feeling but has never been differentiated from it.

Is it love/romance we want or is it sex? Wouldn't it be helpful to know, and also to know that we can have the one without the other? Maybe it's preferable to love the person with whom you are having sex, but not necessarily all the time. Sometimes it feels good to have sex with someone who is just a friend; sometimes it feels good to masturbate.

Does that sound like a man? The notion that men masturbate and/or have sex with strangers/whores because men *need* sex in a way that women do not, that they are animals, predators, leads to the opposite notion that women are the poor little victims who are preyed upon. It becomes a self-fulfilling prophecy.

The truth is that some of us are born with higher libidos than others; some of the low scorers are men, some of the high scorers women. Wouldn't it be nice to know what our true sexual appetite is? No one can tell us better than our own bodies.

When we mate, marry, we choose one another for reasons as various as a shared love of dancing, walks in the woods, Chinese food. Wouldn't it make sense to select a partner who has a common interest or disinterest in sex?

Whatever our libido, sex is an energy, a source of life to be felt, enjoyed, and also used to fuel and feed all the other areas of our life—social, intellectual, abstract as well as physical. Some of us are less social, less intellectual than others; we know this and therefore apply ourselves elsewhere so that we may enjoy life more. What a waste of life not to learn from our own bodies the true level of our sexual interest so that we may better know who we are.

Raised to believe that we come alive sexually only when somebody "out there" ignites us, we use sex to get what we want, to capture a man, to make him love us. Sex becomes a means to an end. Once the honeymoon is over, we don't understand why we are no longer interested in sex. We wake up ten years later and ask, Is this all there is? Angry, we withhold sex, still not even aware that the person we may be hurting most is ourself. How could we know? Sex has become something external that we have used up, like money.

We say men are unfeeling, when in fact a man knows exactly what it is that he is feeling. He knows that last night it was sex and this morning he feels great but it isn't/wasn't love. We say men are cold because they won't "commit," a terrible word that sounds like jail, which is just what the man feels women's idea of commitment is all about.

We resent it that men can have an extraordinary night of sex, then bound out of bed in the morning refreshed, refueled, more independent than ever. He will have a better day at work because of his wonderful erotic adventure with us. We loved the night of sex too, but in the morning we are reluctant to leave the bed; we lie there waiting for him to stop whistling around the bedroom and come sit beside us, touch us, reconnect. We want him to say what he said last night and to tell us when we will be together again. We don't have a better day at the office; we are less focused on work because we are listening for the phone, his voice, the words that will say when and where. Far from being refueled by a night of sex, we are weakened, having left part of ourself in that bed.

Men are no crueler than women. They simply approach sex and love from a different point of view. Let's say the man waits four days to telephone. Not because the night was like any other but precisely because it was so very special. He needs to regain his sense of independence, of separateness, not because he doesn't like/love us but because he came so very close to those emotions. Men overplay the role of the lone cowboy because women exaggerate their role of being the emotional ones, the sirens who would love to wrap their arms around him and never let go. Or so he thinks.

Who could not want the transcendency of wonderful sex? To enjoy that deep, powerful sense of loss of self in the other person, to be able for a few moments to drop the iron controls by which we all live—that is a human wish, exclusive to neither sex. But only the person with a strong sense of identity can emerge whole and happily walk away from the bliss of transcendency.

For many women it isn't a matter of choice. We can't emerge from the deep pool of togetherness. It's as though we never really left this sweet place. He is gone, but even without him we can keep ourselves in the trance. We listen to romantic music; heartbreaking songs of desperate yearning are what we crave; quivering violins, voices that break under the weight of the soulfully killing words mirror exactly what we feel and keep us connected to him and the night.

It is not the sounds, smell, and sweat of abandoned sex we want to re-create; it is the union, the oneness, romance, love. We sip a brandy, light another cigarette, giving ourselves over to it, wallowing in it: Without you I will die, the music says. And we will, or so it feels.

"Better not get involved with men," many women say today. "I feel good about my life, and every time I start up with a guy, I lose that. Who needs it?"

We don't need men the way we used to. Many of us don't need them to take care of us, pay for our food and the roof over our heads. We don't need them for an identity or a place in the community. Economic independence is indeed thrilling: discovering in our twenties or later that we can actually make it all by ourselves.

When I was writing *My Mother/My Self* fifteen years ago, I thought economic independence, more than anything, would help grown women throw off the emotional need to

50

lose themselves in relationships. Ideally, emotional separation and individuation is something that should be learned and practiced in the first years of life. But if we didn't get it then, all is not lost; it is harder later on, but we can teach ourselves.

What I didn't realize in the mid-seventies, however, was that women would confuse economic independence with honest emotional separation. How separate are we if we cannot risk a relationship with a man out of fear of becoming enslaved to romance/love? We worry that sex with a man would turn into that desperate *"I need you"* that destroys our control over our lives. Before you know it, there would be a lovers' quarrel and he would slam out the door, leaving us once again by the telephone while he roamed the streets, picked up women in bars, maybe even went to a whore. Chances are he would do none of this, being as in love with us as we are with him. But he could. He could have sex out of anger, he could have sex for the sake of sex because he doesn't confuse it with love.

We denigrate men for going to whores, for feeding their masturbatory fantasies with pornographic magazines. Could part of our devaluation of men be envy, an angry resentment that they have access to a life from which we feel barred? Envy is a bitter, destructive emotion; the envious comparison makes our lives feel shabby, empty. We cannot abide it that the enviable one has certain freedoms, power, pleasure, that are unavailable to us. Some part of our psyche wishes, hopes that the enviable person will come to a bad end. Only then can our own life regain some of its pleasure.

Envy is such a destructive emotion that most of us deny it. "Who me, envy men?" we say. Absolutely not! Men are uncaring, power-crazed, overly competitive, sexual animals who degrade women. The trouble with the world, we say, is that more women don't have the power—a transformation that would automatically make the world a better place.

And so we punish men with a guilt-free heart, so sure are we of our virtuousness opposite the Brute; we leave men out

51

of the act of creation, the most powerful act in human life: we have babies by ourselves. We say there are no good men around, when in fact we are getting back at men. We are not thinking of the child; we are thinking of ourselves.

We control our lives only through the exclusion of men. Maybe in the workplace we can see ourselves as equal; even if we haven't yet found economic parity, we can compete with men for it. But when it comes to sex, we are not equal at all. He is not a slave to love. He owns his sexuality and we do not.

Here now is the heart of the issue, what this essay is about, and what we must take in if the next generation of women is to be more integrated, more independent and sexually responsible: We can learn economic independence at any time, but *age has a lot to do with learning to believe in one's sexual independence, learning the difference between love and sex.* Cash in the hand that pays the rent on a repeated basis, month after month, year after year, becomes a cold fact of life that tells the "littlest" woman she doesn't have to be taken care of. But it is very, very difficult to learn to believe in ourselves as sexual entities, with responsibility for our sexuality, late in life. Adolescence is late.

The best time is the first years of life and the best teacher is mother. There is no better way to learn the lessons masturbation teaches than as a baby learns, at the beginning. If mother doesn't allow us to believe that our body belongs to us alone, that we own it and are therefore responsible for it, then anything we do with our body later will refer back to her, reawakening our need of her, reawakening her attitudes, her judgment. When we have sex and don't protect ourselves, we are her bad little girl.

Here are two letters I received from readers of *My Mother/My Self.* They capture in a highly personal and, I think, charming way how very present mother is in our most intimate sexual moments.

The first letter is from a woman in Holland:

Somewhere in the middle of your book I did have to get some sleep and during that night came the following dream:

I was traveling by train. My mother was with me and we were sitting at a little table by the window. We both had the same little red handbags—almost like purses. My mother wanted something from her handbag and took the wrong one from the table. She opened it and saw it was mine.

"Mom, you have my bag."

"Oh, do I, well never mind, they are similar anyway."

"But I have all my things in there."

"Oh, well, if you are being so childish about it . . ."

And there, as she absentmindedly gave me my way, she wrote her name in my bag! I couldn't utter one word in astonishment. Case closed.

Hours later I realized in a shock what those intriguing red purses meant—she had stolen my sexuality and my person with it. She stole them so easily as if they meant nothing at all. And I just sat there and let her do it.

(In Dutch there is an old fashioned word for purse that is also used for vagina in slang.)

This was all. I couldn't resist sending my simple, beautiful and shocking dream to you.

The second letter is a poem sent to me by a man.

Here is a poem I wrote for you, Nancy:

Cuntrol—Mother or Daughter?
If I were an artist, I would draw for you and send
A picture of Everygirl, nude from bend to bend.
No pubic hair nor slit, but in that fire place
A recent, sweet photograph of dear mother's face
Smiling out at every guy, her lips stretched West to East,
Inviting him to her home for their sym-bi-ot-ic feast.
What mother has between her legs
Is anybody's guess.
If you are smart you'll never part
Them—for grandma's there to bless.

HOW MUCH HAVE WE REALLY CHANGED?

It is important to distinguish the three levels of change: Attitudes change most easily. Behavior follows at a slower pace. But our deep, unconscious feelings about what is right and wrong require generations to change, if they change at all.

We angrily deny that our own grown-up sexual behavior has anything to do with mother. As declarations of our independence and difference from her, we wear trendy, sexy clothes, talk the latest jargon, and genuinely believe we are light-years ahead of her. These are superficial changes, and they happen quickly, often overnight. We read a book, see a film, sit next to a brilliant, articulate stranger at dinner, and the next day we abandon the attitude about sex we've had all our lives. Suddenly adultery in a "meaningful" relationship doesn't sound so bad. Our attitude has changed.

It may take a bit longer before we act on our brave new opinion. We have an adulterous affair. But when we wake up in the stranger's bed after a night of abandoned sex, we feel dirty, guilty. We don't understand why. We have not taken into account the intractable unconscious.

We get our moral code, our deepest, often unconscious sense of what is right and wrong, from our parents, who got it from their parents. For example, when women who think themselves sexually independent and responsible nonetheless become pregnant, they may be acknowledging their unconscious guilt—that what they did was wrong. They may not have taken into account the third level of change.

In my eagerness to defend masturbation as a healthy, pleasurable, educational act, I do not mean to suggest that it should take the place of intimacy with another person. Some of the women in this book who talk of masturbating three or four times a day might be labeled compulsive by those who like to label—even if their masturbation is more life-enhancing than the five hours a day of television that much of society admits to watching.

Nor do I mean to lay yet another command performance on women who may choose not to masturbate. The operative word is "choice." Let me put it this way: I can imagine a sexually responsible woman who doesn't masturbate, but it sounds like the hard way.

Touching ourselves is the fundamental lesson in anatomy; learning what is "down there" makes us intelligent owners, more in control of what is ours. (It is sad but not surprising that many women say they don't use a diaphragm because they are afraid to touch themselves.) Being able to give ourselves an orgasm *is* sexual independence; though it's nice to have a partner, it's important to know that for sex to take place it isn't necessary. Giving ourselves an orgasm is the sexual equivalent of being able to pay our own rent.

THE CLOACA CONCEPT

What makes learning to masturbate so difficult late in life is that we have been raised to believe that the area between our legs is untouchable, dirty. We have come to loathe the sight and smell of our genitals, which are to be touched only in the process of wiping ourselves clean. It is an unnatural, learned revulsion that has been deeply and dutifully taken in as part of the early mother/child love exchange. Nothing was said, nothing need be said. The mental clitoridectomy is done in the name of mother love and with the full accord of society.

In time, the sight and smell of menstruation—the humiliation of possibly "spotting," soiling our clothes, publicly announcing what we have always felt, that our bodies are dirty—reinforce our feelings of repugnance. The secretive, folded design of our genitals further underscores our certainty that we were not meant to explore that area. We never solve the simple puzzle of our compact, really beautiful design because we have taken on the appraisal of the first person who removed our exploratory little fingers, who toilet trained us, and whose body is like ours. Once again it was not what she said. It was how she felt. She didn't like the sight and smell of our genitals any more than she liked her own.

When a boy enters our lives and wants to touch us there, of course it is unthinkable. We couldn't do such a thing. Why should he? Why does he want to? That a man dreams of parting our lips with his fingers, looking at it, putting his mouth there, is so upsetting to some women that no honey-tongued lover could convince us otherwise. The clitoris, urethra, vagina, and anus have come to be thought of as one filthy, indistinguishable mass "down there." This kind of thinking is called the Cloaca Concept. *Cloaca* is Latin for sewer.

I can't remember the name of the doctor or analyst who first used the term Cloaca Concept, but I remember my own emotional jolt of recognition. I was gathering material for *My Secret Garden,* and I could imagine the women who were contributing, oh so hesitantly, to my research twenty years ago feeling just that way about their genitals—a "sewer," something to be touched with the utmost hesitation.

In those days, we felt guilty about sex, acted guilty, and our sexual fantasies, focused mostly on being overpowered and forced into sex, reflected our deepest, unconscious feelings of guilt. I was so disturbed by the enormity of guilt in *My Secret Garden* that the day I finished, I wrote an outline for *My Mother/My Self,* which in its working drafts was titled *The First Lie.* There was never any question about what I would write next: I had to know the source of this terrible anxiety women felt not about something they had done but about the images in their minds. Who could possibly know what they were thinking?

I bumped into mother right away. Not an ogress, not a bad person (though some are), but a daughter herself. Mother usually passes on the wisdom of her own mother's day.

If I were writing *My Mother/My Self* today, I would put great emphasis on the role masturbation might play in our lives, how it could be one of the acts of self away from mother and into our own identity. I would explain how the exercise of touching ourselves affects self-esteem, which means having a good opinion of oneself. How can we think well of ourselves if we harbor a sewer?

But I couldn't write about the significance of masturbation fifteen years ago because I didn't yet know what the women in this book have taught me.

WHAT IS A REAL WOMAN?

You, the women who have encouraged me to continue thinking and writing about sex, tell me how much strength and self-knowledge you gain from your sexuality, and you say you understand the importance of masturbation. "A person's masturbation seems so, well, 'secret,'" one of you writes me. "It's about the most intimate thing one can talk about, the most revealing of one's hidden self."

You have taken courage and self-confidence from the women who came before you, the voices in *My Secret Garden*. I am always amazed at how those voices, now almost twenty years old, still speak to you and unlock your secret sexual selves. No man, no male voice—no matter how sweet and seductive—could have opened you up to accept your sexuality like those other women.

We are born of woman, we are ruled by woman. When another woman hurts us, leaving us momentarily out of the Nice Girl world, which was our refuge growing up, it pains and humiliates us more deeply than anything a man could do or say. When other women encourage us, there is nothing we cannot do.

The meaning of what it is to be a woman has never been more open-ended and therefore more filled with anxiety. We want to be independent/we want to be taken care of. We want men to treat us as sexual equals/we want men to sweep us away into sexual oblivion. We seduce men/we expect them to know, without being told, what it is we want done to our bodies. Men do their best, some better than others, but all work in the dark.

There is someone who does know what we want. Another woman. Who better than someone whose body is like ours, someone who understands what it is to be a woman? No lesson in geography needed here. No need to break the spell with the giving of cold directions: "Touch me here, kiss this, lick that." She already knows. Nor is there any sense of shame, anxiety about smell or taste; it is all familiar to her. And she is tender. She will take care of us as no man can, at least in fantasy.

No surprise then that the fantasy of sex with another woman is the most popular theme to emerge since the publication of *My Secret Garden.* Women who call themselves heterosexual, bisexual, and lesbian find something particularly arousing in reveries of lying beside another woman and enjoying sometimes tender sex but just as often sex as abandoned as anything imagined with a man.

When I was preparing research for *My Secret Garden,* there was little available for the chapter on sex between women. The material simply didn't surface. I believe the great popularity of this fantasy today reflects the growing complexity of women's real world, where we no longer know what we want, what a woman is; men, knowing even less than we, fail to live up to our increasingly angry expectations. It is as if we are staring into the mirror in some of these fantasies, trying to find ourselves in another woman's body. Part a search for solace and confirmation of our womanliness, part also an angry rejection of men, we turn to people who are like us for sexual release.

Only when the women in this book have children of their own will we see how genuinely they believe in their right to sexual freedom in general and masturbation in particular. Will they be generous enough to wish their daughters something better than what they had? In all of human life no one has more power over another person than a mother over a child. Mother does not have to be perfect. Nobody is. We learn to masturbate by ourselves. The only rules that need be taught are the rules of privacy.

But perhaps the most generous act of all is that mother free her daughter to find her own sexual way, to be different from her, to emulate and copy another woman. Being different from mother will always feel like betrayal unless mother genuinely means it when she says: "My daughter right or wrong. My daughter whether you masturbate or not." It must be said out loud. The daughter already knows how mother feels about everything. It is the courage and generosity, the honesty of mother saying the words that frees the girl. Nothing binds us closer to mother than lies.

The message might go something like this:

"I have problems with this business of sex, my darling. You know that. You know how I grew up. But I want your sexual life to be a wonderful one, and because I love you I want you to take care of yourself. Masturbation can teach you so much about yourself. Enjoy that part of your life. Go with my blessings."

Mother, let your little girl masturbate.

PART III

The Fantasies

A WORD ABOUT THE WOMEN
AND THEIR FANTASIES

Individual women have always tried to break out of the traditional constraints placed on women's sexuality, but in so doing, they did not feel any kinship or solidarity with femininity as a whole. They were adventuresses, scorning other women as tame and submissive. They may have been courageous, but they were alone in their desires, sociological dead ends. Nor were they role models for other women because their search for sexual satisfaction was outside what the society of their time still defined as feminine. "She thinks like a man" may have been meant as a compliment when said about Catherine of Russia, Edna St. Vincent Millay, or George Sand, but it was dismissal, too. It meant she wasn't womanly.

The women in this book, whose fantasies follow, come out of a unique time in history. The past twenty years produced an expression of female emotion that previous generations of women never dared to show. Anger, rage, competition, lust, and iron determination to control their own lives became street emotions, available to any woman to pick up and try on. Popular books like *Fear of Flying* and *The Women's Room* explored these raw feelings in a new, strident female voice. Articulate, defiant women were heard on television, their words appeared in magazines like *Ms,* and if a woman didn't want to see the film *Deep Throat* or take her clothes off with the other hedonists at Sandstone or Plato's Retreat, she knew these ideas and places existed.

After generations of limits, suddenly there were no limits. Sexual freedom was fresh and believable, and women trusted the new images and words of other women saying it was all right to be sexually in control and powerful. Discover your true sexual nature, the voices said; we, your sisters, promise maternal support and will catch you if you fall. The women in this book heard these new voices declaring there were No Rules, and out of this unstructured, limitless erotic ethos, the fantasy of the Great Seductress was born.

This desire to initiate and control sex—indeed to continue sex until the woman's full sexual appetite is satisfied—is the underlying theme of these new fantasies. There are other ideas, whole thematic chapters that might have been included here, such as Young Boys, Incest, Spanking, the Need for Approval, Romantic Interludes, Golden Showers, the Living Out of Fantasies. And of course, there is the fantasy of being raped/forced into sex, which still remains a major theme, along with its opposite and new counterpart, forcing/raping a man. These themes are explored in great length in *My Secret Garden* and *Forbidden Flowers.*

The themes in this book not only are new but also are the most prevalent in my research. They reflect changes in women's real lives, and they strike a consistent chord, revealing a depth and range in women's erotic nature that society is still loath to acknowledge.

Although the fantasies that follow tend to run long, don't take an elaborate scenario as the sole definition of a fantasy. It is possible, indeed inevitable, to enjoy brief erotic images throughout the day. The smell or sight of something that stimulates the imagination provokes a sexual picture in the mind. It is only when we begin to talk or write about these images that layers of detail emerge.

Many of these women have led quiet, even conservative lives. Some have had very little real sexual experience. It is in their fantasies that they try to free their sexuality from the iron rules that have always been clamped on untamed feminine eroticism to keep it from threatening the presumed needs of both men and society—which until recently have been synonymous. Above all, in fantasy they desire to escape at last from the guilt an erotic woman has had to carry if she fulfilled her nature. Though most say they have got beyond their mother's asexual training, none ever forgets the humiliation and fear of having been shamed by her for the earliest expression of sexual feeling.

Until now, until this generation, there has been in the conventional view no such thing as feminine lust. Locker room wisdom—as well as the consultation rooms of many psychiatrists—said that only men were capable of separating sex from emotion; women could enjoy sex only if presented to them within the context of an ongoing, emotional relationship. These women, of every age and socioeconomic class, say otherwise; their favorite erotic scenario is not about their husbands or lovers but about a man they will never see again, someone with whom there is no relationship.

Women want to change; a small fraction of the most courageous are changing. Men are not. The best women today find they are alone out there on the sexual frontier because the men who should be exploring that exciting, unknown place with them are still reluctant to abandon the missionary position and everything it stands for. Even if these men know how limited and suffocating life can be with a submissive woman, they nevertheless are not sure what the new woman is asking of them. Men's resistance to change is not totally without reason, given women's own confusion about their sexual identity. Out of this paralysis, a sullen resentment has grown between the sexes.

Having started the sexual revolution, women are responsible for finishing the job—for defining exactly what it is we want, and doing it in the most specific, sexual terms. For the next step to be taken, men must come to see women as other than some aggrieved, amorphous band of unhappy people with a lot of diffuse, unresolved demands. Instead, women must so enlarge their own conception of themselves that men will gladly exchange the false ego benefits of "masculine superiority" for the real satisfaction of sexual life with the kind of women they never imagined could exist.

Recognizing they have more to gain from mutual reinforcement and self-recognition than from age-old feelings of competition, the women in this book have established sexual community. They do not see one another as a threat but as people who are expanding the definition and limits of their sex. They know that their search for what it means to be a woman is shared by others—"Thank God I'm not alone, not the only one!" If most women are still afraid to use the new freedoms these pioneers have won, nevertheless there is not a literate woman alive today who is not aware that it is only her own choice that keeps these freedoms from her—and that if she is still afraid of them, most likely her daughter will not be.

The women in this book are searching for erotic choices in their real lives, trying to understand what prevents them from fully realizing these possibilities. Without social inhibitions or pretty language, their sexual fantasies deal with various strategies they have developed to get them past whatever it is in their earlier lives that stands in the way of exploring the limits of their true eroticism.

CHAPTER ONE

SEDUCTIVE, SOMETIMES SADISTIC, SEXUALLY CONTROLLING WOMEN

THE GREAT SEDUCTRESS: THE POWER OF THE PLEASURE GIVER

Ah, the joy of seduction! To take a man, lay him down and you on top, orchestrate his sounds of slow surrender with the shifting of your weight, the forbidden dirty words whispered in your female/mother voice, watch his gradual loss of control—no, control his loss of control—until ultimately, with the pressure and release of delicate vaginal muscles on his swollen penis, he comes.

What power to give another human being an orgasm. No, let me change the verb because it is important, what this chapter is about: What power to *make* someone come. "I'm the dominant one doing all the work and he's the receptive one," Sue describes her seduction. "My pleasure is in knowing what abandonment he has felt . . . seeing him change from cool sophisticated male to a man in the throes of sexual release."

I love this opening section of women who dream of leading a man into orgasmic pleasure, reversing the old roles and for a change assuming the position and power of the one who controls the transcendency of fulfilling sex. If I elaborate here at the outset of a chapter that runs the gamut of control, from pleasure to pain, it is because like many other women, I resonate to the idea of chartering a man's pleasure.

Have you seduced a man? Thought of it? Perhaps the idea doesn't appeal. Being the one in charge isn't a universal fantasy, doesn't even appeal to all men, though seduce they must, at least in reality, or fail as "real men."

The timid boy, genetically and temperamentally shy or simply not cut out for seduction, given the early environment in which he was raised, must do the most frightening thing when adolescence erupts: make the first move, pick up the telephone and risk the torture of rejection. In time, he will lead a woman into what he hopes is a proper restaurant, where he must pay before maneuvering her to a car, an apartment, a sofa, eventually a bed, where carefully, expertly he must conduct a seduction of a person raised to say no even when she means yes.

I can remember such a shy boy from my earliest adolescence. He was at least four inches shorter than I and had been ordered by his mother to take me to our first Yacht Club regatta dance. For months I had dreamed to the sound of recorded music that another boy, Malcolm, would be my date. Malcolm, a born leader whom other boys followed as naturally as girls followed me, the captain of their team and president of the class, the tomboy who had led them to the top of the highest trees.

There is an even earlier night in memory—a party on a beach, a game we girls and boys had played countless times. The game was Red Rover, and when your name was called you would race across the beach toward the opposite team, who stood arms tightly linked, and attempt to break their line. Breaking the line out of sheer, unladylike determination wasn't new to me, but what I felt that night early in my adolescence was a unique rush, a sexual desire to claim, capture the boy of my dreams and victoriously take him back to my team. I chose Malcolm, of course.

And I would have gladly chosen him for that wretched Yacht Club dance, telephoned him without hesitation—yes, even risked rejection. Mine was the heart of a leader, already used to the wins and losses of childhood contests. Though I longed to rest my head against his shoulder in the first dance, I would have assumed my share of responsibility in exploring the mysterious pull toward him that I had felt on that palm-swept beach. I am not talking about sexual intercourse, for which I wasn't ready, but about the first innocent steps of the mating ritual, in which I was ready to be an equal partner.

But the rules of adolescence didn't permit me to follow my nature. The night of the dance I took my first step backward into passivity, a stance of acquiescence alien to the girl I was. I went to the Yacht Club with that poor, timid boy, who was as unhappy as I. He left me there an hour after we arrived, and I stood against the wall the entire night watching the dancing girls whose leader I had been. The only action I took that was true to my nature was to refuse to retreat to the ladies' room until someone's father finally drove me home.

With iron determination and out of terrible need for the love of boys, I learned quickly to squeeze myself into the small stereotypical female role. I bit my tongue, slowed my pace, learned to wait, and waited. There was no room in the Nice Girl mold for most of the abilities I had spent my first eleven years perfecting.

I left the best parts of myself back there on the brink of adolescence, the risk taker, the assertive, confident girl who believed in a self she had made by hand. Eventually when sex did occur, I didn't act on my true responsible nature but on the false self I'd constructed to conform to The Rules of female adolescence: I used no form of contraception, allowed someone else to take responsibility for my sex, my life.

I realize that things have changed and that adolescents today no longer treat each other as aliens, which is good. But the frightening rise in teenage pregnancies says that in their sexual lives, they are as confused as we were. They punish themselves by using no contraceptive protection, and we, the grown-ups, punish them for not being able to figure out how to live in a society that is brazenly sexual on the outside and deeply puritanical and twisted about sex on the inside.

Technically, I remained a virgin until I was twenty-one. It was fool's luck that I didn't get pregnant considering the sexual games I played, loving the heat of everything-but-full-insertion sex. Terrified of getting pregnant, dreading a too early marriage that would cut short my dream of seeing the world, I jeopardized everything again and again. Addicted to men, I shed my responsible self every time I shed my clothes to lie down beside them and allow myself to be Swept Away, not like a woman but a silly, acquiescent little girl.

I saw the world, and along the way I learned to use a diaphragm and then the pill. But it wasn't until I became a writer that I began to understand how my destructive relationships with men were patterned on what I wished I'd had with my mother; in handing my self to them—without contraceptive protection—I was asking them to take care of me in a way that she never had, the way a baby needs to be taken care of.

In choosing to write about the forbidden subjects of sexuality, mothers and daughters, jealousy and envy, I was trying to recapture some of the early bravery that was my nature, and which I had worked so hard to unlearn. Today is the best time in my life; I feel I have finally come full circle, having reclaimed the brave girl of my eleventh year.

I've told my story at length because I believe there are millions of women who begin life as brave as their brothers. The women in this chapter represent a generation that hasn't felt obliged to deny assertiveness, the desire to initiate and control sexual pleasure if only in fantasy. When the man Mary desires doesn't respond in reality, "his rejection of me makes me more determined to experience him sexually . . . So in my fantasy, I'm in control, I call the shots. I explore every last inch of his body, and do every pleasurable thing to him that's imaginable . . . I'm the pleasure giver."

The heart of the risk taker, the responsible one, the great

seducer, is not broken by society's rules, only quieted and waiting for the voices of other women, perhaps mine and these women's, to reassert itself. Women like Celia, still too shy to practice seduction in reality, rehearse in fantasy: "I tug at his shirt, popping off a few buttons in my hurry," she says. "I feel like an animal; I'm different from how he has always seen me. He's inspired by my hunger, carried away by lust."

While men are usually bigger and stronger, they have no monopoly on courage. I don't know where these new seductresses learned to practice bravery, but if they take it in so that it becomes part of their trusted selves, they may pass it on to their daughters. And if mothers raise their girls to take the initiative rather than wait, we may eventually have a generation of women more responsible for their sex. When you set your sights on the man you want, know why you want him, and accept that he might reject you, you are already more in charge than the woman who waits to be picked like a cookie on a platter.

If a woman has seduction in mind when she begins an evening, she is more likely to bring along her diaphragm as well as her wallet and keys.

Most significant events are preceded by a fantasy of what will happen. If the fantasy is one of being chosen, being kissed, being led like the walking blind into a dark chamber where, magically, the romantic feeling of surrender is made to happen, how can a woman break the spell by introducing the sexually responsible act of getting up and going into the bathroom and inserting her diaphragm?

If the fantasy begins, however, with, First I will telephone him, and if he says yes, I will suggest this cozy restaurant, followed by sex, skillfully orchestrated by me. Then, of course, I will have along my diaphragm because I don't want to get pregnant and have to either get an abortion or end my adventure as the Great Seductress.

"Younger guys are much more open to the assertive woman, having grown up with the women's movement," says Cassie, who translates competition with a man in the workplace into sexual tension. "My successive climbs up the corporate ladder provoked incredible arousing fantasies where I'd subdue my opponent and make firm but tender love to him. I know it sounds crazy but I became orgasmic for the first time during these fantasies!" As the women in this section attest, being the one in charge can be a great high, so much so that Cassie actually seduces a younger man with whom she works. "My seduction of him was motherly and nurturing, not sadistic," she says, "and he *really* cared about pleasing me. Our freedom to reverse roles and express our real selves made intimacy soar."

I wonder how men will respond to these fantasies, since they often dream of a woman as sexual as they who, for a change, takes care of the man's seduction, his orgasm, everything. Of course, the man is controlling his own fantasy, which is what allows him to let go in the hands of such a powerful woman. Ideally, sex "is a mutual experience," says Liz following her fantasy seduction of a man: "He kisses me gratefully, and I kiss him with equal gratitude." In these happy fantasies, power too is ultimately what makes the woman come.

I have saved my comment on Gabby's fantasy of initiating her son into sex because she is the only mother in my research to admit to the idea, though I imagine it commonplace but quickly repressed. Fathers have much less day-to-day contact with their daughters than mothers have with sons, yet how much more readily we admit to a man's incest fantasies, an idea discussed and written about throughout literature. Perhaps mothers' incest fantasies are seldom heard as explanation for their stepping back emotionally and physically from their sons because mother doesn't step back, withdraw, not ever.

A mother has total physical and psychological access to her boy while he lives under her roof. Men tell me of mothers who crawled into their beds to sleep beside them, who kissed, touched, held them whenever, however they chose. It wasn't sexual intercourse, but it was a complete sexual seduction. Many men never escape their mothers' hold over them, though both mother and son would be loath to call it a sexual hold. Certainly she stars forever, in various disguises, in his fantasies.

A boy cannot tell his mother where to draw the line—a part of him doesn't want her to—nor does society scold her for acts a father would be jailed for committing with his daughter. The line can only be drawn by mother herself, a line that is probably harder than ever to draw in single-parent families. But draw it she must; otherwise mother love can slip into an invasion of privacy, an erotic intrusion that distorts the boy's growth into his own sexuality separate from her, his first Great Seductress to whom no future woman can ever compare.

Cassie

My fantasies are, I think, particularly liberating, as they concern being assertive. First, information: Age—29; job—middle manager for investment brokerage firm; marital status—single; education—MBA.

My fantasies really started as I moved up the corporate ladder and competed with men. With my MBA, job offers were no problem. I picked the one that I found most interesting. Well, very soon I found myself in the new (for me) position of competing with and supervising males. This is an increasingly common and complicated issue in business and the professions today, as you know. Let me just write about how (to my shock) it affected me sexually. I found that when I was in a competitive or supervisory capacity with guys, a real sexual tension entered into the situation. I started to fantasize the situation in sexual terms. If a guy my age, or younger, and I were competing for an assignment or promotion, I would imagine us in a sexual encounter in bed (if the guy was attractive). Our competition was symbolized by each of us wrestling to get "on top" of the other sexually.

My successive climbs up the corporate ladder provoked incredibly arousing fantasies where I'd subdue my opponent and make firm but tender love to him! I know it sounds crazy but I became orgasmic for the first time during these fantasies! I became bold and found I could be multi-orgasmic if I chose; a frightening discovery at first. I had no idea I could be so sexual! Through your books and others I learned female sexuality was okay, even a positive good! A complementary fantasy appeared when I was supervising guys—mostly recent college grads younger than I. This new situation was represented in fantasies of guys being "under" my sexual tutelage. The more assertive my role in these fantasies, the wetter I got!

This was true, too, in the office. I'd be instructing a male trainee in his duties and I'd feel this *rush* of sexual pleasure; it's fantastic! I couldn't wait to go home and masturbate. I felt no guilt! Well, there was only one more thing to explore—*acting out!* Did I have the nerve? Not with my conservative upbringing, but it's well known that romantic/sexual attraction makes one bolder; we usually think men have it, but it works for women too. It's nature's way of getting people together.

Well, I took particular fancy to one male trainee who is younger than I. He is quite shy and deferential to me. Younger guys are much more open to the assertive woman, having grown up with the women's movement. This guy was so sweet that I practically had to order him to call me by my first name rather than Ms. Blake. We really liked each other in a delightful sort of older sister/younger brother way. I took the lead, asking him to lunch to discuss business and he seemed in awe of my power (and my American Express card) the way women have traditionally fallen for successful men. Needless to say, I had never been the object of male adoration before, and I *loved* it. I took the lead in our romance and *he* loved it! I'd give him an affectionate squeeze around the shoulders and I could feel him tremble. We gradually became more and more intimate, at my pace. And I do mean *intimate,* not just sexual—there's a *big* difference as you know! In bed, my seduction of him was motherly and nurturing, not sadistic, and he *really* cared about pleasing me. Our freedom to reverse roles and express our real selves made intimacy soar. Anyway, we're still together even though I make twice the money he does. We don't care! The older sister/younger brother aspect is really wonderful. I'm his mentor and he adores me.

Mary

On impulse and feeling as though I had nothing to lose, I gave my fantasy to my fantasy man to read.

Before giving it to him I explained that it was only my fantasy, and hoped that he would not be angry or upset with me after reading it. With a big, wide grin on his face he assured me he would not become angry or upset.

Needless to say, the rest of the day and entire night, I was nervous, hyped out and very excited. I fantasized his reaction to my fantasy, and to me, and his comments on how descriptive my fantasy was. When I went to pick up my lengthy fantasy, I was very sexually aroused, and truly expected he would make my fantasy a reality. But, true to form, he remained in control but very flattered, and I left his office consumed with disappointment.

I did explain to him that, knowing he read my fantasy, I was less obsessed with wanting to make love to him. I told him I felt more relaxed, as in my mind I did make love to him, in the only way he would allow.

But dear God, I still crave him, and desire him every time I see him. I've noticed a change in him toward me, he's more guarded, and I have not received any more winks. But I am not going to give up, because I'm certain that if I just wait, one day it will be the right time.

I am a 32-year-old college graduate and the mother of a 9-year-old son. My husband and I have been married for eleven years, the past five years being very happy and satisfying years.

I was born in Georgia, and when I reached the age of 10, my parents uprooted my two older sisters and me, and moved us to Florida. I am a good old Southern girl, and although I have lost most of my Southern accent, there is still a noticeable trace, which becomes more pronounced when I'm excited. My Southern roots, accent, and family ties are, I feel, the things that are responsible for making me who I am.

In physical appearance, I am what some men and women would consider "cute." I am very small-boned, petite, have an athletic body, am five feet and weigh ninety-seven pounds. I'm dark in coloring, caramel colored with a tan, and have dark brown eyes and short brown hair with golden streaks all through it. Being tiny in stature has never presented any deep psychological problems for me. If anything, my smallness, even into my adult life, has only gotten me positive and favorable attention. Ironically, I am not the dependent, shy, unsure type of person one would attribute to someone who is mothered by others. I am very outgoing, make friends easily, enjoy people and working with the public.

It seems the men who become interested in me usually do so because they misread my friendliness and believe I am "coming on" to them. If I like or enjoy a person, I express my feeling through touching, hugs, as I love to make body contact. However, my outward signs of affection are usually nonsexual. I am very selective and have been attracted physically to perhaps four or five men in my adult life. When men, and also a few women, misread my friendliness and become aggressive sexually toward me, I'm always surprised, and am awkward when I try to clear up the crossed signals. I do enjoy the feeling of being the "one in control" in these types of situations.

Which leads me to my most frequent and favorite fantasy, one which I use over and over and over, whenever I masturbate manually (several times a day) or when using my Water Pik shower massager. All I have to do is close my eyes and focus on my fantasy man, and I immediately become excited, and I have to touch my already very wet pussy.

The man in my fantasy is a real person, with whom I have a friendly, working type relationship. He is a few years older than I am, a professional, large-framed, and has somewhat of a potbelly. He is definitely not the Romeo type, and is not flirty or aggressive with women. He doesn't radiate sex appeal, like some men, so not all women are drawn to him like a magnet. Except me. Ever since I met him, I have been drawn to him physically and emotionally. He is extremely sexy to me, with his shy, boyish charm and his big brown eyes. When he looks at me, he makes me feel as if I'm naked. That's all he's ever done to me is look at me. I have been very open and obvious in my attempts to seduce him, but he is not the least bit interested in me sexually. He is flattered by my interest in him, and desire for him, but he just isn't interested in having a physical relationship with me. His rejection of me makes me more determined to experience him sexually, and I am obsessed with desire for him.

My womanly instincts tell me that I have a positive effect on him, that he's attracted to me, and probably wants to fuck my brains out, if only to find out if I'm as good as I appear to be. I have only to see him or have him wink at me as we pass one another, and my pussy starts to tingle and the crotch of my panties becomes sopping wet. He has never said or done anything to me, being always very careful not to lead me on. To finally have his hard cock inside me, wanting me, would be the ultimate for me. But try as I may, I cannot break him down, he's just too strong for me, and has too much self-control.

So, I hold back when my mind and body tell me to go on, grab his crotch, rub him until his cock is rock hard and ready to burst out of his pants. But in my fantasy I'm in control, I call the shots. I explore every last inch of his body, and do every pleasurable thing to him that's imaginable. In my fantasy, we have hours of raw, physical, bedrolling sex that I want to have so badly.

My fantasy man is in my home, we're all alone, drinking wine, and having a casual conversation. Having him *all to myself*, without outside interruptions, so near to me, has put my hormones in a frenzy. He's telling me about an old back injury, and how much pain it gives him when it flares up. He confides in me that his back is hurting him now. After another glass of wine, I convince him to allow me to give him a back massage, and I promise him that I won't bother him sexually. He's skeptical, hesitant, but follows me into my spare room where I have a four-poster bed. He pulls his shirt out and raises it up to the middle of his chest. I know he's anxious about being in my home, alone with me, and the fact that I will soon be touching his body. I know he's wondering if he will be able to control himself and keep his emotions intact. He lies down on his stomach, complaining to me that he really shouldn't be here. I begin to massage his back, my hands are so strong, and feel so good, all lotioned up, moving all up and down his shoulder blades all the way down to his lower back. I feel him relaxing, his muscles becoming less tense, and my firm hand movements become very slow and deliberate. Soon I hear his breathing become heavier, and I know he has fallen asleep, thanks to the wine and my soothing massage. Very quietly I reach under the bed and pull out four large scarves, hidden there earlier, just for this happening. I very skillfully tie his wrists and ankles to the posts on the bed, making sure that each scarf is loose enough, so he will be able to lift and move his limbs.

I climb back onto his back, and continue with the massage, knowing full well how angry he will be when he awakens, but not really caring. Of course, he wakes up, feeling my body weight pressing on his back. I continue with my massage, listening to him laughing (as it's comical to him at first), then complain at my tying him up. He tells me the joke is over, now to please untie him, but he's not as angry or upset at me as I thought he would be. He struggles to pull his arms free, but realizes his attempts are futile, as he's tied too tightly and securely. I tell him not to resist me, to let me do what I want to do and I promise I will untie him, but he has to be a good boy. Besides, since he is tied up, I tell him he might as well relax and enjoy all the delicious things I am going to do to him. I remind him that I am in control now, not him. Then, I remove his socks and shoes.

I begin to massage his left foot, rubbing the top of it lightly, and scratching on and around his ankle. I feel him relax just a little. He still doesn't trust me. I move my mouth down to his toes and begin licking and sucking on each toe, moving my mouth up and down, as if each of his toes were a tiny cock. He moans a little and asks me why do I want to do this? I tell him that I love his toes, and how excited it makes me. Oh God, he says to me, I've never had anyone do this to me before, I can't believe how good it feels. I spend at least ten minutes loving his toes and ankle, making sucking noises as I slowly move my mouth and lips up his leg, pushing his pants leg up as I explore. Feeling more confident, and hearing no negative comments from him, I reach under him and unfasten his belt and unbutton his pants. I'm so excited now that my hands are visibly shaking, but as big as he is, I manage to pull his pants down to his ankles. Once again, I straddle him and begin to caress his lower back, and using butterfly strokes, massage his buttocks and thighs. I start kissing his lower back, licking and nibbling on him, as I slowly move down to his buttocks, and then to his thighs which are clasped very tightly together. I use my nails on his thighs, scratching them very lightly, and I start moving my tongue between his legs that are still closed tightly. I notice that as he opens his thighs an inch or so, I can move my roving tongue more deeply inside. He's wearing white boxer shorts, and I unfasten them, and very slowly push them down. He lifts his hips, helping me in the process. Oh my God! I see his naked buttocks, gorgeous, plump cheeks, for the first time, and I'm so excited that I actually scream out in pleasure. I feel my juices seeping out of me, flowing onto my inner thighs, feeling sticky, but I love it. I tell myself to calm down, that I'm the pleasure giver, that later, if things work out as I've fantasized they would, I will get as much as I'm giving.

I grab and squeeze each cheek, and bury my face in his ass, licking and kissing it all over. When I stick out my tongue and lick his crotch, gently at first, then more forcefully, he begins to moan in pleasure and squirm. I ram his hole with my tongue and move my mouth down to his tight, firm balls. I take each ball in my mouth, sucking gently, and lapping them up and down with my tongue. He's covered with my saliva and I use it on my fingers, as I delicately massage the area between his asshole and balls. Now, he is up on his knees, so excited that he is moving his body front and backwards. Tiny as I am, I am able to crawl up under him, although he is still tied. I begin to lick his very erect nipples, going from one to the other. As I suck on his nipples, scraping them lightly with my teeth, he lies down on me, and I can feel his by now fully erect, hard cock pressing into my stomach. He begs me to unfasten his wrists so he can touch and fondle my breasts. He still hasn't kissed me, but our faces are so close that I'm dying to taste him, suck on his tongue, and eventually taste my juices in his mouth. He tells me to untie him so he can feel and touch my pussy, so he can see how wet I am, and see how ready I am. So I relent and untie not only his wrists but also his ankles, as now he is more than ready for me. With his hands free, the first thing he does is pull my thin T-shirt up and over my head, revealing my tanned, swollen and erect breasts and nipples. He gasps, as he grabs one of my breasts, cupping it, and rubbing the tip of my nipple with his thumb. He pulls my breast into his mouth, sucking so hard on it that I almost cry out in pain. He flips me over onto my back. Now, he's really excited, breathing heavily, his eyes are full of his want and desire for me. He moves down, unsnaps my shorts, unzips them, and pulls them down and off me. Now his hands are caressing my lower body, gently at first, but then more forcefully. He tells me how he loves how firm I feel, muscular, yet so womanly.

I move my hips back and forth, feeling his dick head against my swollen clit. I feel his entire body tense up, and his heart is thumping from the want of me, but I'm not ready for him. I'm still the pleasure giver, and I want to suck and taste his cock before he shoots his come deep inside of me. He flips me over to where my pussy is in direct contact with his swollen, ready love tool. I wriggle out of his hold, and move my face and head down to his lower stomach and start licking and sucking on and around his navel, sticking my tongue directly into it, digging in, and jabbing it. I start kissing his pubic hair, making sure not to make contact with his cock, which has been hard for almost an hour, and he is becoming impatient. I know he can't stand it anymore, so I very quickly lick the head of his cock with my tongue. He screams out at me in anticipation and excitement and grabs my head with his two strong hands and pushes my mouth down on his ready to shoot cock. I love to talk dirty when I have sex, and I tell him how much I love his cock, how good he tastes, and how I've waited for this day, this moment, for so long. I can feel his cock growing bigger in my mouth and I know he is ready to shoot his thick creamy come down my throat, as I deep-throat him. When he orgasms, he comes in spasms, which makes his whole body shake. I love the way his come tastes, just like I dreamed it would, and the way it shoots out of him and spurts right down my throat. After he calms down, I lap up what come seeps out, because I want it all.

His breathing becomes quieter and his muscles less tense, all except one muscle, his cock. I lie down on top of him, covering him with my body, burying my face in his neck and shoulder. I begin to tongue-fuck his ear. I tell him how much I want him, and how I want to feel him inside me, filling me up completely. As I bite and suck on his neck, he takes my face in his hands so gently, and presses his open mouth down on mine. He tongue lashes my entire face, even pushing the tip of his tongue up into my nostrils, and around on my eyes. *I love it!* Every nerve in my face is tingling alive. My pussy is throbbing and twitching now.

I'm so hot, I can barely stand it, and he knows it, as I can't keep my hips still. I wrap my firm thighs around his hips, and position my pussy to where he can penetrate and enter me. I bear down and, more determined, push harder against his cock, this time causing him to enter me. Once he's inside me, he pushes harder to experience all of me. He starts to move his cock very slowly in and out—tormenting me. I can't stand it, and I tell him to fuck me, please, baby, fuck me hard—*ram* that sweet, hard cock all the way in—up to my heart. He begins to move faster, thrusting his cock deeper and deeper. I love it so much that I lift my knees all the way up, until they're pressing against my shoulders. I'm opened wide for his big, hard fucking tool, and our bodies move together in perfect rhythm. The sound of our thighs slapping against one another and the feel of his balls against me drive me crazy. When I yell out that I'm coming, he rams his cock faster and harder, faster and deeper, and I have my first shattering orgasm. He keeps riding me, working on his second orgasm. I keep telling him what a good fucker he is, how I love his hard cock, kissing him, tonguing him, loving him. I flip him over, and straddle him, keeping his still die-hard cock inside of me, not allowing it to slip out. I begin to "milk" his cock with my vaginal muscles, gripping it, and letting it slide in and out. I do this several times with my snapper-tight pussy, and after the third time he screams and has his second orgasm. I can feel his come shoot into me. Now I'm ready for a second orgasm and I begin to move my hips, but as I do this, I feel his cock slip out of me. I wriggle down to lick him clean, and to taste and lap up my love juices. We're in a 69 position, and I feel his tongue on my swollen clit. I feel his tongue push into me probing like a tiny cock. He begins to suck and lap my cunt, sucking his come right out of me. He lifts my legs over his shoulders, burying his face in me. He nibbles, bites me, sucking me until I yell out that I'm coming. Oh my God, it's so good, I can't stand it. He slowly licks me after I come, and I reach out for him. We lie in each other's arms, savoring the moment, holding each other. We know that this afternoon, as fantastic as it was, will be our last together. It will have to live in our memories. We don't talk about it, but we both know. We had to be together, to experience one another so we can get on with our lives. As I walk him to the door, he turns and hugs me up to him. He asks me how I learned to do that with my pussy, that no woman had ever done that to him before, milked and gripped his cock. I smile at him and say, I told you I was good, and after being with me one time, I'd get into your blood. He winks at me, and looks deeply into my eyes, and I get that old familiar twitch and tingle in my pussy that I thought after our afternoon together would be gone.

Lynn
I am 17, soon to be a high school senior. I lost my virginity at 15, which seems to be representative of most young women in my school.

When sex in its many glorious forms was new to me, my fantasies were simply replays of my most recent sexual encounters. I am now with my second lover—also 17— whom I had the pleasure of debauching, and the two of us enjoy exploring new pleasures together. We have found, for example, that an occasional "toy," such as ice, Kahlua, or cherry pie filling can add spice to our lovemaking. (We like to think we are sexually a step above our peers, who are struggling with zippers and guilt complexes in dark, cramped back seats.)

There is something delicious about the idea of sleeping with one's teacher, that respected role model, that pillar erected by society to represent all that is "moral" to the corruptible youth of today. Some male teachers possess a certain cerebral sexiness that tempts one to fuck not only their bodies, but also their scholarly minds, as if they could simultaneously fill the cunt with semen and the head with knowledge. Vicarious education. I would not like to see this fantasy lived out for the obvious problems it would present when grades were to be given out.

Other fantasies of mine deal with a mentor/pupil theme, and I can play cither role with equal satisfaction. As a pupil, I create an attractive, older man who could teach me all about world literature, philosophy, art history, politics, social problems, everything . . . including, of course, sex. When I play the role of mentor, I envision myself as a woman somewhere in her twenties or thirties to whom virginal young men seeking an exciting but gentle introduction to sex could come for patient, personal instruction. I would, of course, be in great demand, but I would not accept any money for my services. After selecting a new student that I wish to nurture, I talk with him about anything and everything, allowing him to test the water, to get comfortable with me. When a rapport was established, I would proceed to introduce him to the physical: kisses, caresses, massages, shared bubble baths. Then off to the sexual: mutual masturbation, oral sex, intercourse. I would guide him at first, then allow him to take the lead. At last, I would pat him on the ass and send him out into the world with a better emotional and sexual understanding of women than many men.

One of my recent fantasies was created to entertain my lover. I'm not sure where it came from:

A man (who is faceless and therefore interchangeable) is about to make a speech to a large auditorium full of people. It is an important speech, and he has prepared it painstakingly. The audience eagerly awaits to hear him. He steps out to the podium. He speaks earnestly for five minutes or so, then slowly realizes that a pair of hands, warm and soft, are tugging at his zipper and stroking his pants between his legs. He tries to step back from the podium, but I hold onto his leg. To avoid appearing awkward, he stays. My hands continue their work. Trapped, he grows hard. Now he wouldn't dare step from the podium.

I set his cock free and take it into my mouth. My tongue, lips and hands perform better than ever before. He struggles to appear calm as he approaches his climax. His face is flushed and he is sweating profusely, but he continues to speak. The audience is enthralled. His hips begin to actively thrust his eager cock into my mouth seeking even greater sensations. Faster. He can't hold back anymore. He comes, screaming out the last words of his speech, and the audience goes wild, giving him (us) a standing ovation.

Liz

I am 22 years old, a college graduate (business), single, divorced already, but living happily with my boyfriend.

Just about ten minutes ago I settled myself at my desk, scooched down in my chair, put my right arm down by my side and under the desk, pulled my blue jeans skirt over to the right side a little and due to the nice slit up the front and my lack of underwear, proceeded to finger myself as I thought of a teacher who taught at my high school. He was dark and virile looking with a luscious moustache. I knew he was attracted to me; we joked and laughed and kidded all the time, with the sexual innuendos centering in our eye contact and excited laughter. This teacher also had a combination storeroom/office in which he would go in behind me and lock the door. We would kid and joke and finally he would come up behind me and play with my breasts and tease my nipples into attention. We would rub a lot and get all hot and bothered. We never actually did it there in his office, he was afraid we would be found out, but believe me, I surely wanted to as badly as he did.

One of my fantasies takes place in a public restroom, the kind with one lavatory and one stall. I see from my office window a construction crew across the street from the building. They are installing a concrete sidewalk. They are all pretty muscular and naturally wearing ragged, holey blue jeans and no shirts. They notice me standing in the window watching and make a few catcalls and jeers, but this doesn't bother me since I'm interested in one guy in particular. He is gorgeous as most construction workers seem to be, golden tan, defined muscles, cute-cute ass, golden curly hair, strong rugged face. He keeps glancing my way and I continue to watch him work. This goes on for a few days. I wave to him when the crew arrives in the morning. I watch him a lot during the day. When I drive by in the evenings I wave and he looks at me and waves slowly with meaning (or so I imagine). Well, finally one day he stops my car and asks my name. I tell him and I learn his name is Wayne. I suggest that we get together for lunch sometime. Sure enough, the next day he comes over and gets me. We have a nice lunch in the cafeteria next door and talk about each other, the usual stuff, family, hobbies, etc. Discovering that I am really turned on by just sitting near this guy, I begin to squirm a little in my seat as I feel my wetness start to spread. He presses his smiling face across the table to me and breathes heavily while at the same time putting his hand on my thigh under the table (either his arms are unusually long or the table is short . . . well this is a fantasy . . .). He scooches his chair closer to the table and is able to just reach my juicy wetness and stroke his fingertips through it. All the while he is grinning at my efforts to continue my meal. I suggest that we walk back to my office via the "back way" which is a long deserted hallway where the restrooms are. I stop in front of the ladies' room and say that I have to go. He volunteers to help me with my zipper and we both giggle and crowd through the door. Once in the stall, we kiss and fondle one another. He turns me around, lifts my skirt and pulls his dick from his pants. From the rear he slides in around my crack and over and around my juicy cunt. I am bending over with one hand on my knee and one hand on the wall and am barely able to stand the excitement, knowing that at any second he is going to plunge his throbbing rod into my willing, twitching pussy. At that second, he does! It is ecstasy! He pumps and grinds in a circular motion and then changes to hard thrust-thrust-thrust. It doesn't take very long for both of us to come as he has been stroking my clitoris at the same time. We shudder and hold on for dear life as our abdomens stiffen, our legs stretch, and our backs arch as we groan in pleasure. Silent except for our heavy, contented breathing and sighs of relief, we slowly dress each other, caressing and lingering. He kisses me gratefully and I kiss him with equal gratitude, for it was a mutual experience. We walk to my office and he delivers me to my door with a lusty look in his eyes that promises more delicious lunches to come.

Gabby

My strongest reactions to your book *Men in Love* came when I read the last chapter—I suddenly started crying. I was surprised since I am a psychiatric social worker with many years of therapy, etc. Why was I crying?

Well, for one thing, I am furious at having been a virgin so long myself. I was brought up with sexual restrictions, having been born in 1936 into a rigid Protestant family—the first child. The big thing in my household was to prevent my getting "knocked up"—plus I was supposed to marry well and up everyone's social status. While I was taught that sex had negative consequences—primarily unwanted pregnancy—I was also quick to seize upon the fact that my vagina was my power!! No one was making such a fuss over my high IQ!! I am now a beautiful and sensuous woman and have fought for my sexual rights and freedom to enjoy what was so long denied me—the pleasure of sex. And it has been a fight but worth it!!!

Not only did I think of myself as a virgin teenager who was fearful yet longing to know what all the fuss was all about; but I now have three beautiful, sensual teenaged sons. I assume they are all virgins, but who knows? The 16-year-old has had opportunities, I'm certain. I'm pretty sure the 14-year-olds are, even though they have healthy attitudes toward their young girlfriends, and are able to touch and tease them freely in front of their parents (us). This is probably because my husband and I touch each other and are openly affectionate in front of our sons—unlike what I saw in my household when I was growing up. (It is part of my fight to break these patterns in my children also.) Anyway, I sense that my boys are the boys in your pages, with similar longings and desires. How can we adults make it easier? How can I assure my sons that they will measure up—that they are wonderful and desirable? How can I tell them I would like to help them some way? That I feel powerless to instruct them any more than I already have. I would like to instruct them in intercourse—in my fantasy I teach them how to be lovers and how to enjoy this aspect of living, as I have taught them to eat and to use the toilet and to answer the telephone and lock the door and build sand castles and swim and look people in the eye when you say hello! Why do we leave the important things to chance? I know my sons are healthy emotionally and will make good choices in sex. This is an area in which I as a parent am shut out. I accept that this has to be—in order for them to leave me and become involved with appropriate females of their own age. In my fantasy I am their teacher and break them in, noting how their penises have grown since they were little and assuring them that they are adequate in size and now able to compete with Daddy. Who knows, without actually measuring, maybe they even surpass him? I assure them that their size is adequate and get them forever rid of that particular hang-up. Then (actually this is all done one at a time so as not to have any competition) we try all kinds of positions. They get to experience a woman's taste and smell via oral sex even though they are not as interested in this as much as penile penetration. I assure them that oral sex is a delight for the woman even though some women are at first shy until they try it and like it. I then perform a delightful blow job on the one with me. He likes it and understands the delight of being passive and just receiving pleasure from another person. There goes another hang-up. Then we gently try some anal coitus, which is hard for me because I was abused with enemas as a child. I explain how this can be very sensuous but is often painful and needs added lubrication like Vaseline.

We go over all the places that one cannot normally see. I explain what is the vulva, the lips, the clitoris, the vagina, and which parts have sensation. I show them a vibrator and explain how it works and how to use it for additional sexual enjoyment. This is all very natural and free and they learn this as easily as they learned to swallow Pablum. I tell them that while I am their teacher I am not their woman. They will have to find their own woman. I trust it will be easier now because they will know a lot more about women. They can help the woman (or girl) to be freer and to just enjoy.

I would like to do this in real life, but will not because I am too afraid of any negative consequences and having my boy's libido tied up with me. I feel assured that just my fantasy of doing this and wishing for them to be free as well as to be able to leave me will be unconsciously transmitted. I also visualize my husband having some part in this education—perhaps by fucking me in front of them at the end to assert his own manhood and reestablish the generational boundaries. I know he would want a part in this as he is a very special father. He has been actively involved in their upbringing, not turning over his sons to me in a "here, you raise them attitude" (which I would not have allowed).

I want to tell you of one experience I actually had which illustrates how hard it is to be a sex educator to your own son in real life.

One day when I went in one son's room to get his hamper, I walked in on him masturbating. I quickly grabbed the hamper, then ran out the door. Somehow a voice within me cried out, "Stop running away, you idiot—deal with the situation. Don't you dare run out on his penis!!" So I stopped at the door and turned around and walked over to him by the bed. By now he had the sheets pulled over his nude body and was looking embarrassed. I sat down and said (with a smile and a cheerful voice), "Well, I guess I walked in on you masturbating. That's very exciting!" (His eyes grew wide.) "I mean, this is the beginning of your sex life. Later on, you'll do other things but for now, that's a very healthy thing to do. In fact, everyone does it—even Daddy and me!!" (He seemed shocked by this. I didn't know how much further to proceed. He was only 13.) "Anyway, I want you to feel free to do this—to masturbate—and to enjoy it. I would like us to be able to talk about sex when you want to." Then he said, "I don't want to." (That kinda clipped my wings.) Then I said, "Well, I wanted to, but I will respect your rights for privacy and leave so you can finish." Then he said, "Well, I've read this," and he reached over and showed me his copy of *Love and Sex in Plain Language,* which I knew he was reading. I asked him if he would like me to read it and we could talk about it and he said "Yes." Then I left. From then on, he kept on masturbating with the door closed and I walked in on him again but we never really discussed much about sex.

Now it's a year later from the time I discovered his masturbation. After a period of distancing himself from me and his father, this son now tells me he is a favorite with the girls. He has begun to lock the door. He spends hours combing his hair and flexing his muscles. He receives lots of telephone calls, so I feel he is not too fearful of his sexuality (as I was) but would rather not discuss it . . . at least not with me.

P.S. I am 44 years old, white, female, married nineteen years to the same man, and have three sons (including twins). Graduated in 1958 with a BS. Graduated in 1978 with a MSW, attending a psychoanalytic institute in the fall. I am a psychiatric social worker with a private practice in Seattle. I am also a certified Yoga instructress.

Ellen

I would like to explain some of the details of my job as it is richly involved in the major part of my sex life and fantasies.

I'm a 27-year-old white, college-educated female. Although I care for my husband and we are relatively happy, I consider him just a friend. He is a chemist, and although he is very good to me, I find his personality very dry. For some time I have worked in sales at a Pepsi-Cola bottling company. I am the only person that sells pre-mix and post-mix product in tanks. There are six drivers that deliver it for me. As part of my training I had to go out on the route with a driver for the day. Kevin is twenty-four and has only been married ten months. When we were put together we scarcely knew each other except on sight. I'm considered very beautiful and self-assured, while he is somewhat shy and quite inexperienced in life.

After several hours of having the physical stimulation of bouncing along in a truck and being in such close proximity to a man I felt extremely attracted to, my nervousness started to be obvious. I couldn't quit glancing at Kevin's beard and the mass of blond curly hair at the neck of his shirt. We joked through the day and exchanged information about each other's lives. I started to have hope when he started asking questions that would give him some idea of how unhappy I was at home.

During the day my drivers call me with any kind of delivery problem or question they may have. I also have radio contact with them throughout the day. Kevin began to contact me frequently, and I could barely keep my train of thought straight. Two other drivers would regularly stop in my office at the end of the day and Kevin would watch the interaction to see if I was interested in anyone else. My expression showed nothing although I do fantasize about this sort of situation.

I imagine that I am sitting in my office and two of my handsome young drivers come in to discuss an account with me. I am speaking on the phone so they must wait. One glances down at my feet. I am wearing straight-leg pants but am wearing very sheer black silk stockings and five-inch heels. My toenails are deep crimson and my big toe has a tiny gold star on the nail. One comments to the other how long and attractive my legs are and that he thinks I have very sexy feet. I recline somewhat in my chair, all the while carrying on a telephone conversation. I can see an erection rising in Dave's pants. I motion for him to come closer. Our eyes meet and he gives me a half-grin. His lips brush my neck and my pussy starts to get wet. With his hand running through my hair he bends his head to my low-cut shirt and kisses my tan chest just at the top of my cleavage. Every movement is so gentle and teasing it is nearly unbearable. Being waist high to him, I put my hand on his firm young ass, working my way to the other side. Phil asks me if he should leave and I shake my head no. My arms are bare and Phil extends that arm not holding the phone and gently kisses the inside from wrist to shoulder until I am squirming in my chair. Dave cups a breast and says how firm and nice it is. With my arm around him I start masturbating his cock through his uniform pants as he teases my clit behind the seam of my tight pants. Phil is watching and smiling. I feel so helpless, completely unable to comment while on the phone. Just as I approach orgasm, my caller reminds me I promised him a backrub. As I writhe in my chair I say, "Come to my office when you get in and I'll rub you, Kevin."

In actual experience Kevin and I become so stimulated being around each other that after about three weeks we met for drinks on a Saturday. As attracted to me as he was, he was hesitant because of the possibility of discovery. We sat at the table staring into each other's eyes. After several drinks I was feeling very aggressive and decided that I must apparently make the first move. I touched his face, running my hand over and through his beard. I told him I liked it. He invited me to go out to his Scout. Once in the car he kissed me passionately. The taste of cigarettes and the scent of his aftershave were extremely exciting. I thought I would die if his cock didn't press against me soon. The console was in our way and a bit uncomfortable. I was nearly in his lap. He told me he couldn't understand what I saw in him. It seemed to him that I already had everything. Perhaps the thrill is in having someone with a lifestyle I'm not accustomed to. I find coming down a few notches quite thrilling. It's also exciting that I can teach this young man a few tricks he might like.

By the time his hand and lips found my breasts we were both moaning. It may be hard to believe, but he seemed unable to go any further. I think I scared the hell out of him. We parted in that condition, with the promise of seeing each other again. It has not happened yet, but Kevin calls me several times a day and is always in my office. I suppose he is torn by love for his wife and the thrill of having me choose him to make love to me. Here I sit waiting for the inevitable.

Pat

I am 25, single, live alone and have had few relationships with men, none of which have been good, and I've never orgasmed with a man unless I did it (masturbated during sex). I have much hope, though, that I will get into a caring, mutual, trusting, fun relationship that will be sexually fulfilling and exciting. One of my fantasies is to live out my sexual fantasies in the "safety" of a good, committed relationship.

Here's my latest (most rewarding) fantasy.

There is a man I am attracted to who works in a small restaurant here in town. I've made an appointment to see him after closing hours to show him some drawings and other artwork for a new menu & logo for his business. I bring the drawings in my car & put them in the back, which is accessible by a hatchback door at the rear of the car. He comes out to help me get the drawings. I am wearing stockings held up by garters plus crotchless black lace panties under a very short skirt. With him behind me, I open the hatchback of my car & climb in to get the presentation materials. My skirt naturally hikes up, just enough so that he can see my bare ass. I hear him gasp at the sight but pretend not to & go about collecting the drawings. I get out of the car & together we go into the restaurant. It is very late at night & no one is on the street. However, the restaurant is glass-fronted & the possibility that someone might come by & see what follows makes it anxiety-provoking but heavenly exciting.

I take my drawings inside and proceed to line them up against a far wall on the floor. I bend from the waist with my legs slightly spread so that I am exposing my cunt which by now is glistening with juice. The man (I'll call him David) is stammering about how much he likes my work, and I can tell from his breathing that he is getting excited but he is too shy to act on it. I am in control here.

I turn around and notice that he has removed the apron he previously had tied around his waist and is holding it at a curious angle & distance from his body in order to hide the bulge in his pants. I then proceed to either sit down against the wall with my legs drawn up & my clit fully exposed or else sit backwards in a chair, my legs spread. I talk about the work, pretending that nothing unusual is going on but I am so aroused I can hardly stand it. My nipples are erect under my blouse, my cunt is oh so wet and all I want to do is fuck. I move from the chair to a small bar where the cash register, etc., sits, and hoist myself up, again drawing my knees up & spreading them. My skirt hides me somewhat. Next to me on the counter is a chocolate cake, and I dip my finger in the icing & slowly lick and suck it off, asking David what his favorite icing is. He hasn't taken his eyes off me the whole time. He gasps out, Chocolate, and this time I take another finger full, lift up my skirt and smear it over my throbbing clit and then invite him over to taste it. He throws down the apron & I can see his straining crotch. He walks over to me in about three steps and I proceed to smear his mouth & mine with more icing. He grabs me furiously and kisses me hard (his shyness has disappeared) and I kiss and tongue him back frantically. He proceeds to kiss me on the neck with my head flung back, which I love—also kisses & sucks my ears. He rips open my blouse and falls on my small tits exclaiming all the while how much he loves them. I let this go on until at one point I lift his head up & tell him my cunt is waiting. He doesn't hesitate one moment but dives his tongue into my clit, licking off the chocolate icing noisily and expertly nibbling and sucking. I have never been so hot. I am writhing & moaning on the countertop with his lovely face buried in my bush. From my pocket, I pull out a small vibrator and work that on myself in between his nibbles. In no time at all I come fantastically, yelling and heaving. Now it's his turn & I slide off the counter and unbutton & unzip his pants to free his waiting cock. It is beautiful, sticking out of his pants with a lovely head and a reddish purple hue. I reach up to the now decimated chocolate cake and grab icing to smear all over his cock. I then begin to suck & lick, telling him what a wet beautiful cock he has and how I'm going to suck him till he explodes. He is moving his ass to propel his cock in and out of my mouth while holding on to my head. He comes in ecstatic relief and I swallow all of his sweet load which is tinged with a chocolate taste.

We're not through yet & he picks me up & carries me to the kitchen and places me upon the worktable & goes down on me again while fucking me with a carrot that will later be used in some unsuspecting soul's salad. I want to be fucked by him and love to be entered from the rear so I turn over on the table on all fours and beckon him up, spreading my cunt lips with my fingers. He jumps up and enters me in one stroke and pumps me vigorously, his hands on my hips, his balls flapping against my body. The noises of fucking are a great turn-on to me and we are very noisy. I masturbate myself while he continues to fuck me grandly, sometimes pulling almost completely out and then pulling me down on top of him. He fucks forever & howls like a dog and tells me how we are fucking just like dogs. I come again & again & again. This seems to go on forever.

P.S. I do have an active masturbation life and use fingers, vibrators & Water Pik shower massage heads in the shower. Now I'm just waiting to include a real cock & body in my sexual activities.

Sandra

I am 21 years old. My steady boyfriend and I are both third year university students. We have been seeing each other for one year and plan to be married within the next three years.

To begin with, our sex life is wonderful. We have sex as often as we can. To tell you the truth, I have never been so sexually fulfilled. My past lovers were never compatible with me. However, I am my boyfriend's first sex partner. He was a virgin when I met him. Even though he has never had any past sexual experiences, he knows exactly how to capture my interest, and keep it, for that matter! It is as if we were sexually made for each other. Our relationship is very open, so we can talk about our own sexual fantasies and wishes.

My favorite fantasy: I have just met a great guy. He is gallant, sexy and most of all, innocent. I love baby-faced, innocent-looking men; they have that pure, virginal look about them. Anyway, Tom (my present boyfriend's name) is a virgin. Therefore, I am secretly trying to seduce him. We are getting acquainted over dinner and drinks. He sensuously sips his wine and casually looks into my eyes. This turns me on. I can't wait to get back to my apartment. While leaving the restaurant, he invites me to his home for a nightcap. The drive home seems endless and I begin squirming around in my seat. Upon arriving at the doorstep of the house, he takes his keys from his trousers and clumsily drops them on the ground. As he bends down to pick them up, I get the most wonderful sight . . . his ass is looking right at me. My heart skips a beat and my hands casually touch his round, firm buttocks. He squirms within my grasp; I can see he's loved my gesture. We walk into the house and he goes straight to the bedroom without even looking back. Of course, I follow. He quickly sits on the bed and motions me to come. He passionately kisses me and, to my surprise, runs his warm hands over my breasts. I am still standing and so I have a clear view of the stiffening bulge in his pants. I slowly begin to undress him (I love undressing him when he is wearing a suit—the process is slow and sensuous!). He is still sitting on the edge of the bed but he is now completely naked. His hard, virginal prick is staring beautifully at me, teasing me. It wants me. It wants to feel the tightness of my steaming cunt. I take his hot prick in my mouth. I begin sucking it gently while my fingers wanderingly tickle his balls. I run my tongue over his whole genital area. I can tell he is enjoying it. Tom now lies on the bed with his feet hanging over the edge. I am kneeling at his feet and the simple sight of his rod, balls and asshole increases my circulation. I slowly move up and sit earnestly on his prick. He moans and groans with excitement. I begin pumping up and down on his cock; faster and faster. My cunt is now wet and steaming hot. I am soaking his pubic hairs with my juices. He starts moaning louder and soon begins to scream (I love loud sex!). I begin pumping harder. Tom is really enjoying his first fuck and I feel like my head is going to blow off. Suddenly, he pushes his cock up deeper into my cunt and screams, "I'm coming, I'm coming," as his rod shoots its boiling load up my hole. Almost simultaneously, I come all over his trembling prick. Our juices start dripping from the shaft of his now glistening penis. I get off his cock and start licking the hot come from the tip of the red, pulsating organ. He is in ecstasy. I now realize I have just fucked an inexperienced, innocent virgin, and you know, it's the greatest feeling in the world!

Sue

I'm 34; married thirteen years; with 3 daughters. I'm a survey technician (land surveying) and I work exclusively with men. I've found that macho men are indeed *rare* and that most men want to be liked. I've found that a warm smile and a word or two melt down the most tough "macho." I like men. They have, as a group, a sense of humor that's great fun in the work arena. I've also learned to appreciate men's sense of self-appreciation. They can be homely, old, ugly, or dirty from a day's work and not be reluctant about trying to get a woman's attention. Men seem to like themselves better than women like themselves. I've learned to appreciate myself much more after working with men in this nontraditional career I've got.

Here's a fantasy that is half true:

We were surveying in timber country. I'm the only woman on the crew. We're about twenty-five miles from town. We've reached a point in the woods where we've set up our equipment and it's lunchtime. The three other crew members go back to our trucks for lunch & a snooze. I stay with the equipment & so does another crew member. He's physically very appealing. Late 30s. *Very* hairy. With hair all over his chest, back, neck. Thick beard. Fantastic intense eyes with wrinkles around the eyes where he squints in the sun. He starts taking his shirt off, boots, jeans; under his jeans he wears cutoffs. He's very brown, not Mr. Universe, but a very good-looking body, large muscular legs, very powerful arms, his hands are especially beautiful. He takes good care of them. I always notice a man's hands. I like to see well-formed hands, clean nails, well trimmed. He lays his clothes on the ground & rolls his cutoffs up to his hips. The cutoffs ride just above his pubic hair. And I believe he deliberately likes to show himself off to me. We joke about him looking like a bear or Bigfoot in the woods. He grins showing big white square teeth. He's never made any come-ons with me. Always treats me as an equal & a friend but he's very erotic. Whenever we work together he takes his shirt off & usually wears the cutoffs. I take off my boots & socks, roll up my jeans and tuck my T-shirt up to get sun on my back and legs. He says he'd like to take the cutoffs off. I say, "Go ahead. I won't look—oh, yes I will." We laugh. Then I say, "Don't worry, you're safe with me." He says, "But are you safe with me?" He lies down to sunbathe. Now the fantasy begins:

He lies down & closes his eyes. I'm sitting on a stump watching him. He's very brown, and sweat is glistening in his hair. He has a large knot in his pants and I can tell he's not erect but has a large scrotum. I watch him for a while & he knows it. I walk over to where he lies, bend over and kiss him very softly. He's docile. I kiss him and put my tongue in his mouth and guide him in a French kiss. He groans and says, "Oh no. Are you sure this is what you want?" "Yes."

He continues to lie back. I move my face all over his hairy sweaty body. I grab his arms and pull his hair. I pull his head back and bite his neck and chest. For some reason in this fantasy he's not a sexual powerhouse. I'm the dominant one doing all the work and he's the receptive one. He has a rather low libido and I turn him on by my strength. He's got this naturally large cock and rare erections but today, in the woods at high noon, he gets a rise like never before. I climb on top and just sink down on it in one fell swoop. He groans, startled. I sit on it and pin his arms down with my feet and I pin his legs down with my arms and fuck him like he's never been had before. He's out of control. Eyes rolling back in his head. Moaning & writhing. When he comes his face is contorted in an ecstasy/pain expression. My pleasure is in knowing what abandonment he has felt . . . seeing him change from cool sophisticated male to a man in the throes of sexual release. Afterward he is pale & shaken. He must get himself together before the rest of the crew returns. His face tells me everything I need to know. End of fantasy.

Even though I'm happily married with a wonderful husband & super sex life, I'd like this fantasy to come true.

Brenda

I just read my first book of yours, *Men in Love*. What sweet, sensual beings the men appear through their fantasies, when they seem worse prudes than women in reality.

I'm 32, white, middle class, and live in my hometown, a city in the Southwest. I have a master's degree, a dull, secure professional job. I live with my mother, also a career woman, and am single. I enjoy my situation, but am kind of ashamed of it, too. I have traveled widely in the U.S. and Europe, love reading and films, and hate sports and most group activities. Sexually, I'm a typical Southern woman, very sensual, but outwardly a nun. I'm a demi-vierge, loving fellatio, ready for anal sex, and anything in between, but have not dated for ten years. I can't understand this last, because I'm cute, really, well-built, and friendly.

As you can imagine, fantasy and masturbation are big items in my life, for all yearnings toward anything else seem fraught with dangers: singles bars (Mr. Goodbar, herpes, AIDS) or marriage (debt, alcoholism, wife-beating). I love sex, and the look and feel of the male body if in reasonably good shape, though the look of overmuscled men terrifies me.

The most vivid and complete fantasy is one I began this year. I have worked it all out happily to the last detail, but it consists mainly of one situation. It is 1942, and I am 16 (my favorite year and age). I am a maid and waitress for the summer in a hotel in a small town where a movie is being made. Starring in this picture is my absolutely favorite actor, a great male star of the forties, gorgeous, masculine, gentlemanly and talented. He is also polite, tall, very well endowed and adored by women, and even straight men, for his perfection. Rooms are very short at the hotel, and the female lead (a young all-American type starlet so popular in the forties) suggests that I camp in her room so that she can study my type for the part she'll play.

One noon, I rush up to change uniforms in the bathroom and walk right in on him, nude, and I nearly faint from embarrassment, but it is also love at first sight for me. He is amused, really, but I am fascinated by his lovely build and even more by his gorgeous cock. The lovely accident of his being in the bathroom, he tells me, consists of his sharing a suite with the female lead because of the shortage of rooms. He is very sweet as I apologize for my mistake. I walk around in a daze the rest of the day, and luckily, the gutsy and experienced female lead takes pity on me and suggests me to him as an interesting pastime. She is actually eager to go to bed with him herself, but cannot do this and concentrate on her film role.

When our lovemaking begins, and as it continues over that month, I go from terror of rejection to confident love, to loving but complete power over him. The first time he enters me goes like this: We are both naked. The blood is pounding in my temples. I lie back on the bed, closing my eyes. He puts his hand, large and warm like his penis, between my legs, touching me gently at first, and then more roughly, until I groan. He talks to relax me, and, feeling the wetness between my legs, climbs onto me. Then I can feel it naked between my thighs, tickling them, and it feels wonderful. Instinctively I move my legs as far apart as I can, tilt my pelvis up, arching my back. He shifts, whispering now, and slides his hands under my back. "I've got you—I've got you now," he says. His cock moves ever so slightly, the head, the knob, finding my slit, and I slide my arms around his back, smelling his scent. He comes inside me then, huge, but I welcome him. The pain becomes pleasure immediately. He whispers to me: "You're so small, you're perfect." He is not all the way in yet, and kisses and strokes me until I totally relax. He then slides all the way in, and I gasp, almost fainting, for his lovely cock is twelve inches long. Now I sigh, holding him to me, triumphant that he is in me. He means to be gentle, but gets carried away because of my size, and comes again and again, collapsing from exhaustion, and I cradle him on my breasts.

The next day he feels very guilty because he is married,

100

and because of the differences in our ages (I wasn't a virgin). The female lead has given me some advice on technique, however, and I get him into bed, and go down on him all night. After this, we lapse into weeks of sex of all kinds, the most exciting for me when he bottom-fucks me, and I wish, somehow, that I could give him the same feeling, of totally helpless surrender.

The impetus arrives when his lover, a producer, arrives on the set for the last day of shooting, and a cast party.

This producer is famous, bisexual, influential, and the major force in the star's career, and also excitingly handsome in his own right, but very cruel. He truly, jealously loves the star, however, who really prefers women, and after this month, prefers me sexually to anyone. He has sex with the star at the cast party, which, the star admits guiltily to me later, he intensely enjoys. The star leaves the party, angrily bursting in on me, hits me, and collapses into sobs, admitting he is still under the producer's spell. I comfort him, and, luckily, having caught the exciting word "Fist-fucking" in someone's conversation that day, deduce the meaning, and proceed with the help of Vaseline to fuck him with my arm, not really painful to him because I am very petite, my hands as well. He loves this, and I go on and on, as he comes again and again, and, finally, after some washing up, we collapse into each other's arms, me holding him very tenderly, and we sleep.

Celia

I'm a 25-year-old black girl, middle class and single. I spent a wonderful summer with Derek, a man a year older than I. He's going to be married now, but I still think about him a lot. I sometimes fantasize about having sex with him in unusual places.

At the Metropolitan Opera House, in the parking lot, are two bathrooms for men and women. I've often gone there and seen no one on duty. He doesn't know where we're going and looks surprised when I pull him into the women's bathroom. (I don't know whether the men's has stalls.)

Once inside a stall we start hugging each other frantically.

I tug at his shirt, popping off a few of the buttons in my hurry. He's wearing a T-shirt underneath and doesn't protest when I start tearing at it. It comes apart with a satisfying ripping sound. I feel like an animal; I'm different from how he has always seen me. He's inspired by my hunger, carried away by lust. Abandoning restraint, he pulls down the top of my dress; I'm wearing one of those black lace skimpy bras underneath. He flicks his tongue all along the edge of the bra, even sucking my nipples through the lace. I love the sensation, running my hands down his back, into his pants, cupping his buttocks (so nice!). He pulls my bra down with his teeth, leaving it tangled, almost pinning my arms. He bites gently, gently, at my nipples. It's hard enough to make me gasp but not enough to hurt. We don't have much time—someone may come in. My hands are sliding around his pants and I jerk them down. He's eager to help, gripping my buttocks tightly and raising me to meet his rock-hard erection. It presses into me with one sudden thrust, causing me to cry out. I'm not quite wet enough for him yet, so he has to shove harder than usual to move into me. But I don't mind, it's what I want. Standing up, there's barely room to move. The constrained space means we're banging against the walls, arching our bodies together, slippery with sweat. We're both out of control, giving vent to stifled yells and feverish kisses. My legs are wrapped tight around his waist; he couldn't throw me off even if he wanted. I want to have his cock deep inside me. More, more, harder, I whisper in his ear. He silences me with a kiss, but his thrusts become even fiercer, if possible.

Pulling my hair back so he can see my neck, he rains kisses on it, moving down toward my breasts again. I reach down and rub his cock when it partly comes out of my cunt. I bring up my own fingers dripping with my own juice and smear my nipples with it. He opens his mouth wide around the nipples, taking in as much of my flesh as he can, sucking as if he wants to swallow me. I'm gasping, nearly sobbing with pleasure. He was groaning out my name; now he's just groaning. It's so hard for us to keep quiet even though we know the necessity. He kisses me hard, thrusting his tongue down my throat (we're definitely quieter now!). We almost come together; he continues to push into me urgently, pleading for me to help him. I twist against him and feel more orgasms shuddering through me. Finally he comes, his stiffened body grinding me into the stall door. We almost fall down, both of us exhausted by our violent love play. We pull on each other's clothes, wipe our bodies with the toilet paper and slip quietly out of the bathroom. Even knowing that more awaits us at home doesn't dampen the contentment we both feel.

Annette

I am a WASP female, 33 years old, an only child, with classes in psychology. I am five feet six inches with a pretty face, an okay body and very nice legs. I've never been married or even been asked. I've had only one lover (in secret) because my family (conservative) is very much against sex out of marriage.

My fantasies primarily revolve around cocks but not when I masturbate. I can take my fantasies anywhere with me during the day; i.e., at work, lunch, etc. without making it noticeable. I'll start with my earliest recollection of that magnificent instrument, the penis.

I was 6 and my girlfriend's brother was 3 or 4. I visited them over a weekend. We bathed together and I got my first sight of a boy naked. I liked his dick so much that when we were playing Hide & Seek in his bedroom we stood behind the bed and I got him to open his fly for me.

A few years later, in fifth grade, we had a storytelling time in class and the book was *Peter Pan*. (For movies & such he's usually cast as a nonsexual being but not in my mind—he's all boy.) I remember waking up from a dream one night where I was the little older girl who had to take care of him. He fell from a tree or something and he hit his dick. I had to rub it gently to ease the pain. I got a charge out of that one.

From time to time throughout high school and college we had health classes with pictures in the books and lectures on Freud and sex. But I never saw a real man's cock until I was 25. The man I loved was almost twenty years older than me and very experienced; he had even been a surrogate lover in a sex therapy clinic at one time. He was very patient & gentle with me and was very surprised that I was a "complete" virgin. By that I mean that I had never touched myself "down there" or ever done anything with boys except kiss. No one had ever touched me mentally, physically or morally before. He talked to me about sex and the concept that all the body is a person's sex organ and that nothing expressed is wrong providing that it is always clean and gentle.

The first time I saw him naked he lay down beside me and told me to have a good look and touch what I wanted. After a little shyness I reached out for his penis, of course. He told me the length & diameter of his own and the averages of other men. He held me close by his side and masturbated for me so I could feel the passion and arousal. He ejaculated while I watched in avid interest. He then told me to scoop some up in my hand and taste it. The cum was just like my own secretions, nothing different.

I didn't have intercourse for six months because I didn't want to give up my precious virginity, but I learned a lot about oral sex, which I enjoy. My love is gone now but I have two favorite fantasies to share with the next man in my life:

(1) I imagine that I'm waiting for my man to get home because I'm very horny. When I hear his key in the lock I've already stripped down naked and run to him. I can't wait for him to relax awhile after work, because I've been so hot all day. I undress him as quickly as I can while he stands there in amazement. I take everything off but his jockey briefs (always briefs) and I see he is tumescent. I kiss him passionately and rub up and down his groin to get his hard-on. I urge him to lie down on the living room floor with me and fuck me through the hole/slit in his briefs. I just love it!

(2) My man has been out with the "boys" for the weekend, camping, fishing or something, and they didn't catch anything so he's very, very hungry. I've prepared his favorite meal (my old lover liked a rare steak, a baked potato with lots of sour cream and a fresh salad with crisp veggies and

Coke). I show him the meal and tell him to sit down so I can "serve" him. I set the food before him and then tell him there is something else I want to give him. While he is eating this delicious food I tell him I want to kneel under the table & suck his cock. He agrees and we begin. In a little while he can't take the stimulation anymore and wants to fuck me so he quits eating. I stop sucking him and tell him he must finish all the food that I have prepared just for him or I won't keep his cock hard. He goes back to gobbling his food down and I lick his shaft and head and his balls. He finally finishes the food and leans back in his chair to watch me. I get up and sit on his lap facing him and receive his hard cock in me and hump to rapture and orgasm. (I don't know if it would be that easy in a chair but I'd try it.)

I want to say in closing that I don't have a special man or penis in mind when I fantasize—just a regular guy who is wild about me and loves me tenderly. I don't watch crotches because I know that every guy has a cock and someday some guy I'm crazy about will have a cock just for me.

Elaine

I've had sexual fantasies as long as I can remember, and had my first memorable arousal while playing with the water hose at age four. From that pleasant surprise I progressed to water play in the tub, but was aware from the start that my parents would disapprove. They are still very prudish and give the impression that sex except from a puritanical marital state is completely amoral. That kind of upbringing may have contributed to my wilder and more intense sexual drives; perhaps it is my desire to rebel in the one way they would disapprove of most.

I'm 34, married for twelve years with three children, and am a retired public school teacher. My husband won't admit to having fantasies beyond basic desires of oral sex and screwing. I can't bring myself to tell him my wilder fantasies, either, for fear of shocking him! I don't think he would like to know that I want sex with other men. I was a virgin until the age of 18 and have only let him heavy-pet and screw me, so after sixteen years of only him and his lack of imagination, I fantasize a lot! It would hurt him and make him more jealous than he already is. Also, I fear that it might make him turn off sex with me. I'm always horny and ready to screw or try anything, and he's just the same old predictable guy who likes the same old predictable screwing or "slam, bam, thank you, ma'am." To me, variety is the key to sex, and all of ours is at my insistence. I've never had an affair, but if it weren't for my fear of God's reprisals, I'd have one in a heartbeat! (Thanks a lot, Mom and Dad, you did a number on me all right; I have a conscience and I wish I didn't!)

One of my fantasy themes is of being fucked by animals who allow me to be as totally uninhibited as they are about it. I've let animals lick my pussy and asshole, and have sucked a dog's cock in the futile attempt to get him horny enough to want to fuck me. I rolled him over on his back, unsheathed his penis, and sucked and licked him until I was creaming down my leg with desire to fuck him. He enjoyed the attention but didn't get the message to fuck me, so I finally straddled him and slid his prick into my pussy, riding him for all I was worth. I climaxed, but it was from imagination rather than the actual feel of a dog's cock fucking me.

In fantasy, I imagine I'm in an exhibition arena for scientific experiments and I am told to entice the male gorilla into screwing me so a movie can be made to document it. I'm led naked to a room which is like a cage in a zoo. The gorilla watches me and takes my nakedness for granted, so I crouch down and gradually inch my way near him. He seems to respond to that position so I turn my back to him and raise my ass to let him see my pussy from behind. From between my legs, I watch him as he extends a finger to touch and probe my cunt. He sniffs his finger and puts it in his mouth to taste my juices, then fingers me again with increasing interest. I remain still, but watching, as he bends his head between my crouched legs to get a closer look and a sniff at my pussy. He repeatedly fingers me and licks off the juices like dipping in a honeypot. I see that his huge, hairy dick is getting harder and erect, and when he begins to lick my cunt and force his tongue up me, I am close to wanting to scream, *"Fuck me, oh please, fuck me."* But I don't say anything because I know he could be frightened into hurting me or ruining the experiment. A dozen or so scientists stand watching on the other side of the glass, taking notes, and nodding their heads as the ape grabs me around the waist from behind and pulls my cunt onto his face. He is slurping and gulping my pussy as though he is never going to get enough of it. Finally, I glance at the clock on the outer wall and see that he has been licking and sucking my hole for over two hours, during which time I have been coming and coming until I am exhausted. The scientists note the ape's terrific hard-on which is twelve inches long and two inches in diameter. I signal that I would like a break to use the bathroom, but the doctors feel it would upset the ape to let me leave the area when he is so aroused. He has been unable to mate successfully with a female ape on his own, and they are trying to teach him how, using me as a surrogate. They will take his semen from my vagina and inseminate a waiting female ape if the experiment is successful and he does fuck me. I am very professional and I love my work, so I understand I will have to relieve myself as best as I can with the ape holding me and tonguing my hole every few seconds. I need to pee so badly, I decide to let a little trickle out the next time the ape moves his tongue out of my pussy. As I tinkle a few drops onto the floor, my crotch stings and I know the ape has rubbed my pussy lips until they are chapped, but I see his hard-on and I know when he does fuck me I'm going to remember it the rest of my life. As the piss puddle widens, the ape sniffs at it and carefully watches between my legs to see where it's coming from. As the last of the piss is released, he carefully licks my little pee-hole and cleans me of the urine. He lifts me under his arm and carries me to a corner of the room, hiding me from the scientists and the camera out front; I know I must re-position us so they can all see my pussy when the ape enters me. I also know I must somehow lubricate that huge penis and my cunt or penetration won't stand a chance of success. A special opening in the wall has been supplied with ointments for this purpose, and a lab technician waits on the other side to assist me and photograph the closeup shots of my vagina as it is when the ape has finished the first stages of foreplay. I inch myself closer to the wall and the ape follows me, never taking his eyes off me. He watches as the windowlike opening slides to permit the assistant's hands into the room as I back my ass up to them. (The lab assistant, Sandy, is a punk kid who has had the hots for me since he arrived and he hates the idea of me letting the ape fuck me and eat me, but he gets to finger me and lubricate me for the ape's entry, and he makes the most of it.) He is very gentle and slow as he squeezes the warm, fruit-flavored ointment into my pussy and rubs it across my crotch and asshole. He can't resist running his gloved finger into my asshole and diddling my clitty under the pretense of preparing me for the experiment! The ape has not noticed my clit much, nor my asshole, and I feel myself relaxing and wondering how many fingers Sandy will use before the ape's patience wears off. The ape is still watching me and has begun to jack himself off slowly. The scientists are busy noting this as well as watching the monitor which is showing a close-up of the ape's penis with a split screen of the close-up shot of my wide-open cunt.

Sandy gently and slowly has put three lubricated fingers up my asshole and is rotating them around in circles. I turn around and stand up very slowly, pressing my crotch to the opening in the wall. Sandy quickly puts his mouth on my clit and flicks his tongue across it as I feel his warm saliva run down my pussy lips to further add to the slipperiness I feel from my asshole to the top of my hairline in front. I know Sandy will be in trouble for eating me out and fingering me for his own satisfaction during an experiment of this magnitude, but I hate to make him stop! I see the red warning light going on above my head, which signals me to return to my arousing of the ape. He is creeping toward me with the most enormous hard-on I have ever seen. He isn't any longer than the twelve inches he was before, but he is fully three inches in diameter and looks like he has a pair of small coconuts instead of balls below! I am beginning to fear him, but I must not let it show or he might hurt me. I crouch back down and turn my ass toward him, and I see his eyes light up when once he sees my cunt. No longer hesitant, he knows what he wants and comes right for it, drooling, with his prong sticking out with all his masculine glory. The scientists hold their breath as the ape reaches me and pulls my pussy open with his lips and tongue and eats me with renewed vigor. As his nose finds the fruit smell, though, he gets confused and begins to nip and bite, and then nibble at my asshole. I'm not in pain, but am scared as well as aroused by him as he thrusts and works his tongue into my asshole where Sandy's fingers have taken the fruit-flavored ointment. The scientists discuss this unusual turn of events and note that the anal eating is not usual in apes.

By now, I have been aroused to such an extent that I want that big ape prick in my pussy, no matter what I have to do to get him to fuck me. He has no idea what to do about that part though, so I have to guide his huge rod if there is to be any mating. I reach down and locate his prick, stroking it gently but firmly. With that new feeling, he stops eating and sucking my crotch and waits to see what I am doing. I take the pouch of Vaseline Sandy has given me and slip it over the end of his penis, greasing him down as thickly as I can. I quickly run my hand around my cunt as well to give us every chance of penetration. The ape is sitting down and I turn to straddle him, hoping to lower myself onto his dick and use my body weight to force it into my pussy. He reaches out and fingers my clitty, then leans forward to nibble at it gently! I let him suck the fruit from it before I squat and grab his penis with both hands and stroke it. He grunts and arches his back and I can reach him well enough to fondle his balls as well. He is ready and so am I, and at a nod from the scientists, I lower my cunt to the tip of his penis, rubbing it across the opening of my pussy. I feel his lubricating fluid coming from the end of his dick, and I begin to push his huge cock into my cunt! I must go slowly and work it in gradually while I concentrate on relaxing my cunt muscles so I can take him. He is very still but I can feel the tension in him and his great power. His cock is filling me and the heat in my crotch is growing so I am more than eager to have him fuck me any way it can be done. I am amazed to feel my pussy stretching to receive this enormous ape's cock without tearing; the sensation of being filled so completely makes me feel like the ape and I are making ourselves into one being instead of two. He is too large for me to take his entire length, and I have reached my maximum in length, so I begin to hunch him and his penis slides in and out, in and out, in and out. The scientists are cheering and clapping and congratulating themselves on my successful fucking with an ape. I am getting the screwing of my life and I know it, so I am not surprised that the ape is enjoying it too! After fifteen or twenty minutes I am finished, but the ape hasn't shot off into me yet and I know I must ride him until he does. I've a very wet and throbbing pussy, so I decide to change positions. The ape thinks I am going to run away from him and he grabs me from behind and knocks me to my knees. He rams his cock into my pussy and I cry out with surprise. His hands have found my breasts and he squeezes them in his passion to hold me to him and satisfy his lust for mating. The camera is running out of film and the men are reloading a second and third camera in case we will be fucking several hours. I am exhausted but feel more like a woman than any other on earth, and I am proud of myself for the job I have accomplished. The ape's penis makes huge throbbing movements as his come squirts into my cunt in huge globs. I smile and concentrate on feeling it inside me, knowing that it is a prize the scientists eagerly wait. Satisfied now, the ape's penis shrinks and he pulls it out of me, licking my swollen, wet, and come-laden pussy gently. His tongue feels so good on my aching cunt, but I am beyond further arousal and it is more like a warm, comforting cleanup after a very satisfying fucking. The ape moves away after a while of licking my pussy, and falls asleep in his corner. Sandy comes in and lifts me up and carries me into the next room where the doctors and scientists wait to clean me of the ape's semen and use it to fertilize the female ape. When they finish, Sandy gives me a douche and an enema to clean me of all the ape's secretions, and then I take a nice hot soak in the tub. I'm too tired to desire any more sex, and I expect to be sore for a few days at least, but I thank Sandy for his care of me and promise to call him the next time I'm horny! I go home and go to bed *so satisfied!*

GOOD MOTHER/GOOD ORGASM

A man enjoys lying on a woman's breast. Being held, suckled, even babied, the staunchest man may relax his iron control and allow himself to be lulled back to an infantile time that has a special, primitive sexual pleasure. A woman would like to hold him longer, enjoying from her side the thrill of power, but once satisfied, he pulls away. Sweet as it is to lie in a woman's arms, every man remembers that once, the breast/woman controlled him totally. If he surrenders a moment longer, he may lose his strength, his superior status. The woman sighs, lets him go, feeling her power go with him, knowing she is again resigned to waiting and waiting for the man to return to her breast, her control.

No more waiting! cry these women. No more suckling, cosseting, except on our terms! No more pretending that the mother power is not *the* power, woman power, and that our breasts, our wombs, to which our vaginal muscles suck you men back during sex, are not indeed the beginning of all power! These are new days, gentlemen, and patriarchal society/religion/missionary sex are up for reexamination . . . at least in fantasy.

These erotic explorations of maternal dominance didn't occur in *My Secret Garden* because Mother Goddess power was just beginning to be written and talked about in the 1970s. Not until women received permission from other women's voices, saying it was good to use, indeed flaunt Earth Mother dominance over men, was this particular aphrodisiac transmitted to women's erotic reveries.

Central to this reevaluation and celebration of the beauty and power of the female body was women's new and unabashed physical embrace of one another. When feminists demoted the penis as the source of all sexual power, women's eyes were opened to the erotic possibilities of their own bodies. Women focused total attention on their own sexual satiation, an erotic oral hunger that can go on and on—which is, of course, one reason men shied away from celebrating the multiorgasmic Mother Goddess. Now women want their men to pay specific attention to their maternal power.

The women in this section are determined to make men recognize where power begins and whom they are dependent on for life and orgasm. They tease men with their breasts, playing good baby/bad baby with their life-giving secretions; alternating kisses with spankings, they teach men how to fuck and suck; occasionally they try, as Jane does, "to lure him back into my womb" . . . with squeezes and caresses from the inside.

For the most part they are gentle, doing what they must "for his own good." They often sound like little girls with their dolls: long ago when the woman was little and mommy had punished her, she would replay the painful scene with the doll baby, playing either good or bad mother opposite the doll who symbolized her. Today most of these women are again rewriting history, playing mother as they remember their own fate at her hands; or they rework the memory of childhood sexual abuse by men or women. Whatever the painful childhood memory, in these fantasies of playing Ruler of the Nursery opposite the dependent manchild, everything is magically made right—and orgasmic—in their role as the benevolent mother.

The charm of fantasy is that they control everything. They write the script, design the sets, select and direct the actors, and they are always the star. There is no such thing as a bad opening night because they are the critic, too: Applause! Orgasm!

Some of the women enjoy living out their fantasies; the dominant Good Mother role fits them just fine and they have no trouble finding men in reality, usually younger than they, who also enjoy a relationship in which the woman takes the maternal lead.

"For the first time in my life I'm exercising power over a male," exalts Theresa, a former nun who keenly resents the patriarchal system. "I tell him women's power is here and he'd better learn to accept it." Her fantasy is quite straight-forward: "To make it clear to my lover that *I'm* in charge— and then to 'mother him.' It seems the perfect fantasy for the coming feminist era."

In my research on men's sexual fantasies, the two most popular themes were being seduced by a Red-Hot Woman and punishment/humiliation at the hands (actually at the feet) of a dominant woman. These fantasies, however, came from a different time, an era when hot, aggressive women weren't actually prowling the halls at the office, sitting next to a guy at dinner or on top of him in bed. In the 1970s men went to prostitutes for their domination/humiliation and gladly paid for it because only an economic transaction assured the man that when his erotic novelty was over, he could put on his pants and return to the status quo, meaning him on top.

While my contributors to *Men in Love* may have dreamed of being taken over by a woman, I can't help being reminded of the old proverb "Be careful what you wish, lest all your wishes come true." But I shouldn't be too quick to think all men will be put off by these women who want to infantilize them. Johana, for instance, cannot wait to live out her fantasy of suckling, bathing, and diapering her husband until that ecstatic moment when "I open his diaper and find he is a man and tell him so." When her absent husband reads her fantasy in a letter, is he upset? Absolutely not. He is desperate to get home from his business trip and into his diaper. Ah, the wonderful complexity of human nature.

That some of us, men and women, are sexually aroused by the idea of baby boy being brought to erotic life by a loving mama shouldn't surprise anyone. Don't we all begin our sexual adventure with the same maternal disciplinarian?

Jane

I am 43 years old, in the process of divorcing my husband of twenty-two years, and the mother of three children.

I have a master's degree in a health profession and am working on a second master's in neurosciences (behavioral-experimental psych.). A large area of interest is in journalism, photography, graphic arts.

I seldom masturbate anymore, see my lover at least once a week for the past seven years, and have never yet experienced anything close to orgasms with any man, including my husband.

I have had a very creative fantasy life as long as I can remember. When my mother read to me about Jason and the Golden Fleece, I masturbated while imagining a gorgeous, golden-haired youth. After seeing a movie about a slave girl, I imagined myself tied to my bedpost and beset by some sheik (or whatever) "against my will." In my early school days, my mother was puzzled that I managed to tear the front of so many slips . . . in truth, I tucked them between my legs and gently (or not so gently when I really got into it) pulled back and forth to provide stimulation as I daydreamed in class, imagining myself flying while experiencing wonderful sensations.

The truth is that I got very little out of intercourse with men—they seemed to move too fast to let me get into the feelings I had grown to associate with orgasm. I was sure that my early devotion to self-stimulation was the cause of my "frigidity" but figured I'd done the damage and would have to live with it.

At any rate, one of my college-days fantasies was recurrent, and I had embellished on it over many years until it was able to produce very intense orgasms. It involved an African tribal ritual in which the young men "come of age"

114

by initiating their manhood in a secret ceremony in which, strapped to an altar (shaped much like a GYN table), I am the object of their lust. Since I am tied and vulnerable to being hurt, but know I will be killed if I don't cooperate, I learn to control these men with my insides. I either hold them so tightly that they can't thrust so hard, or I lure them with squeezes and caresses from the inside as I would otherwise have done with my hands and mouth. The last young man to perform the ritual is the extra-heavily endowed chief's son. I know he can hurt me a great deal if I let him thrust, so instead, I grasp the head of his penis so tightly that he has no choice except to burst in a magnificent climax that takes me with him. Naturally, since he doesn't want to lose the source of so much pleasure, he keeps me as his own.

This fantasy finally led me to "dare" to sleep with a black man. In fact, I had the first orgasm I ever experienced with a man when I finally convinced him that moving at my speed rather than driving into me so hard would be worth his while. At any rate, almost as soon as I began to climax readily with him, my jungle ritual fantasy was replaced by another.

In this one, I become a sort of earth mother who is fully versed in the pagan "women's mysteries" involving men and life and cosmic consciousness, etc. As we make love, I take more and more of my lover's sex into me as deeply as he can penetrate. I cover the head of his penis with honey from some special source I have inside, making it extremely sweet, smooth, and slippery, so that all sensation will be subtle and widespread. My lover becomes a sort of "everyman" as I begin to lure him back into my womb. As he tries to thrust, I hold the head so tightly that he can feel my pulse beating on it like little caresses. Alternately, I open myself so invitingly that although he wants to pull back, he's helpless to do anything but fall deeper into me. I begin to draw him into the mouth of my womb in waves, pulling him, overcoming him with the woman power used by all women from the dawn of time. As he feels himself lose control, we climax simultaneously and magnificently. As he finally leaves me, I imagine him "born again." I have never told my lover what I am fantasizing while we make love as I do not want to scare him, but, amazingly, he has several times cried out "Oh no, Mama" or just "Mama" as he climaxed.

Beatrice

I'm 19, a college psychology major and honor student, fairly attractive (I get a lot of second looks, whistles, and propositions) but not stunning. I plan to be a sex therapist and I'm also a feminist, but I believe men have much to be gained also by pursuing equality for the sexes, and I don't like to hurt or unfairly accuse men to help women get ahead. My friends say I'm a considerate, outgoing, sensitive person and I'd never harm anyone in reality. In my fantasies I don't really bring pain to my lover, I just enjoy controlling things.

I've been masturbating since I was in training pants as a little girl, and after being taught it was a "no-no" I continued in private. I began by just rubbing my clitoris, both with my fingers and small toys, and in more recent years I began using objects for penetration. As a young girl, I remember being angry that some women experience pain during their first intercourse, until I learned that a gynecologist could cut the hymen beforehand, if necessary. Then I also read that it could be slowly and painlessly stretched by a woman herself, so I did it. I started with narrow objects (tampons) that slid up my cunt easily and progressed to larger things. I never experienced any pain. When I use objects simply for pleasure, I prefer shorter, thicker phallic shapes; I think the thickness stimulates my clit more. Plump, firm cucumbers are ideal! I guess technically I'm still a virgin because I've never made love to a guy before. Premarital sex is against my religion, although it's a tough rule to stick to. When I'm married I plan to be a very active, assertive partner.

I fantasize about sex often, and sometimes it gets in the way (like when I'm supposed to be taking notes during a lecture). But I get good grades and have wonderful relationships with the people in my life. Throughout my life I've fantasized about many different men, but my favorite now prevails. He's a singer in real life and I have the most fantastic orgasms while screwing him in my mind as his songs fill the room from my stereo. He is actually a sweet, sensitive, often shy, attractive and bright man; tall and slender and intensely sexy. I'm also tall, and in my fantasies he's just a few inches shorter to match my height exactly. It is sort of like a series when I fantasize, and I'll pick up one day where I left off the last. Sometimes I'll get bored and "change the channel" but the new "show" still involves this man and he always belongs to me.

Here it is:

Whatever the setting, I usually put my man in a situation where he's either a slave, servant or member of an inferior group. I find or buy him in a pitiful condition. He's been beaten, raped, starved, prostituted and humiliated extensively before I get to him. I briefly fantasize about him being brutally gang-raped by several women and sodomized with sticks. I don't dwell on this because I hate the real pain and fear I can see it on his face. What I love is taking over. He is trembling and frightened as I carry him home. I try to comfort and reassure him, speaking softly and handling him gently as I bathe him and bandage his wounds. He screams and pleads with me not to give him an enema or touch his genitals because of his being raped so cruelly, but I know if I don't give him an enema he'll have a harder time without it. So very tenderly I hold him over my lap and slowly slide the nozzle up his ass. He sobs and writhes but I keep him down, and eventually he submits. When the bottle is empty I put him on the toilet and he clings to my legs as the water rushes out. Throughout the night I feed, dress and caress him until he falls asleep in my arms. I include a lot of detail and can spend hours just taking care of him, trying to get him to trust me. He's always obedient, though reluctantly at first because he's still afraid of me. I'm kind but firm, and he knows that he belongs to me, so he's submissive to my desires.

The next few days are spent buying him clothes, taking him to doctors, etc. The doctors are always women and he hates such visits, especially the shots and rectal exams. They offer me another chance to hold his shaking body and calm his fears. I don't try to have sex with him too soon because I know his past experiences with prostitution and being raped still haunt him. I work up to it over several days; at first with caressing and holding him, then with kissing and fondling. One night I start making advances as I'm holding him in bed and he thinks I'll stop where I did the night before. When I don't, he starts crying and begs me not to do "it" to him. I keep going but he gets hysterical so I stop and comfort him, telling him I'll wait until he's ready. The next night he tearfully informs me that he's ready for me if I want him. The truth is, he's still scared to death. But he knows that I can do whatever I want to him by law, and since I've been so kind to him he feels guilty that I've been ignoring my own needs for his sake. So, although he's still frightened, I begin making love to him.

I spend a long time kissing and nibbling his face, neck, ears and chest, and eventually move my tongue into his mouth. I move slowly so I won't startle him. He still cries softly and admits that not only does he think it will hurt, but also that he isn't capable of pleasing me. I assure him that I'll be very gentle and that if he just relaxes and does what I say he'll please me. I slide his shorts and T-shirt off and kiss him all over. Through his crying, light sighs and gasps also escape his lips. He lies still on his back and I move onto him, licking and sucking his ears and neck again while I hold his head back firmly. Then I work downward along his ribs and belly, and finally in between his legs. Spreading them wide apart, I lick his soft inner thighs and balls, and then take his hard cock into my mouth, sucking slowly and deliberately. He moans and whispers my name over and over . . . "Oh, Beatrice, please don't. . . ." I want him to tell me when he feels himself coming because I want to be fucking him when he comes. When he calls out between gasps, I move back on top of him and push my dripping cunt onto his cock, moving up and down and squeezing rhythmically. We french again, and as I climax time after time I feel him buck and cling tightly to my body. His moaning and breathing get heavier, and as he screams during orgasm, I kiss him forcefully. My cunt sucks hungrily at his cock and milks him dry, and he gives me everything he has. We both come again and I continue loving him throughout the night. In the afternoon glow, he lies naked in my arms and feels safe at last.

After our first night of sex, I am still kind to him but less gentle. I teach him how to hold his ejaculation until I want him to release it, and occasionally I have to paddle his bare ass to get him to try harder. He eventually becomes very good at it, as well as at sucking my breasts and clit exactly how I've taught him to. He is still shy but wants desperately to please me. We screw in dozens of different settings and hours of the day: during breakfast, in the pool, the garden, the bathtub, even a dressing room as I help him try on clothes. Whenever I want him, I take him. Once in a while he has trouble getting hard, and he cries, ashamed. When that happens I assure him that I still love him and we turn to oral sex and masturbating each other (which I always control). He thrives on being dominated by someone he trusts, on having me discipline his life, knowing how badly I want him during sex and not knowing what might happen next. He knows I would never actually harm him, but sometimes he disobeys and he gets his little butt paddled, hard. We both love how hot and intense sex is after we've both been turned on by his spanking.

Sometimes I'm very rough when I fuck him and I slam down on his balls too hard. Afterwards I'm careful to be extra gentle and I suck them soothingly. I also like to stick my finger up his ass or squeeze his buttocks together as we're coming. Other times I slide a vibrator up him and keep it there as I screw him mercilessly. At first, the size of it scares him and he's tight as he pleads with me not to force it in. But I tie his wrists to the bedpost and push his knees up to his chest and slowly inch it in, always well lubricated. He is very noisy when I do anything sexual to him. Also, when I fantasize while listening to his music, just as each song hits

its peak we too explode in a frenzy of climaxes. Sometimes I "rent" him out to other women or a male friend, but I am always nearby watching to keep them from abusing him.

Those are just a few of the many things I do with my favorite guy. I include a lot of detail and my fantasies are very lifelike. This is one I'd love to act out, but alas, my man is a celebrity and out of my reach.

I think it's important to note that some women fantasize about sexually dominating men, just as men fantasize about being dominated. I've never had a rape fantasy. Rape angers me, but I understand the psychological reasons both men and women have such fantasies.

Maud

I'm 30, single, and crazy about men.

About four years ago, I had a boyfriend who liked to wear my nightgowns to bed. I enjoyed pleasing him by cooperating, and bought him his own in a size large enough to fit him well. It also sparked my own latent interest in the "kinky"—it was new, different, exciting!—and I bought him more items of feminine attire. Soon I was more interested in transvestism than he was, and after we broke up, I actively sought out other, more hard core transvestites. I was able to meet them only through personal ads in kinky contact publications, but meet them I did, and most were desperate to find a woman who would even accept their cross-dressing, much less be turned on by it. After four years of placing and answering ads, I have a network of all sorts of kinky friends from coast to coast, and some overseas.

I drifted from transvestism to S/M (female dominant) through contact with submissive transvestites. It took a while for me to become comfortable with the dominant role (I was raised to be the ideal old-fashioned passive lady) but I actively relish it now, and, under a "pen name," am well known in the S/M world.

Another of my favorite activities is infantilism (as the "mommy"). I have no biological children, but nonetheless possess strong maternal feelings, and have found infantilism to be the perfect solution. Many transvestites (the submissives in particular) are quite susceptible to the pleasures of "playing baby," and I am genuinely turned on by it, too: it's a unique combination of mother-baby coziness and total domination.

I group my current fantasies into two categories: brief fantasies and more elaborate fantasies. I tend to employ the brief category during masturbation (I like to focus on one or two images) but use the more elaborate fantasies (which are ongoing, as I work on them, adding and changing, all the time) for daydreams only.

Of the longer fantasies, I have chosen one. It is not my only fantasy of being a vampire, but is the most erotic:

The members of a world-famous boys' choir lived in a large, comfortable house not far from the cathedral in which they regularly performed. It was in that cathedral that I had, a month before, become infatuated with the sweet-faced boy who was soon to be my own. He was a soloist, and the moment I heard his pristine child's voice ring out, I determined to possess him. Tall and slender, he was poised on the brink of young manhood, and yet without the gracelessness which so often accompanies that age. He had the head of an angel, surrounded by soft golden waves of hair, and his huge gray eyes reflected the innocent wonder with which he regarded the world around him: the plush, sturdy world of 1890s Vienna.

I sought out every opportunity to see him: "chance meetings" in the street and before and after the choir's performances. I knew, as I looked into his eyes, that he had become fascinated by me (mortals are powerless against my gaze), and that already his childish sleep was troubled by strange dreams. I then began actually visiting him at night, as the rest of the house slept. He shared a room on the uppermost level with another of the older boys. Keeping his roommate in a deep sleep was accomplished merely by my willing it, after which I sat by my favorite's bed and watched him as he slept. I allowed him to waken briefly, and he had dreamed of me so often that finding me there frightened him hardly at all. I spoke softly to him, stroked his face, kissed his dewy lips with my own. This had gone on for many nights, when finally the time was ripe for fulfillment.

I stood at the foot of the boy's bed for the last time, and all that had gone before flashed through my mind. Never again would I have to roam the streets seeking him out. After that night, he would be part of me, living through and for me.

I moved toward him and he stirred fitfully. His brow knitted even as he slept and his soft lips half-formed a sound which I could not make out. I sat on the edge of his narrow bed and caressed his downy cheek and throat. The eyelashes —far too long for a boy's—fluttered and his immense gray eyes opened. Confusion flashed across his exquisite features, but then, as he watched my eyes, his head rested back against the pillow and he touched my hand as it lay against the pulse of his warm throat. His gaze never left my face, and the bond between our eyes intensified his pulse and I saw in his face a fire which he felt keenly but little understood. He pulled my hand away from his throat and pressed it to his mouth. Moving nearer him on the bed, I unbuttoned his nightshirt and noted the contrast between the severely starched garment and his delicate skin and slender androgynous body. Wildly dilated pupils nearly obliterated the gray of his eyes, and he reached out to touch my shoulders, face, hair—first tentatively, then hungrily. He was drunk on this new sensation, no "victim," but a willing participant in a rite the meaning of which he could only begin to guess.

The border between dream and reality had blurred for him of late, as the strange images which increasingly preoccupied him had intensified, and now he surrendered himself entirely to my world, where the two are one. He had no fear of my cold white flesh and sharp teeth. So naive was this infatuated boy that he hadn't an inkling of what might follow a kiss, and he accepted unquestioningly what would have terrified an adult.

His gentle fingers on my breast were tentative as a soft breeze. Watching the pulse against his fine, pale throat, I noted the blue veins near the skin's surface and heard his breathing intensify. Passion rising within me, I moved on top of him and kissed him full on his ripe mouth. He moaned and wrapped his arms around me, returning my kisses now. I reached up and pulled out the pins holding my hair back, and let it tumble down around his face and over the pillow. As he had dreamed for so many nights before, he buried his face in its red-gold mass and whispered, "I am yours—take me!" I felt his hardness against my thigh and moved my lips from his mouth to his silken throat. Slowly licking the tender flesh, never touched by any lover, I smelled with my sharp sense the sweet musk of his young body. As my sharp canines pierced the warm flesh, his body stiffened and he moaned again, deep and hoarse, and then was perfectly silent, except for the gradual slowing of his breathing. Slower, slower—and my drinking, first rapid and eager, then softer and slowing. His vibrancy and life flowed into my body, warming my limbs and swirling my keen senses into a swoon. But I did not drain him to the point of death: I rarely kill my victims, and this youth was far more to me than sustenance.

I held him close, my breasts which had been cold and pallid now warm and rosy. He began to say something, but I gently touched his lips with my finger and he lay back weakly on the pillow. His angular body was limp now, the fair curls damp against his forehead. I knew that though he was barely conscious, he sensed his own feelings and my presence with a vibrant awareness unknown to him in his short child's life. He was strong, and he would live to know this drama again and again with me, until he was ready for initiation and eternal life himself.

How could this boy have known what he had asked me for when he moaned, "Take me"? Ecstasy—pain—death to human life—eternity! What can this mean to a child of 14? But after his own vampire initiation, he would understand, he would know.

His eyes closed slowly and he fell into a deep and dreamless sleep. I buttoned his nightshirt, fastened my own bodice, and pinned up my hair. Wrapping the boy in a heavy blanket, I picked him up from the bed and carried him out into the autumn night. I hardly felt his weight as I held him close beneath my cloak. He was mine—mine, body and soul, for all time!

The beautiful Christopher is with me still. With his frankly effeminate features and mannerisms, he has attracted many choice men to our lair. Dressed in black satin and lace, his wide gray eyes heavily painted, pale cheeks rouged, and full lips glossy with scarlet tint, he never ceases to fascinate even my jaded tastes. Physically he will always be 14, with his silvery voice and golden halo of curls. But within he is a 90-year-old vampire, my companion on a journey through endless night. . . .

Johana

I am a 26-year-old housewife with a Science degree, two children and a husband I adore. My husband is a petroleum geologist and often spends months on end at an oil-rig site.

Recently I wanted desperately to have sex with my husband, but he was away, so I sat down and wrote him a play-by-play of what I would like to do sexually with him. I'd never written an X-rated letter and was nervous about how he would react. Well, he loved it, and now he writes sexy letters to me. I think it turned him on just knowing I had more on my mind than baking brownies. It makes me feel like a million knowing he has these wonderful sexual fantasies involving me.

Here is a fantasy my husband and I plan on acting out as soon as he returns. It is the ultimate for me.

I put on some sexy lingerie. I have prepared a cold bath for him. (He says the cold makes his penis smaller which makes it better for both of us while enlarging it.) I tenderly bathe him. I lead him into the bedroom and tell him to lie on the towel. I tell him that I must shave his hair (pubic) because little baby boys aren't supposed to have hair. I spray a pleasant-smelling shaving foam on his hair. As I shave him, I occasionally tease him so he will become stimulated. When I am through shaving him, I place a fresh towel under him and with a basin of water and sponge, I gently wash his pee-pee. Then I rub strawberry lubricated jelly all over his penis, up and down the crevice of his ass and all over his bottom and then powder him. Before diapering him I tell him how sweet the jelly smells and take one breast at a time out of my nightie and massage my nipples with it. While I do this I tell him my nipples get so hard from having him suck on me and need the jelly to soften them up. Then I diaper him. After that, I spread my bent knees apart and seductively slide over his body until my breasts are at his lips. Then I say, "You get hungry for some when you see my tits hanging out, don't you?" I place one breast in his mouth, he sucks for a few seconds and rejects it. I try the other one, but the same thing happens. I get up, squeeze my tits and find my milk has dried up. I tell him to lie still and I go into the kitchen and squirt whipped cream on my nipples. I return to him with my whipped-cream tits hanging out and ask him if he'd like a special treat tonight and he nods yes. He sucks and sucks on my nipples while I seductively rub my legs along his diapered penis. I begin to act stunned when I think it's enlarging. I open his diaper and find he is a man and tell him so. I ask him if he feels sore with pleasure and ready to burst. He nods yes. I take more jelly and rub it on him. Then I lie on my back, knees bent and spread, and apply jelly to my vaginal area while he watches. Then I mount him, softly sliding my vagina onto his hard penis. I ask him if he is ready to burst and he shakes his head no. So I rub, rock and roll all over his penis until he comes.

Then I put his lips to my vagina. I tell him to taste how delightful our juices taste mixed together. After I orgasm, I take his head and caress it on my breast and fondle his penis tenderly with my hands and tell him his penis has given me the greatest pleasure I've ever known as he fades into dreamland.

Theresa

A few years ago I was, literally, a different person. I like to think my story is a metaphor for what so many women face today. My story starts with me as a teaching nun, yes, a nun! I was teaching in a Catholic junior high. I had a strict Catholic upbringing and the decision was natural. Several friends also became nuns. What led me out of the convent were my sexual feelings. I was horrified to find my sexuality making itself known, intensely, *after* I had entered the convent. Up to that time I had only suffered through a few horrific teenage dates and proms and had imbibed the theology that "good girls" didn't think about that. If I had had those feelings earlier I would never have become a nun in the first place. As it happened, my sexuality hit me, like a bomb, in my 20s. I found I was having sexual fantasies about my male students. I was terrified and guilt-ridden, but repressing them was a losing battle. They were just too pleasurable. For the first time in my life I masturbated. My fantasies centered on a 15-year-old named Mark. He was very cute, as only adolescents can be, and the class flirt. My order was liberal enough for secular dress (no habits), and this made me less otherworldly, I guess, because Mark even subtly flirted with me.

My sexual awakening was related to changes in the Church, society, and the women's movement. Women, even nuns, were no longer afraid to assert their rights and to be openly critical of patriarchy. And what could be more patriarchal than the Catholic Church? I found myself caught up in all of this. I began to question the Church's prohibitions against masturbation, birth control, women priests, etc. These policies had been, and are, maintained totally by men. Totally! I began to see that, for instance, my sexuality was normal and even good, and it was silly to be guilt-ridden. This was a great change for me in a very short time. I no longer feel guilty about exploring my sexuality. That's when I discovered *MSG.* What a revelation! Other women, many others, had sexual fantasies and masturbated. I wasn't weird or sinful—just normal. I even got the courage, finally, to buy a copy of *MSG* (sandwiched in with several other books I didn't want) at a bookstore! I was delighted to find how liberated my fantasies were. Enough background— now for the fantasies.

I keep Mark, my student, after school. I tell him his flirting with the girls is degrading for us as women. I tell him women's power is here and he'd better learn to accept it. As I'm giving him the whole feminist lecture, I'm getting *very* excited. For the first time in my life I'm exercising power over a male! I'm also noticing how cute he is in his tight blue jeans. As punishment, he has to do some chores at my apartment (I had an apartment, even then, first sharing, & when my roommate left the Church, by myself). Driving over, Mark seems chastened by his encounter with the new woman! He apologizes and says he's learned his lesson. I'm not sure whether or not to believe him, but he seems sincere. By the time we get to my place I realize Mark's already learned his lesson. So that at my place my feelings for Mark, though still strongly sexual, become maternal as well. I decide to cook him a nice dinner but he has to help and do his share. After we sit on the living-room couch and talk, I feel sexual, fantastic. I so badly want to possess this boy, sexually & maternally. To assert womanpower by conquering him sexually, but also to maternally nurture him. Despite his big talk at school, he is completely under my control—naive and vulnerable. I have him rest his head on my lap & I stroke his hair. Soon he has his head buried in my skirt, moaning softly. The lap is sensitive for us women, of course, and this pacifies me further. All of a sudden I am smothering him in kisses. He is so young! Finally I take his hand & lead him into my bedroom. We sit on the bed & I give him an incredibly loving hug. I feel my power as a woman as I envelop his trembling body in my arms. Then, clothes on, we get under the covers. I hold him in my arms like a baby, kissing him & stroking his beautiful hair. We drift off to sleep with Mark snuggled in my arms.

Well, that's my fantasy. I've never needed others. Of course, details and characters can vary but that's basically it: to make it clear to my lover that I'm in charge—and then to "mother" him. It seems the perfect fantasy for the coming feminist era. It is, finally, my sexual identity. In dating I find myself very attracted to the new, androgynous male—shy, sensitive and vulnerable. Usually my type is easy to spot, young, shy, "cute" rather than handsome. I can tell in five minutes of conversation whether he likes an assertive woman—and you'd be surprised how many young guys, resenting the male stereotype, do! Perhaps, as a former nun, taking charge comes naturally to me. Privately, young guys have told me how much Women's Lib has done for *them*—freeing *them*—and how turned on they are by the liberated woman. With my degree, I'm making more by far than my lover (I'm 26, he's 23). It doesn't bother him a bit! Nor does my sexual assertiveness—his fantasy was to be seduced by his older sister—so you can imagine the fun we have! My fantasies are my sexuality. Otherwise, to me, it's like thinking how much you'd like a steak with onions & getting to the restaurant & ordering a salad! For example, if I don't feel in control of a relationship—in a loving but assertive way—I simply don't get vaginal lubrication. Since I've ventured into *My Secret Garden,* I've changed so totally. In some ways I haven't changed—I dress & act conservatively—but in some ways I have. I left the life of a nun & the Church. Even as a nun I followed & identified with my Episcopal sisters in their desire to be priests, and I admired the way that church was open to them. I am now an active Episcopalian—I don't know about priesthood—but it's good to know that door is open to me if I so choose. I'm mildly active as a feminist, though I think it's something every woman has to define for herself.

"ALL I WANT IS TO CONTROL EVERYTHING"

How did women keep themselves small for so long, lower their voices, shorten their steps, compress their emotional selves into the stereotypical Nice Girl?

Yes, I can understand the temperamentally quiet, undemanding woman finding this livable, but what of her more demonstrative, assertive sister, who would rather lead than follow?

Since I was there in an earlier life, I shall answer my own

question. Women did it because all women did. There was no choice; the universality of female passivity made it mandatory and bearable.

No longer.

Other things may change, but so long as women have some economic control over their lives, those who want a bigger life may act upon their choice. And their lives will give permission to others to also make up a life that suits them.

The desire to lead, to control, to be aggressive, is human, exclusive to neither sex. Ideas of domination, seduction, omnipotence, roil the collective unconscious, which knows nothing of our societal wish to divide emotions between the sexes. Even when we consciously choose to act a certain way in reality because of moral/ethical/religious codes, in the dreams we dream at night as well as in our sexual fantasies, our unconscious selves demand expression.

Why then didn't the women in *My Secret Garden* abandon the rigid, stereotypical Nice Girl role and in the safety and privacy of their imaginations try on the persona of the seductress, the sexual initiator who controls everything? The answer as always is that other women hadn't as yet given them permission. So afraid were women of breaking The Rules that they denied their fantasies even to themselves. I have no doubt that ideas of control were there, perhaps even enjoyed in fantasy, but then post orgasm, once the woman had returned to full awareness, the image of herself as the dominant one was "forgotten," suppressed like an unacceptable dream just beneath the surface of consciousness.

Instead of fantasies of erotic dominion over men, women in *My Secret Garden* who may have had very controlling natures in reality, nonetheless invented elaborate fantasies of so-called rape. It was all they dared allow themselves. Just a few words—"I am forced" to do the following—permitted a woman to create the most abandoned, unfeminine scenario while at the same time maintaining her Nice Girl status.

129

Then, once *My Secret Garden* was published, overnight the rape fantasy was rejected by the women in this book who wanted to exercise total power over and domination of men. The idea suited them. Which is not to say that the rape fantasy does not still abound; today, however, there is no effort to disguise that even as "victims" they are controlling everything that happens.

Nothing is new to the erotic unconscious. That these emotions of erotic domination, even sadism, appeared so quickly on the heels of *My Secret Garden* says that they were always in women's imaginations as well as in their real lives. Women were simply waiting for the jailers—other women —to say it was all right to make them conscious.

In this particular group of fantasies, there is no desire to hurt the man; simply, women want to make it clear that all power sexually rests with them. That the need to be in control doesn't by definition involve cruelty or pain is a distinction worth making. We've all known people who have to control life, their own and that of everyone around them too. The women in this section need to be in control in order to feel the loss of control that is orgasm. "I like to be totally in charge of the whole situation," says Judith.

Many of these women have not had much sexual experience, and they know this has something to do with their need to be dominant in fantasy. Unlike the generations of women before them, they have been educated by popular books on female psychology, women's magazines, and feminist teachers to look to their own lives for the answers to their sexuality. They know they are sexually naive, lack self-confidence, and feel guilty about sex, and they are not reluctant to name the sources of their inhibitions. Some have had strict religious training. Others feel they are overweight or just too plain to be sexually attractive to men. Yet another group realizes that the fact that mother called them a whore for masturbating isn't irrelevant.

In earlier days, these women would have been certain candidates for the rape fantasy, forced into the sex they want but fear by a faceless stranger who comes and goes in the brevity of an anonymous fuck, leaving them satisfied but blameless. Instead, they make a giant leap from the inhibitions of reality into Technicolor fantasies of masterful and total domination over their partners. The unattainable man of reality is made in fantasy "to do what I want for a change."

"I'm a rather quiet, homely person and a bit shy," says Samantha. "Sexually . . . I'm untouched. However, in my fantasies I'm anything but." In fantasy, she takes an event remembered from reality and replays it, but this time she's the aggressor, the sexually confident one. In no way does it interfere with her still thinking of herself as "a good Catholic girl."

The goal of these particular fantasies is not the man's humiliation but the woman's own sense of total sexual control. It is not about him but about her working out her own sexuality. Fantasy becomes the bridge between reality and the future. Anything imagined is safe because the women hold the reins.

Guilty as they may be about sex in real life, they never question the right to their erotic dreams. The men they dream about are not faceless strangers but men whose identity helps make the imagined fuck and the woman's own prowess more real. These women acknowledge they are a transition generation with one foot in the old world, one in the new, but they are emboldened by the sight and sound of real life, by articulate, successful, sexual women who tell them they are entitled to their sexuality.

This is important ground women have gained. Fifteen, twenty years ago, women I interviewed, who were far more sexually active than these, were unable to even think that their fear of sex came at mother's knee. Simply admitting to their fantasies was felt to be a betrayal of her.

These new women own their fantasies. If they can imagine themselves as sexual initiators, is it too farfetched to hope that they might carry this sense of control and power over into their real lives and be more responsible for themselves sexually?

Knowledge is the first step in being able to change our lives. Women used to keep themselves from "knowing" certain things that the women in this book matter-of-factly state as source material for coming to grips with their sexuality. For instance, women may not like the fact that their earliest relationship with mother influences their adult sexual lives, but today it is part of female wisdom. Women fifteen years ago didn't have this knowledge. When I was writing *My Mother/My Self,* there was a popular book (Seymour Fisher's *The Female Orgasm*) that stated that women's orgasmic potential was linked to their relationship with their father. Nothing about mother.

Painful as it may be to look at the maternal relationship, women now know they must if they are to be sexually free. Denial and suppression eat up too much energy, and a woman today needs all she's got.

Beth is only nineteen, but she wants the right to make her own decisions regarding sex "without an authoritative voice (unconsciously) booming over my shoulder." In reality her mother listens in on her private telephone conversation with a friend when they are discussing the pros and cons of virginity. Feeling violated and reduced to the state of a little girl whom mommy controls, Beth reclaims her sexuality in fantasy. She seduces her teacher, who does not see her "as a shy high school girl; he has been especially chosen . . . and I am transformed into some wonderful sexual being." By taking the lead, "making him come," if only in imagination, she transforms herself from little girl into a separate, independent person.

This is role reversal. The most popular theme of male fantasy also reverses reality. How burdensome and tiresome it is for men to always have to make the first move, be responsible, in charge, and how understandable that they should wish to flee from all this hard work and imagine women happily taking on all the sexual initiation, giving the men no choice but to lie back and be done to for a change.

It is equally burdensome and tiresome for some women to play passive little girl. It requires a great deal of effort and not much happiness if the role doesn't fit. Some women have always had the In Charge fantasy and repressed knowledge of it. No longer.

Jenne is a woman who in reality is nonorgasmic and only able to imagine a man "wanting to make love to me" if he is in mortal danger, meaning out of control. Only then can she step in, save his life, and think of him as in her debt, meaning in her control. Kay, on the other hand, is so angry and distrustful of men in reality, so frightened of rejection she can't even imagine sex unless she is the in-control seductress.

If we begin with the understanding that orgasm is the giving up of all the rigid controls that Nice Women must live by, we can see why some women, terrified of falling apart in reality if they lose control, cannot reach orgasm until they've imagined themselves as the ones who run the show.

". . . I wish notions of good and bad, right and wrong were quicker to change," says Danielle. "I do enjoy my sexuality and I prize it, but I must at the same time preserve my innocent appearance for society. And I'm being so hypocritical! I only hope things will be different for my children." To be sure she doesn't lose control of her precarious footing in both the "modern and traditional" worlds that vie for her allegiance, Danielle fantasizes herself as the powerful one who decides the sexual fate of someone crucial to her own moral self-indictment: she seduces a priest.

I'd like to close this section with two fantasies, one from Carol, thirty-four years old in 1981, and the other from Gale, who wrote to me in 1990 when she was twenty. Both women resonate to the idea of sexual dominance, assertiveness. It is fascinating to hear the older woman describe her inner struggle with the morals/ethics/traditionalism of the time in which she grew up, to emerge the responsible, sexual initiator she has always felt herself to be. "The elements of seduction, romance, aggression and equality . . . the food of life and earth mother . . . are all parts of me." Parts she would like, halfway through her life, to actually become. In fantasy, she realizes, "we create situations to suit our

133

needs." And Carol wants desperately to reclaim those dominant, assertive parts of herself she once abandoned in order to live by society's ideas of what a woman is.

For women like Carol fantasy becomes a way of going back and rewriting history so that this time it comes out right. "It's taken a year and a half and dozens of books to reach the threshold of my home," says Carol. "I'm returning . . . I'm coming home. Home base is my sexuality." I do not find it in the least surprising that in fantasy, where she returns is to adolescence. She goes back to where "we were in high school, at the reawakening of sexual desire . . . But this time I'm the instigator."

When she was an adolescent, seduction, aggression, and equality were not allowed women. Now she knows that these qualities and acts describe her. Imagining herself seducing her teenage boyfriend isn't just a stroll down memory lane. Adolescence is the most logical place in the world for women to return in order to recapture qualities, skills, characteristics, the natural, spontaneous gestures that had to be abandoned so that the stereotypical mold would fit.

When we reach puberty, the sexual energy released isn't only expressed in or limited to sexual acts. Many of us are not ready for sexual activity. But out of society's fear that sexual self-acceptance will lead to sexual activity is born a denial, a fear of what is happening to our bodies and minds. The fear inhibits far more than sexual expression. All the energy that could be fueling our social, intellectual, and psychic maturation is dampened, cut off in the name of keeping us Nice Girls. For those of us who didn't emotionally separate in the first years of life, adolescence should be our second chance.

When Carol fantasizes—changing her adolescent role into that of the Great Seductress—she is awakening all the parts of her assertive self she buried back then. How often have I heard recently divorced or widowed women say that being on their own again is like being back in adolescence? On a date with a man, they feel thrown back onto the adolescent rules. Grown women with children of their own, they have no internalized rules for themselves, no idea of themselves outside of a relationship. They went from a symbiotic relationship with mother into the same kind of dependent, safe, controlled relationship with a man. Of course women go back to adolescence to pick up the pieces.

"Unless you change your lifestyle completely," warned Carol's mother, "no man will *ever* have anything to do with you. You're going to be *alone*." Ending up alone was the worst fate that could befall a woman of Carol's generation. The irony is that many women have now learned that they choose to live alone; others know that they are sufficiently seductive and assertive to never be alone. I can't help but wonder how Carol turned out. I certainly loved her fantasies and her spirit.

Gale grew up in the 1980s and her demons are different. Since she is "into being a strong person" in reality, she's not surprised that "power has become the main theme in my fantasies." She has no problem imagining herself a man in her first fantasy: "Maybe it is because men have traditionally had more power, but for whatever reason I get a kick out of sometimes pretending in my head that I am a guy." A lesbian wish? Don't be too quick; this is 1990, and if you read the fantasy closely, isn't she both the dominant man and the woman?

Being a religious person, Gale takes the more enlightened contemporary route to sexual acceptance within the rules of her religion. Rationalizing all the way, she allows herself more and more acceptable sexual exploration in reality and in fantasy. Continuing her theme of dominance, she imagines herself a Mother Goddess because, as she says, "the ultimate power, of course, is to be a deity." Very powerfully and with the educated 1990s woman's knowledge of ancient mother goddess religion now taught in universities by feminist teachers, Gale imagines an elaborate fantasy of total control, with two men fucking her and their two wives licking her breasts. "At this point in the fantasy," she concludes, "I myself and the goddess come all over the place."

Carol and Gale are consummate Sex Controllers; what

separates them is an extraordinary decade of permission given by women to one another.

Carol

I've been called an enigma, and though it makes me feel defensive I think it's true. I *am* a hodgepodge of a woman, 34 years old, following her own plan at her own pace. There's nothing wrong with it but it bewilders the people around me. I understand their bewilderment. I buried myself deep within for over a decade. When the sham became life-threatening I started taking baby steps away from it. They've increased in size and speed to the point where I found the courage to say to my husband: "I hate housewifery. I hate volunteerism. I hate the way we live. This marriage has been a disaster for years; we live separate lives in silence. No more. I'm going to work part time. I'm going to school full time. I'm partly to blame but enough of this shit. Come grow with me or I'll wave good-bye."

It's taken a year and a half and dozens of books to reach the threshold of my home. I'm returning; I'm not coming out, I'm coming home. Home base is my sexuality. The other parts of my life are rooted to it.

I've always loved men and have been fortunate enough to have had two close male friends during my life. The first was a boy who started as a friend and grew to boyfriend status before we deepened our relationship platonically. It was at the start of our adolescence and lasted four years. When high school ended I refused to see him again. It was the biggest mistake I made at that time. If ever two young people belonged together, we were they.

The other was a friend I made when the first was firmly pushed aside. We shared more experiences together than I can count. This one, too, was platonic. The sad outcome was that when I married, the friend faded from my life. He is now half of a fond image: two young people sat side by side in a darkened room of kinetic sculpture. They were mistaken for art by the patrons. There may still be some people who think we were art. I do.

As for the first friend, were I to see him now I think I'd

still love him for himself. I do in my fantasies. We sneak away from our high school reunion together, but the attraction is not purely physical. This is where we were in high school, at the reawakening of sexual desire. At the reunion we carry it through. But this time I'm the instigator. While dancing together I tell him he has been in my bed, my best fantasy, whenever my husband enters me. God, he can't stand it. I feel him go weak in the knees, his erection almost bursting his pants zipper. He laughs in embarrassment when I reach up and touch his neck. I ask if he's still sensitive there. The heat rises. I use my fingernail against the tightly curled hair just above his collar. He shivers and the smile becomes passion. He puts my hand on his shoulder and tightens his hold around my waist. My long hair rests against his cheek. The smell of him—cologne, man and sex—electrifies me. His neck looks vulnerable, at odds with his broad swimmer's shoulder. He's so familiar to me, yet now he's a new experience.

We leave.

In the car I sit close enough to finger his neck. He, in turn, keeps a hand on my knee. I won't allow him to go any higher, not now. At the stoplight he tries to grab me, but I won't let him do that either. I lightly caress his cheek and he just has time to kiss my palm before the light turns. I have to remind him to drive. The motel is a block away.

He checks us in and we walk to the door touching arms. He seems to know I'm in command. I am the first in the room.

He stands with the key in his hand, clacking metal against plastic. I check the heating unit, turn it up and suggest he get us a bucket of ice and some mix. He looks hypnotized. I kiss his sensuous lips gently and ask him again.

"We don't need them," he says.

"Please?" I murmur in his ear.

When he comes back I'm free of my shoes and coat. My dress is a shirtwaist of a slinky material. I've unbuttoned another button, freeing me from girlishness without seeming wanton. I'm smoldering. He sets the bottle and the bucket down and loosens his tie. "Take it off, baby," I tell him. He does. It slips over the shirt fabric with a singing, swishing sound and falls silently to the dresser top.

"And the coat?" I suggest. He shucks it and lays it next to the tie.

I move closer to him and run my hand over his shoulders. "God, I love your shoulders," I whisper hoarsely. I bring his hand up and suck a finger while unbuttoning the sleeve. Then the other. I put his hands on my hips while I run my hands over his chest, unbutton his shirt, play with his stomach. He reaches for me but I tell him to wait.

"Take off your shirt. Your T-shirt."

I gasp. His shoulders are broad, his arms long-muscled. He moves with the grace of a dancer, each motion rippling along his body—not the body of a young boy but of a man. He has filled out. There's a thatch of hair peeking over his belt. I can see it in my mind beneath his clothes, a soft road leading to his cock.

My mouth is watering. I want him to strip. My belly aches with its building tightness. We are equalized. I move back a step and sit on the edge of the bed. His pants are stretched with his erection. I put my hand on it and it jumps.

"Come here," he says. I have to.

"I'm coming," I say and I mean it both ways. I'm in his arms and he's kissing me. My neck and face are love-flushed. My cunt is soaked.

With skill he undresses me while I unfasten his pants. They fall and I see he's wearing bikini briefs, his bulge barely contained.

That does it. I can't control myself. I lunge for him but he won't let me take the briefs off. He strips the bed, his erection poking from his briefs at the elastic top. I start to strip myself of my own bikini but he won't let me. "You're not ready yet," he tells me as he presses against me.

He lies down. With a finger he pushes under the leg band and into my cunt. It's dripping. He removes his hand and sucks it. He holds me so I can't move and cups his hand on me outside my pants while breathing higher up on my clit. I can't move but I have to. I'm shaking all over. I force myself to stop. I grab a blanket and shade the harsh light next to the bed.

"I want your cock," I tell him. "I want to see it." I kneel on the bed next to him and force the briefs over his hips. The hot luscious meat catches on the elastic and then springs out. Oh, hot damn, it's big—big and fat—and a few drops of come glisten on its head.

"Sugar man," I whisper as I drop between his legs and lick it up. "Mama's got a sweet tooth. Give me more . . ."

He sits up and strips his briefs from his thighs. There's a mark on his legs where they'd been, where I'd been. I throw mine off. Before he can move I straddle him and ride and ride and ride. Each time I push down I come, and now he does too. I can feel all of him filling me, spurting hot syrup, running out and covering his balls. I watch his face in that special ecstasy resembling pain, so free.

It isn't enough. There's more. We call each other everything that comes to mind. We tell each other to fuck, to suck, to come, to eat—whatever we want. The world's reduced to the room. The room reeks of sex scents and sweat and I want to stay in it forever. We suck ice before we touch each other with our tongues. It makes hot hotter. We are special ice cream dishes, he a cone and I a banana split. I could go on and on . . . with him there is no end.

What makes it so great is that it could happen. If the attraction was real—in person—I'd make this one come true.

The important thing about this fantasy is that it's nothing like any of my others. It's almost closer to a daydream and it's definitely closer to what I want in my own life. The elements of seduction, romance, aggression and equality . . . the food of life and earth mother . . . are all parts of me. I want hints of the bedroom outside the bedroom (in public). In bed I want the fucking with its juices, noise, talk, experimentation, joy, sharing and lusty gusto. I want my cunt to runneth over, and over and over. I want humor and I want to be cuddled. In other words, I want a lot more than I'm getting.

Gale

I have been fantasizing since I was 6. I'll be 20 next month. For a short while (my senior year in high school) I was trying to rededicate my life to Christ, and I was having a really difficult time reconciling my nightly pillow-between-the-legs escapades with my search for higher spirituality. Then I decided to give up guilt altogether. I feel it is only human to masturbate and fantasize, and it does not prevent me from treating others as I would like to be treated or loving my neighbor as myself. It probably makes me less judgmental.

In junior high I drank alcohol at social events (unchaperoned parties) but all other drugs (pot, LSD) had a big, bad *No!* sign in front of them in my mind. It was the same way with sex. I considered non-virgin girls as "fast" or "slutty" in the same way I considered any kind of illegal drug use only fit for losers. I was waiting until I was married because it was the "Christian," "moral" thing to do. It was all black and white to me.

In high school I still drank, but did not do any other drugs. I had friends who smoked pot, but I didn't consider them losers. I just didn't understand how they could do it, and I knew it wasn't for me. I saw girls who had sex in high school as weak. I have always been an independent person. I always say what I think, I never compromise who I am, I try never to be fake. To me that is all a part of being "strong," and I pride myself on being strong. I saw girls having sex because it was "in." I saw girls having sex because they needed to be validated by having a boyfriend. I saw girls having sex to prove they were grown up. I thought it was weak of girls to be having sex due to insecurities rather than desire.

I scammed in high school and as long as it didn't get any further than his mouth on my tits and my hand on his penis I was able to look myself in the face the following morning.

I am black and most of my friends at the time were white and Asian. I am not ugly but I am overweight. So every time I tried scamming on a really cute guy and I was successful, it

140

was like a trophy. I would love bragging to my friends about it to show "Hey, I'm not gorgeous but look what I caught!" I was with those guys to validate my own attractiveness, not out of desire. I felt bad about being weak enough to need validation from others.

When I was 18 I went to college. My girlfriends who were having sex were all telling me how *different* it was from anything else. They would all tell me that oral sex and petting and dry fucking are all one thing but when someone is inside of you it is so personal, so intimate that it just isn't like those other things. I wanted to wait and give myself away to only my husband, only let him see that special place inside of me (literally and figuratively). Secondly I realized that all the things leading up to sex are not at all on the same level as sex itself. This epiphany released me from feeling guilty about the things I did with guys short of sex. It liberated me to have more fun with guys as long as I wasn't fucking them. Even so, as a freshman I knew I wasn't ready to fellate or to be cunnilingued.

I've sucked one dick since then. It was the dick of a friend of mine who lives in the same thirty-six-person cooperative as I do. The entire situation was totally comfortable. We are really good friends. He understood that I didn't want to have sex. This allowed me to not have to hold back for fear of letting it go too far. It was also comfortable because I knew that whatever I did with him that night wouldn't make me feel guilty in the morning. I was free to have as much fun with my friend as I wanted. But most of all it was comfortable because I was ready. Somewhere between freshman year and second-semester sophomore year I wanted to fellate the next guy I scammed on. I was curious about it because one of my girlfriends (one of the very few saying she did it for reasons other than his pleasure) said it gave her a total sense of power. So I was totally ready. When I sucked dick I did everything my friend said she did. I really got that sense of power she talked about. It made me hot and incredibly heady. I would purposely suck more lightly or more slowly than I knew he would like. Then I would make him beg for me to do it harder and faster. The sound of his begging was an incredible turn-on. I stopped before he came and he got on top of me again and thrusted like mad. It felt so good that the whole time I just kept thinking, "If dry sex is this good, real intercourse must be heaven."

And therein lies the problem. I feel now like I am ready to have sex, emotionally and maturity-wise. But I am not married or even in love. So I scam when I find a friend who I feel comfortable around who is willing.

Since my first fellating experience, power has become the main theme in my fantasies. Since I am so into being a strong person this surprises me not. Here are my two favorite fantasies having to do with power.

Fantasy Number 1:
Maybe it is because men have traditionally had more power, but for whatever reason I get a kick out of sometimes pretending in my head that I am a guy. Sometimes it will be guys I know, Sting, David Bowie, etc. Sometimes it will be totally fictional guys. Either way, all the women are at my total beck and call. They have to do anything I say.

Fantasy Number 2:
The ultimate power of course is to be a deity. In this second fantasy I am a goddess in one of the ancient mother goddess-worshiping societies like in the city of Anatolia. I come down in the flesh to the awe of the citizens. I make my appearance in the temple set aside for my worship and housing my marble throne.

I stand and signal for quiet. I say, "I have come to give you many gifts of my knowledge. I will live among you like one of you, but you must respect my fleshy body and keep it from harm.

"The first gift is a chance to tap my primal waters. The men who need more insight will drink from me. Let each head of the household come forth, bringing her husbands after her."

Now what I had with me was a drug, powder mixed in a cream. It was only effective if imbibed. And I was immune. It was a hallucinogen where hardly anyone had bad trips. It was very potent. I had put this cream in my vulva and had set the jar aside on the throne, out of sight.

The women came forward, the high priestess's husband coming first. He was cute so I used him in a demonstration.

I beckoned him to the throne. I put my hands on his shoulders so he would kneel. My dress had buttons down the front so from my belly button down I unbuttoned. I stepped right in front of him and anxiously leaned his head into my vulva. He kissed once and the drug got into his mouth. He immediately felt pleasure and began to lick more thoroughly. The drug began to do its job. When he was so high that all he was doing was babbling about his visions, I told the high priestess to lead him down the steps of the throne and kiss him. She did and the drug got into her mouth too. She began to trip as well.

Everyone looked on in awe. Women edged their husbands forward to partake in the revelation. They bade me to take their husbands to drink of my primal waters. I arbitrarily picked the good-looking young ones.

The second one I picked was a young husband of an elder leader in Anatolia. The elder leader was honored. She bowed down at the foot of the stairs of the throne in reverence to me. Her husband bowed down as well, and when I bade him he crawled up the steps and I praised him for his humbleness.

When he reached the last step he kissed my foot saying, "This is for a blessing for my wife." Then he kissed my other foot saying, "This is for a blessing for my wife's children."

Then he raised himself up to a kneeling position. He wasted no time. As soon as I stood up he was partaking. He delved his tongue eagerly into me. He swiveled over every crevice, every valley, every heated peak. I gulped and let my head fall back. He snorted, grunted and groaned as he licked even more fiercely. The drug took effect, and his hallucination just made him want more of me.

Women were bidding me now, more than ever, to pick their husbands next. I smeared some of the drug on my breasts and my yoni (ancient Indian word for vagina). Then I bid two women in the back of the crowd to come forth.

They and their husbands kneeled at the foot of the throne and then began to crawl up the steps. They all kissed my feet for blessings. They all kneeled in front of me, waiting. I could see the women hoped to lick me personally, rather than through their husbands. I smiled down at them.

With my foot I teased the loincloth of the cutest of the husbands. He leaned down to kiss my foot, but I wouldn't let him. Instead I continued to tease. His erection wasted no time as he watched me lick my lips seductively. The other husband got an erection watching me tease the first husband.

I stood up and the cutest one leaned toward my yoni. He held onto me and caressed my buttocks and thighs as he licked. I took the other one's chin in my hand and raised him to my breast. I took his hand and placed his fingers on my nipple. He stimulated it with soft touches. Then he began to suck it and the drug with it. His tongue was so nice. But he only had one, so I took the chin of his wife in my other hand. I led her mouth to my other breast. I told her she and the other wife could take turns turning on this one breast. The two of them were into nibbling. They were wonderful.

The first husband came all over my foot. I got up and walked to the sacrificial altar and lay down. This gave the second husband a chance to go down on me and his wife got a breast to herself. He started by kissing my inner thighs, then working his way down. The first wife fingered my clit while he worked his tongue up to my vulva lips. He would stop and just kiss my soft, warm flesh with his lips. He would, with his tongue, retrieve cream from deep within me. My back arched, sending my breasts up farther into the beckoning mouths of the wives. They engulfed my breasts and tantalized my nipples by swirling their tongues over them and tugging at them with their teeth.

The second husband then climbed up onto the altar and took off his loincloth, unveiling a huge, uncircumcised, gleaming cock. The wives each grabbed one of my knees and pulled my legs into splits. Then the second husband entered me. He had a slow rhythm and he drew his cock nearly all the way out and shoved it all the way in each time. His wife was rubbing my clit up and down in time with his rhythm. Both the wives began leisurely licking my breasts. At this point in the fantasy I myself and the goddess come all over the place.

Alison

I am a 19-year-old college student. I am single, and I live at home with my mother and father, two sisters, and one brother. I had intercourse for the first time when I was 13 years old and I have had only fourteen different sexual partners since then. It seems that in the past year or so sex has become of increasing importance to me, both physically and emotionally. My imagination gets more and more vivid with each passing day and I masturbate quite frequently. I have a number of fantasies—being tied up by my lover; tying up my lover; performing cunnilingus on my best friend; having *ménage à trois* (with me, another girl, and one man); and one that is of increasing importance at this point in my life—dominating a transvestite. You see, I am in love with a 35-year-old man that I have been dating for almost a year and a half. He is my best friend, and our relationship has never been sexual until recently. We have had sex only twice so far. The first time, he tied my hands behind my back, taped my mouth shut, and thus proceeded to be the best fuck I ever had. The second time, he wanted me to tape his mouth shut and tell him what a "good girl" *he* was. After that experience, he opened up a lot more with me and shared that he was a transvestite at heart. He wants someone to dress him up like a woman, teach him how to be a "good girl" and basically dominate him during sex play. For some reason, this gets me extremely hot. It is his dream— much more than merely a fantasy—for this to happen to him; and I intend to help him fulfill his dream. It's not charity, as you may have guessed, because I have been having this fantasy about dominating him since we talked about it (I just want to say that *I love you,* Johnny, and by the time you read this, your dream will come true!).

I come home from work to find him fast asleep in bed. I

pull the sheet down to find him naked. He is a beautiful man—tanned, built, tall—and hung! I wake him up and ask him to accompany me to the bathroom, where I proceed to teach him how to shave all the hair off his legs. We then go back to the bed. I tell him to lie down on his back and be quiet. He is starting to look a little nervous, but he trusts me so it's okay. I find some rope we have used before and gently tie him to the bed—spread-eagled and with a pillow under his ass so that I can have a better view. By this time, his cock is starting to quiver. I get a shopping bag that I've been hiding from him and pull out a bottle of perfume and some pink nail polish. I strip down to my lace underwear and bra and go to work painting his toenails and covering him with perfume and kissing every inch of him while he squirms and begs me to stop. After the polish dries, I go to my bag again and proceed to dress him up in black stockings, black lace underwear and bra, and a black garter belt. By this time he is as hard as a rock. He tells me that he wants to be a good girl and he'll do anything I say. So I untie him and tell him to get on the floor, on all fours, close to the bedpost. I then retie just his hands together and then attach the rope to the bedpost so he can't really move too much. I go to my bag once more, and then I kneel down next to him. He is shaking a little, so I tell him softly that it's going to be all right and that he's being an extremely good girl; and doesn't he look sexy in his black outfit, better than most girls; and that he's making me very happy. I then take the baby oil that I've purchased and pour some on his back, just close enough that it dribbles down the crack of his ass and drips onto his testicles. He moans softly and I tell him he better be quiet or else. I then rub the oil all over his buttocks and the backs of his thighs, moving slowly around to the fronts of his thighs. I lean way forward to kiss his penis before I christen that too. Then I cover the fingers of my right hand well with the oil. I reach around him with my left hand and start moving my hand slowly up and down his shaft while I press the outside of his anus with my right hand. Again, I tell him he is being a very good girl for his master and that it will all be over soon.

I press my fingers further into his asshole and speed the rhythm of my other hand. He begins to moan louder and I move my hands in sync, back and forth, in and out, until he begs me, "Don't stop, don't stop," and finally shoots his load all over the rug and collapses in front of me.

I have made myself come many times to this fantasy—and this is only the tip of the iceberg. He also wants to try makeup, cross-dressing in public, and more. I'd like to try a dildo myself.

I also want to marry this lover of mine, and not just for sex, obviously. He is my teacher and my best friend and I love him more than I thought I could love anyone. He makes me feel more like a woman than anyone else ever has.

Danielle

I am a 20-year-old junior at a private Catholic university, fourth in a family of five children, and the essence of innocence and purity to my family and most of my friends. Recently at school, while my friends and I were all a little drunk, we started to talk about our sexual experiences. Everyone was shocked to hear I was not a virgin. I lost my virginity at age 17 to a man of 26. To me, he was the epitome of the "sex symbol," and the third time we went out I went to bed with him.

Ever since then I have become quite sexually active. But this bothers me. I really feel like Teresa in *Looking for Mr. Goodbar.* Boy, did that book hit home! By day I am sweet, innocent Danielle, but by night I am more promiscuous than anyone I know. What I really enjoy though is the fact that men I meet think of me as innocent, and most men are quite surprised to discover I am as old as I am. I guess my size (I am only five feet two inches and small-boned) and my general appearance are to blame. But because I appear innocent, I love to prove myself otherwise. But most of the men I sleep with I don't want a relationship with. I mean, I dream of falling in love but not having sex until the wedding night.

I guess my promiscuity has made me feel that sex is dirty

and I certainly hope I can overcome this feeling when (and if) I fall in love. Luckily, my innocent appearance has saved me from being considered a "slut." Most of the guys I've slept with have displayed a real liking for me and believe that when I've gone to bed with them it is only because I like them so much. But if I did, I wouldn't want to have sex with them, really, I'd want a romantic relationship. I guess I'm trying my damnedest to be modern and traditional at the same time.

I don't have any detailed fantasies, but I have two fantasy situations that I really want to happen. First, I want to have sex with a virgin. The men I've had sex with have all been four to eight years older than me and always the aggressors. I would like to seduce a virgin and be his "first one."

Second, I would like to seduce a priest. I am a Catholic and went to a private Catholic school until high school and I am now at a Catholic university (chosen because it is a prestigious school, and not for religious reasons). After reading *The Thorn Birds* I started having this fantasy. I have always been a little rebellious toward Catholic ideas and ways and I think the vow of celibacy for priests should be eliminated. I have two uncles that were once priests but have since married and I support them wholeheartedly, contrary to the rest of my family. I'd love to modernize the whole Catholic Church but since I can't I'll settle for seducing a priest.

In closing, I would just like to say how much I wish notions of good and bad, right and wrong, were quicker to change. I do enjoy my sexuality and I prize it, but I must at the same time preserve my innocent appearance for society. And I'm being so hypocritical! I only hope that things will be different for my children.

Samantha

I'm 18 and single, a virgin, a college student, and live at home. You might say that I've lived a sheltered life—not strict, though. My mother died when I was 6 years old and my father raised me and my brothers and sisters by himself. My dad wasn't overly strict, though we all had our special chores. I'm a rather quiet, homely person and a bit shy. But, contradicting myself, sometimes I'm bold and assertive.

Sexually, as stated earlier, I'm "untouched." However, in my fantasies I'm anything but. I became aware sexually rather late—at about age 14. My dad never told me *anything* when I entered puberty. (I suppose he was embarrassed.) So I learned through books and magazines. (I was too shy to ask my friends and we weren't taught anything at school.) I remember with amusement and a touch of bitterness my first period—I thought I was dying and made out a will. When I finally became aware of my sexuality I started masturbating (I only rub my clit, never enter my cunt—don't need to) and having accompanying fantasies.

My favorite fantasy stems from a real experience. When I was at the library once, I went to the back to get an old book I wanted to read. While looking for it, I heard panting. Curious, I went a few aisles farther down and saw a man sitting on the floor, with a girlie magazine spread out on the floor in front of him, masturbating. I quickly hurried away, cheeks flaming. But I fantasize about this man. I imagine myself approaching him and masturbating him myself, or taking his cock into my mouth and licking its head—then sucking it all the way in my mouth. All the while my hands massage and tickle his balls. I thrust a finger in and out of his asshole. He grabs my head, thrusts his cock farther down my throat and finally collapses, moaning as he comes. I continue to suck in and swallow his hot salty sperm until there is none left. After I lick him dry, I take off my shirt and bra; my breasts stand firm, nipples erect. He stares at me, breathing heavily, his cock hardening. He reaches for me and squeezes my breasts, then takes one in his mouth, suckling like a baby. I laugh throatily and pull his head against me harder. He fumbles with my pants and I assist in pulling them down. His fingers find my cunt pulsating already. I look down at his cock—hard, red, and straining upward toward my dripping cunt. I reach down and give it a gentle squeeze with my hand; he moans, shaking with pleasure. Impatient, he grabs my buttocks and pulls me roughly down on his cock. We both gasp in pleasure at the feel of his smooth gliding entry. I start to pump, sitting on his lap, impaled on his glorious cock. My fingers dig into his shoulders as I throw back my head and bite my lips to keep from screaming. (After all, this is the library—one's supposed to be quiet.) As my body arches in ecstasy, I feel his cock shoot its come deeply into me as we both groan. We collapse together. I get up shakily as he lies in the same position, eyes closed, cock now limp and pale. I dress quickly and leave him as he now sits up dazedly. I go get the book I'd been originally searching for, check it out and leave the library with a satisfied smile on my face which tells anyone who looks at me that I'd gotten what I'd been looking for!

Judith

I am a 17-year-old girl and am in my final year of school. My parents were divorced when I was very young, and I live with my mother.

When I was 13 I attended a weekly boarding school, and had lesbian relations with a girl of my own age. We were not "in love" or anything, the relationship was purely sexual. We didn't do very much though. We would rub our vaginas together and kiss each other all over, but we never got to the stage that we sucked each other, only each other's nipples and breasts. When I was 14, I was sent to an all girls' boarding school situated between two boys' schools. I am still at this school now.

I became a real "guy's girl," and very popular between the two neighboring schools. I lost my virginity two years ago when I was 15. I have not had intercourse since then, mainly because I didn't feel a thing (I don't think he was very good at it) and also because he virtually dumped me straight afterwards, and I'm very romantic and am all for "long-term relationships." I'm always looking out for the right guy, so to speak.

I have very strong physical urges and tend to be very dominant and aggressive when "getting off with a guy." I love it when a guy and I perform cunnilingus on each other because it's so sexy. I'm also really mean and tease a guy like crazy so he's begging me to do something to him. I like to be totally in charge of the whole situation.

I've never had an orgasm, but it doesn't worry me. I don't masturbate very often. When I do it's usually in the bath or in bed, and I just rub my clitoris and close my eyes and dream. . . .

I am excruciatingly beautiful. I am at school and all my teachers adore me. I am not at all popular with my classmates, but have an indefinable power over them. I am about to start the world's first sex center. This is for guys and girls, and they enter the center to be taught how to make erotic/passionate love—by me. There is one wing for the guys, one for the girls. The two sexes are never allowed to meet, and the culmination of the fantasy is when they actually do make love.

My fantasy only involves teaching the girls how to fuck. People are only allowed into my sex center after they have passed certain tests. I line up all the girls in my class. I automatically choose those whom I dislike or who are wimpy and naffish. Usually they are pretty attractive. They then have to remove their clothes while I inspect them, although not intimately. Once I have chosen the girls (about ten) they are ready to enter the center. The only things they bring with them are their bras and pants.

Everything in the center is white. It's kind of clinical. The girls go into a room and sit down while I tell them the rules. They may not leave at any time. They have to go bare-chested and not be embarrassed about their bodies. It is preferable not to wear any underpants either, but if they so wish they may wear transparent plastic G-strings which will be issued to them. Lesbianism and masturbation are encouraged at all times. If two girls want to make love or masturbate they may do so at any time, provided they do it in the corridor where everyone who wants to can watch. When meeting girls in the corridor, it is essential that they stop and greet each other with a kiss or by fondling the breasts. They sleep three each in one bed.

The sex lessons take a variety of forms. Each girl undergoes an examination by all the others. They are shown porno films and books and are taught to enjoy pain. I demonstrate the art of fucking in many ways, with dildos, hairbrushes, bottles, fingers, etc.; I also perform cunnilingus on them and show them how it is to be done. Those who I make love to are very, very honored.

If need be, they are punished. This is usually by making them drink a drink which has Spanish fly in it. The offender is then taken to a dark cold room and strapped to a wooden table so that she cannot move. She is so overcome with lust and physical craving that she cannot control herself, and my pupils take turns taunting her.

As I said, the climax of the fantasy is when they finally make love with a guy I have chosen for them. All in one big room. I stand and watch them and give advice.

Beth

I'm 19, soon to be 20, living at home, white, middle class, with one year of college behind me. I come from a broken household (both parents remarried), living under my mother's roof. Under my mother's roof there is a lot of unspoken sexual guilt combined with my mother's outspoken "no." Since I was 17, which also marked the beginning of any sexual activity, I've been struggling with the morals of "right and wrong" in terms of full-fledged sexual experience. I am currently not involved with anyone, am hoping to break away from the family, and finally make my own decisions regarding sex—without an authoritative voice (unconsciously) booming over my shoulder.

Perhaps I should add that while I was "breaking away" at 17, my mother listened in on a telephone conversation in which a girlfriend and I were discussing the importance of virginity—rather, losing it, and should I go ahead and "give in" or stay the "nice girl"; that type of thing. That, I think, has worried me more than any dictum that it was nasty to masturbate. I don't know why, but it seemed unfair to be violated in that way.

At the present moment, I am still a virgin.

One of my fantasies: I decide to consent to a night in bed with my girlfriend's 23-year-old brother. It is in the basement. The pullout couch is already out. The television is on. (It is about three in the morning.) In reality he drew me onto the bed. In fantasy, I'm lying on the bed, wearing a nightshirt, as he rises to turn off the television. As his back is turned to me, I get up from the couch, lift the nightshirt over my head and walk over to him, stark naked. He turns, pleasantly surprised, embraces me, and we proceed over to the couch. In the fantasy, I am not at all inhibited or frightened by the thought of bedding down with this girlfriend's brother. (Not that she wouldn't approve of the situation—she'd probably cheer me on—but I've only known him through her, and then, just talking.) I'm getting more and more excited, and less and less inhibited. If he is still in his cutoffs by the time we're in bed, I reach for his zipper. But I have become this extraordinary sexual being, uninhibited by any advances on his part, or, for that matter, any moves on mine. I do all of the things which ordinarily send me off and running in the other direction. The result is this wild, exciting night spent with a "stranger," of sorts, who I know has taken many of his sister's friends to bed. In fantasy, that does not concern me. I am too wrapped up in the whole thing to worry about "Will he still love me tomorrow?"

The latest fantasy involves an old high school teacher on whom I had a mad crush. He is tall, dark and handsome; 34, pretty well built. We have come up to my grandmother's house for a visit. The house is roomy, comfortable, and full of beds. (It figures that I'd choose this setting, but it, too, lends itself well to fantasy.) He is staying in one room (my mother's old room, I just realized—Freudian slip), and I am in the room across the hall. I go across the hall to say goodnight. He is lying on the side of the bed closest to the door, making it easier for me to get at him if I want to. He reaches for me first, and pulls back the bedcovers. I tell him that I will be right back—having to prepare myself for this "monumental event"—and go back to my room to put on a little perfume, a little makeup, and maybe put on something a little more suitable. This will not only be an important experience to me (because it is my first time), but it will also be important to him from the standpoint that he knows he is helping contribute to my full maturation. In reality, this teacher was very helpful in getting me out of my shell, finding out where my talents were (I hope to be a writer), and gaining more self-confidence. Naturally he has been specially "chosen" for this event. I am not seen by him as a shy high school girl; I have been "transformed," in a sense, into some wonderful sexual being.

I had an interesting experience with someone whom I dated when I was 17. He is two and a half years younger. We'd gotten into bed, and he, "experimenting," slipped down in the bed and attempted to perform cunnilingus on me. All in all, that experience was a disaster. About a month or two later, all full of new and different ideas, I went down on him. But something strange and wonderful happened; *I let myself go.* It worked. If he was surprised, I was even more so (he had, before, assumed the "dominant" role). I myself had made the first move. It gave me great satisfaction to see that I made him come; always before he had simply masturbated in between the heavy petting activity. I couldn't get over the experience. Even in the midst of the usual type of adolescent experimentation, there was some room, I discovered, for just being yourself—breaking loose from the standard procedures. What a relief! Could I really be that person who made the first move? Who made *him* come? I felt wonderful. I had finally "asserted myself" the way I wanted to; it really could happen if you just relaxed, let yourself go, and acted on your "unladylike, not-nice-girl" instincts.

Kay

I am 21 and single. The way I was raised, I always was (and still am) intimidated by men and the (apparent) freedoms they have in their lives. Recently I've realized the differences

154

and similarities between my mother and myself. She and her older sister raised their children under the pretext that they should be seen and not heard, especially if you were a girl. Growing up under that influence and the fact that all my cousins, save two, are male, I've had a hell of a time finding my identity as a woman/female. I was a tomboy, always sneering at the "sissy" games of dolls, etc., so I played with my older brother and his friends.

I was an extremely shy child, emotionally at least, once I started school. I was tall and quite plump for my age, and was extremely self-conscious about it. Kids always teased the hell out of me until I learned to fight back with my "wall of indifference."

I'm glad the way my parents raised me, except in the way of emotional expression. It was rare that I was hugged or kissed, and the only time it was done was when relatives visited. I was always told to "kiss your uncle" or "aunt." I didn't want to, being unused to and uncomfortable with physical contact, but did it anyway because "Mother said so." I grew up feeling that men were complete idiots who couldn't do a damn thing for themselves except have fun with no responsibilities, no emotions like girls have. The women in my family have all controlled everything in running the lives of their families and houses.

In my teenage years, I fantasized how I wanted a man to be for me. I always thought of a handsome tall dark man with whom I'd have a perfect understanding, like he was my other half emotionally. Physically, I always envisioned it to be like the characters in Rosemary Rogers's novels. But in reality, I always imagined that the first man I ever had sex with would be all I've imagined physically, *but* a complete stranger, that I'd never see again after we slept together. That way he couldn't laugh at me for being a virgin, nor at my vulnerability. He wouldn't see through my facade of the cool and collected woman of the world who was really just a scared little girl. A girl who thought that since she was tall, flat, had big ugly feet, and wasn't "picture perfect," no one would want her, let alone touch her.

When I was 20 I fell in love for the first time. I wasn't overwhelmed by him. I felt safe. No threat to my vulnerability. He and I got to know one another as people before we slept together. The first time we did, I felt the old dreads and inhibitions creeping in. I was afraid that if I had sex with him, his interest would wane and he'd leave me in the dust, as in the past. So I started rationalizing my fears, stifling them. He made me feel that he desired me, found me likable and attractive, which blew my mind. He taught me desire, showed me parts of myself I never knew existed. And he came back. I fell in love, but I realized that once my heart is involved, my spontaneity dissolves. The person is too close for comfort. I'm no longer in control. I'm involved! The earth shakes and I feel like he's got me at knife point, aimed at my heart. Distrust distorts and stifles my response. I don't want him to touch me but I want him. I can't seem to make it clear to either myself or him that there's a war going on inside me.

I want to touch him, I have to be in control of our sex relationship. I take the initiative always. When he tries to, I push him away. He's too close and I don't want him to see it. I feel that if he knows, he'll run away. He can't handle it so don't shove it at him, when, in reality, I can handle it. I won't drop the barriers and let go. I'm scared. I'm vulnerable.

That relationship ended last year. I was emotionally devastated to the point of a breakdown. For the longest time I couldn't even bear to think of his name. I obliterated him from memory. At least I tried like hell to, but no success.

Since then I've come to know myself better. All my life I've been dominated by men, surrounded by them, yet I never, until now, have taken into consideration that they have feelings, insecurities, problems, too!

It's like everyone is in a game, a race to prove they can outdo the other. They are invincible and don't need anyone. I must say that it's nice to feel that I can *share* my life, knowing that I can take care of myself, but not isolate myself emotionally because other people feel, too! Not everyone is really out to destroy others for the sake of their own security. That's all I think it is—the need to trust, feel secure that you can be yourself and *feel* without worrying that someone's lurking in the shadows to nab you when you're not looking.

My fantasies now vary according to my emotional moods. If I am calm and at peace inside, my fantasies involve having a relationship with a man who doesn't feel the need to play games. He's honest about his feelings and shares it. If I'm insecure, the fantasies have me being the "seductress," the one in control. But in all my fantasies, the man is older than me, and he always loves me entirely. He holds nothing back, he isn't "somewhere else" when we make love and I always surrender myself to the sensations of him touching, kissing, loving me entirely, inside and out. I am sensuous more than sensual. I get such delight out of touching and loving a man the way I like to be touched and loved. The thrill of being totally alone with a man without fear of intrusions is my ideal. That way there is only him and myself to deal with.

The idea of having sex with more than one man at a time excites me when the old insecurities surface. We all get fucked to our fullest without threat of emotional involvement: It's understood that it's all just for physical pleasure, nothing more. I desire one man, physically appealing to me as well as emotionally, who won't be afraid to surrender to his desires with me without becoming aloof on either of our sides. We are both sexually and emotionally involved.

Louellen
I love reading your books before I go to sleep. It totally relaxes me and sometimes creates quite pleasant dreams.

I am a single, 20-year-old female. I was raised a Catholic, and I still attend church when I can, yet I don't believe in everything the Roman Catholic Church does (like the ruling about surrogate mothers, artificial insemination, etc.). My boyfriend and I have sex as much as we can. I love it. Sometimes he ties me up and I fantasize I am being raped.

157

(Good little Catholic girls can't be held responsible for such pleasure!) But here's one of my favorite fantasies:

I become a successful career woman. I work 9:00–5:00, own a great sports car, and a nice house in a not very populated area. My friends and family wonder why I don't go out more, they think I work so hard that I just come home and pass out. On the contrary! Little do they know that I employ fifteen male housekeepers. Some are blond, some brunette, some Italian, even a couple of black housekeepers. They are all different, yet they are all gorgeous. They all have very nice builds, are very well endowed. My male house-keepers wear just a black tie. They all can't wait until I come home from work, they've been preparing for it all day. When I get home they all line up to greet me. I go down the line giving them kisses and my hands go roaming all over their bodies. Most of my housekeepers are already hard and throbbing. They're praying that I'll pick them tonight. You see, I pick only three a day to have fun with, the rest of them have to go back to their household chores. I pick one to serve me dinner, one to give me a massage and relax with, and one to share my bed with me for the night.

After I pick my three playmates for the night, the other twelve housekeepers go back to dreary chores while the special three gloat in their victory, teasing, "Well, maybe you'll get her tomorrow if you're lucky!"

When dinner is ready, my first chosen man gets me and seats me at the table. No one else is around. The dining room is always just candlelit. I take a couple of bites, and my "maid" just stands there with a huge hard-on, waiting for my next command. Sometimes I command him to lie on the table and I eat my dinner off of him, or sometimes I sit on his lap, feeling his maleness through my clothes while he fondles my breasts during dinner. Sometimes I just tease him. I just read the newspaper, seeming indifferent to his naked excitedness, and he gets so frustrated that he shoves everything off the table and lays me there, pumping me so hard that everyone in the house stops what he's doing to listen to how hard and loud I'm screaming tonight. You see, when I'm not around the house, they all compare notes on what gets me really going. It's like a contest with them, "Oh yeah, well I gave her five orgasms this week!"

After dinner, I move into the den to watch the evening news. My second man strips me (dinner sex is always just a quickie, I never have all of my clothes off) and massages every part of my body. He starts with my neck and back, moving over my buttocks, lingering near the back of my thighs. Since he sees me squirming already, he moves to my calves and my feet. He turns me over and smiles when he gets to massage my breasts. (I have very big boobs.) He doesn't knead them like dough, as some men do to us women with big breasts, he starts with just gently swirling around the nipples and widens his circle every time he goes around until he's circling my whole breasts, alternately sucking and licking and nibbling, too. My massaging man never has intercourse with me, he just sort of warms me up for my bed partner that night. He just drives me so wild that I practically have to *run* to my bedroom to get totally fulfilled.

That's where housekeeper number 3 comes in. He's already waiting for me in bed, sipping on some champagne and anxiously awaiting my arrival. Sometimes I just run in and get on top of him and fuck his brains out because I'm so horny I can't control myself. Most of the time he just waits for my orders: "What would please you tonight, ma'am?" Then I tell him either to eat me out until I come, or I feel like a 69er tonight. But once in a blue moon they get fed up with taking orders, and man number 3 will just pin me down and say, "Let's do it like this tonight, this is how *I* want it!" Or sometimes they'll shove their cocks down my mouth, they *know* I can't do a thing about it. I mean, they know I would never fire them!

Jenne

I am 45 years old, have been happily married for twenty-one years and have two children, 19 and 14. I met my husband at the age of 22 years, and he was the first and only man I have ever had sexual relations with. I had been frigid all my life (it took me many years to come to that conclusion) and, when I finally gathered enough courage to tell my husband, just a few months ago, it was he who went to the library to get Masters & Johnson and Helen Singer Kaplan to try to reverse a lifetime's bad habits. Up until that time, the only orgasms I had ever had were upon waking from sleep and a dream (which dreams I could never recall). Together we're working on it, with some success, but I feel that I am and will always be a sexual retard for having gotten started in sexual activity at such a late date (23 years). I tried masturbating when I was a teen, mainly because I had heard that all kids did it, even though they were not supposed to. I never could get any agreeable sensations out of it and quit trying. I cannot remember my parents being particularly repressive or punishing me for anything of that nature that I might have done at a young age, but I do remember a nurse in summer camp telling several of us that we would get cancer if we "abused" our bodies.

I am indebted to you for your book, not only because it showed me that I was not unnatural, as I had feared, for having a rich fantasy life, but also for showing me that my fantasies were rather unusual in that I was never able to imagine anyone actually making love to me. My fantasies are almost exclusively concerned with my saving some handsome and virile man's life and then, as a result of this, his wanting to make love to me. I have been particularly attracted to astronauts, and each time a capsule, space station, or shuttle has taken off has been for me a particularly fruitful time for these fantasies. I imagine that I am particularly attracted to one of the men on board— someone who is very clean-cut, dark and quite well muscled. Then some emergency arises on board, an electrical fire or a leak, and somehow I am the one who risks life and limb, getting burned or whatever as a result, and saves the lives of everyone on board. As a result of this the gentleman that I am particularly attracted to is so grateful that he wishes to make love to me.

ANGRY WOMEN/SADISTIC FANTASIES

The angry voices of the women in this section are long overdue, and I welcome their appearance, these embittered females—yes, even the sadists. It is time we acknowledged that some women are as mean and cruel as some men. Continuing the fiction that women are the loving ones while men alone are the Bad Guys doesn't really serve women so much as restrain them. Denying women's anger is equally confusing to men, who are increasingly surrounded by aggressive women who compete for their jobs and want their hearts, too.

Twenty years ago there wasn't even a whisper of women's rage, which shows how well the defenses were working. The women in *My Secret Garden* felt they had no control over the images that swam into their minds. It was as if the woman were a piece of blank paper on which the unconscious scribbled its messages. Why so many of her fantasies were couched in themes of rape and force was beyond her ability to comprehend or her will to change.

This new generation is not so passive. Wendy's fantasies are literally updated before our eyes as she goes from the standard rape fantasy she's always had—and of which she is ashamed—to a more current fantasy in which she is the dominant, powerful one. She is speaking in the year 1980; women are marching for the Equal Rights Amendment, Sherry Lansing has become the first woman to head a major motion picture studio, and a Gallup poll reports that women have become more at ease picking up the tab when dining with a man. With so much history in the making, one can sympathize with Wendy's disenchantment at being aroused by images of herself as a slave girl.

As if to correct her self-portrait in midsentence, she offers another fantasy, "which is the one I am in the mood for lately," in which the roles are reversed and she is now the dominant master. "I don't make love to the slaves, or even to the guards," she states. "In it I only want to control the fate of the male slaves. I will admit, though, my victim is someone I am angry with, like my last boyfriend. I want to make them hurt so bad that they pray for death . . . or make them feel so good that they wonder what is left, since they have reached their absolute peak in pleasure."

But even an imagined act can take courage. That is what I applauded when I first read these fantasies in the early 1980s, when they were most prevalent. It was exciting to hear women recognizing their anger and fighting back instead of accepting life's adversities as victims.

Maybe this is why I have such mixed emotions rereading these fantasies today; a number of years have gone by and I've seen enough female hostility to last me a lifetime. While bravery remains something positive that I still struggle for in my own life, now when I read one woman's fantasy of holding a knife to a man's throat before fucking him, even though it is an imagined way of "dealing with my rejection," I'm left asking myself whether such an act—even an imagined one—doesn't leave the woman with some moral responsibility.

"The conscious mind allows itself to be trained like a parrot," Carl Jung wrote, "but the unconscious does not— which is why St. Augustine thanked God for not making him responsible for his dreams." How much of what goes on in these fantasies is consciously selected, how much unconsciously? So long as they are not lived out, do questions of morality enter in? Some of these ideas and images of revenge seem to be willed by the woman into the picture frame; others, selected by the unconscious, force themselves into focus.

Paloma, for instance, is in reality frustrated; she likes anal sex and her husband does not. In her fantasy, he is raped anally by a woman who is ". . . me?" she questions. She doesn't know. Or does she?

These new retaliatory, coercive voices, along with the well-known nurturing, loving voices of women, complete a whole human being. Let me add that most of these women

162

have not yet found either the words or the courage to express their anger in reality, though they have good reason to feel it. It is in fantasy where they feel safe and where there is that mysterious capacity to eroticize anger.

Because changes in sexual fantasy reflect changes in our real lives, it is important to understand not only the sources of women's anger but also why it was suppressed for so long and why it finally emerged so forcefully with the women in this book.

In the past, traditional women denied their anger, internalized it; they suffered migraines, depression, ulcers, and worse. But anger is a universal emotion. Feelings of assertiveness and aggression are also human, experienced by both males and females. It wasn't until the late 1970s that behaviorists began to question the long-held theory that high levels of male hormones separated men as the true aggressors. Today the argument continues, but many scientists now agree that neither genetics nor testosterone alone produces an angry, hostile individual. Equally, perhaps more important are early family background, conditioning, and socialization—for both males and females.

Feminists have argued that women's economic and sexual freedom would free men, too. I agree and add that the admission of women's capacity for anger, revenge, even sadism, will also free both sexes. What has been missing in our understanding of women's anger is that their assaults have usually been psychological. That doesn't make the abuse any less traumatic.

For centuries the patriarchal system denied certain truths about women that would undermine male superiority. Most important was the denial of motherhood's power, meaning that women's role in the nursery could only be seen as benign and nurturing. To recognize that mother was sometimes cruel, even violent gave women the potential to feel and exercise the full spectrum of male emotion; it gave them the power of men.

When I began to hear these angry new female fantasies in the early 1980s, I had hoped that they reflected society's readiness to explore and accept the full range of woman's character, good to bad. In the last few years, however, I have been hearing fewer and fewer of these mean fantasies. The falloff parallels women's increasing return to motherhood. My worry is that as women reassume their traditional role, the one that more than any other defines their womanliness, their anger will once again be repressed. They will feel it; they will act on it, but they will deny that anger is what motivates them. Their faces will be red with fury, their fists clenched, but the words on their lips will be "Who me, angry?" What we will have is women in the workplace, mothers in the nursery, angrier than ever but refusing to admit that they are, and denying responsibility for whatever acts of cruelty they commit.

Too harsh? I don't think so. No one, ever, has as much power over another human being as a mother over a child. Alas, not enough men have yet successfully invaded the nursery to alter my view that it is still women's territory; we cannot have women returning to their almost total dominion over that female citadel without coming to terms with the fact that the mothering role is the most important and powerful in all of human life.

My heart sinks as I read an article in this morning's *Wall Street Journal* on pregnant women in the workplace. Citing the "resentment," "intolerance," "discrimination," and "unhappiness" of fellow workers toward pregnant women, along with a sense that they are being "punished" for their imminent motherhood, the article goes on to quote the female editor of a new book on working women: "There is something about motherhood that makes the woman herself and others feel she is less important. Motherhood isn't a powerful position."

Haven't we learned anything? Haven't the past twenty years made women big enough, smart enough to question their own defenses, as well as society's, against the envy of the power of motherhood? No one will suffer more from mother's denial of her power than the child. Yes, some people are resentful of pregnant women—but not because motherhood is a weak, powerless position. Quite the opposite. Perhaps some of the envy the pregnant woman feels stems from her own projection: she would be envious if she were in their place. Indeed, the author of the above article admits to having felt resentment of pregnant women herself. Aren't rich people always imagining that others want to do them in because *they* would if the roles were reversed?

Women are strong enough today to accept motherhood for what it is: a lot of hard work, responsibility, and sacrifice yes, but also naked power and control. If mothers don't come to terms with their omnipotent role in the nursery, they will continue the traditional denial—"Poor mothers, we have no power"—thus leaving themselves free to use that power however they choose on the people who are only too aware of how big the Giantess is, the children.

I have heard mothers' lullabies and I have heard their angry voices, too, humiliating their children in public, screaming at them in the booth behind me in Howard Johnson's. Until the mid-seventies, mothers with children were the only angry female voices one heard, except for the odd shrew, the witch, the *stronza,* the woman of whom my mother used to comment, "She sounds like a fishwife," meaning lower-class, out of control—not the way I, a Nice Girl, would ever want to sound.

It wasn't until women collectively raised their voices fifteen years ago with loud, legitimate demands that the world began to take their anger seriously. As more and more defiant women marched for equal rights, had their ultimatums pubished in newspapers and books, their voices heard on TV, only then did history begin to record the effectiveness of women's anger. Abortion was legalized, women started to get elected to high public offices, and as more and more women sought economic independence, divorce rates reached an all-time high.

The women who effected these historic changes were not Nice Girls who bit their tongues. They played the full scale of human emotions out loud, and the women in this chapter heard them. Maybe they themselves were still too young to articulate their anger, but for the first time in my research, their retaliatory feelings became eroticized in sexual fantasy.

Here are some of the sources of real anger that they mention:

1. The hypocrisy of society, which tells them sex is okay but doesn't really mean it.
2. Parents who tell them sex is bad but themselves practice the fashionable adultery of the 1970s and 1980s.
3. Mother, who punishes them for masturbating, making it clear that any sexual life, other than a repetition of her own asexual life, is wrong/bad/sinful.
4. The church, which would separate them from their sexuality.
5. Envy of male power—economic, sexual, and social —as well as of the freedom from the fear of pregnancy that men enjoy.
6. Dependence on men who hurt and humiliate them.
7. The double standard of sexual behavior for men and women.
8. Last but not least, the men who sexually molested/ raped them when they were little.

No matter who is the source of their real anger, the people these women attack in fantasy are always men. Even when mother calls them a slut, a whore, setting them at war with all good feelings about their bodies, it is men they punish in fantasy. Men may not yet have actually entered their lives, meaning they are closer to childhood than maturity, but still they go for a male target, always safer than a female.

For instance, Anna is twenty-one and has never had a relationship with a man. It is her "old world" mother who doesn't approve of her dating. Is she angry at her mother? No, she would not dare. She may be afraid of her mother's retaliatory anger (as a tiny child would be), or that the love between her and her mother could not stand her fury (as children fear) and she would die without her mother's love (as a child would). Instead, her fury strikes out against an innocent man.

Twenty years earlier Anna might have fantasized a powerful brute forcing her into the forbidden sex she desires, leaving her blameless, a victim, still her mother's Good Girl and safely unaware of any anger whatsoever (except the anger of Bad Guys, of course). But Anna is speaking in the early 1980s. She grew up watching Gloria Steinem angrily debate her opponents. She may have read Marilyn French's *The Women's Room* and was probably taught by feminist teachers. In fantasy, Anna gets on top of her man and "comes down on his penis . . . until he's begging for mercy."

Anna has learned from the example of other women's lives that it is okay to be angry. However, she goes for the wrong target, albeit the safer one. Having reached her orgasm, she "leaves him there on the floor," her toy, her doll, punished as mother would have punished her.

The women in this chapter tie men up, starve them, infantilize them, gangbang them, treat them as "sex objects," and then finally, to show men what they really think of them, turn their backs on them and seek sexual gratification with other women. This is real revenge, the final devaluation/elimination of the male.

I have always thought of fantasy as that safe playground where we can privately play out any ideas we choose without self-recriminations. But ideas of woman as rapist had never turned up in my research on women's fantasies until now. Women like Ruth seem determined to preserve the image of themselves as more sinned against than sinning while at the same time taking on the very qualities of men they have always claimed to hate. Ruth is both angered and aroused by one of her young male students, who flirts with the girls in her class; she soothes her outraged feminist sensibilities by imagining that she shows *"him* what it's like to be treated like a sex object." In fantasy, she lures him to her house, forces him into sex, thus showing him what a "real woman" is. Only Ruth knows whether the fantasy is something she "consciously" wishes to live out or something she already has. If fantasy, it may not be that far from reality. Indeed, only recently the trial of a New Hampshire schoolteacher who was convicted of seducing one of her students and then convincing him to kill her husband made national headlines.

Few women have the bulk or strength to overpower a man (though real physical rapes by women have been reported), but women have always had their own way of getting back at men. Usually the revenge inflicted is psychological and goes unrecorded in legal and medical annals. But the memory of humiliation lasts far longer than physical pain. One way men react to the psychological pain they've suffered at women's hands is to turn around and actually rape women.

In the early 1980s a man wrote to me asking if I'd ever heard of a "muscle fuck." He knew of a young woman on his college campus who had developed the talent of painfully fucking a man dry by using her vaginal muscles and thighs; the word on campus was that she was tired of macho studs and had developed her muscle fuck as revenge.

I welcome the full-frontal appearance of the bitch; there is some of her in all of us. (But I must admit that the muscle fuckers scare me; the image of the killer woman has always been more terrifying to both men and women than that of the killer man.)

It takes practice to express rage in such a way that others listen and take us seriously. People, men and women, have always listened to male voices more attentively than female voices. If these angry young women in the early 1980s sound a bit out of control, it is because their voices are still untrained. Anger begins with infantile rage, a baby's uncivilized scream at the universe. Only with repeated practice and acceptance from others more powerful do we learn how to express anger. When these young women lash out at men in their fantasies, we can hear the unaccustomed rage jerking and soaring in the larynx.

We may not like anger in men, and certainly not all express it in civilized terms, but men are more at home with the spontaneous verbal jab, the blowing off of steam; early on, life taught them that they wouldn't die for daring to show anger. Mother tolerated her son's first show of might: "Such a little man."

It's a different story with a daughter. Would that mother got out the verbal boxing gloves and practiced healthy anger/competition with her daughter. But mother's mother didn't let her express anger; instead of changing the legacy, women too often "forgive" their mothers when they hear themselves repeating with their own daughters what they hated most when they were young.

Many of these young women say they love men. They also hate them. They are the first generation of women to feel free enough to voice this ambivalence. Anger is, after all, love's other face. Until recently, however, women could literally not afford to know this. Economic dependence on men kept them locked into the Nice Girl roles, where they had been taught—long before men entered their lives—that anger could be their undoing, lose them everything.

Nothing was more difficult for me during the writing of *My Mother/My Self* than coming to terms with the idea that our hottest furies are reserved for the people we love most. I lost my hair and wrote the last chapters of the book lying on the floor, my back in spasm, accepting for the first time in my life that I had any anger at my mother.

Men have always been more aware of their love/hate relationship with women. It is not coincidental that men have been more independent, more sexual, more economically powerful. They could afford rage. Women were "the ball and chain." "Take my wife, please!" The tired offensive jokes still get a laugh because they air everyone's pent-up anger at women.

Like other women I resisted for years the notion that men saw us as powerful. Even when I was the breadwinner in my former marriage, I maintained the illusion that a man was taking care of me. To keep him big and me little had a crippling effect on my independence, my sexuality, and my professional growth. Only when I began to write about jealousy and envy did I realize that women see men as the

NANCY FRIDAY

powerful ones—and resent it—and that men do the reverse. Writing that book was the beginning of my ability to drop the defensive posture of little girl.

Why would men have gone to such extraordinary ends to keep women dependent, asexual, and boring if they were not mindful of how small a woman had once made them feel? Putting women on a pedestal, far, far above mere mortal men's heads, had the soothing effect of blotting out men's rage and envy: How could one resent a madonna? She was literally out of his world, too remote for rage and envy.

Deified, idealized, paid lip service on the institution of Mother's Day, an angry woman adjusted her halo and wondered what to do with her bile. She bit her lip, took a drink, practiced denial—"Who me, angry?"—then vented her spleen in the only place where she had absolute control, the nursery. And so the system perpetuated itself.

Now the witch is out of the nursery and the fury of women, feared by men and women alike, is loose in the land. Not as much as it was ten years ago—I'm sorry to say—but at least we've seen and heard the angry witch in people like Margaret Thatcher, Golda Meir, Germaine Greer, and Madonna, who've shown us that the aggressive/hostile/sexual side of women can be aired and the world doesn't end.

The scary witchy side of women is power we gave to mother long ago when we were children and needed to maintain a single loving image of her. We split off the angry mother/witch from the nice mommy, leaving ourselves with the all-loving person upon whom we were dependent. The idea of emotional separation and individuation isn't just the ability to see ourselves whole but to see her whole as well—good and bad. Otherwise we grow up in years but stay emotionally tied to her as children.

There are no pedestals for the new woman. By definition an independent sexual person must recognize her assertive, angry self. Kicking and thrashing all the way, like it or not, women are going to have to accept their mean, cruel parts . . . or find new forms of denial, which by necessity will be even more destructive to themselves and everyone around them.

Separation and individuation are difficult emotional pieces of work which don't require going home and shaking your poor old mother by the shoulders until she admits her former sins. It is work we do alone because we are the ones who want to change, to understand why a few critical words from her, a telephone call, can destroy us in a way our husband cannot reach us. If we don't honestly accept what we had with her and ultimately let it go, then throughout life when the inevitable anger does erupt, it will be out of all proportion to what has happened; the target of today's anger—our husband, our children, our friends, coworkers —will get the full force of fury never expressed long ago at the appropriate time, at the appropriate person.

Is Linda's fantasy, so full of rage and sadistic revenge, a scenario of a man and a woman? The punishments, the language, the anger itself, are rooted in the nursery. The fantasy sexualizes the relationship of a naughty child and a mother. This time around, however, Linda is the powerful mother and the man stands where she once stood: dependent, begging, obedient, ultimately loving. She spanks him, scrubs him fiercely in the tub, gives him an enema, washes out his mouth with hot water, and convinces him in other "loving" ways that "from now on you're mine and mine alone."

"Yes ma'am," he replies.

Those of us who grew up prior to the permissive 1960s had an advantage because what our parents and society said about sex was in complete agreement with how they felt deep down inside: Sex outside of marriage was wrong. If we didn't like it, at least we had their absolutist stance, solid ground from which to push off should we choose to rebel.

While the young women in this book were beneficiaries of our liberation, they were also casualties of our hidden agendas. It takes generations for society to change its mind on the deepest, often unconscious level about something as significant as sex. These women rightfully harangue the duplicitous world around them that applauds sexually explicit women on one hand, then labels them sluts for having sex. "I'm appalled by our society's hypocriticalness," cries Chere, who has read all the books and acted on the permissive messages on the billboards that paper her world.

Angry but not about to take it passively, these young women imagine retaliatory scenarios in which their sexual high is that "I control everything!" In fantasy, Susie seduces an innocent young guy in front of everyone, then abandons him on the dance floor, "with his jeans hanging open."

Tina "corners" her boyfriend, threatening to "spike him" with her high heel if he doesn't let her perform fellatio on him.

"I guess I believed those books where the heroine is independent, sexual and the man marries her," says Chere. "Hah, . . . the man would use her, then throw her away like a toy." Chere takes anger and desire in hand and conjures up a fantasy of the most powerful, handsome man in England, who could have any woman he desires. "I'm not a virgin, nor do I play games!" she shouts at him, then climbs aboard, "descending on him with several orgasms." Like a punch in the nose, those orgasms. Does anger rebound and destroy her, does he leave her? Absolutely not. "He rushes me off to the nearest priest, vowing never to lose me or my love."

These young women assume that the men they have sex with are as liberated as they. The truth is that it was women, not men, who changed in the 1970s and early 1980s. In my own 1981 survey on college men, as well as in subsequent surveys, the number of men who preferred a virgin bride always hovered around the 25 percent mark. Men's fragile sense of masculinity wavers at the thought of comparison: How many other guys has she known? Were they better lovers, meaning to the male, who measures masculinity in inches, did they have bigger penises? Comparison kills.

In an earlier time, a young woman like Nina would have taken her anger at her parents for confusing her sexually and turned it against herself. "They pressed me into believing sex was bad," she says, "but both were having their affairs on the side." Their actions told Nina one thing—sex is exciting—but their moralistic preaching conveyed the opposite. She got a red and a green light and acted on both.

Instead of turning her anger into the traditional fantasy of being forced, overwhelmed into sex, Nina refuses to be a victim. Vulnerable and scared in reality, she nonetheless becomes "as aggressive as hell," picking up men for one-night stands "so that I wouldn't be conquered by my fear." In fantasy, she sexualizes her rage, imagining a rapist whom "I always fight off and practically kill in the process. I have an anger toward men that I release by thinking about being violent toward one."

From past experience I assume that some critics will accuse me of encouraging women to act like the worst of men. That is too simplistic for our time. Women are already "acting like men" in many traditionally male roles. All the sex roles are up for redefinition, and it's not a bad thing either; loosening the stereotypical straitjackets on women may also free men. Nina, for instance, sounds like generations of young boys who feel pressured into macho sex before they are ready; they, too, have had to conquer their fear by being "as aggressive as hell." Terrified of not measuring up, they take out their anger on the easiest target: the young women they fuck.

Which brings us to the many women in this book like Nina, Terri, and Dawn who were sexually molested when young. It is a violent enough crime to make anyone angry for life. These women do something very new with their rage: They sexually abuse/molest/rape men in fantasy. With the wisdom and omnipotence of Solomon they isolate the event that has outraged them in reality and then create a fantasy punishment to suit the crime.

There is more than a hint here of the limitless uses of erotic daydreams, the versatility and elasticity of fantasy to take almost any real event and shape it into a satisfying, orgasmic scenario. If a woman can reverse painful reality into fantasy and feel that revenge is complete, that is therapy. Is it good therapy or bad? Psychiatrists and sex therapists to whom I've shown these fantasies have differing opinions. I've shifted my own over the years, but of one thing I remain certain: It is time we acknowledged woman's cruelty, her mean side as well as her more celebrated good side. Admitting to the destructive bitch completes the picture, makes woman a whole human being.

At about the same time these women were writing and talking to me, a Yale University study was published on the subject of men who were actually raped by women. Says sex therapist Dr. Philip Sarrel, who wrote the study along with William Masters of the Masters and Johnson Institute, "The men who have told us about being raped, sexually assaulted or strongly coerced by a female have found the experience enormously upsetting. They have experienced immediate and prolonged after-effects similar to the traumatic reactions experienced by female rape victims, including the suspension of social contacts and disruption of sexual response. Once we recognize that men can be sexually assaulted or intimidated by women, both physiologically and psychologically, we realize that men and women are much more alike than previously thought."

Here are a handful of angry fantasies from angry women to which I've devoted a great deal of space—some might say more than they deserve, given that rage and sadism aren't themes that turn up as often as they once did in women's fantasies. But that is precisely what bothers me. Where did the anger go? It is certainly still being felt by women, who might even feel they have more to be angry about than they did in the early 1980s. But anger was popular then; it was in vogue for women to march in the streets, argue loudly over feminist principles at parties, and speak whatever righteous anger they felt, even if they spoke it badly, having so little practice.

I'm not nostalgic for the rape fantasy; what I miss is the healthy evolution from the old feminist battle cries into a new, powerful, intelligent female anger focused on the real sources of injustice. We have lost sight of the need for socially sanctioned ways in which women can express the inevitable rage. Without popular approval and support for women to at least try and get it out there, to air their fury, we will go back to splitting the world into White Hats (women) and Black Hats (men). In fact, we have already begun to return to that deluded, destructive thinking.

Enter the New Denial.

Sometimes a book is published, in this case a review of a book, that says it all. Nothing much came of *Love, Envy and Competition Between Women*—you probably never heard of it—but the book, along with the woman who gave it a positive review, waved a bright red flag at me. Speaking of the two women authors, she wrote in 1988 in the *New York Times:*

"To [their] credit, they do not fall into the 'ready-made masculine ideology' that says women have to learn how to compete as individuals in a competitive world. They struggle, as do the women whose stories they tell, to find ways of holding onto valued feminine capacities for empathy and connection while allowing individuation and self-development to proceed. The ideal for women, the authors say, is 'separated attachments and connected autonomy.'"

What does that mean? What baloney to say that competing as an individual is "ready-made masculine ideology"! Men didn't think up competition, nor is the effectiveness of an independent person in a competitive situation a Machiavellian male invention. As for losing our "valued feminine capacities for empathy and connection," I would say that until we are independent, we cannot choose to be empathetic. The pivotal word is choice. The empathy an independent person chooses to offer is more reliable than that of a person who lives through attachments. It is lack of independence, and addiction to connections, that makes us mean, bitchy, and less than empathetic when we fear that the connection to our best friend/husband/lover is threatened.

My only comment on "separated attachments and connected autonomy" as a goal for women is that it is another semantic jungle guaranteed to discourage women from the difficult task of real separation and independence. Separation is separation. Attachments are attachments. Inventing compromises like "separated attachments" makes an unhealthy compromise sound like a feminine victory.

Sociologist Jessie Bernard once said to me, "The whole world is angry at mother." Hers is the often thankless task of socializing, disciplining, while simultaneously providing the only font of love, tenderness, and goodness. It is not because I argue with Dr. Bernard but indeed agree with her so wholeheartedly that I grieve the loss of that brief period of time in the 1980s when so many angry voices were raised, promising women finally a variety of outlets for anger other than within the powerful role of mothering. If we are, as Dr. Sarrel suggests, more alike than different in our reaction to being sexually hurt/molested/raped by the opposite sex, doesn't our examination of men's more familiar and public crime of assault against women dictate an equally honest examination of how women turn their rage against men?

Today's moguls of advertising and the media have seized upon babies, family, and parenting as a selling tool unprecedented in potential since the sexual revolution; in fact, sex and babies are selling products simultaneously and it would seem with little conflict of interest. In a recent issue of *Vogue* magazine, a full-page color photo shows a beautiful blond woman in stiletto heels bending over the breakfast table, her back to the camera. Her miniskirt is raised to her crotch. A young child, shirtless, stands beside her; he/she is what, maybe six or seven years old? This is a fashion photo for a dress, but if you tore it out of *Vogue* and showed it to someone, it could just as easily be labeled kiddie porn.

Are we in for a major new idealization of motherhood, and if so, are women any better equipped to handle anger than their mothers were? Sue Miller's best-selling novel *The Good Mother* was published in 1986 and is the story of a divorced woman who is sexually awakened for the first time by her lover, Leo. By the story's end she has lost her four-year-old daughter, Molly, in a custody battle to her former husband, who accuses her of being a bad mother for having allowed Leo to commit a "sexual indiscretion" in front of Molly. Anna is not a bad mother but indeed a very good one. Understandably furious, enraged, Anna takes a gun and fires it into the sand.

The reviewer, Christopher Lehmann-Haupt, wrote in the *New York Times,* "She throttles her rage, faces the reality of her loss, and decides to accept the humiliation of seeing her daughter on her former husband's terms." It is a decision that left our reviewer puzzled and he continued, "Why, it occurred to me on finishing Sue Miller's novel, could she not have written *Medea* in modern dress, and made Anna fire that pistol with more tragic effect? . . . The answer to my question was supplied by a couple of shrewd women I know. They pointed out what I'd failed to recognize, that *The Good Mother* is really an attempt to dramatize the common female fantasy that if a woman lets herself go sexually she loses control of her world, including her ability to mother. Anna's loss of Molly is her punishment for allowing herself to be sexually awakened by Leo. She accepts her penalty with shoulders bowed and fires her pistol into the sand."

I don't know whether Sue Miller would agree with Lehmann-Haupt, but his "shrewd" women friends' explanation disturbed me so deeply I kept the review and print it here. Twenty years ago traditional women did not let themselves go during sex out of fear that having lost control, they might not regain it. They especially feared masturbation and oral sex, where clitoral stimulation all but promised orgasm, loss of control. I suppose Anna's passive expression of rage saddens me because it suggests that women have already returned to the traditional stance where motherhood is antithetical to sex and where there is no place to put rage except inside themselves, to swallow it. I, too, would have thought that by 1986 we could afford a fictional modern-day *Medea.* I am against murder and suicide, but I would have welcomed, given the injuries the heroine had endured, a response that fit the crime against her.

So long as women deny anger, they deprive themselves of

a large part of the sexual pleasure that comes from being the demanding, aggressive partner. Anger is not incompatible with sex; the freedom to be aggressive is passion's core. Women feel like the passive victims of sex when they deny their anger and project it onto men. Having made men the Bad Guys of sex, they experience the excited thrust of the penis as an attack. What a pity to be left out of so much aggressive pleasure. Women are not holes, merely receptacles for a penis, unless that is the way they choose to think of themselves. It is the abundance of emotion, from tender to sadistic, that we bring to sex that will determine how much passion we feel.

Linda

I am a 26-year-old single female, raised by my parents to think sex was not for nice girls. I have had limited sexual experience, and feel a certain anger toward men. I am a heterosexual and enjoy looking at pictures of the nude male or taking my own.

My fantasy has always been to dominate my partner. First off I call him up and tell him to drive over. He is to arrive in only a jockstrap, nothing more. And he is told to be there at a certain time. When he arrives, he is five or ten minutes late. I push him forward over the back of a chair, so his face is pointing down toward the chair seat, and his rear is in the air. Pulling off my belt, I give him fifteen hard smacks for being late.

"Get on your knees and ask my forgiveness," I tell him, "or you'll get fifteen more." He doesn't want any more, so he obeys. I allow him to beg for a while before giving in. I grab a handful of hair, pulling his head upward. "You belong to me," I tell him. "From now on you're here and mine alone." He says, "Yes ma'am."

I pull him by the hair to the bathroom. As he strips, I turn on the hot water. He climbs into the shower, but stays back away from the hot spray. I grab a brush, the kind you scrub tubs with or other such stuff. I strip and climb in, & as I do, push him under the water. "It's hot," he cries out. "Has to be," I tell him. "To wash off all of those other women." I use the brush to scrub him as he complains. I scrub his right hand and fingers, then the back of his hand, up his arm, then down the other side and back up the other side. I scrub every inch of the right hand and arm, even the palm and the underarm, before moving on to the other arm. After his arms, I move to his face, his neck, chest, stomach, back and shoulders, then his legs. Last I scrub his penis and balls, I scrub hard, as he cries out. "Bend over," I tell him. I move close to him, pressing my legs tight against his back, forcing his upper body tight against his legs. I grab the sprayer, bend forward over him, part his cheeks and push the sprayer up his rear. He cries as I push it in farther and allow the hot water to clean out his anus.

As he begins to stand up, I grab ahold of his hair, holding his head down. "Open your mouth," I tell him. As he does, I shove the sprayer in and move it around cleaning out his mouth.

As he towels off, I tell him once again that he's mine, all mine, and if he ever even looks at another lady, I'll kill him slowly, very slowly. He assures me that he's all mine, that he likes a lady who takes control.

I grab ahold of his penis, dragging him to the bedroom. "On your stomach," I order. Then I tie him spread-eagle and begin to whip him. I don't stop until I bring blood, then I give him five or more good smacks. I hit only the rear, upper legs and lower back. I untie him and tell him to make love to me. The pain has excited him and he has a hard-on and eagerly obeys. I moan in pleasure as he begins to kiss and caress me. He can't seem to get enough of me. Finally, as I am about ready to explode, he enters me. I grab a large thin normal dildo and shove it in his rear as he enters me. He moans as I shove it all the way in, but the pain pushes him onward. I thrust the dildo in and out of his rear, as he thrusts his penis in and out of me. The pace quickens as we both reach a climax. I shove the dildo all the way into his rear, as he climbs on top of me. I move up a little, and his head ends up on my breast. I tangle my hand in his hair, and we sleep. My second fantasy is to deal with a strong, powerful man and to break him down. I hold a gun on him and order him to strip. If he bucks me, I take a shot at him, but most times he obeys and strips. I shove him in a closet. I keep him there for three days, without food or water. I open the door on the third day and tell him that he can have a nice juicy steak if he eats my pussy first. If he refuses, I close the door, if he agrees, I allow him out and keep my deal. Afterwards I shove him back into the closet, and three days later we repeat the scene. It goes on and on until he breaks and agrees to do whatever I want, so long as I don't put him in the closet again. And at that point he's mine, and the fun begins.

Erma

Let me start with a brief autobiography. I am 27 years old, single (but not for long), have three years of college, am white, Catholic, and work in the medical field. I was born in San Francisco to immigrant parents. My father died when I was 3 years old, and my mother never remarried or dated. I attended an all-girls Catholic school for four years, then a coed Catholic school. Finally in high school I went to a public school. I have one older sister. We both had a very strict upbringing. Neither one of us was allowed to date until the age of 17 (which was okay, since I did not like the boys in high school, and the college boys scared me. Perhaps due to a lack of a male image while growing up?).

My mother never really spoke about sex, except negatively. When I was in grade school, I did have a Sex-Ed class. My mom's theory on sex was that you only did it if you were married, and only to your husband, when he wanted it. It actually sounded dirty the way she described it. Well, fortunately (?) for my sister, she was a virgin when she got married. She was the "good girl." I, not sorry to say, lost my virginity when I was 18 years old, to someone I thought I was in love with. My mother was quite infuriated when she found out. She told me that I had better fake being a virgin if I wanted a good man (or my husband might think that I was a whore). So, year after year, date after date, I faked being a virgin. (I really knew that these guys were not for me.) Finally, I got smart and quit faking.

When I was 21, I decided the hell with virginity. If a guy could fool around, why couldn't I? I decided then that perhaps Mom was wrong, and every guy really didn't think the same way that she did.

My mother also tried to instill her ideas on masturbation, oral sex, anal sex, etc., in me. Her idea actually was pure and simple "only prostitutes did those things!" (Boy, do I love going down on someone!!!!!!!!) Every time that I did masturbate, I would feel very guilty, and swear that that was the last time that I would ever do it, but it felt so good, especially when I realized how well my mom's hand-held back massager worked.

Even though it took some time to slowly release the guilt whenever I had sex or masturbated, it wasn't until last year, when I met the man that I am to marry, that I finally realized that all of it was all right, that there was not anything wrong with sex, or fantasies. He really enjoys listening to my fantasies, which I never thought that I had until I read your book. I never knew that *my* fantasies could turn someone on so much. I had always thought that they would sound stupid. At first, I did feel awkward telling him anything. But with his encouragement, understanding and ability to help me explore new subjects, I have come a long way. I can recall having fantasies at the age of 11. I definitely do not feel the guilt that was once there.

Now I would like to share my favorite fantasy with you:

I use it when I am having a difficult time coming, it makes me come very quickly. I'm straddling a man (faceless) who I know thinks that he is using me. He has his hands on my buttocks, and is maneuvering me at his will. In the back of my mind, all I need to do to come is look at him and think, "You think that you're using me, you lousy fucker, but little do you know that I am the one that is really using you!" That's all that it takes to make me come.

I guess that our upbringing really can have traumatic effects on our lives. All that we need to do is to take that first step and really be ourselves. Women are human and have sexual feelings, too. Don't let any man ever fool you otherwise. We need our sexual gratification, too!!!!!!

Mandy

I am 23, single, and have lived alone for the past two years, since moving out of my lover's place. I do not remember anything sexual when I was a child. I lost my virginity with my best friend, and he with me, when we were 15. We had a wonderful time trying to figure out how to fuck, and I often think of seducing a schoolboy of about 15. I live next door to a boys' school, so maybe someday. Because I have not had any sex whatsoever in the past two years, fantasies have kept me alive. My favorite fantasy is about a singer-songwriter named Peter. I have been a fan of Peter's for about eight years, and I've been jerking off to fantasies of him for that long.

Anyway, here's my fantasy: Peter and I are friends, and when in town, he drops by for dinner and small talk. Peter does not write about typical things like love ballads, but rather things he feels strongly about. Talk turns to an article in the paper about rape. He tells me that it disturbs him greatly, but he couldn't write about it because he has never been, and being a man could never be, raped. Conversation moves on, and when it gets late he bids me goodnight and leaves. All this time I have been forming a plan.

The next night when I'm sure he's not home, I slip into his hotel room and hide in the closet. When he arrives I wait until he is in the bathroom and then I creep out of the closet and wait for him to come out of the can. I sneak up behind him and hold a knife to his throat telling him if he does what I say, no one will get hurt. I have him lie down on the bed and I tie his arms and legs to the bedposts. Because I am dressed in black, and have on a ski mask, he doesn't know who I am. At first he thinks I am joking, but he soon realizes my intentions are not at all honorable. He starts squirming and yelling, telling me that I won't be able to do anything because he won't get hard. I slowly undress him, nibbling at each new exposure of flesh. I lick him from head to toe, pausing once in a while at something delicious, carefully avoiding his prick. I get a towel from the can and blindfold him with it so I can remove my mask, the better to eat him. Then I get a pillow and place it lovingly under his buns. I reverse my course, licking him from toe to head and I nibble at his nipples, neck, earlobes and lips. I begin to whisper obscenities in his ear, telling him what I am going to do to him. I climb up and sit astride his face, and I tell him to eat me. He sticks his warm tongue deep inside my cunt and twirls it round and round. He's a great eater! After I've come a few times, I get off and I start kissing him and licking my juices off his face, something that amazes him. I lick my way downward again and I begin to nibble on his buns. I LOVE HIS BUNS! I take one ball into my mouth and twirl my tongue all around it before gently releasing it and moving on to the other one. Then I start sucking up the side of his half-hard shaft, all the while playing with my dripping cunt. He is still trying not to get hard, but I will take care of that. I tell him to suck on my finger, telling him the wetter the better, as I am going to stick it up his ass. He gets it very wet. I gently insert it up his asshole and when I touch his gland he becomes instantly rock-hard. I have never seen such a magnificent column of flesh! I quickly tie a thin strip of leather around the base of his prick so I can keep him hard for as long as I want. I suck his balls and buns some more, and out of the corner of my eye I can see a drop of his nectar at the tip of his penis. I lick it off, and keep on licking. When I can't stand it anymore, I climb on top of him and slowly impale myself on his glistening rod. I begin to rock slowly back and forth pulling him deeper and deeper inside me. I suddenly realize that he is helping me a bit and softly moaning. The moaning gives me a rush, as I love his throaty voice. I have, and who doesn't in their fantasies, an earth-shattering climax. After a few minutes I climb down and stand on the floor beside him, looking at his beautiful, sweaty body. He tells me how cruel I am because I won't let him come too, and that his balls are beginning to hurt. I untie his prick and give him a deep blow job, drinking in all his juice as we come together. I've wondered for so long what he tastes like, and believe me, it was worth the wait! Then when I'm sure he's asleep, I carefully release him, and leave.

The next day he calls me and says he has to come over right away. When he arrives, he tells me all about what happened to him the night before and how scared and helpless he felt. I can't help but notice the huge bulge in his jeans as he tells me all this, and become very wet. We fuck like sailors on shore leave in the living room for what he thinks is the first time. Afterwards he has this funny look in his eyes, knowing. But neither of us says anything.

I am an artist, and for as long as I can remember I can only do my creative work listening to Peter's voice. I sort of keep myself in a constant state of arousal because I listen to tapes of Peter at the office, in the morning when I am getting dressed, all weekend, and when I get home from work. I have been doing this for a long time, and each song is still as fresh as the first time I heard it. That's why I appreciate his work so much. I have a friend who knows Peter and who promised to introduce us the next time he is in town. Believe it or not, it was not my idea. My friend feels we would get along because he says we have similar tastes. He is due here in the near future so I am keeping my fingers crossed, but I doubt I would fuck him without knowing him better. I guess this is my way of dealing with rejection from someone whose music is so important in my life.

Kelly

I have two special fantasies but first I'll tell you about myself. I am 16 and still a virgin. I am proud I am a virgin. A friend "spent" hers on a piece of trash and I'm not about to do the same. Still, there is a certain guy who I would like to lose it with (and soon!).

My fantasy is that I come in on my boyfriend in his bed with another girl. I am dressed like a circus animal trainer. Sequined shirt, boots and whip. I grab the girl and tie her to the bed, arms and feet apart. I take my boyfriend and tie his arms behind his back and lie him next to her. He has the opportunity to watch as I degrade his little whore. I strap on a dildo and climb on top of her. I brush the dildo right over her hot cunt. She really wants it. I tease her for a while and then all of the sudden poke it in. Then I pull it out before she realizes what has happened. She starts to cry. I hit her leg with the whip. I turn to see my boyfriend is thoroughly turned on. By the size of his erection, he looks like he is ready for his punishment. I put a scumbag over his dick and then tie it tight around the base. He looks like he is going to explode. I straddle his face and put my cunt onto it. I pick myself up every time he tries to lick me. Then I take him over to his whore and say to her "Eat him, suck him, now." I release the rubber band and take off the scumbag. I grab his dick and point it just below her open mouth. The semen misses. They beg for forgiveness and I release them. I start to fuck my boyfriend as she lets him eat her out. It becomes a familiar event.

Paloma

I am 29 years old, married happily with four children ages 9 to 2.

I've never shared my fantasies with anyone, not even my husband. I regard my fantasies as *mine*—my own little world apart from reality. If I shared them with my husband, I feel they would not be mine to control and use as I choose. Sharing them with you seems different somehow.

I have had an affair with one man during my ten years of marriage. It hasn't been a constant thing. He was a good friend of mine when we were young. I suppose we got into this affair to recapture our reckless youth or prove we were still attractive to others besides our spouses (he's married too—ten years). He can't last very long, he's not very well endowed, not as romantic as my husband, and not very creative. Man, I don't know why I even bothered with him (except the foreplay and teasing was fun) at the risk of being found out and jeopardizing my character, for what? A lousy fuck!

Well, getting back to my fantasies. I suppose I fantasize to escape, I don't use them to masturbate. But I like to use them when my husband is going down on me. I like to just lie in bed in the morning before I get up and just think of a good one. Or at night if I can't sleep, with my husband's warm body next to mine, and me in these wonderful sexy situations, in my mind. Of course if he should want to make love I'm hot and ready! One of my fantasies involves one of the men from the church. He's about 50, kind of a silly man, a bit of a dork; he comes to my home when everyone's away (conveniently). And confesses to me that he desires to put his cock in my mouth and come in it. He begs me to forgive him and tells me I should punish him. He tells me I should spank him on the bare butt so he pulls down his pants. He's already got a tremendous hard-on, and I kind of smile at him. He bends over my lap, and I begin the punishment. I whack him really hard several times, and he begins to sob. I tell him I forgive him. As he stands up, his cock is throbbing and bobbing right in front of my face and I can't help but put my mouth around it. He explodes almost immediately. I look up to him and just smile. He kisses me sweetly and walks away.

As a youngster, my minister at church had a thing for me—I suppose because I was young. His wife was very heavy and not very pretty at all. He would tickle me and roughhouse with me. Often he would drive me home from church. After he'd lock up we would go to his car, talk and play around a bit (tickling and pushing), and then he would hug me or push up against me, and I could feel the bulge in his pants. I suppose if I had encouraged him he would have persisted. I carry this reality into fantasy here: He pushes me against his car and lifts my dress, puts his hands in my pants and rubs my ass and hips and then he pulls his rod out. He's so excited he's breathing hard, almost gasping for breath. He tells me he is going to fuck me and lick my pussy dry. He thrusts his large cock in me and bangs hard against my body, moaning and groaning. Then he comes and drops immediately to the floor and licks me and sucks both our juices up. This gets me really going and I pull his head, thrusting him into me more, and I come and come.

I like to be fucked in the ass, I like the incredible sensations, although we don't do this very often. Jeff doesn't like his rectum played with so . . . I fantasize he is being raped by a woman (me?) who has tied him up on the bed. She strips him, takes off her clothes and rubs her breasts on him (which he loves) and he quickly gets a hard-on. She goes down on him and then, when he is screaming and happy, she pours oil all over his cock and ass and strokes his cock with one hand and puts her fingers up his ass with her other hand. He tries to squirm away but to no avail. He cries for mercy and she goes for her vibrator. She slowly inserts the vibrator (vibrating) into his asshole and then proceeds to mount his cock, which is as hard as a two-by-four. He's going crazy by now and comes as he shakes uncontrollably in orgasmic spasms.

Anna

I'm a 21-year-old college girl with Old World parents. My mother doesn't approve of my dating an American guy, not even a college student; as a result, I've never had a relationship with a guy, or even enjoyed a guy's company. I wonder if I'll ever be able to.

There is this American guy who sits behind me in chemistry; he's small and very attractive and I've wanted a piece of his ass ever since I first laid eyes on him. I'm not very attractive and wouldn't have a chance at a college guy, so my fantasy centers around raping him. In my fantasy I encounter him alone one afternoon, sitting under a tree all by himself, and go over casually to talk to him. We talk for a while, then go off into the deserted basement of the nearest building to study. After concentrating on the books for a half hour I ask him, "Steve, will you do me a big favor?" "Sure," he says unsuspectingly. "Drop your pants," I order, much to his resistance. I spring on top of him, pin his arms to the ground, hold his legs with the weight of my body, and manage to pull his zipper down and get his penis out, which is already hard. I wiggle myself out of my shorts, get on top of him, and come down on his penis. I fuck him and fuck him, having many climaxes, and totally wear him out, until he's begging for mercy. I leave him there on the floor in the same shape.

Dawn

Here goes re my background: Age—22. Schooling—high school; I took courses in child care, home ec., etc. Marital status—single. Employment—I have had many, many brief jobs. Right now I run a nursery at church, and I baby-sit for two families.

Other notes: I am the oldest of three children, the only daughter. When I was 13 I was molested and *yes,* I'd known the man all my life and *no,* I never told anybody until recently—I spilled it to a close friend who believed, accepted, consoled. It is, for now, my decision not to tell anyone else—the son of a bitch is dead, and except for that, I cannot think of one bad thing about him; he never drank or cheated or any other awful thing—he raised a houseful of kids that weren't his: i.e., his stepchildren.

In reality my threshold of pain is so low it's embarrassing. A tiny cut or bruise makes me hysterical, and I cannot stand to be tied or restrained in any way. My mother told me I went crazy at age 1 when she buckled me into a high chair; she never did it again.

In Never-Never Land I think of tortures and handcuffs and chains. I used to be aroused by reading about torture—well, I still am, actually, and yet graphic violence in a movie turns my stomach, I will not watch it.

I didn't start really making up fantasies till I was 19—they started out just being re-creations of something I'd read; I'd add my own ideas. You can think up all kinds of stuff after reading *True Romance* or a Harlequin novel. Or that's how I started, because I didn't know "nice people" thought about things like that.

Certain ages bring up certain memories. When I was 8 I realized that rubbing against Raggedy Ann or a pillow felt nice. My mother raised hell, so I waited till she wasn't around. I didn't connect what I was doing to sex until I was 13—I *said* I was retarded!

By the way, my mother's attitude has relaxed quite a bit. I don't think I felt guilty—how could something that felt so good be wrong?

At 14 I saw a movie, lots of boys in *tight* jeans. I felt real strange and then I thought, "So this is what a wet dream is like." Afterward I thought of myself walking along that line of boys, calmly picking which one I wanted.

Here's my current fantasy: I live in the woods, and since it's all a dream, I have electricity, etc. A man walks across my property. His age varies—if I feel maternal, he's 19 or 20; if I feel "usual" he's 26 or so; and if I feel upset, he's anywhere from 30 to death, just so he's able to do whatever I want.

So he's been lost for a long time and I see he's hungry and dirty. I invite him in but say he cannot eat until he's had a bath. My house has a nice big bathtub, and for some reason he has no shyness, he just removes his clothes and I conveniently misplace them. Sometimes I just watch him bathe, mostly I wash him and end up in the tub with him or in a bed. I tell him what to do and he obliges till we're both satisfied.

The violent ones: I chain him or tie his hands and tease, tease, tease, but he can't come till I decide, and I don't decide till he's miserable. Sometimes no sex at all, not really, I'm just slapping him, pulling his hair, and coming like crazy. Sometimes out of boredom and to hear him yell I shave his legs—always with soap, nobody should have that much pain. He objects and I move north, removing every hair and threatening more if he isn't perfectly still. I never castrate him, but he can never be sure, so he resigns himself to losing some hair.

And, the $64,000,000 question? I am a virgin so everything is purely invention—for now.

There's one more thing; I've been baby-sitting for five years, over one hundred kids and I have *never,* repeat *never,* had a little girl ask, "Why does your chest stick out?" Every little boy I know asks eventually. And men talk about penis envy! P.S. The kids I refer to are aged 3 or 4, if age matters.

Susie

My name is Susie and I'll turn 17 on October 14th.

I lost my virginity when I was 15. Since everyone was "doing it" I wanted my first to be someone that I didn't know. Someone that couldn't go around bragging about how he was my first. And the guy I chose was a Marine. I'd met him once before. He told me a lot about himself and kept asking me if I had changed my mind. I couldn't understand why he was trying to discourage me from doing this. But he couldn't get me to change my mind, and I guess he figured if it wasn't him it would be someone else . . . and so he introduced me into the adult world. We were really close and I know he loved me . . . and now he's telling me that I was just his little whore for six months.

Oh, I know what you're thinking!!! You're thinking the same thing every other adult does. You're thinking, "What the hell does a 16-year-old kid know about love?" You're thinking of how foolish we young kids are. Right??? Don't deny it . . . because that's what all you adults think. Why don't adults believe that we feel the same kind of pain that you do? Why don't you believe that we can care about someone just like you can care about someone?

I don't have a very high opinion of myself. I figured if everyone thought I was a slut . . . I could be one. But it hurts. I feel trapped now. I don't feel like I have the right to tell a guy no. But I'm changing. I want to be able to respect myself again. I tell all my friends to stay virgins until they love that guy . . . and then I feel sad because so many told me that, and I didn't listen. It's true what they say, "That once you do . . . you can't go back to holding hands." And the other day I got mad, and finally told this one kid that I had no desire to jump into the sack with him—and I was surprised that he didn't hate me for refusing.

I'm waiting now for someone special to come along again. I admit that I get the urge to just go find someone and fuck his eyes out. It's hard. It's hard to change. I'm only 16, and I can't go on screwing everything that comes along. The hardest part is getting used to being without the sex.

Here is one of my fantasies: I left the restroom and joined the hustle of the dance again. The scene was refreshing and exciting. The colored lights danced off everyone's faces, and most of the people were moving in beat with the loud music.

I wore a blue dress that came down to my mid-thighs. It shimmered under the effects of the disco lights. But the best part of that night was how I felt, and what I was planning to do. For my devious mind was thinking up little schemes and I felt wicked. Only I knew that under this blue dress there was nothing else: no panties, no bra . . . nothing. And it made me feel as if I were intoxicated by the mysterious excitement. I felt nasty and naughty, knowing that if I moved wrong, someone might get a fantastic show of my bare body.

I sat at a table that put me in a good position to see a group of guys that were standing near the wall watching the dancers. I checked them over and decided I would make my move on the one that seemed to be the least interested in the dancers, and I thought of how to distract him.

While sitting, my dress rode further up on my thighs and most of my legs were exposed. I stared at that guy. I once read that if you stare at someone they feel your eyes upon them and look your way. . . . Would it work?

Eventually, his eyes came in my direction and he looked at me. I let a trace of a smile come to my lips, then shifted slightly in my seat. His eyes followed the shifting movements of my body, and I separated my legs so he could see up my thighs. I watched the expression on his face register shock, but then he just stared at my pussy as if disbelieving. The way his eyes bore right into me brought a throbbing to my cunt, and he brought his eyes back up to mine . . . and I smiled seductively. I could imagine just then how aroused he must be. After all, it's not every day you have someone showing you their cunt in the middle of a crowded public place.

I got up and walked over to him and asked him to dance.

He accepted. The dance floor was so crowded that we kept bumping into everyone if we moved too far apart. Therefore we danced very close to each other, bodies moving to the music.

After a few songs he put one of his arms around my waist, and I rubbed my body up against his. I pushed my hips up against his huge hard-on . . . and we swayed to the music. He must've realized that no one was really paying much attention to us. The place was crowded with people overflowing everywhere, but they were all having a good time laughing and dancing and doing their own things so that no one even noticed us. He still had that one hand on my waist, but I could feel the other slipping its way inch by inch up my thighs. He was like a virgin schoolboy who gets really excited and can't contain himself . . . and he wedged a finger up my cunt. He kept stroking that finger in and out, and I grew wetter and wetter. He'd slide his finger in, slide it out, then slide in two, then slide them out, and slide in three. He had big hands and huge fingers . . . and with three fingers it felt like a very short but thick cock sliding in and out of my pussy, and I was getting excited. I started shifting up and down, sliding myself along his fingers in rhythm with the music. I placed my hand on his hard-on and could feel through his jeans how extremely hard he was. He was big, and I wanted that fullness up my cunt now, not any more of this finger-fucking that gets me started but leaves me craving more. I unfastened his jeans, and started jacking off that beautiful cock. I found it fascinating that people were dancing all around us . . . and no one caught on to what we were doing.

I was begging to feel that cock travel deep inside me, and just thinking about it had my cunt all wet and aching. I placed one hand around his neck and with the other jammed that throbbing cock up my pussy. Right now I didn't care who saw what, I stood in front of him, legs spread and brought myself up and down on that cock real vigorously. Harder and harder I pumped, and he kept penetrating deeper and deeper.

All the people around just added to the excitement—and ours was boiling! I could feel his cock pushing its way deep up inside me . . . that fat prick filling my heated passage . . . and *oh,* he felt so damn good, so wonderful. I squeezed his dick with my muscles and I think he could have fainted from the sensations it produced in him. He brought his hand down and began to massage my clit. The music drowned out the strangled cries of my moaning, and he began to thrust into me with such a savage hardness that I feared he would surely bruise me, but the pleasure overcame the pain . . . and I rode up and down on that slick cock . . . and he was diving into me with such force my pussy began to contract . . . taking ahold of his cock . . . squeezing that cock . . . right here in the middle of this dance floor I was coming . . . and no one knew!

He kept thrusting and my pussy kept contracting, and soon I felt him shoot all his come into me. He forced my hips still so that I couldn't pull away until he was done squirting his load of juice into me. Then he retreated and I was soaking. His come began descending down my thighs.

I looked at him, gave him a sweet smile. Gently, I kissed him on the lips . . . then turned and left him there on the dance floor with his jeans hanging open. . . .

Tina

I am 16 years old, Caucasian and in the eleventh grade. I live in a small town in Canada. I have been dating for almost two years. My mom is pretty open about sex but she didn't want any of her girls dating until she felt we were emotionally capable of having a boyfriend.

My sexual experiences began when I was about 9: masturbating—masturbating with my sister, dogs, etc., until I turned 11 years old. Then I realized that these things are not acceptable in our society. Unfortunately, or fortunately, I fell in love with the right man too young—we both were. He was my first boyfriend and our relationship lasted for about one and a half years. We had a fantastic time. We lost our virginity to each other, and I have never regretted it.

193

I have talked to other girls who wish they were still virgins, but I feel sorry for those having such a poor experience for the first time.

Teenagers my age feel a lot of pressure to be "in." That includes the drugs, the alcohol and the sex. How a person feels about himself is reflected in his actions. The "in" crowd usually has more insecure and confused individuals than the crowd that just stands on the sidelines.

When I lost my virginity, it was because I wanted my boyfriend to be my first. He was sensitive and gentle and in love with me. These ingredients are important. Unfortunately, other youths don't have these chances, and the guy is pressured to be laid and the girl is pressured to be innocent. This circle is vicious. I blame this circle on the ignorant parents who promote it. How can teens do what they want to do when their parents are trying to fit them into a pre-formed mold? When a girl has a strong sexual appetite, she's labeled a whore. A 17-year-old guy is labeled a fruit if he's still a virgin. Sex should be and is a sensitive matter between two people. The choice should be made freely.

The boyfriend I have now is a bit older than I am but more inhibited. What I'd like to do is to dress myself up in garters, crotchless panties, a skirt, spikes and a silk shirt, then corner my lover in the bedroom, threatening to spike him with my high heel if he doesn't comply with my wishes. I've always wanted to perform fellatio on him as I don't think he's ever experienced it. Once I've got him hard and horny, I'd have him undress himself and me, but leaving on my garters and panties. Then, have him fuck me doggy style, traditionally and anally.

Debby

I am a 21-year-old married woman from a lower-middle-class background. I have had three and a half years of college and limited office work experience. I am now unemployed, being seven and a half months pregnant with my first child.

I was raised in an environment where any form of sexuality was repressed in a completely unstated manner. I find myself in the all too typical group of women who were conditioned to equate sex with love and never to consider sex as the pleasurable activity it can be. This has led me to become almost constantly insecure about my own sexuality even though my husband is a very tender, loving and passionate man.

Up until age 20, I had engaged in no sexual activity whatsoever. I lost my virginity to a rapist. Whatever feelings moved me to do so after that event, I spent the next several months in the bar scene with a female friend who considers herself to be a nymphomaniac. She would pick up men/boys on every possible occasion, while I went through the motions of doing the same, though I never really had the courage to actually have sex with any of the men I had met.

Once I became an office worker, I found myself getting involved with a married man, fearing any emotional ties in a sexual relationship. I then graduated to actually picking up two men before my sexual relationship with my soon-to-be husband began. All my sexual relationships preceding my husband were the "get it up, get it in, get it on, get it out" type. Since my husband was a virgin until he met me, we easily adapted to each other's sexual appetites. Our lovemaking is very satisfying to us both, although I have yet to have an orgasm from any of his stimulation. He tries very hard to please me but to no avail orgasmically. This has led to deep insecurity on his part. He was already insecure when I met him, fearing the size of his penis could never please any woman. I have gone to great lengths to reassure him, though I have never faked an orgasm for his benefit.

Needless to say, my inability to come has made me a bit ambivalent toward sex at times. I am able to enjoy numerous ecstatic orgasms through masturbation but do not seem able to release my self-control in my husband's presence. Hence one of my fantasies.

I come home from a friend's house earlier than expected only to find my husband in bed with my above-mentioned nymphomaniac friend. I am just in time to witness him coming violently inside of her. I pull her off of him with such force that she flies across the room. I announce to them both that I am going to show just what a real woman can do.

I proceed to rip off my own clothes and sit on his face, rubbing my shaven cunt vigorously back and forth while I grab his prick firmly with my mouth, licking and sucking it while one hand fondles his balls and a finger fucks his asshole. Naturally, as this is a fantasy, I come repeatedly, while my friend watches in awe. When I have brought him close enough to his orgasm for it to hurt if I stop, I do just that and instruct him to get his prick in my cunt from behind while one of his hands slides beneath my abdomen to massage my clitoris (a position we actually refer to as making puppies). I tell him to fuck me slowly until I find that I am close to my own orgasm. Then he fucks hard and fast and deep until he and I both come with a tremendous shudder.

I do not anticipate the realization of this fantasy since (a) I have yet to have an orgasm with my husband, and (b) I could not tolerate the very thought of adultery. Let me also note that my "friend" has designs on my husband, but he takes his wedding vows very seriously and would never agree to any proposition on her part.

Wendy

I am tired of hiding my feelings. I call it my Secret Side.

I am 25, three years out of college, majored in art education; Girl Friday to the vice-president of product development in a small company; single with no dependents; never been married; overweight.

My sexual fantasies are usually acted out in a manner of which I am ashamed: that of being a helpless, but rebellious and strong-willed slave girl. I was introduced to this idea for a fantasy by the "Gor" novels written by John Norman. I fantasize myself as sometimes being a beautiful, blond-haired, green-eyed, slim, tall and healthy woman.

I am captured here on earth and taken to Gor, where I am inspected, collared, branded and then forced to make love to a man who either is a guard or someone (man) who owns me. I'm worked, trained, beaten, loved; but I am always rebellious and have to be worn down into submission.

I'm a woman who has only participated in sexual intercourse twice in my life, once when I was 19, and then again at age 23. I have a fear of it for some reason. Please don't think I don't like men. I have dated, and am dating now. Up until the young man I am dating now (who happens to be six years younger) I have never really been cuddled or kissed a great deal. The others were (or seemed to be) afraid of women. This is understandable as I was normally the first woman in their lives. I was also the more aggressive partner, in that I chose them and instigated all physical contact. The man I am seeing now instigated this deal. "Deal," because I have no romantic interest in him. I thought I was in love with the others; this one is just a friend. He is the aggressive partner, which throws me off guard. I'm not used to being touched or kissed in the middle of the day while I'm working. (We both work in the same department.)

A more recent fantasy, but not the first time it has ever happened, is where the slave-master roles are reversed. In this one, which is the one I am in the mood for lately, I am the owner of an island I call Dark Awl. On this island I am a slave mistress. I have both male and female guards under my service and we train male slaves to be pleasing to women.

This fantasy is different because in it I don't make love to the slaves, or even to the guards. In it I only want to control the fate of the male slaves. I will admit, though, my victim is someone I am angry with, like my last boyfriend. I want to make them hurt so bad that they pray for death just so they can be released from the pain and humiliation I am causing them, or make them feel so good that they wonder what is left, since they have reached their absolute peak in pleasure.

I reward those who please me with a job suited to their interests and education, or I can make them do the dirty jobs and suffer from the pain of the strenuous work. I can give them slave girls to fulfill their physical needs or tempt them cruelly by letting them watch slave girls dance, but not touch them.

This one interests me because I don't understand why I use it. The first one is easy to understand. I feel it is typical, I have heard a lot about this type of female desire to be forced to do what she outwardly didn't want. But the second one, where I don't even sexually use the men—it puzzles me. I can't afford to figure it out, I don't have time, and I am afraid to.

Terri

I've always worried that my fantasies (which I wasn't conscious of having until my early 20s) were not "typical" of what I imagined most people's were. This is because I derive about 95 percent of my sexual excitement from the *man's* excitement instead of my own. Most of my fantasies revolve around seeing a man, usually someone known to me, become increasingly aroused sexually to the point where he loses all inhibitions and has a very dramatic orgasm. I guess I like the idea of being able to excite a man to such an extreme that *he* loses control. This in turn really arouses me. I only fantasize for the purpose of achieving orgasm through masturbation. During actual intercourse (or sexual activity) with another person I do not find it desirable to fantasize, as this distracts me from the person I'm with and detracts from the experience itself. I've never had a real inclination to "act out" any masturbatory fantasies with another person, probably because I doubt they'd be very satisfying in reality.

As for the fantasies, they are usually confined to these themes: (a) being seduced by a very assertive, sexual, sensual older man who ultimately "loses control" and "abandons himself" to me; (b) listening to an attractive, sexy man tell me all kinds of sexual things he'd like to do with me, experiencing his growing excitement, and watching/listening to him masturbate himself to orgasm; (c) imagining myself as a high-class prostitute who excites older, conservative men to the point of orgasm. I also fantasize a lot about men's sexual "talk" or moaning & crying out as this excites me a lot. As I said earlier, most of my fantasies center around what the men are experiencing —my excitement is thus vicarious, and that's what worries me.

This seems especially odd, since my *mother* was always a very sexual, sensual woman who never let her motherhood role interfere with her sexuality. She carried on an active sexual relationship with all of her four husbands and always made her satisfaction a priority. While sex was not usually discussed in my family life, it was never hidden either. I often heard the sounds of lovemaking emanating from my mother/stepfathers' bedroom(s), which is probably why sounds like those are so important to me when it comes to getting aroused. Another possibly relevant factor in my family life & later fantasies was that I was sexually approached and physically molested from ages 10 to 13 by my first (& longest-lasting) stepfather. While at the time (& for years later) these experiences were very frightening & confusing, & produced much hostility (& distrust) in me toward men, ever since my early adulthood, & since my stepfather's death, their memory has taken on an erotic quality. I now fantasize about being seduced (not molested) by my stepfather, and enjoying the "power" I fantasize having over him to excite him & make him lose control. He was an extremely authoritarian, domineering and sadistic/punitive man who alternately had a warm and charming side. I thus believe he had quite an impact on the ultimate development of my sexual fantasy life. I just wish I could learn to fantasize more directly about myself instead of being so focused on men and their sexual reactions.

By the way, I'm a 29-year-old WASP, single, never married. I have a graduate (master's) professional degree in one of the mental health sciences/arts, and I work full time, in my professional capacity earning $18,000 yearly. Thanks for listening to all this. It was helpful to me to write it all down.

P.S. I guess I should say that I basically distruct & often dislike/disrespect men in general—and that your book *Men in Love* has helped me feel a lot less down on them as a group. It was lovely to see that they don't seem to despise us (women) as much as my experiences have told me they do.

Chere

I've read sexy novels since I was 13 or 14. I was never really interested in sex with someone (I didn't think I'd ever find anyone who cared) until I was 16 or 17, when I met a guy who liked me and was a special person. I'm really an attractive woman, but in high school I didn't date. I'm 20 years old, white, and just got dumped—or used—again. Oh, it's okay if a woman likes sex with someone she loves, cares about and trusts enough, but that's not the woman a man will marry. I guess I believed those books where the heroine is independent, sexual and the man marries her. Hah, nowadays we all know the man would use her, then throw her away like a toy. This is my fantasy:

I'm an American beauty visiting England. I charm my way, by honesty and frankness, to the upper crust of the nobility. Some fantastic blond, blue-eyed hunk becomes intrigued by my unusual honesty & beauty. I'm 20, with brown hair and beautiful hazel eyes. I'm proud of my sexuality, although my relationships end unhappily for me (but not unhappily for my boyfriends—they dump me). This man (Jason) could have any beauty in England. I have the qualities these beauties lack, I care, love and tell the truth. He approaches me in the midst of a crowd of admirers, taking me off. He suggests we go see his ship. On board his ship is a spacious bunk, which we sit on to talk. I'm appalled by our society's hypocriticalness. It's okay to be sexual, but then when it comes to marriage men want virgins, or nonsexual women. I think men & women are beautiful whether they have clothes on or not.

Jason suggests wine. We drink a bottle or two, I knowing full well he wants me to get drunk, but I don't.

"If you wish to make love to me, just ask! I'm not a virgin, nor do I like to play games," I shout.

By his surprised look, I know Jason had expected me to get drunk, then he would have seduced me. Instead I slowly undress him. I eat him gently and slowly as he undresses me. He grabs me, caressing every part of my body. He makes sure I'm ready by eating me, while I watch his loving eyes.

Next he asks me how I'd like to make love (I hate men who don't treat you as a partner, just a thing to use). I crawl on top of him. I make love to him wildly & passionately, enjoying his smiles. He teases me, making me laugh despite the rushes of pleasure I'm receiving (I love to laugh & have fun with my boyfriend in bed, it's not as big a deal as some people think. Married couples on the average make love about an hour a week!). He jerks up in climax as I descend on him with several orgasms (the true test of love is that most women who feel relaxed & loved enough will have orgasms). He rushes me off to the nearest priest, vowing never to lose me or my love.

Ruth

I'm 21, a college senior and student teacher. I have just one gorgeous fantasy-into-reality.

One of the brattiest of my students is a 15-year-old boy. He makes life miserable for the girls, flirting with and teasing them. I didn't like him and had to speak to him often, but for some strange reason he attracts me sexually. Perhaps not so strange—he's androgynous, like a young Mick Jagger. I found I liked punishing him when he'd tease the girls—like *I* was a girl he couldn't push around. I found great sexual tension in dealing with this boy. I found I really enjoyed humiliating him in front of the other students and loved the seething resentment he showed. It was the first time I ever had sexual feelings for someone I disliked. I found myself getting off at home thinking about making him have sex with me. I've been lonely lately, and masturbating has been a great comfort to me. Anyway, I determined to act out my fantasy. One day after this boy had been particularly bitchy, I had him come home with me after school (my parents are often away abroad). He had a lot of bravado with the girls, but I sensed he was terrified of a real woman. When we got home I changed into my aerobic outfit and gave him some work to do while I worked out. I started to flirt with him and he didn't know what to do. He had never been in the submissive position before. I lectured him, telling him I'd show *him* what it was like to be treated like a sex object. I

201

told him what a cute behind he had and that he deserved a good spanking. I made him pull down his jeans and lie across my lap in his shorts. He has a gorgeous ass and I love spanking it. He gets a violent erection and I start teasing him about it. Then I tell him I know a cure for it. But first he has to satisfy me. I sit on the couch in my aerobic suit and tell him he has to kiss me wherever I say. I make him start on my back and it is so fantastic. I am in complete control and have him doing what I want. Finally, when I get really lubricated, I have him do cunnilingus through my aerobic suit. I press his head into me and finally I have this fantastic orgasm. Then, to his amazement, I make him give me several orgasms, each one better than the last! I had never been this sexual in my life and *it's fantastic because I'm in control.* I can do whatever *I* want! When I am satisfied, I make him put his hands behind his back and I tie them with one of my stockings. Then I play with his penis and tease him—finally making him climax when *I* want him to. Then I hand him his pants and tell him never to give me or the girls in school any trouble again. He leaves and I lie down on the couch, triumphant.

P.S. He's been so cooperative since. I guess he's learned about liberated women!

Nina

I am a 17-year-old female.

I was molested by two different men (both neighbors and "friends") when I was 6 years old. My parents found out, and severely punished me. For years, this was a major block for me. Men scared me, and I felt that it was my own fault I was molested. For years the thought of sex disgusted me and I vowed never to "do it."

Later I had a mutual masturbation incident with a female friend, and another sexual incident with one other female friend. I was about 14 years old, and masturbating regularly, although I never came.

The first males I was close to were homosexuals, and my first lovers were male homosexuals. The first man I ever

202

touched, gave oral to, and later had sex with, was extremely gentle, kind and encouraging. I pride myself on being extremely "good," especially at giving oral (since I learned it from gay men), but it bothers me when a man refuses to give me oral back. For thrills, I used to pick up men for one-night stands. Internally, I felt too vulnerable and scared, so I became as aggressive as hell to prove to myself that I could, so that I wouldn't be conquered by my fear.

I feel that I have worked things out better with myself now. I have had one lover (and only one lover) for a year now, and he is the most wonderful man I have ever known. With his help, I came for the first time. He and I have gotten extensively into expressing ourselves in our lovemaking, and we have tried many things, including bondage (both ways), oral and anal. He is 19 and had never even kissed a woman until me.

With this lover I have found that most of my fantasies can be lived out. We have a game where we play different characters; for instance, once he played a tutor and I played a student he seduced. There are some fantasies, though, that he just can't live out with me. I was with two men once, and they were both concentrating on me. It was delightful, and I would love to try it again. Also I have fantasies of seducing virgins who are just dying to have me climb onto their stiff, dripping pricks. I think a lot about what it would be like to be a man and make love to another man. I know that I could have kept my one gay lover if I had only had a penis. But I love my body—my large, firm breasts, my beautiful, aromatic twat. I resent men (and women) who don't see the beauty in it.

My lover has a fantasy that I would like to help him fulfill. He would like to see two women making love to each other. I am willing, but the lesbians I know do not take sex lightly, and I love them for their minds, not their bodies. Somehow, it would seem like an affront to approach them on a sexual basis.

My parents were confusing to me when I was younger. They pressed me into believing sex was bad, but both were having their affairs on the side. Now they are divorced, and it is a bit more out in the open. I wonder often if my mother comes regularly, and how much enjoyment she gets out of sex. She never discusses it with me, and when I try to discuss it with her she gets embarrassed and changes the subject.

I have fantasies about being attacked by a rapist. In these fantasies I always fight him off, and practically kill him in the process. I have an anger toward men that I release by thinking about being violent toward one. I could hurt someone who is trying to hurt me.

Do many of my fantasies focus on dominating a man? Several men have told me I act very mannish, and I have been criticized for it a few times (although I have also been complimented for it).

I have also been called a slut, whore, bitch, nympho . . . I wish men would quit judging me. The men who tend to do the name-calling are extremely sexual themselves. I *love* men, their bodies and their minds, but sometimes they make that love so difficult. Sex is "making love" to me, and it has to include gentleness, tenderness and caring. Men are generally the ones that attach ownership, domination, violence. I don't want to be owned, dominated or beat up by *anyone.*

I am an honor student at school and have been accepted for this fall term at a private college in the Midwest. My family is poor, but I have received a full scholarship. I want you to know this so you are aware of the fact that I am not stupid. Education is extremely important to me.

"LOOK AT ME!" THE POWER OF THE EXHIBITIONIST

No chapter on women's power over men would be complete without mention of the exhibitionist, she who draws men's eyes to her body and holds them, captures them, controlling what they are feeling until that time when she alone decides the show is over.

When I began writing books twenty years ago, the scientific word from the behavioral world was that men were the voyeurs and women the exhibitionists. Since I had always been a voyeuse, first, guardedly, as a young girl, and then more blatantly as feminism gathered heat, I bit my tongue but assumed there had to be others like me. I remember the first television show I appeared on in 1973 and its host, David Susskind, dropping his clipboard when I announced, apropos of my new book, *My Secret Garden,* that I was an incurable crotch watcher.

By then I knew I was "not the only one" who enjoyed looking at men in their skin-tight jeans, shirts open to the navel; men in the 1970s were beginning to taste the pleasure and power of being admired not for their wealth and professional status but for the beauty of their bodies. As women began to move more steadily into men's turf, the workplace, the power balance between the sexes was adjusting accordingly; men began to allow themselves some of women's traditional power source, looking good. And women looked. In 1972 *Cosmopolitan* ran its first nude centerfold—of Burt Reynolds—and in 1973 *Playgirl* published its first all-male nudie issue for women. Initially the experts grumbled that women were simply not aroused by looking at these naked men, and *Playgirl's* shaky first years bore them out; it took time for women to learn to look, to relax sufficiently for the circuitry between visual focus and sexual arousal to run its natural course. Today we voyeuses gaze unabashedly at the beauty of the naked male and get warm all over.

As our consumer culture recognized the money to be made by including men in the business of beauty, the media, the grooming and fashion industries, and the advertising that goes with them began to encourage men to pursue beauty as an end in itself.

It was a healthy move. Narcissism and exhibitionism are a basic part of life. They are the reasons some people want to be famous, or other people perform philanthropic works. On the most primitive level, there is a need for us to feel we *exist* in the eyes of the people who are significant to us. My own books are exhibitionistic; the majority of women who contributed to this book signed their names because they wanted to be real to me. Even if I have published their fantasies under pseudonyms, they can still point them out to their friends and say, "See—this is me!" It gives them a feeling they exist and may even be admired in the world beyond their known boundaries. In the face of the existential indifference of the universe, our exhibitionism gives us a sense that we matter after all.

Long before an infant can talk, we can feel our mother's and father's loving gaze directed at us. It is like being warmed by the sun. The more we see ourselves reflected adoringly in our parents' eyes, the more we interject the idea, make it a part of ourselves. It is the beginning of a lifelong feeling of value. From our parents we learn as children to love and admire ourselves. When we grow up, the feeling lives within us still. For women this inner sense of value makes us better able to take the later, inevitable battering of the female ego every woman occasionally suffers in the automatic comparison with other women, a competition fueled by the billion-dollar energy of the fashion and cosmetic industries.

There will always be someone more beautiful than we. If our narcissism was fed enough when we were little, we may still find ourselves a bit envious, but it will not depress us or fill us with feelings of worthlessness. Fantasies of exhibitionism fill this gap. They tell us that we are beautiful, that we have a right to love.

I have a great affection for the women in this chapter. In many ways they show a healthy determination to give themselves the attention they feel they are not getting from the world, refusing to be drowned in self-pity for past deprivation, demeaned or diminished because the face they see in the mirror is not as beautiful as their neighbor's. In their fantasies, they *are* their best friends.

If you believe you are beautiful, the people around you are likely to think so too. It is not easy. Our culture is a legacy of our English inheritance: it puts a premium on understatement, self-effacement; there is a terrific penalty attached to bragging, "thinking too much of yourself." When a politician wants to win votes, he starts out with a joke at his own expense. When a woman wears a beautiful new dress, she quickly deflects the very compliments she sought, assuaging envy by telling others that "this old thing" is a hand-me-down.

In a woman's exhibitionistic fantasies, all limits are removed. Her talent for putting on her clothes in reality is surpassed only by her expertise in taking them off in fantasy. If the real world crowns her Priestess of the Garment Industry, her unconscious knows that is not where it's at. Clothes do not a woman make. In her fantasies, she gets approval and applause at the core, where it counts: naked, bare-assed, bared cunt, fucking al fresco.

No wonder so many women enjoy exhibiting their naked bodies to the cheers and applause of all around them in fantasy; women spend their lives juggling how much to show, how much to hide. A bit more cleavage and they are daring, a wow. A bit more, and their husband grows angry. Fashion is powerful because it gives women social approval for revealing what all other women are revealing that year; it tells them to hide what all other women are hiding. In fantasies, women don't need this permission; all anxieties are removed.

When feminism was building strength twenty years ago, beauty was outlawed. Feminists realized if there was ever going to be an army of women, competition over beauty had to go. But even at the height of the revolt against the fashion and beauty business, the human need to be seen, to be looked at and recognized as someone special, did not go away. The competition went on. Only the rules were changed, the standards reversed. It became a badge of honor (but also a proclamation of youth) to eschew makeup, wear old jeans, a shapeless dress, and generally turn your back on the entire ethos that made a woman's looks her only riches. If *Vogue* magazine beauty was out, strange, bizarre, funky, and freaky were in. While seeming to resign from the beauty contest, women didn't stop running at all. They demanded that their souls be seen behind the ugly metal-rimmed spectacles, their true worth discerned behind the "irrelevant" dimple, curl of hair, or curve of breast. And yet the parties of those years, populated by women in costumes that denied the importance of the flesh, were also the ones that most often ended with the same women taking off all their clothes to show more flesh than the law allows.

Before we can be loved, we must be seen. If there were ever a real Invisible Man, he would go mad and cease to believe in his own existence.

Basically, there are two different forms of exhibitionistic fantasy. The first is exhibition of oneself—to gain personal approval and admiration. The other great theme is performing sexual acts where, accidentally or not, the woman is observed. In these, the approval the woman seeks is the right to her sexual desires, feelings; her ability to arouse an audience shows what a "real woman" she is. In some fantasies, the public fucking or masturbation goes unobserved; no one at the cocktail party points a finger of shame. At other times, as when the woman imagines herself a stripper, the audience is meant to look and applaud. While the two themes may be combined in one fantasy, they should not be confused. The first is admiration for oneself. The second is approval of the woman's sexuality.

Take the female striptease, a performance usually misunderstood in reality and extremely popular in fantasy. Strippers are not so much performing a sexual act as involving the audience in their own narcissism. Most men who frequent burlesque houses are true voyeurs; they don't want sex, they want to look, to feast their eyes. They enjoy a kind of pregenital stimulation they get from seeing the woman strip, just as much as she enjoys their admiration. She doesn't want sex from them; they don't want it from her. That is the bargain.

The angry feminists who stand on street corners yelling at passersby to sign petitions against the "bad people" (men) who disparage women in so-called pornographic films and magazines would have us believe their fantasy: No woman would flaunt her naked genitals in front of a camera lens unless coerced by men. These embittered women would do a greater social service turning their outrage against the seventy cents women earn to men's dollar. This is real belittlement of women. Why don't they go to Washington and demand better day-care centers? That is not, however, the fantasy that arouses them.

I am sure there are some evil people in the skin business who take advantage of women. But every industry has its share of creeps who humiliate others, its bullies and perverts who beat up on people littler than they. The "bad men" who make "sex objects" out of women are as likely to turn up in a blue-chip corporation as in the photography studio at *Penthouse.*

What is generally overlooked is that the great majority of women in burlesque houses and in the pages of *Playboy* and *Penthouse* have chosen to be there. These women like to take their clothes off and spread their legs in front of an audience. You don't see big-breasted women with great legs picketing burlesque houses or joining their petition-waving sisters on the street corners, crying, "They made me do it!" No one made them do it. That is probably what is driving the angry feminists crazy—rage not at the entrepreneurs but at the naked women who dared to break The Rules against exhibitionism on which all girls are raised. How dare they! How dare they get into that power all little girls swore at mother's knee never to use, the power of their naked breasts, the hint of what lies beneath the dirndl skirt, between the carefully crossed legs.

How dare these exhibitionistic women use this power to excite and enslave men, thus proving themselves more womanly, more powerful than all the other girls. What the naked, smiling women with the full lips and tousled hair are doing, God forbid, is opening the doors to competition, goading other women to "show theirs" too. Untenable! Unacceptable! But do the angry feminists attack the exhibitionists? Absolutely not. Women are too frightened of the wrath of other women, of tapping into the pool of rage that would open the floodgates. As always, they go for the easier, safer target: men.

The women with exhibitionistic fantasies refuse to live by women's asexual rules; they have needs to be met that are stronger than the need for other women's approval. They want admiration of their lovely behinds, their beautiful breasts, a vagina that drives men mad, approval of their naked, most vulnerable selves.

Some of these women place their exhibitionism in the most public scenes they can imagine, thus flirting with the delicious thrill of scandalizing everyone. One would expect cries of outrage and shame. But instead of rejecting the woman as she has been taught to expect, the people watching her do not act shocked, they do not think her strange or outrageous. She is everyone's heroine, so splendid that they applaud and even join in.

"I get off on inadvertent and 'innocent' exhibitionism," says Shelly, "and almost all of my fantasies revolve around someone viewing some of my naked charms and being driven to a frenzy of lust at the sight . . . The thought that I'm showing this man exactly what he's dying to see is more than my little pussy can take."

"I am a small-boned, thin, petite woman who generally dresses rather conservatively," says Helga, "and probably would not be considered sexy by the man on the street due to my small stature, small boobs, and non-slutty appearance. I am not one to attract attention to myself (read: a nice girl). However, one of my favorite themes of fantasy is that of exhibitionism. Many times while making love, when I feel like I am ready to build up to an orgasm, I imagine that our lovemaking session is being filmed or being watched by many horny men who are masturbating. Sometimes I imagine that I am being posed and photographed for a man's magazine or that I am masturbating and being watched through the window by a horny male neighbor."

On behalf of both the voyeur and the exhibitionist, let me

add that for every woman who cringes when the construction workers whistle at her passing, there is a woman who anticipates the attention halfway up the block and would be crestfallen if heads didn't turn. Yes, it is embarrassing and humiliating to have obscenities yelled, unsettling for anyone, male or female, to be stared at too long. But it can also be a very heady power trip to be able to draw people's eyes and hold their attention, even control their behavior with your body. The women in the fantasies that follow have glorious orgasms imagining people being aroused by their naked bodies. Sometimes the fantasy is so delicious it slips over into reality.

Donna takes great pride in "flaunting" her breasts in reality; she wears tight, revealing clothes that say, Look at me! In fantasy, she imagines a group of men watching her have sex with another man, "enjoying the sight, sounds and smell of me and Bobby so much that they're beating off. What a rush of power I felt at that moment—to know that I could do that to so many men at once!"

In Susan's fantasies, she undresses men she's seen and admired on the street. One night, in reality, she asks the manager of a strip joint if she can "try my luck." She starts dancing, taking off her clothes, and as the men cheer, "I had juice running down my legs . . . I never felt so powerful before!"

While the women in *My Secret Garden* also loved the thrill of exhibiting themselves in their fantasies, they did not have this conscious sense of power these new women refer to again and again. Those earlier women may have been aroused to orgasm by what they were imagining, but it was the thrill of the forbidden, rather than a sense of having created a situation where they had some control, that excited them. It is a very significant difference of intent.

I am not sure whether women's new sense of the power of their beauty extends to a sequential awareness of their responsibility for the erotic wheels they have set in motion by drawing attention to themselves. My own observation is that not enough time has yet gone by for women to responsibly admit, "Okay, now that I've spent two hours putting myself together, I can graciously handle the commotion I'm going to stir up when I enter the room."

Traditionally, a woman would spend those same hours in front of a mirror; she saw the transparency of her blouse, the ass-tight fit of her skirt, but when the hard hats on the street whistled, she was ill at ease, frightened, even angered. Why were they looking at her that way? she wondered helplessly. Raised to cultivate her beauty, to draw men's eyes to her so that one would pick her and take care of her, she was simultaneously conditioned not to use her beauty, not to be aware of it. "Beauty is only skin deep," mother warned her little daughter, even as she tugged once more at the girl's skirt, recombed her hair, and polished her face.

When the Wicked Queen calls for Snow White's heart, because her mirror has informed her that she has been outstripped in beauty, the fairy tale warns little girls, even today, that there is danger in beauty. Fairy tales carry the wisdom of the ages; that is why they last and are passed down from generation to generation. So long as the most beautiful woman got the most powerful man and men were women's only source of power, the role of beauty was too crucial to be discussed. It is only since women have developed alternative sources of economic security and identity that the taboo subject of the power of their beauty has begun to be researched and written about.

Because women now buy their own beauty products, they can look in the mirror with more honest scrutiny. They want to get their money's worth. Having paid for it, a woman begins to feel beauty is something she can use. That is an unladylike idea; I'd go even farther and say it is very unfeminist and not at all politically correct. There are still societal forces that resist the notion of women using the power of beauty in an up-front manner. What we have today is a war not just between women but within the woman herself: How consciously should a woman admit to beauty and use it to get what she wants?

Maybe now that men have entered the beauty arena, the

question will be forced. I recently read a survey where the great majority of men admitted freely to using their physical assets to whatever advantage they could. Without women's early training in the denial of beauty's power, men see their looks as cash in hand, money in the bank.

"Don't hate me because I'm beautiful," says the gorgeous woman in a popular advertisement. If we are ready to sell beauty products through an admission of envy between women over beauty, perhaps we are close to also admitting to women's ancient competition for the eye of the beholder, not as a mindless sport devised by wicked men to set women against one another, but as a powerful force in natural selection, one that is built into the species. What has always made the competition so deadly is women's denial that it exists.

Which forces the unkind but necessary question as to whether the wrath of the enraged women on the street corners hasn't something to do with the choices they have made—not to look good, not to compete. Maybe mama didn't adore them when they were little; maybe their sister was prettier, or daddy didn't tell them they were lovely at adolescence; it could be that they were once so damn beautiful they couldn't stand the envy of the other girls and so decided to put on weight, leave their hair unwashed, and join the enemy rather than compete.

Whatever the reason for their present rage, they certainly don't have that *inner* vision of themselves as irresistible which is what the naked women in the skin magazines share as they make love to the camera lens, totally convinced that the eye of the beholder adores them.

I remember Clare Boothe Luce saying near the end of her illustrious life that what she missed more than all the honors she'd achieved was "my beauty." She was a tough competitor, an honest exhibitionist who refused to deny the power of her beauty, for which sin, it has been noted in one of her biographies, she was never welcomed at the famous (not very pretty) Algonquin Roundtable.

If only the women on the street corners got it. The women in this chapter certainly do.

A POSTSCRIPT: This is not an inconsequential afterthought but is set apart because it is so very important. I refer to the double standard of exhibitionism, and more specifically, to how inappropriate, even dangerous it is today, when men's and women's roles have shifted so dramatically.

Consider the man who exhibits himself publicly, who opens his raincoat and exposes his genitals. He is labeled a pervert and is jailed. What then are the rules, the law regarding the woman who decides to leave her panties at home and spread her legs on the crosstown bus, or who stands naked in front of the window while she masturbates?

Throughout this book, and in this section in particular, women speak of exhibitionism not just in fantasy, where it is safe, but in reality, as if there were no responsibility or danger attached. They describe these ideas guiltlessly, inno-cently, because they think they are safe; they act like children in their real exhibitionism, because childhood is where they were first lied to about the reality of the power of women's beauty.

The naked female body, the blouse unbuttoned, the braless breasts, buttocks cheeks, labia lips apparent beneath the chic body suit, certainly the exposed female genitals, are powerful forces that often set certain irreversible actions in motion. Men are raised to take these signs as very significant indications of sexual interest, even an invitation to sex. What do men know or care about the latest "fashion statement"? The woman, on the other hand, slavishly follows the current trend, enjoying the new permission to show more than was allowed last year. She has been raised to deny the power of her body even as she uses it; she flashes, she teases, and when the man responds beyond *her* limits of what is acceptable, she cries "Criminal act!" She honestly feels humiliated, violated. What does she know of her responsibility in the powerful role of women's beauty in the man/woman relationship?

The double standard of exhibitionism was informally, nonverbally agreed upon in patriarchal society, when wom-en had little else but their beauty with which to barter. It was a time when men's anger at women was more controlled, defended against, a time when men had economic power over women's lives. Men put up with "cockteasers" because that's how "girls" were—pretty little things who needed a man to keep them in line, take care of them.

But the great majority of women in this chapter aren't waiting for a man to provide for them. Nonetheless, they still like "to show off what I've got," as Edie puts it, "without being obliged to fuck." Should a man grab her breast, try to shove his penis in her visible vagina, she would cry "Rape!"

I am, of course, against rape, and there are certainly instances of violation that have nothing to do with physical appearance and exhibitionism. But precisely because the crime is so heinous, isn't it imperative that we try to understand the role exhibitionism can play? The mixed signals, the complicated mating roles and rituals that have their roots in earliest childhood can often contribute to that terrible act of adult anger, especially to what is called "acquaintance rape."

Women's beauty and exhibitionism play a major role in the mating ritual. It is time we acknowledged the function and importance of beauty in women's lives not as a "male plot" but as a pursuit women enter into in their earliest female-to-female competitions. The power of exhibitionism, should we choose to use it, is our responsibility.

Susan

I am female, 28, a college graduate (though currently a housewife with two children) and married for almost six years.

My sexual experiences started at age 16 years 1 month. It was a total disaster—Mark was only a year older than I and no more experienced. He only got his penis in an inch when he came. I was truly disappointed. I figured if I was "going all the way" there had better be bells or something, but all I felt was used and unfulfilled. We eventually broke up and then I met THE MAN WHO TURNED ME ON TO SEX.

We had wonderful times in bed together—in a few

months I was able to have an orgasm during sex with just his penis stimulating me. I've never had an orgasm since then without using a vibrator.

I always felt that my relationship with this man was the turning point in my life. My orgasms with him (Look, Ma, no hands!) so affected me that I wanted more just like it. Now I have masturbated to orgasm since I was a small child. I remember masturbating before I was even in kindergarten. So it is not like I had been unfulfilled, but I *enjoyed* it so much more when the man was able to pleasure me, rather than doing all the work myself.

My husband, Jim, has always been turned on by strippers, and he told me that while he had been in Vietnam, during a trip to Saigon, he and several officers had been drinking beer and smoking dope and ended up in a strip joint (and a little more). The stripper was doing an act where she was giving blow jobs and letting guys fuck her. Jim said one of the officers bet him that he (Jim) couldn't do anything that could top the act that was going on. Jim grabbed the girl from some guy who was screwing her, laid her on her back on the table where he had been sitting, and proceeded to eat her pussy out, come and all.

When we passed a strip joint that night, I made him stop and we went in. We had a couple of beers (we had been smoking dope earlier) and I asked the manager if I could get up and try my luck. The manager agreed and I almost wet my pants from excitement and/or dread. Jim had a hard-on that I thought would bust his zipper. I got up and started dancing to "Queen of the Silver Dollar" (a Country Western tune) and I started taking off my clothes. The men were cheering and I had juice running down my legs, and the whole time Jim looked like he was about to cream in his jeans! I never felt so powerful before! When the record was over there was twenty-five dollars in tips on the stage; not bad for three and a half minutes of work! Jim could hardly get me out of there fast enough after that performance. We had to stop twice on the way home so he could eat me and fuck me. We kept it up till the sun came up. It was fantastic!

We talked about my performance for months. I fantasize about it when I masturbate.

Donna

One evening, while I was reading *Men in Love,* my husband asked what I was so engrossed in. I guess he had seen the smile occasionally cross my face and the twinkle in my eye when I read a fantasy that particularly appealed to me. We took the chance to really talk about our sex life and how it had fizzled out these last few months. (He couldn't last long enough for me to enjoy it and it was always the same. So why bother?)

After hours of trying to get to the reason he no longer enjoyed sex it finally came out. He had been fantasizing about repeating an experience he had with a man a couple of years ago. (I knew about the experience before I married him. So what?) He actually thought he was going gay because he thought about it so much. He talked of the guilt he felt because "I actually did that." Then I let him read *Men in Love.* What a change it made in him to know he wasn't alone. He realized that it was a fantasy and not something he really wanted to repeat.

His endurance improved and he was able to ask me to do things to him that he hadn't the guts to ask for before. Just simple things like sucking his balls and putting a finger or dildo in his ass when I give him head. (I guess he thought I would think he was weird or something.)

I am a 23-year-old housewife. High school is as far as I got before joining the navy for four years.

I was brought up in a fairly strict household where sex was rarely, if ever, discussed. (I even heard my father once call it "monthly rape.")

When I was in junior high I developed faster than most girls my age. In one year I went from a nice 36B to what I am now, a 38D. (You should see the stretch marks!)

I had to adjust quickly to all the attention my prominent figure was getting me. At first the jokes made me cry. As I got into high school I had developed a good sense of humor about it (or them, I should say). I had a comeback for every tit joke anyone could throw at me.

This is such a breast-oriented society that I took great pride in what nature had bestowed on me, and started my long adventure in flaunting my breasts. I wore tight sweaters and low-cut blouses that proceeded to drive my mother crazy. So when I joined the navy at 18, and was free from that heavy hand of guilt over me, I went crazy.

Everything I owned showed off my tits. They were cut to show the greatest amount without getting me arrested. Even the coveralls I wore for work in the engine room had a great zipper in front. I used to wear a low-cut Frederick's bra and unzip the coveralls to the small band of material that held the cups together. I loved the distraction I created.

Needless to say, I was never without a lover while in the navy. (With the odds of two hundred to one when the fleet was in, how could you lose?)

The navy is also where I developed this little quirk I have: I love to fantasize I am being watched when I'm making love or masturbating. It started because of a real experience that was part of my sex life for almost two years. When you live in a barracks with hundreds of other people you learn to take sex where you can get it. Of course it is against the rules to have anyone of the opposite sex in your room after taps but no one cared. It happened all the time.

My lover and I used to sleep on some cushions on the floor of our friend's room in the men's barracks. (There were always extra bodies around. Usually friends off the ships.) The usual occupancy of the room was two, but this particular night there were two extra, not counting my lover and I (all male of course). Two were in bed, one on the couch and one on the floor.

After a long night of partying we shut off the lights. Everyone gets into their own beds for the night after taking off their clothes. (Unfortunately I'm slightly night-blind!) I've never known a sailor who wears pajamas to sleep in.

Anyway, my lover (Bobby) and I are not really tired. I lie there trying to get to sleep but it's no use. I reach over to Bobby, who's on his side with his back to me. I press my tits against his back and reach down to his cock. It's as hard as a rock. He's not asleep either. He rolls over and gives me a long, deep kiss. At the same time he runs his hands down to my twat and starts playing with my clit. The room seems hot as we throw off the blanket. We don't say anything. We just lie there for a minute, stroking and fondling each other.

Bobby moves from my mouth to my tits, sucking in all he can get. He goes from one nipple to the other, running his tongue around it then sucking and biting them when they stand up for him.

He slowly travels down my stomach to my thighs, licking and kissing as he goes. He gets between my eagerly spread legs. I know what's coming next and I'm so hot I can't stand it. When it comes to eating pussy, Bobby is the best there is. I call him "the fastest tongue in the West." I love for him to eat me. I can never get enough of it.

Bobby proceeds to tease me. He licks the inside of each thigh and around my hot mound. I can stand it no longer. I grab his head and press it into my wet pussy. He tongues my clit again and again, pausing just for a second to push his long, hard tongue into my vagina. He goes back to my clit and proceeds to lick, suck and bite it. (That drives me wild!)

While he's eating me I play with my tits. I pull on my nipples and roll them around. (I can put one in my own mouth if I want. Maybe I'll do it and let my husband watch one of these days.)

I got totally involved in what Bobby was doing to me and forgot all about the other guys in the room. My breathing got faster, I sighed and moaned and finally screamed with my final shuddering climax.

Before I can cool off Bobby moves up and slips his throbbing cock into my burning pussy. He fucks like he's never fucked before. He drives me wild with his movements. Maybe he knows something I don't. The way he's going you would think he was performing. The light bulb goes on in my head. I distract myself enough to open my eyes and look around. Three of the guys are watching us, the other has his eyes tightly closed but is listening very carefully. I look a little more carefully and find that all of them are enjoying the sight, sounds and smell of me and Bobby so much that they're beating off.

What a rush of power I felt at that moment—to know that I could do that to so many men at once. To know that they wished it was them I was enjoying so much. Wishing it was their cock in my responsive cunt. It really turned me on.

I went back to the business of fucking my lover, enjoying it more because I knew it was giving pleasure to so many others, too. Finally, as I heard sighs and moans coming from all directions, I had my last climax. It was the best one I can ever remember. My whole body shook. I felt that tingle start at my spine and go throughout my body. I became dizzy and lightheaded. It was wonderful.

Bobby's orgasm was like none he had ever had before either. He shook as he unloaded what seemed like gallons of cum. I could feel it filling me up and running down my thighs and the crack of my ass. It felt so good!

So whenever I need a little help climaxing with my husband or I'm masturbating, I imagine I'm back in that time and in that room fucking my brains out with a happy audience.

By the way, I should tell you Bobby is now my husband. My, how things change.

Shelly
I get off on inadvertent and "innocent" exhibitionism, and almost all of my fantasies revolve around someone viewing some of my naked charms and being driven to a frenzy of lust at the sight.

My real life is something out of every woman's dreams. First and foremost, I've been married for ten wonderful years to a very loving, trusting man, and our relationship just seems to get better and better. I constantly marvel at how lucky I am to have found such a wonderful man so early in life. (We were married when I was 22). My husband is constantly horny and always willing and ready to make beautiful love with me. He is very unselfish and seems to derive his greatest pleasure from watching me scream, writhe, and shudder in sexual ecstasy as I have orgasm after orgasm. We make love almost every day—anytime, anywhere.

I love being horny and fantasize to make myself horny. We live on a very private secluded estate in the country, so I can wear very sexy clothes at home—or no clothes at all—without fear of being intruded upon. Sometimes my fantasies and/or wearing my sexy clothes get me so horny that I masturbate when my husband isn't home, but most of the time I try to hold off until he's home so that we can both take advantage of my horniness and make sexy uninhibited love together.

I also seem to attract attention wherever I go; my friends tease me about it. Since I'm still basically shy, even though I'm now 32, I never dress or act in any way that should knowingly attract attention. But somehow men seem to stop and stare when I go by: sometimes it's downright embarrassing. But these other men become the objects of my fantasies. After I realize that a man is interested in me, I imagine myself alone with the man, letting him "accidentally" see my wet pussy or my hard nipples. Then I imagine him pulling up my short dress so that my pussy is completely exposed and him rubbing my clit until I'm pushing my pussy up in the air as far as it will go and screaming with ecstasy and begging him not to ever stop! At this point in my fantasies (and in real life), I always come. Never fails. The thought that I'm showing this man exactly what he's dying to see is more than my little pussy can take.

Bea

I am a good-looking 42-year-old divorced woman with two children in college. I was married for twenty years prior to my divorce. My first sexual encounters were when I was 5 or 6 and it was a hot summer day—my mother did not have us wear panties that summer because of the heat. I must have been wearing loose-fitting shorts because, as I was waiting to see my friend, her puppy came to me and licked me several times on my little cunny! From that day on, I wished for the opportunity to happen again, but it never did (while I was little). I also remember a day (must have been hot, because of the same type of shorts!), a number of boys from the neighborhood and I were sitting on the ground, legs outstretched, playing games. The boys across from me began giggling and looking at me and it took a while to realize that they could see my little cunny perfectly well! I remember feeling the same thrill I felt with the puppy incident. I also remember sitting in a big chair with a little boy next door, and wishing he would touch my cunny, but he had no idea. I still think of these things happening when I masturbate. I imagine myself working in my garden, wearing no undies, and stooping and bending and being very aware that the little boys next door can catch glimpses of my pussy, their very first looks!

One of my favorite fantasies involves nice old men, the type who have been married to housewife-looking, heavy, kindly ladies for many years, and who still enjoy looking, but would never have a chance at a young woman again. I imagine myself at a winter resort on the beach, with a row of these nice little guys sitting up on a wall away from the beach, just passing the time of day. I am in a bikini and am no more noticed than all the other girls on the beach. Then I decide to change into a mini-skirt and T-shirt under my towel. One guy begins to watch as I hold up my towel and slip into top and skirt—he nudges the guy next to him when he realizes that I have on no panties, and they all start watching me to see if they can catch a glimpse of my pussy. I am aware of this but pay no attention. Then I crouch down to fold my towel and give them all a great view of my dark pussy. My other version of this is to then walk to the floor of the shower area, and as I am rinsing my feet of sand, I lift my legs, one at a time and again give them a good look at my puss, all the time giving no indication that I realize what I am doing.

I also fantasize that I'm on a sailboat with a kindly old professor and some others, and that the others and the old man have gone below for a nap. I have been entirely modest throughout the sail, wearing my bikini, but never acting outrageously. I decide to sunbathe, as I am alone. I take off my top and spread my legs. My breasts are not as great as I would wish, but I do have big round brown nipples, which make my breasts look larger. I am half asleep when I am aware of the old guy coming on deck, but I remain motionless. He never touches me, just looks, and it is the first stimulating thing that has happened to him in years and he never expected to see such a beautiful sight as those brown titties and that mound of pussy pushing against my bikini bottoms.

I also dream of working in a nursing home and again, feeling sorry for the old men whose minds work like a young guy's but the old body does not perform anymore. It has been years since they have seen anything except in an occasional TV show. I pull up my nurse's aide dress and let them look at and fondle my pussy—they are so grateful, and it feels good to me, too.

My favorite place to fantasize is on my deck, where I sunbathe. I take off my top and let the hot sun warm my breasts and my pussy. This is where I am when I think about the things I have mentioned before.

One time I was waiting for the phone man to come to my home, and I put on a bra that did not cover my breasts, but just pushed them up. Then I wore a very thin blouse that allowed my big dark nipples to show right through. He sat and had coffee with me and I saw him looking often at my breasts, and I was very turned on because it was just what I was hoping to happen.

Watching dogs licking each other makes me very horny. Just seeing them marching around with their balls and cocks jiggling will make me masturbate as soon as I can get a chance. It even happened when I was driving my car once. There were several dogs sniffing and licking a female when I drove by. I would have liked to stop and watch and couldn't for fear someone would see me. I drove only one mile before I had already gotten myself off. I would love to have a female dog and when she was in heat tie her up in the yard and watch the males come and sniff and lick and mount her while I would be up on my deck masturbating.

Toby

I am 24 years old and a virgin; not by choice, just circumstance. I live at home with my two younger sisters and my parents due to lack of a permanent teaching job and lack of money. I do not have a boyfriend at the moment, but there are people I occasionally go out with. I am slightly overweight and I attribute my lack of dating to this fact. Maybe I am sexually frustrated due to the lack of sexual encounters.

I consider myself to be a very sexual person. I need to be with someone regularly, as I am always horny. When I was in college, I saw my boyfriend every night of the week and never tired of it. While we were together we did everything but make love for hours—not for lack of trying on his part. He asked nightly and could get me very aroused, but I have always had this silly little girl's dream that a good girl waits until she's married, and I have always been a "good girl." I am sorry now that I didn't go with my feelings. At the rate I'm going I may never get married.

As I said before, I am an extremely sexual person. I think about sex a lot and can become horny if just the right word, sound or suggestion is made. I masturbate at least once a day, sometimes three or four or more. I never tried to masturbate until I was a sophomore in college. I don't know if I didn't know how to do it or what, but I just never tried it. I have always used my hand until recently. I had a muscle massager that had a bulbed head like the end of a cock. When I noticed that, I wondered what it would feel like in my cunt, so I tried it. I about had an instant orgasm. I use my hand now only if I am without the massager. Just hearing the whir of the batteries gets me turned on. I have never used anything else (vegetables, hairbrush handles, etc.). I also never have my fantasies when I am with a man in bed. I concentrate wholly on trying to bring him to ecstasy or enjoying what is being done to me. While masturbating, my fantasies are essential to my reaching an orgasm.

Many of my fantasies involve men that I know through

work, former college professors or acquaintances that I am sexually attracted to and my seducing or turning them on. I am very large-breasted (42E) and for most of my life this has bothered me. My clothes never fit right, etc. As I've become older, it has been to my advantage, as many men are turned on by big tits, and believe me, I often notice them looking! My new boss is also aroused by my titties and that turns me on tremendously. He finds many excuses to come into my office every day. Because he has been so obviously interested, I wear very low-cut tops and bend over next to him while he is sitting down. I press up against his back when I can, etc., and believe me, he looks! His wife is also in the office, so he probably won't try anything, but since he stares at my titties all day, I am in a constant state of arousal. I think he looks more at my nipples (which are usually hard when I'm talking to him because I know he's looking) than he does at my eyes. I can't stop fantasizing about going into his office where he is playing with his big prick (I've checked it out and through his pants it looks to be a nice size!). Since I have no underwear on, I climb onto that beautiful tool and we fuck right there in his chair while he sucks my titties. I can hardly stand to be around this man. I have this constant desire to grab his cock and work him up, but I can't because I adore his wife. If he ever tries to touch a tittie, believe me, I won't stop him. I rush home from work every day and masturbate myself into two or three deliciously wonderful orgasms.

Another fantasy is one where my "husband" (a man who I am strongly attracted to at the time), a friend of his, and I are all at a cozy little restaurant in a secluded booth in the corner. My husband and I are exchanging gropes under the table; I am stroking his cock while he is fingering me (I have no underwear on). My husband's friend is away at the restroom (I find out later he went to jerk off because he is so turned on by my large breasts, which I keep exposing to him as I lean forward in my very low-cut dress, and by what we are doing under the table). While he is gone, I drop my napkin on the floor. As I am leaning to get it, I fall off the bench and onto the floor; just then the friend returns to the table. He asks where I am and my husband tells him I went to the restroom. He asks my husband if he may talk personally for a minute about something he has been dying to ask. He tells him how I had him so turned on that he had to go jerk off and offers himself if we ever want to have a threesome. Finally he asks what I am like in bed and if I give good head (which I do absolutely love to do). Before my husband can answer, I have unzipped the other man's pants and have started sucking his huge, beautiful cock in response to his question. He just moans quietly in answer because, after all, we are in public. Of course, so my husband doesn't feel left out, I go down on him too, just the way he likes it. We are all very turned on by now, so we pay the bill and go back to our house for a rip-roaring threesome.

Iris

I'm 23, white, single, oldest of five children. I have a BA in psychology and work in the executive world, and I'm quite obese.

I fantasize all the time. I masturbate frequently during the week, usually for several hours on my day off. I really didn't start masturbating until I was 14, after I got my period. I only had two encounters when I was younger, with an older neighbor boy. I was 5 or 6, he was 11 or 12. We were swimming and he wanted me to take off my bathing suit to see my pussy. He told me he'd show me his penis. I ran away. To this day I have fantasies about this boy. Secondly, I was caught playing doctor with some friends. I was about 7. All of my encounters when I was young, 10 to 13, were with my girlfriends. When I'd sleep over we'd pull off our panties when we were in bed and casually caress each other's pussies. Another girlfriend and I would do striptease-type dances, each taking a turn. Or we'd go in the bathroom and take off our pants and spread our legs and examine each other one at a time.

In my early teens, I was obese. I didn't have boyfriends or dates. At first I would just touch my breasts—that was fine for a while. Then I'd put my hands in my panties. This was all at bedtime, of course, caressing and fondling places where I felt good, then I'd rub myself against my pillow. That was real stimulation, I could always have orgasms, usually multiple. Then I tried sticking small things partway inside me, pulling them in and out, things like mascara tubes, but then I wanted to go further, so I had this hairbrush. I used the handle end. I would lie in different positions to feel it in me in different ways: standing, squatting, straddled, sideways, stomach, on my back, even doggy style to get different feelings. I tried all types of objects, toys, sticks, toothpaste tubes, later, carrots, anything I thought would feel good. Some people I used to babysit for had a vibrator. It was so big and fat I thought it would never fit, but it did and I loved it—orgasm after orgasm. It was fantastic. Later, I had a brief encounter with an older man. I was 17, he was 28. We didn't fuck. I wouldn't let him. I just held his penis the whole time, preventing him from entering me. He did eat me out and it was fantastic. I did suck his cock for the very first time. I really didn't know what to do with it in my mouth. He seemed to enjoy it.

I'd love it when no one was home because I could take off all my clothes and masturbate in front of windows, in different rooms, while I watched TV, just playing with myself for hours. I later found a book that had a chapter about lesbians—and did it turn me on! I read it over and over whenever no one was home, and I'd masturbate with it.

I fantasize about doctors fucking me on a gynecological table, about a man fucking me on a motorcycle, about being tied to a four-poster bed, about being on a nude beach being fucked over and over, about having two men, or one man and one woman, on a patio of an apartment building a few floors up, or in front of a sliding glass door with curtains open, or in a drive-in movie with the people next door watching, or me fucking someone while my boyfriend watches, or inside a dump truck with a dirty truck driver, or a semi driver I pick up at a local rest stop.

I fantasize about wearing a very mini mini-skirt so they

227

can see my pussy when I sit and walk, and blouses and shorts that show my large breasts and even my nipples.

I fantasize about having someone taking pornographic pictures of me in all kinds of clothing, all kinds of places, with all kinds of men.

I love giving men views of my breasts; being obese, it's impossible for me to wear mini-skirts, but easy to let them see my breasts. I like to casually rub them in front of men. I've seen erections appear.

Edie

I'm 16 years old, and a sophomore in high school. My parents have always been pretty lenient with me, so I have no sexual hang-ups.

I'm a female who's dated strictly males, but lately I've been having a few lesbian fantasies during masturbation. (Of course I wouldn't tell anyone this except you, because I don't know you.)

Once while at a party, a boy put a XXX-rated movie in the VCR, and turned the TV on. I agreed with the other girls that it was gross and disgusting, but we all watched it anyway. I think everyone in the room felt like masturbating, but of course no one did. In my fantasies, we all masturbated in the room together.

I often wonder if my fantasies are normal. Sometimes I have fantasies about showing my body off to some cute dude without being obligated to fuck. I'd like to somehow show off what I've got and let the watcher think I don't know I'm showing it. During masturbation, I often picture in my mind another person seeing me nude and masturbating while thinking of me.

I also fantasize about seeing other people masturbate. I wish this fantasy could come true. I'd like to watch a man and/or woman masturbate. However, I'm too shy to ask anyone to. In the XXX-rated movie, I saw a woman rubbing her pussy with a vibrator, but I'd like to really be able to spy on someone real. I'm interested also in how a man jacks off, and what he looks like when he climaxes that way. I mean,

I've had sex a few times, but what I'd like to see is a cute dude playing with his own prick because he's too horny to stop himself. The whole concept of masturbation amazes me. I do it two times a day unless I've got too many things to do.

Monica

I am a 26-year-old single, second-year medical student. Thought that I'd take another study break tonight and tell you of a frequent sexual fantasy of mine.

Fact: About a year ago, I ran into a man named Ron at a party. I knew him only slightly, and enjoyed chatting with him that night. The drinks were flowing freely, and joints were being passed around. When I was ready to leave, Ron offered me a ride home, even though I live only half a block down the road. I asked him in for a drink, and we sat on the couch, drinking and talking. I was just high enough to feel bold, and as we were talking, I told him I was hot, and pulled my sweater off over my head. He smiled and pulled me over onto him, took off my bra and sucked my nipples as I zipped down my jeans. He reached into my undies, slid them off, and carried me into my bedroom. He and I sucked and fucked throughout the night until the sun began to come up. I am very orgasmic, and this was turning him on. I also love to masturbate in front of a man and then tell him explicitly what I want him to do and what I will do to him. Well, my "bedroom manner" was exciting Ron. He kept saying, "God, I've never heard a woman say that before," and telling me how beautiful I was and how big my clit was growing and how he loved to fuck my fat pussy.

Now, my fantasy is this. I'm sitting in my living room when I hear a knock at the door. Answering it, I find Ron standing there with a large, good-looking black man. He (Ron) is carrying what looks to be a movie camera. I invite them both in, though I'm feeling a little nervous. Ron tells me that he was telling this black friend about me, and his friend said that he was anxious to come try me out. I start to protest, but the friend walks right over to me and says that he plans to ram his cock into my cunt if I like it or not, and I may as well enjoy it. With that, he picks me up, puts me on the bed in the bedroom, and takes out his cock for me to see. "This little momma," he says, "is going to go for a nice long ride with you." It's huge and hard, and he undresses me, all the while making great remarks about my body. I now notice that Ron is in the room, on the bed, taking movies with his movie camera. It's as though he's directing a play, telling the black man to "spread her lips," "suck her good," "make her suck your cock" and so forth. The idea of fucking this beautiful black man and "performing" for Ron and a movie camera is all very exciting to me. I like men who are very dominant in bed. The black man stays hard for a very long time and brings me to orgasm after orgasm, fucking me from the rear, with him on top, making me ride on top of him, etc.

Helga

When I first heard about *Men in Love,* I thought "Nancy Friday—she's so FREUDIAN!" And considering all the damage Freud has done to female sexuality with his ridiculous notions about vaginal orgasms and penis envy, I was reluctant to read your book at first. But my curiosity and desire to better understand the male mind got the better of me. Now after all this as an introduction, I must say that I enjoyed your book very much; and much to my surprise, I enjoyed your interpretations even more than the fantasies. To sum it up, you've restored my faith that Freud was not all bad.

I grew up believing that sex was for men, and if they wanted it, certainly there was no need for guilt. It was we females who were not supposed to want sex and to feel guilty, or abnormal, if we did. I learned that masturbation was something that boys did (even though I knew I did it), and what's more, they all knew they all did it and it was all right because they had penises and that is what you did with a penis.

When I was a little girl (my earliest recollections are in the third grade) I had sexual fantasies (called "dirty thoughts" in my church) and masturbated all the time, and even though I truly believed I was the only one who did such things, there was very little guilt. Later in life, masturbation may have made me feel lonely or sad, but never guilty. And the same is true for my fantasy life. I am a small-boned, thin, petite woman who generally dresses rather conservatively and probably would not be considered sexy by the man on the street due to my small stature, small boobs, and nonslutty appearance. I am not one to attract attention to myself (read: a nice girl). However, one of my favorite themes of fantasy is that of exhibitionism. Many times while making love, especially when I feel like I am ready to build up to an orgasm, I imagine that our lovemaking session is being filmed or being watched by many horny men who are masturbating. Sometimes I imagine that I am being posed and photographed for a man's magazine or that I am masturbating and being watched through the window by a horny male neighbor.

My fantasies get old pretty fast, and I am obliged to come up with others to take their place. Fortunately I have a pretty good imagination and come up with a lot of variations on my favorite themes. I fantasize all the time during masturbation and in lovemaking when I want to climax. Other times during lovemaking, I just enjoy what is going on and keep my mind on my partner and the wonderful things he is doing. But to me, having an orgasm is work, not like falling off a log (even in masturbation), and it requires participation of my body and mind (i.e., I need mental stimulation in the form of fantasies).

I am a 30-year-old white woman. I consider myself a feminist, but a moderate. I was raised Catholic, although I never agreed with church dogma, even as a child, and am university educated and work in a professional job.

Faith

For several years now, I have enjoyed undressing in front of my bedroom window. An older man next door employs young men age 16 to 28 to do odd jobs for him. They are always walking by, so I am positive that they notice me.

At 18 my figure is okay. My measurements are 38–25–38, which sounds good, yet I have always felt that my thighs are fat, especially because I have the common female problem of cellulite. Presently I am attending college as a freshman.

I am technically still a virgin because I have never allowed anyone to enter me, but my boyfriend and I have explored each other intensely, so I am not sexually frigid in any way. I just want to make sure I find the right man to share everything with.

I fantasize that I am in my room with my curtains pulled open for a good view. I have just arrived home from a night out. As I begin to undress to get ready for bed, I slowly pull off my skirt to reveal my smooth legs and lace panties. Taking my time, I unbutton my blouse to reveal my large tits as I watch myself in the mirror. My stomach is very flat because I spent years in a ballet company; its snow-white skin is as smooth as satin and as soft as velvet.

Slowly my hands caress my stomach up and down. I play with my belly button. It is so deep and soft. Gently my hand moves up to find my breast. I feel the lace of my bra beneath my fingers, my hands search for the clasp, and soon it falls onto the floor. My nipples are big and pink, not yet erect. I lick my fingers and squeeze a nipple between my thumb and forefinger. I don't have enough lubrication so my hands glide down to my pink panties that are wet from my cum. I can feel the presence of a man watching me outside my window.

I look so beautiful in the mirror. As I pull down my panties I reveal my dark thick hair which is as soft as a cloud above my heaven. I get down on my knees. Watching myself in the mirror, my fingers separate my lips to find my clitoris. I excite it by softly rubbing it back and forth. I use one hand to play with my now hard titties as the other moves up and down over my entire cunt. I'm so warm. I dream of feeling a man inside me as my middle finger enters my moist heaven.

Just as I'm about to climax, a man enters my room, the

handsome man from the window. He has an intense look that I can feel deep down in my soul. He is slightly dirty and sweaty from labor, but he looks so good. His muscles are bulging. He moves closely behind me. He gets down on his knees behind me. He pulls off his shirt so that I can see that his nipples are as hard as mine. He pushes them against my back as he begins to fondle my tits. His hands are so big and strong. I can't help but breathe quickly, he excites me beyond belief.

His lips brush against my neck. Soon they find my ears. His breath is rapid and hard while his tongue moistens my inner ear. I turn my head to meet his lips. They are as soft as rose petals.

My hands unfasten his jeans, and I can see his cock, not long but thick, the way that feels good between my hands. We fall together onto the floor. Now I can feel the warmth of his entire body. My legs glide against his while my hands explore his chest. They feel his entire chest until they reach his cock. The skin is incredibly soft. My hands move over the tip while I watch some cum ooze out. I lick my finger; he tastes sweet. Then I put my hands back on his dick and glide it into my pussy.

He feels so strong, I can feel his heart beating throughout his body. My fingers start to tingle. He is trembling like a child. Suddenly, I feel him as he reaches orgasm. I am filled with delight.

He squeezes me next to him, and kisses my face. His lips soon find my tits. He licks them with tenderness. I can feel him suck on my nipples, and with all the excitement I push his shoulders down hard and raise my hips.

As his mouth searches for my cunt he reaches my belly button and kisses it. His mouth smothers my cunt with kisses while he uses his hands to feel my soft hair. He pushes against my skin with his fingers. God, it feels so good. He parts my lips while his tongue explores my cunt. I can feel my skin wiggle while he sucks me in and out. His tongue enters my vagina. Oh, I can't stand it. He moves up to tickle my clitoris. I move back and forth with my hips smashing my cunt into his face, but he loves it. I love him. When I climax my cum moistens his face. He licks everything. Then I lift him up so that I can taste the sweetness of my pussy on his lips.

I'll never forget our experience, and always from then on I will leave my curtains open and do a special dance just for him.

CHAPTER TWO

WOMEN WITH WOMEN

"ONLY ANOTHER WOMAN KNOWS"

There is something uniquely satisfying in a woman's body that cannot be had with a man. As sexually exciting and elegant as a male body may be, it lacks the obvious physical attributes of our first source of love, mother. It isn't just the breasts; it's the texture of skin, the smell, the whole mysterious aura of that first body we lay against, which fed, warmed, and overwhelmed us with its power. We loved her power, we envied her power, for it was hers to give or to take away at any moment of her choosing. How could any of us, male or female, ever forget that relationship?

We don't. In memory, we long for a taste of it, so important is it still to our sense of well-being. We yearn to be loved, nurtured, and adored whether we had it or not. It is so primitive and obviously associated with infancy that many of us repress the longing out of a sense of shame that these are baby needs. Though tough guys may deny what they are responding to when they rest their head against a woman's breast, suck on her nipples, and explore that mysterious area between her legs from which they issued, men nonetheless have always been able to re-create the earliest mother/infant satisfaction whenever they lie down with a woman. They need not know it is their mother's breast they still want; they don't have to put a name to their frustration because it is satisfied—guiltlessly, unashamedly, easily, without having to ask for it—every time they take a woman in their arms.

Men have a straighter path of psychosexual development than women. While for both sexes the first love is the same, boys continue to love their mother's sex—women—for the rest of their lives. A girl is expected to cross over. This new attraction to the male means a break with the past, a loss of contact with those early, warm, life-enhancing satisfactions. At the back of everybody's unconscious is a memory of Eden—mother's body and breast.

Whatever sexual pleasure women may find with a man, they cannot get this primitive physicality with him. It has been argued that men are not sufficiently tender and nurturing in their lovemaking; but even the most tender of men cannot offer the unique satisfaction found in a woman's body. Nor should he be expected to give it. When women try to turn the male/female intimacy into a mother/child relationship, they are doomed to disappointment.

Society has always condoned, even smiled upon the ease with which women touch, hug, and kiss. Perhaps this easy permission stems from our knowing that women suffer a certain deprivation in the pairing of the sexes. The penis can only offer so much, extend so far; it cannot make up for what the breast offers. And so we look at women lying together on summer riverbanks, walking arms entwined, we stare at the countless painted masterpieces of naked women in languid, even suggestive groupings, and we accept what we see.

But there have always been women who want and need more than the occasional embrace from another woman. Judging from my research, there are far more of these women today than ever before in modern history. Their voices began to be heard in the 1970s when women were encouraged to turn to one another for acceptance, self-discovery, for everything, at times even to the exclusion of men. There are many things we left behind in the 1970s and the 1980s. As other issues grabbed the headlines, memories of women's consciousness-raising groups and open physicality seemed to diminish along with the enrollment in NOW. But the women's voices in this chapter and throughout the book say in their insistence and lack of self-consciousness that women have never stopped the emotional and sexual turning to one another that began twenty years ago.

I am so accustomed to the familiar picture of women embracing that, until this research, I have been blind to what is going on beneath the surface, the heated exchange of desires and needs that many women today feel can only be met by another woman. It goes beyond homosexuality. Men fail women, society fails them, they fail themselves, having created new roles in which they do not feel as womanly as their mothers did in theirs. They feel chilled, cold, unable to give their traditional warmth and unable, still, to find with men the tender, nurturing love they always wanted.

In a song lyric written by Dory Previn, the singer anxiously asks the man she's just met to stay the night "and save my life." Does this sound as if sex is really what she wants from him? Has she some apocalyptic orgasm in mind? I don't think so. The women in this chapter know who can more appropriately "save their lives"; they want sex, yes, but they also have a nameless memory of a lost kind of physicality, softness, breasts, smells, a female tone of voice, a way of being tenderly held and touched.

"Women know how to make love to another woman, all the time, not just when it is time to go to bed, time for a climax," says June. "Men so often miss this important fact although women say to men, 'I need to be held and snuggled and touched and sucked on without needing a climax every time.' It is called tenderness, nurturing, caring, loving, sharing."

How much revenge on men is built into women's fantasies of the ultimate sex experience with another woman? Most of these women do not speak of it that way, but the implication is there: "Since a man will not give me what I want, I'll go to an expert, someone who really knows how to please a woman."

Lying in another woman's arms, a woman gets back at men by usurping their position. She, too, will have a woman. She'll steal some of this female heat he thought was his. She imagines sex with a woman and does quite well without him. Women have told me of fantasies of sex with a woman for whom a man left them. In these fantasies, the man is made to watch the two of them make love. The two women are not enemies, they are lovers. And *he* is the one left out.

Even the women in this chapter who love men unequivocally realize that there are things a man cannot, will not give them. Years of passivity, of waiting while he plays the field, also lead to anger. Call it a "spite fuck." But a more contemporary reason to have another woman, if only in fantasy, is for the woman's own pleasure. "Who me, angry?" these women say. "I'm not angry, it's simply that a woman can give me the world's greatest orgasm and he can't." These fantasies say to men exactly where women put them on the scale of Great Lovers: at the bottom.

During the years the women in this book were talking and writing to me, a series of books has been published, unremitting in their criticism of men who do not give women what they need: *No Good Men, Men Who Can't Love; Men Who Hate Women and the Women Who Love Them; Women Men Love, Women Men Leave*—to name only a few. Beginning in the 1970s and continuing to this day, women's magazines, along with the book-publishing world, have lashed out at men for their inadequacies.

Opposite all this disenchantment with men is the sisterhood, people who understand a woman's needs in a trying time when women's lives are changing as never before. The manifestos of the many women's groups read like giant menus, offering everything many women have been dreaming about all their lives. Here it is, the menus say, and it's OK, in fact good for you. Yes, absolutely, these women respond, here it is and I didn't even know I wanted it or that it isn't weird to have it.

The menu reference is intentional: there is more oral gratification in these fantasies than was ever hinted at in *My Secret Garden*. Even men's fantasies, with their loud choruses of praise for the ultimate oral orgasm, fade in comparison with these new women. "More tenderness, more soft skin, more holding, much more breast, please!"—these women place their orders, and as for oral sex, well, it clearly takes another woman to do it justice.

If women are tired of waiting for men, they are even more tired of waiting for sexual satisfaction. What makes women most tired of all is having to fake it. The debate about clitoral versus vaginal orgasm goes on. Regardless of what else it has done for human sexuality, all the talk has accomplished one monumental achievement. It has convinced women that orgasm itself does exist, that other women are getting it, not only guiltlessly but as their due; other women are so replete in their sexual wealth that they are even arguing about which type of orgasm they prefer! Out of all this comes the final message: The clitoral orgasm is *guaranteed*—*if* you are with someone who knows his business. Or hers.

Most men don't know where a woman's clitoris is. Not surprising, if you stop to think most women don't either. We all know the general location, of course, but every woman is ever so slightly different in the way she is built. Eventually a woman may lose hope in a man's ability to locate the magic button, but she believes that another woman *must* know where it is. Other women always know everything. When a woman gives up her dream of a knight in shining armor finding the grail, she has fantasies that another woman can.

But I am getting ahead of myself. First things first: All fantasies with other women begin and end with tenderness. When women are with women, they do not rush sex. However aggressive the sex may become later, it begins with a slow and loving seduction.

"She's very tender, so tender I can't stand it," says Paula. "We lie on the couch embracing each other firmly, but with a tenderness I've never experienced with anyone before." Certainly never with a man, perhaps not just because he is not good at tenderness but because the quality of tenderness wanted is a nurturing closeness that predates the entry of men into women's lives. Not only would a man not be able to give this kind of maternal closeness; in her mind it would not be manly for him to try.

Lindsay's fantasy of an orgasmic high from sheer closeness reminds me of the unconsummated sex in the heated nights of my adolescence—hours and hours of holding and kissing, the car windows steamed, the radio's romantic music lifting me and the boy up into a heartrending oneness. Ultimately I would return home, lace-trimmed white panties drenched but not a breast touched (God forbid the sacred area between my legs). "Right there on the sofa, we both feel so emotionally and physically intense," Lindsay says, "that we both have a thunderous orgasm—fully clothed. End of fantasy."

Did we girls drive the boys to "blue balls" distraction? I've always thought those extraordinary nights of passion in parked cars weren't altogether pleasureless for them. Certainly we found in their arms a virginal orgasmic high that we'd been waiting for since we left our mothers' arms; based in part on physical sexual contact, it had far more to do with the emotional re-creation of symbiotic oneness, the swooning loss of self in one another. Most women never outgrow this desire for romantic oneness, which many men fear and others tire of.

Tenderness may not be all that is wanted in these fantasies, but after the last bite has been taken of the nipple, the final juices swallowed from "her sweet, dripping cunt," the last dildo inserted "up her delicious pink ass hole," then once again the women return to the all-important cuddling in one another's arms. "I again place my arms around her to draw her as close to me as I am able," says Gemma. "We fall asleep in each other's arms."

Though men have been left out of these fantasies, they could learn a few pointers from these women, who are so consistent in their yearning for certain demonstrations of love and desire. Take for instance the emphasis put on the early steps of seduction, the importance of setting, ambience, as described by Paula. The winning over of the beloved with talk builds trust. Only then come sexual gratification, the oral pleasure (described here so vividly and expertly), the passion, the insistence on *mutual* pleasure, that each partner be satisfied before the denouement. Then comes the all-important return to the overture's tender, final embrace in each other's arms, with God forbid, none of that cold, unfeeling postcoital rolling over and going to sleep, leaving one's partner to spiral down to earth alone, abandoned, staring at the ceiling.

Not every man's cup of tea, these romantic imbroglios, but they are rich in advice for anyone interested in knowing what women want sexually, much of it readily adaptable to a male lover. Men may have real mental and physical problems with women's desire for prolonged foreplay: physically his penis has been hard for what seems like hours, and mentally he feels more manly thrusting than cuddling, which he associates with the maternal arms he fled to find his manhood.

Still, I would urge men to get past the myths of their sleeping too long in women's arms. While there is a component of anger at men behind these fantasies, what most of the women are saying is that men aren't even making an effort to understand their emotional and sexual needs.

I understand that women are not always expert lovers themselves, but if I were a man who loved women, I would take these fantasies, with their splendid directions, to heart.

At the same time, women could benefit from better understanding men's sexual anxieties and some of their new anger at having had the world, as their fathers knew it, turned upside down.

A man spends his life proving his manliness. "Be a man!" father orders his four-year-old son no less sternly than a sergeant orders him to take a beachhead twenty years later. A woman never has to prove she's a woman.

In their fantasies, women can be excited, friendly, foolish, lighthearted, or simply erotic about other women. They can accept homosexual fantasies as an expression of affection, curiosity, and exploration, while the same fantasies arouse enormous dread and anxiety in men. In these fantasies, women do not have anything to lose. To put it another way, if a woman does not have an orgasm in ordinary inter-course, she does not assume that means she is a lesbian. But if a man fails to have an erection every time, right on time, he immediately falls prey to fears of impotency, weakness, and above all, homosexuality. I am left with the notion that women have a surer sense of their sexual identity than men.

In the end, sexual fantasies of other women cannot be understood if we do not recognize that even more than to men, the female sex is an enigma to itself. After centuries of taking each other for granted, women's eyes have been opened to the mystery that is woman; women find they do not know each other at all. They look as if into mirrors; they see but cannot touch. If the woman is basically heterosexual, as are the vast majority in this book, she probably has examined and known more male bodies by now, more closely, than even one woman's. But the unknown is the essence of romance.

Brett

It is a relief and a joy to know I'm not the only woman who has outrageously sexy fantasies or who masturbates to them regularly. I am 21, married almost a year to a man I love very much, with no children (thank God). I model, am considered very pretty, have a high IQ and enjoy many hobbies like writing, drawing, playing piano, painting. I'm hyper—I have a burning desire to see and do everything in life, live out every fantasy, capture every dream. I grew up with my mother and sister as my dad split when I was in fourth grade. I consider myself to be pretty liberated and uninhibited.

I think my fascination with the male genitalia began when I was 5. At that age I was reading on a fourth-grade level and was flipping through the *How and Why Wonder Book of the Human Body.* I had already established that the sperm must encounter the ovum to produce a baby, and so on, but was at a loss as to how they were put in the situation to meet. I used to ponder that quite thoroughly and could not achieve a satisfactory answer on my own. Thus, I approached Mom. Age 5, now. Needless to say, she told me in very adult terms.

Penis, vagina, all that. My parents never baby-talked me or my sister. I asked Mom what Daddy's penis looked like and she asked him to show me. I remember seeing an enormous purple stiff appendage jutting from beneath his towel. In retrospect I realize I was not seeing my father's organ in its flaccid state! Of course, then I couldn't know that. I was fascinated. Wow! So that's how they made babies. Amazing. At age 8 or 9 I used to sneak his *Penthouse* issues and *Forum*. Touching myself was considered very taboo by my strict Catholic mother, but I did it anyway. No earth-shattering results until much later.

What amused me very much when I read Daddy's *Penthouse*s were the women and the men's descriptions of women's bodies and responses. I used to gaze for hours upon the luscious bodies of the women therein and end up with the tight tingling in my pussy that seemed ever present. I used to get so horny I'd get my sister to lie on top of me and press her pelvis against mine. This was exquisite. That's all we ever did, though, never anything else—probably because we were still typical sibling archenemies. My cousin and I, however, used to dry-hump each other at every available opportunity.

My husband, Justin, is a very loving, considerate husband. Sexually, he's great, but penetration has never excited me. I've always had lady troubles though, so maybe that's why. But I do come when he eats me, but only if I fantasize. At 16 I began fantasizing about women much more than men, and I came like crazy when I did. My own hands are the best lover I've ever had. My orgasms are from clitoral stimulation only.

My fantasies were excellent, involving many assorted women, mostly black and *ugly*—obscene—forcing me into eating their sopping wet pussies, suckling their enormous distended boobs. I have other fantasies, too, where a spectacular, well-endowed blond beauty seduces me, and I her. But it's the thoughts of women that get me off.

And now finally I am about to be with my first woman. She looks nothing like the women in my fantasies. She's the butch type who has been chasing me for months through letters and phone calls—I'd met her a few months ago. She lives about three hours away and she has seduced me over and over in both our minds. I'll see her in a month. I am obsessed with her. I love my husband and we have a great married life, but this woman excites me beyond belief.

Now—a fantasy. This is based on a woman I met when I was a door-to-door cosmetics saleswoman and she was my customer. She admitted to me in the brief two hours of our acquaintance that she was bisexual and loved eating women. If only I'd encouraged her! But being in love with my husband I felt at the time that I would be doing him a disservice, to say the least.

I approach the door and knock lightly. It's a cool, crisp day and the breeze stiffens my nipples to hard little peaks. I am wearing no panties beneath the skirt, only a garter and stockings. And no bra beneath the proper silk button-up blouse. A tall, buxom heavy-lipped black woman, fairly young and very pretty, answers the door. We exchange pleasantries and she invites me into her home. I go through my presentation. As I'm doing this, I notice that she gazes at my milky-white tits as they thrust against my blouse. She offers to smoke a joint with me. We catch a good buzz and relax some. I see her glistening mouth and the pink tongue within, and I am getting turned on. Her low-cut top allows me a healthy view of her lovely boobs. I strain to see her nipples. No luck. Her great big shepherd comes bounding in from outside and rushes up to me. As most dogs do, he pokes his head up my skirt and begins to sniff my musky femaleness, taking a few licks with his long, slick tongue. I squirm, I am so hot, but I try to pass it off as embarrassment. The woman scolds him and he retreats. I can see my odor has aroused the dog, as his thick red cock is distended. I am trying hard to appear unruffled when in fact I'm so horny I could die. I carry on with my presentation. She says she can't hear me too well over the noise from the street, so she moves to the couch where I am sitting. I can now see the sweat between her tits, the mole on her neck, the just-shaved smoothness of her ebony legs. She leans forward slightly as if

244

to hear me better, draping her arm over the back of the couch (I'm one of those women who like to chase someone very, very subtly until they think they've caught me. This comes across in my fantasies I think). I tell her I have cotton mouth so she goes to fix me a tall refreshing glass of sangria. While she's in the kitchen, the dog sees his chance and once more begins to lick my quivering clit. I lean back and spread my legs slightly to give him better access. He licks more slowly now, lazily, as though he were well versed in the delightful art of teasing a woman.

I strain against him, mentally begging him to lick faster. I writhe against him, panting, grinding, feeling the first waves of orgasm approaching. I fondle my tits beneath my shirt, and my skirt has ridden up my thighs, exposing my cunt. I hear a gasp and look up horrified beyond words to see her standing there, mouth agape, watching me get eaten out by her pooch. I frantically get myself together. Suddenly she hisses, "Sit down!" Too stunned to reply, I obey. She kneels before my still spread legs and spreads my lips, pouring the cold sangria over my steaming cunt. "That'll teach you to try to fuck my dog, you disgusting cunt!" She begins to lick the juices up off my thighs, and once again I am aflame. I clutch her soft hair and push her face into my cunt. Oh, please, eat me, suck me, make me come! She stands up suddenly, leaving me unfulfilled. She hikes up her skirt and shoves my head to her. I plunge my tongue into her wet cunt, savoring the slimy, mushy wetness. She comes almost immediately. "Now for some real fun," she says. She grabs my wrist and yanks me off the couch and into her bedroom.

She ties me up, spread-eagle, to her huge four-poster bed. I am still fully clothed with my skirt up to my waist and my top half undone. She undresses slowly, enjoying my help-lessness, and kneels down over my face. "Again!" she commands. I begin to eat her again, lapping furiously, feeling her muscles clench as she rocks in orgasm. Her juices flow down my face. I feel the dog between my legs again, going to town. As I am about to come, she orders him to stop. Climbing off me, she trades places with the dog. She tells me to let the dog fuck my mouth. He rams his rod into my mouth. I smell his maleness, can feel his black hairy balls slapping my face. Meanwhile, she is eating me. But she won't let me come! I am so frustrated, so aflame with desire. The dog is humping my face furiously and his cum squirts down my throat, and he's hard again. "All right, bitch, you wanna fuck my dog?" I can't answer, my mouth is full of him. Yes, yes, yes. She orders the dog back between my legs. "Now tell him to fuck you!" I tell him to, beg him to, I plead. He positions himself over me and plunges into me, bucking like crazy. It feels like he's trying to crawl in. Her breasts are dangling over me. I suck her nipples viciously, hungrily, and suddenly I am coming and coming and coming.

Where we used to live, there was a public swimming pool. I was about 10 or 11, and I remember seeing a beautiful woman who lounged by that pool almost all day long, every day, during the summer. Since the girls I knew were such gossipmongers they all had things to say about everyone. I remember standing next to the Pepsi machine, and one of those silly females was telling me that the bathing beauty was a lesbian—all this said in horrified, hush-hush tones, you understand. At the time I would watch her for hours thereafter, fascinated beyond belief that this shimmering creature was a lesbian. Never found out if this was true or not, but the lady has been in my fantasies ever since. I do wonder if she was actually as fabulous-looking as my memory insists she was, or if the years have merely enhanced the object of my oldest and dearest fantasy.

My fantasies of her are very adult although my first reactions to her are childlike. Possibly because of how young I was when I first saw her. Anyhow—

In my fantasy I am lying on the pavement sunning myself by the pool. It is hot, so hot, outside. I remember the whole pool area in remarkable detail. Anyway, here she comes through the gate, clad in the briefest of French-cut bikinis that shows her undulating (yes, undulating) body off to perfection. I always loved her legs—so long and shapely and golden. Sexy! The pool area is crowded and she wants to catch some rays, and the only available spot is the one next to me, of course.

Terrific, isn't it, how fantasies just sort those things out. She spreads her towel out, lies down on her back and closes her eyes. I keep stealing looks at her. She even has golden downy fuzz on her belly below her navel. I get restless, and for lack of something better to do I begin massaging suntan oil onto my legs. I also try in vain to apply it on my back. She sees my difficulty and offers her assistance. God, her voice is so low and husky. I comply and lie back down on my belly. Her long slim fingers begin rubbing the lotion into my skin in slow small circles. I feel myself getting wet. Her hands move up and down my sides and make brief contact with the sides of my ample breasts. I don't take this as a sign of encouragement—could've been accidental! She's rubbing my lower back now, my legs, with the same maddeningly slow movements. My thighs now, the insides of them. Her fingers lightly but firmly graze my pussy lips through the fabric of my swimsuit. Once. Twice. Yet again. I'm going crazy trying to pretend I'm not noticing her deliberate touching.

"Your turn!" She smiles at me, hands me the bottle. Her green eyes sparkle, lit with an aura of devilment! She lies on her belly, I begin my delicious task, touching her in the same way she touched me. I want to lean down and kiss the back of her neck, her knees, lick up her thighs, suck her clit. But I appear calm and unruffled. I notice suddenly that her bikini bottom is soaked at the crotch. I am now almost beside myself with lust. She says it's hot, invites me up for some iced tea. "Sure," I say. We head for her place.

It's cool inside, so breezy and airy, and my nipples poke right out. Hers do as well. I can't help but stare. We sit on the couch, chatting away. She goes to get me some tea—I offer to help. She smiles that cat smile. I join her in her tiny kitchen. She bends over to pick something up and her gorgeous ass strains against her suit. I am enthralled. She looks up, sees me staring, smiles. We wander back into the living room, the air is charged with tension, with two aching pussies.

She hands me my tea and lets her fingers linger lightly over mine. Somehow I think she must be much older than me because of her confidence and ease of manner. I am feeling so ruffled and nervous, like a small child—here she is, so suave and cool. Anyhow, she smiles enigmatically and bends to kiss me slowly so as not to scare me off. Her lips are so soft and sexy. My mouth opens and we french kiss lightly, yet with passion. And she then proceeds to make love with me over and over.

In my fantasy I am in awe of her face, her body, her breasts. She is so beautiful, almost ethereal-looking.

My fantasies, as you can tell, are of women and dogs. It used to bother me, but mainly because I was afraid of what people would think of me if I were a lesbian, which I'm not. Men fascinate me, and I love my husband to distraction.

But in the past six months this woman I mentioned, who is a lesbian, has come on to me many times. Of course I pretend I'm not entirely available, but I am joining her in a month when my husband goes to California for a few months on his job. I will miss him terribly but I'm looking forward to my time with this woman. After much soul searching I realize I am bisexual, and am eagerly anticipating my first encounter with a woman. Even now I find I've always been attracted to certain women, and that my moral self found excuses to part company with them. My sexual self kicks me in the butt a lot for it now.

Natalie

I am 28, single but engaged (I'll be married in September), and heterosexual (in practice at least; in my fantasies, however . . .). I'm originally from the East but have been living in St. Louis for three years. I have a BA from Sweet Briar, a year's graduate work in psychology at the University of Michigan, and a law degree from Michigan. I presently work in the legal department of a multinational corporation but will be leaving shortly to join my fiancé in the Denver area. David is also a lawyer; he's five years older than myself, divorced (no children), and a wonderful man and lover. I am what they call "average-looking," maybe a little better (a "six and a half"?), five feet five, slim but not skinny, dark brown hair, gray eyes, good complexion, nice smile— altogether, healthy and pleasant looking but hardly an eye-popper. I have had several lovers in college and afterward but do not go in for casual sex. I am unmarried by choice and will marry by choice, since I am doing well enough not to need to marry at all. Aside from the usual teenage girl-lay, I have never had a sexual experience with a woman. I'm not absolutely averse to one, but the right situation would have to arise, and so far it hasn't.

Probably every woman thinks she's oversexed, but in my case this became a factor in my career choice. It didn't lead me to law, but it did force me out of psychology. I just became too "interested" in the case histories I read about. I think I'm what you'd call a "psychological voyeur."

A person's masturbation seems so, well, "secret." It's about the most intimate thing one can talk about, the most revealing of one's hidden self. My fantasies involve masturbation—watching or being watched, or masturbating together with someone else. Very often, usually, in fact, they're about other women, women I know, or don't know but have seen, or else women from my past. I masturbate about two or three times a week, always at night so I can drift off to sleep after I come, *never* at work. In college I was more adventurous about times and places, and in my year of graduate school I became absolutely shameless. Now, as a corporation lawyer, I am more demure, but I enjoy it as much as ever. I am sure I will never stop. David enjoys watching me masturbate and I enjoy being watched, but that's just another form of sex play. It's not something that will replace my private masturbation. My fantasies are my own and I want to keep them that way, though I am more than a little excited by the prospect of telling them to you.

One of my favorite fantasies, which I still entertain rather often, draws on my psychology background. I am reclining on a psychiatrist's couch and you or someone like you (an interviewer or an analyst, I'm not sure which) is having me describe my sexual fantasies in detail. The analyst sits behind me in a chair, notebook in hand, and takes down everything I say. I can't see her, but I know she is wearing a suit and sits very professionally with her legs crossed, listening to my every word. I am embarrassed and at the same time strangely excited, as I talk about the details of my fantasies and of masturbatory practices. I can feel myself getting wet and find I have an uncontrollable desire to masturbate then and there. I ask the analyst if she would mind if I do and she says, "No, of course not. Please go ahead." At first I am very shy about it and simply undo the waist button of my pants and slip my hand down inside, but soon I am so excited that I remove my pants and panties altogether and masturbate myself just as I would if I were alone. In fact, I even put on a bit of a show. All this time, of course, I am continuing to relate my fantasies, which I assume the analyst is taking down. On a hunch, though, I look over my shoulder and see that she (you) has hiked up her skirt and is busily masturbating, too. Somewhere around here I usually come, so my fantasy doesn't continue into any overt lesbian activity. I don't think I'm repressing my secret homosexuality, though there's certainly an element of that in my fantasy. The main thing is confessing my masturbation and being watched while doing it—and watching, too. About the only thing needed to complete this fantasy would be for me to know that you masturbated as you read this.

My fascination with masturbation, mine and other people's, goes back to some experiences of my adolescence which I still use as fantasy material. I'll describe the experiences themselves, since the fantasies are just one or another variation on them.

The first one dates back to when I was 13 and in the seventh grade and my friend Cindy and I used to sleep over at one another's houses and talk about boys and sex, about both of which we were very ignorant. I remember how we would undress quickly in front of one another and cast furtive looks at one another's cunts to see who had the most hair (I did). Then we'd push the beds together and spend hours giggling about what we'd heard about sex (neither of us knew anything firsthand). It was on one of these nights that we discovered masturbation. Cindy had seen her first erect cock and was describing it to me. I remember feeling very "itchy" as I listened to her, and I instinctively lowered my hand to my crotch till finally, to my amazement, I came in a loud chorus of moans. Cindy was astounded and made me tell her how it felt and how to do it. When I couldn't explain, she made me turn on the light and lift my night-dress and show her. I vividly remember sitting up in bed with my thighs parted trying to find the spot again to show Cindy. No one had ever looked at my cunt so intensely as Cindy, nor has to this day. I took her hand and placed it on my clitoris (my love button, I thought of it then) so she would know what to look for, then she spread her thighs and we felt around till we found her clitoris, which proved to be bigger than mine. She was wet now, too (neither of us knew anything about that—who would have told us?), and I watched her and masturbated to a second orgasm (a real veteran now!) as she tentatively stroked herself to her first. Altogether, I think we must have masturbated six or seven times that night, including two sessions of mutual mastur-bation which we both enjoyed tremendously but felt a little guilty about. There were several other evenings like this in the next year before Cindy moved away.

The other experience from my adolescence that I like to fantasize about concerns my summer as a junior counselor at a girls' camp in Vermont. The counselor I worked under was a Swiss exchange student named Uta who was studying at Bennington. She was 20 or so, I was 8. We all idolized Uta, who was tall, full-bodied in an athletic (but not really muscular) way, and very European, down to the hair in her armpits which she refused to shave (she did shave her legs). My bunk was right across from Uta's so in addition to all the common opportunities for seeing Uta nude (in the showers and so forth) I saw her dress and undress every day. Even now I don't think I've ever seen a more perfect or, at any rate, more sexual-looking body. Uta was like a splendid female animal with all the smells, hair and secretions that belong to femaleness. She obviously enjoyed her body, too—the things it could do, the pleasures it gave, the tastes, everything. She was made for sex, but unfortunately there wasn't much around at a girls' camp in the Vermont woods—Uta was strictly heterosexual. Partly to relieve herself but also, I think, because she loved any kind of sensuality for its own sake, Uta would masturbate every second or third night or so, when she thought all the campers were asleep. They might have been, but I wasn't, though I pretended to be. I would lie on my stomach with my head turned toward Uta and my hand underneath me between my legs, and I'd lie there for what seemed like ages waiting for Uta to begin. Uta slept nude but usually under a sheet, so all I could generally see was the outline of her legs parted and slightly raised and the motions of her arm between them. Uta had trained herself to be as quiet as possible—not, I think, because she was embarrassed about masturbating (I'm sure she wasn't) but because it didn't seem a thing eight-year-olds should know about. Quiet as she was, though, she couldn't help thrashing around a little when she came. I learned to follow her rhythms and to time my orgasm to coincide with hers. The best nights were those which were so hot that Uta threw the sheet off her and lay there nude in the moonlight. With her body all silvery and glistening with sweat, she looked like a goddess of sorts. She moved more freely too on those nights, and sometimes she would turn on her side (toward me!) and raise her left leg so that her whole cunt was visible in the moonlight. Her bush, which was blondish brown in daylight, looked like spun silver. Those nights were agony to me because I wanted to look at her but was afraid to open my eyes for fear she'd know I was awake. I was also afraid she'd catch the movements of my hand beneath me. I developed a kind of squint for those times and learned to bring myself off with the most delicate, undetectable motions of my forefinger on my clitoris. When I fantasize about these nights I change the scenario a little and make myself bolder. I, too, throw my sheet off and lie facing Uta with my right leg up and we each masturbate as we watch the other. Sometimes now, on summer nights when I'm alone, I relive those times by tilting my dresser mirror so that it faces downward toward my bed. I watch myself in the mirror as I sensuously masturbate and pretend I am Uta looking at me, or me looking at some other woman. The moonlight makes it beautiful and surreal —also guiltless. I am sure I would make this fantasy a reality without a second thought if the situation presented itself. Sometimes I substitute one of my friends for Uta in my fantasy, or occasionally an actress like Dominique Sanda— did you see *Voyage en Douce?*

The following fantasy is my current favorite. Here goes. My friend Ann and I are biking in the woods. It's a beautiful June day and we have packed a lunch and a bottle of wine and are hiking along a seldom traveled path. We have had a lovely day of it, but on the way home we find we need to go to the bathroom. It's still about three miles back, but out of modesty I decide to wait. Ann says she can't, so we go a way off the trail and find a hidden spot, and Ann walks ahead of me and takes off her jeans and panties and squats down to pee. Her back is toward me, and as I recline on the pine-needle floor I watch the stream descend from the secret place between her legs. I have never seen Ann nude before, and I am surprised by how lovely her ass is.

The stream trickles to a halt and I get up to go but Ann asks me to wait a minute. She lowers her buttocks and bears down. I can see her anus open and close and open again, and a large turd slowly descends to the pine-needle floor. Ann looks over her shoulder to me and laughs apologetically, "I hope I'm not grossing you out." I don't answer. I can't. I never thought it could excite me to watch anyone defecate, let alone another woman. But there I am, decidedly aroused. I can feel the wetness between my legs (this is getting awfully difficult to write). Ann bears down again and two more turds drop down. I long to touch myself but I don't for fear Ann will turn around. I don't think I've ever been more aroused. I am not into toilet games or anything of that sort, and I have no desire to wipe Ann clean (she's very clean in my fantasy—no mess, no smell). It's the intimacy of watching her that arouses me. What she's doing is such a *private* act. It's usually done alone and indoors, not here in the woods on a beautiful sunny day.

Ann finishes and pulls up her panties and jeans. "Ready?" she asks. But now I need to go—or rather I want to. I want Ann to see me. I want to open myself to the sun and the woods. I ask her to wait, and I turn and face her. As I drop my panties I catch her eyes on my navel, then my bush, then my cunt lips. Our eyes meet and she blushes a little. I squat down facing her and begin to pee. Her eyes drop to my cunt, and this time there's no embarrassment, only interest and desire. "Mind if I watch?" She smiles. She drops to her knees a few feet from me and in response I part my thighs further and open my cunt lips with my fingers so that she can see everything. My clitoris is erect, as it is now, and I wish she would reach out and touch it, but she doesn't. I finish peeing but remain squatting. "That's not all, is it?" Ann whispers. "No," I answer. I tighten my muscles and push and my bowels empty their fullness on the forest floor. Ann walks around behind me and stays there for a minute or so. I recall how she looked from the back and am excited to have her seeing me. A shudder like a small orgasm goes through my loins. (All right, I give in. I am masturbating a little now between sentences. I wish I were a one-handed typist.)

Ann comes around in front of me again and bends down and kisses me tenderly on the lips. Then she undresses till she is nude from the waist down. She sits across from me Indian fashion. Her cunt lips are parted and between the wondrous chestnut brown hair I can see her clitoris and the sheen of her wetness. "Is there more?" she asks. I nod. "Do you mind if I masturbate as I watch you?" I whisper no but that hardly expresses my feeling. Ann moves her fingers slowly and rhythmically over her clitoris. She holds them out to me now and I sniff her scent. I hold her hand to my nose and lips and bear down again. I'm finished now but also just begun. "Oh, Ann, do me too," I plead. Ann returns her right hand to her clitoris while her left reaches out to find mine. I gasp when she touches me. She is close to coming now, and I drink in every detail of her movements and sounds. Her lips are parted and her eyes are half shut. She is rubbing her clitoris rapidly now. I'm almost there, too, and I put my hand over hers to give me the rhythm I need. We reach out and our lips meet again and we twine our bodies together as we pump ourselves to orgasm, squeezing out every little corner of it. At the end we're not using our hands at all but are scissored together with our cunts touching, clit against clit.

Well, now I will have to go and finish myself off. I'm amazed I held off this long. I guess I just enjoyed describing my fantasies so much, I feel a little guilty about it.

Marla

I'm a 24-year-old lesbian currently living in Japan. I got a degree in Japanese and Asian studies from Vassar, and am currently a translator/interpreter for a large Japanese company. I have always known I was a lesbian since eighth grade, but never actually had sexual relations with a woman until college. All that stuff people say about lesbians is really untrue. I had a very happy childhood with parents who also had a happy life. I view my lesbianism with pride but am still in the closet, mainly for economic reasons—but also I think a person's sex life is a private matter.

My lover is still in the U.S. We plan to live together forever. I have never been interested in anyone else.

Most of my fantasies involve power. In one of my favorites I am the absolute ruler of a tiny Middle Eastern kingdom where women control everything—the men are the servants. Some women are straight, and they are allowed freely to marry men. I love to have huge feasts of lamb, wine and fiery dishes. After one lovely meal I am deeply in love with a talented woman artist of the kingdom. She has just shown me my official portrait. I take her hand and kiss her passionately and she responds. It is a long kiss. We have more wine and I order a servant to play a harp as we make love. She kisses me all over and I her. Afterward we have more wine and I gently touch her beautifully nude body.

In another fantasy, it is the Middle Ages. This time I'm a cardinal in the Catholic Church—this church only has women priests. (I really am still a Catholic, by the way.) Since marriage is forbidden, the women are allowed to have passionate love affairs—and these are only sinful if they aren't truly love affairs. After a ceremony in which I officiate at a beheading of a man who tried to seize power in the Church, I am carried back to my château on a portable throne by several lovely women—all have short blond hair and strong features. They take me to a room filled with silk pillows and lay me down gently. A lute and a recorder can be heard in the distance. The most beautiful of the women slowly disrobes and takes off my cloak and hood, all the while caressing my thighs and breasts with her hands and then her mouth. Food is brought in—a big turkey, grapes and lamb—and she carves the meat and we eat, all the while touching each other and whispering endearments. After the meal, we kiss deeply and I lie on top of her—I rub her all over until she orgasms, and she does the same to me.

Other women come in and we all make love and feast. A blind man enters and brings more food. I think food is very sexual; after a good meal, sex is always terrific. Two women artists show me the latest illuminated manuscripts they have created for me. One is highly erotic—the story of Sappho and her poetic community. I give the artist a bag of gold coins in payment and she kneels and kisses my ring in gratitude. The other woman shows me a golden chalice with a cross embedded with rubies on it. I give her a bag of silver coins. Suddenly she professes her love for me and so we go off to a private room and have a long talk. We talk about art and the love of women, and in the end we make love. I give her a backrub and then kiss her shoulders and neck. Neck kissing always excites me. Her hair is soft and long and it falls on my face as she lies on her side. She whispers that she has never before slept with a woman and I am excited at being the first to make love to her.

Well, these two have many variations, but I like the Middle Ages and Middle Eastern customs. Oddly enough, I've never had fantasies about Japan. The women here do not attract me at all—they have no fiery passion in their eyes.

I think men have no idea how wonderful love between women is. They think we all have dreams of being dominated by them! Actually, my lesbian friends and I often dream of ruling the world and at the same time remaining loving and gentle in our relationships with women. I don't go in for kinky sex and don't like oral sex all that much, but I do love the warmth of being with another woman intimately —even having a wonderfully long intellectual discussion with another woman turns me on. Love without good talk is nothing.

It is rare when I see men and women who are in love truly talking about things. The men just make the women listen to them and admire them. Even my straight friends (those select few who know I'm gay) sometimes tell me they're envious of gay women because they can be so close to another woman. My straight friends say that although they love men they are still at a distance from them—still unequal. Someday all women should discover the joy and peace in loving other women. Only when we learn to love and trust each other will we be able to overthrow the centuries-old patriarchal structure!

I think you tried in your books to be fair and understanding, but I still could sense your inner anxiety about gay sex. If you think of the violence men do to women—plopping on top of them and shoving their penises into a small hole— maybe you'd see that lesbian sex seems perhaps gentler and more humane. When women learn to live without men then we'll grow in freedom and confidence. As long as we sleep with them we are giving them aid and comfort. I think if women thought of the political implications of sex with men they'd think twice about jumping into bed with them!

Stacy

I am a 19-year-old female, presently going to college, single, upper middle class, heterosexual (I think). I am very preoccupied with sex, think about it a lot, and do it whenever I can. I love to masturbate, even when I have a steady sex partner. Sometimes I think I lean toward being a nymph. Men seem to be attracted to my surface innocence, and they love it when they find I'm a tiger in bed. I love to wear my tight black leather pants and let my titties practically fall out of my shirt and watch them stare at me and try to take me home.

My first sexual encounter was with my cousin. We were both about 7 years old. We would play "doctor" at every opportunity—she would lie down on her stomach and I would explore her ass and hairless pussy, then she would do the same to me. Later on, when I was about 13, my friend, a 10-year-old girl, asked if I knew how to French kiss. She would lie on top of me and we would "play" for hours. One time I masturbated under the covers while we were kissing.

I guess my present fantasies are created from these early lesbian experiences. It is strange that I feel repelled at the thought of ACTUALLY touching a girl sexually, yet I fantasize about it all the time. Whenever I masturbate I think of this one: I am hitchhiking on a lonely road when a gorgeous, sexy girl picks me up. I try to stop myself from looking at her nipples poking out, and her soft, full lips. She asks me to stay at her house. We arrive a few minutes later. She gives me a bikini and tells me to go swimming, that she'll be out shortly. The bikini barely covers my pussy and ass; there are hairs hanging along the inside of my legs. The top is nonexistent. I get in the heated pool and reach down to feel my pussy. It is slick with my juices. Then the girl appears in a bikini like mine. After swimming around for quite a while, I realize that she doesn't share my sexual thoughts and I try to think about other things. Finally she lightly brushes past me, then offers to put some baby oil on me. She starts with my shoulders. She is giving me the most sensuous massage. Then, her fingers trail lightly down my back, softly rubbing and squeezing. Her hands travel further down to my thighs. God, I want to turn around! But I don't move, thinking she might stop. I feel those hands inch toward my ass; finally one finger slips in the crack. Her lips softly kiss the back of my neck. I can't stand it any longer; I turn slowly around. She says, "Let's get out and dry off." I follow her, wondering if I blew it by turning around. On the way to her room, she grabs two big fluffy towels. "Lie on the bed," she says, "and let me dry you off." Soon I feel her exquisite hands as they untie my top. Ever so slowly, she continues to sweetly torture me with her hands and lips until she says, "Turn over." Her lips travel up my inner thighs until they tease my pussy lips. I am going crazy for her tongue. I grab her blond head and press her into me. Oh, it is so nice! At this point in my fantasy, I come all over the place.

June

I am a lesbian, not bisexual. I don't hate men in general, but I definitely would not go to bed with a man. I've been there, I'm a widow. It's a case of being brought up not to think sexually. If I had had that freedom I never would have married, I would have just had my son and lived with a woman. I'm 43, my son is 17 now.

Women know how to make love to another woman all the time, not just when it is time to go to bed, time for a climax. Men so often miss this important fact although women say to men, "I need to be held and snuggled and touched and sucked on without needing a climax every time." It is called tenderness, nurturing, caring, loving, sharing.

Now about my fantasy. I thought it might interest you to read one that is not quite so wild. I am a butch who loves her mate a lot. We try to satisfy each other. I can climax fantasizing about making love to her when I'm by myself. I climax just masturbating and thinking about sucking on her breasts or cunt. I climax thinking about her responses to my

259

lovemaking and her giving to me. Usually I'll climax making her climax, but then she will follow through by loving me, fingering me, kissing me. It is fantasy when I get so horny when she is not around and reach orgasm with her in my head. But it is also my reality most of the time, so maybe it isn't a "fair" fantasy.

I guess the real fantasy was making love to a woman when I was married—that fantasy is a dream come true.

Incidentally, I was brought up a Connecticut WASP but a natural renegade to that! College degree (AS), electronics technician; have always loved women from as far back as I can remember but did not do anything about it until after my husband died. I'm happier now than I've ever been. It's terrible, in a way, that it took someone's death to set me free.

Sandy

I am 21 years old, single and heterosexually oriented.

I grew up in a middle-middle-class Canadian family. As an only child I have enjoyed the exclusive attentions of my mother, who has been very generous with her love, concern and time. She is an intelligent, open-minded woman, and I consider myself fortunate that this woman is my mother. She has never closed any doors to me; in fact, she has opened many.

My father, on the other hand, is a closed-minded, uninspired soul with whom it is very difficult to communicate. I cannot remember being fond of him, although I've been told that when I was a preadolescent, my father was the focus of my world.

At age 16, I left home to escape my father's authoritarian nature. I moved in with a man whom I regard as the most positive influence in my life (next to my mother). We plan to live a stimulating, adventurous and fantasy-filled life together!

I have wondered, "What meanings are inherent in my fantasies?" but I have never felt guilty about fantasizing or about the content of my fantasies. I am fortunate that I love a man who loves and appreciates the very essence of me! He is interested in every facet of my being . . . including my fantasies.

All of my fantasies revolve around a central theme: my sexual involvement with other women.

As a child I experienced various sexual encounters with female peers. I remember feeling quite stimulated during these infrequent adventures.

At 16 I had my first and only homosexual experience since my childish explorations. I found it to be a boring and unexciting encounter. As a result of this, I have since then refused similar invitations. Nevertheless, I continue to have frequent and stimulating "lesbian" fantasies. I fantasize when I masturbate; on a few occasions I have fantasized during lovemaking.

My most frequently recurring fantasy begins with my presence at a gay bar. I am dressed in a slinky black front-slit skirt and a brief black bodysuit.

A beautifully exotic woman approaches me and inquires if I would like to dance. I turn toward her, appreciate her obvious loveliness and accept the invitation. We begin a slow and sensuous dance movement. Our bodies slowly draw together until I am overwhelmed by her scent. As I place my damp hands on her delicate waist, she tenderly rests her own hands on my shoulders. I feel the thrill of eager anticipation as we gaze into one another's eyes. As our dance continues, I slide my right hand toward her crotch and playfully toy with the opening of her front-slit skirt. She emits a throaty moan as my hand parts the curtain of fabric and my fingers begin to caress the softness of her pubic mound. I then allow my index finger to descend from her mound to her equally delightful cleft. As my finger loses itself in her wetness, my own excitement becomes undeniable and I feel an insistent pulsation in my cunt.

By gently parting her dangling lips and stroking her soaking slit, I explore her pussy. My digit gravitates to her now protruding clit, where my finger lingers to tantalize and tease; I release her breasts with my free hand and eagerly place my mouth on an erect nipple.

After bringing her to orgasm in this manner, I allow her to

reciprocate. She slips her cool hand into the cup of my bodysuit, where her fingers lightly graze my breast. Groping more forcefully, she kneads and pinches my nipple until, longing for release, I guide her hand to my crotch.

Kneeling in front of me, her hands part the flap of my skirt and she begins to nuzzle my mound with her delicate nose. My hands caress her silky dark hair as her jutting tongue delves forcefully into my swelling cunt; luring her to continue her assault, I press her head more tightly to my pussy. As my arousal mounts, I open my eyes to watch her. Holding my breath, I feel the first tinglings of orgasm; as the sensation builds, I gasp for air. My orgasm peaks and I explode in her awaiting mouth.

Priscilla

I am a high school senior on an exchange program from England. I attend what must be a typical suburban American high school consisting of mostly middle-class kids, but it is very different from my all-girls "public" school in Sussex. I come from a middle-class family in the south of England. Both my parents are in the theater business.

I have been attracted to girls since early adolescence so I suppose I must be a bisexual, but I'm not worried about labels. I think most people have fantasies about those of their own sex, but they are rarely acted out.

I would like to describe an early sexual experience. When I was 14 I accompanied my best friend and her family to their holiday home in the south of France. She had a younger brother and sister and an older sister, Mary, about 19.

One evening the family went out to the local cinema, but Mary and I stayed home. It was a cold and rainy night. We sat in front of a huge fire in the living room of this old rustic farmhouse. We settled down with our books and Mary went to get some wine. She returned with two glasses, poured the wine, and we resumed reading. After some time I glanced up in surprise to see Mary really upset. I moved over and she said that something in the book conjured up memories of her ex-boyfriend, who had just dumped her. She was emotional, and I put my arms around her.

She started describing this guy and how affectionate and warm he used to be. It was really cozy in front of the fire, and I was beginning to get a little lightheaded from the wine. I could feel her breath on my neck as she snuggled further into my shoulder. She told me how wonderful and gentle he was and what he used to do when they made love. I could feel her breast pressed against my arm. Strangely, I became aroused. It was a lovely feeling but I was very confused, as you can imagine. I could not make sense of my emotions, but the warm, prickly sensation between my legs was real enough.

Mary rose to refill our glasses and came back, sitting very close to me. Her skirt moved up and I caught a glimpse of her panties, which really turned me on. I could not understand my emotions but I felt drawn to her. She wasn't wearing a bra and her breasts were visible through her thin blouse. I had an instinctive urge to reach out and touch them. Mary asked me in a husky voice if I knew what it was like to be really kissed.

Without waiting for an answer she moved a little closer, parted my trembling lips with her warm, moist tongue, and at that moment I almost died with pleasure. It was the most wonderful feeling. We kissed for ages. She undid my blouse and stroked and kissed my small breasts. I felt as though I was in heaven. Mary wanted to go further but I was too scared. Although nothing else happened, this event remains so powerful for me and is the basis for a recurring fantasy. I often dream of making love to Mary now that I feel confident about who I am and what I want.

Most of my fantasies revolve around girls my own age but there is a teacher at my school here whom I find very attractive. She is the typical American blonde, very athletic, very pretty. I often find myself wondering how she would make love to me. I would love to kiss her. I imagine nothing will happen, though, but I wish she would try to seduce me. Yesterday I casually sat with my legs slightly parted so she could see up my dress. I imagine that put her off her teaching stride a bit. I wonder if she was shocked. I hope it made her interested because there is no way I can make the first move.

I have long legs and a good figure. I am a dancer and do aerobics every day. I love the feeling of a tight-fitting leotard on my body. I think the sculptured outline of a woman's body is quite beautiful. I play squash regularly and always wear a white blouse and short, pleated skirt. I love the way a skirt swishes back and forth revealing crisp white panties, so I spend a lot of time watching girls play squash.

I'm really turned on by underwear and always wear the softest, most luxurious things. I often wonder what the other girls who wear baggy jeans and huge sweaters have underneath and if they have the same feelings about underthings. When I see someone I'm attracted to I try to imagine what she has on (I always look at panty lines) and then imagine undressing her slowly and letting her try on my silky underwear. Sometimes this may lead to caressing and kissing.

I often wonder why clothes are so sexual for me. For example, sometimes when I move on my seat in class the slight pressure of tight nylon on my vagina gives me a lovely feeling—particularly if the teacher I was telling you about is teaching the class.

I'd like to tell you about an incident that I often think about. One night last year I was in my room and there was a knock at the door. It was one of the girls on the squash team. We were not special friends but I liked her and, to be honest, fancied her a bit. She wanted to know if she could borrow a skirt and shirt for an important match the next day. I got the things out and suggested she take off her uniform and try them on in my room.

She took off her blouse, skirt and slip, remaining in panties and a lacy, wispy bra. She looked so good. I suggested that she try one of my sport bras. She asked me to help her with it and I slowly undid her at the back. As her bra fell off her shoulders, she turned around and we both looked at each other. She had lovely creamy breasts and her nipples were standing out. I was feeling very aroused and my mouth went dry. I didn't know what to do. However, she moved slowly toward me.

Before we were aware of what was happening we were kissing, tentatively at first, and then slowly, deeply. My hands moved down her body. I shivered as I felt her smooth skin. I felt around her thighs, up her back and then down her tummy. I traced the outline of her panties, massaging the silky fabric over her bush. I could feel her getting moist and her breathing becoming raspy. My finger went underneath the elastic and inside her. She was so wet. By the way, this is making me feel really horny, I'm typing with one hand and the other is under my dress. My other hand caressed her buttocks. I led her to the bed. I lay between her legs, put my hands under her bum and started licking her inner thighs. I slowly, very slowly, moved higher and higher until I reached her vagina. My tongue found her clit and I started sucking until she had more orgasms than I could count. We have been lovers ever since.

Here are some short fantasies:

I am the house mistress at a school. I have been assigned to check that the new girls are wearing the regulation underwear. When I discover that three of them are wearing high-cut sexy panties instead of school briefs I make them come to my study and undress each other and masturbate whilst the prettiest girl fingers me.

I am teaching an aerobics class. In the class is a beautiful, feminine boy about 16. I ask him to come to the front of the class. Soon he has an erection, visible through his black tights, from watching me exercise. I dismiss the rest of the class. I take him home, dress him in a skirt and panties and then suck him off. Afterward he tries on my leotard and then fucks me in the bum.

A friend and I are double-dating two boring guys. During dinner I kick off my shoes under the table and slowly start rubbing the inside of my friend's leg. I slowly move up her thighs and rub my toes against her vagina. She's obviously really enjoying it but doesn't suspect me. The next day she tells me what her date was doing and how she enjoyed it. I tell her it was me.

I would like to be seduced by a really beautiful, light-skinned black woman with a fantastic body. I'd like her to make love to me on the beach. Afterwards she takes me to her beach house and shaves my pussy. She straddles me, parts my legs and starts licking me with her warm pink tongue. All I can see is her bum covered by nylon panties.

Paula

I am 17 years old.

I've been gay as long as I can remember. I say "gay" because the word "lesbian" turns me off. I recently graduated, as an honor student, from high school.

I use this fantasy when I'm in the shower. My fantasy alone brings me to an orgasm without actual physical contact. I'm very attracted to women. My favorite fantasy centers around a famous rock singer. (I won't say who, because I wouldn't want to make her uncomfortable should she ever read this.) If it's possible to be in love with someone you don't know personally, then I'm head over heels. Here is my fantasy:

I have just been to a rock concert where my idol was the main act. After the concert, I manage to meet her and we hit it off instantly. She's exactly how I imagined her to be. After talking to her for what seems like hours, we decide we want to see each other again. She tells me she has a week off from touring and would like to get away for a weekend. She decides to rent a cabin and go to the mountains. I'm all excited when she asks me to go. We go on the long drive to the cabin. When we get there, the snow is falling. For me, this is the perfect romantic setting. We unpack after we find that there is only one bed (lucky for me). After we get settled and get used to the idea of sleeping together (which doesn't bother me one bit), I cook a big dinner complete with wine (you might say I wanted to seduce her). After we're both a little blitzed we move to the couch in front of a roaring fire. Our conversation moves toward sexual experiences. She's surprised when she finds I am a virgin (probably the only one 17 years old). After drinking a little more wine, I see she's as hot as I am. As I sit watching the fire, I am (pleasantly) surprised when she leans over and kisses me passionately on the mouth. I smile and she sees that I enjoyed it. This time, the kiss is equally initiated by both of us. We lie on the couch embracing each other firmly, but with a tenderness I've never experienced with anyone before. She quietly suggests that we move to the bedroom. At first I am apprehensive because I have never made love to a woman before. She tells me not to be afraid, that she will show me what to do to give her the most pleasure. We enter the bedroom and slowly begin to undress each other, stopping once in a while to caress and kiss each other. We slide between the cool sheets and lie in each other's arms. She's very tender, so tender I can't stand it. I kiss her, but she becomes more aggressive. She presses her lips firmly against mine and parts my lips with her tongue. I begin to trust my own intuition and begin to slowly caress and kiss her breasts. She moans. I start to flick my tongue across her nipples and suck them. My hot breath makes her even more excited. She tells me to kiss her all over, and I'm happy to do what she asks. I kiss her lips fully, then I slowly plant tiny wet kisses on her eyelids and nose. I nibble on her ear. I move down and kiss her belly until I reach her beautiful crotch. I pass over it and move to her feet. I begin to kiss her feet and suck on her toes while rubbing the insides of her thighs. I lick up the insides of her legs. Then, finally, I part her lips and begin rubbing her clitoris. She begs me to kiss and lick her. I start flicking my tongue across her clit. She takes a deep breath and sighs and comes. I continue licking and probing with my tongue. At the same time, I caress her breast. I rub my finger over her erect nipple. I increase the speed of my tongue, she tenses and has an orgasm (at the same time I'm having mine). She lies on the bed, completely exhausted, with her arms tightly around me. She slowly runs her fingers through my hair and softly kisses my face and neck. Her hands move and she starts rubbing the back of my neck. Chills are running through my body. She gets out of bed and goes into the bathroom. I hear her turn on the shower and she comes back out and takes my hand and leads me into the shower. The water is hot, and I start to relax. She embraces me and starts nibbling on my shoulders. She takes the soap and starts lathering up my body. I'm terribly excited, and the thought of doing this gets me even hotter—I take the soap and lather her up, spending a lot of time on her beautiful firm breasts. The warmth of the massaging water, combined with her feeling me up, brings me to a climax that can never be equaled. We get out of the shower and dry each other off. Then we crawl back into bed and fall asleep in each other's arms.

Giving *her* pleasure is the most important thing.

Suzanne

I am 20 years old and have been married since I was 17. I have never been able to achieve an orgasm during intercourse, and I have been sexually active since I was 15. I only achieve orgasms while masturbating.

I have a lot of lesbian fantasies. I have never been sucked off by a woman, but I think I would love it. And I would probably come! Wow! I have, however, sucked off another woman, and I loved making her come! I can remember how she felt and tasted. I would like to tell you about it, and hope someone else can enjoy it too!

Joan had come over to our house to visit me. We began drinking (Joan, my husband and myself) and we ended up very drunk. Joan dared me to pull out my husband's cock and suck it. She even offered to help. I laughingly agreed. But before I knew it, I was sucking and licking while she held his cock for me. My husband came all over Joan's and my face. Then I offered Joan to my husband, and I watched them fuck till she screamed. Then my husband was sucking her pretty tits, and I couldn't take my eyes off her beautiful cunt. I couldn't resist anymore, and I went in after it. I spread open her legs and placed them on my shoulders. I spread open her cunt lips, and I went down on her. I licked her just like I would like her to have done to me. I probed her cunt with my fingers, first one, then two, then three. She loved it, every minute of it! It got me all hot when she came! She put her hands on the back of my head and bucked up to meet my tongue.

This threesome went on for about three weeks. Sometimes my husband would fuck me while I snacked on her cunt. Or she would suck on my husband's dick while I took her. She never did me, she couldn't bring herself to do it, but I often fantasize about her eating my cunt now while I masturbate.

I fake orgasms with my husband (wrong I know), but I don't want him to think it's because he's not good. I feel he is. It's probably just me. I don't even get my rocks off when my husband goes down on me because he's a little too rough, and hell, it's not the same.

Kerry

I am a black female. I was married at the age of 16 and had my first child at 17. I am in my early 50s now and I have three children. Two are teenagers.

Besides my husband, I've been with only one other man and that was at the age of 14. (By the way, I'm quite embarrassed using such words as cock, cunt, pussy, etc.) Believe it or not, I hardly know anything about sex, intercourse, foreplay and the like, even though I've been married more than 30 years and have produced three kids.

Let me explain: I'm a battered wife and have been for all my married life. I'm going to try and be open with you— though I never can be with anyone else. Getting married was the biggest mistake of my life. I have no sexual attraction to my husband whatsoever. To this day I have no idea why we got married. Although he says he loves me, his treatment of me makes me wonder. After all these years he is still sexually attracted to me, yet I don't know why. We have intercourse nearly every night. He always makes the first move, otherwise there would be no sex.

I have no idea how to turn him on. I guess it's because

deep inside me I don't want to. I don't want him touching me or vice versa. You could say I've been faking it all this time. We would have some terrible fights where I would wake up the next day all sore and black-and-blue. His way of apologizing was through sex. That turned me off even more, but I've never said no. I did once, but he accused me of being with or wanting other men. He would always come— but I had to fantasize to get an orgasm. He would try anything to excite me, from licking and rubbing my cunt to anal sex (hurt like hell).

I discovered masturbation when I was around 12 years old. It started with me and a few other girls masturbating each other. The more we did it, the better it felt. Then I discovered that looking at female breasts excited me. I've never touched another woman's breasts, but I do fantasize about it.

I met my husband at age 15. He despised the fact that he hadn't been the first, yet he still wanted to marry me. My life with him was pure hell. He says he won't eat me anymore because I might get interested in women sucking my pussy. He doesn't allow me female friends for the same reason. I have neither close female or male friends.

I must tell you one thing that has been bothering me. While I'm masturbating I fantasize about women. Women always seem gentler, and men quite the opposite. One fantasy is of me sitting on the lap of a big fat black woman with huge juicy breasts. She's completely nude and she undresses me like a baby and takes me in her arms and flaps her huge nipple in my mouth to suck. While I'm sucking, she spreads my legs and starts rubbing my cunt till it's hot and wet. She continues to finger my cunt and rock me in her arms like a baby. After that she cleans me up and puts me to bed. I don't think I'm homosexual but more bisexual.

Renee

I am 18. I was born under the triple cusp of Taurus, making me strong-minded, extremely stubborn, highly sensuous, bold, and I guess a bit of an extremist. I'm a fashion model, five feet ten, dark blond hair, green-eyed, full-lipped, and almost full-blooded American raised Italian.

As a young teen, I was curious and completely self-minded much to the dismay of my suburban middle-class parents. I went to a continuation high school after being kicked out of the public high in the first month of my freshman year as a result of cutting classes and fighting.

I had started having sex toward the end of the summer between junior high and high school, but had been raped as a child by my step-grandfather and approached and fondled by a number of elderly men before the age of 10. The scene with my grandfather ended around that time too. By that time (after several years), I'd started to protest and scream and cry. (My mom became pregnant by her grandfather at age 14, and her mom was also molested as a child by her grandfather.) Weird?!? Coincidence?!? Bullshit, disgusting!!! I never really got to be a virgin. The part that hurts the most though, is that it bothers me more to think back about it now than it did then.

So, I went to high school across town. I ended up freebasing large amounts of cocaine for about one and a half years. I became extremely disoriented, anemic (115–117 pounds at five feet ten) and hated everything, everyone, but myself most. I attempted suicide. In the emergency room I realized I only wanted to kill the beast I had turned into. I saw a vision: a Paris street and myself sipping wine in a cute sidewalk café. I felt the extent of the happiness in my ultimate goal, to be able independently to pick and choose and make my own decisions in regards to fulfilling my life as a fashion model. (I had just begun to find out about modeling.)

I got out of school three and a half months later with the equivalent of a high school diploma. Approximately three weeks later, I was stoned and came home around 2 A.M. to my mom, awake and drunk. I ended up telling her about my grandfather (who is virtually impossible to live with, but we do). I told her if she told my father his father raped me I couldn't handle it. Two days later she said she had told. I didn't ask any questions, I moved out that evening. I moved to the city and tried to kick drugs and be a professional model. My boyfriend—a photographer—had me living in some of the sleaziest hotels in the downtown area and we had no money. I got a few good breaks in modeling and left him.

I fantasized from a young age. I was probably 3 or 4 when I had my first fantasies. I played with girlfriends and imagined and pretended all sorts of different things and situations. At the age of 11 or 12 I began to jack off in the shower with the Water Pik. I have glorious, shuddering orgasms using this method. With my lovers I am always the one making it a great fuck. (Many of us women share this certain talent, I might add!) I started to fantasize more during sex to excite myself, as well as give the guy a memorable experience. Sorry if I seem sexually conceited, but I truly am a hot piece!

I found that I love to suck cock, and as much to my surprise, swallow cum . . . ummyumm!!

Lesbian tendencies I always had, and I vaguely expressed them with my roommate, a motherly type infatuation. My favorite, most exciting fantasies are all about women. I love the feel of a woman, it's so electric yet so ultra soft.

I imagine myself flying somewhere and a beautiful redhead with a tantalizing British accent and lovely, flawless complexion, who is one of the stewardesses aboard, approaches me. She says something about loving the shade of eye makeup I'm wearing and could she impose on me to show her how I had applied it. We go into one of those small bathrooms and of course, end up having a great fuck. (Gets me hot just writing it down!!)

I've had dreams and fantasies of a surprisingly beautiful, ultra dyke rescuing me from being raped by a bunch of hoods in some alley in the city. The twist to this one is I turn out to rape her! She's handcuffed and begs me not to hurt her. I tell her to shut the fuck up, that I can see the scars she's got from fighting and being the rowdy bitch that she is. I tease her and ask her how it feels to play the part of a woman, for a woman, unwillingly. By this point I'm so hot I can barely concentrate, I guess the focus point in this one is victimizing this brutal dyke who has saved me.

I love to fantasize about deflowering young girls, although in real life I don't have the patience to date virgins of either sex. I gave it up; it's exciting but they just end up getting my twat too hot, and giving me a headache.

Gemma

I am 23 years old, Catholic, and come from an upper-middle-class family. I attended parochial school until eighth grade and came away with a whole set of ideas on how the world should be. Although I had a decent upbringing, there were a few things that bothered me. For one, I recently "came out of the closet," and as homosexuality is not condoned in the Church, there was a lot of adjusting for me to do. Another problem (a particular fear of mine) is that I never learned how to deal with affection of any kind. In my family, the only emotions shown are anger (never temper) and amusement. I used to worry about being a "cold fish" but as the following fantasy hopefully proves, these fears are unfounded.

A little background. My fantasy concerns the first woman I ever knew who ever told me she was gay, Liz, and her lover Camille. I used to work with Liz, and after I got over feeling guilty over being gay, the three of us used to go out to the bars and such. (They have since moved.) I, unfortunately, fell totally in love with Camille, and even though they both know about my feelings toward her, our relationship has not changed that much. It might even be stronger. We still visit each other occasionally. Anyway, on to the fantasy.

I am visiting Liz and Camille at their apartment. Liz for some reason is on her way out the door. I have never invented a reason why Liz is leaving, but we all know it will be for a while. Anyway, Camille and I are sitting on the couch; we're not doing much, just watching TV or reading a book. Camille leans over and gives me a small kiss on the cheek. I give her a disapproving look that clearly says, "I can't believe you did that." We go back to watching or reading, and after a while, she kisses me again. I don't react as before, but instead kiss her on the cheek. She puts her hands on my shoulders and gives me a gentle kiss on the lips. I respond by putting my arms around her and returning all her kisses. Soon we are lying on the couch and exploring each other's faces with our soft kisses and caresses. As natural as holding each other seems, we both realize that we truly want to be closer. We move to the bedroom.

After undressing, we again lie in each other's arms. I start our lovemaking by softly tracing the outline of her eyebrows, eyes, mouth and chin with my fingertips. The route of my fingers is followed by my kisses as I softly kiss her brows, nose, and gently pull on her bottom lip after a long kiss. I next run my fingers down her shoulders and arms. I place my arms underneath and around her and hug her as close to me as possible in an effort to make us inseparable. I then take her hands and rub the backs of her fingers across my face. Her hands are very small and delicate. I kiss each fingertip and palm. I next caress her thighs, legs and feet with a gentle touch, just barely touching her skin. Camille continues to hold and kiss me. I then lightly cup the outside of her vagina, as I move my kisses down to her breasts. I tease her nipples with my tongue until they are erect, while slightly increasing the pressure of my hand on what it is holding. I trace a line with the tip of my tongue down to her belly button. I circle it with my tongue and kiss her stomach. My path continues down to her vaginal lips, which I separate slowly. I kiss and circle her clitoris with my tongue. After teasing her this way for a few minutes, I put my tongue in her vagina. I start slowly moving my tongue around and in and out. I continue to caress her legs and stomach with my fingers as I speed up the workings of my tongue. Without warning, she comes, as I keep using my mouth on her; I drink as much of her as I'm able. When she stops moving, I stop my actions; I trace my path back to her mouth with my kisses and light caresses. She gives me a sweet kiss and gently tugs on my bottom lip with her teeth. I again place my arms around her to draw her as close to me as I am able. We fall asleep in each other's arms.

As I have said, both Liz and Camille know my affection for Camille. They prefer to call it "infatuation" while I maintain (to myself) that it is love. I think they would be surprised to see how much and vividly I fantasize about Camille. I do love her.

Lindsay

I am an attractive, athletic, 31-year-old woman, high school graduate and some college, married for two and one half years, no kids. Presently I'm taking a break from working as a secretary and am enjoying being a homemaker and taking exercise and art classes.

I have been masturbating off and on since I was 14. I also have a rich fantasy life, especially now since I'm not working and have time to think about my desires and feelings. I was a lonely, introspective adolescent with no friends and many secret thoughts. I thought I was the only girl in the world who had "dirty" thoughts and who touched herself into getting that delicious, wonderful explosion "down there." Pleasure accompanied by acute guilt, though I thought I was doomed to hellfire but I just couldn't stop.

Older women attracted me rather than boys. I fantasized about getting close to my teacher, Mom's friends, and later, my work associates. Boys liked me because I was cute, but I wanted to be with a woman and went from one crush to another.

Thus, my first sexual relationship was with a girl one year older than me, when I was 18. We met in church; she had just moved into town and was staying with her brother. I was instantly smitten with her. Her intense, penetrating green eyes choked me up so that I couldn't look at her straight for fear she could see what I was thinking. I wanted so badly to kiss her on the mouth and fondle her large breasts. So we became friends. Eventually she moved in with us (I was still living at home) and we shared my bedroom, and soon, my bed. At night we would touch and feel each other and go a little further each time. Under her pretext of "getting to know each other and she teaching me about females, since I didn't have any sisters," I got to act out my fantasies, and so did she. She said for me to pretend I was her baby and suck her nipple and fondle her breasts, which I did gladly. One night, after weeks of being titillated to the very brink, I had an orgasm (she had been stroking my pussy). It scared us both because we (or rather, she) had not meant to really "do it." I apologized and said I couldn't help it and we held each other tight. After that she made me come every night—the feel of those big, soft tits bouncing and rubbing against my chest and her touching my pussy never failed. For some reason I never figured out, it was months before she would let me make her come. By then, of course, we were more than teacher and student, we were genuinely crazy in love, obsessed with each other. To this day I'll never know how we remained unsuspected by my parents. If they only knew what went on in my room all that time!! It was rather difficult for us to face them in the mornings and act casually—we both felt really guilty.

We eventually got jobs and our own apartment together and lived as lesbians for nine years, loving each other, protecting each other from a cruel world that was anything but understanding of people like us. It was nine years of gut-splitting highs and lows, happiness and hell. It finally ended when she got attracted to an older woman she worked with and left me for her. For months I couldn't get through the day without breaking up and the hardest was that I couldn't share my grief with my co-workers or family. But the wounds did heal and I will NEVER forget my years with her.

I am now married to a darling man three and one half years younger than me. Our marriage is happy, peaceful, and we get along fantastically. The only area that isn't as great as I would like it to be is our sex life. Before we got married he introduced me to the joys of straight sex, and I went WILD! I was insatiable, and even became multi-orgasmic. But after marriage, his ardor tapered off steadily and now it's almost nonexistent. Our marriage is more one of companionship and friendship than lovers. He is content, he doesn't fool around on me, and likes being home. This is okay with me, but I get rather frustrated because I am very physical and want sex very much. I don't nag my husband about sex because he is so great in everything else. So, I have resurrected my fantasy life, and once again am starting to get attracted to older women.

Currently, I'm taking an art class and my teacher stimulates me no end. She's somewhere in her 60s and she just radiates life and vibrancy. When I look in her dark eyes (still tastefully made up) I can feel that familiar excitement in my body and mind. She's very witty and so am I. I'm wondering if our verbal sparring contests leave her as turned on as they do me. My fantasy is:

After the next class she asks me to drive her home (she doesn't drive) and I jump to it (God—I'd carry her if she asked me to!). When we get to her house she invites me in to see her paintings. By now my chest is thumping, I feel lightheaded and can hardly concentrate on her paintings. Her shoulder and arms keep leaning against me and her head tilts toward me and her mouth is only inches from mine. It's almost too much for me to resist. Then I spot her grand piano in another room. I rush over to it and begin to play, softly at first, then casting off all restraint as I let my emotions come out in the music. My jumbled feelings of love, desire, fear, torture and excitement come pouring out, filling the old house with intense, beautiful, unleashed sounds. I play myself into a trance, and when I come back to earth and stop, it's deathly quiet in the room. I turn around and see my darling sitting on the sofa watching me, with a look in her eyes that makes me go over to her in a rush. She holds out her arms, tears coursing down her cheeks, and I am in her arms, kissing her face and mouth, caressing her, both of us crying as our love comes pouring out. Right there on the sofa we both feel so emotionally and physically intense that we both have a thundering orgasm—fully clothed. End of fantasy.

I wish with all my heart that this fantasy could come true, but I'm afraid her interest in me is purely professional, and I don't want to shock her or scare her away by coming on too strong. So I guess I'll have to be satisfied by daydreaming about her. It sure is hard to act casual in class though. When she looks at me with those intense, dark eyes of hers, I think I read more into them than there really is, and it's very hard to face her.

Deidre

I'm 19 years old, have blond hair, blue eyes, a 36-27-36 figure, weigh about 125-130 pounds, and I'm bisexual, although I've only been with a woman once. I've been masturbating since I was about 11 years old when I found out the joys of taking a *long* shower, with my mom's vibrator.

As for my upbringing: My mom and dad got divorced when I was about 10 or 11, I don't remember exactly, but they were pretty open-minded. I've been partying and doing drugs since about 12. Sex was never a taboo subject in our house. I heard the story of the birds and the bees when I was 6 or 7, when Mom explained it to my older sister. I learned a lot of the rest of the story from my dad's collection of magazines, ones like *Playboy, Penthouse,* etc., which I read every chance I got. By the time I was about 15, my mom and I started really discussing sex. I mean, we talk about different things to do and different ways of doing it, from straight one-on-one sex to lesbian one-on-one sex, to threesomes. And over the years I've had a lot of fantasies.

I didn't really get started on explicitly detailed fantasies until my first husband wrote me one. I wrote him back, and I've had many different and varied fantasies since then. My present husband likes to hear my sexy thoughts, but we've only acted on two of them. We've had another guy with us once, and another woman with us once. But the guy didn't work out the way that I had hoped it would. See, I have this fantasy of seeing Mark sucking and/or fucking another guy, and also one of him being sucked and/or fucked by another guy. But neither of these fantasies came true. He says that me with another woman is more natural than him with another guy. But I don't see what the difference is. Anyway, the fantasy I prefer goes like this:

There's this singer named Tiffany (I guess you've heard of her by now), and the first time Mark saw her he fell in lust. Recently I wrote him a letter about how I'd like to set it up so that me and her could get together and give him a show while he hides in the closet so that she doesn't know that he's there. This is how the story goes in my head:

Mark has brought me a new "toy," one of those that vibrates, gyrates, and all that. I also have a collection of "toys": large ones, small ones, two-headed ones, etc. I've set this up to where Mark is in a closet with a full view of the couch where the singer and I will perform for him. I have a VCR and two tapes, one about two girls who share an apartment with this guy, and one about two girls who got stood up by their dates. Tiffany hasn't arrived yet, but I put in the tape about the roomies and I have my toy with me as I watch this gorgeous Oriental devour a delicious blonde from her head to her toes. Watching her go down on the blonde gets me wet and horny, so I start rubbing my pussy and slide two fingers into my juices and lick it off while looking at Mark, who is hidden in the closet. He loves to see me lick my own juices.

Then I get my new toy and get on my hands and knees to where my ass is facing Mark. I oil up my toy and place it so that the vibrating tip is at my asshole. I slowly work it in, inch by delicious inch, and then gently work it in and out, letting Mark watch it disappear into the depths of my ass. I turn over and spread my legs wide, and while the toy is buzzing away in my ass, I spread my dripping snatch open and let him watch me sink two fingers into my slippery cunt while playing with my clit with the other.

Just as I'm getting ready to have this terrific orgasm, the doorbell rings. I know that it's Tiffany, and I have to quit so that she won't suspect anything. She comes in and asks what I'm doing. I say, "Getting ready to try out my new toy."

"What new toy?"

I show it to her. "Would you like to try it out, too? I'll use

279

it on you first." She says okay, and we go sit on the couch and watch the two girls screw themselves with a double dildo. The longer we sit there, the hornier we get.

I kneel in front of her and unbutton her blouse and unfasten her skirt and remove them. I now have her in a white lace bra and G-string. I gently kiss her lips and caress her chest and stomach. I nibble her ear, and kiss her neck and shoulders, slowly working my way to her chest. I unfasten her bra and expose her firm young breasts with their perky rosebud nipples. With my mouth, I capture one, rolling it between my teeth and flicking my tongue over the very tip while caressing the other breast with my hand. Then I move down to her feet and kiss them and suck her toes. I gently nibble and kiss the tender flesh of her inner thighs while she squirms and raises her ass, trying to get me to kiss her pussy. Very gently, I remove her panties and position her on the edge of the couch.

I slide my thumbs down the length of her slit and back up the inner lips, splitting her juicy pink wetness open for Mark and I to enjoy. I tease her lips with the tip of my tongue, then I let the warm fullness of my tongue slide from her asshole, up between her lips, and up to her swollen clit. I circle it with slow, lazy circles, and then I capture it in my mouth, teasing it, nibbling it, sucking it gently but firmly, the way I like to be eaten. Then I begin to tease her lips and ass with my fingers, and before long she has her legs wrapped around my head and is begging me to fuck her with the new toy. I slip two fingers into the entrance of her love hole, just enough to make her beg for more. "Please! Don't stop! Fuck me, please!"

I push my fingers into her as she raises her hips to meet my thrusts, and a rhythm begins. My mouth is still teasing her clit, and with a loud "Ohhh," she comes all over my hand and face. But I don't stop there. I keep on fingering her and eating her and soon she is about to come again. But just as she reaches the peak, I stop for a moment. Only long enough to get my toy and slide the head of it into her. She arches her back for more, but I tell her to lie back and relax, and then, slowly, inch by inch, I slip it into her until the full length is inside her tunnel. I lick her juices from the lips of her cunt and work my way to her ear again, and I put my fingers to her lips and let her taste her own come.

"Do you like having the toy inside of you?"

"Yes! Oh, yes! Please don't stop!"

"Just wait until you find out what else it can do."

I reach down and flip on the vibrator and she screams in pleasure.

"Just relax. There's more yet to come. Just enjoy it."

I get back on my knees and begin licking her clit again and fucking her with the toy. As she begins squirming with her building orgasm, I turn the toy fully on. She now has a vibrating, gyrating, throbbing "cock" in her with me pumping it in and out of her juicy pussy, and my mouth is giving her clit a licking and sucking to remember.

"Oh God! It feels sooo good to be sucked and fucked at the same time! Please! Please! Don't stop!" And I don't. I slowly increase the pressure and the tempo of her fucking, and she cries out.

"Harder! Faster! Oh God, fuck me! Please! Make me come!"

I start pumping her cunt and sucking her clit for all I'm worth and I'm fingering my own cunt at the same time. Suddenly she starts bucking up off the couch and grinding her pussy on the toy and into my face and screams, "I'm coming! Oh God! I'm coming!"

And I come all over my own hand just listening to her and feeling her wetness all over me.

We rest for a minute and then I send her into my bedroom to see if she can find any other toys she would like to try out. While she's gone I roll a joint, and when she comes back I get her to go in the kitchen with me so Mark can come out and stretch.

When we come back, I put in the tape about the girls who got stood up and light the joint. We relax and talk, and by the time we finish smoking, she says, "Who needs a guy anyway? We've got this."

And she pulls out my double dildo. She pushes me back on the couch and slips my robe off my shoulders. Then she

NANCY FRIDAY

sits back and caresses my breasts, my stomach, and she
lightly touches my bush. She leans over and kisses my right
breast, flicking her tongue over my nipple before capturing
the whole thing in her mouth and swirling her tongue over
the nipple. She takes turns and then works her way up to my
neck and my ears and whispers, "I'm going to give you an
orgasm that you won't ever forget." And she works her way
down to my navel. She licks the very edge of my bush, down
the inside of my thighs, which I part eagerly for her. But she
goes very slowly, kissing my tender skin and eventually
working her way to my slit. She opens my lips with her
tongue, and she sucks and teases my clit with her teeth as she
slides her finger into my steamy hole. She takes turns
licking, sucking, and fingering me, sometimes sliding her
tongue deep into me and fingering my asshole.

Soon she takes my toy and slips it deep into me, letting it
vibrate and gyrate and throb inside me while her mouth
again fingers my secret place. And God, does she ever know
how to kiss me there. I guess that women just *know*.

Before long I'm begging her to fuck me—to fuck me hard,
fuck me fast, fuck me deep, and then I'm coming all over her
hand and her face. But she doesn't stop. She pulls the toy
from me and starts playing with my asshole again. She licks
it and fingers it, gently working her middle finger into it and
stretching me open so that she won't hurt me. Then she
coats the double dildo in oil and slowly works it into my
tight hole, only the head of it, stopping to let my muscles get
used to being stretched so far. Then she rubs my cunt with
her other hand while she works the dildo in deeper. Then
she slips the other end into her pussy and our clits grind
together, and her breasts press into mine as we kiss. We then
get on our hands and knees, and I get so that I can see Mark
in the closet.

I mouth the words "What do you think?" He answers by
pushing the door open far enough to let me see him stroking
his throbbing, straining cock that is purple from the pressure of the come that is built up in his balls. I reach back and
start fingering Tiffany's clit, and as I touch her, Mark sends

282

thick white jets of come into the air. And seeing that, and knowing that it was seeing me with her that caused it, I come like I never have before, and that sets Tiffany off, and all three of us are dripping come and we're all deliriously happy.

Tiffany and I go to sleep and Mark slips out to call and say that he's "on his way home." We get dressed and when Mark comes in, she doesn't suspect a thing. But Mark and I know, and she'll always be welcome to "come" for a visit, and to experiment with my toys.

I really would like to be with this girl and do these things, and not necessarily with Mark watching.

"AM I GAY?"

Freud was the first to document early childhood sexuality, the Oedipal years, roughly from age four to seven. For this "discovery" he was all but ostracized by his profession. Before Freud it had been assumed that there were no sexual stirrings until puberty. No one wanted to think that little four-year-olds have sexual feelings; many people still resist the idea, especially in their own children, who very much need the parental recognition of what they are going through.

Like many of the women in this chapter, one who wrote to me vividly remembers her first sexual encounter at age seven, with her female cousin, and then one with another girl, at age thirteen. "I guess my present fantasies are created from these early lesbian experiences," she says. Though she feels "repelled at the thought of ACTUALLY touching a girl sexually . . . I fantasize about it all the time."

These memories of early sexual exploration with another girl become the seed from which today's erotic daydream is born. Such adventures are common enough at young girls' sleepovers but are often forgotten or repressed; for many of the women in this chapter, however, the incident remains an important clue to their sexual identity. Priscilla was fourteen when she had her first sexual experience with another girl. They innocently kissed and touched each other's breasts, "but the warm, prickly sensation between my legs was real enough," says Priscilla, and "although nothing else happened, this event remains so powerful for me and is the basis for a recurring fantasy."

Because they are the first steps into our own sexuality and independence away from parental rules, these early sexual experiences resonate with the thrill of the forbidden and can retain a lifetime of explosive energy in memory. Often nothing is ever again quite so exciting as that first arousal. When it was with someone of the same sex, it can be a reassuring, loving memory, as it is with many of the women in this chapter, or it can retain forever its original "sinfulness and excitement," as we learned earlier.

Women seem to have a far easier time than men living with the memory of their youthful sexual experiences with people of the same sex. For many men the early sexual encounter with another boy becomes not so much an exciting recollection from which to create adult fantasies as a nightmare. No matter how many women the man seduces, or how many years go by since the childhood incident, the indelible label can remain nailed in memory: homosexual.

The young boy may know nothing of our society's homophobic preoccupation; he learns it quickly enough and labels himself. Consider an article in the *New York Times* published in 1984 and titled "Sexual Fantasies: What Are Their Hidden Meanings?" Within the article, the journalist referred to a paper given at the American Psychoanalytic Association. The doctor who wrote the paper "contended that a person who has homosexual fantasies, but does not actively engage in homosexual activity, is homosexual— even if his homosexual fantasies are unconscious."

I have the yellowed piece of newsprint in front of me as I write, along with my heavily penciled exclamation and question marks. I am dumbstruck, angry that anyone calling himself a doctor could say such a thing. How could we label someone a homosexual for what he thinks? It is the police state carried to the wildest extreme.

Women's fantasies of other women present one of the most powerful themes in my research since *My Secret Garden,* where it was barely a murmur in the garden. It began gathering steam in the early 1980s and has remained a favorite fantasy—no matter what other themes of fantasy the woman may enjoy—to this date. I doubt it will ever disappear now that it is with us, since it offers so many women not only sexual excitement but also a mirror into themselves.

Twenty years ago I was surprised that my research didn't turn up more of these women-with-women fantasies. I knew men enjoyed watching or being with two women, both in reality and in fantasy. And I knew women very often had early sexual experiences with other girls. But it wasn't until women got the endorsement from other women in reality, to turn to one another for support, for identification, for everything, that the sexual fantasy of women together emerged and took off.

It would be misleading, however, to say that all the women in this chapter are unthreatened by these ideas. Ours is a culture obsessed with labeling everything and everyone. It's an inhibiting, limited view of life, one the labelers intend in order to scare others away from exploration that would enlarge and enrich their lives. Labels exist because they make life tolerable for those who have already slotted themselves into the narrow, safe life; this kind of person can live with his puny life, born out of fear of trying anything new, only if he can keep others from leading lives that would remind him of how boring and bloodless his own life is. Labels, especially derogatory labels, allow the envious to sleep at night.

So it is not surprising that some of these women label themselves out of fear, anxiety at what others must think of them. "I call myself bisexual," says Molly, "but this is really a technicality for a society that insists on a person wearing a label. By and large I prefer women, but men can be fun in bed too. I am a hopeless romantic and for serious romance, for love, I prefer women."

I believe we begin life with the potential for feeling sexually attracted to both sexes. With time most of us become more strongly oriented toward one sex or the other. Although I have never been sexually attracted to a woman, on the right summer night I could be; to think otherwise would limit life. We are all "latent." Listen to Maya attempting to figure out whether she's latent this or that (and for whom? For the labelers): "I don't actually consider myself homosexual because I don't prefer women to men," she says. "I suppose I like them just as much, although it would appear I like women more, but not necessarily, it just worked out that way. I imagine it would be safe to say I am bisexual, for I believe that given the opportunity, and if the circumstances were right, I would again be involved with a woman."

I have decided not to organize this material into hetero-sexual, bisexual, and lesbian fantasies. The women often don't know what to call themselves: "I have this fantasy a lot and sometimes worry that maybe I'm some kind of re-pressed lesbian or something," says Gwynne. Since she and others in this book are already unnecessarily worried, I'll just call these fantasies women-with-women and let the women speak for themselves. What the women in this chapter do say about their real lives is that 70 percent of them either have had a sexual experience with another woman or would like to. As for guilt and anxiety, it was most frequently expressed in the early 1980s, as with Libby: "When I think about the pairing off of two people of the same gender, it usually makes me want to throw up. I don't feel I am homosexual or even bisexual. I just want to make some loving contact with this wonderful girl!" By 1985 most of the guilt and anxiety over labeling had disappeared.

For some women it is crucial to establish in their fantasy whether they are the sexual initiator or the passive one who is taken. For instance, for those women who worry that their imagined sex with another woman may label them a lesbian,

286

anxiety magically disappears when the other woman's role is clearly stated to be that of the aggressor, she who is in charge. "I have this fantasy a lot and sometimes worry that maybe I'm some kind of repressed lesbian," says Gwynne. Since the fantasy is her creation, over which she has total control, Gwynne makes up a woman "who knows me so well, she knows just how to kiss me, and I know she can feel me surrender. I want her to take me . . ."

The purpose of fantasy is to arouse us, get us past all the barriers that inhibit sexual surrender. The mind, being a marvelous creative force, knows our sexual needs and primitive fears even before we are consciously aware. These women do not speak of their fantasies as pieces of fiction they sat down with pen and paper to consciously create; fantasies, like dreams at night, get their most important story lines from the unconscious. When the women close their eyes during masturbation, what swims to consciousness may derive in part from recent events, new people met, but the exquisite obstacle that must be overcome, the forbidden ingredient that gives fantasy electricity—this usually comes from earliest childhood and is most often unconscious.

Lilly's real sexual life is with men, but her fantasies are only about a woman, "who does everything a guy could do to me (except screw) only better, because she's very gentle and loving." Lilly's need for love and tenderness predates the entry of men into her life, but the fantasy frightens her because "if my parents were to find out what I think, they would probably disown me and friends would shun me." The anxiety of being loved by a woman is softened by the creative distinction that it is the other woman who "ravishes my body," the other woman who takes responsibility for shy Lilly's seduction.

In certain ways, this definitive assignment of passive and aggressive roles reminds me of the traditional rape/force fantasies with men, where it was essential to stipulate that the woman was being taken against her will. In Georgina's fantasy, for example, "a butch, but attractive, lesbian has cajoled me into coming home with her." The woman then proceeds to aggressively undress her, orders her to play with herself, spanks her, taunts her, "C'mon you cunt! Let's see you come!" And come she does, "in great spasms." After all, she has no choice—the big bad woman made her come.

In reality, Georgina describes herself as "quite a proud, dignified person. I could never let myself 'go' like that— least of all with another woman!" But in real life, Georgina can't let herself go at all, not with the traditional, conservative older men with whom she's had sex; only in the safety of fantasy, where the unconscious answers her needs, is the necessary sexual partner created, an aggressive older woman who gives her no choice but to submit and reach her shattering orgasms.

How often these women specify that their fantasy woman is "older." When Caroline orders up "a warm and friendly lady who wants to take me under her wing," it isn't someone her own age she wants for sexual satisfaction but rather the breast of a maternal, "middle aged" woman. ". . . I see how good it must feel to a man when he sucks a woman's nipples and I also want that feeling," she says. Why not? For some people the idea of being "mothered" is anathema to sexual arousal; for others it's the ultimate sexual pleasure, if it is made clear that the other person has initiated, taken responsibility for the act.

The parallels with the early, powerful mother of childhood are obvious. Sometimes, within the fluidity of fantasy, the woman moves from being mothered/loved/disciplined to playing the role of mother herself, not unlike what a small child does in play therapy.

Most emphatic about their role are the aggressors, those women for whom being in charge is everything. "I want to feel that I'm in control of the situation/woman," says Marybeth, who describes herself as a lesbian. "I want to be the boss. I like to be the one who sees 'em when I want to—not them." In her case, fantasy mirrors reality. But for many women I have interviewed, whose "biggest fears are of rejection" in real life, fantasy becomes the place where they can safely experience being "the aggressive one." Imagining themselves giving their partners as much pleasure as possible, they not only reach orgasm, they get there in the role they would most like to own in reality, that of the seducer who never gets rejected.

It would, of course, be overly optimistic to suggest from my own research that women have refused to wear society's homophobic labels any longer. The women in this chapter are the youngest group in the book, on average in their early twenties. We don't yet know whether they will maintain their self-acceptance and tolerance of others as they enter the more conservative years of marriage, motherhood, and career establishment.

What will be interesting is to see if men's traditional fantasies of women together have remained as popular as they were in *Men in Love,* where men loved the image, both in reality and fantasy, of two women ravishing each other's bodies, expertly bringing each other to climax, strapping on dildos with an enthusiasm that used to reassure men that women loved sex as much as they did. Those were the days before women had gained any economic strength and sexual independence. Given today's real women who want men's jobs and their love, too, are these fantasies of women sexually awakening one another destined to excite or to dampen a man's libido?

Georgina

I am a 23-year-old woman, a lecturer and doctoral student at a large Canadian university. So much for real life—now on to sex and sexual fantasy: I have had only four sexual partners, all of them older men, very traditional, very conventional. Masturbation and orgasm are two things I've only discovered over the last five months or so. The fantasies I use while masturbating vary considerably—they're either about simple, straightforward encounters with men I know and am attracted to or they are about domination at the hands of an imaginary man or—more often—woman. I'll relate a current fantasy in its complete form, although merely dwelling on segments of it is enough to make me come.

A butch, but attractive, lesbian has cajoled me into coming home with her. On the way, we stop at a department store where she makes me try on outfits of her choice. She watches me try them on. She brings in a delicate beige camisole and tells me to try it on my bare skin, without a bra. I comply. She is standing behind me as I face the mirror, and suddenly she reaches around me, placing one hand on my breast, one on my pubic area, and kissing me on the neck. Then she orders me to put on my own clothes on top of the camisole—she's forcing me to shoplift.

We arrive at her apartment, in a skyscraper. We take the elevator (she lives on one of the highest floors), and as the doors close, she shoves her hand aggressively under my skirt, obscenely clutching my cunt (she confiscated my panties at the store) and forcing her tongue into my mouth. Her body pins me firmly to the elevator wall. I protest. "Chris,"—Chris is usually what I call her—"not yet! What if someone comes in?"

"Then they'll think you're a dyke, like me. Everyone knows I am." She drags me by my arm to her apartment. Once in, she presses me face-first against the wall as she kicks off her shoes, then mine. She pushes me toward the living room, where she fondles me and taunts me before pouring herself an aperitif and sitting down on the couch.

"Take your clothes off," she orders, as I stand in front of her. I remove them piece by piece, until I am wearing only the "hot" camisole. "Turn around!" I do this, shyly. (I do look quite shy and feminine, standing there, seminude, my long curling hair tied with a ribbon at the nape of the neck.) She makes appreciative, but crude, comments about my ass and legs.

"Now bend over. Touch your toes." I cringe as I do this. I feel so humiliated, so vulnerable.

Next, I'm told to turn around and ordered to play with myself. I sigh deeply, but finally comply, deeply humiliated, so vulnerable.

"Come here. Kneel." I obey. She smiles wickedly at me, "Don't you know that it is wrong to diddle yourself like that? Don't you?" She pulls me onto her lap and begins spanking me. At the same time, she rubs my clit with her other hand. Her hands are bringing me closer and closer to orgasm, and she assaults me verbally for this. (Variations: Sometimes the ribbon from my hair is used to tie my wrists, sometimes she makes me guzzle her aperitif, licking any spilled liquor off my chin and neck.)

She tires of spanking me before I am able to come and makes me crawl to the bedroom, where I'm forced to undress her in a slavish way (unfasten her fly with my teeth, etc.). She puts a dog collar on me and fastens similar bonds on my wrists and ankles. These bands can be attached to each other or to the straps on the four posts of her large bed. I kneel meekly by the foot of the bed, wrists chained to the post behind me, while she stands before me and rubs her cunt all over my face, then orders me to lick her clit. All the while, she threatens me to do it exactly right, or I'll be punished. I do my best, and she humps my face, coming two or three times. Sated, she kneels and licks her stickiness off my face. She tells me gently that, although I did my best, it wasn't good enough, and I must be punished. She slaps my saliva- and cunt-wet face, then refastens my wrists, one to each post at the foot of the bed, so that I'm kneeling on the floor, arms spread, facing the bed. She shoves a leather ottoman between me and the bed, stretching me uncomfortably. She takes a stiff leather paddle, rubs my face with it, makes me kiss it, masturbates me a little with it, forces me to lick my secretions off it. I must beg her to spank me with it, which she finally does. I'm forced to ask for it again and again. Her crude humiliating comments turn me on immensely. Also, the strength in her strokes drives my cunt right onto the edge of the ottoman, and I try to rub myself surreptitiously on the footstool. She notices this and begins taunting me cruelly: "You sleazy cunt! You're humping a fucking stool. You low cunt, fucking furniture. You horny bitch. Here, let me help you fuck your precious stool," she says, dropping the paddle to hump my ass with her cunt. She continues her crude comments and pinches my nipples as she humps me into the ottoman. "C'mon, you cunt! Let's see you *come!* I want to hear you coming, fucking that chair!" I can tell by her voice that she's close to climaxing, too. I try to defy her and hold back, but it is no use. I come in great spasms, and she glues her cunt to my ass as she comes with me. She leaves me chained this way as she rests.

This is usually the end of the fantasy, but I sometimes continue it, for variety's sake. I imagine her sitting on my face, while I'm tied spread-eagled to the bed. Or my crawling behind her on my hands and knees as she leads me (on a leash attached to my slave collar) in front of the picture windows. Then she straps me to the bed again, bringing me just to the brink of orgasm using various (humiliating) things, like her foot, her nipple, the paddle again, until I lose all dignity and beg her to let me come. She does this, finally, with her thighs as she lies full length on top of me. She comes this way, as well.

Reflections: In this fantasy, I am only allowed to come when it's demeaning or humiliating—either during corporal punishment or after I've begged for it.

Nothing I've ever done in real life has come even remotely close to what happens in this fantasy. I'd never attempt to realize this fantasy; I'm really quite a proud, dignified person. I could never let myself "go" like that—least of all with another woman!

Yolanda

I am 19 years old, have one and a half years of college behind me plus a short-term experience in a rock band, am now signed up in the Army and am single.

I've been consciously masturbating since 4 years of age. I still do it the same way, and so far it has allowed me intense, multiple, and early orgasms. That is why it is so hard for me to imagine frigidity and the inability to orgasm in a woman. I accomplish my orgasms by fantasizing and reading sexual excerpts from books and magazines and real-life encounters, while I cross my legs, stiffen them, and release them. As orgasm nears, my movements (or thigh twitches) quicken. Great pleasure suffuses my clitoris. I realize that it feels like "fucking" yourself. It has always been my way of relief, going to sleep, etc. . . . I usually feel sexual tension a week or so before my menstrual period begins. (Not that I'm not usually horny all of the time—it's hard to be single—my loins certainly feel it.)

My earliest sexual encounter was at age 5. I didn't know what sex was then but I remember a certain blond boy my age whom I met on occasion just to drop my britches momentarily with. We would balance ourselves on a stone wall and walk quite a distance to an old neighbor's graveled garage/shed. There we would take turns or simultaneously urinate. It was an unusual thrill at the time to just watch each other; it gave us an innocent excuse to examine each other's privates.

My parents caught me stretched out on the coffee table "making my legs stiff," and they told me not to make them stiff anymore. Looking back, I'm sure they realized what I was doing was experiencing a sexual pleasure, though I was too young to understand (though I did think it unusual, and because it was "down there" where my sensations sprang, I felt somewhat ashamed and embarrassed). That was my first lesson that what I was doing was "wrong," "unnormal," and forbiddable. Nonetheless, I did it and gave in to my whims of enjoyment through my entire life so far. I sometimes wonder if that is why I've become so promiscuous. At age 9, a boy even caught me wriggling in my seat and he said the same thing in my parents' unique phrase, "Don't make your legs stiff." I didn't think he understood what I was doing, though. That's just what it looked like.

At 9, I also realize, like today, I must have had lesbian tendencies. Once I took a girl younger than myself behind some shrubbery and seduced her with, "I'll let you see my 'down there' if you let me see yours." She refused. Then, once a pretty blond friend of mine and I were atop a long slide, and when we both reached the top, she asked me if I would "kiss her down there." The idea, I remember, some-what excited me but it seemed too wrong and nasty at the time. Then, I said no.

I lost my virginity at 16. It was in a cute, maroon Fiat, with a big, muscular tennis buff. He also went down on me; it was so exciting, me being so young and the first time. I do remember though that he didn't get it all the way in and that I hurt so much I was thinking of some gentle lesbian girl "saving me" from this, although at the same time I was very excited. (Sex is so confusing and hypocritical for me.) Well, anyway . . . I have never or rarely said no.

I sometimes feel ashamed to say I have had about twenty lovers (mostly one-night stands). I guess, in pure definition, I am not a "nice" girl. I've always felt I should take what I can get. It's not that I'm homely; I'm fairly attractive, am into fashion and I guess I am a bit narcissistic at times.

I am a lesbian in most of my fantasies; I think it is mostly because lesbianism is one fancy in sex I relish and it has so far been unfulfilled. It's like having things but always wanting more because you don't or can't easily have them. I have had a black man; it was the interracial experience I wanted. Literally, it was indifferent. Sex is sex . . . it was just society's condemnation I wanted to personally rebel against, besides my own contrast in color. I loved his black, near-velvet chest; such a smooth body . . .

Anyway, I fantasize about my friend Jeanne. Once, after smoking some grass, me and her boyfriend did try to seduce her, but she wouldn't give. Oh well . . . I have a feeling she would like to with me. We always talk and read about sex aloud, and she always manages a lot of "melting" eye contact . . . I think there's something . . . maybe some-day . . .

I dwell on famous figures, too. Some of these include (quite a range) Deborah Harry, Diane Keaton, Jane Fonda, Brenda Vaccaro, Marianne Faithfull, Britt Ekland, Donna Mills, Xaviera Hollander . . . I usually imagine sweet, sensi-tive moments in someone's home, on the beach, in a sauna. I wish I could just blink my eyes and make them appear as desirous lovers. I usually imagine us holding each other, passionate kissing, finger-fucking, cunnilingus, bathing; ménage à trois turns me on too.

I love loud, lewd, passionate sex. I like to hear my pussy sound like an aquarium filter, loud slushing. I want to eat pussy. I also have thought to enter a girly bar in Montreal (one that I've been to) and have the strippers turned on to me; I enter the bathroom, and one or more of them follow me in. They notice my femininity in contrast to all the horny old males and ask me if I feel funny being the only female customer. I say yes, and they put me at ease by welcoming me readily, by touching me, brushing their lips against me softly, and saying they love women. The crowd of males whistle and catcall; they look forward to another performance, but it is delayed because of my presence in the bathroom. (An extended version of this goes beyond, to the point I am one of the strippers—they turn me into one and teach me how to move, dress and dance.)

Molly

I am a single, bisexual, college graduate, age 23. I was raised, an only child, in a small town by conservative yet lenient and understanding Christian parents. My parents know of my sexual preference, but our relationship is strong and close anyway.

I call myself bisexual, but this is really a technicality for a society that insists on a person wearing a label. By and large I prefer women, but men can be fun in bed, too. I am a hopeless romantic, and for serious romance, for love, I prefer women.

In my fantasy there is a young woman with whom I work. She is beautiful—shoulder-length, wavy, golden-brown hair, high cheekbones, turquoise eyes and a figure to die for. In reality, just the sight of her in a snug skirt and tailored blouse sends my pulse racing and soaks my panties. She is very heterosexual.

At any rate, back to the fantasy. Karen is riding to my apartment with me in order to pick up some books she wants to borrow. It is snowing heavily, building up until at last the streets are impassable and we must abandon the car and walk the remaining two or three blocks. We go in, shed our coats and wet, cold shoes and socks, and I light some candles and open a bottle of wine. (This is not an attempt to seduce her through atmosphere. I know she is straight, this is my favorite setting for quiet relaxed chat with a friend.) I get a fire going in the fireplace, and we settle in front of it on big comfy pillows to talk and get warm. As we talk, she seems distracted, but I attribute it to the weather and being stranded and don't mention it. Then, suddenly, she stops talking and just stares at me, her turquoise eyes solemn and uncertain. I ask her what is wrong, and she says, "Well, I'm not sure how to say this . . . but I want you to make love to me. Ever since I found out you like women I've thought about it and . . . well . . . but if you don't want to . . ." She drops her eyes, and I take her hand in mine and gently lift her chin with my other hand until our eyes are level again.

"Are you sure?" I ask, for as much as I want her, even stronger is the desire not to hurt or frighten her. (In reality she is not only straight but a virgin as well.) She nods, so I move closer, take her in my arms and cuddle her, stroking her back. After a moment I pull my head back, look into her eyes again, then kiss her, gently, but firmly. Without breaking the kiss, we undress each other, and I lay her down on the pillows. As I kiss and nibble her lips, ears, and throat, my hands caress her beautiful body, stroking her smallish, firm, round breasts and massaging the soft mound between her legs. My fingers probe slowly deeper, and I find she is wet and warm. My mouth leaves hers and migrates southward, pausing to kiss and nibble her breasts and plant a kiss and flick of the tongue in her navel. Then I am at her crotch. I separate her lips and bury my face. My nose is in her pubic hair, my lips sucking her clitoris, my tongue flicking in and out of her. She squirms and whimpers with growing excitement, until finally her muscles tense and her back arches, and I thrust my face even deeper into her warm pussy as she comes.

When she has relaxed again, I lick off the rest of her juices and crawl back up beside her, taking her in my arms for a reassuring cuddle. She looks into my eyes, and a small smile forms on her lips. "Your turn," she whispers and begins giving me the same treatment. Gentle fingers caress my breasts, warm lips surround my clitoris, soft hair slides over my thighs. In what could be an eternity, or no time at all, I have a heart-stopping orgasm. Then she crawls back into my arms. We snuggle close and fall asleep in the firelight, with the snow still falling silently outside.

When I masturbate while fantasizing this scenario, I always have a wonderful orgasm, followed by falling asleep feeling very warm and contented inside.

Robin

I'm a 19-year-old sophomore at a women's college. I'm very shy, especially around guys, although I'm reasonably pretty and have a slim body that other girls have always envied.

If men and adolescent boys only knew what dirty minds some girls have! They would feel so much better about their own dirty minds. I fantasize about sex a large part of the time, whether I'm sitting in a boring class, or in church, or watching men (discreetly, of course) in a shopping mall, and of course when I masturbate.

I've been masturbating at least once a week, and often more, since I was 15. Sometimes I do it several times a day. My most often used method is to lie on my stomach in bed and rub my bare cunt up and down against the sheet. (This method is also easy to disguise as merely sleeping if someone comes into the room.) I can have very intense orgasms this way, especially if I don't do it too often and if I tease myself by bringing myself to the edge again and again before finally letting the climax come.

I had my first orgasm when I was 15 by trying something that was inspired by a card I saw in Bloomingdale's (I'm serious!): I reclined on my elbows in the bathtub with my legs spread and wrapped around the faucet while a stream of water poured onto my clit. I have had agonizingly intense orgasms this way, and they are different from the ones I have using the bed method. Different still are those I have by stroking myself with an oiled finger. (Less intense.)

I'm still a virgin, though I came pretty close to losing it with the boy up the street when I was 11 and he was a year or so older. We had progressed from "playing doctor" at 6 or 7 to oral and anal sex and *attempted* vaginal intercourse by the time we hit puberty. We were so ignorant. It frightens me now to think of how close I came to possibly getting pregnant if he'd succeeded in "really" fucking me. Of course we both basically knew the "facts of life," but that knowledge was very muddled.

The first consciously sexual pleasure I ever remember feeling was when the boy was licking my cunt one day (I was 10 or 11) and I started to feel this really good sensation; instinctively I tried to verbally "steer" him to where it felt the best, though I didn't know what my clit was for until years later.

We also used to pee in front of each other a lot, but I don't ever remember being consciously aroused by it. I do remember being very excited by a picture in a porno magazine we found that showed a woman squatting and peeing in a tall glass with ice cubes in it and a twist of lemon on the rim.

What all of this is leading up to is the fact that when I masturbate, I always fantasize about women urinating.

The other thing that really turns me on when I masturbate is fantasizing about lesbian sex. I don't think I'm a lesbian, though, because the women I'm surrounded by every day don't arouse me at all. Only imaginary women do. I think I would like to experience sex with a woman sometime. Maybe I'm bisexual—that thought doesn't threaten me at all. In fact, I think it would be fun. I also enjoy fantasizing about straight men being seduced into gay sex.

OK, finally, at great length, I get to my actual fantasy: The woman was lying with her legs far apart, the glistening pink lips of her cunt spread wide open. She had a thick, dark bush and huge tits with big hard nipples. She wore a white lace garter belt and white silk stockings, white elbow-length gloves and white spike-heeled pumps. She reached down with her hand, stroked her bush, and ran a gloved finger between the lips of her cunt. Her other hand caressed her full, round breasts, lingering over the upthrust points of her nipples. A young blond girl knelt on the bed, wearing only a pair of white silk panties. Her pussy hair showed around the edges of the panties, and the lips of her cunt were clearly outlined by the sleek silk. She had high, firm tits with small nipples that were hard and jutting.

"Pee for me," the woman said. "I want to watch you wet your pants. Pee in your panties, and I'll let you have it," she said, stroking her clit and spreading her legs wider so the girl could have a better view of her cunt.

The girl wriggled with wanting, but got up on her knees, with legs spread wide and hips thrust forward a little. Her mound was full and tempting under her panties. She urinated a little, enough to make a spot on her crotch. The woman smiled. She let go a little more, and the wet spot got bigger. The woman arched her back and lifted her hips, thrusting her cunt toward the girl. "Do it more," she whispered. "Soak your panties! I want to see yellow pee running down your thighs!"

The girl kept teasingly dribbling pee in her panties until the silk was quite wet. But she held back, watching the woman stroke her pink, swollen clit faster and faster. She was excited by the sight of the woman's juicy, glistening cunt and by the lovely warm wetness of her own panties. She peed again, more this time, and felt the urine soak through the panties and run down her thigh in a hot trickle. But she was still nearly full; the pressure was still there. She cupped her breasts in her hands, pinching the hard pink nipples; she trailed her fingers down her stomach to the edge of the panties, slipping a finger under the elastic to stroke her pubic bush.

The woman groaned with desire, thrust her crotch upward. "Oh God, do it, do it, let go all the way!"

The girl did. She leaned back a little, thrust her hips forward, and let go a torrent of urine. She moaned as her hot stream spurted out of the crotch of her panties onto the white quilt that covered the bed. Urine poured down her thighs in golden streams and made pools on the quilt. When she was finished peeing, she pulled her pee-soaked panties down her thighs, and with her bush still dripping urine, thrust her throbbing cunt over the woman's mouth, while the girl's mouth found her hot, slick cunt wide open and waiting. They licked and sucked frantically at each other's cunts, nibbling the clits, tonguing the lips, squeezing each other's tits, until they exploded together in an incredible orgasm. They lay together exhausted for a few moments, the girl savoring the wetness of her urine, the bright yellow crotch of her panties, the fierce heat of her cunt.

Heather

I have feelings and thoughts of shame that are completely out of my control these days.

I am 22 and just married one month ago and expecting a baby. I come from a broken family (parents divorced at 16), and I am the only child. As far as my family goes, I had it OK monetarily. Mom was an alcoholic—Dad, a workaholic. My support system was obviously not at home!

My fantasies have always been of heterosexual experiences, and they still are but they have taken a twist that really created a discomfort in dealing with everyday life. They are of homosexual origin. I can recall when I was 16 years old having oral sex with my boyfriend and seeing a cunt in front of me instead of a cock. I got so terrified by this that I made him leave, and I spent a tormented couple of weeks trying to figure it out. It disappeared. Then about eight months ago I went to visit my father to meet his fiancée, and she was very beautiful, and I can recall getting nervous around her because I was really "looking" at her. After that I never thought of any one woman, but it started appearing in dreams and even fantasies while masturbating. I would look at women during the day to see if I was turned on by them, because I was so confused and still am. I look at their crotches to see if anything happens psychologically to

300

me. I've seen psychologists about it, and of course all that really comes of it is, "it's a conscious choice to be gay, not something that just happens without your consent." True, it is. I *don't want* to be gay, the thought of it makes me almost suicidal! I've openly discussed this with my husband, and he is always very comforting; he says it's natural. He says he's thought of things like that but he knows he never could be. But with me, I am so ashamed that it just goes over and over in my mind that "what if I'm gay and I'm married and expecting a child?" It seems ludicrous at times, and then it seems a possibility.

Enough of that, I just felt it necessary to explain that my fantasies are not at all something I accept, and many women, I bet, feel like this too, shame instead of peacefulness with their thoughts. Here goes: my fantasies are really three different kinds:

FANTASY NUMBER 1:

I am at the doctor's office waiting for my gynecologist to come in and give me a pap smear. He walks in with his nurse (which is not the usual procedure). He is really cordial. He introduces his nurse and tells me after I've put the sheet around my hips, covering everything I possibly can, to lie back and relax. He tells me to lie back and put my legs in the stirrups, and he puts the light directly on my cunt and swings his stool over to me and begins. He asks me how everything has been going, while his nurse is also watching him work on me. Slowly he places his fingers on my clit and presses it lightly and says, "OK, you are going to feel my finger first." Then he starts rubbing his pointer finger in a circular motion and says he's just checking to see if everything is OK. By this time I'm squeezing my butt up and squeezing my thighs to create that familiar feeling I make for myself on my bed. I start feeling myself getting wet, and I'm not understanding what kind of checkup this is but wouldn't say anything, because it was simply ecstasy. All of a sudden the doctor's head disappears under my propped legs, and I feel his hot breath real close to my cunt as he says he has to get a little closer to watch every movement and see if any changes have taken place from last time. As he breathes, I suddenly feel a little soft, wet stroke up the length of my clit. It is so light that I can't be sure that it was a tongue or just his finger. Then there's no mistaking that hot, wet tongue penetrating me as he separates my lips and sucks on my clit "softly." He knows how sensitive it is and knows just how to make it feel. Then he tells his nurse to come down and see if everything looks OK to her. She looks and can't resist putting her mouth on my dripping cunt, and she sucks me. Just before I come, I'm moaning and saying that everything feels so good, and I ask the doctor to fuck me. He took his tongue off my clit and stood up with his cock bulging out of his zipper (he had been beating off and was ready too) and forced it into my little cunt. He ripped me open, and I just screamed with pleasure, and the nurse checked the door and locked it again. She took her clothes off and climbed on top of my face, arching her skinny body back, causing her breasts to stick out, and made me lick her pussy. I just feel like I'm in heaven, and that's how it ends.

FANTASY NUMBER 2:

Actually, this fantasy was one that my husband kind of created for me—he talks to me and tells me stories during foreplay. It starts with him in a hotel room and me being in the room next door. The mirror between our rooms (on his side) is transparent for me, but he cannot see through to my side. He starts by saying he hears knocking at the door, and I watch him walk over to answer the door, and it's two girls. One with long blond hair (of course!) and one mulatto with long dark hair. They come in and drink some champagne together. The women start undressing my husband, slowly his cock grows, and I can see it through the transparent mirror. They begin to take turns sucking him until he is ready for them. They undress down to their bras and panties, which they save for him to strip off. He does so slowly and begins lightly licking their nipples one at a time while they stand erect like stones. He then pushes the girls forward to lean on the wall over the headboard, with their firm asses sticking up at him. He spreads one girl's ass open and begins to lick her asshole, and she's moaning as she comes. Then he does the same to the other, only he rubs the clit of this one while he's sucking her ass. The women lie on their backs now, and he puts one hot clit at a time into his hot, wet mouth and sucks them both off to orgasm. Meanwhile I'm watching and getting so wet as I'm masturbating myself. I can't take it anymore, so I go next door and knock, and he answers the door, saying, "I know you were watching, come in and take your clothes off." He looks at me like he loves me and he doesn't even know me. I take my clothes off, and he pushes my head over his swollen cock, and I suck him until he gets to a climax and stop so he doesn't come . . . yet. Then he tells me to lie with my legs apart and orders the girls to suck my cunt and my tits. I lie there in ecstasy. Then he comes up behind the girl licking me and he fucks her up the ass. She screams while she is enjoying the new sensation of anal intercourse while licking me. Then the other woman sits on top of me and rubs her dripping pussy all over my face, and I lap it up like a dog. My husband then comes up to my face with her pussy juices all over it and he cleans my face and then sends the girls home. Then he makes sweet love to me, and we love each other forever.

FANTASY NUMBER 3:

This one doesn't have much substance, but it brings me to orgasm when I think about it. When my husband and I make love, a man walks in and watches us as he beats off. He walks over to both of us and rubs his hot hands over our bodies, feeling my moist cunt and my husband's bulge. He then mounts my husband from behind and fucks him up the ass. My husband doesn't like it at first and then he begins to relax as we reassure him it's natural to feel excited, even if it is another man. Then this guy turns around and sucks my husband off until he comes in his mouth. I just get so excited when I think about men getting it on together. I guess because I want my husband to know what it feels like to get fucked.

Marybeth

I was reading your book and I started wondering what somebody like me would have to say about sexual fantasies. I'm a senior in social work, have already been professionally employed in a children's group home as a houseparent and as a counselor for clients in another group home. Have returned part time to college. I'm just off an Indian reservation. Grown up on reservations almost all my life, except two years I lived in California. Am a "closet heterosexual," as some female gay friends told me once. I think that describes me a lot.

I was barely 19 when I first had a homosexual affair. It lasted two years. She was black, a nursing student I met out in California. That was the strongest commitment I ever had. At the time we both were seeing other people. She had a boyfriend, so did I. I saw and met another girl during that time. Propositioned her over a pool game one night when I was lonely, hurt and angry. I was still 19. Now I'm just 24 and at number seven. I think six out of the seven all told me and believed that they were straight. I think three of them had had one other female lover before me. Still, they're straight! Just three of them—I was their first. It is really fun to see whether a so-called straight woman will be with me or not. It really is a challenge. Ego trip, too.

I guess in that way I have really good feelings about it. But there is anger afterwards. It's like it goes in stages. I've seen the anger, all the pain of realizing what happened—guilt— the whole trip. It's pretty predictable. People put themselves through such grief. Women really do want commitments and promises over these things. The ones I've been with need to feel they trust me to know what to do, etc., feel close to me before it's sexual. I don't believe women can be casual like many men. To me, it's like you gotta be able to reach their mind, their emotional side before they let you make love to them. A lot of talking.

There's one woman that I do have a fantasy about. I was introduced to her by mutual friends (who I later found out figured that if anyone, I could seduce her and prove that she would "do it"). We spent that whole evening talking. I talked about working with kids and what makes it so valuable to me. I never tried hustling her. I met her about seven months later. She knew I was in town, and my best friend called her. She said, sure, she'd come meet us for a few drinks. She came in, so beautiful. Guess I have a thing for blond good-looking women. My best friend wanted her too, for longer than I.

In my mind, I replay what happened, my fantasy/reality: The whole evening is spent with my best friend trying to win Daisy. I laugh and watch in agony. She carries herself so well. All three of us are laughing so hard. A great time. Up to now I hadn't ever made any indication that I wanted Daisy. I'm just being mellow. Later, we go up to the jukebox to play some music. She is standing, reading song titles, close to me. I understand what being physically attracted is, now. Her presence is so overwhelming. I wonder if she can feel it too. Really sensual. I can sense that feeling even now nearly a year later.

We take Daisy over to our new apartment. My best friend still trying to win her love. I not only want her body, but all of her. My best friend has to crawl in a window to get us in. While we wait at the door, I tell her that "—'s not the only one who wants you." She smiles and takes a drink of her wine, saying, "I'll have a drink on that." My best friend comes and lets us in. It's late. After a while, all three of us are sitting on the floor. For the first time we begin to ask Daisy how come she is with us. It's funny, we're all laughing, but my best friend and I have never done this over a woman, ever. Daisy's laughing, telling us we really sound like two guys hustling her. She says she knew what she was getting into by being around us. She says that she knew long before what both of us were and that eventually she would have to deal with us individually. She says she hasn't ever done this sort of a thing before.

I tell Daisy not to bother with my best friend, 'cause I'm the one for her. She's telling us both no, but her body is telling us yes. I believe that body language tells so much more than words. Finally, my best friend gives up and leaves the room. I'm alone with Daisy. I keep talking. She tells me she doesn't know if she could handle a situation like that. I'm in love with a stranger. I tell Daisy that I want to hold her. That's all, just hold her. She jumps up, says she has to go, and I see how scared she is suddenly. I tell her I don't want her to leave, but to stay, talk to me. I ask her to stay, please. She sits down and stays, to my amazement, 'cause she's free to go at any time, ain't nobody gonna stop her if she wants to go.

She talks a lot. We're fairly close. I want to hold her so bad. I tell her I wanna hold her. I'm close to her now. I feel brave, tell her I want to kiss her. Daisy has been protesting all along, softly, saying she's never done this . . . I tell Daisy again, I want to kiss her. She says, "No, I might like it." It hits me! That was a yes if I ever heard one. So I move in. I know now that words can't help, only action. She lets me kiss her. She responds. Just as good as I thought it could be. I feel so good. She is kissing me back and pulling me closer. I ain't no fool. I do as she wants! Success. I don't even need anything more than the knowledge that I won. That she kissed me and not my best friend.

I tell Daisy I know she's scared, so am I. No more words, just kissing. And feeling good. Knowing she feels what I do. It's even sweeter when my best friend walks in and sees that Daisy's kissing me, holding me close. I see Daisy pull away suddenly and get up to go after my best friend. If I had a fantasy come true, it'd have to be that, all over again. Just like we did in reality. Just to be able to go through it one more time with Daisy. All sensual, nothing any more physical than it was.

It might have developed more between us had other people not wanted Daisy to "cross over" so badly. I want

Daisy. I know people have used, abused and hurt her. I wish for her to know what it's like to be treated well. And I know how to treat someone. Respect, caring and gentleness.

With just about every other woman, I've always wanted to see if I could seduce them. To boost my ego. I feel intensely proud of it. I think that my attitude doesn't go along too well with others. I really can't handle a woman dominating me, except someone like Daisy, and then only a little. I want to feel that I'm in control of the situation/woman. I want to be the boss. I like to be the one who sees 'em when I want to—not them.

I've had three *sexually aggressive* women, and it's been difficult sleeping with them 'cause it threatens me sometimes. I need space. I have to keep some distance because I don't want to get too involved or hurt. Women sure are dangerous. They can melt their way thru walls, and if they wish—they can crush a person. Women are something beautiful, and so many, all around. Gotta get going. Someday my fantasy will come true, Daisy, someday.

Mickey

I am a 22-year-old college student who has an active sex life. I'm involved with a man I plan to marry after graduation (he's 26), but prior to our relationship, I had many lovers. I've always been told I was a good lover, often "the best they'd had," so I feel sexually confident, but I admit I have fantasies I've never been able to act out.

One of my most frequent fantasies that I indulge in while masturbating (I don't fantasize when with a partner) is having sex with another woman.

She is not someone that I know . . . usually she is slender and dark, very exotic looking, with cascading black hair and small breasts. I'm alone in my apartment, lounging about in revealing short shorts and a skimpy T-shirt without a bra. (I have large, full breasts.) The woman is a casual acquaintance, and she knocks on my door. I let her in, and we begin talking. She produces a joint, which we smoke, and I complain of muscle tension in my shoulders and back. She offers to massage me, and I comply. The massage is very stimulating, as I am lying on my stomach while she perches on my ass and manipulates my flesh with her fingers. I then tell her it feels good, very good, and that I am tense all over, with sore and tender breasts also. Immediately, she turns me over and removes my revealing T-shirt and begins to gently massage my large, aching breasts while sitting astride my hips. Oooh, it feels so good! Her hands work magic, and I become soaking wet with arousal. Deftly, she pulls aside the crotch of my shorts and inserts a finger into my slippery slit. (I am naked beneath the shorts.) My hips begin to undulate to the movement of her finger, and I begin to moan. With her other hand, she fingers my clit, almost bringing me off, yet stopping just short of my climax. We are both breathing hard as she continues to finger-fuck me and play with my clit. Now she has four fingers of one hand jamming in and out of me while the other hand rhythmically rubs my clit till I come in a screaming climax.

But we are not yet through. She slides my shorts from my hips and strips herself. She then buries her face in my pussy and tongues me right there. Oh God, I'm losing it! She swings her ass and cunt over my face while I furiously eat her out . . . I have to stop now and masturbate—I am that horny!

I've never had a lesbian affair, although it intrigues me. Were I to meet a beautiful gay woman like the one in my fantasy, I would surely try it. I probably have bisexual tendencies, but I don't care; it turns me on and makes me come, and that's the whole idea, right?

Caroline

I'm a 22-year-old. I'm married, but now separated, with two children. I finished school.

My fantasy is to go to bed with a woman. Don't get me wrong, I love to have sex with men, but I see how good it must feel to a man when he sucks a woman's nipples and I also want that feeling. I want my lady friend to be middle aged, color doesn't make a difference. First, when we meet,

I'll be so shy. Then we'll go to her place and sit and talk, sipping on a glass of wine. She'll walk over to me and start kissing me. As she starts kissing me, I'm so timid. Then she starts unbuttoning my blouse and eases it off my shoulders and starts kissing my neck and shoulders, and by this time my nipples are hard and alert. I run my fingers through her hair, I am ready to return her affection. We undress each other and lie down on the floor. She starts sticking her tongue down my throat. She licks my cunt, and I'll finger her ass.

I want to meet a warm and friendly lady who wants to take me under her wing.

Beverley

I am a 19-year-old college student. I have been sexually active since I was 15 years old. I masturbate regularly. I started masturbating when I was about 8 or 9. I used to rub myself against my dog's penis until I climaxed. I also used to spread butter or mayonnaise around my clitoris and nipples and have the dog lick them off.

As I got older, I was much less interested in the dog. I then used to manually masturbate myself while reading some form of erotica. I would also use a stream of water or rub against pillows to achieve orgasm.

My most vivid sexual memory was when I saw my brother masturbating. I clearly remember hiding and watching him rub his very large, purple-tipped penis. I was so incredibly turned on by this incident that I came while watching.

I have a lot of sexual fantasies. My favorites are mainly between me and another woman. I am by no means a lesbian. I am very much a heterosexual. I am just very curious about what it would be like to make it with a woman.

My fantasy goes like this: I am a foreign exchange student in France. I am staying with a very wealthy French family. My room is very close to the maids' room. I knew they were lesbians because I would sometimes hear them having sex.

One night while I was sleeping, one of the very pretty

maids comes in my room and lies next to me. I cannot see her because I am facing the wall. I pretend I am sleeping. She begins by rubbing my arm. She then lifts my silky nightgown and proceeds by rubbing my back. I am beginning to get very aroused. I let her do whatever she wants. She is now caressing my stomach. Soon she is fondling my breasts. My breath is quickening. She is rubbing her vagina on my buttocks. I want to touch her so badly. She then starts to touch my vagina. She finds the exact spot that makes me come and masturbates me. I cannot stand it any longer. I turn over and start sucking her breasts, stomach, and soon I am eating her out. She is moaning and writhing all over the bed. She pulls me up, and we rub our clitorises together and come. She then slides down my body and continues to eat me out. I come and come. I do not think there is anything wrong with masturbating. I love it! I love to rub my body and make myself feel good.

I don't think I will ever tell anyone about my fantasies. It's a very private thing.

Libby

I'm 19, a high school graduate, saleswoman—notice, not salesperson—and single.

I have been sexually involved with one wonderful man for a year and a half. At this time, he has been in another country for three months, and there is still another three to go.

I have found that thinking about homosexuality in people disgusts me. When I think about the pairing off of two people of the same gender, it usually makes me want to throw up.

But: I have a friend that I also work with, and we have talked intimately about sex. As a matter of fact, I love talking about sex!—with anyone who will listen!

Anyway, one day we talked about breasts, and then I asked her if one of her breasts hangs lower than the other. She said yes, and then we talked about nipples and she said that her boyfriend teases her about her nipples hanging downward! I feel this is terrible, since the breast is such a beautiful, maternal object. This was about five or six months ago, I suppose. Anyway, ever since, I have thought about my fantasies, and I realize that I do have a fantasy about kissing this girl and sucking and feeling her nipples and breasts.

I don't feel I am a homosexual or even bisexual. I just want to make some loving contact with this wonderful girl!

Gwynne

I'm 16 and will soon be a senior in high school. I have never fucked anyone but I think about it a lot and wonder what it will be like. I masturbate when I'm horny, which is often, and I'm really fascinated (obsessed?) by sex.

I *did* give a guy head once and I thought it was bitchin! I liked the feeling of that hot, hard rod in my mouth! I think I would like to have a guy go down on me but haven't had the chance.

Anyway, the fantasy I just have to tell you about is one about my best friend—a girl. I have this fantasy a lot and sometimes worry that maybe I'm some kind of repressed lesbian or something. Oh well . . . It goes like this:

My best friend has just broken up with her boyfriend over the phone in her bedroom when I walk in and find her sitting on her bed crying. She doesn't see me, and I hesitate at the door—not sure what I should do. I've never seen her cry before. Finally, I walk over and awkwardly put my arm around her shoulder. She puts her arms around me, crying, and after a while her crying tapers off. I'm really trying to think of something comforting to say, when she kind of pulls back and looks me in the eyes for what seems like a long time. I can't describe the look she gives me, but it makes me "cream in my jeans." She knows what's happening and, without saying anything, she tells me it's alright. Slowly her face moves closer to mine . . . before I can think about what I'm *doing,* she kisses me. Oh God, her lips are so soft, warm, and moist—I can't help it—I just kiss her back. She knows me so well, she knows just how to kiss me, and I know she can feel me surrender. I want her to take me . . .

I've never really developed this fantasy further than this. I think I'm afraid I will start wanting to make it come true. Who knows?

Maya

I am 22 years old, single and on my own. I have been involved with three women (two of them strictly gay) and one man, with whom I'm presently involved. I don't actually consider myself homosexual, because I do not prefer women to men. I suppose I like them just as much, although it would appear I like women more, but not necessarily; it just worked out that way. I imagine it would be safe to say I am bisexual, for I believe that given the opportunity, and if the circumstances were right, I would again be involved with a woman.

My favorite fantasy is one with a woman, a specific woman to be exact, Rita Mae Brown, a fiction novelist. I've read all of her work that I can get my hands on, and I'm absolutely enchanted with this woman. In my fantasy I'm older, wealthier, more powerful, successful and beautiful. I'm alone on an elevator, and she gets on. We don't say much because obviously we don't know each other (I don't recognize her). The elevator shorts, and we are stuck between floors. Both of us are somewhat annoyed, for we have meetings to attend. We're informed through the emergency phone that it's going to be a while before they can get us out, so naturally we make the best of it and begin talking, getting to know one another. Our conversation is relaxing and self-revealing, we respond to each other as if we've been close friends for a long time. Slowly, the conversation begins to pick up a suggestive tone, and we agree to meet for dinner as soon as we're able.

Time moves on and eventually we have dinner, and since I'm out of town on a business trip, I invite her back to my company's penthouse that I am staying in. She agrees, and once there, we again are caught up in a somewhat suggestive conversation. It eventually comes out that the suggestive comments are not entirely meant in jest and there is a mutual attraction between us. Finally, she reaches out and touches me, the electricity that begins pulsating through my body is incredible. She moves closer, and I reach up to touch her face. I feel myself whine in anticipation. Our lips are inches from each other's, and we kiss. Gently at first, then fiercely with a hot passion. I run my fingers through her hair, grabbing a lock in the back as if I'm forbidding her to break our bond. Her hands gently begin to caress my body, running over my breasts and up my inner thigh. She eases away, and I lead her into the bedroom. We begin making love to each other, exploring each other's bodies completely with our eyes, hands and tongues. She brings me to orgasm with the mere way she fingers me, but it's incomparable to the orgasms I experience when she goes down on me. Kissing my very soul, like no one had ever done before. This woman knows every spot to kiss, lick and touch to make me cry out with pleasure. Then it's my turn to please her. We continue on into the night until we're both exhausted and fall asleep in each other's arms.

My favorite part of the fantasy is, surprisingly, at the end when we part, promising to keep in touch. She hands me a folder and tells me to read it later. When I do, I discover it's full of beautiful poetry she has written to me. It's so full of emotion and feeling, I almost cry to think I have affected someone in such an intense way. I'd like to reread her real poetry and pretend it's written to me, but unfortunately I haven't read any in such a long time for I can't find the books in print anywhere! So if by some bizarre chance you are reading this, Rita, there's someone out here that would desperately like to know where you're hiding your books!

Meg

I'm 21 years old, married a little over a year. I'm a housewife and happy with my life. I had my first orgasm about six months ago. For the longest time I was depressed and felt like I could never achieve an orgasm, and I didn't enjoy sex all that much. I finally decided to try seriously to masturbate. I picked a day when I was home alone and wouldn't have any interruptions. I took off all my clothes and lay down on the bed with a mirror, a jar of Vaseline, and some items I thought might feel good in my pretty pussy. I grabbed some of my husband's "girly magazines" and read a little bit and looked at the girls in the books, with those pretty pussies, and then I got my mirror and looked at my own pussy. I took some Vaseline and spread it all over my little cunny. I found my clit for the first time, the Vaseline made it very slick, so I rubbed over and over, and I discovered my cunt muscles squeezing and I was really getting wet. (Most important, I took my time and I was relaxed.) I stuck the small end of a cucumber in my pussy and I just kept rubbing my little clit bud. I rolled over on my stomach and had the urge to slam it in farther and harder and I had my first orgasm.

Since that day I've learned that my body is beautiful and masturbation is a natural and a beautiful act. That has made me realize I, too, can enjoy orgasms as long as my clitty gets equal time. My sex life all the way around is better.

I have so many fantasies while I masturbate, but my favorite one comes from the following:

A friend of mine tells me about a woman she knows who is older and married who has never learned to masturbate or climax and is very distraught. Loving women's bodies the way I do, I agree to help her. She comes over, and we talk a bit. I gently touch her thigh, and she smiles. I feel it's okay to ask her to the bedroom. I tell her to take off her clothes and lay on the bed, I join her. I have her look at my pretty cunt and explain that my cunt, like hers, is a thing of beauty and can give great pleasure. I then suck her titties a bit and caress her thighs. Finally I make my way to her pussy. I spread her legs wide and tell her how beautiful her cunt is, while I grease it up a bit. I insert my finger, and she squeezes a bit. I then gently lick her clit, and my lady friend moans. I lick a little harder and harder still. She tells me it's feeling real good. I tell her I have a surprise for her. I take out my big vibrator, add a little more grease and tickle her clitty as I slowly insert the big dildo, which is whirring like crazy. She is loving it and finally, after a good, sincere fucking and clit work, my lady comes and kisses me with a tear and a thank-you.

I must tell you I have never been with a woman and I love my husband very much, but since I've learned how to masturbate I've longed to gently bring off a woman who really needs it. Until then I'll be masturbating with my vibrator, which I feel is a must for every woman. (It beats the hell out of water on your clit. When you can finger your clit and jam a big cocklike dildo in your little cunny, it's a much better orgasm.) And I'll dream of a woman coming over and letting me bring her off.

I want women to know from me, an average woman, that it's okay to masturbate. Get in touch with your body and you'll feel great.

Chris

Let me tell you about myself before I tell you about my sexual fantasies. I am a 23-year-old woman who recently graduated from college. I grew up in a medium-sized town with my mother and two sisters, both older. Sexually, I was a late maturer and didn't have a full growth of hair on my pussy until age 18. I was a virgin until age 19 and experienced my first orgasm at age 20, which, by the way, was through masturbation. Ever since then masturbation has played a big part in my life, and I masturbate to orgasm *at least* once a day. During my private masturbation sessions, that is where my fantasies come into play.

Most of my sexual fantasies are about myself engaging in lesbian acts. I did have one lesbian experience in my life and I enjoyed it very much. It happened in college, and if I ever had the chance again, I would probably jump at it, even though I would never go out looking for it.

My first fantasy starts with me in a large department store, shopping for sexy lingerie. I end up picking up a garter belt, stockings, a pair of French-cut panties, and a matching bra. The saleswoman, who is in her early 30s and very attractive, asks me if I would like to try my outfit on before I buy it. Thinking this a good idea, I let the woman take me into the dressing room. The woman left as I began to undress. When I just finished putting on the outfit, I heard the saleswoman ask if everything fits okay. I felt the juices in my cunt as I said that the bra was a little tight. The saleswoman stepped through the curtain and said that maybe she could help. She unhooked the bra from the front and asked me to take it off.

As she was adjusting the bra, she mentioned that this outfit was very pretty and that she owns the same thing. I asked her if she thought I looked good in it, and she said yes. I asked her if she had any problems with her same outfit, and without saying a word, she unzips her dress and lets it fall to the floor. To my surprise, she has it on. The only difference is that she is not wearing any panties. I stood there motionless, and she said that, no, she never had any problems. She also mentioned that she didn't wear any panties because she likes to masturbate during her breaks. With that comment, I started uncontrollably rubbing my exposed tits. She asks me to sit down in the chair and says that she will do me a favor. She could tell how turned on I was.

As I sit down in the chair, the saleswoman removes my panties and comments on how beautiful my pussy is. I want to give her a better view of my cunt, so I take both my hands and spread my pussy lips as wide as they can possibly go. The woman kneels on the floor and starts to explore my now soaking cunt. I beg her to eat me, and without any questions she starts to tongue my clit. While she is licking my love button, she is working two of her long fingers in and out of my cunt hole. I look down at her beautiful pussy and notice that she is working on her own clit as she licks mine. The sight of her playing with her own pussy makes me close to orgasm. The woman senses this, and without warning, she removes the fingers from my pussy and puts one of them up my anus. I reach a violent orgasm, and we both get dressed and leave. I thank her very much, and she says any time.

You don't know what writing this down is doing to me. So before I continue, I am going to have to go masturbate.

I am back now and have just masturbated to two wonderful orgasms. One with my fingers and the second with my vibrator. For years, I just masturbated with my fingers but just discovered the joy of dildos, bottles and my hairbrush. Sometimes I work the object in my pussy with one hand while I rub my clit with the other hand.

The second fantasy that I would like to tell you about does include me masturbating. This fantasy starts with a group of ten women who want to learn to have an orgasm. I am not the teacher but an assistant. All the women are nude, including the teacher and myself. We are all in a single room which has a double bed with chairs all around it. All the women, the students, are eager to learn to have an orgasm and request a demonstration through masturbation. The teacher instructs me to lay down on the bed and spread my legs. As I do so, the teacher points out my clit and cunt hole to the other women. I am then told to show how I bring myself to an orgasm through masturbation. I use one hand to stroke my clit and the other to finger my wet pussy hole. I arch my back so that I can give each woman a good look at my cunt. When I reach my orgasm, the women all cheer and want to try themselves. The teacher tells them all to lay down on the floor and spread their legs. As the women begin to play with their pussies, the teacher and I go around and make sure that all the women were masturbating correctly. We would help the women find their clits and sometimes assist them by rubbing their clits for them and fingering their pussies. I usually reach my own orgasm at this point, and the fantasy ends.

I probably could go on for hours but I feel the need to go and masturbate again. Yet before I do, I feel that I should thank you for your previous books and for letting me tell you about my fantasies. It was a relief to see that women can be open about sex. I have a lot of friends who say that they do not fantasize or masturbate. I, on the other hand, have told many of my friends about my fantasies and have even admitted to them that I masturbate.

I am very proud about my sexuality, and if my friends or

other women do not fantasize or masturbate, I feel sorry for them because they don't know what they are missing.

Lilly

I am very shy. If my parents were to find out what I think, they would probably disown me and my friends would shun me. When I used to go to my shrink and told him what I am about to tell you, he said it was a "stage I was going through and as long as they're just fantasies, it is okay."

Like everyone else, I have sexual fantasies. They're usually about the same thing: me having sex with another female; whether it be with someone I know and like and am attracted physically to or with an attractive stranger whom I don't know. The dreams become so intense that at times I question which sex do I really prefer. It scares me because I've been dating for eleven years now, and while I'm attracted to men, I never fantasize about having sex with them or even with strangers.

I am usually the passive person in the lovemaking, and my partner ravishes my body. She does everything a guy would do to me (except screw), only better, because she's very gentle and loving. I've never been an initiator in sex; my boyfriends would "help" me (e.g., undress me, fondle my breasts, etc.) because I am shy and rather undemonstrative, though I enjoy showing affection to those I have feelings for. While I enjoy taking an active role (e.g., participating in sex and not "just lying there"), I love having my body savoured, where I can just let go, regardless of whether I climax or not.

In these fantasies, I always reach orgasm because they turn me on enormously. The fantasies have not become real because: (1) I cannot approach my friends or a stranger to whom I am attracted to satisfy my curiosity and desire. (2) I'm afraid I may enjoy it and choose that way of life permanently. (3) I'm afraid. Pure and simple. Period.

It's safe for me to fantasize because it's my own private world and no one is intruding upon it. I would love to make my fantasy come true, however, but I'm really afraid.

By the way, I am 26, single and am dating a few guys now who I really like. I've never told anyone what I have just revealed.

THE OTHER WOMAN AS MIRROR

Having suggested that men could learn from these fantasies what it is women want, let me add that it is not by chance that women have left men totally out of their scenarios. It would be a rationalization to say that these women are turning to other women simply because men disappoint them sexually. The magic of fantasy, after all, is that we control everything. Why not conjure up a man in fantasy who has the mouth, the tongue of an angel if it's just oral satisfaction that is wanted? Why strap a dildo on a woman if all that is wanted is to have a phallic object in one's vagina or anus? No, for reasons conscious or unconscious, a woman is selected over a man as fantasy partner because something is desired that only a woman can provide.

Dottie says that none of her male lovers have taken the time to stimulate her to orgasm. Though she plans to marry and have children one day, is it her "dream" husband she conjures up in fantasy to nibble "on my fiery hole," to put his warm tongue "on my throbbing knob"? Absolutely not. It is a woman she creates: ". . . very beautiful and toned, feminine but butch . . . She parts my lips and presses her mouth on my swollen clit . . . Who else would know better how to jerk me off besides another woman?"

The recurring theme of this chapter is Dottie's line that "no one can satisfy a woman like another woman." But doesn't that imply any woman could do the job? These women have a very specific kind of woman in mind, someone who is in touch with her own body, on intimate terms with the erogenous crooks and crannies of her genitals, her breasts, and for many of these women her anus, too. How many women are there out there who fit this bill?

Either these women are being overly optimistic about

what people of their own sex are willing and equipped to offer, or they are simply too damning of men. It is simplistic to suggest that only other women can satisfy one another when in truth each woman, with her own individual set of needs, has her own custom-made fantasy woman in mind. Only sex with that particular woman, imagined while her hand explores her own body, then becomes a trip of self-discovery, a way of seeing herself, finding out about her own sexuality.

Women have always had this need, but in the past it went pretty much unfulfilled. To whom was a young woman to look in real life or in her imagination? *How* was she to look, given she had no permission to be a voyeuse, to see and feel another body like her own that would give her a clue about female sexuality?

Mother as model was out of the question. Even if mother had a modicum of sexuality, there was the family taboo against seeing one's parents as sexual. Chances were, before the 1970s, that the model of womanhood, femaleness, that mother presented to her daughter was that of a nice asexual woman. And the ladies next door, the women in the greater community, replicated mother like cookie cutters. There were, of course, Marilyn Monroe and Elizabeth Taylor and before them other femmes fatales, but that's what they were: fatally flawed, destined to excite men but to live in that forbidden community on the outskirts of Nice Women.

The young women in this chapter are the first generation to take for granted that sexuality is part of women's identity; therefore, they must literally make themselves up, invent themselves. There are no blueprints on which to pattern themselves as economically and sexually independent, feminine people who are sometimes wives and mothers too.

Today mother as model is more complicated than ever. While mother as good provider who works outside the home may be useful, the image of her as sexual can be as threatening as in the past; the old family taboo still exists. And what if she is too sexual? Many of these women were raised by separated or divorced mothers; the issue of sexual competition between mothers and daughters is more real than ever but still remains one of the last unexplored and untalked-about areas of women's identity.

Who then to give a young woman a picture, a feel of female sexuality in this first period in history when it is correct for a woman to be sexual, as well as all the other things a woman must be today? Enter the other woman of fantasy, often older, who opens her arms and bares her breast. What safer and more private place to investigate another woman, "whose body is like mine"? "I like the feel of her body, and my ability to arouse her seems to bring me closer in touch with my feelings as a woman," says Eve. "I feel so very feminine as I rest my hot mouth on her enlarged clitoris."

The average age of the women in this chapter is twenty-two. They were raised by a culture, by media that pretend to applaud the sexually explicit woman; many of them have been educated by the feminists who dominate so many college campuses. They have been led to expect a lot, not only in their sex lives but in their roles as professionals and mothers too. Beginning in the early 1980s and up to this date, every study I have read indicates that this new generation of women is convinced that they will succeed in their chosen careers, earn top dollar, and find egalitarian husbands who will share in the housework as well as the raising of the children.

Realism has already begun to enter. While young men on campuses may choose their future wives as much for their earning ability as for their grace and beauty, a man is hard-pressed to urge his wife to compete harder than he; should she earn more than he, the relationship is often in trouble. A lot of how we define masculinity still has to do with being a good provider, a better provider than she.

Professional success, should she find even a fraction of what she anticipated, is encouraging but it doesn't make a woman feel more womanly. Today a man is so confused about his own role as a man, he has trouble reassuring a woman about her tender, female self. But another woman could and would do it better, being a woman herself.

This need to see one's sexual womanliness in another

woman's body became popular in fantasy in the early 1980s, when women literally covered their feminine selves in the mannish dress-for-success suit, sending up flags to men that they were not women at all—Just treat me like one of the guys, please—but internally sending up flags to themselves as well. At the same time, women were learning to pay their own way, open their own doors, and compete with a man for his job. How was a woman to be reassured she hadn't lost her essential female core that cried out to feed and to be fed?

Enter the breast, symbol and substance of this chapter.

When these women talk about breasts, there is little doubt that something more than genital satisfaction is being sought in intense loving relationships with other women. Whatever else may go on, the breast reigns supreme. "Her breasts can't fit into my hand because they are too big," says Jenna, "and the brown nipple is so high upon her tittie she can almost reach it herself with her tongue which is now caressing my own breast through my silk blouse."

These breasts are not judged by size alone; what is wanted is a "good enough breast." While Jessie's fantasy devotes most of its time to clitoral excitement, the meal begins as always with the breast: ". . . she takes my breast out of my black under-wire bra and begins to nurse. She pushes me onto the floor, rips off my panties, exposing my pussy in all its wet, juicy glory. 'Ah, the main course,' she moans, and goes right for my cunt."

When I began writing twenty years ago, the wise men in the behavioral world told me that the reason we sexualize our "baby needs" is that we are ashamed of them; the sexualization is a disguise. Perhaps that is true for men, who must defend their manliness on an almost hourly basis. But these women don't seem in the least embarrassed getting their "baby needs" met. They don't go out of the way to mask the need for nurturing; nor do they make up euphemisms for nursing and sucking on the beautiful breasts they have created.

Jenna's fantasy woman sits on her lap while another woman spanks her, eventually "fucking my cunt with a huge dildo she's strapped on. It feels nasty and delicious. She says, 'You want to be fucked, don't you little girl? You like me to fuck your cunt hard and deep. Your little virgin cunt hole is spread open now, baby. Tell everyone what a bad girl you are, tell them!'"

These fantasies make it clear how deeply our adult sexuality is rooted in the first years of life. So many of women's problems go back to the difficult years of toilet training, where they first learned from mother to believe that their genitals were dirty, untouchable. Today, to believe that their vaginas and anuses are acceptable, even beautiful, it is to that problem-filled second year of life they return; they rewrite history with another woman.

I have always believed that a woman's sexual development would be so much easier if a man, as well as a woman, were involved in these first years of her life, both in discipline and in nurturing. Men bring less rigidity to toilet training, to the "bad" smells and sights women associate with bodily functions.

There is a bias in the family structure worth pursuing, since it touches on the scarcity of warmth and tenderness not just between women and men but also between parents and children. If women believe men are incapable of providing affection of a soft and comforting sort, how can they believe men are good in the nursery, where women say they desperately need men but are loath to relinquish their territory?

At certain anxious moments women say they want genital/sexual satisfaction from being in bed with a man. What they really desire is mothering instead—the closeness and primitive unseparateness they had as infants. It is a quality that rigid psychoanalytic theory, and some equally rigid women, would say only a woman could supply. But this is an unnecessarily sexist idea. Not all women are good mothers. What is needed at this time is summed up in the psychoanalytic concept of a "good enough mother." Not the perfect mother, not even the real mother, but someone who can do the job.

323

The idea transcends gender. It is a certain quality of love and tenderness that, yes, either a man or a woman can give. Either a man or a woman can give it to an infant as well as to a lover in bed; I believe a man who has this quality can bring up a child better than a woman who doesn't. In time, that child will become a grown man or woman who is comfortable with the idea of a man as both a passionate and a tender lover.

The burden placed on women that each be a good mother is similar in unreality to the burden put on the penis that it always be erect, on demand. Psychoanalysts' offices are filled with people who feel worthless because they have failed in these iron structures. We ought to question instead whether the demands themselves aren't crazy.

As roles within the family continue to shift and change, we will have to either stop using the word "mothering" in its narrowest, female-oriented sense or invent a new one. It puts men off. I'm not advocating that men become more like women, any more than I am saying that women must become more like men. It is a balance we are striving for; if women go too far in some unconscious desire to turn their men into warm, cuddly, nurturing comforters, they will have gained a mother but lost a man.

The capacity to be a nurturing, emotional parent can be found in both women and men. There are certain physical attributes, of course, that only women have, and vice versa. But there are also emotions which are not divided among us by sex, and which can be expressed by either sex. We are getting past the notion that bringing a good appetite to the table is a male trait; in fact, we've learned to enjoy women who bring gusto to anything. We should get past the idea that the ability to be a "good enough mother" is something limited to women. Only then will women find in men the tenderness, along with sexual satisfaction, that they say can only be found in another woman.

A young duckling who is removed from his mother before he opens his eyes will become "imprinted" on the first living thing he sees, and will contentedly follow a cat or dog around. If a dog can raise a duck, is it too much to think that an emotionally flexible father can be a "good enough mother" to a child?

Or to a woman who needs him in that role now and then?

Reluctant as we were twenty years ago to accept that our sexuality begins in the mother/daughter relationship, women Jenna's age grew up on that knowledge, which had been assimilated into the culture. She is now twenty-three, in love with a man, and clearly not in the least embarrassed by her "bad little girl" erotic dreams. Given her fondness for "nasty photos of women sucking each other's breasts and fingers pressed gently in and out of pink pussy lips," she may have also seen the films *Entre Nous* and *Emmanuelle,* which graphically embraced sex between women and were very popular in the early 1980s.

A new library of films and books produced and written by women was created in that decade and flourishes today. The 1970s wisdom that women must turn to one another for understanding and identification began with the camaraderie of consciousness-raising groups and quickly evolved to actually lying down together. "Okay, even if you're heterosexual," went the party line, "and you prefer men sexually, women need another woman, too." For women who want this kind of encouragement, it's very much a part of today's culture.

The women in this book would laugh at the behavioral world which used to state categorically that women were not voyeuses, were not aroused by looking at sexual scenes; how often do these women speak of the excitement they feel looking at porno films and at photos of nude women in men's magazines. They take for granted the masturbation that generally accompanies their voyeurism. They are the first generation of women to know the guaranteed orgasm that comes from clitoral stimulation. And when they close their eyes and masturbate, how much more tender, loving, and exciting to imagine not their own hand but another woman's mouth bringing them to orgasm.

For women oral sex in reality and in fantasy came alive in the late 1970s and 1980s. The surveys on women's sexuality that have been published in recent years indicate again and again women's preference for oral sex. Ah, the miracle of change, for I remember the women in *My Secret Garden,* who were terrified at the loss of control that came with oral sex; and I remember the men in *Men in Love,* who dreamed and prayed for their women to let them go down on them. Nice Women, raised never to lose control, used to fear that if they ever let themselves go in the weightless, limitless voyage of clitoral orgasm, they would "die," never to return to consciousness.

Nowadays young women wish their men in reality had the expert tongues of their fantasy women. Men might learn if women told them exactly what they wanted. But women hate giving instructions to the man, telling him what to do, what it is they want; getting involved in their own seduction makes them too responsible, breaks the mood of being Swept Away. Instead, they dream of a woman who doesn't have to be told, who has been created "knowing" by the woman herself: "Tentatively I put my mouth to her cunt," says Dana, "and drink in her beautiful juices. She holds her labia open with one hand as I move in and lick her clitoris up and down—in long strokes that cover her entire cunt. From her streaming vagina up to the top of her cunt, I lick her again and again, getting faster and faster."

Again, whatever "natural" expertise another woman may have in oral sex, it is significant that these women choose *not* to create a man for the job. What many of these fantasy partners provide, in addition to orgasm, is an idealized image of the fantasizer herself. A fantasy woman is created to embody the characteristics the woman longs for; she is the fantasizer's ego ideal. Elizabeth, for instance, is "very insecure" about her looks; presto, her fantasy woman is slim and beautiful. Jackie feels her breasts are too small, but in fantasy, the breasts of the other woman are "the biggest titties I can suck."

In a society such as ours that is riveted on big breasts and equates thin with beautiful, it is hardly surprising that these women choose to see themselves in the mirror of their created "others" as reed-slim with perfect breasts. Sometimes the fantasies read like fairy tales, where the woman closes her eyes and imagines her "imperfect" self transformed into the beautiful princess whom she then proceeds to adoringly ravish.

". . . I work my way down to her breasts and just feel their beauty," says Debbie, making love to the woman she herself would love to be, ". . . taking in all the pleasure as if it were my own body being touched." This is just one step removed from a narcissistic fantasy, where she might be embarrassed loving or exhibiting herself. Substituting an alter ego gets her past the taboo. Even more important, loving the other woman—while she is masturbating, touching herself—becomes an exploration, the investigation of a mystery: "Kissing her stomach *slowly,* working on the whole body, discovering, still discovering."

In the past, when women found their economic security in men, and thus their identity, too, they would look into their men's eyes for an image of themselves. "Tell me about her," they would urge, meaning the woman before them, who was a clue to him and therefore also to themselves.

These new women know better, and while most do not express anger at men in so many words, there is the insinuation in their rejection of men as suitable fantasy partners that men have somehow failed them. These women are the transition generation. In their understandable confusion and disappointment that men do not "measure up," are they punishing men by leaving them out of their fantasies, just as in real life some women leave men out of the act of procreation, preferring to go to a sperm bank rather than mate with an "inadequate" man?

The fantasies in this chapter are filled with woman power. Throughout the book I have wondered how men are going to react to this naked display of sexual power: Will they be pleasantly surprised? Or will they say, "I knew it all along—these bitches want to take us over, control us, even leave us out!"

Whatever men's reaction, women must decide how much compassion they want to show men. We are the more powerful sex. Early feminists' refusal to even consider men's point of view critically hurt their cause; they lost the support of the majority of women who wanted to live in a world with men.

It has always been easier for women to be angry at men than at women. I believe it is also easier for women to compete professionally with men than with women. Isn't it time women acknowledged that part of this new erotic enthusiasm for other women is a way of denying anger and competition with them?

Ironically, some fantasies of making love to another woman *do* begin with fear of competing with her. Notice how often the other woman's beauty is discussed—that area of competition between women that has no beginning and no end. If we can't beat her, we join her, sexually and literally. "I'm not angry at you," these fantasies say. "In fact, I love you; let me lick and kiss every part of your body."

Scattered through this book are fantasies of women who reach orgasm imagining their men with another woman. They remove themselves from the picture so that they don't have to compete with the rival. In a sense, they *are* her.

In our sexually permissive times, women remain the final heart of darkness. In their fantasies, they explore one another at last, and thus themselves. Just as women gaze so carefully at the naked women in men's magazines, seizing the opportunity to satisfy their curiosity about how other women are made in their every sexual part, their fantasies of other women open secret doors closed against them since the time they pointed their fingers at their mothers' naked bodies and asked, "What is that?"

These fantasies allow a woman to feel the other woman's skin, know her desires, hear her sexual cries, compare her appetite. They tell the woman she is not alone. The other woman's touch is doubly attractive, familiar and reassuring, yet taboo and erotic. With her the woman gives herself permission to act as freely in reality as she does in fantasy.

In the end, these dreaming images of beautiful, naked,

erotic women become a kind of ideal, loving mirror of the woman herself, as she had hoped she would grow up to be. They are images of her secret, longed-for womanhood— images that her mother, from whom she once yearned to receive sexual permission, sternly felt she must deny her. Even a woman who feels sexually sure about herself, and who can give sexually liberating and sensible advice to someone else's daughter, often does not feel free enough to do the same for her own child.

In these fantasies, the woman is both mother and daughter, the rival and herself. Magically, they are lovely, they see that they are the same, and they see that the other does not grow angry that they are rivals at all. In these secret, girlish fantasies, her mother smiles at her again as she lies at her breast. "Yes," she says. Instead of the frown her sexuality once aroused in the past, on mother's face now are "the lineaments of gratified desire" of which William Blake wrote so mystically, and which she dreams of growing up to wear one day herself.

Ultimately there is, of course, more to women's fantasies of other women than the inevitable psychoanalytic return to mother. I believe one of the desires they grow out of is to learn from other women how we might more happily live with men.

Elizabeth

I am a black 22-year-old virgin. Even though I am a virgin, there is nothing I would like better than to have a man's big hot cock sliding in and out of my wet pussy. I have always been very shy, even though just about everyone tells me that I am pretty, and I have always been very insecure about my looks and have never had many boyfriends even though I get propositions.

I suppose that I started to learn about my sexuality at about the age of 6. A younger playmate and I used to rub our cunts together and get wet and excited. It used to feel so good. About four years later, my family moved and I stopped seeing my old playmates and I stopped masturbating, but I did start reading pornographic materials that my sisters and brother used to hide between the mattresses and in their dresser drawers. As a result of reading these books and magazines, when I was 16, I started to masturbate again, but this time by sticking things into my cunt, like soda bottles, cucumbers, bananas, vibrators, and candles.

I hardly ever fantasize while masturbating, but I fantasize in order to put myself in the mood for masturbating. While in the act itself, I like to read dirty books and look at nude pictures, and I get especially excited if the pictures are of two women making love.

I have never been with a woman before, but this is one of my favorite fantasies and I would love to live it out one day. Most of my fantasies are of white women who are slim and beautiful (I am currently thirty pounds overweight).

My favorite fantasy is about me and two roommates whom I'll call Sherrie and Laurie. The three of us are watching 1001 Tales of Erotica on the Playboy Channel, where the three harem girls are making love to each other in front of the sheik. Afterwards, we start to talk about what we just saw, and we discover that we all have fantasies about making it with another woman. After the movie is over, we go upstairs to my bedroom and talk about what sex with another woman would be like and decide to experiment for ourselves.

We all sit around on the bed after taking off our clothes, uncertain as to what to do next. Then I take the lead, and I lean over to the left and I kiss Sherrie on the lips while holding Laurie's hand, and I lean over to my right, and Laurie and I start to kiss passionately, and then Laurie and Sherrie kiss while I start to suck Sherrie's tits and finger her cunt until she comes, while Laurie does the same to me. We are in a frenzy of passion and soon start to lick and tongue-fuck each other's cunts, bringing one another to orgasm after orgasm. Then I get out a large penis-shaped vibrator, which I keep hidden away, and I strap it on and I start to fuck Sherrie's cunt with it, while she moans with pleasure and tongues Laurie's cunt. When she comes, I fuck

Laurie's cunt with the vibrator, moving it in and out of her hot and wet pussy faster and faster as Sherrie sits on her face and has her cunt eaten. Sherrie and I are facing each other, so we kiss passionately and suck on each other's tits. I bite Sherrie's tits from time to time. She loves it and starts to come as a result of this and Laurie's tonguing her cunt.

I pull my mouth away from Sherrie's tits and start to concentrate on making Laurie come. I drive the rubber cock in faster and faster while I look down to see it going in and out of her pussy. The rubber cock is soaked with her juices, which also soak her cunt hairs and run down the crack of her ass. Finally, she can stand it no longer, and I start to finger her clit. She comes with a violence that I never believed was possible.

Then it is my turn. Sherrie unstraps the big rubber dick from my hips and straps it to her hips. While she is doing this, Laurie is kissing me all over. She reaches my pussy, which is boiling over with passion, and starts to lick and tease with her tongue. Just when I can't take the teasing anymore, she starts to tongue me with a fervor that I have never known before, and I love it.

Then Sherrie gets in between my legs and drives in all nine inches of rubber dick with one stroke and starts to fuck me like no man ever had. My head has been propped up on pillows, and there are mirrors on the walls and ceiling, so I can see her ramming the rubber dick into me from all angles. While Sherrie and I fuck, Laurie leaves the room, and returns with a selection of sex toys, which include a double-headed dildo. She straps on a rubber cock, which is about seven inches long, and forces Sherrie to turn me over so that I am on top while Sherrie still fucks away at my pussy from beneath me. I grind my wet cunt down on the big rubber cock that she has strapped to her hips. Laurie by now is putting K-Y jelly on the rubber prick that she has on, which is in my asshole, and she slowly drives it inside. There I am being double fucked by two beautiful white women and loving it. I am in heaven. As we near orgasm, the tempo speeds up. We are fucking so fast that I think I will lose my mind from pleasure. Then I come with Sherrie fucking my pussy, and Laurie fucking my ass. If God should strike me dead at that moment, I would die with a smile on my face.

I am a college graduate who works as a manager in a large Southern department store chain.

Jenna

I am 23, single with a strict Catholic upbringing. I have a beautiful fiancé whom I adore. I have LOTS of fantasies — many of which include other feminine women. I don't feel lesbian, because I enjoy my man so much and have no desire for a masculine woman, but I do definitely enjoy daydreaming about other women.

I remained a virgin until 20 and have shared my body generously ever since with my fiancé. He is very experienced and has the body of a Greek god and the heart of a saint.

Anyway, since I'm a fairly creative person I thought writing a sexual fantasy would be interesting and titillating. I'm very nervous if anyone should see I wrote this.

I often daydream very vividly and graphically (I am a fine artist, also the child of an alcoholic and have heard these may contribute to a vivid fantasy world, I suppose escapism). I love to see nasty photos of women sucking each other's breasts and fingers pressed gently in and out of pink pussy lips, lipstick ladies with tongues deeply tasting feminine juices.

One fantasy is that I am on a flight from Italy to Germany to Ireland, and the plane can't depart from Germany, so the airline pays for an extra night in Germany. No one knows me there, so I get very adventurous and go to a lesbian club. I am a model in reality, so I imagine myself after being made up with lots of full hair, all wild. I know I'd be shy in this situation, so I see myself as kind of hanging behind a beautiful blonde with a large bust and rounded ass until she invites me to follow her. We enter the playroom, which is full of women loving each other. Since I don't speak the language, she motions for me to watch and sit down while she spreads her legs, takes my hands and motions me to undress her. I gently rub her nipples through her sweater first, and it's obvious she wears no bra, because two points rise up as I rub them with my two fingers. Then I pull her sweater up and she is exposed. Her breasts can't fit into my hand because they are too big, and the brown nipple is so high upon her tittie she can almost reach it herself with her tongue, which is now caressing my own breast through my silk blouse.

Now she takes the glass of ice water next to her and slowly pours it all over my silk blouse, so my own tits rise, cold and dying to be sucked, but she won't yet. Now all the women have encircled us, watching and playing with themselves, knowing I'm new and young and wanting to watch our love play. She sits me on her lap and pulls my skirt up so that everyone sees my white underwear and smells my muff. She just takes another girl's middle finger and rubs it against my clit through my underwear, which is sopping wet now. The girl licks her pretty full lips, she's young, around 16, and loves her sexuality. She has on a shirt that has been pulled up above her young breasts, so we all see her rounded breasts and wide nipples. She kneels down in front of my chair, pulls my underwear to one side and holds her tit to my cunt lips, stimulating them with just her nipple. Another older woman sticks her finger, which is wet with her cunt juices, in the girl's mouth and makes the girl suck it as she plays in my cunt with her tittie.

The blonde pulls off my blouse and places her hand under my breast and bounces it up and down, her vision concentrated on its movements. She is still underneath me, so she motions two black twins over, and they each get one to suck and nibble. My underwear is pulled down in all the lust, and I feel two different women's fingers together pushing up into my cunt hole, which is so wet they add a third. A vibrator is applied to my clit and the woman underneath me has wet her finger in another girl's cunt and plunges up my own asshole, wet with a pretty girl's cunt juices. I cum again and again and then get down to eating other women. One woman spanks me and tells me what a bad girl I am, then makes me kneel in front of her with my legs so wide apart she can count my cunt hair. She pulls up her dress and tells me to explain what I see graphically, I say, "I see your cunt lips, I can see them so clear with fine blond hairs teasing me, hiding and inviting me to those fat pink lips." She puts her knees up on a chair so that now she has her cunt spread apart. "Now I see your cunt so clear, you are all pink with a brown clit that hangs out." She tells me to bend over, I do and before I know it she's fucking my cunt with a huge dildo she's strapped on. It feels nasty and delicious. She says, "You want to be fucked don't you little girl? You like me to fuck your cunt hard and deep. Your little virgin cunt hole is spread open now, baby. Tell everyone what a bad girl you are, tell them!"

Jessie

I am 21, single (and like it that way), am a singer/songwriter/ musician, and come from a very strict upbringing. My parents are very young (still in their late 30s), but have a very "fire-and-brimstone" attitude about premarital sex. But nonetheless, I am a very sexually oriented person and have slept with twenty men so far. When I was 17 I lost my virginity in the backseat of a large Toyota station wagon to a boy by the name of Jim. I cared very little about him but was in very desperate need to find out about sex for myself. It was the basic "Wham-Bam Orgasm," and I was left saying, "That's It?"

When I went to my mother to tell her about it, I was told I was a whore, a slut, you name it, I was it. So from that day on, I kept my sexual exploits to myself. (I only tell my two best friends.)

I am a heterosexual, but when I get hot and horny, I almost always fantasize about making love with another woman. It is a subject that, even if I was ever offered a romp in the hay with a lady (and I have been), I would most likely refuse. But it is enticing. . . . So let's get to the fantasy shall we???

I envision myself performing at a nightclub where most of the audience is made up of males in gold chains and ladies of the night. (I have always looked up to a woman who actually gets PAID to do it.)

I am singing "Burning Up" by Madonna (and incidentally I do sound and look a great deal like her—apart from the fact that I'm a little on the heavy side), when this beautiful Marilynesque creature hands me her phone number and says she is "burning up" with desire to eat me. I quickly finish the set, and she is waiting for me. We leave the pleasure palace to go home—to MINE.

The woman is beautiful—platinum hair, large bust, and a very slender body. I am trembling all over. The thought of her painted red lips on my vaginal lips makes me almost come. She says, "I'm hungry," and proceeds to kiss me.

She slowly kisses my neck, and I start dripping, oozing, sexual juices. I take off my blouse and jeans, and she eagerly does the same. We start kissing again, and she takes my breast out of my black under-wire bra and begins to nurse. By this time, I am moaning with pleasure. She pushes me onto the floor, rips off my panties, exposing my pussy in all its wet, juicy glory. "Ah, the main course," she moans, and goes right for my cunt.

She knows exactly what she is doing, and she spreads me apart with abandon. I am screaming "Eat it—EAT IT!!" Her tongue is extremely long, and at first she is teasing me by nibbling my clitoris, and then fucks me full force with her long gorgeous tongue. Faster and faster she licks and pumps it into my cunt, till I am writhing in ecstasy. I scream at the top of my lungs and squirt my love potion all over her beautiful face and swanlike neck. Come is dripping from her chin as she kisses me full force on the mouth, letting me taste myself, and this makes me come again. I tell her to get into doggie position, and she does so with no argument. Her pear-shaped ass is up in the air, and I part her and start licking her clit as if I had done it for years. I ram my tongue up her sacred vessel, pumping and shaking my head as fast as I can. I stick my finger up her asshole, fucking her with it, and she comes instantaneously. Oh my God, does it taste good. Her cunt juice is running down my neck and onto my D-cup tits. I lick her clean, slide down on the floor, and we do a 69 until we just can't come anymore. Afterwards, we part ways, but she promises to come and hear me "sing" again.

I am dripping wet right now. If my mother only knew . . . I am going to dream tonight of my "Marilyn" having her "last supper."

P.S. I just want to explain that I have a very healthy, active sex life with men, and I enjoy men a lot. I enjoy their pricks in my pussy, I enjoy giving blow jobs. But I enjoy them eating me more than the actual fucking itself. I also had an abortion some years ago, and so I think that the act of oral sex with a woman is a pleasing thought to me because you cannot get pregnant that way, and I absolutely love to have my pussy licked, sucked, nibbled on, etc.

Dana

This fantasy keeps me very warm on my nights all alone in the big city.

My best friend Laurie and I go to the beach; it's actually a very special beach, because it's a nude beach. When we arrive there are very few people around—just dark blue sea, bright blue sky, hot sun, and a wide expanse of sand.

We lie down side by side on my long fleecy towel, and the sun starts to warm us. As it sinks into my skin, I get hotter and hotter and decide to take off my suit. Then I lie totally naked and I feel a little chill as I realize, one more time, how much I want my dear friend.

She starts to pick up my vibes, comments on how hot the sun is, and removes her suit as well. The beach is blessedly deserted.

As we lie there, only a few inches apart, I ask her if she would put some oil on my back. I roll over on my stomach, and I feel her soft hand come stroking down the length of my spine, smoothing warm oil all over me. Her hands move over my body as she bends over me, massaging my shoulders, my shoulder blades, my ribs, and down to the small of my back.

Then I feel the weight of her body as she sits squarely on

top of my thighs. She massages my ass with a little more oil, gently lifting each cheek in her hands. By now my cunt is getting wetter and wetter, and I roll over on my back. We look at each other, and I can see how turned on she is. She asks if I want oil on my front, and I nod.

She slowly pours it over my breasts and my stomach and rubs it in gently, in soothing, circular strokes. By now I am massaging her back with some oil. She bends down and lovingly kisses me, her tongue probing into my mouth. I respond, and we kiss and kiss. As her body rubs up against mine, I can feel her breasts press against mine.

She has the most beautiful body, which is now wonderfully slippery in the pool of oil on our skin! She slides her body over mine, kissing me hungrily, and I reach down and caress her vulva! It's wetter than I ever imagined it could be, and as I start to stroke it, she leans back and invites my body to come on top of hers. I slowly slide my body down until I can kiss her stomach, her thighs, her pussy.

She opens her legs very wide and begs me to eat her. I take some oil in my hand and rub it over her thighs, her buttocks, her cunt. Her juices are pouring furiously, and as I look up, I see her nipples are erect and beautiful.

Tentatively, I put my mouth to her cunt and drink in her beautiful juices. She holds her labia open with one hand as I move in and lick her clitoris up and down—in long strokes that cover her entire cunt. From her streaming vagina up to the top of her cunt, I lick her again and again, getting faster and faster. She is breathing harder and harder now. Her pelvis is shaking and jerking, and her lips part as she cries out. With my mouth buried in her mound, I can feel the juices wetting my face, running over her ass, as my own hips are contracting.

She pulls back and suddenly throws me down. Now she's on top of me, slipping against me—thrusting her tongue deep in my mouth. She takes out a dildo she has with her and shoves it up inside of me—I am so wet it nearly slips out—and it's a good eight inches long.

She starts shoving it up inside of me while playing with my clit. She then rolls me on my side, and produces another, smaller dildo she shoves up my ass—with both going, I can barely stand it.

The rhythm builds and builds, the dildo in my vagina going deeper and faster. She then takes it out, pushes me down on my back and buries her face in my cunt. With my legs up in the air, she covers my entire pussy with her licks, bites and kisses—moving her tongue in circles around my clitoris until I can't stand it a moment longer and I come and come and come, crying out violently.

I watch her masturbate herself to an orgasm then, sliding her dildo in and out, while circling her clit with her fingers. It's fast and violent. We then crawl together on the towel and curl up in each other's arms. We fall asleep in the sun.

Just for the record, I am a 26-year-old woman, single and an avid heterosexual. I have never made love to a woman, but think about it often. My wonderful boyfriend has his eye out for a suitable woman for us to ménage with, as do I. I look forward to the day when I can complete my fantasy.

Incidentally, I was raised in a very expressive, affectionate family and have freely masturbated since age 14.

Tracey

I am 26 years old, Caucasian, dark blond hair, light blue eyes, single, and a lesbian. I was raised in a family with one brother (four years older than I am), a passive mother and an alcoholic father who was physically and verbally abusive, although the abuse did not include sexual assault.

The following is a fantasy I had while masturbating with my vibrator (noninsertable kind) recently. In reality, I have met a woman, I'll call her Ann, and though she's not a raving beauty, she turns me on something fierce. When we first met, she spoke with a German accent, and her voice was so soft sounding that it got me wet! She asked me some question, and I was so excited that I didn't hear a word she said. She noticed my lack of response, asked if anything was wrong, and I responded, "I am one flustered woman!" It wasn't the most appropriate response, especially for a first meeting, but she engaged me in conversation quite easily.

She has a lesbian lover and so do I, and from what she has told me, I am not the only one having problems in my relationship that seem unsolvable. The fantasy goes like this:

We are coming out of a social rap group we both attend, and she offers me a ride home. I have been fantasizing about her all evening and so I eagerly accept. The conversation in her car is light—we discuss the cold Wisconsin weather, how well the meeting went, and finally, she engages me in deeper conversation as she opens up about how unhappy she is in her relationship. I tell her that I, too, have been having problems in my own relationship. We pass a restaurant, and though we are near my apartment, she suggests we stop for coffee there. It is crowded inside, and realizing that the walls have ears, we agree to leave and head for my apartment. My heart has increased its tempo at her suggestion, but I try to remain calm and casual, outwardly showing no signs of the emotional passion I feel for her. Once in my apartment, I put on a classical music station, and, thankfully, they are playing romantic music with lots of strings. I ask her to make herself comfortable and offer to make coffee, which she accepts.

We continue to discuss the problems we have with our partners until, tiring of the dismal topic, I ask her if she has ever had an affair. She says she has not. I then ask if she would consider having one now. She asks, "With you?" And I answer her by leaning in real close, touching her cheek and kissing her full on the lips, using all the passion I can muster. She looks surprised when I pull away, and I say, "Ann, I want you so badly," and kiss her again, this time wrapping my arms around her and pulling her close to my body. To my joy, she starts kissing me back, and soon I am all over her, kissing her cheeks, her forehead, and dwelling on her earlobe, my tongue darting into her ear, until she asks if we can get more comfortable.

I take her hand and lead her to my bed, and we neck for what seems like hours, fully clothed. She nibbles lightly on my neck, and I come, pressing my crotch into her thighs and moaning, "Oh, Ann, oh, that feels so good, oh my God!" Then she licks my ears, gently pushing her tongue in and pulling it out again, like a penis with a vagina. I come a second time, and she cannot believe how sensitive my neck and ears are. Realizing that she has been neglected, I am upon her, licking my way down her cleavage, into and around her bra. I can stand it no longer, and I quickly unbutton her blouse, deftly unhooking her bra with one quick movement. I bury my face in her ample succulence, licking and sucking hard, and she begins to groan. I push them together, gently, so as not to hurt her, and begin licking in side-to-side motions, getting both nipples at the same time. She is writhing now, rubbing her crotch against my thigh, which is between her legs. I remove her jeans and underwear and go down, having been soaked to the knee with her drippings. Parting her, I breathe gently upon her clitoris, then lick it, using just the tip of my tongue. She begins hopping up and down, and I grab her hips and hang on, never losing contact with her passion fruit. Her breath comes in rapid "Oh, oh oh's" as I increase the speed but not the light pressure, and soon my face is flooded with all that she has to give me. I continue to lick, making occasional journeys to her labia, and just as she is reaching to pull me up, she says, "Oh Jesus, I don't believe it!" and she begins to come again. Finally, both of us exhausted, I bring my face close to hers and we kiss, her juices still on me. We fall asleep in each other's arms, content.

Debbie

The only fantasy I have is a lesbian fantasy . . .

Her name is "Stevie" and she is beautiful. She stands in the living room, looking so sexy with her long, curly blond hair, dressed in tight jeans and a blouse that buttons down the front. (She happens to be a dear friend. She has no idea what I think of her in a sexual way, but she is such a beautiful person both inside and out, I suspect that she has or had some lesbian feeling, but I would not want to endanger our friendship by "making a pass.")

She turns around and smiles at me. I stand in the corner just looking at her. She asks me if I would like to take a hot-tub dip with her. I agree and we go to the hot tub. I go to put a suit on, and she tells me we should skinny dip. We get in. (There's wine and a little pot on the tray by the tub.) First, we both have a glass of wine and a puff. Then we start to talk to each other. The whole thing is so emotional. We both have a great desire for each other. She leans over and kisses me. I try to say, "I've never done . . ." She puts her finger over my mouth and tells me not to talk. She gently leads me out of the tub and into the bedroom, where there is a round king-size bed with bright red satin sheets. (We lie down and she becomes the aggressor, but I want to make love to her.) I sit up and ask her if she could lie back on the pillow and just let me look at her body, that I just want to explore her for the time being. She agrees and just relaxes and lets me discover.

As I touch her, I start asking questions about how this and that feels, what first made her sexually interested in women, and questions like that. (Dealing with the fact that I might be a lesbian makes me feel ashamed and embarrassed. Sometimes when I masturbate, I suddenly stop because I'm thinking about women!) Then we kiss long and lovingly. My hand moves slowly as I work my way down to her breasts and just feel their beauty, taking in all the pleasure as if it were my body being touched, with such deep satisfaction. Kissing her stomach, slowly working on the whole body, and discovering, I push her legs apart and feel the tender wetness of her "private part"! I move my face down in between her thighs, but I am not licking her, just looking. Watching her move to the motion of my fingers, touching her. Then slowly I lick her, feeling the softness of a woman's cunt instead of the roughness of a man's cock. I move my fingers all along her, from her cunt to her butt. She comes, and I finally taste her sweet love juices instead of the bitterness of men's "cum."

Although I would really like a woman to make love to me, I find it impossible to do. I'm not sure why, but I just can't.

341

Also, after reading what I've written, I've discovered that the feelings I have are not just fantasy. I really desire a woman's tenderness.

Deena
I am a college freshman, will be 18 in a few weeks, and am engaged to marry a 28-year-old man of Italian descent whom I love very much. He is the first and only guy I've ever slept with. I used to feel sort of deprived—you know, here is this world full of gorgeous guys and I have only tried one—but finally I realized that Dan is the only one I want to sleep with now.

I have fantasies involving Dan, myself, and my best friend, Elena. Most of these fantasies happened when I was first being initiated into sex. Elena and I were and are so close that I'd be lying there with Dan inside me, thinking, "Wow! She's wonderful, she should be experiencing this." A fantasy evolved where she would be experiencing it, and I was lying in bed beside her watching the expression on her face and her reactions. It was like watching myself make love, only with the added feeling of being able to share it with another woman. (I don't think I'd be interested in lesbian sex, though. The thought doesn't turn me on at all. That's interesting.)

Jackie
I have been married and divorced two times. I am 28 years old. I have a boyfriend now who is four years younger than me. We have a great sex life. He makes me very horny (and satisfies me very much); I love sucking his dick and balls and asshole. He really doesn't like me to lick his asshole. I don't understand why. He fucks me so good, in fact, my pussy is very wet right now, just thinking about it. I would like to tell you something I have been dying to do. I don't know how to go about it or where to go, or who to ask. I want to have sex with a woman, real bad. I want her to have the biggest titties so I can suck. I want to know how a pussy tastes. I am not lesbian, I just want a woman out of curiosity. I want a woman to suck on my boobs too and to suck on my pussy. I

342

would like to rub our cunts together. I would like to have a two-sided vibrator, so one end could be in my pussy and the other in her pussy while we hold each other and suck each other's tits. I've been really, really horny for a woman with huge tits. Where can I go, who do I ask? I'm kind of embarrassed. I've been thinking of answering an ad in one of those porno newspapers.

I'm five feet two inches, black hair, bust 36B, waist 26, hips 37. My nipples are bigger than silver dollars. That is a big turn-on to a lot of men I've had, even though my tits are small (I think they are). I think that's one of the reasons I want to be with a girl that has huge tits. I'd do anything to have a chance to fuck around with a girl.

Eve

Your writing allowed me to open my subconscious self, as I've been inclined to suppress my physical desires in the presence of others. I always thought I was the only female who masturbated by means of a running bathtub water faucet. What a wonderful awakening.

I am 23 years old, single. I come from a broken family. My father has been married three times. My last stepmother was so insecure, to the extreme that she interpreted the close father/daughter relationship between Dad and myself as incestuous. This conception of hers couldn't be further from the truth. She was a victim of insecurity and jealousy, which originated with her low self-esteem. The incest was all in her imagination: I was Daddy's little girl, who thought the world of her father. *However,* this implication of hers managed to brand me with a strange sense of guilt as far as my sense of sexual identity goes.

On the other hand, my innate sexual desires didn't go unrecognized. I have recollections as early as *age 6,* when I would rub my teddy bear up against my clitoris area, and I even tried the same thing with my dog when she was laying down. No one ever introduced me to this activity/behavior —it was simply my own initiation.

I have practiced a consistent and satisfying method of masturbation since age 11. I lay in the tub and bring my

343

crotch up to the end of the tub—below the faucet and let the warm running water trickle/dance/pound (depending on how horny I am) on my clitoris and vagina area. I achieve far better climax here than I've ever experienced with a man. The only time a penis really gets me hot is when it's just ejaculated, is warm and sticky with sperm. At this time I like it to run over my vagina area and circle my clitoris until I can't take it any longer.

I lay back and let the warm water do its thing to me. Fantasy comes into play—although I'm not a lesbian, I wouldn't turn down the opportunity should it arise. I imagine an attractive woman that I admire (usually famous) performing cunnilingus on me and me on her. I like the feel of her body, and my ability to arouse her seems to bring me closer in touch with my feelings as a woman. I feel so very feminine as I rest my hot mouth on her enlarged clitoris and run my tongue in a vertical and horizontal fashion, very slowly. She is doing the same incredible tongue work on my clitoris, and I am escalating. We are both absorbed 105 percent with each other, and there's no turning back now; climax has hit both of us simultaneously, and we rest our mouths on each other's throbbing clitoris and proceed to slowly lap up each other's labia/vagina area, savoring every juice.

Dottie

Your books have made me realize I am normal! I masturbate a lot, always to orgasm and usually with my fingers (once with a candle and a few times with those lovely fat pickling cucumbers!). I always fantasize when I masturbate—never have when I'm with a man. I am single, 25, white and college educated. I've slept with a total of eight men, and lost my virginity on my 22nd birthday to a 46-year-old man (it was a delightful, fun time!).

My first experience with masturbation took place in fifth grade with my girlfriend. We used to sleep over at her house in one full-size bed, and while lying on our backs next to each other, we'd hold each other's index finger and guide it all around each other's puss. She'd rub my finger all around her clit, trace her lips, and put it in her a bit. She called it a tour and would talk to my finger as she moved it all over her bumpy cunt.

I have never had an orgasm during sex and in fact have never had one with a man *present* in the same room. I am very shy about verbalizing my requests and say little more than my lover's name a few times and moan with the pleasure of just feeling him in me. But none of my lovers have taken the time to stimulate me to orgasm. Sometimes I can't wait for him to leave so that I can lie where he was and dip my finger in my hole and smear my clit while using one of my favorite fantasies. Sometimes I just read an excerpt from one of your books and jump right into the scenario.

Almost all my fantasies lead to lesbian thoughts. The thought of a woman touching me sexually and actually licking me, nibbling on my fiery hole and putting her warm tongue on my throbbing knob makes me wild and soaked (like I am now!). Here are some of my favorite fantasies:

1. I often stand naked before the mirror and play with my nipples as though I were being photographed several times for a *Penthouse* spread. I bend forward and hold my pussy lips open from behind so that I can see the silhouette of my lips in the mirror. I usually bring myself right off there and observe closely my face as my body quivers with orgasm.

2. A woman, very beautiful and toned, feminine but butch looking comes over to have my first lesbian experience with me. (She knows this is for me to live out my lesbian fantasy.) She is very experienced, and I am very inhibited. She talks softly to me and tells me to relax and get comfy. I put on a sexy, snug negligee top with pretty panties—the top shows off my firm, large tits. She takes off her coat and has on a one-piece, crotchless black negligee. She stands behind me and hugs me from behind—massaging my nipples while pressing her crotch into my rear. I throw my head back and grind into her movements. I am dripping now, and my crotch is soaked. She moves her hands to my wet spot and teasingly presses on my clit. She turns me around and lays me on the bed. She sits on my belly (straddling me) and her juice is flowing onto me. She dismounts and gives me a long,

deep, fiercely passionate kiss—licks her juice from my belly and kisses me again. She tells me I am hot and creamy and to prepare for a soaring climax. She parts my lips and presses her mouth on my swollen clit—she circles it with expertise and tells me I taste marvelous. Her tongue darts in and out of me, and I feel an orgasm coming on—I hold off while she kneels next to my head and reaches down to my cunt with a huge dildo in her hand. She rubs my clit with the head of it and, as I tell her "I'm coming," she thrusts it in me and uses her other hand to stimulate my clit. All the while watching my face. She tells me how sexy I look when I am in ecstasy and then licks me clean. We continue to fuck around all day long until I can clearly say what I want her to do to me without any inhibitions.

In real life I'd be too nervous to have a lesbian encounter (everyone knows everyone), but it could be great. Who else would know better how to jerk me off besides another woman? I plan on marrying and having a family one day. I will work on unleashing my inhibitions when I find the man I plan to marry. Until then I plan on counting on myself for those beautiful climaxes—unless a lover is very candid with me and encourages me to guide him to bring me off.

Alexis

I have found that most younger, liberated women are simply astounded to discover that we older women without partners not only think about, fantasize about, dream about having more idyllic sex before life ends, but also that some of us pleasure ourselves by masturbating, reading *Playgirl* and Anaïs Nin, and watching cablevision's steamier early-morning offerings.

Let me give you an encapsulated version of my life story. I am a widow, 61, live alone and am not employed but instead consider that I am "perfecting the arts of leisure."

My husband died thirteen years ago, after we had been married nearly thirty years. We had married when war marriages were common occurrences; I was 19, he was 26. His only prior sexual experience was a single visit to a prostitute shortly before our wedding; I suspect his Air

Force buddies encouraged that visit in order that he should not be embarrassed with me, as I had been married at 17, divorced at 18, and had a child.

I did not know I had a clitoris until about seven or eight years into my second marriage; then I decided I must be missing something, and so I bought that staple marriage manual by Van de Velde, *Ideal Marriage.* After that I quickly learned that I am multiple orgasmic, and the marriage bed became an even more heavenly arena!

When my husband was 48, he had a serious heart attack, and that put an end to our idyllic sex life. He lost all interest in making love with me, became withdrawn, noncommunicative, depressed, and from then until his death from coronary artery disease eight years later, my life with him became a hell of frustration and torment, wanting him, feeling the loss of his wanting me as rejection of me, yet remaining faithful to him because I still loved only him, and because I had vowed to be his in "sickness and in health." I know this sounds old-fashioned now, but it was my choice then.

I had been so hurt and embittered by what I then interpreted as his rejection of me (though I now understand more completely what was behind it) that after his death I made a deliberate choice never to allow another man into my life—no more hurt, no more vulnerability, I thought. For a dozen years I repressed my sexuality, barricaded out that whole aspect of my personality, busied myself with other interests, turned myself into an asexual, neuter-gender being.

Then, last spring, something wonderful happened to me: nature will not forever be denied, so I fell in love! It came as quite a shock to me, since I believed myself immune, to discover that I was strongly attracted to a much younger neighbor (37), whom, until then, I'd considered merely a friend. Instantly, it seemed, all the desire and passion I had successfully repressed returned with such force that I became as horny as a 20-year-old. Within months he was offered a better job in another city and moved away.

I am once again permitting myself to be a sexual being, a

whole, complete woman. Those complacent years when I was half alive (which also reads "half dead") are over and never to be repeated. While I do not currently have a partner, I am, or consider myself to be, sexually active, because I have finally mastered the art of masturbation, at age 61, and it has given me a fabulous sense of my own worth and my own sexuality. I am now "youthing," as Sondra Ray calls it, instead of aging. A new woman friend commented to my daughter that I am "the youngest person she has met since moving to this city." I have never felt better about myself or my life!

My sexual fantasies began around the age of 10, when an aunt and an older cousin, suspecting that my puritanical mother would never tell me the "facts of life," took it upon themselves to supply me with stacks of old *True Story* and *True Confessions* magazines. Though tame by today's standards, those publications were tantalizing to me then; they seemed to titillate me with all sorts of hints of future bliss, and I buried myself in their pages for one whole summer vacation, becoming in imagination the leading lady in my favorite stories.

Throughout my school years and during my working years I must have fantasized about dozens of boys and men—fellow students, coworkers, librarians, ministers, teachers, friends—wondering what *it* would be like with them, yet remaining faithful to one man whom I loved at the time. I have had sex with only three males, two of them my husbands, yet I have by now enjoyed hundreds in my daydreams and fantasies.

Lately, though I have never had a sexual experience with a woman, because all of my new women friends are younger lesbians, I have begun to fantasize about them, or about some younger woman I may meet through them. Given the handicaps faced by selective women of my age in finding a suitable male partner (age taboo, or married, or gay, or with a younger woman, or already dead), I believe a lesbian relationship is a promising option for the older women, though I shall never lose interest in males. It seems to me that a close, loving relationship is what matters, regardless of gender. My daughter is a lesbian, and I have had gay friends all my adult life, both men and women, so I feel very comfortable in considering an alternative sexual relationship for myself.

I wonder how many other women past 60 might be out there fantasizing as I am doing, or how many may still bear effects of Victorian attitudes of their childhood, which do not permit their imaginations to roam at will, lest they should sin.

CHAPTER THREE

INSATIABLE WOMEN:
THE CRY FOR "MORE!"

I've always suspected that women have richer, wilder fantasies than men . . . Men are only beginning to perceive the true nature of woman's being. They have created a false image of her. She is neither an angel nor a bitch in heat. If she is no longer an enigma, she is certainly an everlasting source of wonder and rich in unexplored possibilities in every domain of life.

HENRY MILLER, 1973

When Henry Miller wrote those words in a letter to me after reading *My Secret Garden,* he was voicing a suspicion that patriarchal society had tried to keep under wraps since its inception: that women's sexual appetite might be prodigious, beyond men's comprehension and ability to satisfy. I regret Henry Miller is not alive to comment on the fantasies in this chapter; that first collection expressed a ladylike appetite compared to these new women, whose voracious quest for ever more erotic stimulation poses any number of problems, not the least of which is, What do you do with a woman for whom one man is not enough, whose sexual identity is structured on breaking the rules, defying authority?

These are, of course, just fantasies, but I would point out how many of them have been lived out and how many more the women say they would enjoy experiencing. Listening to these sonorous voices as I sit here writing in a world still strongly defended against women's sexuality, I can't help wondering how these women deal with the cultural split in which we live. Even as they talk of sex with four men, they must know as well as I that there is a persistent, dug-in part of our society that refuses to admit that they, these women, exist. But perhaps that is part of the excitement of being the fastest girl on the block while all around, the Nice Girls (mother) purse their asexual lips. Never underestimate the thrill of the forbidden.

THE THRILL OF THE FORBIDDEN

My own fantasies tend to fall here; they have always centered around defying authority, taking an enormous risk by secretly stepping outside the role of Nice Girl, by which I still define myself. My fantasies play with guilt like a spool of silken thread that strings out my pleasure and teases me with ecstasy; I have no doubt that breaking the rules, risking loss of my Nice Girl status, was essential to my emotional separation from my mother and into my own identity. That this theme of fantasy has remained with me all my life— despite whatever obvious identity I have established in reality—will tell you how much we all remain our mother's/ society's daughter, or to put it another way, how crucial the role of sexuality is to our full identity and, therefore, how carefully it should be nurtured and developed from our earliest years. Had I felt that my sexuality, my body, my genitals, were lovely when I was a very little girl, that they were as highly prized as my good manners and excellent grades at school, and that, in particular, masturbation was acceptable, would I, and the other women in this book, have had to fight so hard and break so many rules to overcome guilt and regain what is ours?

My fantasies, like Cara's, often occur in public places; they contain a constant element of time running out and the possibility of being caught—before my orgasm, of course.

Cara's masturbatory thrill of daring to go down on a man in a public restaurant clearly has its origins in her defiance of parental attitudes about sex. Cara hasn't actually done anything; that is, she is twenty-two and a virgin. But she is deeply guilty about her sexuality and fights to own it in her fantasies.

Some men find it very exciting to act out the kind of fantasies women like me have. Some men find women who gamble, take risks, to be the height of excitement. Others wouldn't touch us with a ten-foot pole. It is so unlike what they expect. In a word, it is *unladylike.*

A sculptor who discovers a flaw in a piece of stone will change his design in midstream so that the seemingly intractable gnarl or crack becomes incorporated into a larger conception of the work, giving it a feeling of un-planned spontaneity. The ingenuity of women in this section—and of many throughout the book—turns the hindrance of sexual risk and danger into the advantage of sexual excitement.

Our desires for the taboo are born out of the emotions left over from the time when we came in conflict with our earliest authority: mother. She taught us we must not wet our beds, we must control our infantile frustrations. If she won then, we are going to get our own back now. Even when we were children, the best games included the thrill of getting away with it. In fantasy, the thrill is especially strong when the person to be fooled or eluded is an authority figure—as in Sheila's fantasy, where she only has to think of the "prudish" antisexual things her mother has said to her and she has a "great climax."

Why do we so often think of our mothers not as women like ourselves but as prudes? Mother has worked so hard to keep the sexual dampers on us that she has come to live in our eyes as some kind of vegetable life. Without thinking about it, the younger woman has already thought about it, and has unconsciously decided that her mother's sex life is long over. It happened in such a dim, distant past that mom cannot possibly remember or understand the trembling excitement her daughter is feeling. It is very difficult for us at any age to envision our parents in the sexual act. If you don't believe it, close your eyes right now and try to summon up the picture.

If part of the thrill of the forbidden is the defiance of someone else's authority, a second, more affirmative part is based on a reverse desire to establish our own. Getting what is forbidden is a way of struggling to grow, to achieve autonomy. To reach for what we've been told is beyond our grasp is a way of testing our limits to the full. We are determined to master our own circumstances.

The height of excitement for Andrea is to secretly defy the very learned and public institutions in which she has been educated and now works; she masturbates late at night in "my own public/private space"—an empty library, concert hall, or museum.

Sue Ellen's rebellion against early authority is expressed first in her fantasy of sex with another woman, which quickly includes a dog, a man, then two other young men, and ultimately a priest and a nun. Men have always felt free to use forbidden, religious figures in their written descriptions of sexual adventures: Sade often described scenes of virgins being raped by monks and priests. Casanova's writings abound with stories of sex with nuns. In contrast, women thought of religious figures only in their most saintly context. Traditionally, women needed the authority of the church to help them tame men. Many women today want to be less tame themselves.

Fantasies like Sue Ellen's show a new desire on the part of women to reject the church as repressive sexual authority. Her anger at that authority is apparent in the cruel way she ties up the religious figures in her fantasy. She forces them to perform sexual acts against their will, and when they find that despite themselves they love the feeling, Sue Ellen is condoned for loving the feeling too.

Religion puts us into conflict with our own sexual desires; the way most of us experience religious instruction, sex comes out as dirty or holy. Either way, we must not do it, which makes many of us angry. People like Sue Ellen will no longer suffer this without protest. In fantasies like hers, we see women rehearsing their new determination to achieve control in areas of conduct where they feel it has not been permitted to them. If part of Sue Ellen's thrill in her fantasies is a childish thumbing of her nose at authority, the other part is the expression of a grown woman giving herself permission to stop letting others tell her how to run her life.

Women used to feel that if reinforcements of sexual scarcity (like religion and marriage) were swept away and sex were made psychologically and economically free, we would have nothing to offer. Our sex, our virginity were "our greatest treasure." After marriage the withholding of sex became our greatest power. In a free sexual world, without a partner to whom we belonged and who belonged to us, we feared we would be invisible, devalued. Instead, sexual freedom has been our salvation. We have learned that our value is in the world, not in the role of sexual inhibitor.

Writers like Dickens, Proust, and Dostoyevsky had the ability to intuitively penetrate the guilt barriers and descend into the deepest layers of the unconscious. Many of the women in this chapter do not recoil from the steamy jungle of emotions they find there. If Dostoyevsky could look within himself and recognize the emotions of patricide and child molestation, these women are unafraid to face their own desires for sexual domination, incest, pedophilia.

We used to ask why more women did not produce works of art comparable to *The Brothers Karamazov.* The larger part of the answer was clearly social conditioning. In the past, culturally sanctioned goals for women did not include explorations of the unladylike emotions with which literature deals. "Anonymous is a woman," Virginia Woolf said. It was her speculation on why some of the finest poetry that has come down to us through the centuries has been unsigned.

No longer. As economic, intellectual, spiritual, and yes, sexual limits have been removed, more of us have had access to the limitless pool of energy that is the creative spirit.

I have heard writer's block described as "mother sitting in the unconscious with a blue pencil." She sits there still, but with identities of our own, more of us can look her in the eye and decide what are *her* judgments of good and bad, right and wrong; what are ours.

Don't misunderstand me; these fantasies are not literature. But each is an individual woman's fingerprint, a burst of creative energy, a form of self-acceptance with which literature must begin.

Andrea

I had my first orgasm when I was 2½. I know this because we moved house shortly thereafter and the fantasy which gave rise to this thrilling discovery occurred in our first house. It was a tiny dark apartment in the depths of an industrial city. I had once seen cows in a field on a day out and had been taken by the farmer to the milking barn. I watched the hot steaming animals munching on what was described as a "cow cake." I could see their breath, smell the milk, dung and straw, listen to their contented chomping and the hiss of the milking pumps, and feel the all-pervasive warmth of their bodies. It was the machinery, the polished steel milking apparatus, the long pink rubber pipes, the pulsing vacuum and the soft suck of the pumps which were attached to the "udders." The word still makes me shudder. Soft, velvet pink bloated sacks with pendulous fingers. They arouse me. Back home, remembering the cows and the milking barn made me feel excited. I thought it must be very pleasant to be a cow, and as I found myself pretending to be milked, my arousal increased. I stole some wheatmeal biscuits from the larder and broke them into little pieces to simulate the "cow cake." I put them under my pillow until nighttime came, I ate them without using my hands. I imagined having the cold metal suction device on my genitals. I thought of the smells, sounds and heat, and I came. I didn't even touch myself, but swayed gently like a beast in a stall.

My second fantasy came later, about 4 or 5, when I had

discovered and mastered the art of masturbation. Cows were replaced by horses. I became a knight, riding into battle. A brave, fair handsome youth. I imagined being prepared for battle by my squires, who washed me with oil and balm, swathed me in soft undergarments like bandages and then riveted me into the cold metal armor. It was heavy and protective, but beautifully engraved with gold and silver eagles and griffins. It both enhanced and protected my youthful body. It made me powerful; a hero. I was hoisted onto my shiny black charger, my lance, shield and sword strapped into place, and I was off, at the very front of the brigade. The horse flew, lunging toward the enemy, faster and faster, till I was dizzy with fear and excitement. Of course, I fell with the first shower of arrows, having been pierced through the heart. My horse fell with me, panting and snorting in its death throes. I lay injured, feeling the warm blood running down my chest and arms inside my armor. Before I died, a young knight stopped by my side, opened my visor and unbuckled my breastplate. He kissed me, stopping my wound with his bare hands, but it was too late. Dying was orgasm.

These days it's more difficult. I've tried violence, rape, whorishness, striptease and every conceivable combination of multiples. I'm left with my imagination and its unpredictable and infrequent vaults. Perhaps I know too much. Perhaps I have experienced too much.

But, if I go late at night to an empty place, a museum, old schoolroom, library, concert hall or deserted house; a place where there are usually people, or where people used to be, then I can masturbate in my own public/private space. There I am, in front of a full auditorium, hiding behind the stacks in a thoughtful library, or in front of my favorite painting or a beloved teacher. It's a ritual affirmation of what we all have but which we will only ever know of our individual selves. The perfect oneness.

I am 40 years old. English. Born and educated in the cold North. A city dweller all my life, until recently, I studied art history and theater and got wound up in the workings of medieval stage machinery for a while before becoming a

painting conservator, onetime museum director, and thereafter a chameleon of faux techniques: a limner.

Sheila
I am 20 years old, masturbate several times every day, and
have absolutely no trouble at all bringing myself to fantastic
orgasms in minutes. But I have two very close girlfriends
who not only don't masturbate at all, but change the subject
every time I try to talk about it. Neither one has ever had an
orgasm. One of them is a virgin, but the other, Karen, has
had sex with a man several times and still has never
masturbated or had an orgasm. She can't even bring herself
to put in a tampon, so she uses pads. I think your books may
help women like my two friends to become aware of the
fantastic pleasure that their bodies are capable of giving
them.

When I am with a guy I don't fantasize that much, but
when I am masturbating I love to fantasize. My fantasies
enhance my orgasms so much and they are never ever boring
since I can always think up something new if the usual ones
get tiresome. My mother is a prude in the truest sense of the
word. If she knows a girl has even let a guy touch her breasts
she calls the girl a whore. Crazy as it seems, I can have a
great climax simply by thinking of the stupidest, most
prudish things my mother has ever said to me. In real life I
find these sayings of hers revolting, and I think I get the most
intense pleasure out of them at orgasm time, because I am
thinking, "Ha! Ha! You make me sick, but look at the fun I
am having," or something like that; something to the effect
that I am "showing her." Why, I don't know, but I no longer
worry about it. Anything that works is just fine with me.

I love sex, sexy books, movies; etc., and everything
connected with it and have a sexual drive which makes it
necessary for me to climax several times a day. I only wish
our society was different and that women had different
socially sanctioned roles than they do. Men are supposed to
enjoy everything and women are not supposed to enjoy
anything. I love to do everything with a sexy, nice man, but
most of them get turned off by the way I enjoy it so much

and think of themselves as having gotten something from me, having used me. I don't understand why they think anyone has used anyone, or why they don't think it was me using them. I hope the world changes very soon, or at least that I will finally meet some men who do not think that they are the only ones who love sex.

Sue Ellen

I am 24 and have been married for three years. Like most of the women in your book *My Secret Garden,* I have kept my fantasies to myself. Because they are my own personal Secret Garden, I want to share them only with you. After reading your book, I am relieved to know that I am not perverted or different. I am confused about my sexuality, even though I have only been involved in heterosexual relationships. Now to my fantasies.

All of them begin with me driving a van, alone, down the Pacific Coast. I always pick up the same beautiful woman, who is hitchhiking. One of my favorites is, after picking her up, I tell her that she can clean up in the back of the van and get some of the dust off. She leaves and undresses in the back. She has a marvelous figure. (I am watching through the rearview mirror.) When she starts washing her pussy, I get all turned on and start masturbating. She notices what I am doing and tells me not to waste an orgasm on myself, that she would like to share it with me. I pull the van to the side of the highway, and both of us race to a large field with tall grass and flowers. She lifts up my skirt and tells me what a beautiful pussy I have and how hungry she is. She then starts licking me and sucking on my clit. We are both undressed in the tall grass, and in a 69 position, devour each other's juices.

Unbeknownst to us, a young, good-looking guy with a German shepherd dog is watching us moan and groan with delight. He masturbates the dog until it is ready to come and leads him behind my girlfriend, who is on top of me. I notice the bright red tip of the dog's cock as the boy mounts him on my partner, who is unaware of his presence. Finally, she (the hitchhiker) realizes what is happening and squeals with delight. I take my mouth off her moist cunt and start licking the dog's balls, which are hanging over my face. Meanwhile, the boy drops his pants, exposing a huge penis, kneels in front of my partner and slowly slides it into her frothing mouth. By some miracle, we all come at the same time.

Another fantasy I have quite often is being in the van with the same woman, parked near the beach. After mutually masturbating, she says she needs a good fucking with a man, so we look out the window for some prospects. Two boys in their early 20s come up from behind a sand dune, carrying surfboards. We invite them into the van, offer some wine, take off our bikinis and start to casually play with each other. We can tell the boys are turned on because their swimsuits are bulging. Before long, we each select "our boy," and with them sitting side by side, we proceed to suck them until they explode in our mouths. Shortly thereafter they fill our pussies with their youthful come. After the boys are through and decide to leave, my girlfriend tells them the party isn't over and tells them it is time for them to amuse us! Much to my surprise, she pulls out a pistol and threatens to kill them if they don't cooperate. They are scared to death, and are told to assume a 69 position with each other. To make sure we won't be cheated, she and I masturbate them while they are sucking. This assures us that they will come in each other's mouths. I have multiple orgasms when I feel "my" boy's cock pulsating and jerking, and I watch the startled expression on his buddy's face.

I have saved my best one till last. It involves picking up a stranded priest and nun at a bus stop. As we move down the highway, my beautiful blond girlfriend takes out her pistol and makes them handcuff each other with their hands behind their backs. We pull over to a lonely stretch of beach and strip them. The priest is naked, but the nun has her headdress on. The nun is then forced to sit on a small side table with her knees up and her ankles pressed to her thighs. Her ankles are then tied to her hands behind her back, exposing her virgin pussy for all to see. My girlfriend performs cunnilingus on her until she cannot resist anymore while I fellate the priest to get him ready. After the priest's cock is hard as a rock, we stand him up next to the table. I guide him into the nun's now moist cunt as my partner pushes him from behind. The nun begins moaning in quiet ecstasy as I suck on her hard nipples, and my friend slowly moves him in and out of her by pushing and pulling his hips. He tries to hold back but he can't, and after he comes, I finish her off with my tongue while drinking in his still-warm, liquid gift to her.

I have many other fantasies but must stop now as my panties are drenched (you know how icky that feels), and I must "take care of myself."

Lititia

I'm lying here in my bed on a sensual Saturday afternoon—sensual because your book has me quite aroused.

I'm a tall, long-legged blond woman, 31 years old. I have quite an active fantasy life, yet I find it difficult to meet men I'd really like to fuck. Usually my lovers have been foreign men or men from different racial backgrounds than I. I have never been married and have no children. I live in the suburbs of an East Coast city and have a college education. I am originally from "the Bible Belt," where *I* was as a child the religious one of my "redneck—good ol' boys" family. I was quite pious. I was quite prim and proper, taught Sunday school and Bible school, and was "saved" properly.

I was a virgin until my 22nd year, when I moved to the city and asked the first urban man I met to teach me to fuck. He obliged, and we had a great time. The next man I dated was another uptight religious one who judged me for not maintaining my virginity!! Anyway, I concentrated *all* of my sexual energy (and I have *a lot*—I'm very much the Aphrodite Woman) into seducing the religious one, and of course I did. After that I sampled the wares of many different men and had several relationships. I've been in therapy to deal with fear of emotional intimacy and the residue of fundamentalism that shamed my core self. So—today I accept

360

and love myself as I am and get off with my great fantasy material from the fundamentalist days:

I am approximately 14 years old, long, lithe, with small high and round tits, and an aching cunt I just don't know how to handle. I'm a member of a small church on the outskirts of town, and today is the annual spring cleaning. So I get to church, and the minister's pretty wife assigns me the second-floor closet. I'm feeling *so* horny, so as I sort through the piles of old books and papers, I start to play with my nipples, feeling them harden, and rubbing my clit through the outside of my tight jeans. Suddenly, I'm aware that the minister's wife is standing there watching me! Horrified, I stop, but she comes over and puts her hand on my shoulder and says, "Don't worry, honey, we have ways to help you with these problems of lust." She tells me to come back on Sunday afternoon at 3 P.M., and states that it is important that I wear all white.

So at 3 P.M. on Sunday, I enter the quiet church where the preacher had belted out a brimstone and hellfire sermon a few hours earlier. I have on a lay conservative white dress, white gloves, a white hat, white lace panties and bra, white stockings, and white high heels. My long straight blond hair is shining as I walk in looking for Natalie, the minister's wife. She greets me. She is a tall, thin, angular-featured woman with dark hair, almost masculine in appearance. "The reverend is waiting for us," she says. Oh my God, I think, she told him of my problem!!

We walk into the minister's study, with all his religious paraphernalia and books around. He is wearing the long robe he wears to preach. He is tall and broad shouldered, with blue eyes and blond hair. (Like the minister I had when I was 16!! Who I *know* was attracted to me—ah missed opportunities.)

The couple are in their mid 30s. Natalie tells Andrew of my lust problem. He raises an eyebrow, then asks me if I've been letting boys touch me. "Of course not," I reply. He explains that with his training as a minister, he is qualified to help me release the lust from my body and give it away, but I must desire the help with all my being. He must "examine" me to see how bad the lust problem is. He tells Natalie to unzip my dress, and he takes my hat off himself. She removes my dress, and I stand before him in my slip. I begin to breathe a little heavily as his eyes examine all of my body, lingering at my tits, and traveling downward. I feel my cunt coming alive, my clit swelling, and the achy feeling in my hole. With just his looking, my nipples harden, pointing out through the thin sheerness of my bra. "Take her bra off." Natalie complies. With his fingers, he reaches out and encircles each nipple. I gasp. Waves of arousal are washing over me. He seems to examine each nipple, closer and closer, until his tongue is on me, sucking and licking. Natalie stands watching, but I hear her breathing increase. Slowly he runs his hands around my hips, still licking my tits, and begins to pull off the white stockings. I kick off my shoes, and the stockings are off. I stand before him in my little white lace panties. Sticking his finger partway under, then stopping, he pulls the waist of the panties just a little way down and kisses me softly just inside my pelvic bone. I see Natalie on the couch, her dress pulled up, she is strumming her clit like crazy. "See—you help us *all* with our lust," the preacher coos. His big strong hands are suddenly inside my panties, touching all my hot and wet parts. He sinks his fingers into my hole, and I moan. Then he rubs my clit, which is as hard as a small rock. Natalie comes loudly. He then asks her to come back over, pulling my panties off while he talks. His eyes take in the full view of my cunt as he has me stand with my legs apart. He is on his knees. Natalie stands behind me with her arms around me, stroking my nipples. He tells her to lift my cunt lips so he can see better. She does, and my clit sticks out even more. Slowly, he comes closer and begins to lick my cunt. He runs his fingers through my straight blond cunt hair. He puts two fingers in my moist hole, withdraws one, and sticks it up my ass. Natalie lifts me up and down on his fingers as he licks my clit. My legs are practically around his head. As he continues to suck my clit, he tells Natalie to lick my asshole and finger me alongside his fingers. As I feel her tongue up

362

my ass and his on my clit, I come so hard that my body feels projected into the heavens!

Sometimes this fantasy is enough to make me come. I have other variations: the minister fucking me up the ass to maintain my virginity; he fucks his wife while he eats me; he teaches a teenage boy "to relieve my lust"; he spreads me on the altar and licks me to orgasm there; he fucks me on top of his desk; he tells me to come back when Natalie's not there—AND IT'S ALL IN THE NAME OF RELIGION!!

Because of the shame the church gave me, I never even masturbated until I was 30 years old! Crazy! Those churches have a lot of frustrated people in them, let me tell you. I'm so glad I woke up. Today I am getting my master's in feminine psychology. Perhaps there's still hope for me to change the old attitudes, at least in myself.

Cara

I'm 22, single, white and Catholic. Right now I'm a junior in nursing school. I've also gone through two years of college. I prefer men, but do have fantasies about women though I've never been with one. I do think, given the chance, I would go for it. Let me also say now that I am a virgin. The furthest I've ever gone with a guy is giving him a hand job and getting me frustrated. I've had a middle-class upbringing, and there aren't many things that I've wanted that I haven't gotten. So I guess you could classify me as a spoiled brat.

My earliest memory of a sexual encounter was when I was six. I had a very close girlfriend, and we would strip and rub our little bodies all over one another and kiss. We didn't know what we were doing but we knew it felt good. At about 9 years old there was this little boy who lived next door, and we used to do the same thing. I have felt guilty about these encounters as long as I can remember and used to pray never to see these two people again for fear they would bring up the subject. Gratefully, I no longer feel this way and would love it if they would bring it up so I could see how they feel about it.

Until I read *Men in Love* I thought men derived little pleasure from going down on women. I am so happy to be wrong. Though I've never had this done to me (except by my dog), the thought of a guy sucking and licking me blows my mind. I masturbate a whole lot, and oral sex is usually the main theme of my fantasies. I also like the idea of sucking a guy off. I've never done that either, and I'm not even sure I know how, but if someone would teach me I'm sure I'd prove to be an apt pupil. My only hesitation about oral sex comes from the fear that my cunt smells. I have smelled my own come and tasted it and it does absolutely nothing for me. But after reading what you said about males having a natural liking for it, I'm willing to take your word for it. So when the time comes and the guy's willing, I won't hesitate.

I have a liking for Orientals. It started with my "hard-on" for American Indians. For some reason those dark foxes make my juices flow. Since I was little, every time there was a Western movie on, I'd be glued to the TV in the hope an Indian would appear. My father thought I was interested in the history of the American Indian—the noble savage. He used to buy me book after book about them. The truth is those books were never read, but if there was a picture of an Indian on the cover, he saw more of my cunt than I ever have. (If Daddy ever knew what I was doing with those books!)

From Indians, my attention was drawn to Japanese, Koreans, Chinese and so on. I'm at the point now that any fairly decent looking guy who even looks remotely Oriental or American Indian sends shivers down my spine and straight to my cunt. I have one main fantasy.

I go on a date with my brother's best friend, whom I've had a crush on since I can remember. We're seated in a pretty secluded area at a table with a tablecloth over it. P. sits across from me and is dressed in a black tux and looks great. I'm wearing a black strapless dress that's fairly short, and I have on black spike heels. After we order and are sipping our wine and talking, I slip my shoe off and place my foot right between P.'s legs. He is quite shocked by this and looks at me for some explanation. I smile and begin rotating my big toe around the bulge in his pants. At this time the waiter comes over with the order, but this does not faze me in the least, and I continue my ministrations. P. is having a hard time keeping a straight face and moves in his chair a little so no one will see my foot. After the waiter leaves, P. opens his zipper, and I continue to manipulate him with my foot. After a while, P. is nearly jumping in his seat, so I "accidentally" drop a spoon on the floor and go under the table to search for it. No one sees me go under, and they think I've gone to the ladies' room. In the meantime, I give P. the best blow job he's ever had. In my fantasy, the biggest turn-on is my control and the expressions on P.'s face while I'm giving him a blow job. Him trying to look normal, eating and drinking while I'm under the table with his cock in my mouth, drives me crazy.

Connie
I am 18 and met my boyfriend in the fifth grade, and immediately we fell in love. This past June we both graduated from high school. We have been together the whole time, and he's never dated or screwed anyone else, and nor have I. I was his first and he was my first. The whole time we were in school we wanted each other but we didn't actually fuck until tenth grade. I was 15 and he was 17. (He is now 20.) He lives with his grandparents, and our first time was on a Wednesday, late afternoon, in his grandfather's garden shed. (Next to the garden fertilizer and lawn mower.) We had a bottle of baby oil, and we masturbated each other and had oral sex. It was fantastic! That was enough for us for that day. We didn't actually fuck until the next day, on the couch at my parents' house. Ever since then, we've had a very happy sex life and we've always had a happy relationship. We never tire of each other. All through high school, we'd fuck in the car or at a friend's house during a party or at a motel.

It was so exciting the first time we openly talked about masturbating. I have been doing that ever since I was 3 or 4. (Maybe I wasn't that young, but I do know it was before kindergarten.) We used to set a time, say 10:30 P.M. or 11

P.M., and when we were both in bed (at our separate houses), we would masturbate and then tell each other about it the next day at school in letters we'd write to each other.

I would get so wet and worked up I'd have to slink to the girls' room and wipe the juices from my snatch so they wouldn't seep through my pants. When we started making love, he admitted to not masturbating as much, but I still do, and I love it even more when he does it! Sometimes I'll do him for the fun of it. I love to give him head! Even when he's not feeling up to it, I'll beg and plead for him to let me unzip his fly and suck him dry. I simply love to do that.

Here is my fantasy:

Any policeman makes me wet, hot, horny, and wild for sex! Black men don't particularly turn me on, but if he had a uniform on and drove a white car with blue lights on top, color wouldn't matter. (I don't wish to fuck a cop, the idea just turns me on.) In my fantasy, I would be driving down a long deserted country road with forests on both sides. With the sunroof open and the music high. I don't realize that I am doing twenty over the limit. It just catches my eye that there are blue lights flashing in my rearview mirror. "Shit," I say and pull to the shoulder of the road and stop. He (oh God I'm getting so horny as I write this) steps out of the car about ten feet behind mine and slowly walks up to my car, shaking his head in disapproval.

"Ah, ma'am, did it ever occur to you that you were doing seventy-five in a fifty-five zone?"

All I can see is my reflection in his mirrored sunglasses, and I don't know where he's looking. His eyes could be savoring the firm roundness of my tits or the tantalizing curves of my smooth tan thighs, just barely covered by my tight white skirt.

I start to shake I am so scared, and all he's doing is standing as close to my door as he can (I'm wondering if he's doing this on purpose) and looking down at me with his head leaning to the side and his arms folded, the bulge of his load just peering over the metal of my door. (The window is down.) He tells me that he has to search me and take me in.

He opens my door for me (how nice) and I slowly step out, baring my whole leg all the way up to my sweet crotch. He has now removed his glasses, so I can see where his eyes are looking. They start at the delicate curves of my white spike high-heeled shoes and move up my bare, smooth, tan leg and reluctantly skip over my white mini and up my stomach to the tight cleavage between my tits. I begin to wonder what he has in mind, and this starts to excite me. I fully step out of my car.

"Turn around and spread your legs and lean on the car with your hands and arms apart," he says, and I obey. My bikini lace panties are just barely hiding my pink rosebud, and my love juices are caught in the lace. My clit begins to tingle and burn. He slowly bends down and places his hands around both my ankles and slowly starts to go up, tightening his grip when he reaches my thighs. He moves his hand around in front of my thighs and gently pulls my lace panties to one side and titillates my clit like a marble in oil. I can hear his heavy breathing and feel his rigid cock against my ass. Pressing harder and harder, he places his hands over my tits and squeezes. My nipples harden under his palms. He tells me to get into his car. Taking my hands down from the roof of my car, he pulls them behind me, and then I feel the cold metal rings of the steel he is putting around my wrists. He then walks me over to the door of his cruiser and opens the back door. I get in and savor the sweet, strong smell of leather while I gaze helplessly at my car through the black, small-holed fence in the middle of his car. Pushing me over to the other side of the seat, he gets in behind me, puts his hand right beneath my neck and slowly pushes until I am laying on my back. He removes my shoes and parts my legs, revealing my barely covered honeypot. Reaching over my waist, he pulls up my skirt. Taking a pocketknife from the floor of his cruiser, he gently cuts through the lace panties at the side of my hips. Taking them off, he slides down and puts his tongue into my pussy, separating my lips to find my clit as he goes up. Sucking hard, he reaches down and pulls out his cock. I am writhing with pleasure at this point. He stops and takes off the rest of his clothes and climbs on top of me, pushing his throbbing cock in my vagina. I push my hips up to meet his speed. He is pressing his pubic bone down awfully hard on my clit, and this leaves me delirious with pleasure. He tears open my blouse and sucks my uncovered nipples. Electricity shoots up and down my body as I feel him straining. I can feel his balls banging wildly against my ass, faster and faster as he thrusts into me. My muscles begin to tighten, and I hear him groan and feel his cock pulsate deep inside me. His hot come splashes against my vaginal walls. Just then I feel my orgasm coming in a wave high with pleasure and release. My sweet juice covers his cock and balls.

He unlocks my hands from bondage, and we clean ourselves up.

He then says, as he kisses me sweetly, "There. Maybe that'll teach you to obey the rules of the road!" We then go our separate ways.

I've been driving for about a year and I've never been stopped by a cop for anything. Every time I'm next to one at a red light or something, he'll casually look over at me, and I'll just smile in a devilish way and wish he could read my mind.

Kimberly

I am 19 years of age, lost my virginity at 18 (at college), am single (but seeing a wonderful guy), and politically conservative. I put that last part in because it seems odd to me to be conservative in one aspect and to be so liberal with the thoughts that go on inside of my head.

My family consists of a dad who is over 55, a mom who is over 45, a brother in his late 20s (married—lives away), and myself. My parents are the *real* religious type, which sometimes can be very unnerving (for instance, when I go to breakfast with a smile on my face after having a wonderful fantasy, and then they start to have devotions—guilt time). I guess that is part of the reason that I never told anyone about my fantasies. I prefer to enjoy them all by myself.

As for sexual preference, I have always been heterosexual; I find the male body too stimulating to look elsewhere.

I began having sexual fantasies at about the age of 10. I was in fifth grade, had begun to have my period, and was physically more advanced, so to speak, than the other girls in my class. The boys in my class would tease me about my growing breasts, the hair on my underarms and legs, and my rounding hips. After they would comment on this, I would go home and try to think of what it would be like to have an inanimate object explore my body. Here is what I fantasized.

Fantasy Number 1:
I am lying on a steel slab, totally nude, being pulled along by a conveyor belt. There is no one around, just me and the machine. The machine has a rectangular opening (where the belt runs through), but other than an on/off switch, has nothing on the outside. As I am finally pulled into the machine, a mechanical hand reaches into my vagina, and a green light above the hand goes off, meaning I passed the test of having a satisfactory vagina. The second arm manipulates my clitoris, and again the green light goes off. A third arm (all the while I'm being pulled through the machine by the belt) comes out and inserts a cold yellow rod up my anus, and the green light goes off. The fourth and last arm fondles my breasts. Here a red light goes off, the arm fondles some more. Then I find out that the light is stuck on red and the arm just keeps on fondling. By this time I was usually asleep, since I fantasized before going to bed. I feel it worthy of mention that at this stage in my life I would not masturbate or have an orgasm, I was just *thinking.* With my strict upbringing, I thought masturbation was "sick, evil, wrong . . ." and had no knowledge of what an orgasm even *was,* since my parents did not even say the word SEX or tell me what my body was like (or for).

Enter the high school years. During high school I never dated much, and if I did, it was rarely the same guy more than twice. I resigned myself to the fact that the "cute ones" were busy elsewhere, and I would have to figure out something to do on my own. And figure I did!!!

Fantasy Number 2:

I am invited to a "teen dance" by a guy that I really find attractive, John. John is older than I am, has a car, and can therefore drive us to the dance himself, rather than having to ride with his parents. John pulls in, in a red Mustang (odd, since I *hate* Mustangs!). He comes to the porch to escort me to the car. My parents are astonished he would be so polite! After we get to the dance, the band begins to play a s-l-o-w song. I am wearing an almost-sheer pink dress, off the shoulder, and short in length. He is wearing a black suit with an enormous overcoat. While we are dancing close, he puts his hand into the bodice of my dress, and proceeds to play with my nipples until they are very hard. As I brush up against him, I can feel a very tight bulge in the front of his pants. He pulls me in closer to him, covers us both up with his overcoat, and pulls down my panties to rub my clit, and I unzip his pants and play with his erect penis. When the slow song is finally over, John and I are so close to coming that neither of us wants to stop. But we must, at least for the moment, because as we look around we realize that we are the only ones out on the floor, and people are watching us rather strangely. We zipper up, readjust our clothing, and make a mad dash to the parking lot. We climb into his car, and look around to make sure that no one is near to us, and we both undress. We throw ourselves into the backseat, and he continues to rub my clit and fondle my breasts, and I am giving him a hand job. We keep this up until I begin to moan loudly (in real life, I am very noisy when I come), and he tells me he is about to go too. I arch my back as his fingers find their mark, and I scream in ecstasy as he ejaculates into my hand. He wipes off my hand, his penis, and then, ever so slowly, wipes my clit and cunt clean. He takes me home, and my parents commend me on such a fine choice for a date. I look at John, then at my parents and say, "Yes, going out with John can be *very exciting!*"

This is the first time in my fantasies that I had (Yea!) an orgasm. I can still remember how good it felt! Again, I was just *thinking* this, and they say the mind is a powerful tool!

My college years were when my real world became *almost* as exciting as the fantasy world. I remember the first week I was at school I had a guy come up to me and say that he would love to hear me moan while he "ate me out." Boy, I thought, college life will be *great!!*

College was the first place I masturbated. I was not in full view of my parents, and I guess the new freedom I was enjoying made it easy for me to do it. Five of my friends and I (three guys, two girls, and me) decided to watch a movie called *Body Double,* which contains a few scenes wherein a woman masturbates. Let me tell you, until that movie was over, my cunt was dripping wet! Of course the guys were making cracks about how big her "cunt lips" were and how her "tits jangled," and that didn't exactly help me feel less horny! After the movie was over, about 11 P.M., I gave the excuse that I was getting rather tired and was going to bed. Well, when I got back to my bed, I decided to try out the "technique" I had just witnessed. I laid down on my bed and put two pillows under my pelvis. I took off all of my clothes and began to rub my clit with my right hand. Gosh, it felt so good I decided to rub a little against my cunt too. When I finally put the palm of my hand over my clit and inserted my ring and index fingers into my cunt, the sensation was fabulous. After a few minutes, I had a terrific orgasm, and I came all over my hand. I was so relaxed I fell asleep as I was, nude and postorgasmic, and woke up the next morning with a devil-made-me-do-it smile on my face. I now masturbate (always to orgasm, luckily) almost daily.

Now it's time for one of my favorite fantasies.

FANTASY NUMBER 3:

This involves a cute guy, Charlie, who told me himself that he would love to go down on me. He has never done so, although he has felt me all over. Charlie comes into my dorm room and asks me to join him out in the hallway. I find this a bit unusual, since the hallway is crowded with my frat sisters (I was in a frat) and we cannot possibly hear each other talk. Nevertheless, I follow him out, and he tells anyone who happens to be listening that he is going to fuck me in the hall and he doesn't care who knows it or who watches. He yells for me to take off my clothes, which I do willingly. My roommate, Carol, is rather shocked that I would be so blatant about this, but goes on about her business up and down the hall. Another sister, Karen, asks Charlie if he would like some pillows to prop up my hips or a blanket to lie down on; he says yes, and she brings satin pillows and satin sheets, which she spreads ever so carefully down. (This is rather unusual, since Karen is a lesbian and does not enjoy men at all.) Two other sisters, Brenda and Cassie, proceed to rip the clothes off of Charlie's body, much to his (their) delight. The sisters move off in a kind of circle around us. Some watch, others continue to pace the hall. Charlie tells them to watch closely so that they will see a "genius" at his "best" work. He pries my legs apart so that I feel I will soon be ripped in half. He then kneels on his hands and knees and rubs his nose (which is rather large) over my clit. He then flicks his tongue over, around, and into my cunt. Charlie is all the while getting a hand job from Karen (again, strange). Charlie then leans a bit against Karen so that he can get a hand free to rub my cunt and insert a pinkie into my anus. I begin playing with my breasts (which are rather large), and look down to see Charlie's face moving closer, then farther away from me. I tell Karen to stop because I want to have Charlie all to myself. She obliges, and I ask Charlie to sit down with his legs spread apart. I lower myself onto his erect penis and bend his head toward my nipples, asking him to gently suck on them. I grind my hips, cunt, clit against him and pump and pump and pump. Charlie asks me to stop a minute and actually *feel* the blood coursing through our bodies. I do, but it is not very long until I just *have* to move. As I do, Charlie grabs on to me and we both can tell we are going to go soon. As his hot semen drives into me, I can feel my stomach muscles as if I was going to explode, and the next instant my come is drowning his cock. As we kiss, lip to lip in sweet abandon, we realize we are alone in the hallway. We just look at each other and smile.

I have masturbated alone in my room, in the shower (I could never get the stream-of-water orgasm exactly right), watching TV, driving to work (what a way to start the day), and talking to men on the phone. I adapt the fantasy to the particular mood that I am in. I do not enjoy masturbation without fantasy, so I have several to "make the moment." When I told a guy a little about my fantasies, he replied that I was just an "oversexed bitch," so needless to say, I now keep my mouth shut. Maybe someday I will find a man open-minded enough to share my fantasies and reveal his, but until then I will continue to enjoy what goes on in my own mind.

Just writing this has really absolved me of the guilt I carried with me for so long, relating to my dreams. It has even made me smile a little to know I "had it in me" to do it in the first place! (Write to you, that is!)

WOMEN WITH BIGGER APPETITES THAN THEIR MEN

In this chapter, women say things that shake the patriarchal system at its foundations. "I feel that women are much hornier than men and desire sex more," says Sophie, setting the tone in the 1980s for women's acceptance of their true sexual appetites. Whatever time in history you may be reading these words, remember that sexual fantasies are never "dated"; all erotic literature—*The Story of O,* the books of Anaïs Nin and Henry Miller—continues to arouse because there is nothing new in human sexuality; only the curtain of repression rises and falls.

Sexually adventurous women like those whose fantasies follow have always existed. But never so vocally, in such

numbers as today. They speak with the supportive knowledge that they are not alone in their sexual curiosity. They
began to "come out" in the 1970s in response to the sexual
permissiveness specifically asserted by women. The identification women found in the words and images of other
women's sexuality set a historical precedent: for the first
time, women were not punished but rewarded for their
sexual inventiveness. To understand how revolutionary this
is, simply turn on the late late movie; there are countless
versions of "wayward" women like Anna Karenina crushed
beneath the wheels of a train for sexual transgressions. No
matter how sympathetic the heroine, if she was an adulteress, she died. It wasn't until the 1960s that Hollywood,
guardian of our morals, became comfortable with scripts in
which the adulteress survived.

Could censorship and repression again return women to
the fate of Emma Bovary? Logic would say that women's
new economic power eliminates a sexual double standard,
that what we've been through in the past twenty years isn't
merely a phase but an evolutionary stage. Like the tide of
women still moving into the workplace—from which economic base this sexual phenomenon emerged—it will never
be reversed.

But sexual repression is not logical; if women cease to
control their reproductive rights, that alone could keep them
"in their place." Men and most women, too, have no idea of
the extent of women's sexual needs; the culture was designed to keep us ignorant. Men continue to ponder Freud's
question "What do women want?" with amused resigna-
tion, as if the answer were a new hat. The timid little man
hiding from the bossy woman in James Thurber's cartoon
hardly suggests that what may be wanted of him is "More
sex!"

Patriarchal society defined itself by the missionary position because only by putting women on the bottom were
men a priori on top, superior. When women like Bootsie
were struggling in the 1980s to wiggle out from under their
sexually boring husbands and flex a few erotic muscles, they

weren't sure how many other women out there were like them: "We have an unusual problem—or maybe it's not, I don't know," Bootsie confesses, "in that I have a more active interest in sex than my husband . . . I just plain like it! He, on the other hand, doesn't have much of a sex drive . . ."

But word got around pretty quickly in the 1980s. It was a decade of sexual information as well as excess, and by the mid-eighties women with low-libido husbands no longer worried that they were the only Bad Girls who wanted to stray. Certainly guilt never disappeared and never will. But women were learning to accept some guilt as a part of life; as figures on real infidelity soared in the early 1980s, more and more women learned that just thinking about something "illegal" provided the zest that took them over the top. "I love sex . . . which my husband never has really cared about," says Joyce, whose fantasy "has always been to make love, deliciously, wickedly, all day long and all night." Following her "aggressive" nature, she turns her fantasy into reality. She has an affair with her minister, which I suppose takes care of guilt.

Bernard Shaw once remarked that the reason for the enduring popularity of marriage was that it combined the maximum of temptation with the maximum of opportunity. Funny enough in Shaw's prudish age. Married or not, the Victorians felt there must be something wicked about sex if only because it felt so good. But today all too often marriage combines the maximum of opportunity with the minimum of sex. We all know the cliché about the couple who lived happily in sin but whose sex life went to hell the day they legally married. Many of us have also read the surveys that indicate that in our society, the wedded state serves men better than women. No wonder that as more women build an identity of their own, they are resistant to marriage.

Given woman's new fascination with the taboo, there is endless curiosity in her mind about the next man, even when there is a current man. The thrill of the forbidden stranger, left over from girlhood, is built into her. Even though today my conscious mind does not want another man and my life with my husband and my work is full, I still have fantasies of this mysterious—who? They almost kept me from marriage, so convinced was I that I could never be faithful.

At its best, monogamy is not something society has imposed on us but an agreement two people freely enter into, one that millions of people have chosen for centuries, so it must have powerful attraction, satisfy real human needs. For myself—and I believe it is true for many other women, too—I remain happily faithful, healthfully monogamous, because my mind is free to fuck whomever I choose. Deprived of sexual fantasy, "treated" by a doctor and trained to think only of my husband while we have sex or when I masturbate, I would indeed find monogamy not an ideal but suffocation, or a reason to avoid marriage.

It would be misleading to say this chapter is just about frustrated women whose men do not satisfy them. Many have full sexual lives, men with whom they are happy and satisfied. Still, they have fantasies of more sex, reels upon reels of sexual imagery, quantities of sex that often bear little relation to reason or reality.

If, in fact, a woman found herself on a desert island with ten naked men, handsome and willing, she would ordinarily become involved and satisfied with one of them and say to the others, "Why don't the rest of you get dressed and pick some coconuts? Harry and I are doing fine."

But in these fantasies, we find women who want two, six, ten, and twenty men at one time, women who not only delight in a single fantasy but have dozens that drive them into ecstasy. Vast appetites are revealed, hungers that rise far above anything a woman could handle in reality. These fantasies express a psychic need, a desire to experience all the possibilities of one's own body and desires, to make up for lost time. Women—limited for so long—want to seek their own true limits. Their fantasies of three and four men suggest they haven't found them yet.

Perhaps more than any other image, that of the Ultimate

Giant Cock can be seen as a metaphor of desire for the larger life some women crave. When I titled this chapter "The Cry for 'More!' " I meant more of everything.

Sex is never unrelated to the rest of life. It is symbolic of what goes on in reality, and the way a woman acts in sex has a relation to the way she sees and feels about herself in society. Women today feel they have a *right* to everything that until recently they could not even admit to thinking about. If a woman is not happy with her husband, she has a right to divorce him. If she is bored with work at home, she has a right to go out and get a job, and if that doesn't pan out, she has a right to return to traditional work. If she feels society has put limits on her sexuality, she has a right to break those limits.

Above all, these fantasies of having more than one man at a time are a reaction to the traditional role of passivity forced on women. Instead of idly waiting for one man to phone her, she creates a situation in which she has a dozen men available to her. No matter what else happens in the fantasy, the focus is on her. Having invented the scenario, assigned the actors their roles, the woman alone chooses what will then happen. The basic nature of fantasy is that she has willed it into being to satisfy her own specific needs.

Take Veronica's fantasy of sex with four men. She is twenty-one and practically on the eve of her wedding. In reality Veronica is having an affair with her fiancé's best friend; her favorite fantasy is of being with not just the two of them but, simultaneously, two of her fiancé's groomsmen. She has ". . . my two luscious holes being filled with the cream of the great loves of my life [which] sets off the greatest orgasm I've ever experienced." Veronica says that once married, she's going to turn over a new leaf; she wants to be a faithful wife. Perhaps the fantasy of her with her fiancé and his best friend, in which no one is jealous or judgmental, is not just thrilling but an absolution of her earlier infidelity. But why then include two more men? To satisfy another of Veronica's needs, voyeurism; this is, after all, her bachelor party. While two men fuck her, she can now watch the two others "in 69 position. This really turns me on, because I've never seen two guys together like this."

Not many women have, to my knowledge. The spectacle of two or more women sexually entwined has always delighted men, but the walls of Pompeii, the *Kama Sutra,* the murals in the gardens of Khajuraho—none of these illustrations of the ancient sexual rites of mankind depict men fucking one another for the delectation of a female audience. The obvious reason, I suppose, would be that early verbal and pictorial records of human sexual delight were all created by men for men.

Certainly nothing has opened women's eyes wider than television, film, and the growing supply of adult films. The many books on sexuality published in recent years are mentioned throughout this chapter, but a picture is worth a thousand words when it comes to sexual education. Enter the local video store. These women describe their sexual appetites as if they were ordering from a giant catalogue. Life has taught them that one man tires too quickly. They want extra men, and they want them with big, big cocks. Many of them faithfully insist that their husband's average-size penis is fine, but if you're going to create a fantasy lover, why not one with truly splendid proportions, so that he may produce "gallons" of come, enough to bathe in, enough to drown in?

Even if size is not central to the fantasy, there is rarely a mention of a penis without the preceding adjective, "Big," "Huge," "Giant." Behind the thought of wanting to be sated, filled, stuffed with a giant cock, overwhelmed by an enormous sexual experience, there is a famous Freudian maxim: "Behind every penis is a breast." It means a woman wants a penis to suck on, to enter her, a giant one that is hers alone to make up for the love, attention, warmth, kindness, tenderness, mother's milk and breast she didn't get as a little girl. When grown men try to find in a woman's body all the good warm things they got from mother—or wish they'd got—we understand their focus on the breast. Well, we all begin life dependent on a woman's body, and if a grown woman's sense of having missed something earlier that was big, lovely, and warm is displaced and sexualized, it can "feel" like what she wants is a giant cock.

Most men cut off all tenderness and affection not only after fucking but also before and during. They separate sex from affection. It is why so many women end up unfulfilled in sexual experiences; even if they have had multiple orgasms, if sex did not gratify their need for closeness and warmth, it is ultimately incomplete. We fuck with more than our bodies. Our emotions must be satisfied too. Some of these women say they couldn't physically endure, take in a man larger than their husband; but the giant warm cock they dream about is very satisfying on many levels.

Perhaps there is also a sense of omnipotence and confirmation of womanliness in these fantasies, especially today when women are trying to redefine themselves as "real women." The fantasizer sees herself as so womanly, so sexually powerful that she can take the ordinary man and turn him into Superman—thus proving she is Superwoman. Isn't there an element of the boast here—almost in the same way a man boasts about his size—that she is such a woman, of such great capacity, that no man is too big for her?

We are left to speculate on why the women in this chapter cannot fantasize directly about a larger life. They want something out of the ordinary and everyday, something so radically different from anything they've ever known that it will push them beyond all their limits, take over their lives. Why does this desire for transcendence find expression through sexual imagery? Perhaps because they cannot emotionally relate to the heroines on television and in women's magazines; what do they know of vast riches and enormous professional success? They have, however, experienced sex. Even if their men fail them, they are artistes of masturbation. They have single-handedly mastered orgasm.

Even the shiest woman can educate herself at the local book and video store. "With the help of a library filled with books (*Free and Female* was my favorite)," says Odette as early as 1980, "a dozen horny guys and a free supply of contraceptives from the campus birth-control clinic, I set about learning all I could about sex." *Playboy* and *Penthouse* to this day remain for women a continuing source of voyeuristic pleasure and information. While the idea of men hungrily poring over photos of other naked men doesn't gel, women have a sexual elasticity: at any time, provoked by images of either sex, women can be aroused. And we wonder why men felt it necessary to repress women's sexuality.

More than any other medium, the home video market literally opened women's eyes to the wonderful world of sexual possibilities. Life has never been the same since the invention of the VCR. In 1980, 805,000 had been sold; by 1990, 65 million homes had VCRs. It isn't just that women can take home films like *9½ Weeks* and *Blue Velvet* for closer scrutiny and instant replay, but as the 1980s rolled into the 1990s, X-rated films became more explicit, more available, and increasingly aimed at the female market. Women's enthusiasm not just for voyeurism but for exhibitionism has also led to the latest video market: homemade sex films produced by and starring amateurs. When the economic slump hit the publishing world in the early 1990s, forcing many publications to close, the most popular category of new startups was sex magazines. With titles such as *Erotic Lingerie, Sexual Secrets,* and *Wet Lips,* what woman could refuse a peek?

Early in the 1980s women like Pauline were mildly concerned about the extent of their sexual appetites. "Will I wind up like something out of *The Story of O?"* she wonders, given her real adventuring, along with her fantasies of domination and group sex as the favored model and plaything of a tycoon clearly patterned on Hugh Hefner. "I wonder what will happen a few years down the road," she muses. "After all, it's not all that many years ago that I was just another good little Catholic girl from the Midwest!"

Flash forward past the publication of *The G Spot,* the reissue of Anaïs Nin's books, Calvin Klein's ever more erotic advertising, to the 1990s and a woman like Laurie, who is so advanced she incorporates watching her home video into her fantasy: "Two women fucking you is quite a 'creamy experience' [while watching] lesbian porno films

[and] using a three-way dildo . . ." Ultimately Laurie, being a modern woman, makes her own home video and "Gordon popped popcorn, opened up three beers and I sat down between them as we watched our performances."

Whether you believe these women are representative or simply a minority of exhibitionists who want to see their fantasies in print, their sexual preferences are conscious choices any woman can make. The information and permission are out there. Censorship isn't going to make Laurie the Nice Girl her mother ordered her to be. The fact is, Laurie's mother gave her no information about sex when she was young, no preparation for puberty, nothing except the words "Nice Girls don't." So much for prohibition. Like many of us Laurie is more sexually excited by what her mother forbade than by anything the video store could cook up.

The women in this chapter aren't just men's sexual equals, they are hungrier than their husbands, whom they often love but who do not sexually satisfy them. They are so hungry that no one man could measure up; many of these women don't just want to be fucked in one orifice, they want their anus filled too, and something in their mouths, both hands full, and not just one sex but male and female together. And they want it all at the same time. They are very hungry indeed.

They make a joke of the old-fashioned double standard. These women are so different and opposite from the sexually inert Doris Day genre—-the ideal of the American woman for so long—that the question poses itself: Was the insatiable woman always there, simply repressed by societal rules and the short sexual leash on which women had always been kept? My own feeling is that the only new ingredient is permission. Women now feel it is okay to express themselves. It gives them a sense of power, a word they use often.

Traditionally, women didn't complain. But Holly's been "pleasing men for so long" she'd like a little attention herself. "I don't know how to be pleasured, only to pleasure," Denise chimes in. Twenty years ago these women

NANCY FRIDAY

would have stifled their frustration, had a migraine, an
ulcer, or taken a drink; there was no alternative, no permission from other women, except to stoically carry on pleasing
others.

Cultural wisdom, prior to the 1970s, declared that men
were animals who needed sex in a way that women did not.
While it served the patriarchal system to set up men as the
active and therefore more powerful ones, it established
destructive role-playing for both men and women, making
sex not a bond but a battle. For those men who were unable
or unwilling to be erect at all times, the role was hell. So long
as all sex was initiated and dominated by men raised to
believe that a Nice Woman had virginal apprehensions,
these childhood lessons became self-fulfilling prophecies:
sex was felt to be against the woman's will (unless the man
went to a whore, where, not surprisingly, his favorite fantasy
was to be dominated for a change).

Of course sex disappeared in marriages once the honeymoon was over; for women, disillusioned at having found
that sex was not the romantic, symbiotic oneness they'd
dreamed of, sex became a bargaining chip. The withholding
of sex was called "women's greatest power," meaning she
doled it out when she wanted something like a vacation and
withheld it when she was angry, which was often (though
suppressed).

These new women make a mockery of such passivity.
Very much in touch with their sexual needs, they represent
their husbands as being the ones who put sex last on the list
after the laundry and bill paying. Allie's husband is certainly
not the first man to want sex with his wife "to be sweet and
nice and gentle. I know he wants other women, and buys
men's magazines and fantasizes about other women, so
why," Allie contends, "can't he give me a good sound
fucking like he imagines he does to them?" Maybe Allie's
mother could live with her husband's whore/madonna problem but not Allie, and not Janie, whose lover tires before she
does: "After about four hours I can still keep going," she
matter-of-factly admits before calling in fantasy reinforce-

382

ments, again not one but two men who "tease and fuck me until I can't take any more."

I have always thought fantasy to be one of the great aids to monogamy, as it allows us to remain faithful in deed while transmitting to the people we are with all the excitement that has been fired by our imagination. In our real love relationships, we often come to know one another so well it is as if we live in one another's pockets; intimacy can be reassuring on the deepest level, but is it sexually exciting when the right hand caresses the left? For the spark of sexual fire to ignite, distance is required. It is why sex with the stranger is so thrilling: There is no relationship. It is sex without strings. I applaud fantasy as an aid to fidelity and wince when I read—as I once did in a scholarly report—of therapists who consider their patients "cured" when they fantasize only about one another during sex. It is a prescription as medieval and mind-controlling as the dictum of olden days that categorically stated that women did not have sexual fantasies.

The women in this chapter know that if their sexually lazy husbands are leaving certain areas unattended, there are two or three men in fantasy land who know just how to please them. Most women understand it is wise to keep these "expert" lovers to themselves; telling a fantasy is risky business. First, it may lose its zap once aired; second, our partner may not want to know that we dream of his best friend(s); third, if we think our lover should accept our fantasy as a test of love, that is blackmail. Last, I would advise anyone considering the living out of a fantasy to remember that we cannot control things in reality as we do in fantasy.

Perhaps women are getting wiser in this regard. In a survey in *Esquire* magazine, an overwhelming majority of husbands admitted that what they *didn't* know about their wives were their sexual fantasies. Unless one's fantasy is something that cries out for real fulfillment, like oral sex, my advice on the subject of sharing sexual fantasies is to think twice and then think again.

Sophie

I feel that women are much hornier than men and desire sex more. I am mostly speaking from my own desires, but from talking with female friends I get the impression they are also very horny, and quite frankly do not get enough sex from their husbands or lovers. *My own husband has stated that he is grateful he calls the shots in our sexual life, because if I did we would be having sex once a day.* I feel that there are probably a lot of women that do have a limited interest in sex, but for good reason. I suspect that their sex lives are probably very dull, unimaginative, and no doubt include very little foreplay, which is the key to good sex.

Laurie

I'm a professional with a master's degree. I'm a petite, blue-eyed blonde in my mid 30s (thirtysomething). I'm single by choice. Childhood experiences:

My earliest sexual remembrances were around the age of 4. I had older cousins who would play "house" or "doctor." I would watch them as they looked at and touched each other. When I was in the third grade, my next-door neighbor Steve (one year older) was always wanting to feel me everywhere. He would brush my long blond hair and kiss me on my face, neck, chest, and feet. It was during this time that he threatened to tell my parents about a lie I had told unless when I turned 11 I would allow him to "pee" up me with my pants down. I was shocked yet excited at the same time. Before the "proper age" arrived, his family moved away.

About age 11, I had my one and only female-to-female experience. It was with an older female cousin (age 12). She was spending the night with me. We had already had a long talk about boys and sex (that is, what we knew of it). I had been talking about how it must feel, when she got on top of me and started kissing me and rubbing her body over mine. We stopped there because that's all we knew to do. I didn't have the sexual knowledge she did. My mother never spoke to me about sex or sexual feelings except that "nice girls don't." She didn't even prepare me for puberty. I started my period in the fifth grade. I was the first in my class. But again all my mother would say was "nice girls don't," and I didn't.

My sexual training did not happen until I was in the twelfth grade. My friends, both male and female, discovered how innocent and naive I really was. My instruction consisted of reading *The Happy Hooker, Everything You Always Wanted to Know About Sex,* and the film *Last Tango in Paris.* This information was provided by my male friends. My girlfriends related their experiences with guys and how to act, respond, and look. Even with all this, I was still a "nice girl."

College life was one big turn-on after another. I had relationships with several guys—one was a married student who had the most enormous dick. But the most sensual relationship was with my best friend's guy (they're now happily married).

Female to Female:

Even though I'm not a lesbian I have often wondered what it would be like. This is usually while I'm masturbating using my dildo and/or watching two females "eat" each other in a porn flick. (Porn flicks make me horny fast.)

My fantasy is that I've broken up with my boyfriend. I caught him with another woman. I decide to approach her on her own turf. I call her up, and she says to come over. I arrive, and she answers the door with nothing on but black see-through crotchless panties and a sheer black kimono. She is very voluptuous, her breasts are a size 38C and her pussy is dark like her long black hair. She's just the opposite of me—petite, blond, blue eyed, with little tits. I can't help but stare at her. I don't know if it was envy, lust or a little bit of both. She noticed my reaction and started her plan. She sat me down on a love seat with her beside me. She explained how sorry she was about my boyfriend and for me not to worry, because she wasn't in love with him or anyone. She had lots of lovers, both men and women. My surprised "oh" made her laugh. She asked if I had ever fucked with another woman. I told her no. She asked if the idea repulsed

NANCY FRIDAY

me, I said, "No." "Good," she said. She then started kissing me and putting her hand up my shirt to touch my breasts. It was a feeling I had never had with my boyfriend. It was all tingling, warm, and erotic. That was it. I had never felt *erotic.* All my clothes were off, and she was between my legs licking up my sweet juices. Her tongue was going to places "where no man had gone before." And I was having orgasm after orgasm. She then got a dildo and fucked me with it. I stood up, and she was eating me from underneath. This angle touched my clitoris like never before, and I must have had about twenty orgasms. Before I sat down, she entered me doggie style with the dildo, while her tongue licked and entered my asshole. I was surprised how her little tongue darting in and out of my rear could feel so good. She then pulled out a different kind of dildo—it had three different parts: one for my clitoris, one for my vagina, and a thin one for my anus. This was almost more than I could bear, but then she put one in my mouth that squirted spermlike juices. She was sucking and licking my tits while this was going on. I thought I had died and went to erotic heaven. I couldn't stand it anymore. I was screaming, "Stop it, I love it." She pulled out a dual dildo, one on which we both rode and rode and rode . . . It was my turn to do her, but I was nervous. She said that she could fix that. She had another contraption called the Venus Butterfly Vibe and this was placed between my legs. It had garterlike straps and it fitted snugly over my cunt. Attached to it was a remote-control battery pack that she operated. This little butterfly was making my "cream" run over the edge. So while I ate her, she kept the Butterfly going, which made me forget my inexperience. I was just trying to make her feel the way I was. And she said I must be feeling pretty good. Twenty-four hours later, I left her. Except for a couple of hours' sleep, it was nonstop fucking female style. I really didn't know if I would ever see her again, but two weeks later she asked me to come over to meet a friend of hers. I did. It was another woman. Three-way was very erotic, too. More new things to try.

386

Two women fucking you is quite a "creamy experience." We also watched lesbian porno films while using a three-way dildo—three fucks in one shot. Eventually, I met another man and was involved with him, but before Meg and I stopped seeing each other sexually, she came over for a three-way with me and my new boyfriend. Boy, was he getting to eat the cake and the icing, too. My new boyfriend got his ass fucked off. Meg brought a dildo just for the asshole that tied around the penetrator's waist.

Another lesbian fantasy which I've done: I'm watching a porn movie with a three-way or two girls. I call the lesbian Action Line for them to describe in detail what they would do to me if they were present. This is the ultimate masturbation.

Puppy Love:

Once in a while I'll have a fantasy about doing the ultimate doggie-style with a real dog. This is usually with a German shepherd. The fantasy goes like this: One of my girlfriends and I are masturbating. Her male dog comes in and smells her and starts licking up her juice. He then tries to mount her leg. She rolls over, and then he mounts her. He has an enormous nine-inch real dick; that dog kept it "up" for over twenty minutes. My friend was totally drenched in sweat from so many orgasms. I was getting very hot just watching. They did this for about thirty minutes. I had to get off with a dildo while watching them. They finally stopped, and the dog laid down for a much-needed rest. After about ten minutes my friend said, "Your turn." She came over and started eating my pussy—just enough to get my juices going. She fucked herself with a dildo and rubbed her juice on my tits. Rex (the porn dog) was called over. He smelled his mistress on my tits and started licking them. Rex then went for the puss, and that big tongue licked me deep and dry. His dick was sticking out, all red. My friend put him up with his front paws on my stomach so I could not only feel, but see the whole thing. Rex's dick felt like no one else's— hot, thrusting, huge, and never ending. We both climaxed over and over again. We kept Rex busy for hours. Afterwards, he got a nice warm bath and got his dick sucked off. The three of us lay on the bed too exhausted to move.

FANTASIES OF BOYS:

I have a friend who married a man with two boys. The older seventeen, the younger fifteen. It's customary for all of us to kiss hello and goodbye. The fifteen-year-old Kevin always gets a hard-on when I touch him; so does his dad (Gordon). Gordon comes to me with a strange request. Seems like Harry (the older boy) and his (Gordon's) wife were away for the weekend. He wanted me to teach Kevin about "life"— the facts of life firsthand. I was at his house when this was suggested. We made a bargain. Kevin was gone on an overnight camping trip. So we had the whole place to ourselves. Gordon said this was a practice run for the next day. I agreed. The dad was going to be hidden in his room with a video system setup—this was to be a "training film" of sorts. Kevin got home very glad to see me. He thought we were alone. I suggested we go out to the pool for a swim. I put on my new thong-bikini (hot pink/black). I was floating on a tube when Kevin came up between my legs, I caught him there and let him lick me over my bathing suit. He then started sucking my fingers, toes, and earlobes. I "accidentally" fell out of my bathing suit top. He was ready to suck them. I let him for a while, then I laughed and said, "Go for it." I pushed his head back down between my legs. I had slipped my suit over to expose my pussy (which his dad had shaved for me the night before). Kevin ate and ate my "puss" until I thought he was going to drown from not coming up for air. I pushed him away—removed the rest of my bathing suit. He needed no instructions. He removed his own suit. Much to my pleasure, his dick was a pretty good size—not his dad's size yet, but hey—it was getting there. I stayed in the tube, and he locked legs with me. We fucked this way for twenty minutes. When he had his first orgasm, I thought he would drown. I was coming so much—I almost went through the tube, too. We then left the pool, he wrapped his manhood in a towel and got me one, and he picked me up and put me in the lounge chair. We fucked five different ways in that chair. Kevin on top, me on top, sitting up face to face, doggie style and 69-ing it. Inside on the couch I instructed him on how to properly eat pussy. His tongue became the devil's tool. He could dart in-out, go deep or just hit the surface, go the whole length of my vulva to my anus. He loved the taste. I then showed him how I masturbated. This prompted him to do so as well. We then licked each other "dry." I showed him many sexual devices, especially my dildos. He learned how to operate them on me. I even did a small ass one on him. My dildo that squirts penis-like juice I placed in his mouth so he can feel what I feel. I then took him into his bedroom and sucked his balls off. I did the butterfly flick, the silken swirl, the hoover, I even gnawed and chewed on them. I then put candy briefs on him and on me, and we ate them right off each other until we were down to eating each other. We then took a bubble bath. After that I went into his bedroom to give him a massage. I wore black crotchless panties and red tassels on my tits. He liked playing with my tassels. He also liked my "finger express" undies. His dad, Gordon, had been watching us from his bedroom on the video system and decided to let Kevin watch himself on camera. He was enthralled. Gordon and I went upstairs. My reward was to be fucked by the master himself, Gordon. We were so carried away that we didn't hear Kevin enter. He had been videotaping us for quite a while. When his dad finally saw him, Kevin grinned that big smile of his, "Gotcha, 'Smile, you're on *Candid Camera.'*" Gordon and I were aroused like mad. Gordon winked at me and said to Kevin, "Son, come here, you're about to get firsthand experience on how two men can fuck one woman." Kevin set the camera up and jumped in. Kevin watched as his dad fucked me on top. (Kevin was sucking my tits, and I was sucking his cock.) Then Kevin would eat my pussy while I "deep-throated" his dad's dick. After an hour Kevin left with the camera to preview his training film. Gordon popped popcorn, opened up three beers, and I sat down between them as we watched our performances.

Odette

I am an unmarried 23-year-old legal secretary and aspiring writer. I have a degree in broadcasting and am working on a second degree in creative writing. For the past two months, I've been working at an environmental law office.

My parents were silent concerning sex as I was growing up, and I interpreted this lack of direction to mean they thought I was intelligent enough to make my own decisions. Even if they had been a bit more puritanical, I have a feeling I wouldn't have listened to them very much. I was always a terribly independent, precocious child who insisted on her own way. The thought of being controlled by another person makes me uneasy. My mother has always worked, and I learned self-sufficiency early in life.

You wrote, "Men often shy away from the boredom . . . of hit-and-run sex . . ." This is so true—not just of men, but also of women like myself who have led unrestricted, sexually active lives. In my late teens I went through a promiscuous period I called my "Sexual Coming of Age." With the help of a library filled with books (*Free and Female* was my favorite), a dozen horny guys, and a free supply of contraceptives from the campus birth-control clinic, I set about learning all I could about sex.

My level-headed approach at the age of 18 still amuses me to this day. At 23, I consider myself sexually experienced— but love, well, that's an entirely different subject. Despite my pretended world-weary air of having been everywhere and done everything, I've never really been in love. I guess I never thought I was mature enough to commit myself to a serious relationship; but that may be changing as I get older.

Many of my friends (both male and female), who a year or two ago were fucking anything that looked good in Levi's, are now settling down into monogamous relationships. Many, myself included, are choosing to remain chaste for periods of several months to a year while between partners (or, in my case, while trying to figure out what I really want in a man).

What I'd like is a relationship with a man with whom love can be playful as well as highly erotic. I want to laugh and cuddle and scream and wrestle and toss a Frisbee with someone. Not a man to complete me, for I've been on my own too long to want a "mommy," but one who can enrich my life, enhance it. And I'm willing to wait.

I masturbate once a week or so and enjoy it immensely, with or without fantasy. When I do fantasize, it's about a man I see on a daily basis: my boss, Michael. He's 38, divorced, and a warm, funny mixture of outdoor jock and gentleman lawyer. His job involves protecting the legal rights of endangered species. We have a friendly, easygoing relationship with just the right amount of sexual attraction to keep me from getting bored. I admire him; I respect him.

Here is my fantasy: We exchange sexual secrets, the kinkier, the better. I tell him I'd like to make it with a black man and a white man at the same time, with a collie on a waterbed, with another woman onstage at the Greek Theater in Berkeley. He tells me he'd like to give a young, innocent girl her first sexual experience. I decide that, as a surprise to him, I will help him play out his fantasy.

I borrow my cousin's old school uniform from the Convent of the Sacred Heart and wear it to work. His eyes widen as I walk into the office, locking the door behind me.

"I love it!" he laughs, showing lots of straight teeth. "You look about fifteen." I spin around, showing my legs under the short skirt, and plop onto his lap. His hands snap under the elastic in my knee sock as he strokes my calf.

"You're a nut. Do you know that?" he says. I'm wearing a white cotton blouse, a pleated wool skirt, and a navy blue cardigan sweater with "Class of '74" on it. He reaches under my skirt to catch the waistband of my panties and pulls them down to my ankles. His warm hands roam between my thighs.

"Virgin cunt," I say, "and it's all yours." He strokes me gently, delicately, with one finger. I moan and squirm against him, abandoning myself to the warmth that spreads upward from the pit of my belly to my flushed cheeks. His hand moves regularly, evenly—my body tenses, and I come, cradled on his lap in the big swivel chair. As my contractions fade, I look up at him and we both grin.

Joyce

I'm 32, married with two kids. I was married at 15, my husband was 18. We have lived all over the Southeastern United States, as well as three years in Europe while my husband was in the service. We came back to the Midwest, where we were raised. My husband is a skilled worker making $30,000–35,000 a year. I work part time as a social worker. I have some college and would like to get a degree in home economics and psychology and work in family counseling. We own a new car and an old van for camping. I guess basically we're the "typical" young family—but I hate that stereotype. We have been regular churchgoers, but I'll go into that later.

My fantasy has always been to make love, deliciously, wickedly, all day long and all night. I love sex. I can't remember ever thinking of sex as anything but desirable. I grew up with three older brothers. Two of them enjoyed having a baby sister to play with, although they did little more than use me as a turn-on for masturbating, doing hardly any touching. I knew I enjoyed it. I knew I shouldn't tell anyone, which I never have—you're the first. I really don't remember a whole lot about it except that it happened. I do remember one brother asking me to suck on his pecker, but I didn't do it. Strangely, none of these things "educated" me to what would happen when I finally had sex with my future husband. I saw my brothers' orgasms and yet didn't know what happened the first time with my husband. In fact, I didn't even know what a "hard-on" was.

My general fantasy was just lots of sex, which my husband never has really cared about. Sure, he enjoys sex, but not like I do. I have always been the aggressor in our relationship. Even as a naive 14-year-old, I knew he was going to make love to me before I left on our date the night it happened. I have never turned my husband down sexually. He turns me down regularly.

I masturbated as a young teen but I don't think I ever orgasmed. I think my first orgasm was after my second baby, after reading *The Sensuous Woman* and buying a vibrator. I now masturbate frequently—always with a vibrator, I can't do it without the vibrator. My husband can bring me to orgasm with his fingers, tongue or pecker.

About three years ago we got tied up in the usual marital problems, building a house, kids, work, etc., etc., and sex always came last. I turned to another man. He happened to be our minister. He too felt about sex as I always have—the more the better. However, his guilt got in the way. We never had vaginal sex. He really got turned on by my aggression— he'd never been propositioned before. I always performed oral sex on him, and he brought me to orgasm by hand. I always felt like I gave in that relationship more than I got. But the turn-on was always our mutual fantasy of an endless day and night of sex, even though it never happened. He was really hung up on me eating him—I think that was his fantasy before he met me. His wife had turned him down on it, after a discussion.

My favorite fantasy has to do with my preacher friend. The first time we realized each other's mutual desire we were away at a conference together. We sat up and watched a late movie in my hotel room together and we got into a childish "tickle" fight. Nothing happened and nothing was said, but we both knew what the other was thinking. That night when he left my room, I put my arms around him and kissed him, a deep prolonged passionate kiss—anyway that's how I remember it. And he left. My fantasy is always that he doesn't leave but that we have the long night of lovemaking.

I don't know what it means, but I've analyzed my fantasies thus: When my husband is in the fantasy, he does things to me; when it's the preacher, I do things to him.

I'd really like to make it with a woman, but I'd like my husband there too. Sometimes I suck on my husband's navel and pretend it's a woman's pussy. I'd like to form a circle with another woman. I occasionally fantasize about two men. I love to suck peters. I'd like to suck off a man and have another man in my vagina.

I have a theory on why a woman wants to make love to another woman. My husband is terrific in bed but, like I said, not always as eager as I am. I think another woman would be as eager as me. Not some young innocent but someone really as turned on as I am. She wouldn't turn me down, she'd know what to do and how to do it because she feels like I do. I doubt if I will ever have my "threesome" fantasy but it's a turn-on just to think about it.

Even though my husband and I were married young and there has been one involvement outside the marriage, we have a good marriage. We love each other, and it is successful. And we're intelligent people and ambitious. We don't like average, we like "better." The other thing is all of this is real—except the fantasies.

Pauline

I am 23 years old and a law student at a very prestigious school. This letter may ramble a lot—I'm trying to unscramble the history of my fantasies.

I discovered my clitoris at 12, but until I was 16, I only masturbated by rubbing my pubic area against a wadded-up pair of panties or the corner of my pillow. This hurt the pubic bone, so I pretty well gave it up. When I couldn't have vaginal orgasms with my first lover, I convinced myself that if I could bring myself to clitoral orgasms, some sort of Freudian magic would transfer them into vaginal orgasms during sex. That never happened (though I can have vaginal orgasms with most men), but my fantasy life really started then.

Mostly I fantasize while masturbating, or at least that's when I do what I consider fantasizing. Frequently during the day, I'll think about being in bed with a specific past, present or (if I'm lucky) future lover and what lovemaking with him was/is/might be like. Usually I don't have sexual fantasies about men I know. My favorite fantasy is really a life I have

394

constructed, and I'll plug into this life at any given point (from about age 15 on) when I masturbate. Here it is (for some reason, I tend to think about most of this in the third person, but the sex usually happens in the first person, so I'll switch back and forth).

She is brought up with only her father and older brother; mother is dead or divorced. She was always very mature & sexy, and at the age of 9 or so, one of her father's friends (or sometimes her male piano teacher) introduced her to sex. By the time she was in junior high school, she was fucking all her brother's friends. During high school, she slept with all her (male) teachers to get passing grades and spent lots of time at the local university fucking the students there. Sometimes she'd take on a whole fraternity house or sports team—I'd lie on my back with my legs spread, and they line up to fuck me. Once a guy came, he went to the back of the line, and if he wasn't hard by the time he got to the head of the line, he was "out." The guy who lasted the longest got me for the rest of the night (a variation of this—usually performed with rock groups—has me sucking the guy who's next in line to fuck me, to get him all that much harder).

At 15, she's out shopping someplace, and meets the Man. He has no name, but he's perennially in his early to mid 40s, with steely gray curly hair on his head & chest, blue-gray eyes & Grecian nose, muscular body that's in very good shape for his age, and so forth—his looks aren't clearly defined. He is the head of a huge commercial empire, including a *Playboy*-type magazine & several business enterprises. They all operate out of the same high-rise building, which he also owns. Anyway, she and the Man have an affair that lasts the rest of the fantasy, though neither is by any means faithful. For my 18th birthday, he sets up all his photography equipment, fucks me on satin sheets and then photographs me for the centerfold of his magazine. Thereafter, he sets me up in the penthouse of the building he owns, and I service him and any of his business associates. They are uniformly middle aged and domineering. In a typical encounter, I am simply pushed back on the bed while the man kneels over me, ties or holds me down and I suck his cock. This turns me on at least as much as it does him, and he puts his hand in my cunt & discovers how wet & hot I am. With no further preliminaries, he simply inserts his cock & fucks me; I come with every thrust.

During this period of my life, I also model for high-fashion ads. The pseudoviolent sexy ads. I will spend the day rubbing up against & teasing the male I'm modeling with. The final picture usually ends with me in a fur coat; I don't have anything on underneath. I manage to rub his cock as the last photos are taken and I suck him, then he just fucks me, still in the fur. The photographer is taking pictures throughout all this.

This is basically where I've got her, though there are variations on the same theme. Until a few months ago, this would have been the end of the letter. But since then, I've met a man with whom I have literally nothing in common but sex, and I've had a chance to play out some fantasies in an environment where I felt safe, felt I could control the situation and didn't have any emotional baggage to deal with. This has been enormously freeing. I enjoy being dominated—I like being fucked, no preliminaries, while tied to his headboard. Once, I did get to play out the fantasy of two men—one cock in my mouth and one in my cunt—with this man & a business associate of his I've never seen before or since. This has spurred lots of recent fantasies; I want to do it again. This is the first time I've ever fantasized about a man I know.

I have a background in psychology (in fact, I used to work with sexual psychopaths!) and have heard countless times that any fantasy is okay, it's acting them out that can give you problems. So I don't have any problems with my fantasies, but I wonder now that I can act them out. Am I sick? Does the fact that I started having sex at 16 and have had a lot of lovers mean that to find fulfillment, I'll have to do continually more kinky things & can never be satisfied with one man? Will I wind up like something out of *The Story of O?* At the moment, these questions don't really bother me too much, but I wonder what will happen a few years down the road. After all, it's not all that many years ago that I was just another good little girl from the Midwest!

Vana

My sexual fantasies have begun to change lately, and I welcome the opportunity to explore the changes.

I am a 37-year-old woman, married and a graduate student. My husband and I have been together for six years. When we got married, we had it all going for us—mental, physical and emotional rapport. Our sex life was the best I'd ever known. I was having orgasms regularly, either from manual or oral stimulation though rarely from intercourse. Prior to meeting my husband, I hadn't climaxed much in any way with men but had always come while masturbating if I fantasized. My masturbation fantasies were of being dominated and forced to have sex by faceless men and, occasionally, faceless women. (My real experiences have been exclusively with men.) I was able to climax with my husband regularly if I used my familiar faceless submission fantasies.

Anyway, about two years ago our sex life began to deteriorate. Gradually it reached the point where my husband could not maintain an erection at all, and we totally stopped having intercourse. I tried everything I could think of from sexy nightgowns and candle-lit dinners, to pleading for us to go for marriage counseling. My husband refused to consider counseling for about a year and then reluctantly agreed to go when I threatened to leave him.

To make a long story short, after some sessions with the therapist our sex life resumed somewhat, but we quit going, and within a month we were down to no sex again. I still love my husband very much and don't want to divorce him, but his sexual withdrawal has left me feeling so inadequate as a woman. I didn't think my self-esteem was this shaky, but then I've never loved anyone as much as I love him. And believe it or not, in every other way he's a great husband.

Last spring I met a man in one of my classes at school. Brian first caught my eye because I liked his looks—tall, thin, blond hair, blue eyes. The more I got to know him, the more I liked his mind, his sense of humor, etc. And I find him incredibly sexy. Sitting next to him in class, I can feel him in every pore of my body. I don't think I've ever been as physically aware of another human being before (although this is probably due to my deprived state). Many times I've come home from school with my underpants soaking wet just from being near him.

Now for the fantasy changes: In the last month or two, my lifelong masturbation fantasies have changed. No more faceless men forcing me to do things I really wouldn't want done in reality. Now I just picture Brian making love to me as I'd really like to experience it, and I have the most incredible orgasms.

Fantasy Number 1:

Brian asks me if he can meet me after class at a park near school. We meet, and he tells me he can't stand it anymore, he's dreaming about me, fantasizing constantly, etc. He's tried to fight it because he's married too, but he had to tell me. We kiss passionately, and hungrily begin exploring each other's bodies. He takes my shirt and bra off and begins sucking on my nipples until I think I've died and gone to heaven. Gradually he reaches down and gently stimulates my clitoris (I'm soaking wet) until I explode into orgasm. I caress his penis (it feels wonderful) and tell him I want him. As he enters me, I climax again, and when he comes in a joyous, noisy rush, I have my third orgasm.

Fantasy Number 2:

Now that we've begun our affair, we start meeting regularly at motels, friends' apartments, etc. One night while sucking on my nipples, he murmurs that he'd like to do this for hours. I tell him to go right ahead. After ten minutes or so of his exquisite mouth, I have an orgasm from breast stimulation alone (this has never happened in reality). Then I go down on him and lovingly perform fellatio until he explodes in my mouth and I happily swallow his semen (something I've never fantasized doing to anyone before. I've never been that crazy about it). He tells me he loves to eat me and performs cunnilingus on me until I have five or six orgasms. We do and try everything, fingers up each other's asses, anal sex—everything. We're both extremely vocal and tell each other before, during and after sex how much we love to fuck, eat, etc., each other. We tell each other our sexual dreams and fantasies about each other and try out every one of them. After we fuck, he always stays inside me and, within fifteen or twenty minutes, gets hard again and we start to fuck all over again. Sometimes in class he'll lean over and whisper that he can't wait to make love or fuck me later that night. Or I'll say it to him, but the important thing is that he wants me as much as I want him.

I have finally decided to try to make these dreams into reality. I'm positive that Brian is attracted to me—he spends as much time as he can with me at school, sits as close to me as he can, we've had lunch together, etc. I don't know what the story is with his marriage—we talk about everything but our spouses—but I'm guessing that he's holding back because we're both married. I don't know exactly what I'm going to do yet, but I want this man! I want to explore all my sexual fantasies with him.

Holly
I am 22 and a single mother of one daughter. I dropped out of high school halfway through my junior year because of drugs. I have "cleaned up my act" since then and have not taken any for about five years now. I have a very active sex life and am quite pleased with the way things are going. I do, however, have one fantasy that sticks in my head. By the way, I do not masturbate. I believe in it wholeheartedly, but I simply do not need it.

My fantasy: I am alone in my house, the lights are dim, the music is low. Suddenly there is a man, about 30, good looking, standing in front of me, totally nude. He gently lifts me up and carries me to the bedroom and undresses me. As he begins to caress me, another man, much younger, around

18 (I like the young ones best!), also nude, comes into the room and also starts caressing me. I'm getting hotter and hotter, when still another man, about 19 to 20, comes in, and then and there they all start doing anything and everything to make me come. The older man is fucking me, the 18-year-old is letting me suck his cock and the 19-year-old is feeling my breasts. They are all telling me how beautiful I am and how much they all love me and want me. Then we all come together and lie there exhausted and do the same thing in the morning, switching places. I have been pleasing men for so long, just once I would like a few of these men to please me the way I want.

Denise

I am an unmarried 20-year-old college junior majoring in the behavioral sciences. I am a Christian (not religious; there's a difference) and come from a strong church background. I do not, however, take the standard "thou-shalt-not" view against sex. I do not believe in sleeping around or adultery, but to me premarital sex with someone to whom you have a deep commitment is something God probably understands. Anyway, I don't expect any hellfire and brimstone for either fantasizing about or participating in sex.

I have only had one lover, though I have dated more than a few men. I was 19 and he was 30. He was in love with me (at least for a while), and even though I could not feel that emotion for him, I wanted him. I was at a point where I longed to know what sex was like, and since he is one of my closest friends, he was the only man I trusted enough for the first time. We had a brief affair that ended by mutual consent because our friendship was in serious danger. We just did not make good lovers. Fortunately we got out in time and today we are still as close as we ever were.

This man (I'll call him Keith) is gorgeous and very knowledgeable where sex is concerned. He instructed me in what to do, always being very patient and understanding because he was aware that I knew nothing more than what I'd read in textbooks.

Keith's only flaw is that he is somewhat self-centered when it comes to sex. Every time we made love it began by me fellating him until he came in my mouth, then he would fuck me (always twice) and we could lie in bed for a few hours and I would go home. He didn't let me stay all night after the first time, a fact I always resented. I felt cheated.

Since Keith was more concerned about his pleasure than mine, my "pleasure" fantasy always concerns two men whose one desire is to make *me* reach orgasm after orgasm. There are various "teams" in this fantasy, but in relating it I'll use the two men with whom I mentally pioneered it, a couple of comedy actors named Tom Hanks and Peter Scolari. Tom is tall and brunette, and Peter is a short, muscular blond. They're both gorgeous, with great bodies. I'll try to explain my fantasy as best I can.

I am a famous screenwriter, living in a lovely home in Hollywood. (I would like to write for films someday.) Tom and Peter are there to discuss a script. They begin to seduce me in some part of the house, usually the kitchen; they both start kissing me, and Tom carries me to the bedroom. Peter follows, joining Tom in whispering how much they want me.

The fantasy really begins when the three of us are in bed together. I am naked, lying under the cool sheets. The men are wearing only tight blue jeans. They begin by kissing and caressing me: my face, my throat, my breasts, my shoulders. This goes on for quite a while. (Keith was never much on foreplay.) In my fantasy this alone almost makes me come.

Suddenly Peter stops. I watch as he moves to the foot of the bed. He pulls back the sheet and, on his knees, crawls in between my feet. "Open your legs," he says gently, lovingly. I do, and he undoes his leather belt, unzips his jeans, and tosses both articles away. (No underwear, naturally.) He is naked, with a lovely cock that is by now quite erect. He starts getting into position to begin cunnilingus on me.

I become frightened. I don't know how to be pleasured, only to pleasure. "I can't—I can't" I say, and start to rise. But Tom is there and gently pushes me down, kissing me and reassuring me with, "It'll be all right, baby. He knows

401

how to do it. Just let him make you come." I am still scared, but Tom's urging keeps me there, along with his constant caressing.

Peter carefully places his tongue on my clitoris. I tense at first, stiffening, but as he works on me—circling my clitoris, pushing deep into my vagina—I begin to loosen up. He knows how to do it, all right; Tom wasn't lying. Peter's favorite acts are quick flicks of my clit with his tongue, or agonizingly slow circles around, or passes over it. Somehow I manage to hold back my orgasm for quite a while, and when I do finally come my back is arched, my head thrown back in sheer ecstasy, and I scream so hard all I can do afterwards is lie there, shuddering.

Now Tom takes Peter's place. It is his turn to kiss and caress me. His cock is as fabulous as Peter's. Tom sits between my legs, rubbing my inner and outer thighs, staring down at me with his sparkling brown eyes all the while and whispering, "You're so beautiful. What an incredible woman you are. I want you, baby, I want to please you." Again these simple acts of affection are almost enough to make me come.

At last Tom presses himself flat on me. He kisses my face and throat, rubs my breasts and kisses them, too. (Peter is lovingly caressing my hair.) After a few exquisite moments, Tom enters me. His thrusts are perfectly timed: long and gentle at first, then building as he goes on and I begin to get into it, until he eventually is putting his entire being into it, into me, his whole fabulous body centered in his cock. Again my orgasm is total, my scream of ecstasy thunderous.

After this they lie kissing and caressing me all night, whispering their love to me. Sometimes I fantasize that I fellate them, an act I enjoy but which causes a few painful memories, since Keith was so preoccupied with it. In the fantasy, though, I do it as a gift to these wonderful men, and it is very sexually fulfilling for me.

From what I've written, Keith may seem somewhat of a monster, and I don't mean him to. He's really a very sweet man, and I believe he truly loved me. I'm glad we had what we did and that my first time was with him. He just wasn't ready to make a commitment with me, and I want a man who is, the first step of which is being as concerned about my pleasure as his. My fantasy lovers fill all my requirements. Perhaps if I prepare for him in fantasy, I won't be afraid when my "pleasure giver" comes into my reality.

Veronica

I am 21 years old, white, female, and am getting married in three weeks. My fiancé (who I'll call Dan) was my first lover (and I was his first), at the age of 16. I had experimented with fellatio and mutual masturbation before I met Dan. Sex was and is very good, but I seem to want sex more often than he does.

Four years ago, when Dan went away to college, I let his best friend, Jack, seduce me, but I really wanted Jack to fuck me, so I guess it was a mutual seduction. Jack's prick is smaller than Dan's, but I find it much easier to perform fellatio because of this. Eventually, Dan came home from college, and we were together again. I told Dan about Jack and I. He got angry and upset, but we stayed together.

I have been making it with Jack every couple of months for the past four years without Dan knowing about our relationship. Jack is much more experimental, and we have had many great experiences acting out our fantasies.

Dan recently went into the service, and we became engaged.

I have been seeing Jack quite often because we both know our relationship will soon end. Sexually I'm much happier with Jack, as we do love and care about each other. It's just that I'm ready for a commitment and he isn't. The thought of a permanent relationship scares him. As soon as one of his girlfriends becomes serious, he "cools off" their relationship. I'm not jealous of his other girlfriends, but he's jealous of Dan, just a bit.

We have recently tried anal sex, and I really love it, and so does he! Dan is just too big to have up my ass, but Jack's prick feels so very fine! A week before my wedding, Jack and

I are planning one last night of wild and crazy sex. I want to be a faithful wife to Dan, so this will be my last fling with my illicit lover.

My fantasy is this: After the wedding reception, Dan and I check into a very luxurious hotel. I ask Dan to leave for a while so I might "slip into something more comfortable." He leaves, and I put on a black satin lacy gown. It's skintight and very effective against my blond hair and light skin. I turn down the lights and sit by the huge picture window overlooking the city from fifty stories up. I hear a knock at the door and get up to answer it.

I open the door, and there stands my husband and three of the groomsmen, still in their tuxedos. (Jack is one of the groomsmen in my fantasy, but he's one in reality too!) I'm slightly embarrassed, but I let them come in.

We all sit on the huge bed and drink champagne and tell dirty jokes. Soon we are all drunk and terribly horny. I undress each of the men, and they peel the black satin gown off my body. Jack sprinkles champagne all over my body, and all four men start licking it off of me. Jack and Dan are kissing my face, neck and breasts, and Jim and Tom are kissing my feet. Then they pick me up and carry me over to the round table next to the window. Suddenly I realize it's only Jack and Dan kissing me. I look down on the floor, and Tom and Jim are in the 69 position. This really turns me on, because I've never seen two guys together like this!

Meanwhile, Dan is sucking and kissing my cunt and Jack is forcing his cock past my protesting lips.

Suddenly, Jack's prick starts throbbing and he yanks it out of my mouth and comes all over the window. I look down on the floor just in time to see Tom's prick entering Jim's asshole.

I turn to Dan and cry "Fuck me now! Stick it in me, please!!" Dan carries me to the bed and places me on my stomach. He stuffs a pillow underneath me and lifts my ass into the air. Finally he mounts me from behind and slips his cock into my cunt and smears my juices all around my asshole and perineum. Very slowly he pushes his cock (all nine inches of it) into my spasming cunt. Jack moves around

404

to my face, and I take his cock into my mouth to make him hard again.

Dan pulls out of my cunt and moves underneath me. I mount Dan and impale myself on his hard shaft. Jack moves behind me and sticks his cock ever so slowly into my asshole. As Dan shoves it into my pussy, Jack pulls his cock away from my asshole ever so slowly. It's a slow and beautiful fuck. Dan reaches up to pinch and roll my nipples between his fingers, and Jack reaches around to finger my clitoris. Tom comes up behind Jack and starts tonguing Jack's asshole, and Jim starts licking and sucking my toes. Finally Dan starts to come, and this triggers Jack's orgasm. Feeling my two luscious holes being filled with the cream of the great loves of my life sets off the greatest orgasm I've ever experienced.

Wow, what a fantasy!

Bootsie

I am a 33-year-old mother of two children. I have been married for fifteen years, but my marriage has been shaky the last two years. We have an unusual problem—or maybe it's not, I don't know—in that I have a more active interest in sex than my husband. So many of our problems go back to this. I just plain like it! He, on the other hand, doesn't have much of a sex drive, which has always been so hard for me to rationalize because he's quite handsome and masculine looking. We are for all outward appearances the "ideal" couple. We are very well off financially and have a beautiful home and wonderful children. We travel a lot and are both active in our careers. My husband is one of those guys who wanted to be a millionaire before he was 30, and he did it! All of this still leaves us with what I consider a miserable sex life. He, on the other hand, sees no problem.

I have begun an affair with a younger man. It's been the happiest two years of my life. I was starved for affection and love and sex, and now I have it. I'd known this younger man for several years on a strictly casual basis, but the possibility was always there. I felt very strongly attracted to him and I hoped he felt the same, but never really knew. I also couldn't imagine him being interested in someone nine years older, so I just enjoyed his friendship.

This may sound totally ridiculous, but it's as if we're two halves of the same person. Our sex life is so perfect, so satisfying. He'd had several long-term, live-in affairs before me, but he says they weren't like what we have at all. I can actually imagine living to a ripe old age with this person. That's what he wants. He has said he'll wait until I can decide how and when to get out of my marriage. The truth is that I really do love him. It's stronger now than ever before. He's my strength. I lean on him. My husband never allows me to need any emotional support. He's such a good man, and I hate that we have what seems like an insurmountable difference in our sexual and emotional needs. Anyway, this may help explain my sexual fantasy. I had never had one until two years ago. My sexual experiences were so limited (I was a virgin when I married) because my husband only wants missionary-position intercourse after a few kisses and very little vaginal stimulation with his finger. Because of this, I really didn't know how to fantasize or what to think about. I would have very vague sexual dreams, but when I awoke, I never could quite remember who was my partner or what we did.

Anyway, my lover introduced me to everything I'd never had. The list of have-nots was great. I'd never been stimulated until I wanted sex—was dying for it. I'd never had a guy go down on me. I'd never given head. I'd never used any positions other than missionary. I'd never made love anywhere except in bed. Well, my lover has a tremendous sex drive. The first six months we did it thirty to forty times a week. No joke. We literally spent days in bed. Even now we have sex eight to ten times a week. So now I have something to think about, and I do. He's made me very aware of my body. I feel gorgeous now. Here go my sexy thoughts. These always happen when I can't be with my lover for several days. It depresses me greatly, so I go off and have these little sexual daydreams about us, or I use these thoughts to put me to sleep.

Whenever I see a guy who in some way reminds me of my lover, either by his hair, face, stance, laugh, or anything really, I kind of zero in on that person. Then in quiet moments I have these little quickie fantasies about how it might be to have him go down on me or if it would be good for him if I did it for him. My lover tells me that's the one thing men want that they don't get enough of. My lover has also made me aware of the beauty of my body. I now fantasize about getting to show it off to total strangers. As I mentioned, he told me that a friend of ours told him he'd love to fuck me. Well, I fantasize about that. This other guy's name is Craig. My lover once said, "Craig's a real tit man. He's always talking about someone's tits and he's often said he'd like to see if yours are as great as he thinks. I wish he could see them. He'd come in his pants. He'd be able to imagine them from then on when he sees you down at the club in shorts and a tight tee-shirt." This male generosity amazes me. My lover seems to wish that everyone could know how good our love making is, so that I now often think of him as watching while I strip for someone or maybe he actually watches me do things with someone. At any rate, it always involves him or things he has lovingly taught me. I tell him I was nearly a virgin before him.

Allie

I am a 31-year-old heterosexual woman, married for six years to a man four years my senior. We have a 4-year-old daughter, and I have been home for three years, raising her. I will be starting medical school next July; my husband is a doctor.

Both of us were raised in extremely repressive religious families. Sex and pregnancy were never discussed in my parents' home, and neither was any other bodily function, for that matter. When I graduated from college and moved away from home is when my life began. I loved my work and came to realize that I *was* likable and fun to be around. I was a virgin until I was 22, and had never had the opportunity to explore myself or masturbate until I had my own place. I didn't have a lot of sexual relationships when I was single, but I enjoyed each one as it came along.

My husband and I are presently going to marriage counseling for a variety of reasons, not the least of which is sex. My husband likes everything between us to be sweet and nice and gentle. I know he wants other women and buys men's magazines and fantasizes about other women, so why can't he give me a good sound fucking like he imagines he does to them? I've not always been responsive to him in the past, but I don't know anyone who would enjoy lying still under a man for maybe three minutes while he pleased only himself. Whenever I suggest something new or behave in some manner other than "cute," he stops cold.

One of the counselors is a man who I'd guess is in his mid 40s and is not strikingly handsome, yet I find him immensely attractive. He told me that it's not necessarily a detriment to a stable relationship to have fantasies; and I suppose I'm attracted to him because I'm grateful to him for giving me "permission" to fantasize. At any rate, my fantasies involve him, and they're the first ones I've ever had that do not involve a current partner.

Here's how they go: I am in his office for a counseling session. He is asking me about our sexual practices and is dismayed by my husband's lack of understanding and concern for me and my needs. He tells me that he finds me very desirable and gives me a good strong kiss. His hands find my nipples, and he begins pinching them. I reach for his belt buckle and undo that and his fly. He's hard as a rock, and he undoes my blouse and sucks and bites my nipples. He lifts my skirt and pulls down my panties, breathing in my scent. He licks, nibbles and sucks on my clit, which by now is as erect as my nipples. He runs his tongue around my cunt and then sticks it in me. (I would love this in real life, but my husband finds it distasteful and seldom indulges me. No matter; he's inept when it does happen.) I almost come right then, and I need him inside me. I push him down on his leather chair and lower myself on his gorgeous prick. We move together a little while, and then he moves me to the floor. All the while he's telling me how fragrant, how wet, how tight I am and how much he wants me. He teases me by putting in only the tip of his cock and rubbing it around the rim of my vagina. I want it all, every inch of it, and arch my back up to meet him, but he moves away each time, keeping only his tip in. I tell him that I want it shoved in, please fuck me. He slides his whole shaft in slowly at first, then faster and faster. I have to bite my lips to keep from screaming as I come. When he feels the last spasm of mine, he comes himself and fills me with a load of warm cream. We rest for a minute, then he wipes me clean with a warm washrag. He buttons my blouse for me and pulls up my panties; I straighten out his clothes for him. We smile at each other and both look forward to next week when we'll meet again.

Maybe next week he'll tie me down on a table, or on the floor, or in his chair and caress my naked body. Maybe he'll use a feather or some silky fabric, or an ice cube, or his hands, or his breath, or his cock, or something rough or warm. Whatever would please me, whatever we wanted, that's what it would be. I would love for my husband to treat me like that, and I sincerely hope counseling opens his mind to these possibilities. I don't know how the counselor would react if I made him aware of my desires, but I doubt I'd ever actually tell him (unless he asked me outright about my fantasies).

I bought a copy of *Forbidden Flowers* and put it under my husband's pillow. Keep your fingers crossed for me/us!

Janie

I'm 21, a female, single but living with a guy that I really love while trying to go to college part time and work full time.

I was a virgin until 18 years of age and have had no regrets since. From the first day of my college experience, I've been sexually active. I seem to enjoy sex so much that I've really never been without a boyfriend during my entire college career.

I've slept with all types of guys and all sizes too. The old myth that size *does* count is all wrong, it's what a man does with what he has, hands, mouth, tongue, and of course penis, that counts.

I have quite a lot of fantasies that I use while I masturbate. It's not that I don't get satisfied enough that I have to, it's quite the contrary actually. Whenever I'm horny and my boyfriend is around, I can get satisfied anytime. It's those times while he's at work and I've been out and seen a sexy guy or something like that I masturbate.

I was sexually abused by a member of my family when I was 13 and I was raped at the age of 18, but I still think that sex is great and that all men are not like those two who abused me. It puzzles some people that I can still think of sex as being beautiful and great, but like I said before, it's just the way I am.

One of my favorite fantasies, which has yet to come true, is about my boyfriend (Jack) and this friend of mine who I'm very attracted to, Ben. Jack and Ben decide to surprise me for my birthday by taking me to a cottage on the lake near my home for the weekend. Just the three of us are there to celebrate all weekend. We go swimming most of the day and lie out on the beach. As we are walking back to the cottage, Jack tells me that he and Ben have another surprise for me. They are going to tease and fuck me until I can't take any more. (See, I usually last quite long, meaning Jack tires first; after about four hours I can still keep going but he can't.) So they got this brainstorm that with twice the pleasure, I'll tire sooner and at about the same time as them.

So we get to the cottage and go in and sit in front of the fireplace. We drink the champagne Ben bought and talk, and then Jack says, "Let's play strip poker, loser not only has to take off a piece of clothing but also kiss someone (the guys me, me the guys) anywhere on their body." Ben and I agree, so the game begins. Needless to say, by the time the game ends (all the clothes off), the three of us are so horny that there are no other thoughts but getting off and having a great time doing it.

So while I'm kissing Jack, he's playing with my nipples, and Ben is kissing his way down to my cunt. Jack is kissing my breasts and telling me how beautiful I am, and Ben is licking my pussy, and you can hear the slurping noise. Then he looks up, pauses and smiles and dives back down. I'm going crazy. I have one man sucking my tits and one man sucking my cunt. As I'm getting ready to come, I'm thrashing all over the floor, but both of them hold on and never miss a lick. And what an orgasm I have too! My whole body is alive and tingling from being touched and petted all over by four hands and two mouths.

As Ben lies down on his back to catch his breath, I scramble around and get down on my hands and knees and take his wonderful, hard throbbing cock in my hands and lick all over that beautiful cock. As I really get into sucking him off, Jack gets behind me and enters me, which really gets me going. While Jack is thrusting his cock in and out and in and out of my dripping cunt, I'm sucking Ben's cock for all I'm worth. As Ben starts to reach orgasm, it makes me worse. So when Ben starts flooding my throat with his delicious come, I'm coming and squeezing Jack's cock, and then all that wetness, and hot, clutching cunt brings Jack right over the edge, and we all collapse in orgasm.

The idea of both these men, whom I love very much, sharing me and loving me together is the biggest turn-on there is for me. No one else knows about this *yet*. I'll probably tell Jack soon and see what he thinks.

Men are not the only ones that can enjoy and talk about sex. Besides, if more women enjoyed and talked about enjoying sex, more men would be happy (women too). Men would relax and know that they aren't the only ones and that pleasure goes both ways.

ONE WOMAN, MANY FANTASIES

I'm not sure most men would know how to handle the encyclopedic variety of sexual images these women entertain. Once upon a time, women were as faithful to their one standard fantasy as they were to their man in reality. In the early 1980s the single-image screen switched to a smorgasbord. Now, as sexual adventuring in the real world has become increasingly unsafe, women seem to be compensating with fantasy. Having savored real freedom of choice, they have switched their fondness for variety to erotic multi-images; any one woman may run the gamut from voyeurism to exhibitionism, animals, group sex, younger men, other women to even having a fantasy of *being* a man.

(A parenthetic comment on women's most trusted friend, the German shepherd: Those who are offended by animal fantasies will be glad to know that they are not as popular as they once were. My explanation is that as women's sexual freedom has increased, they have felt less need in reality as well as in fantasy to call upon the family pet. Twenty years ago Fido served the same purpose as the anonymous stranger: he wasn't going to tell on the woman, judge her, or expect any further compensation except perhaps an extra Milk-Bone. But the well-endowed dog will never totally disappear from fantasy, primarily because the idea so often has its roots in childhood, when a dog's curious nose gave the little girl her first sexual feeling. Until we can teach Rover to keep his nose to himself, there will always be women who include him in the erotic parade along with everyone else.)

Ultimately there is a great sense of power in these multitheme fantasies. Why, for instance, would a willful woman have a fantasy of being dominated? First of all, as one woman wrote, she likes a "good, hard, rough fuck" in reality, a reminder to those feminists who would like to take all the pain out of sex, that without the rough animal abandon—the scratching, biting, thrusting—sex for many men and women is boring. But this woman enjoys a fantasy involving aggression because, as she puts it, "I think I just want to be forced to do what I want to do anyway." By making the man make her have sex, she is putting the thrusting and pounding into the kind of sex she likes. This, too, is power, this ability to create ourselves as powerless even as we get what we want. Then, "in the blink of an eye . . . as you can only do in fantasy," April comments, these women switch positions, switch fantasies, and go powerfully from being "taken" to taking what they want.

Eileen

I wouldn't dream of telling my husband any of my fantasies. He is the original missionary, and I have even begun to suspect, in the last ten years, that he has a real deep problem with sex. He barely lets me touch his penis and rarely does more than touch my breasts. Anyone who can reduce sex to a three-minute Johnny Carson commercial needs help as far as I'm concerned. A friend suggested that I buy the book *The Joy of Sex.* After looking through it, I decided definitely not. He needs a kindergarten primer on the ABCs. Maybe all this is lack of experience. We have been married twenty-two years (since age 19), and I don't know if he has had any other women or not; I suspect not.

I have had several affairs in that time, mostly in the last ten years, and I am grateful. Nine years ago, one very sensual man of 59 made me sexually aware of myself, and it was like coming to life and admitting what I really was. The only problem is that now I am even more aware of the inadequacies at home.

Consequently, I fantasize a lot more, masturbate a lot more, crotch-watch continually and am always on the lookout for a likely looking sex partner. I don't know if I'm frustrated (I suspect so) or if I'm just too oversexed.

My fantasies are great; usually of men I have my eye on at the moment, but they have also included a stepgrandfather I had who made me jerk him off when I was 10 years old and didn't know anything (that fact is real), a dog, another woman, threesomes, groups, and my favorite one, getting a man and myself so hot over the phone that we both masturbate and tell each other about it while we are doing it. The funny part about that last fantasy is that in the last month we have had many, many misdialed calls for a sex hot line whose number is one digit different from ours. Some of these guys don't say hello, they just start telling you how they are going to fuck you. Although these calls are annoying, I do get a vicarious thrill from some of them, and my fantasies are off and running. Someday when I'm alone and I get one of these calls, I might just live out my fantasy.

I have no idea how my marriage will turn out. My fantasies and small affairs are sufficient for now. I have lost all guilt about it somewhere along the way and am just trying to satisfy myself as best I can. I realize I'm not weird or perverted as I used to think I was. I do not intend to be a nun (none) for the rest of my life (I'm 42 and have been told that I am a good-looking woman).

Zoe

Pardon this disjointed syntax, but if I don't mail this now I'll change it, and I don't want to.

I have an IQ of 158–165 (depending on the test). I am a college student, a theater major (technician) and art minor. I am 22, single, and was a virgin until four months ago, and am still dating my first. I have often been accused of living in a fantasy world. My favorite fantasies are dogs and young boys, and sometimes women, although for my personal "moral" and legal reasons these are simply fantasies. I have found myself to be sexually insatiable, although monogamous, and have found myself *considering* sex with almost *any* man. My romantic ideas of one man, one thought, seem to have gone the way of my virginity. I think and fantasize a lot about how different men's penises look and what they might like me to do with them. I have numerous close male friends, and back rubs and hugs are commonplace. I love to glide a long leg between the thighs of an unsuspecting guy and grind my hip against him to give him an instant hard-on. Then to lick his earlobe—mm, mm—and walk away; not to embarrass him, but to make him want me. My lover knows nothing of my fantasies. I would, someday, like to convince my lover to spread honey, say, or melted chocolate all over my body and have him lick it off. I am terribly orally fixated, but he does not seem to mind. I had never given a blow job before him either, but he says it's like nothing he's ever had: "the room spins" (and he's sure had his share).

FANTASY NUMBER 1:

I meet a man, Joe, who is walking his large dog, Butch. The man is tall, broad shouldered and dark haired. We begin to chat, and the dog sniffs me again and again. His owner scolds him and says he's better trained than that, but he's a stud and has not been worked lately. He's been around bitches in heat and turned on a lot, but has not been allowed to come, so he's built up and probably uncomfortable. By this time the dog has been alternating between licking himself and nosing me really hard and whining. I am also excited; that hot pink tip shooting in and out, getting bigger and wetter. The gentleman says that he must really want me—he's done women before—that's part of his training, and he asks me would I be interested? By now the slow throb between my legs is almost unbearable, so we go to his place, where the owner tells me that I must be ready for the animal, as he gets quite huge. I must be lubricated well enough for him to go in all at one stroke so that his "stud qualities" are not damaged. I lie down on a mattress with my hips at the edge, knees far apart. As Butch comes toward me, his huge pink, wet dick shoots in and out of his sheath and dangles almost to the floor with the engorged weight of his come-filled post.

Joe slides back the sheath behind the huge bulge that throbs at the base of that hot shaft, the organ quivers with the animal's anticipation, and drops of clear gel form at the tip and are shaken free with the dog's excitement. Butch, after a perfunctory sniff, begins to sniff and lick and lick and whine in my dewy pocket; his huge tongue in and out, hot and long and wet. Then his cold nose on my thumping clit. Joe checks that I'm dripping wet and ready for the bulge and all the rest. But, he says, he "forgot to tell me"—the dog has been trained that he cannot come until I have! With that he releases the animal's thrusting pelvis, and Butch plunges into me with that hot, long dick and that huge bulge,

415

thrusting over and over, giving a bit of that clear beginning come, spraying it hot into me. As the owner, Joe, says "he's fucking huge—he's gonna go all inside you," and as the dog whines, I come, *hard,* and again as the huge animal empties his wad into me and cries as he pulls out and then licks himself clean, and I come again as he licks and sucks me clean of all that hot come.

FANTASY NUMBER 2:

Later—if I'm up for it again; Butch's owner was so turned on by that scene that he wants some. He licks my nipples, slowly sucking them, biting them softly. Then he stands up and unbuttons only the top of his bulging jeans. The head of his cock pops out, almost purple and slick already with his sweat and the clear, salty sticky dew that comes first. I lick slowly around the head and flick the eye with my tongue. He moans, and I pull open his pants with my mouth as he gets harder and bigger. He lies down on me and puts it in slowly, just a bit, and teases me with just the tip on my clit, asking me if I want it. He teases me almost to tears and as he thrusts, finally, he moans. Butch, rested, comes over with a much more slender hard-on, and his owner reaches down, gets some of my cream on his fingers and rubs it around his asshole—obviously Butch knows what to do and sticks his boner in and starts pumping away deeper and deeper until Joe screams and pumps his heavy, thick, hot come into me, and Butch comes his hot-water doggie come all over Joe's balls and jumps back as I come again. Then, once again, he licks us clean, all three.

FANTASY NUMBER 3:

Next time there are three little boys, 12–13, maybe 14. They all have hairless little hard-ons in their hands. I walk in and stroke each one, teasing and smiling. They all smile shyly, hoping to be chosen. I choose a beautiful young Adonis— Michelangelo's David in blue jeans—which we soon re-move. We go to the futon in the center of the room. I kneel over him, kissing, coaxing as the other boys stroke themselves, sometimes roughly. They want only me and wonder which of them, if any, will be next. Mine touches me, shy and gentle, curious, ravenous. He tests himself—licks, tentatively, my nipples, and kisses, soft gentle kisses on my mouth, his hot tongue on mine, his hands everywhere. Then, his hard-on jumps as I lower myself a little. We both gasp. I whisper, "I have made the right choice." We join and hold each other tightly as he writhes inside me, then he is over me—his long dark hair around his face, his mouth on mine. He pulls out, and the hot, wet tip of his small, perfect maleness begins beating away on my stiff little clit, his young cock softening just a bit to flick me over and over. I reach down and tickle the underside, and he moans, stiffens, and as I stroke his balls lightly, we come together hard and hot. His body crumples, and he sleeps with his hands cupping my breasts to his mouth.

I've found that although my lover can give me wonderful orgasms (which I prefer to self-induced), I can usually give myself harder, faster—sometimes longer O's.

Rereading this I guess I must have some pretty voyeuristic tendencies—and exhibitionist too, eh?!

April

I am 22 years old, graduating from college in just a few weeks (!), single, the youngest of four, Catholic, heterosexuals. I'm from a typical middle-class family, my parents are divorced (after twenty-five years of a miserable marriage). I have only one older sister and two older brothers.

I started having sexual relations after high school. Previously I had a boyfriend for over a year. We had done everything except "it"! (We were both good Catholic kids!) When I got to college, I went on a "Spring Fling"! A few "one-nighters," and I knew that wasn't what I wanted. I then dated a boy pretty seriously for a while. After we broke up (by now I was in the middle of my third year at college), I started dating several guys at once. I was having the best time of my life! I was only sleeping with one of them;

strangely enough, the only one not really available. He was a bartender at a local bar and he had a "serious" girlfriend. He would come over to my place after work (around 2 A.M.), and we would both relieve some tensions. After a while I was sick of men in general, and I dumped 'em all! To be perfectly honest, since then I've been pretty lonely. There have been a couple of "one-nighters" when the tension gets too much, but other than that, nobody interesting. In fact, I think my hormones are dead, or at least hibernating! I would be convinced of this if it weren't for one thing—my fantasies are out of control!!!!!

I have been masturbating since a very early age, and my earliest fantasies had to do with groups of men forcing me to have sex while some watched or participated. This theme has continued to the present time. Sometimes the group of guys come into my room and say that they just want to see my breasts (which are rather large—36C). Then they begin to get excited, and they all begin touching me all over. I usually have sex with all of them, climaxing with the last and most well endowed! Other times I am the only female at an all-male card game. We end up playing strip poker, and I lose, of course. So we begin playing for sexual favors. Me and two other guys end up in the bedroom. In this fantasy, I imagine that I am kneeling over both of them (they are on their backs) and I take turns at taking each of them into me very slowly. I like to watch them enter me, and, as usual, they are well endowed and rock hard with excitement. In the blink of an eye, our position is changed (as you can only do in fantasy), I am on all fours, giving head to one, and the other is entering me from behind, but not anally. (I never fantasize about anal insertion.) We all come at the same time.

I could go on—I have hundreds, from being a stripper or waitress to lying on a beach and being "taken" by a man in a string bikini. In many of them my "mystery" theme is continued, but I never recognize a face, even if I do get to see it. Many of my fantasies have force involved, but never pain. I always enjoy what my fantasy men do to me, and there usually isn't any resistance on my part. I enjoy sex, although so far it has been very difficult to climax with a man inside me. But then I never have let my fantasies take hold while I'm with a man. I intend to remedy that.

Tanya

I have always had fantasies and have been masturbating ever since I can remember, and it is great to know I'm far from alone. I'm 22 years old, a student at a fairly prestigious university, single (I currently have one steady boyfriend and one other lover—my boyfriend also has another lover), and am basically straight. I say basically because I fantasize about having sex with women, but never have. I'm the older of two kids, raised in a nonreligious, but nonetheless sexually repressive home. As I said earlier, I have masturbated from very early childhood, my mother caught me several times, either during the "act" or after the "act" ("your hands smell like dirty hiner"), and I was told this was filthy, disgusting, wrong, etc.

When I was in grade school—before third grade—I had one very good girlfriend. We would go up to her room and lock the door and tell each other sexual situations, like, "what if a man came up to you and asked if he could feel you up, then put his hand in your panties and started feeling you, over that bump, feeling you, feeling you . . ." while we would each masturbate ourselves. By the time I was 10, I was fucking myself with whatever I could: penlights, over-sized pencils, tampons (in the applicator), my fingers . . . I would also give myself douches or enemas. When I was 12, I got this very large stuffed animal, larger than me, with this incredible tail, and you can guess what I did with that tail! I think I fucked that stuffed animal at least once daily from the time I was 12 until I was 17, usually with one of three fantasies: first, that I was some innocent girl thrown into a jail by some evil older women, usually nuns (?!), who wanted to punish me. They send in this man (some gorgeous guy, usually one of several hockey players) who would take pity on me and just fuck me wonderfully. Second, I was an

419

experienced woman thrown into a jail (by no one in particular) with one of my stock males. He is injured, and I save his life. Somehow I get into a position so that I am bent over him, and next thing I know, he has bared my breast and is sucking my nipple. This drives me wild, and we are soon fucking, with me being the aggressor. Third, I am the male in the second fantasy, and the turn-on is mutual—no aggressor. I imagine sucking my own nipples and clit, then change over to the female role when it comes penis time.

Whew! This is hot. When I was 17, I went away to college and had my first real boyfriend and my first sexual experience. I fell madly in love with sex and remain so to this day. I've had about twelve to fourteen lovers, including my current two. I absolutely love new sex—that is, having sex with someone for the first time. The smell of a new man, the feel of new hands, new lips, a new cock—even thinking about it turns me on! I am an avid crotch and ass watcher.

When I fantasize, I will very often write the whole thing down while I masturbate. This makes it take a lot longer. (I can usually masturbate from a cold start to climax in five minutes.) When I'm good and satisfied, I'll crumple the paper until it's soft, wipe myself clean with it, and burn it or otherwise completely dispose of it.

My favorite fantasy requires a few props. I dim the lights and put on my most revealing dress and highest heels, no underwear. I am the only single woman at this incredibly ritzy dinner party, and I've decided to steal the most gorgeous man from his wife and fuck him. I walk around the house for a while, imagining the scene & the guests, walking very sexily, and finally spotting my prey. By now, my cunt is dripping. We're seated at dinner, and I'm across from my man. I put on my most sultry look and make sure I lean over so he can see my beautiful breasts and hot nipples. I know he's hard as a rock and is anticipating dessert. After dinner, I get up and wander off by myself, knowing he'll be following. I stand on this balcony looking out, and sure enough, I hear footsteps behind me. I don't turn. Suddenly, a hot hand has entered my dress and is cupping my tit, squeezing my nipple. Another hand is on my thigh, and there is an unmistakable bulge pressing on my ass. I lean back against him. The lower hand slips under my dress and finds my moist slit. Two fingers go in my cunt, and with his thumb on my clit he brings me to a quick orgasm. Now I turn to him and we kiss deeply. I feel his wonderful tight ass, then unzip his pants and feel his warm balls and finally his smooth, hard cock. I go down and admire it, begin licking the sides gently, taking my time about getting to the sensitive underpart. I take as much as I can in my mouth, suck, use my tongue on it, then back off, sucking his balls (I *love* balls!), then licking until he is moaning and I know he's about to burst. He sits down on an armless chair, and I straddle him, bringing myself slowly down on his aching rod. I squeeze with my cunt muscles, then fuck him slowly, slowly, then faster as I get hotter, and faster and faster until we come together in an incredible sweaty orgasm.

Sometimes this fantasy ends when the man manually brings me off. He kisses my neck then walks away, and I'm never sure who did it.

Veronique

I am a 32-year-old female raised in Southern, WASP middle-class America by "liberal," yet strict parents. My developmental years were very regimented and sheltered, with the myth of the proverbial "Southern Belle" well inculcated into my brain. I have worked my way through college and been very successful in my career.

My biggest problem in growing up may sound silly: being too good looking! I have had to fight most of my life to make men accept me as an intelligent being, to see beyond the hourglass figured, blue-eyed blonde image. Being an active feminist during the '70s, I became resentful toward men in general and in particular of their treatment of me as a sex object. My rather immature reaction was to play their game in reversal . . . to make them fall madly in love with me and then drop them like hot potatoes. To use THEM as sex objects for a change.

Well, this behind me and in the maturation process, I came to the conclusion that I LOVE MEN and have been trying to work toward liberating them and building sound relationships ever since. God knows they need release from their stereotypes as much as we do (or did).

This may sound selfish to some, but for me my fantasies are far too intimate, too personal, and I think deep down I am afraid that by talking about them to a partner I will somehow spoil this special, private zone that is totally mine—a small space that is created, elaborated and edited by me alone, for me alone. Apart from a slight embarrassment in bringing these thoughts to light, I fear that he would always know what I was thinking at certain moments, thereby destroying the flavor of the "forbidden fruit," intruding if you will, becoming a sort of psychic voyeur.

I believe that our fantasies are rooted in childhood experiences. (I can remember masturbating at age 4–6, although I don't believe I ever came, and then losing interest altogether until about age 13.) There is always an element of this first "knowing" or innocence that pervades my fantasies.

In retrospect, I can see a definite pattern to my fantasies. When I was on the pill, I fantasized almost exclusively about women (although I've never had a homosexual experience), and once off it, fantasized purely about heterosexual events. I guess hormones were playing a trick on me!

I have had a great variety of lovers—culturally, racially and agewise. I have been married, but have since divorced and have no children. But my life is far from empty! My current love has opened up a whole new world to me sexually, and I couldn't be happier. When he first asked me to share my fantasies, I told him probably the most notable is to make love in the most unusual places. He said he would eagerly go along with my desire, but I must keep myself ready at all times. So far, we've done it in just about every closet, bath or corner that we've been in, inside and out in public. Often there are many people around, and since I tend to raise my shrieks as his full ten-incher enters me from behind, he usually glides a finger or two in and out of my mouth to keep me quiet(er) and coming in gushes. It is the greatest turn-on for me to be always at his disposal whenever he feels the need, which is often!

On to fantasyland. These I use either while masturbating or while he is eating or playing with me, or simply to keep me well lubricated during the day when he is around.

1. I am 13, still technically virginal (I lost it at 14), but very well built and a cheerleader. My best friend, who is older by a few years and gay (male), is driving me home from a game, when we decide to park for a while in a secluded area. We drink some beer, maybe pass a jay and listen to some hard rock at full blast. Feeling a bit bold, I ask him to tell me about his affairs because I can't understand what two boys could possibly do together. He refuses to talk about it, but climbs into the backseat of the car and invites me to join him. (N.B. the scenario is true up to this point.) He then instructs me to lean across the front seat, which I do, having no earthly idea what he has in mind. He proceeds to slowly pull my lacy panties down to my knees and begins to lick, suck and tongue my ass. However, he is extremely careful never to touch my pussy, which by now in the scenario (as well as reality) is sopping, dripping wet. This stimulation and teasing drives me wild, and I beg him to "touch me there," but he refuses and just continues until I come and come. Usually, that's the end, but if it doesn't suffice . . . he reaches around and pulls on my clit, working it as if it were a pint-sized cock (boom!), always careful to avoid my cunt. Later, when I get home, my stepfather is waiting up for me. I am well past curfew and obviously in a mess. He pulls me roughly toward him as he is seated on an ottoman, runs his fingers up my inner thigh and discovers I am dripping love juice. Infuriated, he takes me over his knee and gives me the spanking of my life (in reality, I've never had one) first on top of my panties, then with them peeled off. That I refuse to cry makes him all the more determined, but I can feel him getting harder and harder under my stomach . . .

2. I'm a young, black African girl, living in a typical mud

hut with many other sisters of all ages, our father, mother, uncle and grandfather. All young boys are required to live separated from us in another village, until they marry. As we are near the equator, the heat makes any type of clothing unbearable, so we are usually nude except for some beads or jewelry. All young girls are in the complete care of older male members of the family, and it is their responsibility to prepare the girls for a full and joyous sexual life without fear or dread, thereby assuring fertility and continuity of the clan. There are many public ceremonies in which the men paint, adorn and tease their girls (usually with feathers on the genital area, etc.). From a very early age, the girl children are kept in a near-constant state of sexual arousal. They are encouraged to play with themselves and others, and the men can do anything short of intercourse, which is reserved only for their wives. In our hut, men stretch and pull at the bald pussies at will and often sleep with their erect cocks between our legs or against our buttocks. When a man from another family enters the dwelling, a show begins, as uncle or grandfather opens one of our cunts fully to his view and begins to massage the enlarged clit until we come. The men laugh and tease us endlessly. At age 9 the girls go through a ceremony in which they are drugged, strapped spread eagle in front of the tribe and then the clit is stimulated with various feathers until fully erect. The official shaman comes forward in a leopard headdress and sucks the little rosebud just to the point of orgasm, and then places a tiny gold band around it and secures it. This supposedly keeps the clit in full view and erect at all times, adding to its sensitivity and beauty. (By this time I've usually come several times, but if not . . .) My older sister and I sneak off one evening to quell our curiosity about the boys' camp. It is so far away that by the time we arrive it is quite dark and all we can see is their campfire. As we sneak up closer, unobserved, we see that they are having some form of festival: passing a pipe around and dancing very sensuously, one boy at a time, nude. At the end of each dance, an older boy leads him away by the hand, places him on all fours and begins to lick his balls and ass from behind, sometimes reaching around to pull on his penis, sometimes entering him like a dog and pumping like mad.

The end.

"MORE ORAL, PLEASE!"

If men fail the women in this book, they do it nowhere so much as in oral sex, where women have finally come of age. Having discovered it, they cannot get enough. It is a fascinating turn of events, given traditional woman's massive problems with the idea of a man putting his mouth between her legs.

Twenty years ago sex therapists referred to masturbation as the great taboo for women. Raised to think of anything outside of a relationship as threatening, why would a woman want to bring herself to orgasm? Even if she knew where her clitoris was, how could she explore the "cloaca" (Latin for sewer), which was how she thought of everything "down there"? If she couldn't touch it, she certainly wouldn't want a man looking at it, smelling it, God forbid licking it!

Then, as women began to learn some respect for their genitals and discovered the thrill of masturbation, the obvious next step was oral sex. They didn't just enjoy it, they expected a man to love, kiss, lick everything between their legs. The women in this chapter speak of their secretions as ambrosia.

Ironically, it is now some men who think the "sewer" smells, tastes foul. Not only does Ellie's husband refuse to go down on her, when he does deign to bring her to orgasm manually, he wipes his hand afterward on a piece of Kleenex. He is only surpassed in bad bedside manners by some of these women's husbands, who enjoy fellatio from their wives but refuse to return the favor.

For generations the penis enjoyed the supreme position—

in women's minds as well as in men's—as *the* powerful, beautiful genital. Because it was external and available for all the world to admire, it was easy for a little girl to assume her brother could control his body better than she could and thus please mother in the difficult toilet-training stage (where so many of our adult sexual problems begin); being visible, out there in the open air, it must also be cleaner than the girl's hidden, moist genitals. Once grown to adulthood —and still never having seen or touched her genitals (except to wipe herself clean)—a woman might take courage in hand, hold her breath, and wrap her delicate lips around a man's penis—though not as often as he would like—but she adamantly pushed his head away from her own private parts.

That was traditional woman. When I was doing research on *Men in Love,* my contributors' fantasies were filled with imaginary heroines who did what their wives/women would not: they not only loved to go down on a man, they lapped up his semen with gusto. By putting her mouth on his penis, bringing it to full erection and then—and this is the most important point—swallowing his precious bodily fluid, the fantasy woman reversed the repugnance a man thought women/mother felt about the part of his body that had never been acceptable. Because men longed so deeply to receive oral sex, they could not understand why in reality, even if a woman gave it, she refused to accept it. How could the man know that unlike him the woman had come to identify with mother's disgust of all genitalia, that she had become her mother?

No longer. Now what I hear are choruses of women longing for oral sex, pleading with their men to go down on them. As unreliable as most sex survey figures are, there is no doubt that more men and women are giving and receiving oral sex than ever before. The fact that the women in this book aren't getting as much as they'd like doesn't necessarily reflect a national starvation; my contributors are self-selected by an already avid interest in sex. But if there are more women out there who are unsatisfied by the oral sex they are getting, it could be that men just aren't willing to give the little lady what she wants for the same reason women used to roll over in bed and deny sex to men: consciously or unconsciously men are expressing anger at the power balance outside the bedroom.

In the minds of some men, that scale is settling danger-ously in the woman's favor; if men are having more sick headaches than ever before, it may be that the withholding of sex is no longer a power on which women have a monopoly. A man can still get his orgasm during inter-course; but going down on a woman—well, he feels more like a wimp than King Kong.

Whether it was the books, the videos, the articles in the women's magazines that gave them permission, women have learned there is no guaranteed orgasm like the clitoral, reachable by one's own hand, by modern machine, but oh, so much sweeter by way of a loving, warm mouth. Practice has taught women that the loss of control they once feared is not dangerous but delicious; and today working women have so many more reasons to want to escape, for a few precious moments, the added disciplines and responsibili-ties demanded of them.

You can only trust that you will return from the other side of orgasm once you've experienced it again and again. When women had no real control over their lives, the prospect of sexually letting go was filled with terror. Now that they have seen the rapturous midorgasm expressions on other women's faces via film and video, they, too, want to give up their iron control over reality. They wonder, Why not me? They read the blow-by-blow descriptions of how to give and receive oral sex and are eager to try it: If you love me, they say, eat me like a peach.

Is there a greater sexual gift we give one another than this most intimate kiss? If a woman has any doubts about the infamous bad smell and taste, it takes only one good man to prove that it's all in her head. One man or one woman. The women in this book are never more rhapsodic than when they are describing oral sex. Erica's husband is a "wonderful man . . . but dull," and so she fantasizes another man "is finger-fucking me, rolling my nipples and sucking my pussy. After about 60 seconds (60 wonderful SUCKS), at last 100,000 flapping quail wings take flight through my body as I climax as he continues fingering, rolling and rubbing, and sucking."

Some of these women are so eager to be eaten they attack their lovers' mouths with their genitals: "Rockets of sensation shot through my body as I thrusted—fucking his face . . ." says Trudi, who switches her fantasies back and forth from women to men. "She started rocking her hips against my face, and her clit hit my tongue. She moaned, 'There. Lick me there!' She's pulling on my head, making her cunt almost swallow me . . . this chick's on fire, riding my face for all it's worth."

For many of these women, one mouth, one tongue, is not enough. "After two years of being together [my husband] confesses that he doesn't really like oral sex and masturbation," says Penny. "I love oral sex and if I didn't masturbate, I'd go crazy . . . Now I'm afraid to ask him to suck me, when it's the thing I want most . . ." Penny solves all her problems with one fantasy: First, she imagines that a man has slipped under the dining table to eat her. Then, to assuage her anxiety, she includes another couple who encourage her not to be embarrassed but "to just enjoy the ride. They rise and engage in gentle caressing of my breasts. I sigh as the man below begins gently, then more probingly, kissing my wet pussy. I begin to moan and my friends bend down to kiss and nibble my nipples . . ." In the end, Penny gratefully eats the other woman and "we come one after the other as the crowd applauds," providing her with the acceptance of her oral lust that her mean spirited husband had withdrawn.

In their search for ever more sensation, these very creative oral women include the anal thrill along with the clitoral. The thinking tends to run, If it feels good to have one orifice aroused, why not all?—a sentiment that requires some ingenious types of two-headed dildos and gyrating vibrators. "I don't know why I came to love the anal thing but I really do," says Tara, an inventive woman who enjoys a fantasy of being forced to have anal sex while in reality she uses two vibrators, one "to tease my clit and shove up my ass while building to the climax and a large U-shaped one with small friction bumps [to use] when I'm finally going to come." All the while she lies in front of a full-length mirror for the final voyeuristic thrill, "so I can see what my asshole looks like during all this."

Anal sex is an acquired taste, as some of these women, who love it more than their men, lament. Throughout this book I've been surprised at the eager curiosity and lack of hesitancy the women show in exploring the possibilities of anal sex. They are almost all in their twenties and bring their generation's lack of shame and distaste to what they assume is yet another position, another erogenous zone to be explored. They don't just want it for themselves, they are equally eager to look at, touch, kiss, smell, probe their men's anuses. But again and again, the men clap their cheeks together with the nervous alacrity of maidens protecting their virginity.

For many men anal sex represents nothing so much as homosexuality. What if he enjoyed it? Yes, it may be a woman actually arousing him, but in his mind, in his fantasy, what if he suddenly imagined it was not her finger but another man's penis? Instinctively, protectively, he pushes her mouth, her hand away.

Ironically, I believe it is the very same logic that has inspired so many of these women to think about the pleasures of anal sex. Before AIDS there was a period when homosexuality was in vogue, in fashion, in its most powerful and pervasive manifestation. How could women who had homosexual friends, who saw homosexuals in films and on television not wonder what these usually very attractive men did together. "Actually," Madonna says in a *Vanity Fair* interview, "it would be great to be both sexes. Effeminate men intrigue me more than anything in the world. I see them as my alter egos. I feel very drawn to them. I think like a guy, but I'm feminine. So I relate to feminine men."

Throughout this book women, in their fantasies, have watched gay men during sex, picturing both the excitement and the tenderness they imagined two men experience together.

Anal sex, for women, has become a part of their own erotic dreams of total gratification. It would, however, be misleading to suggest that women's new fascination with anal sex derives only from curiosity about homosexuality; the anus is a highly erogenous area unto itself and would probably be included in more heterosexual activity if it were not so primitively associated with "bad" smells, "bad" sights, "bad" memories. Before we learned that our excrement made mother wince, it was one of our earliest gifts to her. Our need of her love along with our fears of her rejection over issues involving that small area between our legs became the battleground of our earliest efforts to please her and retain some modicum of the memory of what was once a good sensation "down there." What is strikingly new in this research is how many women have discarded yet another layer of Niceness.

Ellie

I'm 27 years old, and have been married for a year and a half. My husband is 24. Our marriage is very satisfying for me in every way except for sex. Don't get me wrong, he and I make love beautifully—when we get around to it. Our average is 1.5 times a week, which he says is satisfactory for him. I would be happier with 3–4 times a week. As a result, I masturbate a lot.

My husband is very tender and loving during sex, but he will not perform cunnilingus on me. I had a boyfriend once who enjoyed loving me this way, but my husband refuses to even try. He loves it when I go down on him, of course, but he won't bring himself to look at my "naughty bits," let alone kiss them. He will bring me to orgasm manually, but as soon as I have come, he pulls his hand away and wipes it on a piece of Kleenex. Arrgh!

I am about thirty pounds overweight anyway and have

enough trouble thinking of myself as a desirable, sexy woman, without my husband's partial rejection of my most female part. As a result of all this, my favorite fantasy is pretending that my own hand is my husband's mouth, bringing me to climax.

I hope and pray that someday he'll discover that I don't smell and taste bad.

Hannah

I shall write this as if I were writing my fantasies to him:

FIRST SCENARIO:

I'm hoping we'll be able to go this coming weekend. I'm really looking forward to having my cunt rub against the saddle while I imagine that I am riding bareback, my cunt rubbing against the hairy back of the horse, massaging it—feeling the moisture building, realizing that my panties are all wet, wishing I were being fucked.

On the trail it's easy to escape into a world of fantasy and to think and relive some of the scenarios you've related in your past. The scenarios where I come across a clearing—you'd be waiting to assist, of course, as I knelt under the horse to stroke his huge cock, to lick on his big head and to massage his massive balls. And when his cock was fully extended, hard as steel and throbbing, you'd order me on my hands and knees, positioning that steel rod *directly* at my cunt while encouraging this creature to push forward, knocking me flat on the ground. After the first time of being flat on my stomach, you slip a collar around my neck and can now pull my head up by the leash, getting me to my knees as the eager cock slams up against *my* cunt once again. I'm now actually being pushed along, I'm scrambling to remain on my knees.

Realizing that I'm exhausted and the horse is about to shoot his wad, you flip me onto my back just in time to receive a load of horse cum—wad after wad—until I'm one big, sticky cum-covered barnyard tramp, with horse cum all over my tits, my belly, my cunt and my thighs.

Your cock was hot, purple and full, and the only appropriate place to deposit your treasure was on my face. Glob after glob dropped onto my face, covering my eyes, my nose, my cheeks, my lips and my chin.

This is what I'll be daydreaming about should we go riding.

SECOND SCENARIO:

After resting a bit and having another drink, Sylvia and I agree that you and Scott deserve a treat.

While watching us perform, dildoing each other, drowning in each other's juices, being fucked by Wolf and eating dog cum, your lovely cock and Scott's nice cock had swollen until we thought the veins would burst. The head of your cock was purple. Scott's cock was throbbing, both were hard as steel and looked as though they could use a hand—our hands, that is.

You and Scott were sitting on the sofa, completely naked (watching us perform caused your body temperature to rise), with your legs spread apart.

Sylvia and I knelt in front of the sofa, she in front of Scott; I knelt in between your legs, and we began massaging your balls and stroking the cocks, followed by our mouths nibbling and chewing on the hairy balls, licking from the balls up the shaft to the tip and down again.

You and Scott agreed earlier that when you both came it would not be in our mouths but all over our puckered rosebuds, so when it was about to happen—when both cocks were about to explode, Sylvia and I turned around, on our hands and knees with our asses up in the air, and after stroking your cocks between our cracks—you shot wads of creamy, sticky cum all over our butt holes.

Then you and Scott massaged the cum all over our cheeks and all over our cunt lips, and what remained on your hands was smeared on our faces.

It was time to perform once again. First Sylvia knelt behind me and licked your cum off my rosebud and cheeks. I did the same to hers, and we ate each other's cunt, savoring the cum that had been smeared on the lips.

She was enjoying the taste of your cum, while I was satisfying my hunger with Scott's juices.

After we had cleaned each other up we licked cum off our faces. I licked hers and she licked mine. We were like hungry animals—looking for more. That's when we noticed that both cocks were stiff once again, but this time you and Scott asked us to rest the upper part of our bodies on the sofa, kneeling with our legs spread and our hands pulling apart our cheeks so our asses could be fucked.

Scott had no difficulty shoving his stiff prick up Sylvia's asshole—it slid in easily, and he slammed it in deep while holding her hips, in and out while she screamed with pleasure.

It took a little longer for your swollen cock to penetrate my tight opening, but once your head was inside, pulled out and shoved back in several times, it got easier, and before long your cock was buried deep inside, and all I could do was moan and beg you to fuck me hard, to tear me apart if you must but not to stop, and you complied happily, riding my ass as if riding a horse, slapping my cheeks with each thrust deep inside until I began to shudder, feeling your cock erupt, filling my dark cavern with your whitish cream.

THIRD SCENARIO:
So how was your weekend?

I rented four movies on Friday—*Wild Orchid* was one of them. Mickey Rourke really turns me on. He reminds me of you. In fact, as I watched the movie I thought of you. But by comparing it to *9½ Weeks,* well, I prefer *9½ Weeks.* However, after the scene with the black man and woman and during it, of course, my fingers were quite active, and my cunt was as hot as hell during the final scene, just as the girl was.

Yesterday while I was home, I had an opportunity to watch the videotape you gave me.

The last scenario of Volume I—the dark-haired girl. While watching I was absolutely losing control thinking of sucking on your cock, being fucked, etc.

Then in Volume II there were two cocks for a blonde to

433

feast on, and feast she did—as her lunch, which she hadn't had as yet. She went back and forth between the two guys, licking and sucking their balls and big cocks.

One of the guys reminded me of Charlie, so I drifted into fantasy and you and Charlie being the two I was feasting on.

I was soon being fucked from behind while sucking on one of the cocks, then both of you were on either side of me as I sucked each one, back and forth, wildly.

I was on the floor on my side while Charlie fucked me, and you jammed *your* stiff cock into my mouth, and eventually I had my lunch; a mouthful and face full of warm gooey cum, lots of it, a big smile on *my* face and two drained and happy cocks.

Again *I* came many times, using my fingers, three, stroking in and out of my hot, wet, dripping cunt and once using the champagne bottle.

I thought of what it would be like to be out of control, to be deliriously pleasured and abused, hair pulled, ass slapped, tits pinched, cunt punched and fucked in every opening until I was a dripping, uncontrollable bitch who was still looking for more and was told I'd get it.

Why do you remind me of Rourke? Well, listening to your scenarios makes me wet, and sometimes it's unbearable—I want it so bad. I feel your beautiful cock and I *want* more. You tease, excite and make me hungry for more always, even after a delicious handful, 'cause I long to lick off every drop, long to lick and nibble on your hairy balls, long to rim your puckered little rosebud, long to be squeezed with a big bear hug, long to be fistfucked, but most of all want to pleasure you, so I contain myself but wishing always that I could lose control someday with you—to go out of my mind.

Yes, I did say I want abuse, humiliation, degradation and that I would be obedient, subservient, cooperative, etc. But I need the other side of the coin as well—scenarios involving you and me, only of me, you and a special friend. Peter, Charlie or Scott—attention, kindness and cum, as much as you can share.

I'm not complaining mind you. Some days I'm more

lonely than others, some days I wish certain people didn't exist. Some days I'm down, but otherwise I'm okay.

At this moment I'm thinking of you, your lovely cock—how beautiful it was on Friday and how bad I wanted it at five o'clock.

Your worshipping slave, suck-slut, dog fucker, hungry witch in heat, who loves your cum, who thinks you're terrific, who missed you yesterday.

Now picture me wearing black thigh-hi's, high heels, a string bikini—black, of course, and nothing else. I'm surrounded by a group of your friends, including a few familiar faces, their cocks dangling out of their pants as I crawl to each one on my knees sizing them up.

One of your friends told me to crawl to him and try to catch his dick in my mouth without using my hands, telling me how full his balls were. He had me begging for it, grabbed my hair and jammed it into my mouth, ramming it as if it were my hot cunt.

My fat ass was up in the air while I was now being fucked in the mouth—another friend of yours came up behind me and slammed his big cock up my cunt, pumping in and out wildly as if riding a horse.

The friend fucking my face came all over it, and the one fucking my cunt came—filling my cunt full of his cream, so much that it ran down my thighs.

Your other friends loved this sight, began stroking their cocks, and I was crazed for more cum. Getting up, I began to crawl to another but was pushed down flat on my back. A big black dildo was pulled out of somewhere, an electric one, I was being stuffed with it—my legs pulled apart—and ordered to dildo myself silly.

While doing so, each of your friends stroked their cocks till they were hard as steel and ready to spurt, and one by one they shot their wads all over my body, all over my face, all over my puss till I was a big fat gooey blob—wallowing in it like a hog in mud, and my body was shaking with an orgasm—a wild, juicy orgasm as I squirmed in this big, slimy puddle of cum.

435

My hair was covered, my tits were covered, I was a cum-covered slut if there ever was one.

Afterwards your friends left, one by one, and you and I were alone.

FOURTH SCENARIO:

To continue with our scenarios—I'm tied up on the bed with a dildo in my cunt and one in my ass, and you are in the other room. The dildos are held in place by my panties, and as I squirm and move a little, the dildos work their way inside a little further. I can sense the moistness inside my cunt, and as I lie there, helpless, I'm hoping you'll return to pound the dildos into me, hard and fast as you once did in the large conference room while I was on my hands and knees.

I'm chilled and begin to shudder. When the door opens, I turn my head to see Charlie standing beside me, surprised at what he is looking at, shocked that I was left alone, stunned at the pathetic sight of me trying to orgasm by rocking back and forth with the dildos stuck in my openings.

He asked why I was in this condition. I replied that I enjoyed being abused, humiliated, degraded from time to time, and that I was indeed humiliated that he had seen me like this today.

Charlie wasn't happy about my condition. He felt that I should be untied and given an opportunity to relax a few minutes and a chance to warm up, so he proceeded to fix me a drink—brandy—and slowly massaged my legs, my shoulders, my back, my tummy and my tits in order to warm me. His hands were smooth, gentle as they glided over my body, very sensually touching my tits as he aroused the nipples—followed by his tongue, which flicked back and forth across them; first one then the other, and then his mouth was sucking on them, back and forth from one to the other, as his hands stroked and kneaded my back, my hips and my thighs. His fingers were lightly touching my cunt lips.

It was exciting. I was coming, and he hadn't done anything, yet I was warm. I felt wonderful. I wanted him.

While he sucked on my tits and his hands roamed my

body, he told me that it didn't matter that I was older. He didn't think I was fat, but nothing mattered except to be fulfilled, to experience the ultimate, to be fucked in the ass. I told him that I never had the pleasure, and with that he positioned me on my hands and knees. My ass was high in the air, my cunt was dripping with my juices, my thighs were moist, and I could feel the warmth of his body as he pressed against my backside. I could feel his hardness as he slid his stiff cock back between my cheeks, and my excitement increased the flow of my juices as he slid inside my cunt just once to moisten his cock before slamming it up my asshole.

At that point he became an animal as he slammed his hard cock inside my ass, practically tearing me apart. I cried out, but he ignored my cries to stop—the pounding intensified. He felt like a searing hot poker, and my cheeks burned as he slapped them with each thrust into my tight ass.

He had the stamina of a bull, and the intensity of the ass-fucking increased. I was in pain and yet I was expecting more, and I thought of you. I wanted you more than anything—more than life itself—and you were in the other room.

I thought of your lovely cock resting on my lips, my tongue circling your ridge, the taste of your delicious cum—and just then Charlie's load was deep inside. It was running out of my hole and down my legs as I collapsed on the bed, he on top of me.

That's how you found us as you entered the room, saying that you had a surprise for me—another cock to have fun with—another cock that loved to fuck asses bad and who wanted a shot at mine.

I pleaded and begged to be left alone, that it hurt, but you insisted that an insatiable, fat, cum-eating, greedy slut deserves more—she deserves all her holes can hold, and with that I was lifted onto my knees once again, your fingers dipped into my cunt, withdrawing with my creamy juices, held in front of my mouth so I could suck your fingers clean. Then you slam them into my hot twat again, lifting me on the bed.

My ass was up in the air, with my cunt throbbing. A *larger* dildo was being forced inside—it wasn't just a dildo, it was a vibrator, and it was turned on the high speed till I shook uncontrollably.

Just as the cock entered my butt hole, it slid deep inside easily after its initial intrusion. The vibrator was being stroked in and out and every now and then glided over my cunt lips and clit, and as my head was pulled up by my hair—your swollen cock invaded my mouth so I couldn't cry out. I was in ecstasy—it couldn't be better than this, could it? I thought of you—your cum filled my mouth, my asshole, and I was filled again and my cunt was on fire.

FIFTH SCENARIO:

On the ride home on Friday, I thought about Thursday and wondered how it could be more "outstanding." If time had permitted perhaps lifting me off the floor; if time had permitted perhaps fucking my tits; if time had permitted perhaps allowing me to kneel in front of you, allowing me to nibble on your balls or lick the underside of your hard shaft; if time had permitted perhaps shooting your wad onto my tongue. It was enjoyable though, being almost naked, a condition I would love to see you in—standing in front of the door while I sit in your chair watching as you drop your pants and slide your shorts down, exposing your beautiful cock.

Saturday morning I was alone. I went about business as usual after showering, etc. I had breakfast while watching the news coverage of the war, followed by a session with my champagne bottle. I had thought about you so much the night before that on Saturday I was in desperate need of relief—so with thoughts of you, your lovely swollen cock full of life, picturing it between my legs with its head touching my clit—the neck of the bottle resting between my meaty soft cunt lips, sliding inside, my thighs grasping it tightly as I moved and squirmed with my eyes closed, pretending that it was your throbbing cock that was filling my twat.

I grabbed the base of the bottle and stroked it in and out

using my left hand while the fingers of my right hand were busy with my clit, massaging it, pulling it, pulling on it and twisting it.

Both hands then massaged my tits until my nipples were erect as I bounced slowly, feeling the bottle deep inside.

The sensation of the bottle neck inside, coupled with the massaging of my clit produced a nice orgasm—at that point I thought of you exploding all over me, all over my tits, my stomach and my cunt.

Afterwards, the bottle withdrawn, lying quietly on the bed, I could feel throbbing sensations inside my cunt, and it felt swollen.

I continued to think of you.

Yvette

NAME:	Yvette (purely mythological for reasons given below)
HAIR:	Redhead HEIGHT: 5ft. 9in.
AGE:	46 and female (am the second of four children)
DIVORCED:	after twenty years of marriage to an alcoholic
CHILDREN:	two girls, ages 25 and 20
CITIZENSHIP:	Born in Canada. I am a naturalized U.S. citizen.
SCHOOLING:	High school graduate, 2+ years trade school, 2 years college
EMPLOYMENT:	Asst. Systems Manager of an architectural firm. All other employees in my dept. are male. I also do some writing on a free-lance basis.

I was married to an American I fell in love with at first sight. I must have been wearing blinkers, because for so many years I failed to see how much his drinking problem was affecting him, myself and the children. When I did come to that realization I got out of the marriage.

I never felt loved as a child. My older sister created havoc in our household ever since I can remember and caused my parents a great deal of pain. I came into my marriage with very low self-esteem.

I was not a virgin when I married, having experienced sexual encounters with at least four men including my husband.

My first relationship, after the marriage ended, was after eighteen months of sexual deprivation. The gentleman, whom I saw for six months, turned out to be married. This came as quite a shock to me since I'd been seeing him almost every day after work and we went out several times each week, in addition to several weekends away at the beach, etc.

A variety of other lovers have since given me the pleasure of their company. A few have been long-term (seven months –one year) relationships. Some still keep in touch.

My husband was not well endowed but was extremely good at oral sex. I believe he overcompensated in this way because he had a complex about the size of his penis. Initially, it took me two months to let him perform oral sex on me. Once I experienced it I absolutely loved it and can never get enough now.

My husband indicated to me that I was a nymphomaniac because I always wanted sex. After having sex with him, I wanted to follow him around, grateful as hell, for several days until the cycle repeated itself, until he finally had sex with me.

A male friend indicated to me recently that, in his opinion, women are "suckers" or "fuckers"; some are better at one thing than the other. He put me in the "sucker" category after experiencing all my sexual talents. I think I am orally inclined, both in giving and receiving oral sex. I felt the need to prove to him that I was also a "fucker" and soon did so by milking his dick for hours with my cunt. I always did like a challenge.

In the past I have gone for long periods without sex, not wanting to show other people (men) how much I really need it. My pride has held me back. The longest period was just over four years. There were extenuating circumstances: one guy, whom I dated for a year, exposed me to genital herpes, and I felt my sex life was over upon discovering I had the disease. I always have my partner use condoms if I know any kind of outbreak is in the offing. Some men really resent the request to wear a condom.

A man recently told me he is turned on by women who can put a condom on a man by using her mouth. I'm thinking of practicing this with my dildo.

I absolutely love sex. I am turned on by the use of vulgarity in the bedroom, which I only recently experienced for the first time. I am not in menopause yet but am completely immersed in sexual feelings to the extent that I have considered asking the doctor to give me something to make me want it less. I masturbate frequently, sometimes several times a day.

I recently had a wonderful sexual experience with a man, Robert, who lives and works in the Middle East. I've just spent eleven days with him, during which we each got about ten hours sleep, total. We went to the theater, ate out, danced, talked, made love for hours on end. When he left, I was devastated. At present my hope is that he will also want to continue our relationship.

When I'm with Robert, time is suspended. He is fascinated by the amount of come I produce. He is not the only man to have commented on this. He will suck me for hours, fully gratifying my need for oral sex.

I have sucked more cock with him than I have ever in my life. I swallow his come and have learned to deep-throat his large cock. He taught me to do this in front of a mirror. I could see the ecstasy on his face as I performed fellatio on him. Indeed the mirror image turned me on even more. I usually come while sucking a man.

It was the most complete sexual and friendship experience I have ever had and it left me feeling that it would never be the same with another man.

I have two fantasies I would like to share:

I once saw a picture in *Playboy* magazine, a movie scene.

It depicted an enormous "Gulliver"-size cock on wheels, secured by lots of ropes which were being used by tiny "Lilliputian" people in colorful dress to pull the huge circumcised cock along. The reference to the storybook character is my best depiction of what I saw in that photo. It firmly imprinted itself in my mind. This is the Supreme Cock of all Cocks, and as I masturbate, these tiny people are bringing this cock to me to finally satisfy all my wants, needs, and desires.

My second fantasy was created after a male friend was arrested for drunken driving. As I drove to pick him up I fantasized about jail and the horny men it held within its walls.

I picture the cells around a main exercise compound. All of the inmates have their pants down at their ankles and are masturbating at the sight they behold in the center of the compound. That sight is another cell, barred on all sides, yet open to the view of all. I am lying in that cell, wearing a skimpy piece of lingerie and masturbating for all to see. They cannot touch me but they can see me fondle my breasts and rub my clitoris. I rub myself vigorously, seeing their excitement, listening to their exclamations of "horny bitch," "cunt," etc., and bring myself to a thunderous climax as they jerk off and shoot their sperm my way.

I wonder if this fantasy is related to the months I spent masturbating when I found out I had herpes. Look but do not touch.

Trudi

Number 1: One day I was lying on the couch in my living room in just a robe (I had just showered). I was bored and slipped a porno flick into the VCR and lay back to enjoy. I was getting really turned on, and even though it was the middle of the morning, I thought, What the hell. I let my robe fall open and casually let my hands move down my body, which was still damp from the shower. I moved to my breasts, which have always been remarkably sensitive. I teased my nipples until they stood out like spikes. From there, my hands grazed over my flat belly to my bush. I parted the soft blond down to get to my hot cunt—already moist and waiting. I covered my mound with my hand, and as my middle finger arched and buried itself deep in my pussy, I rubbed the heel of my hand over my clit. My thrusting got faster and faster as the action on the screen got hotter and hotter. Suddenly, I looked up—above me stood a girl. She had long dark hair and was small, but had very large breasts. She smiled and unbuttoned her blouse and let her skirt drop. She stood in front of me in only a pair of black panty hose, watching as I masturbated. I moaned and smiled back at her. Soon, she was on top of me, and I was still masturbating as she kissed and massaged my breasts. I was covered in sweat. From nowhere, she produced a banana and shoved it up my cunt. I was near the verge of coming as she rammed it in and out, in and out. She moved down and started to eat the banana. This drove me wild. When she was through with the banana, she ate me. She held onto my ass as I bucked my hips off the couch and pulled her face farther into my cunt. She was sucking hard on my clit and, at the same time, humping away on one of my legs. I came like gangbusters, screaming as I never had before—in unthinkable pleasure. She produced a can of whipped cream. She squirted it all over her breasts, and I eagerly licked it off. She was moaning and she pushed me on my back and sat on my face. I started licking her cunt lips through the nylon of her panty hose, aching to rip them off. She started rocking her hips against my face, and her clit hit my tongue. She moaned, "There. Lick me there!" She's pulling on my head, making her cunt almost swallow me . . . this chick's on fire, riding my face for all it's worth. I'm aching for something—anything—to be shoved up my cunt. Suddenly, sensing my need, she straps on a huge dildo—fourteen by three inches—and rolls me over onto my stomach. I get up onto my hands and knees, squirming and waiting. She rams the whole thing into my cunt and starts humping away. In and out, burying it in me to the hilt every time. Then her hands go to work—one goes to my clit, making me nearly faint as orgasm after orgasm washes over me. Her other hand she uses on herself until we both come for a final time and collapse. When I come to, she's gone. The only evidence I have that I didn't dream it is a banana peel lying on the coffee table—drenched in my cum.

Number 2: I'm lying facedown on a towel by the side of a pool. I'm dressed in a pair of bikini bottoms and no top. I'm watching a very handsome man doing laps in the pool. He doesn't realize I'm there. Then he notices me; he gets out of the pool and comes over to offer to put suntan oil on my back. I roll over to reveal my breasts and say smilingly, "How about if you . . ." but I don't have a chance to finish my thought. He drops to his knees and starts kissing me. His hot tongue is going right down my throat. He pulls my pants off, and I loop my thumbs around the sides of his trunks and rip them off. His mouth moves to my tits—rolling my nipples in his mouth and letting his hands roam down to my pussy. He started to move in between my legs and was soon lapping my cunt hungrily. He sucked on my clit, driving me wild with passion. Rockets of sensation shot through my body as I thrusted—fucking his face. I knew what I wanted . . . I pushed him onto his back and mounted him . . . not on his dick yet, but teasing. I kissed him hotly, and he took my hips and lifted me up, setting me down on his hard-on. I'm so wet, it just slides right in. I look into his eyes as I ride his prick and he massages my breasts. He starts to moan and meet my thrusts and soon he comes—buckets of come shooting into me. I'm still not there, but I slide off of his limp dick and lie down next to him, fingering myself and wishing I had a dildo.

The next thing I know, I have a strange sensation of a tongue on my cunt. I turn halfway around and am shocked to see a large male German shepherd behind me. Shocked, but excited, I bend over farther and let him lick my insatiable pussy and asshole. Soon he attempts to mount me. I have to help him guide his rod in, but soon it's in me to the hilt. He's humping away, and soon his knot goes in. We're hung up, and I'm nearly passing out from coming so many times. The dog comes, we separate, and he leaves. I roll over—at last satisfied—and the man and I kiss and sleep.

These are my two major fantasies. Actually, if I'm not really horny and masturbating—which I do a lot—the lesbian stuff really turns me off. I really like female dominance, male dominant bondage (mild), and doggie style. I love to give blow jobs, but I save that one for real life and the others I just indulge myself and my dildo in. Incidentally, I'm 18 years old.

Cynthia

I am 42, married and with two children. I would like to share my fantasy with you. I feel it illustrates how we create situations to suit our needs. Its first appearance was during a period of very low self-esteem.

I am anonymous. I spend the middle of the day in a hotel suite furnished to my specifications. There are no windows and only one door. Viewed from above, it appears a Grecian-urn design, a motif of open-ended boxes of finished off U's. The boxes, however, are of unpainted plywood. At the base of each U on the outside is a straight-backed chair. Inside each is a special chaise fitted for a woman to spread her legs around the base and into the box on either side. Mouth high is a padded opening for tongues—no cocks allowed. There are no curtains covering the boxes, for this is a special gallery. One chooses the cunt by looking at them all. Inside, we women can see no one but ourselves. We describe our sensations to each other quietly so the tonguers can't hear. It keeps us wet, the better to increase our desirability.

I have my favorite tongues, and one of my regular cunt lickers visits at least once a week. I cream when it touches me, each time it touches. I know immediately which one it is, and each time it arrives I want more of it until I think I'll burst having to remain anonymous.

After months of this, the gallery operator finally allows me my silent wish. The tonguer has offered him anything he wants in return for my body for an hour or two. I'm scared but I agree. It is, after all, my decision. But what, I wonder, if the tonguer is ugly or smelly? What if the tonguer can't stand the way I look outside my box within a box?

I'm in a cubicle on a cot. The tonguer opens the door. I see only a shadow. Then a hand, an arm . . . she's so beautiful I can't stop staring at her. She's sophisticated, with a warm, husky voice that matches her tongue. She undresses slowly, folding each garment carefully, draping her dress over the single chair in the room. And then she's on top of me. Her skin is soft and sweet, her nipples taut with anticipation. She is magic. Gentle and soft, she kisses me until there is no place she hasn't explored, no part of her I haven't licked and kissed. We come together, separately, in every imaginable way, and still I can't get enough of her. There is no rush. This is eroticism at its height, breadth and depth. We are the stuff of dreams.

I have always accepted my fantasies as a natural part of myself. I have also kept them close. They are my personal stories, written, directed, produced, edited and reviewed by me. I star in them but I am also the audience. I see them as films to draw on anytime I choose. They are mine to change without consultation. Sometimes I use them while I'm alone. They serve me when my husband is fucking me; I need them then. I have an enormous film library in my head. I spin my Rolodex and summon according to my needs. The exception is the first fantasy I've written down for you. As my husband climbs between my legs, it is always my old friend.

There are other sides to me too. The following variation of the above fantasy has been developed in the past year. I use it as a lead-in to others when I'm high on life:

Outside the suite red neon signs flash, one for each plate-glass window siding the door: "Mama's Ristorante." In the door a sign hangs below the bell. It says "Specialty of the house: Dietetic Lunch." Inside there is a round table for two spread with a red-checkered tablecloth at each box. A Chianti bottle, a glass and a napkin rest on each table.

I loathe fat people but I've always wondered what a grossly overweight man might look like in the nude. (Shades

446

of the past; I was a fat little girl.) I'm not going to find out. My favorite customer is tucking his napkin in his collar. He adjusts his chair and sits, his fat cheeks hanging over the edges of it. His facial cheeks are drawn down; he's not pleased. He'd rather get sucked off, but no one will let him. He can't even pay for it. He's disgustingly fat. My desperate man has turned to Mama. She's the last chance he's got to lose weight. He eats lunch here every day. Nothing but her cunt touches his lips at noon. (As for the rest of the day, he wouldn't dare overeat. Mama wrote him a note. If he doesn't lose weight steadily over the next year or so, he won't be allowed into the ristorante.)

He comes each day and leaves completely satisfied. Over the months, Mama's watching him. He's had to buy new clothes several times. It's becoming apparent that this is going to be one handsome man. She writes him another note. "Exercise. I know who you are, and I'm going to make sure you do it. I'll see you sometime, my lovely tonguer, my going-to-be Adonis. I know how hard it's been, but don't let cock Robin become discombobulated. Mama loves . . ."

It's a year and a half later. When the former fat man comes to lunch there's an old-fashioned scale beside the table. The note on the mirror reads: "Step on it, lover. Mama wants to see . . ." He looks around. No one is there. He does as he's told. The needle jumps, flips back and forth, then steadies at 180. Another five pounds and it'll be over. He eats and wipes his face. Mama breaks her silence. "Five to go, my lovely man. Hurry! Mama can't wait."

Finally the day arrives. My former fat man is lean and in great physical condition. Mama is waiting for him. She sits at the table, dressed to kill. She's sipping a glass of wine, her legs crossed, skirt hitting the knees. He rounds the corner and sees her. "You!" he says in astonishment.

"Who else?" Mama sets the glass on the table. (Mama has been his running partner since he began his exercise program. An enthusiastic crotch watcher, she makes sure she ends their encounters with an eye on his. She never leaves until he has a giant erection. This is part of her philosophy. Mama builds strong bodies in every way.) "Do you think I'd let you hang loose? I adore being your fantasy while you're having lunch. You come to Mama's, but Mama comes first."

Mama pats his erection. "Let's go. We've got reservations."

She takes him by the arm. They go to lunch (salad; what else?). At dessert time, while he's eating cheesecake, Mama has her sweets under the table—Mama always watches her weight. Proving, you can have your cake and eat it too.

Mama loves . . .

Martha

I'm a 19-year-old high school graduate who is currently looking after an invalid grandmother. I have black hair, blue eyes, I'm five feet six inches, and weigh 147 pounds. People tell me I'm exceptionally good looking, but I was never one to judge my own appearance. A very close friend described me once as being "a reluctant Amazon"—a compliment which I cherish.

I've only had sex twice, both times with the same man. I loved it both times and, had I seen the man more often (thirty miles separate us), I'm positive we would have screwed at every available opportunity. I masturbate often —at least four times a week. The first time I masturbated was when I was around 4 years old. I'd lie in bed, gently rubbing and massaging my entire genital area. Around the age of 7, I tried to get my little brother to stick his finger up my ass, but he refused. When I was 11, I had a poodle that *loved* to lick my cunt. For the next five years, that dog was my only means of masturbation. I was around 16 before I finally found out what the vagina was all about—it was when I discovered the candle. I remember one time I got so horny that I used a frozen hot dog, but it was too cold and the frostbite soon quenched my pussy fires. When I masturbate now I get out two very special *Playgirl* magazines. I read a page or two of erotic material, then I commence to screw the candle vigorously. I've broken more than one candle.

If I see a good-looking guy that I find appealing I'll think,

448

"God, would I like to get hold of that," but I *never* fantasize about strangers, no matter how attractive. I can only fantasize about someone with whom I have some sort of an emotional commitment—no matter how small the commitment, be it a friend, neighbor, teacher. I have to know and like the person I dream of fucking.

I'm a very oral person, and if a man's kiss can't turn me on, then there's no need in the relationship going any further. Hours and hours of sensual necking and petting with a super kisser with no sex is rare, but if any woman ever has the chance she'd better jump at it. I've only had the opportunity once and I must admit that the kissing and fondling session left me more satisfied than fucking or masturbating ever could.

The thought of giving the man I care for a blow job makes me that much hornier. I couldn't give just anyone a B.J., but if I really liked the guy, he wouldn't even have to ask me to go down on him—I'd already be down there. The man I first screwed introduced me to blow jobs, and I've gone down on him numerous times. I think I get as much out of it as he does. I think swallowing your lover's come makes you that much more his woman. I *love* the smell of a man's dick and balls. A good, deep whiff leaves me light-headed. I've always wanted to stick my finger up my lover's ass but I'm afraid he would find it offensive. If he gave me any indication he would enjoy this, I would not hesitate.

I've never had a guy eat me out either. I know I would enjoy it tremendously (the poodle), but only if I were clean. Cleanliness in the sexual act is extremely important to me.

I guess you could say I'm an *exceptionally horny* girl waiting for Mr. Right to come along so we can share night after night of beautiful, caring and loving sex, but at the same time I want it to be wild and abandoned, just to add a little spice so neither of us can get bored.

Now for one of my favorite fantasies: Doug and I are sitting on the sofa, listening to AC/DC (a very sexual group) and smoking a couple of joints. Personally, pot is the perfect aphrodisiac!! We're just holding hands and letting the pot ebb slowly through our minds and bodies. There is no rushing—we want to postpone the inevitable. Hesitantly I turn my mouth toward him, waiting for that all-important first kiss, which always leaves me weak. As our kissing progresses, I gently move down his neck, leaving a trail of what I call love-sucks (not quite hard enough for a hickey). As I reach for Doug's zipper, he reaches under my shirt, gently massaging my already erect nipples. By this time, I have his rigid cock in my hands, anticipating the moment when I have his beautiful rod in my eager mouth. Gently, I nudge his head back to mine for another soul kiss. Then I stand over him, looking first into his heavy-lidded blue eyes (from pot or horniness, I don't know), then to his gorgeous dick looking up at me so enticingly. I realize I'm licking my lips because I know what is soon to come (no pun intended). I kneel beside him, taking his burning peter in my hands. I tenderly massage his balls. I ask him in a breathless voice, "Tell me, Doug. Tell me what you want me to do!!!" He grabs me by the hair and pulls my hungry mouth toward his. Doug then kisses me with such abandon, such raw sexuality, that I come instantly. He is squeezing and rubbing my boobs during all this, and I'm still rubbing and stroking that beautiful piece of meat. I tear myself away from Doug's probing tongue and I start kissing my way down. I remove his shirt, sucking on his nipples while I continue my journey. I take off his shoes then tug at his pants. As if on cue, he raises his hips so I can remove them. Not being able to resist, I bend down to kiss the head of his marvelous prick. With Doug totally nude, I then commence to do a little striptease. Doug's cock is so engorged that I wonder if it is going to burst. I look at Doug, smile and ask once more, "Tell me, Doug." He replies, "Suck me, Martha. Suck me, lick me. Take me in your hot little mouth and show me whose woman you are!" With that, I slip the head of his prick between my aching lips. I treat it as if it were some sort of rare jewel to be pampered and admired. Giving him pleasure is my only concern at the moment. I rub my tongue back and forth over the smooth, velvety head. My tongue flicks around the rim mischievously, then I suddenly stick the point tip of my tongue down in his slit. I run my tongue up and down the slit, causing Doug to moan out loud. I then take all of him in my mouth that I possibly can without a gag reflex. (Unfortunately, I can't deep-throat.) My tongue is massaging and swirling around his shaft. I am gently rubbing his balls, and I remove my mouth from his throbbing meat long enough to kiss and lick his balls. I am running my finger around his balls when I hear Doug say, "I want your finger up my ass." I lean forward a little to take a big whiff of his sensational set of genitals. My lips envelop his dick once more, and I start sucking him off—at first gently, but as I get hornier, I can't help but increase my speed. I can feel his peter pulsating between my outstretched lips and, just as Doug requested, I gently stick my finger up his ass. Doug's back arches up suddenly, almost gagging me, but there's no way I'd turn him loose yet! While I'm tenderly moving my finger back and forth, I start to feel his prick go into convulsions. I know what's coming and I prepare myself for the flood. Unexpectedly I feel the hot thick spurts of his cum against the back of my throat, bathing my tonsils in its rich, milky sweetness. I continue to suck Doug until I feel his cock starting to go limp in my mouth. Exhausted, I fall back at Doug's feet. Just as my heart and breathing are getting back to normal, I feel Doug nudge my thighs apart. Needless to say, I have no objections. When I feel his hot, steamy breath on my cunt, I can't help but stiffen in anticipation. As his tongue brands my tender cunt, I involuntarily let out a small cry of pleasure. My legs fly around his head, pushing his face even deeper into my burning pussy. I'm helpless to stop them. He sticks his tongue in my hole as if it were a miniature peter. Then, just as if he is kissing my mouth, Doug frenches my cunt for all it's worth! I come four times before both of us fall back, exhausted once more.

After recovering somewhat, we sit up, lean against each other and smoke another joint. By the time we are finished, we are ready for another round. This time our kisses are brutal and animalistic. Doug is clawing, squeezing and pinching my yearning tits. My fingers are entwined in his hair when he gently pushes me back on the floor. I grab hold of his ass cheeks, squeezing and hugging them, trying to draw him closer to me. Abruptly, he mounts me. I'm yelling for Doug to fuck me harder. My legs are completely out of control, my hands in continual motion, my fingers tangling up in his hair then moving to his shoulders, leaving claw marks on his skin, our mouths still hungrily glued together. As we climax in unison, my cunt clamps down over Doug's prick while I "suck" the cum from him. We hold each other tightly until we catch our breath. Then I nudge him over on his back. In appreciation for the night of love he just gave me, I go down on him again, gently licking off the remains of our love juices that have intermingled. As a considerate gesture, Doug does the same for me. We go to bed, but the afterglow of the event just passed still possesses us, making sleep slow in coming. Wrapped in each other's arms, we talk, but of nothing of importance. Just being together creates a peacefulness so pure and special that words could ruin the entire night. We soon fall asleep, still clinging to each other, and with the morning light shining across our faces, we awaken—still in each other's arms.

Maria

God! What a relief to know that there are thousands of women every age who have fantasies and that many have done the very same things I have.

I am 30 years old, married six years and have a 7-year-old daughter. I had my daughter when I was 22, "out of wedlock." I was brought up in a very strict Catholic home. To top it off, I'm Mexican-American, with very old-fashioned strict parents who never told me anything about sex. I grew up in an all-white community (small, redneck town) in New Mexico. The people here believed that Mexican girls, no matter what age, were always "horny whores." I was the only daughter out of five children. I have several years of college and would like to go back in the near future. My husband and I would be considered your average American middle-class family with a house, kid and pets. I'm determined for my daughter to grow up feeling proud of her body and never disgusted by her feminine functions and odor the way I was for the longest time.

I dearly love my husband and am always horny for him. It still amazes me how much I desire him after this long. I'm sexually frustrated because he just isn't into sex as I am. The most we have sex is once or twice a week if I am lucky. Also, I rarely ever come through intercourse. When he fucks me, he comes so quickly that he has to get me off by sucking my cunt, which I do love. I wish he'd take longer with foreplay and was more imaginative. This lack of interest in sex (or should I say lack of frequency to want to suck and fuck me?) has made me have affairs and/or one-night stands. I enjoyed my flings because I have this sense of control over the man. I fuck him good and make him come long and hard. But I'm always overwhelmed with guilt about it.

I never have a problem getting the attention of men, only my husband's. My husband is extremely good looking, sexy, with a huge cock and a wonderful tongue. He just drives my ass crazy when he doesn't give me what I want, so I need an outlet.

I first discovered orgasms when I was about 5 or 6 years old. My parents had taken me to visit my godparents. I was outside playing in the backyard when I decided to play behind this air conditioner. They had a dog that followed me behind this old unit. When I sat down, he started to sniff between my legs. I remember that it felt good and something compelled me to pull my panties over to one side just to see what he would do. As I watched in amazement, he slowly brought his warm, wet nose down to my hairless pussy. His warm breath drove chills up and down me, and he started slowly nuzzling his nose in my wetness and started licking me! The orgasm I had was incredible! I remember my ears ringing, my vision darkening and this intense throbbing of my clit. Somehow, I knew I shouldn't have been doing this. I suddenly felt a presence and turned around. Well, shit if it wasn't my godfather standing there with this godforsaken look of shock on his face! I quickly tried to act as if the dog had bitten me, but he had fled to my father. My dad came and a few minutes later told me that the dog was dirty and did nasty things. I felt so ashamed, and I've been tormented all these years at being discovered in such a manner. It intensified when I got older and knew what it was all about, but this didn't stop me from letting my own dog eat me.

I can fantasize anywhere and anytime. But when I want to forget about the world today and my life's situation, I'll masturbate in the tub with running water about this:

I have been taken captive by pirates on this ship. The ship is the old kind with huge billowing sails and wood-plank floors that smell of wet cedar. The pirates are all kind of old and nasty looking with ragged clothes and a couple of days' growth of beard. They smell of musky sweat and whisky. There's a big storm brewing, and the ship is starting to creak and rock from the wind and waves. I'm tied up on the dock against one of the poles by my hands, and my legs are left free. I have a long blue dress on, with a very low bustline, and my tits are just about to fall out. My skirt has been ripped up to my waist, and my petticoats and pantaloons have been carelessly discarded to the side of me in a heap. The dirty old pirates have formed a circle around me and the pole. Their eyes are gleaming, and they crudely lick their lips as they decide who's going to have the privilege of going first. They finally decide, and the pirate who's first is kind of fat and drooling with anticipation. He gets on his knees and crawls toward me. Slowly, he pulls my skirt to one side and starts sniffing up my thighs to my muff. His wet tongue slowly licks my outer lips. I can clearly hear him whiffing my erotic pussy fragrance. Then he slides his tongue into the fold of my lips, just licking ever so slowly. This takes my breath away. Then he darts his tongue into my pussy hole. I'm wondering how a maiden like me could possibly respond to such a thing! All of a sudden he changes his mouth to where he has my long inner lips in his mouth and is sucking them and my twitching clit with a steady, tugging rhythm. Every now and then he'll flick back to my hole. By this time in my fantasy, and sometimes actually, I've already had an orgasm. I'm going wild with ecstasy over this old man. The men in the circle have their cocks out by this time, and the storm is getting stronger, which is making the ship rock even more. They are considerate enough to let my throbbing pussy rest before the next pirate, with a crooked cock, has his turn. He then approaches me in the same manner as the first, except his saliva is dripping down his chin like come. This makes me even hornier! He spreads my tan legs even further and reaches for my wet asshole with his very hot tongue and probes in quick wet motions, then he slides up to my protruding clit. I see this so vividly, my cunt so swollen and throbbing. As the boat rocks in intense rhythm, he brings me to a thrashing orgasm. The thunder is loudly clapping, the men yelling and jacking off because they *just can't* stand it any longer. I'm humping my pelvis so nastily and spread my legs even further and cry for more.

As you can see, I prefer oral sex but do wish coming while fucking was easier for me.

Penny

I embarked upon the path to active sex a bit early—I can say that in retrospect—since I had no real relationship with my mother as woman to woman. She never exhibited any sexual feelings or attitudes until recently when she discovered how to enjoy them without shame. You see, I gave her your book when I finished with it. That was six years ago. After a marriage counselor and lots of patience from my father, she can now explore her sexual feelings and those of others unabashedly.

But back to myself. I always loved erotica. Once, when I was lying in some hedges, I found a book, a large paperback called *Orgy 2000* or something like that. My friends and I sat in our playhouse and took turns reading it aloud. I felt embarrassed to read aloud, but I loved the sensation of sexual excitement I felt. We never engaged in any sex play during our periods in the playhouse. Perhaps we were all taught to be ashamed by then. We were only around 8 or 10 years old. I didn't even know about using masturbation to release the tension I felt afterwards until I was 16, though between those years I was exposed to more and more erotica. My older brother, who was quite young for acquiring *Penthouse* and *Playboy,* had an impressive collection in his desk drawer. He first showed them to me, then I'd sneak in and take some to my bedroom to read at night. The pictures weren't interesting, but the fiction was wonderful. So one day I tried masturbating and found it quite nice. When I had orgasms I didn't know what they were until after a long time. I couldn't wait to get home from school to try it again.

Then I began using the shower to stimulate my clitoris. My mother never asked but probably wondered why I took such long showers! I was afraid to be discovered doing this, though I made no effort to curtail my behavior. I wished I had another woman, older and open, to share these desires or apprehensions with. Maybe I would have waited longer in finding out who I was before having sex and needing a man to define me.

I am married now, 23 years old, and I still fight to define myself as Penny, not so-and-so's daughter and so-and-so's wife. If it's hard when you're 15, it's harder when you're my mother's age.

When I met my husband, he knew he had found a woman of intense desires, and he enjoyed sex with me. I enjoyed it, too. I don't mean to put it in the past tense. We still are happy in bed, and sex is fulfilling, but when we were first engaged in our wild activity he was much more creative. He knew how to please me orally and manually. He bit and teased, and I found the most exquisite sensations with this man. Now, after two years of being together, he confesses that he doesn't really like oral sex and masturbation. I love oral sex, and if I didn't masturbate, I'd go crazy. It makes me sad to think that, for him, masturbation is only a last resort if a woman is unavailable.

You'd think that after living with a man for eight months you'd see enough of him to decide whether or not he's your type. Why, after all this time, must I find out such a sad thing? Now I am afraid to ask him to suck me, when it's the thing I want most. We're falling into an abyss of boredom; we have only begun to fall. I'm desperate to do something.

Sex is of major importance in my life, but I love my man, too.

Here is one of my more exciting fantasies: I am in a mansion, dressed in a ball gown with wide skirts and a tight bodice. The swell of my bosom is evident due to the corset. A ball is taking place, and we are all dancing. I find myself at a table, seated with mixed couples, engaged in light conversation. Suddenly, I feel a gentle hand on my thigh and a pair of lips. I try to make no outward sign of having an intruder under our table, but the sensations cause me to become wet immediately. My unknown lover becomes more ardent in his caresses, and I part my legs as wide as I can to accommodate his head as he kisses my thighs and caresses my pussy, by now quivering and wet. I think I shall cry out from this teasing man beneath my skirts, when I see a man at the table and his date have noticed. They tell me not to be embarrassed and to just enjoy the ride. They rise and engage in gentle caressing of my breasts. I sigh as the man below begins gently, then more probingly, kissing my wet pussy. I begin to moan, and my friends bend down to kiss and nibble my nipples. I think for sure I am in ecstasy, then I am driven higher by a finger in my asshole, all wet from my vaginal juices dripping down. His tongue probes my pussy and fucks my clit until I cry out, "Fuck me now, oh please!" I sit on the floor as he reveals a lovely, erect cock for the entire household to see and admire. I am mounted by the other woman, who asks me to please suck her pussy. I oblige as I am being fucked and my tits are being rubbed by the other man, and we come one after the other as the crowd applauds.

Lydia

I'm a 25-year-old black woman name of Lydia, middle class and single. Ever since my boyfriend left me, I've been having varied and exciting fantasies about him, which I never had before we met. Oh, I did have them, but the characters were faceless, nameless without much pleasure or interest for me. If he only knew what he was missing!

We're lying on my bed at home, fully dressed. Mike and I are kissing like mad, clutching each other. French kissing—he's really good at that, it's one of the things he taught me. When I try to undress him, he whispers for me to wait. Pulling off the sash of my dress, he offers to blindfold me with it. The prospect is exciting and a little scary. What is he going to do? I accept and he winds it around my head. He stuffs padding under the sash alongside my nose so I can't peak under it. Once I'm completely blinded, he starts undressing me. His fingers linger along my flesh, leaving fiery tracks in their wake. It's so thrilling, not knowing where he'll touch me next. He runs his hands down my arms, lifting them over my head. Something cold lies against my wrists; there is an audible click. With a sudden shock, I realize he's handcuffed me to the bedpost. I'm startled, but his voice is in my ears: he assures me he won't hurt me. The wildest thoughts are chasing tails through my head. I've lost all fear, but my curiosity and desire are almost uncontrollable. When my blouse is undone, he rubs his fingers around my bare nipples until they're tight. Oh, they hurt, but an exquisite hurting. Whimpering deep in my throat, I arch my back toward him so that he can take them in his mouth. He pushes me back, denying my need. Except for his breath I can't even hear him. His touch has been so soft and gentle throughout; suddenly he hooks his fingers in my panty and rips it apart, jerking it off my thighs. The violence is so unexpected I can't help gasping. He pushes my legs as far apart as they'll go and deliberately strokes up and down my thighs with his fingers. Grasping my ankles, he binds them with some kind of material to the other end of the bed. I'm completely helpless. The restraints allow me some movement but only enough to heave futilely beneath him. He's in control of the situation; there's nothing I can do to stop him. For a few minutes, he amuses himself by licking and sucking on various parts of my body. I'm gasping and moaning by turns. The bed shifts underneath me. He walks out of the room. I can't tell what he's going to do, but my skin is tingling as if acid had been poured on my nerves. I'm

458

impatient for him to return but resist calling out for him. All at once I sense his presence near me; he's managed to sneak back without my hearing. He spreads something cold on my breasts and belly (jelly? whipped cream? onion dip?) and then slowly laps it up with his tongue. As he crouches between my legs, I can tell from his skin against mine that he's stripped, but not whether he's completely naked. Grasping my buttocks with both hands, he raises me up and plants his mouth over my moist cunt. Writhing and screaming, I squirm so hard he almost loses his grip. But he stays with me, forcing his tongue deep into my warm crevice. I shove my body up to him, as much as the bindings will allow me to move. Now his tongue is inside me, probing my inner walls; now the tip is flicking and playing with my clit; it's rapidly licking all along the outer lips. Oh, glory, it's all too much; I could come any minute, but he stops before I'm through. I'm begging him to let me finish, wanting his cock, his long, hard member inside me. Desperation causes me to twist futilely and curse like a sailor. He presses himself on top of me, kissing my mouth fiercely, but he leans back after a moment, torturing me again. Then I feel something prodding at my wet, dripping cunt. It slowly enters me, causing me to groan. It feels—no, it's not quite right. At once I know it's not his cock but something else, hard and stiff, yet giving a little. I gasp, shuddering, for it is *bigger* than his cock, whatever it is. Slowly, inexorably he pushes it into me. My body starts bucking once more. The heated state I'm in makes this pressure welcome no matter what the source. His preparation with his tongue has left me so slick the object glides in with only a minimum of difficulty. But the fit is so tight, the sensation lies just beyond the threshold, but stops short of actual pain. He stops pushing, asking if he's hurting; I can barely find the voice to tell him to go on. Don't stop, I plead, please don't stop. Withdrawing the object slightly, he swiftly thrusts it hard into my cunt. Once again my back arches, as if it would break. I'm screaming in ecstasy, my body shaking the bed with its spasms. Now that he sees I can accept the whole thing, he uses it like a real penis. Firmly, he moves it in and out, in and out. At one point he withdraws it and plays with the tip all around my clit and outer lips (what is it?). When I shriek that I'm coming, he leaves it stuffed inside me and lays the whole length of his body on mine, hugging me as tight as he can. He rides out the storm and caresses my body soothingly, as I lie trembling from reaction in his arms. He doesn't untie me yet, though. He brings his fingers into play again, pulling the thing from my cunt. Even feeling it drawn out is enough to make me grit my teeth. I can feel desire rising in me again like a tide; he senses my reaction and presses both of his hands onto my aching cunt. I feel his sticky fingers smearing my come onto my breasts. He laps at my mounds greedily, almost biting in his eagerness to taste me—he pants that he wants to drink all my juices: spit, sweat, come. I can't believe he's saying such things. Now he's ready for his turn—his cock, real cock, shoves its way into me. He straddles me, now leaning up, now crushed tight against me, head to toe. We strain against each other. His body is now more a prisoner than mine. Winding his legs around mine, he starts moaning hotly in my ear. Nonsense words, sobbings, deep groans, obscenities, everything all mixed up together with pleas to finish him off, help him get it. Some of the words are mine, but I can't tell. The darkness I've been in from the beginning doesn't seem to matter anymore—it's as if it's always been like this, a faceless stranger begging me, at the mercy of my body. He is at my mercy, for he must thrust into my waiting flesh, make up for my restricted movements. My imagination supplies his heaving body, corded muscles, twisted, sweating features, open mouth and tightened buttocks. With a final lunge and ragged cry, he comes, comes, comes. His arms lock around me in the moment of his climax, and I reach mine too; my voice is so worn out I can no longer scream, only sob helplessly. Even though his torment is over, it seems as if his stream of spunk will never end. But it does, slowly. Slowly, too, he unbinds me and tenderly rubs my wrists and ankles. The bedsheets are twisted and stained with our sweat, but we don't care.

Sometimes I picture him making love to me using only his words. Once more, I'm blindfolded and naked but standing up. Still dressed, he walks deliberately around me in a narrow circle, sometimes touching me, sometimes not:

MIKE: You have beautiful breasts. [*Cupping them from behind*] I love holding them, they're like warm, heavy fruit— peaches? persimmons? [*I try to lean against him, but he shoves me back.*] Don't move, I didn't tell you to move. Just keep still. You have these cute little hairs around your nipples, you know that? I bet you didn't think I noticed. Every time I kiss them I pick hairs out of my teeth. [*Laughter*] You think that's funny? How about this? I'm going to squeeze your breasts, I'll lick them all over, especially your hairy nipples. I'll suck off every hair until there isn't any more hair. I'll pinch them with my lips so hard, you'll think I was biting them off. You'd like that, wouldn't you. I can tell; you're shaking; your heart's banging under my hands. Maybe I won't, maybe I'll start playing with your navel. [*Running his hands down my belly*] You've got a really deep navel. I'd like to stick my tongue in it and wiggle it. You've got the most exciting navel I ever saw, it's like a second cunt, it's so deep. I'd like to stick my cock in it, I mean, really poke it so hard you'll think it's coming out your back. Maybe I will, if you're a good girl. You feel my cock poking you from behind, don't you. It's hard like a rock, honey, it's begging for mercy. You want it inside you, say the word, come on. Ask.

ME: [*Whispers*] Yes. Please.

Bets

I am a horny bitch and love reading about sexual experiences and fantasies. I love to masturbate and do it often. I am getting wet and horny just writing to you. I never thought I would write about *my own* sexual experiences and fantasies.

I am white, 50 years old, single and a virgin who loves to play with her tits and clitoris.

When I was 7 years old, a neighbor boy and I would

explore each other's genitals. He loved putting his fingers inside my vagina lips and tickling me there. We found many secret corners so he could play with my clitoris.

When I was in college, I discovered how to masturbate. I learned how to stimulate my tits and clitoris. I found the magic button and zapped myself into ecstasy. Watching myself masturbate in front of a mirror turned me on. I finally felt like a *woman.*

Now for my fantasy:

I'm riding on a bus and a man sits next to me. He pulls out *Playboy* and lets me see the nude pictures. I'm getting wetter by the moment. He leans over and asks me if he can put his hand in my cunt. I say yes and he slips his hand inside my slacks and inside my panties. He tickles the hairs of my cunt and gently reaches inside. He rams his finger inside my vagina and begins stimulating my clitoris. His other hand reaches inside my blouse and slips out my tit and squeezes my nipple, and I come easily. He takes his hand out and licks the juices off his fingers—one at a time. I'm out of my mind with desire.

We stop for lunch, and we hurry to a toilet at the gas station. He takes his pants down, and I pull mine down quickly too. He leans over the sink and rams me from behind. He is an expert at holding back. He rams me for over ten minutes. He expertly stimulates my clitoris so that we both come in an explosion. He then sits me down on the toilet, spreads my legs and sucks me, sucks me faster and faster. His tongue is pure magic as it darts in and out of my vagina. I orgasm over and over. I am going MAD. I am ecstatic. Lunch is over, and we board the bus.

Another fantasy has to do with bratwurst. After a barbecue at a friend's house, the leftover brats cool, and we decide to see how these would feel inside our vaginas. So we take turns slipping them in and out, and finally we ram them in and begin to nibble away at them after we pull them out of our vaginas. I've never done it, but what pleasure it would be.

I believe sex and all that stimulates sexual desire is part of keeping us well and healthy. The more I masturbate, the better I feel. I have masturbated two or three times as I thought of writing, what to write, and now I'm so wet, I can't wait to put my fingers between those lips to explore the hidden and glorious place within.

I haven't felt the need for intercourse with a man, but if that possibility occurs, my cunt is willing and anxious to receive his penis.

P.S. I feel so good sharing my sexual experiences and fantasies with you. I feel so free, so much a woman. Masturbation is *great.*

Daisy

I am 34 years old, overweight, married ten years, and have three children ages 8, 6, and 3. My husband is only the second man I have ever slept with. Neither my first experience at age 19 (with an abortion at 20) nor my husband has been able to bring me to climax. I never had an orgasm until after the birth of my third child, when one day I decided to try to use a vibrator on my clit. I nearly blew my mind. I have been using it ever since. I have tried vaginal masturbation (using fingers, cucumbers, hammer handles, batons, etc.), but—nothing.

FANTASY NUMBER 1:

I am coming back from the supermarket when I am kidnapped and taken to a lavish mansion. After six months of coerced exercise and forced dieting, with plastic surgery thrown in to complete the job, I have turned out to be a beautiful, classy whore for a man who throws orgies day and night. At first, I let any man fuck me who wants to, since it does nothing for me. Then someone realizes what my problem is and performs some minor vaginal surgery, reconnecting nerve endings. What happens then makes me cream just thinking of it. My first time out after the surgery is a mind-blowing and cunt-blowing experience. The kindly doctor decides to give me my first run with the new sensations. After taking off my robe (I am never allowed to wear underwear), he lays me down on the bed and caresses

463

my body very gently. He tells me to lie still, and I let him do all the work. He squeezes my breasts and then sucks them to hardness. He progresses down my body to my cunt, where he gently spreads my lips and lets his fingers do some exploring. After he gets me all juicy he brings his head down and starts kissing, licking and sucking my clit until I scream in ecstasy. By this time I am moving and grinding and very impatient. Very slowly he brings his cock to the opening of my cunt and slowly enters me with extreme tenderness. I now have feelings I never felt before and am ready to die with ecstasy. He continues moving in me very gently so that practically every move brings me to orgasm. As I get used to these feelings, he starts thrusting deeper and harder, and finally we climax together in an explosion. I am exhausted and I fall asleep. When I wake up I have been placed on a magnificent dining room table as a centerpiece during a party. I am fucked all night by men. The next night is oral night, where I give blow jobs willingly in return for them sucking and licking me. Eventually we work up to Ladies Night. The thought of doing it with another woman revolted me, but I was assured that I wouldn't have to do it but only have it done to me. My first experience with a woman was delicious. Being a woman, she knew what she liked and brought me to heights I've never known before. She tenderly separated my lips and, with her fingers, explored every nook and cranny of my pussy. Within seconds her fingers are dripping with my juices, which she uses to rub my clit and anus. She kept my clit going with her thumb while fingering my vagina. With her other hand she is massaging my anus with the juice from my pussy and all of a sudden shoves two fingers in. I cry out in pain and scream "I have to shit," but the shit never comes—only pleasure. With her fingers still up my ass, she proceeds to lick my pussy with her expert tongue—licking, sucking, biting. Her long tongue darts in and out of my vagina. After many orgasms, I have to yell stop because I can't take it anymore. This is when I find I can give what I received, and I am able to bring her to great heights of ecstasy as well. I am able to do this all night. My fantasy usually ends here because I have to take out my vibrator to relieve myself.

FANTASY NUMBER 2:
I am stranded in a stuck elevator with one other person—a very handsome psychiatrist. We spend a lot of time talking and gradually get around to my nonorgasm problem. He feels that it is just a matter of knowing how to screw right. He willingly offers to show me. We undress quickly and start making love. I am understandably nervous as I am afraid to be disappointed again. He carefully massages my pussy and works on my clit until I come, and before I can catch my breath, he tells me to get on my hands and knees doggie fashion and he enters my vagina, aiming right at my G spot, and I gasp and cream and cream. He quickly pulls out before either of us comes and shoves his cock up my ass—it is great—and again before coming, pulls out and shoves his cock up my cunt again, and after a few minutes we both come with a scream. Exhausted, we quickly get dressed and the elevator starts to move. When it stops, we get out as if nothing has happened.

As to my sexual background, I have some vague memories of a girlfriend and I playing at her house when we were 10. I remember each of us experimenting on the other with pencils up our vaginas, rubbing Vicks VapoRub on our clits, making them sting and throb. We would also pinch and clip our clits. I don't remember if we came, but it felt good. Later, when I was older, I would play with myself, but never to climax, no matter how hard I tried. Despite my fantasies, I have never done anything with a woman. My husband on occasion licks me but doesn't keep it going as he doesn't like the smell or the taste. I do give him blow jobs, which he likes.

Erica
I am happily married 25 years to a wonderful man who is very dull, so I fantasize a lot, which helps to arouse me

before sex. The only way I can climax is through oral sex, which my husband likes, so he keeps me satisfied. His sex drive is low, so much of the time he sucks me to orgasm and then goes to sleep. Or he will finger and suck me to orgasm before leaving for work. We also play the "nursing game" during the night, or he sucks my breasts off and on during the night when I want him to. Our three children are in college away from home, and we enjoy privacy and freedom now. After supper we shower together and then watch a program or two on TV, while he sucks my breasts (during commercials and boring times) and I fondle his cock. Needless to say I enjoy weekends and holidays.

I have always been too embarrassed to mention this to *anyone* before, but when my breasts began to develop, at age 10, my two brothers liked to fondle and suck them (we were raised to bathe/shower together). They never fucked me with their cocks, but we engaged in oral sex. I was always afraid that all that stimulating of breasts and clitoris by them until I left for college enhanced the size of my breasts and my need for frequent sex.

This is only one of my many fantasies:

We step out of the shower, and he kneels, opens my pussy lips and runs his tongue over my genitals . . . back and forth . . . back and forth. Going into the bedroom, I stand in front of him, and he looks over my shoulder into the mirrored wall at my big Dolly Parton breasts while sliding his hands up and down my belly, up to stroke my tits around to the hard pointed nipples and then under my breasts to lift them up, and rolls my nipples between his fingers . . . and then slides his large hands down to my pussy to open and close . . . open and close it. Still behind me, he kneels down and licks and strokes my ass cheeks and the crack while stroking my inner thighs and crotch before turning me around. He opens my pussy lips and again he licks my genitals and runs his long tongue back and forth . . . back and forth . . . licking back and forth. He rises to his feet slowly and licks and sucks my lips and French kisses me . . . I suck on his tongue. He pulls up a tall stool, sits down, making his mouth level with my tits. He points again to the mirror, and I watch as he begins licking my nipples and the moons surrounding them. He fondles my breasts and gently presses them together and with a flat tongue, while moving his head up and down and around and around, he licks one nipple . . . then slides over my breasts to the other nipple and licks up and down, up and down and around, while his saliva covers my breasts and moves very slowly down my belly . . . and then slides over to the other nipple and repeats this for ages, until my tits are swollen and throbbing with pleasure and arousal and heat. I hear myself beg, "Oh, please SUCK them, suck them, suck them, please." Putting a nipple and the surrounding moon in his mouth, he sucks and turns his tongue around the moon. He moves to the other nipple with his mouth, but his fingers rub the one just left . . . they are being both sucked and rubbed while his other hand moves up and down my inner thighs until finally, finally a finger slides into my hot cunt about two inches . . . and it moves in and out, in and out, around and around the opening, teasing. He notices my trembling and sits me down on the foot of our low king-size bed and kneels between my opened knees. He licks and sucks my tits for a long time before leaning me back on some pillows, touching my shoulders and motioning to watch the mirror or look down at what was to happen next. Placing his hands around my ankles, he lifts my legs, bends them at the knees moving them up and open wide. He licks his lips, sticks out a pointed, stiff tongue and begins to tongue-fuck my cunt, sliding it in and out . . . in and out and then around and around and then sticking it in deep and wiggling it until a finger replaces his tongue, which has now begun licking my pussy. His other hand moves up my belly and begins rolling my nipple between two fingers. It feels like an electric current runs from nipple to pussy to cunt to nipple and it is wonderful, but when I can't bear it, I cry out loudly, "Oh, please SUCK IT." So now he is finger-fucking me, rolling my nipple and sucking my pussy. After about 60 seconds (60 wonderful SUCKS), at last 100,000 flapping quail wings take flight through my body as I climax, as he continues fingering, rolling and rubbing and sucking. I beg him to let me rest a minute, and he pulls me up by the arms into a sitting position and licks and sucks my tits and strokes and fondles them. We then stand, French kiss, and he sits down on the bed, leans back on the pillows while his big, thick cock sticks straight up and moves while growing thicker . . . a thought of the expression flashes in my mind . . . "sexually active." I kneel before it and stroke his inner thighs and begin licking his balls and very gently sucking-kissing his balls and then suck-kiss under his cock up to the top, where I run my tongue around and around the tip . . . and then slowly, slowly I tongue down the underside of his long cock and then gradually back up to the top, where I begin licking the large knob of his hot cock and keep licking it while saliva wets and runs over everything until he pleads, "Darling, please SUCK IT, SUCK IT." I open my wet lips much wider and slide his thick cock in as far as I can and begin sucking and sucking until I suck him off.

After I return from the bathroom, I see he has moved up higher in the bed and is lying on his side facing the mirror, napping. His once big, thick, hard-throbbing cock is limp . . . looking lonely . . . like a big finger with no bone in it, and I slowly get on the bed so as not to awaken him . . . this time with my head toward the foot of the bed. Lying on my side, I open my mouth and slide his limp cock in and I too begin to nap until I feel my top leg being lifted and a doubled pillow placed between my knees to keep my legs wide apart. With his fingers, he opens my pussy more and places his tongue between my pussy lips, and we rest a little longer. When I awake, I'm tonguing and sucking his growing cock, and he is running his tongue back and forth over and over my genitals and sucking too. He asks me to get on my knees and hands so he can lick and suck my hanging big tits, which I enjoy tremendously. Then, while he sucks, he begins fingering my juicy pussy and then he jumps up and begins fucking me from behind. My ass is high up and my shoulders are low on the bed and my face is facing the mirror so I can watch his wet cock moving in and out and in and out of my juicy hot cunt. He stops for a while and fondles my tits and stimulates my clitoris . . . and then he moves slowly in and out . . . in and out. Then he lies on his back and I straddle his hips and move up and down on his cock as he watches . . . up and down . . . up and down, until I lean over and drag my pointed nipples over his chest. Then I turn around toward his feet, straddle his hips and lean over until my shoulders and breasts are lying on his legs, keeping my ass in the air and move up and down on his cock as he watches it going in and out . . . in and out . . . up and down. He strokes the cheeks of my rear end as I gradually build up speed until I have a cock-cunt orgasm. Usually I can only climax through his sucking and fingering my clitoris, but sometimes I can have an orgasm in this position. He lifts me off his hard cock and fucks me in the missionary position until he comes and calls out that he's coming, he's coming. Afterwards we lie facing each other, and he sucks my nipples and fingers my cunt and pussy, which are covered with his come . . . until sleep comes. About dawn I awake and go to the toilet and when I return we lie in the 69 position and "nurse" each other, on and off until morning. This game of "nurse" has been going on in my family for generations. It's a peaceful way and intimate way to sleep, making you feel close and loved and waiting until you can lick and suck and fuck again.

Tara

My own favorite fantasy is quite detailed and elaborate, and I'd die a happy woman if only I could find the man who could fulfill it. I have actually done this to myself dozens of times, usually every other weekend, when I'm home alone and have *at least* two hours to kill. One time I actually spent five hours masturbating before I allowed myself to come. During that time I talk out loud, both what I'm saying and my lover's words. I use two types of vibrators. One thick, ten inches, to tease my clit and shove up my ass while building to the climax and a large U-shaped one with small friction

469

bumps when I'm finally going to come. One end goes up my ass and the other end up my cunt. I don't know why I came to love the anal thing but I really do. During this fantasy, I have taken dozens of Polaroid shots of myself. My favorites are ones taken with my legs spread in the air, my cunt held open, and the ten-inch vibrator stuck in my ass, with white cream oozing out around it. I always masturbate on the floor in front of a full-length mirror so I can see what my asshole looks like during all of this. But enough—the fantasy!

In my fantasy, I pretend *not* to like anal sex. What I want is a lot of soft, gentle caresses and to have my clit licked until I come. My lover is wonderful at doing that, but *he* loves anal sex and doesn't give me what I want unless I agree ahead of time that he can fuck my ass. One night after dinner, I'm exceptionally horny and start cuddling up to him on the sofa. He suggests running a bubble bath and says he'll join me and give me a night to remember if afterwards he can fuck my ass. Finally I agree, and he does truly treat me extra special, and when I finally come, it's like fireworks.

He continues to stroke and caress me while I recover. Finally, it is his turn, and he has me roll over on my side, knees pulled up to my chest. He leaves for a few minutes and when he comes back, he has a tube of K-Y jelly and rubber gloves. As he puts on the gloves, he tells me to reach back and pull my cheeks apart. He then tells me to push out like I'm having a bowel movement. As I do, he inserts his greased middle finger all the way into my ass. My sphincter muscle closes, and he holds his hand still. Suddenly, he starts moving his finger back and forth inside me and is very unhappy because I'm "full." I swear to him I had a bowel movement earlier, but he says he can't get all of his cock in unless he cleans me out, so we head to the bathroom. He puts me on the floor on my hands and knees with my ass in the air and gives me an enema. Several times he fills me up until at last the water that explodes out my ass into the toilet contains no more shit. We go back to the bedroom, and he "prepares" the bed with a plastic sheet and several absorbent diapers stacked on top of each other where my ass will be. I start to lie down, but he says he's not ready and gets out his homemade "frame" from the closet. I beg him not to use it but he ignores me. It is a frame that sits on the floor but arches over the foot of the bed. My legs get strapped into stirrups, then he moves the frame back a little so that my ass is pulled up off the bed. He places a pillow under my hips so that I'm comfortable. He now sits in a chair at the foot of the bed, eye level with my asshole. The height is perfect so that when he's ready to stick his cock in, he merely stands up. I beg him again not to use the frame and promise I'll do exactly what he tells me. But he reminds me that last time we fucked doggie style I didn't keep my ass in the air long enough. I begin to cry, and he consoles me and promises to be gentle and only use a little cream for lubrication. He starts fingering my clit and biting on my nipples, and soon I'm horny again and lie down on the bed. He then lifts my legs and straps me in. I'm comfortable but completely at his mercy as my ass and cunt are spread wide and I'm unable to move. A board keeps me from seeing anything that he's doing or covering myself with my hands. He leaves the room and rolls in a cart with all his "supplies," to sit next to his chair. I realize he has several gallons of white lotion and begin to panic. I tell him he promised not to do that, but he very gently says, "But baby, you know this is what your Daddy needs, and if you do everything I say instead of fighting me, you'll like it." He begins kneading my cheeks and licking my clit to get me excited again. He pulls open my cunt, and I can feel his breath and know that he's looking at me. Next, he opens my ass wider and tells me to push out. As I do, he drills his tongue into the hole. He occasionally places a vibrator just above my clit to keep me excited but always takes it away before I can come. I hear him pouring some cream into the smaller squeeze bottle with the long pointed tip on the end. He squirts a couple of drops in my asshole, and I gasp as I realize it's ice cold. He's had the cream in the refrigerator in the garage for days. He spreads the cream around a little and pushes his finger in. He pulls it out, spreads my asshole with two fingers on one hand, and tells me to push out. As I do, he inserts about half an inch of the two-inch pointed tip up my ass and then tells me to "hold it" and squeeze tight. This means he wants me to squeeze my asshole in as if trying to *prevent* a bowel movement. All night those are my only two instructions— to either "push out" or "hold it." As I do, he begins to slowly squeeze the bottle and I can feel this ice-cold cream run into my rectum. After squeezing in the whole bottle very slowly, he pulls out the tip and plays again with my clit, again exciting me. "Now we have to begin stretching your asshole so you can take all of my cock." He has me push out and he inserts a smooth, narrow, six-inch dildo. My sphincter closes, and he yells, "Push out! Push out! Push out!" I do, and he moves the dildo in and out over and over again, slowly. Suddenly, I get a cramp and I tell him I can't hold it any longer. Just like the enema, suddenly you know that everything is going to come exploding out of your ass and you know you can't stop it. He pushes the dildo in and tells me to squeeze tight, and I hold it. Finally, the cramp passes. Slowly he removes the dildo, and I can feel some of the white cream oozing out of my hole. He refills the bottle and starts again. This time I can't hold it, and as I relax my ass and give in, my lover shoves the dildo in and out of my ass as fast as he can. Once it's over, I beg him not to do any more, but he says "You're doing great, baby. Each time you'll be able to hold more. The sooner you do what I tell you, the better it'll feel. Daddy loves to see all the cream ooze out of your asshole, and I can't wait to give you my cock, baby. But I need for you to be able to hold a gallon of cream so that when my hot cock is finally fucking that beautiful ass of yours, it'll feel all that nice and cool, clean cream around it." So he then removes the diaper with all the cream on it, bathes my ass with a warm washrag and starts over. This goes on for hours. As we progress, he increases the size of the dildo to stretch me so that I can take his cock. He only uses dildos with a smooth surface so that I won't get sore before he fucks me. His cock is ten inches long, so thick I can barely get my fingers around it and has a large bulb on the head.

This process goes on forever, but he never gets impatient. He constantly tells me that I'm doing great and he continues to play with a vibrator against my clit to keep me excited. I shit loads of white cream probably ten times, but each time I'm able to hold more and last longer. Finally, I'm full of cream and have to take only one more squeeze bottle full to hold a gallon, when I feel a cramp coming on. My lover coaches me and helps by squeezing my cheeks together. "Come on, baby, you're almost there, squeeze it, squeeze it, hold it tight! Tight! Tight!" Slowly the cramp subsides, and he inserts the tip in all the way and quickly squeezes the last bottle, filling me up with a gallon of cool, white cream. "OK, baby, you're doing great. You know this is what Daddy wants. My cock is hard as a rock, and you know you want it too." All the time he speaks very gently, as if I were a child. He stands up and rubs his cock against my asshole. I am nearly delirious from having gone through this for so long and being right on the edge of climaxing. He tells me, "Do everything I tell you, baby, and you'll love it, but you have to listen to me and do exactly what I say or this will hurt you, OK?" I agree and tell him I understand. "My cockhead is right against your asshole and you're nice and stretched now, but Daddy's big head won't go in unless you push out. But you must do it very slowly or you'll push all the cream out." He increases the pressure as he pushes against my hole, and very slowly I relax my muscles and gently push out. Suddenly, his big head pushes past the sphincter and is inside, and I feel cream ooze out all around. He shouts, "Hold it! Hold it! Hold it! Squeeze tight, baby, as tight as you can." He holds very still and doesn't push in any further while I regain control. The urge passes, and he gently strokes my clit. As my excitement mounts, he very slowly begins to push his cock in further. As he does, I start to cramp, and he once again coaches me into holding on. Finally, all ten inches are inside of me and I can feel his balls against my cheeks. "You make Daddy so happy, baby. Does Daddy's big cock feel good up your ass?" He then squirts cream all over my clit and starts rubbing the vibrator in little circles

473

all around it. "Hold tight, baby, Daddy wants his baby to come real hard." Just as my climax approaches, he starts bumping against my ass. He doesn't move his cock in and out but rather presses deeper, deeper, deeper, by bumping against me. As I'm just on the verge of coming, he starts moving his cock slowly in and out, bringing on that crampy feeling. I shout, "I'm going to shit, I'm going to shit, please stop!" But he keeps moving slowly and says, "Hold tight baby until you come—you're gonna come." And he changes the pitch on the vibrator from a dull throbbing to a high-pitched, fast buzzing. That does it. I begin screaming from climax, and he yells, "Push out! Push out! Push out!" I do, and as my asshole opens, he finally has room to fuck me. He pulls his cock out about eight inches and then shoves it back in as fast as he can, all the time, shouting "Push out! Push out!" I'm still coming and suddenly get that enema cramp. Uncontrollably now I let go with a huge "bowel movement" of white cream. This opens my ass even wider, and my lover comes—fucking me in and out as fast and as hard as he can. The climax lasts for nearly five minutes, and when it's over, I'm absolutely exhausted.

I am a 36-year-old, single female, B.A. degree, earning $62,000 in the public relations field.

TAKING IT ALL IN

The power of the pleasure giver. Many of these women have felt it, relished it—for it is an exciting awareness of power—and they dream of working their magic on a man again, of loving him with their mouths and then of viewing their handiwork, the spent cock, the pool of come, the exhausted male. The power of the voyeur.

But this is not a chapter on sadists. These women love to love men's genitals; they are the answer to man's ultimate fantasy, the woman who takes the initiative, enjoys oral sex, and then, because she knows a man needs a little time between sessions, bathes him and naps until he is ready again. Would men include this quality of loving patience in their own fantasies if they didn't fear their inability to satisfy women's lust? The magic of fantasy is that without our even having to be conscious of our fears, the erotic imagination builds a fantasy that covers all bases.

Intuitively, women with big appetites create their own reciprocal scenarios where they happily take care of themselves and the man, too. ". . . we'd make love three or four times in a row," says Babs. "Then he'd drift off to sleep, and I'd get up, go to the bathroom, clean myself up, then come back to him and wash his genitals, dry him off, then curl up in his arms and drift off to sleep . . ." until the next round. If there is a quality of nursery power in these fantasies—the woman as the all-powerful mother opposite the male child —it is because our sexual needs are so deeply fused with our earliest oral, anal, genital feelings.

With what concentration and pleasure Lillian watches a man masturbate and come. Extended, the idea becomes a fantasy of two men "fucking me in both holes at the same time," which extends still farther into "watching two guys fuck each other," a fantasy I'd never heard before this new research. Because it is so new and fascinating—for some women it is the *only* fantasy they have—I include a brief section on this theme later; for now, for Lillian a fantasy of "two guys fucking and sucking each other [is] . . . kind of like watching a guy jerk off, like I'm not even there. I'm just watching."

"Just" watching? She who watches has the power. The power to hold the man in her gaze. "I don't care for pictures," says Blythe. "I want to see the real thing. I crotch-watch all the time, hoping to see a man with an erection, if I can't be so lucky as to catch someone jacking off." Summing up women's voyeuristic coming of age, Babs concurs, saying, "I love the sight of the male body, period. I don't understand why, for years, articles on sex always said the male is the only one who really gets off seeing the opposite sex nude. Whoever wrote all that garbage doesn't know me . . ."

The thrill women feel looking at men, the power of being able to take a man in visually after years of lowered eyes, averted from anything so unfeminine as a focused stare—this is the same power that women have always resented in men who looked, thus reducing them to "sex objects." I would repeat, however, that not all women mind being looked at; the exhibitionist has her own form of power, one that she wields as she demands the man's attention and then controls his gaze and body temperature with what she does, what she shows. Voyeur and exhibitionist, not unlike the sadist and the masochist, often change places, enjoying the power in either role.

Men today say they like it when women stare at them if it's "done in the right way," but they don't like being looked at "like I was a piece of meat." They sound just like women. No one, male or female, enjoys feeling powerless.

Power, the sensation of controlling one's sexuality, is the core of this book. The women in this chapter refer to areas of power never before open to women. Power is thrilling, exhilarating, especially when we generate it all by ourselves. ". . . I believe it is the woman who *makes* herself come," says Cheryl. "My first love thought he had 'taught' me to come. Truth is, I've been making myself come for nearly ten years . . ." Knowing that she controls her own sexuality frees Cheryl to consciously create what I call the "new" rape fantasy; in the old version, women didn't imagine themselves raped in the true sense of the word, but twenty years ago they didn't know *why* they had rape fantasies. Their fantasies often frightened them, even though they also aroused them.

Cheryl, on the other hand, never loses sight of the fact that she controls the motivations in her fantasy. She knows exactly why she imagines what she does. "All of my fantasies are about a contest of wills," she says, "where I am accustomed to winning, but lose to this one man . . . I am seduced or forced, but I always want him, though I feign disgust, hatred or indifference . . . it's my fantasy and I MAKE THE RULES!"

When we are dependent on others for everything, as women used to be, our minds are closed to self-analysis; knowledge is not felt to be revelatory but threatening to the symbiotic oneness to which we are accustomed and without which we feel we cannot exist. The prospect of understanding, and the power it brings, is not exciting but something to be avoided because any power on our part says to the "other" upon whom we are dependent, "I don't need you."

The women in this chapter don't "need" another person in that desperate manner; knowledge has taught them that understanding loses them nothing. On the contrary, it opens them to the strength they didn't know they possessed. Of course they want to know more. They look at their sexuality and analyze it in a way women never did before.

Trish read in *My Secret Garden* that fantasies often have their genesis in childhood; it was an idea that made her remember an incendiary fragment from her own childhood—a memory that gave birth to her own fantasy version of the Prometheus myth. On the brink of her adolescence, her parents shamed her for what was in fact an act of innocent sexual curiosity. The memory of such humiliation never dies, especially when it is delivered by the hands of the people we love most and upon whom we are dependent. Trish understands that it is her own powerful intellect at war with the sexual inhibitions and guilt planted in her long ago that has created a fantasy contest with her opponent, a contest in which she only seems to lose: "My will is entirely broken . . . I am quivering and dying for more . . . nothing but naked, helpless lust."

Because these women understand their lives, they feel powerful enough to look at men, to watch them masturbate, to use words and language that would make their mothers blush, to enjoy the smell of sex, even to be aroused by the sounds of sex: the sound of a man's balls slapping their buttocks, of their own breasts smacking against his chest, the slurping, juicy sounds of a man eating them. These words and noises used to make a woman cringe because they were the sounds of man's dirty world, reminding her of her exclusion from its power and of her own powerlessness.

Where did women learn to express themselves as they do in this book? Not from men, who do not seem for the most part to be as engrossed in detail, in capturing the nitty-gritty onomatopoetic essence of sex. "I . . . love to talk dirty and to be told what to do, sexually, and in foul language," says Betsy. What a tongue these women have to express themselves! And what an ear! Just listening to her husband when he "occasionally jerks off in bed when he thinks I am sleeping" gives Blythe an orgasm, "without any manipulation of myself."

Whether they have completed high school or graduate school, most have an ease in using the full lexicon of sexual imagery that seems to skip not one but three or four generations since *My Secret Garden.* Speech is power. Unless we are performing acrobats, how we look and what we say are the two prime ways of drawing attention to ourselves, making ourselves "seen." To some degree we all want to be seen. It is part of being alive. Little girls speak earlier and more fluently than little boys. At four, six, eight, and ten, mom and dad exhibit their little talking treasures with pride. It used to be that girls abandoned their natural fluency when adolescence came along. Young girls who wanted male approval learned to shut up. I use the past tense although I'm well aware that not everything has changed; many young women are still hesitant to speak up, and in time, like their mothers before them, they will learn not to speak their thoughts. They will not trust their fluency. Speech requires practice, use, so that the circuitry of cognition and articulation between the mind and the tongue does not get rusty.

The women in this book may not always use perfect grammar, but you would never call them "rusty." They have a thought, an image, and it's out there, known. For having expressed it, they feel more alive, visible; when they read their words here, they will feel even more identified. That is part of why they spoke or wrote to me, a process of being "seen."

Trish

I am 32 years old. I come from a family that has the disease of alcoholism; my father is the "identified patient," that is, the alcoholic. I was married once, for six years. I attempted to masturbate from college age on, but it was always just frustrating and boring. At age 23 I met my (now ex-) husband and had my first orgasm during intercourse with him. It was always very easy to have an orgasm during intercourse with him for the remaining six years we were married. However, otherwise our sex life was boring. He was defensive if I suggested anything other than intercourse. Six years after we met, I left him because of this problem.

Until I had an orgasm I felt that I was abnormal for not having one; after having them with my ex-husband during intercourse, I thought that I was weird because I couldn't orgasm by masturbating. Then thanks to reading *Self-Love and Orgasm* by Betty Dodson, about a year ago (two years and three relationships after I left my husband) I bought the most powerful electric vibrator I could find, and have enjoyed orgasms with it almost nightly ever since. This experience had been very liberating as I disliked being dependent on men strictly to "get my rocks off." I still have not orgasmed through manual stimulation, but I'm not too worried about it right now. I don't want to get into an expectation/frustration bind. I'm encouraged by the progress I have made.

My mother explained the bare anatomical facts of sex to me as soon as I was old enough to understand the words. I remember her sitting on my bed and telling me that the man puts his penis in the woman's vagina. I asked, "Does Daddy do that to you?"

"Yes," she replied.

"Does he like to do it?"

"Yes," she said, sounding surprised, "Yes, he does." It's amazing how these things come back to me.

479

When I was near puberty, my best friend and I drew some dirty pictures; cross sections of penises spurting into vaginas and the like. My mother and/or father found them and hung them on the refrigerator to shame us. It was a joint decision on their part, I know, as I remember hearing my father saying to my mother, "Did you put up the artwork?" and she said, "Yes." I yanked it down the second I saw it, of course. Was I ever embarrassed. Now, I still get mad thinking of what an awful thing that was to do to emerging sexuality.

Also, when I was close to puberty I remember her saying, during the course of a conversation I forgot, "Well, I'm not that crazy about sex anyway . . ." which surprised me. Right then and there I know I made a decision; at first unconscious, I think: that I was not going to be like her, and by God I was going to enjoy sex. And it's taken unswerving determination not to "settle for . . ." which I suspect most women do.

I have always read voraciously. At about age 8, I was home sick from school one day. I read a basic account of the myth of Prometheus. What sticks in my conscious mind, as I remember it, is that he brought fire to the cold clay of mankind, for which he was punished by being chained to a cliff—forever, as I remember it. Every day two eagles flew to him and ate his liver, but as he was immortal, every day he grew it anew.

For some strange reason that story gave me a powerful sexual thrill (although at the time I had no idea what the strange feeling was), the first I can ever remember. After I read it, I got out of bed, went to the head of the stairs and called to my mother to reemphasize the story to me:

"Mummy, did the eagles *eat Prometheus' liver?*"

"Yes."

"Every day?"

"Yes."

As I conjure up the image of this extremely important archetypal Christ-like giant-god, I am not surprised that he would have had a powerful effect on my imagination. The "punishment for doing good" theme has to do with my role

480

in the alcoholic family as the Good Girl, Rescuer, Savior (also a typical female trip). Guilt has always been one of my favorite emotions, and intellectually I can see how punishment is to guilt as scratching is to an itch.

However, until I read *My Secret Garden* (I just finished it yesterday) and got to the part about a fantasy flourishing in one's mind ever since it takes root in childhood, I have suppressed this memory, thinking it was some horrible sick beast in my mind.

But now I have had the courage to explore and expand on this fantasy. To date, I have found it the most direct thrill yet, bringing me to orgasm faster than any other fantasies. My repertoire is so far limited; I only started fantasizing when I got the vibrator. I was at a stage where my few fantasies were getting stale, but nothing new seemed like fun. I feel a door has been opened with this Prometheus thing, though.

Here's some of my expansion:

Sometimes I *am* Prometheus, sometimes I am the eagle, and sometimes I am a combination, or an observer.

The god-giant-titan Prometheus, immortal, beautiful, primitive, instinctual, animal, is chained to the lonely cliff as punishment for caring for the fragile, barely surviving human race. Humanity is as yet nothing. The world is raw and new. The gods care for nothing but crude power and satisfaction.

All day the blazing sun roasts him on the bare rock, and all he has to occupy his mind and night—is anticipate the arrival of the eagles, his implacable torturers.

Then he can see them across the empty desert, black specks at first, growing slowly larger as they home in on their rightful meal, that which is destined to be theirs every day, that delicious living immortal meat torn from the perfect breast. (God, I'm getting excited, and here I am at the word processor at work after hours. I can't wait to go home and masturbate. This is fun, delayed gratification.)

Leisurely these stern-eyed predators land on his arms and shoulders. They have all the time in the world; they know the food is there for them. The Titan cannot help straining in his bonds, in anticipation of the daily agony, in the vain attempt to escape. When they have rested a little from their flight, they rip into the chest, exposing the vitals to the burning sun. The reddish dark, vital liver awaits them. Blood runs from the opening down his chest. Slowly, coolly the eagles set about the business of gorging themselves, taking their time, making it last as long as they can. They know when the liver is gone, they must wait until tomorrow for another feast.

Prometheus, in agony, can only think of how he longs for this session to be over. He wants them to hurry, accelerate the pain if need be, take their fill and go, for then he will have some time in the undead, numb state of an immortal missing a vital organ.

But even as they are eating, the immortal liver is regrowing slowly, drawing out the meal. The eagles stop feasting frequently, savoring like people at a dinner party, taking breaks to preen or to clack their beaks and swallow the blood. As birds of prey, they care nothing for suffering. He is in more agony than any mortal has ever endured, because a mortal would have died before now.

Horrible thought—perhaps today they will extend the feeding so much that they will leave some of the liver, so there will be no respite, or else they will never leave at all! (But you see, that doesn't really happen, because I always come, although I sometimes switch to another part of the fantasy.)

Finally the eagles, heavy, sated, gorged, as uncaring as stone, leaving not one shred of warm, quivering liver, fly off slowly from whence they came. They will be back. Tomorrow.

Meanwhile the chained one who should be dead can feel the unwelcome sensations of his life force mending his immeasurably strong, unquenchable body against his will. There is only more pain as he is made whole—only to look off into the distance again, straining to see those black specks drawing slowly closer and closer.

My other fantasies go something like the following; I now think they may be derived from the Prometheus fantasy, although I "discovered" these more realistic (?) fantasies before rediscovering the Prometheus fantasy:

I am strapped to immobility on a medical examining table. An experiment is to be performed on me to see whether a woman can be made to die from orgasming. The scientist/doctor instructs that my current fantasy man (somebody with a gorgeous body; at the moment a coworker who is a bodybuilding champion) must excite me. He eases his huge hard penis into me slowly; it is veined and glistening with my juices as he plunges it back faster and faster, swearing "I'll make you come, you bitch," and the like. But he starts to get excited so it looks like he might come. But he doesn't want to stop. The scientist tells him to slow down, and he does for a bit, but not enough. So the scientist directs two enormously strong, faceless flunkies to pull him off me, which they do, although it is a terrific struggle. Then the scientist starts fucking me. Meanwhile the other fucker has a tremendous hard-on, and is cursing and struggling and foaming at the mouth to get to me. He demands to masturbate for relief; he's in agony from excitement, he wants me so much, but the flunkies have pinned his arms to his sides and won't let him.

Finally, he breaks free of them and tears the scientist off me, repeating his epithets and performance, sweating and straining. The above is often repeated in a crescendo until I come—sometimes with the fantasy man in me, sometimes while he strains in frustration watching me come with the scientist.

Sometimes I am tied up naked in a dungeon, to be burned at the stake as a witch, except that I am at the whim of one man, a gentleman or knight in armor, who comes in occasionally to feed me a little bread and water. I am so physically exhausted that all my defenses are down, and I get excited at the slightest provocation, for my will is entirely broken. The man enjoys sexually tormenting me. Without getting particularly excited himself, he licks my cunt, and he is fully clothed except for his exposed penis, he leisurely brings me almost to the point of orgasm, sometimes coming himself in a rather bored way without caring whether I do or not, and then leaves (although in reality I do get satisfied) so that I am quivering and dying for more and am nothing but naked, helpless lust.

I haven't shared the Prometheus fantasy with my lover, for the reason you put forth—I don't want it to lose its clout! I hope our sex life will get so wild there'd be no fear of that.

Lillian

My background: I'm 21, a college student, white suburban and middle class (though somewhat poorer since my parents got divorced in my junior year of high school). My father is a college professor with a master's degree. He is very old-fashioned (61 years old) and hates women since my mother divorced him. My mother is 50, very cool as a parent, has a master's degree and teaches in a day-care center at the university I commute to. (Suffice it to say when she got her B.A. in psychology and her M.A. in early-childhood education, I learned a lot from her textbooks.) I'm a freshman with no declared major at the University of Indiana.

I'd like to say first that I really love men; they really fascinate me and I try so hard to understand the way they think about life, love, women and sex. Out of about five close friends, four of mine are guys. I don't tell them everything about me, but they all know more about my personal/sex life than my girlfriend. I just find it a lot easier to be totally frank (and sometimes hilariously raunchy) with my guy friends.

I've been masturbating for as long as I can remember but I don't think I ever achieved orgasm until about 10 or 11. Everything I knew about sex then—which was a lot—came from books from a local suburban library. I started reading about sex when I was 9 (fourth grade). I took children's and adolescents' books about sex out of the library on my mom's card. She never objected; I don't think my father knew. I think my mother was relieved that I was getting the information I wanted to know from decent books (I caught her flipping through them a couple of times) so I wouldn't be asking her some touchy questions. I was very relieved to read that masturbation is totally normal, because I'd always done it, not to climax but just because it felt good. But I had to share a room with one (sometimes all three) of my sisters, so I used to do it in the bathtub. In sixth grade I finally got my own room.

My earliest memories of sex/sensuality:

1. I don't know how old I was, but when one of us was sick, my mother would isolate us in the living room on the sleeper sofa so everyone else wouldn't get sick. It was nice to have her to yourself all day, when everyone else was in school. I distinctly remember having her take my temperature anally. I really liked the feeling of having something in my anus; I have ever since.

2. In fourth grade, the boy who sat next to me in class (us two secluded by a bookcase) showed me his thing and I undid the fly on my pants and somehow got my underwear down enough to show him my clit. Also in that year I kissed his best friend, behind the school. It was a very innocent sweet kiss.

3. When I was in sixth or seventh grade, one time early on a Sunday morning, I answered a phone call for my mom. When I went to my parents' room I just unthinkingly opened the door without knocking. Quite shockingly, my mother was on top of my father in her robe making pleased sounds. I shut the door, gave my message, and went back to bed with this inerasable image in front of my eyes. (I knew how sex was done, but I'd never *see* it before.) At that time my parents were really fighting a lot, so when my mom came to ask me if I was "okay," all I could say was, "I thought you guys *hated* each other!"

4. Sometime between 9 and 12, I gave myself my first orgasm. Since from eighth grade until after high school— and even now—I was very shy (also somewhat chubby), I became addicted to masturbating.

My fantasies at that time were mostly romantic, that some guy would finally ask me out, and we would slow dance, and he would kiss me—then I'd finally have a boyfriend. After

I'd got my period in ninth grade, I also had a problem with vaginal discharge, and I thought everyone would smell it if I didn't keep my legs crossed. I never discussed it with my mother because I was too embarrassed. I think it was probably recurring yeast infections. Now that I've been seeing a gynecologist for a few years, I know what they are like. But at the time I thought there was something wrong with me.

Real Experiences: A month before my 18th birthday, I went to a bar downtown with a black girlfriend and got fucked for the first time by this black guy I let pick me up. I did everything I read about that first night, and I was only mildly disgusted by some things, and secretly thrilled that I had finally done them. I was disappointed though, because none of it (oral, regular, anal, and mutual masturbation) led to the shuddering releases I could give myself. I thought maybe sex with guys just wasn't as good as masturbation. It was nice to be held, though, after a long cold adolescence.

Two months later I met my "first love," Jonny. He didn't fuck me the first night; we had sex the first time about two weeks later. But he could excite me with his hands and mouth so good I guess I fell in love, or in love with sex as an activity with no competition in terms of making you feel good. He was the first guy to bring me to orgasms like the ones I was used to from myself. He did everything to me and I loved it. He would eat me and lick me for hours it seemed, and tongue and finger my asshole. We found my G spot and that I could ejaculate, I grew to *love* anal sex, and he loved it when I'd stick my finger up his asshole and rub his prostate gland while I gave him head at the same time. He bought me a vibrator, and we used it on each other or to fuck me in both holes at once. As I said, I'd fallen in love with anal sex the way he did it to me: fucking me in the ass and rubbing my clit at the same time, or using the vibrator in my pussy while he fucked my ass. It was really mind blowing, I could never get enough. I also learned how to give really great head, and since Jonny and I broke up about a year ago, everyone I've sucked off since then says that I give fantastic head. I haven't sucked off everyone I've slept with since him because I won't give that to just anyone. (I have to know that they love eating pussy before I'll give them head, and they have to be a better-than-average lay. Otherwise they just want you to give head for twenty minutes then fuck you for five, and expect you to have a really good time like that!)

Let me just digress about giving head and getting head for a minute. I love to be like lost in space, just totally passive, laying there while someone sucks my clit and tongues and fingers me for a really long time. But I love to *do* that to guys. I love to love a guy's cock with my mouth and tongue and listen to him appreciate it. It sounds dumb but I feel all warm inside when I just go off orally on a guy who'll just lay back and take it. It is kind of a power thing: I love to hear a guy beg me to not stop sucking his cock.

Another thing that I really love is to watch a guy jerk off. It arouses me so much. Jonny's the only one I got to watch (many times) jerk himself off to climax. It's so cool to watch, like he's in his own world and I'm not even there. Sometimes I'd masturbate at the same time. Mostly I'd just watch and then wait for him to get hard and fuck me. It took a lot of coaxing on my part to do it; he thought it'd make him look "faggy" to me. But just the opposite! I loved it, and sometimes when he was just about to come, I'd put my mouth on the head and suck and swallow while he came.

Most guys seem to get a little jumpy when you touch their anus unless you are giving them head at the same time. Although one time recently, also with Jonny, when he was really banging me and I was loving it, I had my hand on his beautiful bun anyway, so I slid two fingers between his cheeks and rubbed his anus in rhythm with our fucking and he really loved it, went even crazier. But one of the things I do at the start of a good head session is spread the guy's legs and get between them and lick a few long strokes from his asshole, between the balls, all the way up the shaft of the cock to the head. They sure seem to love that, too. Seems those guys like to have me pay attention to everything between their legs, not just their cocks.

I've always had a fantasy of two guys fucking me in both holes at the same time, but I've only seen that in pornos. Maybe someday I'll experience it for real, but for now I'm too afraid of AIDS to specifically look for guys to do that with. And I've never told any of the guys I've fucked about that fantasy. I also found out with Jonny that sometimes what you think you like in your fantasies often isn't the same in real live sex. One time I asked him to tie me down, because I've always had some kinds of bondage fantasies. But when we did it, it wasn't too great. Maybe because he was unsure about it and if he might hurt me. I also fantasize a lot about watching two guys fuck each other. I've seen that in bisexual pornos, and it really turned me on, two guys fucking and sucking each other. It's kind of like watching a guy jerk off, like I'm not even there, I'm just watching. I have a feeling I wouldn't just watch in real life. But so far I have no real desire to get in bed with two guys just to see up close how they get each other off. It stays in my fantasies, though.

I fantasize a lot about domination, I guess, things like *9½ Weeks* (the book is much more explicit and kinky than the movie was) and *The Story of O.* One of the things that turns me on about those books when I read them is the whipping and spanking and being chained up like a slave, like the only reason to live is to be fucked in every orifice, in any way the guy feels like fucking you. No one's ever spanked me yet, except Jonny once, and I really did get turned on by it. It wasn't "real" spanking though, not really painful, just the playful stinging slaps on the ass.

I fantasize about going to bed with a woman, too, and I think how I could eat her out and make her come. But in reality I'm afraid of the lesbians at school (the school I go to is just a huge commuter school with about every race and sexual orientation you could imagine). I think I'm afraid of liking it with a woman too much, but if it weren't for societal attitudes, I think I would like to have one male and one female lover. One of my female cousins is/was gay; she's not sure now, I guess. With women I always think of dildos and vibrators and how the girl could use them on me and vice versa, but I don't know if that's really how lesbians have sex or if that's just what the people who make pornos think people who watch pornos want to see.

Blythe

I am 39 years old, twice married, with one son from my first marriage, and I am now raising my four stepchildren from my second marriage. My marriage is very solid as we believe in commitment, and we are faithful churchgoers, very much respected in our church and in our community. I have a college degree in finance and presently hold a job in management for a local firm. No one but my closest friends knows that I secretly have an insatiable appetite for men.

It started for me at a very young age—probably about 8 or 9 years of age. I cannot remember when I wasn't involved with at least one if not two or three or four males. I seem to be drawn to men of all sizes, shapes, ages, colors, and personalities. And they seem to be drawn to me. Many of my relationships with men have been full of love and caring for each other, and the feelings seem to last through the years, even though for some reason or another we decided to go our separate ways. I can remember as a young girl practicing sexy poses and looks in the mirror, learning how to attract men in a very subtle way.

As I got older, I knew that I was very attractive, so I didn't worry so much about attracting men with my looks. I worked more on getting to them emotionally. The problem was that once I got to them emotionally, I was looking for the next man to play with. I absolutely love the mating rituals that males and females go through before they actually consummate the relationship. The sexual tension that builds up between two people is for me the greatest excitement. It is just a matter of time after the sexual acts happen between us until I get bored and start looking for someone new. Many of my past lovers are now my closest friends and we still care for each other, but the sexual relationship is over. I use my marriage as an excuse, even though these men would love to continue with the sex. My husband thinks I am just not interested in sex. I could never tell him that I am as horny as hell, just not for him.

I don't find women at all interesting. I only think about men. I have only a handful of female friends. I also never fantasize about bondage and pain or urination and defecation. My fantasies are either about watching men I don't know masturbate or about fucking men I do know. Some of my fantasies are reminders of actual happenings in my past, only involving different men.

For instance, one of my past lovers always wore boxer shorts instead of Jockey shorts. I discovered that I became very sexually aroused by the feel of the cotton fabric around an erect penis. My lover would lie on his back in his boxer shorts. I would sit by him and just softly rub the fabric around his penis while it became harder and harder. I continued this for several minutes, and I loved listening to his groans and heavy breathing. He would begin writhing in ecstasy as I finally let his penis poke through the fly opening in his shorts and began to rub his penis with faster and harder strokes until he couldn't stand it anymore and rolled over on top of me to fuck my brains out. We both came within a couple of minutes, because the pent-up desire was more than we could control. We would then rest awhile and fuck again, this time more slowly and longer and much gentler, as we whispered loving words to each other. I now find that in my fantasies, the men are always wearing boxer shorts.

Anyway, I find now that a large number of my fantasies are about men masturbating. The very thought of seeing a man with his penis erect in his hand, with the hand pumping it and his face showing the ecstasy he is feeling is enough to get me so excited I can come right away while masturbating myself. I also like to hear the sound of the hand rubbing the penis during masturbation. My husband occasionally jerks off in bed when he thinks I am asleep, and the sounds of him jerking off are enough to bring me to orgasm without any manipulation of myself at all.

Among my fantasies of men masturbating are the following:

1. I meet a man who is buying liquor in a store. He is

either an older man, say in his 60s, or a very fat man in his 30s. He is already intoxicated, and he is ogling me. He starts talking to me and telling me how attractive I am. I ask him if he would like to invite me to his place for a drink. He says, "Of course!" We go to his place, where he immediately takes off his shirt and pants and sits on the couch in his boxer shorts. I sit next to him as we sip on our drinks and visit for a while. He puts his arm around me, and soon I notice that he is breathing harder and harder. I look down and see that his penis is poking straight up in his boxer shorts. I become so aroused I cannot keep from touching it. So I begin to fondle his penis, and he becomes more and more excited. He wants to fuck, but I tell him no because we have just met and I don't want to fuck someone I don't know. But I would love to watch him jack himself off. I tell him to lie on the floor while I stand over him facing his feet so I can have a good clear view of his hand working away at his penis. I hold my pussy lips apart so that he can see and reach up with his other hand and play with it. He reaches up and puts his fingers inside me. I begin to move with his movements, fucking his fingers. He gets so excited watching me that he is panting heavily, and his hand begins to move roughly on his penis. He jerks it and jerks it until his whole body is in spasms and his come shoots in the air. He then passes out on the floor. I wait a few minutes and then I begin to play with his penis to see if I can get it hard again. Since he is passed out, it is very difficult to get it hard, but I work frantically on it until it becomes stiff. He doesn't wake up, but after I work on him for a few minutes, he comes, and I chuckle to myself as he groans in his sleep. Then I leave.

2. I meet a man in a bar. He is not a particularly good-looking man. I find that men with average looks are much more sensual than really good-looking men, usually. Good-looking men are often too much in love with themselves to let any woman get inside of them. Anyway, he is obviously attracted to me as we sit at the bar, and I notice his eyes dropping to my tits and to my legs quite often during our conversation. I am wearing a fairly short skirt

and a low-cut top, with no bra or underpants. Music is playing, and I ask him to dance with me. We go out on the dance floor, and I press my body up against him and rub my tits against his chest. He soon starts to caress one of my tits with his hand, as he grabs my ass with the other hand and pulls me up against his now hard-as-a-rock penis. I rub against his penis with my body, and he lets out a gasp. The music ends and we go back to the bar. He tells me he wants me to go someplace where we can be alone. I tell him what I would like to do is go see a porn movie at the local porn theater. He agrees to take me there, because I am too shy to go by myself, and I really want to go see a porn movie. I am the only woman in the movie theater. The men don't notice that I have walked in. On the screen is a scene with a woman lying on her back with her legs in the air and her pussy fully exposed to the viewers while a man first fucks her with his fingers and then with his penis. The movie camera catches sight of the penis going in and out as the woman's vagina opens to let it in and then closes around it. I hear the men in the movie theater begin to breathe very heavy. Some of them are squirming in their seats. I hear a couple of low groans. The man in front of me reaches for his zipper, and I hear the sound of him unzipping his pants. I see his arm reaching for his penis as he squirms to let it poke freely out of his pants. Then I see his arm start working away at his penis, and I hear the sounds of his hand rubbing the shaft up and down. I stand up behind him and watch him as he continues to play with his penis. He doesn't want to come right away, so he slows down the action from time to time, but soon it is too much for him, and he tries to stifle his groans as he comes in his hand. After seeing this, I am so excited I am ready to explode myself. I lift my skirt up so that my companion can play with my pussy. He flicks his finger around my clit for just a short time, and I come in his hand. He then unzips his own fly to free his penis, which is standing straight up. He grabs it with his hand and starts to rub it. He wants me to jerk him off until he comes, so he grabs my hand and tries to put it on his penis. Teasingly, I refuse to grab hold of it. He is going crazy and can't stop from jerking his penis himself. He is so excited he is leaking semen out of the tip of it, and that excites me to where I can't help but grab it and jerk it until it explodes in my hand.

3. I often fantasize that I rent out the extra bedroom in my home to a young man around 19 to 23 years of age. His room is right next to my bedroom closet, and I have installed a two-way mirror between the two rooms where I can watch him in his room without him knowing. I have put several pornographic books and pictures in the room for him to discover. When he is in his room, I watch through the mirror as he jerks off while looking at the pornographic pictures. At night I sleep with my bedroom door open so that if he walks by my room he can see that I am lying in bed and exposing my bottom to him. One morning he walks down the hallway and looks into my room. He sees that I am naked from the waist down and he is able to see my pussy. He stands in the doorway, just staring. I pretend that I am asleep and soon hear him unzip his pants. I hear his hand rubbing back and forth on his penis. He jerks off faster and faster, I become more and more excited and open my eyes to watch him. I start playing with my clitoris, and as I start pumping as if I am fucking someone, he comes over nearer to me for a closer look. He is pumping furiously away with his hand on his dick, and his knees start to buckle. I scream out as I come and writhe all over my bed. This brings him to his own climax, and he comes all over his hand.

4. I go to work in a pornographic bookstore that has dancing girls who will dance for a man in a booth with just a pane of glass between them. The bookstore owner tells me he has a customer that wants to use one of the booths, and he tells me to turn him on. I take my place on a stool behind the glass in the booth. Soon the customer comes in and sits down. Music begins to play, something like "Bolero." I stand up and begin to gyrate my hips as I rub my hands all over my body. I slowly take off my skirt and blouse, revealing my sexy bra and underpants. The customer has his eyes glued to me. He is beginning to breathe heavily. I reach

NANCY FRIDAY

my hand inside my underpants and begin to play with myself. My eyes are closed, and I show him that I am really becoming aroused. I open my eyes and check the customer's crotch. His pants show a large bulge, and he keeps reaching down to his bulge and pressing against it with his hand. I take my bra off and start rubbing my hands over my tits, playing with the nipples. He begins to squirm in his chair as his hard-on becomes more and more uncomfortable for him. I take my underpants off and lie down with my legs spread wide apart and my feet up against the glass, and I start fingering my pussy. He stands up right at the glass and unzips his pants and pulls out his throbbing penis. He is rubbing the head of his penis against the glass as he watches me play with myself. He rubs it back and forth, and the semen that is leaking from the head is smearing all over the glass. I start raising and lowering my hips as if I am fucking him. He starts to rapidly jerk his penis up and down, faster and faster, gasping for his breath, until he comes all over the glass and I come all over my hand. His time is up and he leaves.

A man's penis excites me tremendously. I don't care for pictures, I want to see the real thing. I crotch-watch all the time, hoping to see a man with an erection, if I can't be so lucky as to catch someone jacking off.

As I said, my fantasies of actual fucking are always with someone I know and have a close relationship with. I make friends with men very easily, and as I become acquainted with men, I always go through a time of dreaming constantly of our first fuck as I masturbate myself. I can bring the fantasy to such a point that I can almost feel the man's penis inside of me as I fuck the air and play with my clitoris at the same time. I can bring myself to wild orgasms that way. I know that many of these men are as excited by me as I am by them. I love to catch them looking at my tits or my legs. If it weren't that I'm married and most of the men I am around are married, I'm sure I would have a variety of lovers to choose from.

494

I can't believe I have gone on so long, but I have really enjoyed writing these fantasies down on paper. I have never done this before. I have really turned myself on as I have written, and I have gone back several times to read over what is here. I am very aroused and will probably spend the rest of the day dreaming about men jerking off their dicks and about fucking someone I know into ecstasy.

Cheryl

I am almost 19, unmarried, pretty, confident, a student at a respected college, raised in an upper-upper-middle-class family. My parents, however, are anything but traditional and conservative; rather, eccentric is a better word. I don't feel entirely comfortable chatting about sex with my parents, but my mother says it's perfectly natural to feel this way. Nonetheless, I know she'd give me any help in this department I requested. The way she sees it: If it's forbidden, you want it more and you go to great lengths of stupidity to get it. Thus, sex has never been a big taboo.

At 16, when I had my first lover, she figured we were sleeping together (we often did it at my house, when my parents were home). She just said, "If you're too embarrassed to buy birth control in a store, I'll be happy to provide you with it." It made me a bit uncomfortable at the time, but now I'm so proud of her, 'cause I'm sure it's a hard thing for a mother to face.

I started masturbating and fantasizing at 8 years old. The first fantasies I can remember involved my 12-year-old girlfriend spanking me. I would actually bend over a chair in order to imagine it more richly. Since then, I have rarely fantasized about women, but the idea of sex with a woman fascinates me and I intend to try it some day. Most of my fantasies involve black, Hispanic, and American Indian men. (I've only ever seen Indians in movies.) I used to feel guilty about the things I imagined and the feelings I had; now I believe it's good for me! I think my cheeks have a prettier, glowing color when I've been having a lot of orgasms recently. Here are some of my present fantasies.

The face of the man in a fantasy is that of my latest fancy or a sort of faceless face.

FANTASY NUMBER 1:

I am lying on my bed in a silk robe, and my hair is making soft curls around my shoulders. There is a scuffling in the hallway, and I sit up and gasp. Then three men in ski masks break down my door as I scramble to hide in the closet. They find me and drag me from the closet, saying, "Pack your things." I pack and they carry my luggage and me, screaming and fighting, to a limo outside, where they give me a tranquilizer.

I awaken in a strange and lavish room where a Hispanic (or black, or whatever) man sits across the room in an unbuttoned shirt, with a drink in his hand and a cigarette hanging carelessly from his lips. I realize I am on a bed in a red gown. I see that he is an infamous and powerful drug lord (or some other white-collar criminal). Drowsily, I ask, "Why am I here?" He answers, "You're mine now. When I see something I want, I just take it." As he strides casually toward me, cigarette in mouth, drink in hand, I spit in his face and call him a bastard or son of a bitch or something. He laughs confidently, setting aside his drink and cigarette. He grabs the front of my gown and pulls me to my feet, kissing me fervently. I struggle, but his effortless embrace holds me. He throws me to the bed and undresses himself. He pins my arms to the bed, still kissing, nibbling my face and neck. I whimper, and he chuckles. "I am going to teach you, because I know you want this." He inserts his fingers into my cunt and then his tongue (I am wearing no underwear). My ability to struggle wanes. Then he fucks me slowly, as though with calculation.

FANTASY NUMBER 2:

In this fantasy I am wealthy and spoiled. There is a yardman working for my family. He has long black hair and strong arms. Although he is a mere manual laborer, he is intelligent and proud. As he works on the yard, I hang around outside, with a ho-hum attitude of nonchalance, yawning, pretending to check the mail or walk my dog, scantily dressed in a purple figure-hugging nightgown. But he catches me staring at him often. All the while, I appear indifferent. When he was finished with our yard after several days' work, he leaves. Some days later, I seek him out and find where he is working in a factory or something. As pretense to approach him, I bring some gloves that I pretend to think he left in our yard. He looks suspicious as I hand him the gloves, "Now, Miss So-and-so," he says in a deep and sly voice, "I think you know damn well these aren't my gloves, nor are they the reason you came here." I am shocked and humiliated, so I slap him on the face with the gloves. When I get home, I see a motorcycle in the garage. Then I go inside, and there he is, smoking a cigarette at the kitchen table. As though with disinterest, he rises, and without hesitation, places a hand on the back of my neck and kisses me forcefully. I pull away and tell him I'm going to scream. "Somehow I doubt that," he sighs. "In fact, I think you'd go out of your way to make sure no one disturbed us." Slowly, he walks behind me and presses his chest and stomach to my back. I try desperately to free myself as he presses his hands against my back, forcing me to lean over the kitchen table. He lifts my skirt and caresses my inner thighs and cunt lips, commenting on how wet I am. Then, still holding me down, he whips out his cock and shoves it deep inside of me, while I cry out in pain and ecstasy.

FANTASY NUMBER 3:
The beginning part of this is always different, but somehow I find out that some man—sometimes a professor, distant relative, stranger, etc.—is a vampire. He knows I know his secret, so he flies through my dorm window. He says, "How dare you, pretty mortal, know my secret? I could kill you with my bare hands, etc." As in most fantasies, I act arrogant and bitchy. "I am not afraid of you. I'm not afraid of anyone." He always pulls me by the hair; it varies where

and how he pulls. Often, he grabs my hair and pulls my face to his, telling me he ought to kill me, but I'm so beautiful that, instead, he's going to make me his mistress. Still holding me by the hair, he pushes me to the floor so I am kneeling at his feet. I look up and see he is wearing only a black cape, and his cock is monstrously large and erect. "Take your clothes off, bitch," he says calmly. And I do. He tells me to get on my knees and beg for my life. I refuse, and he says, "Then when I fuck you, I'm going to make it hurt." He throws me on my back and licks, sucks and nibbles my cunt and large breasts. Then I willingly get on hands and knees, and he fucks me violently from behind and bites my neck. This makes me his and gives me special powers. After that I must seduce young virgins (boys and girls) to keep my powers. By the way, some of my friends told me that real vampires can't have sex with mortals, or can't have sex at all, but I figure, it's my fantasy and *I make the rules!*

Those are just a few, and each fantasy has numerous variations. All of my fantasies are about a contest of wills, where I am accustomed to winning but lose to this one man. He is always powerful, strong, and arrogant; so am I, but not quite as strong as he. I am seduced or forced, but I always want him, though I feign disgust, hatred, or indifference. A lot are "Taming of the Shrew" fantasies, where I am such a wild-tempered bitch that some guy decides to do the impossible: conquer me, make me submit to him!! Making me come is a triumphant feat to the fantasy-man, because my submission says that he has power over me. (In actuality I believe that it is the woman who *makes* herself come, for the most part.) My first lover thought he had "taught" me to come. Truth is, I've been making myself come for nearly ten years.

Betsy
I am 21 years old, white, a high school grad, one year college, single, and currently an unemployed bookkeeper. I am from the East Coast but currently live in the Midwest.

My earliest sexual experience was with masturbation, which I started at age 3. I used to play with myself at nap time at day care. I don't remember if I climaxed back then. I used to rub myself over my underpants. As I got older, I masturbated on my bare pussy and started to use fantasies. My earliest fantasy (around age 8?) was to be felt up against my will by a strange man or boy. I would imagine that my hands feeling my breasts and pussy were the hands of this stranger. Intercourse never entered my mind at this age. I also remember when I was 4 years old, a boy in my preschool class and I used to play "you show me yours and I'll show you mine." I would always show him mine and then he would refuse to show me his. An alert teacher finally put a stop to it. Also in this class, at nap time I would masturbate under the cover on my cot. The teacher, sensing my unrest, would come over and rub my back. I especially liked it when her hand would travel over my bottom. I would often toss and turn just to be rubbed this way. I was raised by my father, so maybe I just wanted pampering from an adult female.

During my early teens, I was introduced to petting but never to orgasm. My breasts were very small (and still are), and I never let a boy touch them until my first real lover, at age 17. He was a fair lover and was very good at eating pussy. He was also very abusive physically and mentally, though he was not this way in bed.

I have had two lovers since then and am currently living with my boyfriend of one year. We are very much in love, and I hope to marry him soon. I have never enjoyed sex so much in my life as I do with him. My favorite thing is to suck his cock. It's about seven inches long and so very soft. His dick head is as soft as a rose petal. I would suck his cock several times a day if he would let me. I also love to lick and suck his balls. I love the smell of his balls. I would love to lick and suck his ass cheeks and crack (anus—I don't know). His ass is small, but so round and firm. He likes to use mirrors during sex, so do I. Our favorite position is "doggie style." I love to be dominated. I like a good, hard, rough fuck. I would like to be tied up spread eagle on the bed and dominated. Pain would turn me off, and I never fantasize about it. Also, I wouldn't want to be called names or humiliated. I think I just want to be forced to do what I want to do anyway. I also love to talk dirty and to be told what to do sexually, and in foul language.

My recent fantasies are about my boyfriend's friends. I imagine that while my boyfriend is at work, one of his friends stops by. I let him in and we talk. Sometimes, he is intoxicated and rapes me. Other times, he tells me about his poor sex life with his wife or how she'll never suck his dick. I tell him how much I love to suck cock, and he starts to get an erection. We have lots of foreplay and oral sex, and he fucks me roughly. Another fantasy is to watch an unsuspecting male masturbate. Sometimes a boy. I often fantasize about seducing a young boy (13–16). I want to make him feel like he has never felt before. Sometimes, but rarely, I fantasize about sex with women. These fantasies occur more frequently in my dreams. It is never a person I know, and she is always very feminine and beautiful. I have never had a real-life lesbian experience and I doubt I ever will. Outside of fantasy, it turns me off. I also fantasize about having sex with two men at a time, but I have never done this either. I enjoy X-rated movies and reading about sex. I think I'm a voyeur at heart.

I also would like to watch two men get it on with each other. Two attractive masculine men. Fags, the obvious feminine types, are a *real* turn-off to me.

Babs

I'm 40, a high school graduate, married for twenty-four years, mother of two grown children, and a 14-year-old still at home. I've been married in name only for thirteen years, but I never broke loose until a year ago, when I met the man I love and plan to marry within the next year or so. At present, he's in a federal penitentiary.

All my life, I've been a dreamer, an intellectual. I never knew what a true man-woman relationship was or could be until a little over a year ago. But I've always had my daydreams, many of which have come true since that memorable day when I broke loose from the "good, decent, respectable" image that had been forced on me since childhood. I was raised very strictly, got almost straight A's in school, married at 16, always conformed to what was expected of me. But even then, in the confines of my regimented life, I lived in a wild fantasy world. Now I can hardly believe I'm the same person. I'm wildly, crazy in love with Jim, and he's every bit as passionate and earthy as I am, also sweet and affectionate, and very sensitive. I bless the day I met him. This separation is hell for both of us, but our fantasies help us tremendously. I'll only list a few of my favorites:

1. I'm in a van with four men, all in their late 20s or early 30s. We all remove our clothes, and I'm in a frenzy of excitement, seeing all those erect penises—all waiting for me. I'm straddling one man, licking and sucking on a second, hand-manipulating another to climax, as a fourth enters me from the rear (something I've yet to experience, but will as soon as my lover is released). Or one man has my legs in the air, sinking his tool up to the balls, as a second straddles my chest while I do a head job on him, and the third is fucking the fourth in the ass and jerking him off at the same time. The variations are endless, but it's always me with four guys. What really turns me on is the idea of all these guys depending on me for release. I guess it gives me a feeling of power. I love watching them lose control, knowing I'm responsible. Also, the sheer visual thing excites me beyond control.

I love the sight of the male body, period. I don't understand why, for years, articles on sex always said the male is the only one who really gets off on seeing the opposite sex nude. Whoever wrote all that garbage doesn't know me, and there have to be other women like me all over the world. Hell, I've been a "crotch watcher" ever since I can remember. And I've been sleeping with Jim for over a year, and every glimpse of his nude body thrills and fascinates me. We shower together, sleep in the raw every night, but it's always new and thrilling for me. I used to wake up in the middle of the night and sneak peeks at him, and every time he walks past me nude, I get the same thrill.

When he was out on bond, awaiting sentencing, and our time together was so short and precious, we'd make love three or four times in a row. Then he'd drift off to sleep, and I'd get up, go to the bathroom, clean myself up, then come back to him and wash his genitals, dry him off, then curl up in his arms and drift off to sleep. I'd wake at least twice each night just to cuddle up closer to him. I'd lie there thinking how much I loved him and wondering how long it would be before he'd come home to me for good, and I'd trace his eyebrows with my fingertips, touch his lips, kiss his chest very softly, then doze off again. I'd wake up in the morning to see him bending over me with love in his eyes, and I'd know we were one day closer to his sentencing date. The reason I'm telling you all this is because I know that if I didn't love him so very much, I wouldn't feel this fascination and wonder about his body. I get turned on by male bodies, per se, but his is familiar and dear and precious, because I love all of him, inside and out. It's mine, his body, as mine is his. A fantasy:

2. There's a sex party at my house. The people may be people I know, or strangers, or a combination. There are about twenty guests present, men being in the majority. Everyone is nude, and I'm getting a charge out of seeing all these erections, all shapes and sizes. Couples are humping away in every possible position, and a couple of guys are jacking off from sheer excitement, watching the action. And I'm enjoying watching those cocks flapping away. I walk out into the kitchen, and this big guy is telling a swishy-type guy to bend over, which he does, holding onto the table for support. The big guy inserts his enormous penis into the smaller one's anus, the gay one begging him not to hurt him. The big guy rams it home, despite the little guy's squeals, and you can tell they both like it. I watch them humping away, their faces tense, then I go into the living room. The big guy is done, you can hear his grunt of satisfaction, then a guy from the living room grabs the gay one, forces him down on his knees before him, tells him to take it

all. He has a medium-sized penis, and he rams it into the gay guy's mouth, up to the balls. He's swaying back and forth, and all of a sudden the little guy starts making all kinds of grunting noises, and I see that his long skinny tool is jerking every which way, and he starts squirting all over the floor. I want to run over and grab it, feel it spurt, but I'm frozen to the spot, all I can do is stand there and watch as he spurts all over the place. This is where I climax.

Again, the out-of-control thing.

GROUPS

There is another very new expression of power for women that belongs in this chapter: According to the sex manuals, anything over three people—a ménage à trois—constitutes a group, anything over seven people an orgy. The theory most often repeated to me in the past by sex therapists and analysts was that group sex was always the man's idea; when women went along, it was either to please the man or out of fear of losing him should he go without her. Not an illogical premise, given traditional woman's total dependence on her man.

With the sexual revolution women began to participate in group sex with enthusiasm; even today, despite the legitimate concern with sexually transmitted diseases, the Lifestyles Organization contends that there are over two hundred swing clubs in the United States. The clubs are defined as "a party house or facility where people go to engage in sexual activities with someone other than or in addition to their primary partner."

In fantasy, too, women like Mary Lee, Sage, and Sarah Jane have a deep and abiding curiosity about the pleasure principle: If one man is exciting, wouldn't that thrill be doubled or tripled with two or three men and another woman as well? These sex groups are very much the woman's idea, a fantasy in which she controls everything, knowing as she does that things can get out of hand in a group unless someone is in charge. It is this sense of being the one in command that excites as much as anything that goes on. "The variations are endless, but it's always me with four guys," says Babs, whose fantasy appears earlier in this chapter. "What really turns me on is the idea of all these guys depending on me for release. I guess it gives me a feeling of power. I love watching them lose control, knowing I'm responsible."

Attracted as they are to variety, women don't want their men getting too excited by another woman, even in fantasy. No matter how many rules are laid down in real group sex, there is no controlling the possibility of jealousy and envy. In fantasy, the woman makes sure these negative emotions never occur. Sarah Jane loves the added thrill of imagining her boyfriend with her best friend; because she loves them both, she can identify with what the other woman is feeling. But when it is time for the finale—when Sarah Jane is near her masturbatory orgasm—she returns her boyfriend's cock to where it belongs, inside her. Then, with the magic of fantasy, she plugs her boyfriend's best friend into her own friend. Complicated? Not at all, so long as it is contained in the mind.

Even in fantasy, adultery can be stressful unless carefully orchestrated; there are not only the woman's own guilty anxieties but a husband's pained reaction to her infidelity to account for. Victoria loves her husband but can only reach orgasm during masturbation when she imagines fifteen men with cocks ranging from twelve to fourteen inches pleasuring her. To assuage her sense of unfaithful preference for men with "enormous dicks, while my husband's is only half their size," she includes her husband in the fantasy. Is he jealous that she has abandoned him or envious of these other men? Absolutely not. "I am sure it is symbolic for my husband to be in the fantasy . . . ," she says, ". . . in fantasy he is not repelled. He is quiet and gives no opinion." And because there are certain loyalties that should be observed even in group sex, Victoria lets the fifteen men come only in her mouth and her anus. Her husband is "the only man to get into my vagina." Now, that is fidelity.

It is also tribute to the power of the mind. People and events are not so easily manipulated when fantasies are acted out, especially group scenes. Sage found this out the hard way: "My husband seems to take over when it's three of us (two women and he). And when we've had a guy join us he always wants it to end when he's had enough." Bad sport. To compensate, Sage invents a fantasy that allows her to fuck another man, and presto, just as the fantasy man is about to come, "he screams he loves me, and my husband hears him say that and forgives me because he knows I need lots of love and it won't take anything from us."

Does Sage need lots of love or lots of sex? Men used to try to explain away their infidelity as "just a one-night stand," meaning it was just sex with no love involved. Women were the ones who confused love and sex. Perhaps they still do, which is why many choose to live alone, without men, fearing that even one night of sex would leave them enslaved, in love with love.

How to combine sex-with-love (women's sex) with men's sex-without-strings? In the early 1980s, before the epidemic of venereal diseases and AIDS in particular, women experimented with this equation, living out in the safety of fantasy their adulterous affairs as never before. Today they continue to try to find the sexual middle ground that has always separated men and women. In the privacy of their minds, it is possible to combine men's hit-and-run adventuring with their own deepest feminine needs for warmth and tenderness. "No one ever caught anything from making love to a hundred men in a hundred nights in her mind," says Sage.

Sage

Women have always been known for being more romantic than men, so it's really hard to believe people think we shouldn't or don't have fantasies. That's the main reason I read romantic books about pirates kidnapping women then falling in love with them. It's a fantasy I can get into, even partly live as I read. I do like to be dominated and to be dominating, but not hurtful. The pleasure is what I'm seeking.

I am 28, married for eleven years, and have one child. I have always fantasized. I think everybody does but just doesn't categorize it that way. I've been sexually active since I was about 14, not totally by choice as my 15-year-old stepbrother molested me. I slept with many partners before I got married at 17. I was never really kinky until after about a year, when my husband and I discussed girls—that really turned me on. I had never consciously wanted a girl before, but I had played doctor with girls. I need a man, but women are pure enjoyment and they feel so soft. I had touched a girl's boobs before. Since my husband and I started talking about girls, they have entered my dreams. The real act so far hasn't been as good as my fantasies. We've had other girls join us on a few occasions. Once in the beginning, I had one to myself, that was the best. My husband seems to take over when it's three of us. And when we've had a guy join us, he always wants it to end when he's had enough. My husband never touches the man, he just watches and fucks me. So I fantasize that it's just this other guy and me and that he loves me and wants me—that he pumps me slowly until he comes inside of me as he screams he loves me, and my husband hears him say that and forgives me because he knows I need lots of love and it won't take anything away from us.

My main fantasy is based on truth. He's my lover and his wife is pregnant. I live with them and love with them. He's mine, she's mine, and the baby is part mine. I hold my lover's wife in my arms and caress her beautiful swollen tummy and feel our baby kick. We all sleep together with her in the center as my lover and I hold her and love her. And while he makes love to her, it's to me too. We are one and she is ours. And when he makes love to me softly and slowly, she caresses me and loves me, and he plants his seed in me. And he loves me. I dream about him every time I'm upset. He's there, waiting for me to be free.

I actually cried when he finally got married. I felt he was

no longer there for me. But I still fantasize that he just married her because I wasn't free, and that if I want him, he still wants me. And if he ever asked me just for sex and wouldn't mess up my marriage, I'd do it! Even though from experience I know there could be a lot of pain for lots of people. I had an affair with my brother-in-law, with my husband's initial OK. But it about broke all of our hearts, and about ruined both my and my brother-in-law's marriages.

Fantasies can be so powerful once unleashed to the living world. So now I'm very careful never to lose sight of my marriage and my love for my husband and child. Fantasies are very normal for me and risk-free as long as they live in my mind, where nothing and no one is out of reach. When real life fails me, I explore the outer limits of my mind where no one can ever tell me no. I should also add that fantasies are Safe Sex; no one ever caught anything from making love to a hundred men in a hundred nights in her mind.

Victoria

I am 20 years old. I was married at 18 to a man I worked with in the U.S. Military Service, and we have a son almost a year old. We have a good marriage and a good sex life. I am the first woman my husband (I'll call him David) ever had intercourse with, but he did have oral sex with several women before we met.

I was always sexually promiscuous. I remember doing myself with a carrot (we didn't have much else in the house to use) while I read my dad's porno books when I was 11 or 12. He used to keep them hidden in a box in my parents' bedroom, and I would keep the book and carrot under my mattress until I was ready to exchange the book for another. My dad finally confronted me with the evidence and told me that he understood, but not to let my mother find out. He never told me to stop, and he never said or did anything more about it. I have always been too embarrassed to bring up the subject, but I did continue for a long time.

I lost my virginity around my 13th birthday, with a friend's boyfriend. We did it three times that day and never met again. He was 15, and I really didn't feel anything. So I kept to carrots for almost another year.

Then one of my little brother's Cub Scout leaders and I did it in a camper (parked in front of his house on a busy street). This time (he was 30) I felt it. He was a lot bigger than the 15-year-old boy. After that I did it with other men, never boys. I wanted to be discreet. Boys brag. No man in his right mind would brag about an underage girl.

I really feel I had a lot of sex so early because I needed affection. My parents split up when I was 12, and I lived with my mother, who was a real bitch. She put down men in general, and I suppose that's the reason I wanted affection from men.

While my sex life with my husband is extremely good, I don't get horny like I used to before the baby came along. In fact, sometimes I only go along with it because I don't want my husband looking elsewhere. I usually orgasm, though due to fantasies I have while making love to my husband. I never had to fantasize before I had the baby. All I had to do was think about what we were doing, how it felt to have my husband inside me and how much he was enjoying it, and I would really explode. The following is my basic theme:

I am in a bedroom making love to my husband on a bed. I am straddling him, with his (I hate to be vulgar in reality, but my fantasies are, so I'll comply) dick in my pussy. We go at it pretty good. Then the fantasy goes one of several ways:

1. A full-grown German shepherd (male) dog walks into the bedroom and starts licking my anus. He becomes excited and enters my asshole with his huge dog prick. My husband and I cannot stop him. In fantasy I feel no pain, but I am sure I would in reality. The dog begins fucking me in the ass while my husband and I continue making love. The dog's master comes in, chasing his dog, and informs me that once the dog gets started there's no stopping him. Then he suggests I suck him off while he waits. I then proceed to deep-throat the man (something I cannot do) until we all come. At this point, in reality, I come.

2. A good-looking, husky Italian man and about fourteen

other men come into the room. The Italian has the biggest dick, about fourteen inches long and really thick, so he is the leader. He tells me he's going to stick it up my ass and then he does (again, it doesn't hurt). All of the other men have dicks at least twelve inches long or more. They proceed to masturbate, rubbing their dicks over my back. One, a black guy, makes me deep-throat him (really impossible with twelve inches or more), and the Italian informs me that I must pleasure all of them at least three or four times each. Then as the men who are only rubbing themselves begin to approach their orgasms individually, they stick the heads of their dicks, one at a time, inside my mouth alongside the black man's dick and come in my mouth. This increases the excitement. The whole time all of this is going on, the Italian is telling me about the gallons of come he's going to shoot up my ass and how I'm going to love it. Then all three men come at the same time, and, in reality, I come.

I am sure it is symbolic for my husband to be in the fantasy even though he is not greatly endowed (six and a half inches long and three inches around). In reality he is the only man I've ever reached orgasm with (and I had plenty of chances otherwise), and in the fantasy he is not repelled. He is quiet and gives no opinion. He is also the only man to get into my vagina.

I have never told my husband my fantasies because I know I would be hurt to find out if he had any that involved other women. I just don't mention it at all. I'm sure he wouldn't appreciate discovering I fantasize about screwing three men at once with others waiting their turn or screwing a dog with my asshole. I also note that all of my fantasy men have enormous dicks, while my husband's is only half their size. I want you to know that I am not very deep and my husband is all I could take! To me, he is enormous!

Steph

Rob and I were married by a justice of the peace in January. We have not seen each other since March 7. Rob was arrested on that last day. He has been charged with possession of stolen merchandise. This is thanks to a "friend" who turned state's evidence against him. I want you to understand that Rob is by no means a bad person. It was just a fact of being in the wrong place at the wrong time. Anyway, he was sentenced to three years in the county jail.

We write each other every day, sometimes two and three times a day. He calls at least every other day (sometimes two or three times a day).

Well, after three months of being apart, I got a very interesting letter from him. He was telling me how bad he wanted to fuck me, what positions he is going to fuck me in and each and every step leading up to it. After I got that letter, he wanted me to write to him the same way. I am a very shy person when it comes to sex (I have gotten over that a great deal since I met Rob), and I was a little shaky at first to write these types of things, but after a few of them, it started getting fun. It was kind of like the only way Rob and I could satisfy ourselves sexually without being unfaithful. I still laugh at the way he put it, as "long-distance fucking." It did actually work. I would always go to my room with his letter, take all my clothes off and just go through the motions with my hands as he put them in his letters. So, I would be sexually excited by just fantasizing he was there with me. He told me that he always gets a hard-on when he reads my letters. He said it was real embarrassing because there were all guys there and here he was walking around with this hard-on, but he still loves reading those letters.

Well, the letters just got better and better. They are still coming every day. Now, we have brought other couples into our fantasies. This is something that took me a long time to grasp because my naive mind just could not do it. Rob has been with other couples before with his previous wife (ten-year marriage). When he asked me if I would like to do that sometime, I was really shocked. I haven't "been with" other men at the same time, or other couples, but with our letters and my husband talking more about it, I get more and more excited about trying it. I want to tell you one of my favorite sexual fantasies that I wrote to my husband. We both always set the scene in our letters to give it a more realistic effect, but here it is:

MOVING DAY

Rob and I have finally found our "dream house," and it is moving day. Our "dream house" is a two-story, four-bedroom house with a Jacuzzi off from the downstairs bedroom and a beautiful lake behind the house.

We are sharing this house with another couple, and they are helping us to move today. They are a very good looking couple, and I have already been checking out the nice-sized bulge between the guy's legs (call the other guy Frank and his wife is Trish). I'm thinking that this is really going to be fun living with Frank and Trish. It's going to be like having your own live-in playmates.

We have been moving all morning and have all gotten to know each other a lot better. We decide to take a break for lunch and try out the Jacuzzi. So we order in pizza and head for the Jacuzzi. The Jacuzzi is in the middle of this elaborately tiled room. There is a well-stocked bar conveniently placed within arm's reach of the Jacuzzi. We all start slowly slipping out of all of our clothes. I catch a glance at Frank's muscular body and also confirm my thoughts of him having a big dick. (I always like the men in my fantasies to have big dicks, and Rob knows that I like them that way.) Oh yes! I want that inside of me bad. Rob starts mixing vodka and orange juice for me and Trish. He throws a beer to Frank and takes one for himself. We are all in the Jacuzzi. I am sitting across from Frank and Rob is across from Trish. We are enjoying each other's close company while we drink our chosen beverage and eat our pizza. We are laughing as the bubbles come up from between our legs, sending exciting little thrills through us all. Then, I feel a new thrill as Frank moves his foot up my thigh and slowly between my legs. He starts moving his foot up and down and around the outside of my pussy, and once in a while he sticks his big toe in my pussy and also tickles my clit, sending spasms of excitement through my whole body. I'm staring across at him, and if anyone else looked at his face, you wouldn't have a clue of what pleasure he was sending through my body as I am pulled closer to what I've wanted all day.

I am now sitting on his lap, facing him. One leg on each side of his own strong legs. He moves his hand down to my hairy, hot pussy and starts rubbing around the outside and then starts tickling my clit with his fingers. I can feel the huge bulge of his dick growing larger and harder, pushing against my stomach. As he thrusts one long finger into my pussy, he also thrusts his thick, hot tongue into my mouth, stifling my scream of pleasure.

I look over at Rob, and he is now sitting next to Trish. I can see the small lump of his tongue exploring around Trish's mouth, and one of his hands has gone underwater to explore the other depths of her pussy.

Frank has now pushed me up a little out of the water with his hands around my ass. He positions me over his huge dick and slowly starts bringing me down on it. I bite my lip to hold back a scream as the head of his huge dick penetrates my hot, tight pussy. For a short moment I don't think I can take it as it feels like he is ripping me wide open, but that short moment of pain turns into pure pleasure as he goes deeper, moving me up and down on his long dick.

Meanwhile, Rob and Trish are still there. Now she has her hand under the water, and I can see the surface of the water move as she massages Rob's dick, both of their faces showing their sexual pleasure. Then, while Frank is still moving me up and down, both of us moaning with pure ecstasy, Rob and Trish slip out of the Jacuzzi and head for the adjoining bedroom. They leave Frank and me in our own fantasy world. I feel every pulse of his dick as he moves deeper and deeper. I feel my pussy throbbing as we reach our climax at the same time. He pulls me up one final time and thrusts me back down as deep as possible as our cum mixes together. I then slip off, and we just relax for a while, listening to Rob and Trish reaching their own climax.

Frank and I then move to the bedroom to join Rob and Trish. They are lying next to each other, and I notice Trish's hairy pussy, just the way Rob likes it. Her breasts are swelling with every deep breath she takes.

I move toward her and put my face between her legs, moving my tongue around her clit, tasting her cum mingled with the familiar taste of Rob's. I then move around into the 69 position so she can also taste the moisture between my legs. As I feel like I am ready to have another orgasm, I move away from her and over to Rob, wanting his dick in my pussy more than ever. I lie on my back, and he mounts me and thrusts his dick into me with such force that I cannot stifle my small scream of pleasure. As he is pumping in and out of me, Trish moves to us and starts licking Rob's dick and my pussy as Rob moves in and out of my hot pussy. Frank is next to us masturbating himself, enjoying the sexual scene before him. He moves to my mouth and thrusts his dick into it as he is about to cum. Trish has her pussy over my mouth, and Frank's dick moves up and down on the outside of her pussy while I suck his dick. We all reach that wonderful point of no return, and I taste Frank's and Trish's hot cum as it runs down my face and spills onto my thighs.

We all just lie back on the bed and bask in the sexual glow of each of our own fantasies being fulfilled.

Sarah Jane

I started masturbating when I was 5 or 6. I guess that I had normal sexual experiences for a girl in early junior high and high school. You know, the usual petting and fingering, etc., but I never had sex.

Until last year . . . and then I met this really wonderful guy who I really fell in love with and I decided that it would be OK to have sex with him. He is the only guy I have had sex with since then, and I still love him, and we are still together enjoying (I think) really good sex.

One of our major problems is that my family is very religious and we can't let them find out about our sex life until we get married (which we intend to do eventually). And his dad would kill him if he found out we were screwing. So a lot of our fucking has been in the car, parked somewhere at a friend's house, at our school after hours, at my house when parents are gone, on picnics, etc. Occasionally we get to do it on a bed, and that is really special.

But, for all our awkward places of screwing, we do enjoy a relatively free sex life. I've learned how to suck him off, and he has gotten to where he enjoys eating my pussy. We fuck in all sorts of positions, but I think that me on top is the best for both of us. He likes to watch me play with myself, and although I've never gotten him to, I'd like to see him jerk himself off. He still won't fuck me when I'm on the rag even though that is when I'm the horniest of all. We are the best at five-minute quickies (understandably!).

I have never told him any of my fantasies, but I have almost finished *Forbidden Flowers* and when I'm done I intend to let him borrow it and read it. I wonder if it will turn him on like it did me? I stay wet whenever I read it! Maybe, when I am done with this letter, I will let him read it. It's not that I'd be embarrassed, but I just don't want him mad at me.

I never fantasized when we were fucking even if I knew I wasn't going to come (which I sometimes don't, don't ask me why, because my boyfriend is a great screw!). My boyfriend is the only guy I really want.

Generally, I think of my fantasies before I go to sleep or when I am waiting for him to pick me up on a date so we can go screw.

My three main fantasies are . . .

1. My boyfriend is away at a football game in his home town in Florida. I drive down to surprise him, but when I open his hotel door, I hear these moans from the bed. I hide so they won't see me and I watch what is going on. Apparently, my boyfriend has gone with this girl he knew (the only other girl he ever fucked) and one thing has led to another. As soon as my eyes adjust to the semilight, I can see that she is sitting on his face while he eats her pussy. She is arching her back and wiggling around on his mouth, and I can feel his tongue on MY clit, like it has been so many times before, and I start to gush wetness in my lace panties. Suddenly his back tenses, and I KNOW that she has just had one hell of an earth-shattering orgasm. About this time I notice my boyfriend's dick jerking away down there. It's actually bumping his stomach in its desire to get into a wet,

juicy cunt. It is all I can do to stop myself from running over and taking it in my mouth. This girl starts to slide down my guy's body until her lips are on the top of his straining prick and she slides her mouth down over it, taking it all in her mouth (something I can't do). Up and down her mouth goes, and I can see by his toes that my boyfriend is loving every single minute of this fuck. Just as he is about to squirt juice down her throat, she lifts her head off and lets it stream down her face and tits. I guess I missed his signal in my own rising passion, but all of a sudden she moves up and sits on his dick, and by this time I've got my finger in my own wet pussy. Anyway, as she starts to ride his prick, he is pulling on her tits and pinching her taut nipples until I just can't stand it anymore. I run to the bed, and before he can even see who it is, I put my now exposed pussy on his mouth. When his tongue starts darting in my hole and around my engorged clit, I just can't hold back anymore and I come in spasms of pleasure just as he shoots off again in this girl's cunt.

2. My boyfriend has this really good friend who is also hung big—I'm talking eight and three-quarters inches!! I imagine that my boyfriend brings him over to my house one day while my parents are gone and surprises me. I'm laying on the couch watching soaps, and in they walk. Unfortunately (?) I don't have anything on but this filmy see-through nightie. Without a single word, my boyfriend picks me up and starts toward my bedroom, motioning his friend to follow. He throws me on the bed and rips my nightie off (under which I have nothing on). With a swift move, he sticks his face in my already moistened pussy and starts to lick my clit. With each stroke over my hole, I get a little hotter until I'm writhing in ecstasy. Then I notice that his friend is just standing by the bed watching and I can see that he has this HUGE hard-on and I tell him with my eyes to put it in my mouth. He unzips his fly and this monster sticks its head out, and when his pants are disposed of, I feel this throbbing dick stuck in my open mouth. As I start to give him great head, he grabs my boyfriend's prick and starts to jerk him off. Suddenly I feel these hot streams of come

shooting into the back of my throat, and my boyfriend, who is still eating my sopping cunt, makes me come in waves of emotion as he too shoots his load, all over my thighs and pussy.

After a brief rest, we finish with fantasy number three . . .

3. I come to after drifting off into a really fulfilled trance and realize that someone is knocking on my door. I yell to them to come in and I shake my two bed companions to arouse them. As soon as my best friend walks in the door, my boyfriend gets this instant erection. I can't believe it, so I nudge him and tell him to go get it if he wants it. I just lay there with this other guy fingering me while I watch my boyfriend undress my friend and start sucking her tits. When they have been lapped into mounds of engorged tissue, his kisses move lower and lower until his face is even with her free-flowing cunt. With two slow licks of his sooooo good tongue, he makes her come. I wonder why he moved so fast until I see them lay down and him spread her legs and open her pussy lips big enough to fit his rock-hard dick in. As he starts to fuck it to her good, I begin to squirm with desire for that prick to be in ME. My hips are moving in rhythm with this other guy's three fingers, and I start a slow come. Before it's over, I feel the fingers leave my aching pussy, and not wanting it to end, I feel around for anything to put in my hot cunt. When my hand closes on a dick, I guide it into my hole and start screwing away. As I feel molten come shoot off and flood my pussy, I climax in groans of excitement. Then I realize that somehow my boyfriend left my friend and found his way to me, and that his friend has just brought my friend to a mutual orgasm on the floor while we did it in the bed. I come again.

Mary Lee

I am 30 years old and am a registered nurse. I am a college graduate who has been happily married for seven years. Here is my fantasy:

My husband and I are vacationing in the Caribbean and are having dinner in a cozy but crowded restaurant, when the headwaiter asks if we would mind sharing our table with another couple. We enjoy dinner, drinks, conversation and dancing with this tanned attractive couple. When we leave the restaurant, we find that our rental car has been stolen—but the other couple offers to drive us to the police station to report it. Obliged, we get in their car only to find they kidnap us and drive us to a secluded part of the island! When we arrive, my husband and I are separated and taken to different rooms. I'm escorted to one room by the woman, and there are two other women there. They order me to take off my clothes—afraid at first, I become more relaxed when I find that what they do is bathe me, give me a manicure, a hairdo, a facial, etc. Then they lay me on a table for a massage; but massage more than my aching muscles from all that dancing at dinner. (I'm not aware of it, but there's a two-way mirror in this room and my husband was taken to the adjoining room and is watching.) The massage turns into a female ménage à four. Then my husband and three other men (with stiff cocks from watching the ladies) enter the room and join us. There's a lot of sucking and fucking going on, and I end up being fucked in the cunt and ass by two guys at the same time. (One guy is black and muscular with a huge cock.)

Jeanne

I am 20, a student and in my second year at university. I was a virgin until the age of 19 (it was actually my birthday) when I succumbed to the wishes of my first steady boyfriend. Since then we have split up, and it is only now that I am getting over the trauma of being rejected. When I "gave" myself, it was a total gift. I never thought it would end. My first affair (and only) was a good one (obviously I have nothing to compare it to), but just by reading the recent erotic literature I realize we were pretty adventurous.

Now to my fantasies (that might seem a very disjointed jump, but I want to start at the beginning, that is, when I first had my "dreams"). When I was very young, about 5 or 6, I think, I used to take great pleasure in undressing at night

(I always wore those thin brushed-nylon pyjamas), feeling cold sheets against my body. By wriggling about, I had the most incredible feelings.

This developed when I was older to placing a pillow (or anything heavy) on my body and spread-eagling. I then used to fantasize that I was a captive of a Red Indian Chief or a Sultan, and he would touch me with his hands very roughly. He would usually be showing me off to a friend. They would have conversations about the shape and firmness of my body (particularly my thighs and buttocks). This went on for many years, the story only ever slightly changing. Often, by the way, if I thought about these intently enough I would fall asleep and my dreams (or the basis of them) would carry on, this time not controlled by me. I would wake up from these quite wet with excitement, often thrusting my hips, though I didn't realize why, and would have the most incredible pulse racing in my vagina.

When I was a teenager, the fantasies varied and, to be quite honest, I can hardly remember the majority. One favorite and recurring one involved "waking up" to find myself trapped in a mechanical machine. It touched my body all over. It was cold and hard—it even had projections which entered between my legs. The picture would then switch to a conference room, long table with about a dozen chairs on each side. All these smartly dressed men would be there, to all purposes discussing the latest trade figures. The majority of them would be middle aged. One man, the most distinguished, would sit at the top of the table in front of a panel of switches. He would then announce his latest pastime. Screens would roll back, and then this metal contraption with me in it would slide high onto the walls, almost from the ceiling across the room until it was directly above the table. All the men would look up and gasp—some would immediately get excited and demand to touch me. Meanwhile I would get this overwhelming feeling of hanging down—the machine was holding me, but it was as if a weight was on my back pushing me down, obviously my breasts were hanging. Through a series of button sequences, the man could make any part of my body come directly to any individual's face. At this point I would get wet and excited in reality, though not reaching climax—which was simply because I was using a funnel or some other object in my vagina, not realizing what a powerhouse my clitoris was. These days I elaborate that scene to men actually stimulating all parts of my body while I squirm, although of course I am loving it.

My fantasies today keep me sane and now include animal ones (particularly large dogs) and group sex—always this involves me being totally dominated, all areas being stimulated. I realize that many of my fantasies are of this domination sort because I feel guilty. I don't intend to get into any psychoanalysis, but I realize a lot has to do with an awful scene when I was quite young (about 10), when my mother caught me masturbating (I was so far away, I hadn't even noticed her in the room). She stopped me, took my hands away from my vagina and told me that I was dirty and too old for that! It has affected me. Part of the reason my boyfriend left me was because it seemed to him that I was disgusted by his suggestions. I know I gave this impression, but underneath I was thinking of scenes that would have absolutely amazed him.

I have come to realize that I am not unusual or dirty in any way . . . just natural. I hope, when I go back to university, to find somebody who will help me forget my guilt and enjoy the whole thing, fantasy as well. Until then I have my "dreams."

WATCHING TWO MEN HAVE SEX

As monogamy and even chastity become alternatives to sexual experimentation, the question arises as to what we do with all the information, stimulation, everything we did and learned in the last twenty years. What we assimilate from the past and what we throw away will be decided largely by women, who have always held the key to sex with their all-powerful No. Now women initiate sex and they are major economic players too. When times got tough in the past, men worked harder and women lowered their hemlines. Because so much of a man's identity lay in being a "good provider," working harder put no more strain on his sense of himself as a real man than going to war.

But women get only a portion of their identity from providing financially, about as much as they get from a rewarding family life (according to a Roper poll); the part of their identity they get from their sexuality is still changing. Simply put, women have a lot to gain from being the sexual pioneers of the future.

Therefore, when I say that the sexual adventuress stands alone on the frontier, it is not meant as a put-down of men. Most men have watched from the sidelines as women sexually evolved in recent years; some enjoyed what they saw, others were terrified, but most, I believe, clung to their old-fashioned dreams of macho dominance, uncertain over what the evolving new woman was suggesting should replace the double standard. The sexual status quo may not be great, these men feel, but it still works for them. Why should they change? Perhaps if they do nothing, if they let the women slug it out together as they are currently doing, things will return to the way they used to be.

Meanwhile a small fraction of the more courageous women continue to explore new erotic roles, possibilities, and satisfactions for both men and women. Many of the women in this book are without men; masturbation is their only sexual outlet. Whether men have failed them, whether they are angry at men, they don't share the destructive feminist "To hell with men" attitude of twenty years ago. These women believe that if they are going to live in a world with men, the opposite sex should be better understood. Perhaps in understanding men, they will know themselves better.

What do men want? What are they like sexually? Why can't a man be more like a woman, more caring, more loving, more tender? In no type of fantasy do women investigate men's sexuality more blatantly and look at men

520

more closely than in fantasies of watching men have sex together.

Men's enjoyment of watching women sexually entwined is very different in quality and purpose from these fantasies. What women bring to this very new category of voyeuristic fantasy is an unprecedented female interest in the up-close investigation of men's sex, not just as an orgasmic high but as a clue to what makes men tick; here are women practicing their famed talent for trying to hold people together, heal emotional wounds, and yes, have a good time too.

In watching two men make love to one another, sometimes as a participant but more often from outside the picture frame, these women look for emotions and sights and sounds in men's sex with one another that will help them understand what is missing in their own real heterosexual relationships. "I feel that I fantasize about two men because I'm tired and bored with seeing women being so loving, caring, free with their emotions; and men being cold, aloof, laughing off situations," says Mona.

Many of these women remind me that I said in *Men in Love* that women are not aroused by the image of sex between men. Well, at that time I'd never heard of the idea; ten years ago women didn't like to think that their men even masturbated without them—it was too threatening. But as times change, fantasies follow accordingly, and women in the 1990s like Bonnie think "It's wonderful when two men I know well are being open, vulnerable and tender toward each other. It signals a new kind of masculinity—men who are sure enough of their manhood that they can show deep emotion in another man's presence . . . [it] makes me feel hopeful about the future, and my clit also approves—it's an optimistic organ."

In the chapter on women's fantasies of other women, I mentioned how often they stated that "no one knows how to please a woman like another woman." In a fantasy of two men, a woman similarly learns how two men expertly bring each other to climax, a lesson she can then take to her own bed with her own man. For Natassia, whose lover will not go down on her, fantasy becomes a form of wish fulfillment where two men bring each other to the oral climax she desires.

In reality, women do not get to adore the male body, nor do they get to see the male body being adored; a fantasy of another woman adoring a man would arouse competition, but with two men a woman can relax, watch, and adore. Meanwhile, of course, either "arrang[ing] the two men according to my desires," as Chloe does, or just holding them in her omnipotent gaze, she enjoys the power of the voyeur. "I find men beautiful," says Diane, "not aside from their sexual organs but with them being a fantastic part of the whole person, a part I enjoy looking at often. Because of the pleasure it brings I sometimes nearly worship it."

Not all the excitement in these fantasies of men together comes simply from voyeurism. Some women find the idea of giving their husband the opportunity to excite another man in fantasy exciting to them as well.

With the knowledge that her mind is no longer a blank piece of paper upon which her unconscious unwittingly scribbles erotic messages, a woman today accepts her fantasies as sources of sexual pleasure and important biographical information, too. Our fantasies are where we learn about ourselves from earliest childhood to the last shameless act before we close our eyes to dream.

Diane

I'm 28, divorced and have a daughter a year and a half old. I went to Bible College for two and a half years. It was dually accredited, which means you took a double major; theology and English were mine.

I was a virgin when I married and never cheated on my husband.

I now have a 19-year-old lover. He is a very special person to me, and we enjoy sex together tremendously. He is very open and often lets me lead, which I enjoy very much.

I've always wanted to try a ménage à trois, but he isn't comfortable with the idea, at least not yet. We'll see.

Anyway, what you wrote about women not fantasizing about two men making love is wrong: at least one of us does.

My fantasy was sparked by a comment my boyfriend made about frostbite (sounds funny, huh?). He is in the Army, and they told him when your face is frostbitten not to rub it but put it in the warmest place you can, under an arm or, if there are two people, in each other's crotches (because it is one of the warmest places in the body). You can see where this takes me.

I envision my boyfriend, Marty (he is tall, thin, light skinned with freckles, red hair and blue eyes), with a very bad case of frostbite, and he is with another soldier, dark haired, brown eyed, tall, but a little huskier. They decide they'd better try out the face-in-the-crotch solution, because it is very cold and their faces are really hurting, so they find a sheltered spot and curl up together. They have their faces down between each other's legs and they begin to warm up.

Only it's not just their faces that are warming up. That sweet face down in between their legs is feeling very nice and warm so close to their cocks that they can each feel the other breathing right through the fabric of their pants. They both begin to get a hard-on. How can they help it?

One of them is a little embarrassed and tries to shift his swollen cock a little, but it only makes it scrape against his buddy's mouth, and his thighs brush his cheeks. So of course Marty squirms a little at this and the same thing happens to his friend.

It feels so good, his friend opens his mouth and, placing it gently over the swollen area of Marty's pants, just blows warmly, heating Marty's penis even more, causing him to squirm against his buddy's mouth. Now they are both breathing hard and very aware of each other sexually, squirming, rubbing against each other. Finally, this close, prolonged contact between them is too much. Each quickly removes the other's throbbing penis from his pants and sucks and sucks on it until they both come in each other's mouths. I am shaking all over just writing this.

I often wondered why almost all people, male and female,

seem not to feel threatened by lesbians and yet are by men who love other men. We're taught all through life women are beautiful, desirable, sexy. Even women think so of each other, and who could be surprised? I find a naked female body just as much a turn-on for me as a male's. I never have had sex with a woman. It has crossed my mind with a few women I have known and really loved, but was put aside as impractical and not really what I wanted, just a thought, but homosexuality neither shocks or disgusts me as it does my boyfriend and so many other men.

A movie with naked women in it is rated R, a movie with a naked man is rated X (right along with movies too violent for children?). Are men's bodies more obscene? I find men beautiful, not aside from their sexual organs but with them being a fantastic part of the whole person, a part I enjoy looking at often. Because of the pleasure it brings, I sometimes nearly worship it.

Even my boyfriend who knows me well finds that hard to accept. Like so many other men, he finds it hard to accept that his body and his sex drive are not only OK, but great. I love them and him.

It's sad. Homosexuality, it is not for me, but it is not fearful or disgusting to me either. I love anal sex, why shouldn't a man? I'd love to use my finger on my boyfriend, but he sees it as a threat to his masculinity, "only guys do it." Too bad. There are too few really great things in this world for men to pass up so many because they see themselves as dirty. Not all women do. I never did. I hope they learn not to. I wish I could teach them all, but I'm only one person. Too bad.

Mia

Although I have had a fairly active sex life for the last seven years, I managed to repress most of my sexual fantasies (without even being aware that I was doing so), for fear of being "unfair" to my partner or "abnormal" in some way. Now I have a rich, satisfying fantasy life, thanks to your liberating book, so I will return the favor with some more data for your research.

524

I am 21 years old, a senior at a large Eastern university. I lost my virginity at 14, to a rough and brutal boyfriend. I was raised in a white, middle-class, suburban American home. Aside from my fairly active sex life (mostly with one partner) and the occasional use of marijuana, I was (and probably still am) a model daughter—"such a good little girl." I have been dating the same man for two and a half years now; we have a very intimate relationship, although I occasionally seek sex elsewhere.

Despite a regular schedule of sex since I was almost 15, I never had an orgasm until I was almost 20! In fact, I never knew women were capable of orgasm until I was 17 or 18, when a girlfriend spoke of her sex life, and I tried desperately after that to achieve one. My current boyfriend, Steve, bought me a vibrator when I was 19, and that finally did the trick. I have never had any trouble since, with or without the vibrator, alone or with another. I think it's a *crime* that I never even knew women could have orgasms, just another form of the oppression we face. Here are my fantasies:

I. The Human Chain: I am lying on the floor, and my legs are spread wide apart. A friend of mine (male or female, but always someone I know) is kneeling on the floor, actively licking my clitoris and working his or her fingers into my vagina and my anus (or any phallic-shaped object in place of the fingers). A male homosexual friend of mine is kneeling behind this person, pressing his huge cock into his or her anus. Meanwhile, I am happily caressing and stroking a woman friend's breasts, while another man enters her vagina from behind. This chain continues on, with every participant's genitals being manipulated in some way, with more and more people joining in all the time. The exact order of the people and what they are doing varies, but several things are consistent: (1) I am always linked to at least one woman and one man. (2) I am either sucking breasts or having mine sucked by a woman. (3) A male is entering another male's anus. (4) Everyone is enjoying themselves immensely. (5) They are all very specific people I know.

This chain can get very long, depending on how long it

takes me to achieve orgasm, but in my mind I am always returning to myself as the central participant. Often it will close itself off, becoming a circle.

II. I often relive a wonderful sexual experience I had the pleasure of having a few months ago. A good friend (and sometime lover) was graduating and had his two younger brothers here for the ceremony. My friend, J., was 22, his brothers A. and K. were 19 and 17, respectively. After a fun night of partying and intimate (not sexual) chatter, we decided that I should be adopted by the M. family. J. was my best friend, and I loved A. and K. as much as they loved me, which was totally. After vowing our total love and acceptance, we snuggled up on the bed, laughing. I'm not quite sure how things got started after that, but soon I was being undressed by all three M. brothers. I can still imagine the throbbing in my body as I felt my clitoris swell with excitement. Soon, J. was sucking my breasts, A. was entering my vagina with his penis and R. was vigorously stimulating my anus with his finger. I am writhing on the floor in ecstasy, groping for J.'s penis in order to suck it in. It is delicious when I finally taste it. Soon J. is fucking me between my tits (I am very large breasted), K. is entering my vagina and A. fingers my asshole while looking on and stroking his erect penis. After J. comes all over my breasts, all three brothers gladly lap it up, while I beg to be fucked, my cunt gaping. By the end of the night, each brother has had his turn in my vagina at least once and has stroked his own penis while I watched at least once. I have had dozens of orgasms (well, in the real-life occurrence of this fantasy, I only had four or five). This scene really happened, and since then I have relived it many times.

III. Male homosexuality interests me very much. I often imagine two men sucking each other's cocks, or engaging in anal intercourse. I have a good friend, (S.), who is a male homosexual and I often imagine him with another guy, usually my boyfriend, Steve. Usually, I picture Steve's penis in S.'s anus. In a recent trip to visit my three adopted brothers in their home city, A. told me that when they were younger, A. and J. often sucked each other's dicks and fucked each other up the ass. Since then, I have often imagined this scene, and I plan to ask them for a show someday.

IV. Although I am primarily heterosexual, I am also quite openminded and adventurous sexually. Until last summer I had not thought much about sex with other women, except for a few dreams that disturbed me at the time. Then last summer, a girlfriend of mine, W., also heterosexual but quite adventurous and experienced, propositioned me. My first reaction was no, but I found myself quite turned on in a way I've never been turned on before. I agreed to sleep over at her house one night, and while we were talking about sex, she confessed that she was quite turned on, and so did I. Relieved, she climbed into bed with me, and we spent several hours gently stroking each other's clitorises and sucking each other's breasts. We each had several orgasms that night. I found it almost impossible not to imagine that it was her each time Steve performed cunnilingus on me. W. and I had several other sexual encounters, several of them with other people (men, such as J., and a few of their male friends). She is almost invariably included in my fantasies, though sometimes just as an onlooker. Often I imagine her tongue taking big, long wet licks over my genital area, especially my clitoris, while she works something into my vagina (such as a vibrator) and her fingers into my ass. I also often imagine me doing the same to her as she screams and writhes in ecstasy. Sometimes I imagine Steve fucking her while she licks my cunt and he puts his tongue into my anus. Just about any combination will do.

Mostly I interpret my homosexual enjoyment as a way to come to terms with my own feminine body and my identity as a woman. I was exposed to feminism at about this same time and have since become quite radical in my (feminist) thinking. Having sex with a woman in a relaxed, loving atmosphere greatly helped develop my sense of female equality. To love other women is to love myself! I'm not denying that I'm "bisexual" or whatever. I just think that such labeling is unnecessary and misleading. Even to call myself a "heterosexual" somehow seems silly.

The only fantasy I had that I would call violent (it actually does disturb me somewhat) occurred once while I was hiking in the mountains. I was totally alone, so I stripped down to my hiking boots to truly experience this outdoor adventure. Upon reaching the summit, I lay down on a huge stone and admired the sky. Eventually, I began to manipulate my clitoris gently. As I got excited, I had this fantasy: I look up and notice that I am being watched by a big brawny hunter in a red-and-black-check shirt. His pants are open, and a huge erect penis, which he is stroking with one hand, points in my direction. Pleased that I have an audience, I allow him to keep watching as I stroke, stroke, stroke my clitoris faster and faster. He is violently jerking off, a pained expression on his face, and finally squirts his jism out onto the dried, fallen leaves of the forest. This excites me terribly, and I beckon to him with my hand. He walks slowly toward me, his wet penis beginning to shrink. I lie down on the rock, my legs spread, my knees bent, my fingers ever stroking my clit, and my wet cunt wide open. Then he puts his gun into my cunt and slowly works it back and forth as I go faster and faster with my fingers and finally come.

Of course he doesn't pull the trigger or anything, but I still find this fantasy disturbingly violent, almost like a suicide wish or something. Maybe it's just a longing for something "dangerous," I don't know. The thought of it now disgusts me. I only had it that one time, in the morning.

Clair

I am 38 years old, divorced twice, with two small children. My first marriage was completely sexless and dull. I was much too young (20) and very immature. I had an affair with a man twice my age and ended the marriage. In the affair I realized what real passion could be like with someone you care about. My second marriage lasted thirteen years and resulted in two lovely children. Unfortunately, he also lacked any of the passion I love, and he enjoyed drinking much more than my company. I am now in a wonderful relationship with a man fifteen years older than myself, he loves fulfilling my fantasies, and our sex life is terrific. We are very committed to one another. I have also realized that I am bicurious. Whether or not I will ever have a bisexual experience is another question.

I never considered writing about my fantasies until now. This particular dream is a favorite of mine.

With the scheduling of jobs and kids, Nick and I don't have a lot of time to get away, but we managed one fall weekend. With no telephones or careers, and the beautiful fall weather, it was perfect.

We were checking into a lovely traditional hotel. As I sat waiting for Nick patiently, I noticed a young bellboy in his early 20s eyeing my legs. I was having a great time doing some flirting when I realized my dress was open halfway up my thigh. It had been a long drive, and I forgot to rebutton it before entering the hotel. When I crossed my legs it left little to the imagination. The young man stood close to Nick while he signed the appropriate papers. During the lull in the paperwork, Nick saw the man was totally concentrating on me, then he chuckled as the man struggled with our bags. We all took the elevator to the fifth floor. While in the small compartment, I pressed my ass up against Nick's cock, letting him know how badly I wanted him. He gently touched my ass and kissed my neck. The weekend was a long time coming, and we were both looking forward to it. What I didn't know was Nick had some interesting ideas for fun in mind.

Our room was beautiful, complete with a large king-size bed. I went to the large windows to enjoy the view as Nick talked to the bellboy and gave him a tip. I knew it was taking a bit longer than it should, but I really didn't pay any attention. We decided to take a long hot bath together, with drinks, and relax. After a short nap, Nick ordered a lovely meal to be served in the privacy of our room. I knew it seemed strange to me that after dinner Nick wasn't responding to my advances. I assumed he wanted the evening to last and was just taking it slow. After all, how often did we get away? It wasn't long before I heard a knock on the door. I was disappointed at being disturbed, but Nick cracked a huge smile. To my surprise, the bellboy stood at the doorway, once again talking to Nick. He was invited in and introduced to me as Adam. He looked extremely nervous but in control of himself. Nick walked over to me and whispered, Adam wants to kiss you and touch your breasts, then he would like you to suck his cock while I watch. I was so turned on by the whole scene I didn't want to wait anymore. Nick instructed me to take off his clothes and then take off Adam's things. They sat on the bed, then I was told to suck Adam's cock while I fondled Nick. He knew how turned on I was getting and decided to move things right along. Nick sat me on the bed and proceeded to lick my awaiting clit. While placing his tongue into my already wet pussy, he fingered my ass. Knowing that I would come quickly, Nick told Adam to caress my breast and kiss me. I was coming for him. I was in ecstasy, feeling him at my cunt. I was so turned on I stroked Adam's hard penis. Nick pulled at my legs forcing me down to his level and motioned for me to suck Adam's awaiting cock. Adam was going wild as my soft lips touched him. Nick and I both stroked and tongued him until he was ready to come. I took over and allowed Adam to explode in my mouth. Nick now kissed me passionately. He caressed and fucked me hard. He was wonderfully strong and secure in his movements with me. We came together as we always seem to do, while Adam sucked at my breasts. He laid with us awhile and then, excusing himself, went back to work. It was a wonderful weekend and a perfect fantasy. Maybe someday it will really come true.

Natassia

I am a white female, 20 years old, single, a full-time college student, pursuing a career in nursing. I lifeguard and teach swimming part time.

Nobody really discussed sex in my family when I was young, and I can't remember having sexual feelings until I was about 15. I lost my virginity at age 16, which to me seemed pretty young at the time (and still does, as a matter of fact). I've been having sex pretty regularly ever since (with the same guy) but have never achieved orgasm by intercourse. I discovered masturbation at age 17 and had my first orgasm soon after.

Even though I don't achieve orgasm during sex yet, I still get a lot of pleasure out of it. I love to go down on my boyfriend's cock and lick and kiss and suck it and his balls until he comes in my mouth. It gives me great pleasure to give him such satisfaction.

I guess not too many women fantasize about two men making it because the thought can be very threatening to the woman.

Well, I guess I'm a minority, but my favorite fantasy is about two men together. I am totally turned on by the male sex and love fantasizing about not only one, but two, three, or four or more male bodies together in sexual ecstasy. The two men are never men I know (and I would *never* want to think of my boyfriend in this position), but total strangers.

These two gay men meet in a gay bar. One approaches the other and asks if he'd like to dance. They dance together for a while, their bodies pressed together, feeling each other's asses and cocks, getting totally turned on. After a while, they walk off the dance floor toward the rest room. One man has sweatpants on, and his cock is sticking straight out for all to see. They squeeze each other's buns as they walk through the room. Once in the bathroom, one man instantly pulls the other's pants down, and his erect cock bounces out. The first man takes the cock in his mouth and sucks long and hard bringing it very deeply into his mouth. The man who is getting sucked is thrusting back and forth, holding the man's head close all the time, as he thrusts faster and faster until, with one last thrust, he comes in the other man's mouth. After he has swallowed all the come, the other man stands up. In the process of sucking the man off, he has taken his own erect cock out of his pants and is rubbing it. He now has the man bend over and proceeds to ass-fuck him, harder and harder until he has his own explosive orgasm. End of fantasy. This fantasy takes a lot of other forms but always involves two or more men in various sexual acts.

I always come with no problem while fantasizing. I think I'd have more luck reaching orgasm with my boyfriend if he would go down on me, but every time I mention it he shrugs it off and says he doesn't think he'd like it. I know he feels guilty about this, because he does everything else imaginable to please me, and I'm sure one day he will be ready to try it. I'm not too worried about it. I hear a lot of women have problems reaching orgasm when they're young. Still, I look forward to the day I have my first oral orgasm.

Bonnie

I am a 26-year-old woman who calls herself a lesbian, though some folks might want to say I'm bisexual. I'm not gonna fool myself and say I'm never attracted to men, in fact, I find myself responding to men much more than I did in the past, either because men have been improving, or I've just started to meet the kind of men who interest me. I have a B.A. in history, which is utterly useless, and do temporary office work. I currently share my life with John, a bisexual man of 35.

My connection with gay and bisexual men got me labeled a "fag hag" early on, and I now wear that label with pride. I sometimes wonder if I didn't decide to align my sexual preferences in a manner so that I would have nonthreatening credentials for hanging around nonheterosexual men. (I.e., "I am a lesbian and not after your body—a safe fag hag, not one that will annoy you.") On the other hand, I do have a definite attraction toward women.

You state that women aren't (or rather aren't to your knowledge) aroused by two men having sex with each other. I am aroused both by the concept and the actuality. When I see two men walking down the street with their arms around each other, I am definitely turned on—particularly if the neighborhood isn't very gay. It takes guts to be that up front, and I'm turned on by that kind of courage. I was also turned on the few times when I have witnessed two men embracing, kissing and sucking each other's cocks. I think it's wonderful when two men I know well are being open, vulnerable and tender toward each other. It signals a new kind of masculinity—men who are sure enough of their manhood that they can show deep emotion in another man's presence and don't need to compete. I really enjoy those men. I sometimes fantasize about men I know having sex together or about male fictional characters whose gayness hasn't at all been established (such as *Star Trek*'s Kirk and Spock) having a gay relationship. Fantasizing about men loving each other freely and more openly than they have in the past makes me feel hopeful about the future, and my clit also approves—it's an optimistic organ.

Lisa

Other women *do* have fantasies and I am *not* strange or sick. What a wonderful thing to know.

I was raised in a strictly religious home. Sex was never mentioned and questions about it were ridiculed. My father was a very abusive man and frequently hurt us. I attended a small, church-supported college and am now a newspaper reporter. I am 25 and consider myself to be open-minded and creative. I have lived with my current lover nearly five years and am not very experienced with other men. Sex is good, all of my fantasy life is rich and varied and a source of extreme comfort.

I have had sexual fantasies since I can remember—long before I knew about sex. One recurring theme in my fantasies has been that of men being gently physical with other men. As I grew older and learned about homosexuality, my fantasies began to revolve around a central scenario.

There is one man—young and very pretty in a girlish way. He becomes the property of two older men, both much larger and stronger than he is. The men are intrigued by their new "property" and tell him he must learn to satisfy their sexual needs. They strip him and handle him, all the time being gentle and considerate. Both of them try to excite him as they become excited. Finally, one man holds him firmly and comforts him while the other penetrates him. At this point, I'm usually masturbating and the fantasy becomes very vivid. I imagine how the boy must feel, with one man stroking his hair and another fucking him. One man comes inside the boy and they trade places, with the other penetrating the boy even better than the first. In my fantasy, the boy always takes great pleasure in the fucking and comes at least once. (So do I.) After both men are finished with the boy, they hold him and kiss him and make him feel very safe and loved.

The fantasy can change as needed. Sometimes I'm there, being touched and fucked and soothed by all three men. Sometimes the boy (younger man) has been horribly abused and is rescued and cared for tenderly by the other men.

We must remember women are as human as men—we feel lust. That's not such a bad thing. I hope if I ever have daughters I will be able to talk to them about the importance of being comfortable with our own needs and feelings.

Mona

You have written that women are not turned on by the thought of two male homosexuals and that they feel threatened by homosexuals because women would not want to compete with other women *and* men for men.

If this is the case, then I must be a rather unique woman. The thought of two men making love turns me on a *great* deal. I feel that I fantasize about two men because I'm tired and bored with seeing women being so loving, caring, free with their emotions; and men being cold, aloof, laughing off situations.

This is why I love *Star Trek*. Captain Kirk and Spock love each other (not necessarily as homosexuals, but as friends). And they are generally unafraid to show their feelings for one another. I fantasize a lot about two guys that I care about being homosexuals. They are both nude, standing beside a bed with the light of the late afternoon coming through half-closed blinds, gently holding each other. The dominant man pulls the other closer to him and kisses him, feeling him shake with passion and a little fear. The dominant then looks into crystal blue eyes filled with tears. As he brushes away a tear, he says, "I won't hurt you." The other whispers back, "I know."

The dominant gently lays the other on the bed, then lies on top of him and begins slowly rotating his pelvis against the other. They smile at each other as they become aroused. After doing this and kissing for a while, the dominant turns the other over on his stomach, sits on his buns and gives him a back rub with some baby oil. Soon, he moves off the other and starts massaging his buns. He moves his index finger into the other's hole. The other moans quietly while hugging a pillow tightly. The other becomes so aroused that he rises up on his knees and asks the dominant, "Lick me, please." The dominant lightly and teasingly licks his hole and his balls. Then the dominant rises on his knees and slowly pushes his penis into the other. Tears come quickly to the other's eyes as he is entered, but the pain soon turns to pleasure.

The dominant pumps him slowly at first, then goes faster as he feels his own excitement burning through his body. Soon their pleasure completely takes control of their bodies and they both come powerfully. The other lies fully in the bed, feeling the warmth of his cum on the sheets and the tears of the dominant lying on the other's back, kissing him.

I'm a freshman in college, going for a degree in math, and am 18 and black.

Jenny

I am a 16-year-old heterosexual feminist. I live in a small town on the East Coast, where I go to school. In my class, I am not especially popular because I am one of the "smart" kids, and not very attractive physically at that, unless one likes original facial features, which is not true for the people in my school.

For some reason, any man-to-man contact is always extremely exciting to me, unless it contains sadistic elements, which are a turn-off in any case. Any kind of kissing, hugging, stroking, and/or sucking between two guys is my kind of turn-on.

I fantasize about sex constantly, every day, but somehow I can't imagine myself doing it with any of the male persons I know. I imagine two guys, in their teens, perhaps, putting their arms around each other and kissing gently and tenderly. Often, the two are best friends, and one of them is gay, while the other is bisexual, leaning toward the heterosexual side. The bisexual guy then lies down on a bed, and his friend puts his hands on his chest and strokes it, kissing it and sucking on the nipples occasionally, causing whimpers of pleasure. The homosexual friend then lies down next to him, and they kiss again. The homosexual friend then spreads the other guy's legs apart and sucks on his cock, caressing his balls. He does this until his friend moans in ecstasy, and the come spurts out of him so forcefully, it almost causes his cock to explode. He swallows the come and moves up to kiss the bisexual guy. There is some come left over on his lips, and so the bisexual friend licks it off and they kiss again, passing it between them. Next, the bisexual guy sucks his friend off in the same manner and also swallows his come. They lie in each other's arms, occasionally kissing and touching each other's chests and backs. This fantasy has many variations, and I use a different one every time.

I want people to know that 16-year-olds do have sexual fantasies, and that "smart" kids think about other things besides DNA molecules and the Pythagorean theorem.

Kristin

I am 19 and am bisexual. I am currently living with my lover and best friend of four years, and I love her so much, we are so close and honest!

I am an incredibly horny person. I have only had sex with a man once, and I don't really consider myself to have had sex with him, but I guess technically we did. We worked together in a health food store in a mall. He was 22 and I was 17. It was summer and I was living with my lover, Anne—

he knew about us. One night after work, he came over and Anne fell asleep. He and I were really drunk, and when I'm drunk, I'm a slut, I am so hot and I can't say no. Before we knew it we were kissing, very wetly and hotly. I had a shirt on that zipped down the front. Slowly it became totally open, and he feverishly kissed, licked and buried himself in my very large breasts. We were on our sides facing each other, and I began pulling open his 501 button-flies. I rubbed the outside of his jeans feverishly, feeling his throbbing dick straining within. Soon his pants were off. I teased him and played with the band of his underwear and rubbed the cotton crotch, squeezing and kneading. He moaned a tortured moan as I finally found his throbbing meat, and he pushed me onto my back. He slowly kissed and licked me, moving his mouth lower and lower, and he began begging and begging me to let him "taste me." I kept refusing because I felt like that privilege was sacred to my lover, Anne. Finally I let him, but for only about a minute. It was enough to get me very wet and slimy. I then went down on him, engulfing his meat in my mouth. Eventually the time came to fuck. I laid on my back and he tried to enter my pussy, but I was too tight. Finally he had me put my legs over his shoulders so my hips were elevated to the perfect angle. Then in it went, so snugly and so slowly. I was begging him not to come inside me and was almost too paranoid to enjoy it. After about four thrusts, he pulled out and squirted his load all over the back of my ass and back.

I really didn't mean to spend much time on that story. I didn't come. I have had so many excellent orgasms with my lover. I felt so guilty about doing it with him in our apartment that I made him leave right away and went and washed my pussy for a good ten minutes. I got into bed sobbing and woke Anne up and told her everything. I felt horrible. She was very sweet and understanding. She's a virgin too and is now 25. We were gonna lose it in a ménage with one guy (someday). I felt so guilty for having ruined those plans.

Anyway I really wanted to tell you about my fantasies. I wish so much that I had a vibrator. I'm always sticking mascara bottles and writing utensils up me while I fantasize, but I know that's dangerous. I'm just too embarrassed to go buy a vibrator.

I have always fantasized about a male teacher rather roughly but passionately taking me—especially a gym teacher. I imagine I'm in the gym alone, the last one there, and am taking a shower. A big coach comes in and sees me washing my big boobs. He can't take it, so he comes over. He takes off his shorts and gets under the water, he tells me to wash his dick. Fascinated with its huge semi-erection, I do so slowly and shyly. He begins to moan and reaches down and begins running his finger through my pussy lips. I begin whimpering in ecstasy (I am having to touch myself now as I write this because I'm so gooey). Here I stand bent at a right angle to him and begin licking his cock. He moans and reaches over to my ass, he licks his big index finger and slowly begins twisting it into my asshole. I moan, quivering with pleasure. He brings my head up, and I'm standing, and he says, "Don't move." He pushes my legs apart and kneels on the floor. He spreads my lips wide with his fingers and slips his hot tongue in. I am dying at the same time he slips his finger back in me, but I begin gasping and get close to orgasm. He sits me on the floor (the shower is still beating down on us). He lays me down and slides his huge meat into me. We begin a rhythm, moaning "Oh God, Oh God." He pulls back and turns me over onto my hands and knees, and we fuck doggie style, lunging frantically in a rhythm together. As we're fucking, he slips that finger in and out, in and out of my ass. I die—he is near coming, and a big black coach enters. He strips—the first coach and I come. The big cute black coach starts jacking his dick off between my tits. When it's really hard, I beg him to fuck me, and he says, "Yeah, baby, I'll fuck you good, you ain't never had a dick like this." He compliments my wet pink pussy and slides in. We roll over and I'm on top, gyrating—riding the black horse. The other coach is hard and hot again, and I get on all fours. I'm getting fucked by the black guy, and he's got a skinny hot wet vibrator up my butt. The first coach, I am eating, and I've got a finger in his ass. We all go at it for hours. The guys even jack each other and love it. One eats my pussy with his fingers in my cunt and ass while his ass is getting fucked by the other guy. God, what a dream it would be.

I just had to go masturbate as I read over this letter.

Chloe

I am a white, 24-year-old, married mother of one. I completed high school with honors (28th in a class of about 450), went on to college, but married after the first quarter. I am five feet seven and a half inches tall, attractive, overweight (but working on it!!). I was very active sexually since the age of 13; this was when I rebelled against my parents' decision not to let me date a 21-year-old guy. Of course, they knew to let me date him would mean I also would surrender my virginity to him. So the inevitable happened. I deliberately set out to screw him.

I met my husband at the college I attended. He was a friend of my sister's current boyfriend. They introduced us and hoped we would enjoy making a foursome with them on a date. My sister and her boyfriend thought we (Mark and I) were both too shy, and this was why they fixed us up.

I felt lousy that day and felt like shaking Mark up. He really was and is to this day very shy. I suggested a walk to the park, sat him down and asked him if he wanted to make it with me. He agreed, but didn't even hold my hand for three weeks. After three months, we eloped.

I often fantasize of two men having sex—fellatio and anal intercourse—as well as fondling, caressing, kissing, etc. Most often one man is my husband. He is in a military setting, at basic training, I believe; as I know he is really not interested in sex with another guy, he either (a) is in a desperate state of horniness, or (b) has just come to realize the male form can be as attractive to him as the female. Each time I fantasize this, different sex acts are performed. Sometimes my husband is out of basic and I am part of a threesome with him and another man. Mostly I don't get penetrated, except orally, in this one, but I am free to touch and arrange the two men according to my desires. I also know I am not the only one to fantasize this way, because my closest friend, a girl my age whom I have known for nineteen years, has recently confided in me her secret desire to see two men make love. My husband is in the process of setting this up with a gay friend of ours.

I used to fantasize of just straight missionary sex until about age 16.

My urge to see two men perform came during a time when I felt I could no longer respect my husband.

I am a well-adjusted young woman in love with sex. I am glad to see that more and more women really enjoy sex and fantasy without the guilt so many of us carried during our adolescent and teen years. Myself included.

IF I HAD A PENIS

Who could fail to admire the design of the penis, worthy of the Leonardo da Vinci award for beauty and versatility, form and function?

Envy begins with admiration; there is that moment, before admiration sours into bitter resentment, when we feel the "Ah!" of appreciation.

Alas, the pages of *Men in Love* were filled with the laments of men whose women would not even look at their lovely penises, much less bestow upon them the long-anticipated kiss of acceptance. In fantasy, men dreamed of women who adored their penises.

Now their dreams have come true. Now there are women who are angry that their men are less interested in fellatio than they. These young women take an epicurean delight in fondling the penis, mouthing it, taking it deep into their throats, swallowing its lovely sticky fluid, and it should therefore not be surprising that they sometimes imagine owning one of the amazing instruments.

They are long past Freud's mistaken assumption that women see their genitals as mutilated and thus envy the superior penis. They don't want to give up their lovely vaginas; they don't want to give up anything. Instead, they play with the idea that their clitoris, during masturbation, gets "larger and larger until it is the size of a penis," as Lally says. "I imagine I can feel the sensations of a man during intercourse. I also imagine that the man is having sex *with* me." Why not?

In a famous paper in 1943 titled "Women and Penis Envy," Clara Thompson set the record straight: "The attitude called Penis Envy is similar to the attitude of any underprivileged group toward those in power." Penis envy, from then on, has been understood to be symbolic, a rationalization for women's feelings of inadequacy in a patriarchal society.

These new women, however, go a step further. They throw symbols aside and make no apologies for imagining themselves with the real thing. Throughout this book women have been strapping on dildos, both in fact and fantasy. Why not imagine what it's like to actually have one of those fascinating appendages that you can really get a hand on, make it go this way and that, write your name in the snow, rub until it gets big as a horse and then actually shoot your come clear across the room?

A vagina has its privileges, but damn it, there is something very assertive and dramatic about the penis. While it is heaven to have one inside you, to dexterously grab it with your vaginal muscles and play it like a flute until the man can't stand it any longer and explodes, how can the mind resist imagining what it must feel like to be the thruster whose "monster" is filling you up?

Young girls like Fran still envy the symbolic power of the penis: "I secretly resent being a girl who has to worry about pregnancy, the pain of the first time, a clean reputation and so on," she laments. "I think guys are lucky to be so carefree." But then she wavers in her desire to be a boy as she remembers the new pleasure of "necking with guys." Fran is fourteen.

Older women, however, appraise their own lives, look the penis in the eye, and see it for what it is: a penis is a penis is a penis. "Look, you slouch," Pam seems to be saying to her sexually uncreative, boring husband, "I'll show you what I'd do if I had a cock. You don't even know how to use that thing." In fantasy, she takes his/her "hot cock" in both hands and admires her "manhood in the mirror (we're talking ten inches long and eight inches around)." Then, as if to get back at all the sexually withholding men she's known, she doesn't offer to fuck anyone with her beautiful cock. Instead, "I think about all the cunts that long for my big cock and how silly they are because I love to jack off and no one can make me shoot my come like my hand." This is revenge, not gender change; in fantasy, Pam keeps her big tits as well as her cock.

Haven't we women been trying on everything male for years? We reinvent ourselves daily, taking on men's work, their attitudes, behavior, even their clothes. Putting aside issues of fairness, we have taken their jobs, their all-male clubs, their double-breasted suits, lace-up shoes; we've even cut our hair, slicked it back, and donned their fedoras in our never ending effort—in the name of fashion—to steal their magic. The question all but poses itself: May I borrow your cock, too? Just for one night, just in fantasy, just to experience what it's like to unzip my elegant Ralph Lauren fly and, as Pam says, see it "spring free."

Complain, complain—that's all we women do, when at times I think a note of compassion might better get us what we want. Consider how men must experience our taking over of their world. One minute we're competing in the office, wearing their pants; the next we're seductively laid out in our minuscule teddy, all heat, seduction, moist vagina waiting to take them in. We have no idea how much breast and womb envy there is out there. Men can't afford to discuss it, to even be consciously aware of it, again. The flight from that first woman's power was never truly completed, since every woman after her threatens to suck him back.

Nor are we up-front about woman power, the magic of the one who carries, bears, and raises the child. Instead, we prefer to paint the mother role in heavy shades of burdensome responsibility and sacrifice. We deny it's powerful at all, meanwhile assiduously guarding our unimpeachable control over the first ten to fifteen years of the whole human race, by which time the child's very soul has been imprinted by the ambivalence of mother love.

No, aside from the transvestites, transsexuals, and some homosexuals, men must deny their desire to take on or imitate any of our female parts. To reinforce their disdain of wanting to be like us at all—to defend themselves even more against conscious knowledge of their breast/vagina envy—they exaggerate the aggressive, brute characteristics we women loathe, but which we secretly dream of imitating. Marge, for instance, sexualizes her real anger at men by imagining the Bad Guys being gang-raped. Even her own fantasy of being raped is a means to an end, which is men's punishment, her revenge on them where they are hurt and humiliated.

When a woman like Marge tires of imagining she has a penis that can actually squirt into her lover, she can change persona and return to her female role. Her lover "is so understanding about how I wish I had a penis." How many women, in the reverse position, would enjoy their lover's fantasies of owning a vagina, a womb, breasts, actually wearing a dress, high heels, and makeup? Men do not have the option to work for a year or two and then find someone to take care of them. Being a man, proving it, is full-time work; put another way, giving up one's manliness, if only for a moment of let's-pretend, can be terrifying.

The power of the penis has been blown out of all proportion not because men have so much faith in it, but to compensate for their envy of the breast, the womb, women's power. The penis must be big, big, biggest because the womb/breast is bigger. Since men cannot say these things, women who love men should at least know them.

My own penis envy goes something like this: I am standing nonchalantly on the afterdeck of my yacht, in my Hermès blazer and white flannels, smoking a cigar and peeing a high arc into the sweet summer air off Cap d'Antibes . . . instead of having to scurry below and half undress to squat over a toilet in an airless cubicle, all the while hearing the music of laughter above as the gents, without spilling a drop of either their martini or their pee, finish the joke I missed.

Fran

I'm a 14-year-old Caucasian female from a repressive home. Most of my former sexual activities arouse feelings of guilt and embarrassment in me. I need a vent for confessing my actions.

I really like to be with boys, but as long as I can remember, I've wanted to be a guy. A guy with erections, fantasies, pleasures and masculine muscles. This worries me. I've no desire to be homosexual. I've no idea why I want to be a guy. I've no desire whatsoever to be a guy just to make love with other girls. I just want to experience all that boys are lucky enough to experience, but sex with girls doesn't excite me a bit.

When I used to be flat chested, I'd wait to have the house to myself, then I'd go on a pleasure binge. I'd make believe I was a boy by balling up tissues in the shape of a penis and testicles, in my plainest pair of underwear briefs. I'd add more tissues to represent an erection, put on jeans and admire my bulge in a big mirror. This was a big turn-on.

Following this unusual, yet "sacred" ceremony, I'd masturbate with myself. (Of course I also had to dispose of my simulated male genitals via the toilet.) I have never, to this day, no matter how hard I try, masturbated to a full climax. The only real turn-on for me was to be a guy. I enjoyed it even if that whole act made me feel guilty, perverse and abnormal. I'd be thoroughly disgusted at the pleasure I could have doing something that "gross."

I turned 12 and resolved to do whatever I could to abstain from these clandestine rituals of mine.

When I started to look more like a woman, I almost enjoyed being feminine with my first menstrual period.

Now I enjoy the pleasures of necking with guys, but fondling their genitals still makes me jealous. I really like boys and even tried to make love with a special one. It was fun for his first time, but not for mine. I secretly resent being a girl, who has to worry about pregnancy, the pain of the first time, a clean reputation, and so on. I think guys are lucky to be so carefree. I wish I could be reborn a boy. I want to watch myself grow into a man because puberty-aged boys excite me, and feeling it for myself would be so cool.

I'm very ashamed of what I've written. I hope whoever reads this will understand and not laugh. It's bad enough having to think of myself as a mentally disturbed pervert. I don't want other people to think of me that way.

Basically, I wrote this so it wouldn't bottle up. I realize that other people might be able to identify with my feelings. In this way, I won't feel as alone in this world as I have been.

Pam

I am 34 years old, Caucasian, married four years (third marriage for me, second for my husband). Between us we have five children from 8 to 19 and one grandchild. My husband is a professional, and I "retired" three years ago to be an "at-home mom."

I do not recall having any sort of sexual feelings until I was 19 years old and a girlfriend lent me a book, the title escapes me. I was very naive to say the least and in addition came from a home that was in constant uproar. In addition, I was everyone's "friend" but nobody's "girlfriend" . . . I now realize that my inexperience was largely due to lack of opportunity.

I married my first husband at 21 and "saved myself" until the night before the wedding. Sex with my husband was "for him"; if I asked him to try something, such as oral sex on me, he went out of his way to avoid complying. Our marriage lasted two years. My second husband was somewhat better as far as performance goes, but I was the constant object of his criticism (he wanted me to have very small, firm tits, and I am a 38DD, sagging with stretch marks). That marriage also lasted two years. From age 21 until age 30 when I married my present husband, I had three orgasms. Not a good average. However, even though I am not pretty, between my last two husbands I fucked over one hundred men. I do not consider myself a prude. I never

545

fantasized or masturbated until I was 25, when my Mormon boss unexpectedly bought me a vibrator.

My husband was a better lover before we got married and when I was "pre-orgasmic." We fucked several times a day, and there was a lot of foreplay, and he never seemed "bored" with me. Most times sex is only on Saturday &/or Sunday morning and it lasts fifteen minutes tops. He has figured out how to bring me to orgasm and goes straight for the cunt or the clitoris. Very seldom do I get "aroused." I long for a little unbearable aching, however, I don't hold out much hope as I know that my husband is not interested in what excites me.

Now to my fantasies. I might point out at this time that I only masturbate about once or twice a week. Sometimes at night in bed with my husband, trying to sleep, but most times in the early morning after everyone has gone to work/school. My fantasies illustrate a very strong penis envy.

1. My favorite: I am a man instead of a woman (although sometimes I also have big tits as well as a cock). I absolutely love my body and at any opportunity I unzip my fly and let my cock spring free. I strip down and stand in front of a large mirror in my bedroom. Admiring my body, but especially my huge cock (we're talking ten inches long and eight inches around). My balls are very large also, and very hairy. I cup them in my hands and hold them against my cock; which by this time is getting very hard. Oh how I love to feel my cock throb and grow and I feel the urgency to finish the job. I hold my hot cock in both hands and admire my manhood in the mirror. Now I can't resist any longer and I begin stroking my cock. I think about all the cunts that long for my big cock and how silly they are, because I love to jack off, and no one can make me shoot my come like my hand. I stand there, legs apart, pumping my meat, and explode. In reality my orgasm is so intense I absolutely shake all over.

2. I am my current age, but unlike myself in reality, I am very curvy and sexy looking, with very large tits with big nipples. I arrange with a teenage boy I know to meet with

him and a couple of his friends in a secluded place. When I arrive there are about ten teenage boys, all about 15 or 16 years old. I am skimpily dressed so that my cleavage and my smooth thighs are showing. I walk around the boys admiring their bodies, even though they are fully clothed. I only touch their faces; many don't even shave yet. I lean up against one of the cars there with all of the boys around me and I announce that the boys are there for my pleasure. I get on top of the car, put on some sexy music and begin to do a very seductive striptease. I watch the boys, no one dares speak, afraid to break the mood. I see a lot of rigidness in their crotches and can hardly wait. As I get down to my lace bra and skimpy lace panties I inform the boys that soon the fucking will begin, but in order to establish the order in which we fuck, they all have to unzip their pants and take out their erect cocks and their balls. But they can't pull their pants down yet. I scan the circle of boys as I continue my seductive dance. There are ten hard cocks of various sizes, but all eager for a release. I tell the boys that they must have a jerk-off contest while I continue my dance. The boy that lasts the longest is the first to fuck me, and so on. All of the boys grab on to their rods and start pumping. I'm amazed and turned on by the various ways they handle themselves. I am terribly excited now and totally nude. I play with my big tits and move my hands down my body to my juicy cunt. I bring my hand out of my cunt and show the boys how wet and sticky my hand is. Most of the boys explode now.

I choose one of the boys; he's about 17. I lie down on the hood of the car and have him eat me. Although he has never eaten pussy before, he is excellent and within minutes has me begging for him to fuck me. Somewhere between the first and third fuck I reach orgasm.

3. I have a fantasy about teaching my 15-year-old stepson the fine art of masturbation and oral sex.

4. Another fantasy is primarily a bondage fantasy, where I'm strapped on a "rack" with padded cushions placed on each thigh to spread my labia. Once I'm spread, I am teased by a stranger (man) with a big cock; then the door opens and a very beautiful shapely woman walks in, strips and begins

to eat me out. She loves my clit as it is quite large, like a small penis. She sucks, licks and strokes it until I come in waves of exaltation. Then she stands back while that huge cock fucks me. The fantasy brings a fairly intense orgasm.

Without my fantasies, I'm afraid I would be very frustrated with my personal sex life. I've shared my fantasies with my husband, and his reaction was very ho-hum, like he couldn't imagine how in the world I could get excited over that. Yet he expects that his fantasies should throw me into the throes of rapture. They don't; yet I can understand his fascination with them. I never fantasize during sex, frankly there isn't time.

Lally
I am 27, single, wholesome family upbringing, heterosexual. I have a doctorate, support myself quite well (I own my own home, etc., in San Diego), have a lover about once a week, masturbate three times a week. I have an identical twin sister—we were always very close but shared no sexual experiences. I did not masturbate until age 22, when I was lonely and miserable in graduate school and found a booklet explaining how to do it! (Until then, I concurred with my friend, married eleven years, that female orgasm did not exist but was a massive hoax by women to attract men!)

My fantasy occurs when I masturbate. It helps me achieve satisfaction.

As I massage my clitoris, I imagine it growing larger and larger until it is the size of a penis. I imagine I can feel the sensations of a man during intercourse. I also imagine that this man is having sex *with* me.

Hence, I imagine I can feel the sensations of both partners at the same time.

Allegra
I was divorced seven years ago and have one daughter. I was raised on a farm and I assume most of my fantasies about urination come from watching our animals (especially horses). I partied frequently in high school with friends who

drank alcohol (especially beer) and have vivid memories of watching the men urinate.

I am incredibly fascinated watching acts of urination, erections and penises. Obviously, I have penis envy and have always wished I could have been born with one, along with my vagina, of course. My fantasy is to watch a tanned, muscular well-built man stand with his legs spread watching his protruding hard, meaty penis urinating (I prefer to call it "squirting"), outdoors on a bright warm summer moonlit night in an open field, completely nude and alone together. He has allowed his bladder to fill beyond belief and is unable to accommodate another drop. I love to watch from all directions (front, side, behind). He is so turned on by my presence and my willingness to participate. I pray it will take him forever to finish squirting. I walk up behind him, reaching around his waist for his hard, meaty penis to help him squirt as I hold and rub it, frequently sticking my finger out to feel his warm stream. He reaches behind himself to tickle my wet, throbbing pussy with his soft fingertips as I stand behind him looking around his side to watch him squirt. My bladder is also full beyond belief, and I squeeze my muscle to keep my bladder from exploding until he is finished. When he finishes squirting, he turns to me and continues to tickle me while I spread (standing) and squirt for him. I am able to squirt a long time. He is so incredibly excited he is unable to stop himself from jerking off. I beg him to finish himself inside me.

I fantasize that my lover will squirt inside me, on me, and that I squirt on him. I love to watch him flex his penile muscle, once he has finished squirting, causing his penis to stand straight up and bounce as he tightens and relaxes his muscle over and over again and again. I enjoy watching a man with a fully erect penis while he walks as it bounces and moves from side to side.

I am equally fascinated to watch a muscular-built horse with a dangling erect penis, spread, squirting. I enjoy their erections as they flex their penile muscle, causing their penises to bounce up and down.

I have always wanted to have a picture of a man and a

horse squirting so that I may enjoy them as I masturbate. I masturbate regularly with a vibrator. I also enjoy my fingers, a plastic soap bottle full of warm water—holding it at arm's length above me, squirting on my pussy in the bathtub as I lie on my back with my legs spread. I also use ribbed rubber fingers (the ones secretaries use for shuffling papers), wieners and rubber animal toys.

Marge

Lots of times I fantasize about a guy getting raped. He is always a bad guy and gets his just desserts. It is always a group rape, and he is humiliated by becoming aroused and ejaculating. I always fantasize the guy's cock going off even if it isn't being touched. Sometimes that makes it better because it just drives him nuts wanting to be touched. Rarely I fantasize being raped myself, but always with brutal revenge or the guy being caught, sent to jail and subjected to the above-mentioned-type rape.

When I think about my own lover I get a little kinky but never cruel. My most recent fantasy has to do with his ass. I love to touch him. He is leaning over our bathroom dressing area, lavatory, etc. I am sitting in a chair behind him. I run my hands all over his legs and ass. I run my tongue up between his legs. I especially like the soft smooth space by his balls. I kind of bobble his balls with my tongue. I love, in reality, to see him masturbate. In the fantasy, he starts stroking the monster slow and easy. I'm massaging his cheeks and part them to get my tongue deep in his ass. While he's stroking, so am I. The point of my tongue is a gentle little penis. The strokes come faster, and I keep pace exactly with him. His knees begin to buckle, and his prick gets bigger by about an inch. When he starts squirting, it's like all of it shoots out of his dick at once. It goes all over the floor. The head of his dick is as soft as silk after he comes, and I love to touch it. I scoot down and get my head between his legs and just touch the tip of my tongue to the last drop of come. (Not because I don't want to touch it but because it is so sensitive now.)

He is the best lover I ever had. He is so understanding

about how I wish I had a penis. Sometimes we use a position with me on top, and I fuck him. He always brings his legs way up and talks "dirty." I always have premature ejaculation. How I wish I would bring him off in that position! (My arms give out.) I think somehow my body would find a way to squirt into him.

Daphne

The theme in my favorite fantasies is actually *being* the man. For instance, I (as my husband) am sitting right next to a strip-joint "runway." A woman struts out, with huge tits bulging out of her bra. She wags them happily in my/his face and says, "Who wants them?" She pops her bra open from the front to display lovely *large* round tits, then comes over and smothers my/his face with them as I fondle them with both hands. I want to stand but must stay seated, because another woman (someone I imagine my husband secretly lusts after) is kneeling between my knees, sucking my very hard, terribly excited cock. I keep telling her (from between the huge tits) to suck harder. Finally, I explode in orgasm.

There are variations on this scenario—sometimes I do stand up and suck her tits, or sometimes I'm bartending and the woman is fucking me as I talk with unsuspecting customers. (My fantasies usually have nothing to do with our current sexual position.) I also get turned on by imagining the following:

1. While my husband is fucking me, a male friend of ours slips up behind him and begins fucking him in the ass, saying how much he's always wanted to do this. He uses filthy language to describe the pleasure. Of course my husband was so close to orgasm by the time our friend arrived that he can't stop to protest. We all climax together.

2. My husband and our male friend are both fucking me at the same time—one in the ass and one in the cunt. (Anal sex has proven more uncomfortable than it's worth, so we don't do it anymore, but I still get a lot of mileage out of it in my imagination.) The friend tells my husband how much he's always wanted my cunt—they talk to each other about how good my various orifices feel, as if I'm not even there. I feel

primitively and thoroughly desired. We all come together, of course, and collapse.

3. I'm a man in this one—no particular man, sort of myself but with a cock. My hands and feet are spread and somehow attached to the sides of a doorway. Three other anonymous men are involved, all of us wildly aroused. One is fucking me in the ass, the second is sucking me, and the third is watching, masturbating, and ordering no one to climax before he's ready. I don't try very hard to obey, though, because I am the observer at the same time. Ah, the magic of fantasy!

I've never been able to reach orgasm using my (or anyone else's) hand. I've always masturbated by crossing my legs and squeezing, using the pressure to trigger orgasm. It can take less than a minute this way, and the orgasms are very satisfying. I can masturbate in a roomful of people and no one knows!

During sex, we both lie on our sides with my husband behind me and my crossed legs between his. (I lock one foot all the way around my other ankle.) It sounds awkward, but it feels delicious.

Karen

I am a 24-year-old woman, married, with a 2-year-old son. I have three years of college and intend someday to finish. My husband is in school, and I am the breadwinner.

I've read your books of fantasies and have enjoyed them very much. I am, however, disturbed by the fact that I was extremely aroused by most of the men's fantasies, while in the main, the women's fantasies were merely fascinating.

I've wished I were male, off and on, since I was quite young. I greatly enjoy being female, though—being pregnant and breastfeeding were exciting experiences, and I like to look at myself wearing lots of makeup and tight clothes. Knowing that I look sexy makes me feel good. It doesn't matter whether men or women look at me.

Sometimes the things I read suggest to me that my husband and I are not typical in our sexual desires. He is very straightlaced—it has taken me almost six years to talk him into letting me suck him, and he becomes very angry if I suggest him climaxing in my mouth. This is the only mildly kinky thing we do. He likes to have me on top, but I hate it.

I am aroused by very weird sex stories. I would like to try almost everything. I suppose I am bisexual. I am more turned on by the pictures in *Playboy* than any nude males (though I seldom get chances to see those!). Only once have I touched another woman sexually—it was very brief. I wish I knew how to go about finding a horny, beautiful woman who would like to be with me.

I am getting very bored with my husband sexually. We may split up for that and many other reasons.

I've never been unfaithful, although I don't think I would feel guilty over a lesbian affair. Just thinking about touching lovely nipples and tonguing a soft, sweet-smelling cunt makes me hot! Women are soft and silky. (My husband's personal hygiene leaves a bit to be desired.)

This is not to say I am not turned on by men. Most of my fantasies are heterosexual. Here are a few:

1. Against my friends' advice, I go to a biker bar alone. I wear a very tight tube top, which shows off my round, tight tits. My nipples stick out. I also wear jeans so tight they slip up into my ass and outline my cunt in perfect detail. (Actually, my breasts are very large and saggy, though I'm pretty slim and I usually dress conservatively.) I order a White Russian and sit sipping it. I feel eyes on me. I look up and find myself surrounded by men wearing black leather over bare hairy chests. They all smell faintly of grease. They all have *huge* bulges in their pants.

One of the men suddenly puts a hand on one of my tits. I smile. Then they all begin feeling me with their big hands. My pants are unzipped for me, and they feel my ass and cunt. Pretty soon an enormous cock is shoved down my throat and pumped in and out a few times. I am placed on my belly on a pillow on the floor, and a second cock is slowly pushed into my ass. After a bit of that, I am getting so hot I'm going crazy.

All the men stand around me in a circle, their pants down

and their (huge) cocks pointing at me. One of them mounts me and fucks my cunt furiously as they all play with their cocks. Finally he comes, so do I, so do they. I am ecstatic and exhausted, and they have shot their come all *over* me. God, what a thrill.

2. An audience has gathered in a huge symphony hall to hear me do a recital. (I'm a talented amateur.) I come out and sing an aria. They applaud. A tall, handsome baritone then appears and we sing a duet. More applause. Then, during an overture by the orchestra, we take each other's clothes off, pose naked for the audience, and then fuck like mad right on the stage. The audience is stunned, but soon they begin to applaud again, shouting "Bravo!" and "Encore." When we come and stand to take our bows, we see that many of the audience have become so aroused that they have also taken their clothes off and are either masturbating or fucking each other all over the hall.

Quite a night at the opera, wouldn't you say?

I also have what I think of as "weirdo" fantasies.

I like to think about having a great big cock and either fucking a woman with it, or fucking a man.

I often wish I could watch gay men. This probably sounds odd, but I like to think about lips with mustaches touching each other, or two cocks rubbing together. Gay men are almost the only men who show any love for each other. This fantasy is the one that regularly stars my husband. He has a big cock and is macho looking, and it sets me on fire to imagine him tenderly making love to another man. He'd die if he knew, because he thinks gays are not quite human.

I also like to imagine the perfect lesbian lover; sometimes it's a woman I know who I suspect (and desperately hope) is gay. If she is, maybe I can be with her sometime. I also imagine pretty conventional sex scenes with two or three of the men I know I am attracted to.

A dear friend of mine is one of the sexiest men I've ever known. If I ever get a divorce, I'll be begging him to fuck me. I already know he is attracted to me but is holding back because I'm married.

Sometimes I have a fantasy that goes something like this: I am divorced and I go over to Ed's (not his real name) house. I tell him I love him and beg him to fuck me. He kisses me, and says he loves me, too, but he's gay and it's against his principles to have sex with a woman. I am told he's waiting for his lover. I convince him to let me watch. His lover is also a good friend of mine. When they undress, so do I. They both kiss me tenderly and then they devote their attention to each other. When they start to fuck, I stroke both of their bodies. They take turns mounting each other, then get in 69 and suck each other's cocks for a while. Finally they turn face to face and they gently kiss each other on the mouth until they come all over their bellies and chests. I am allowed to squeeze between them as they rub their come into my skin and kiss each other and me. They tell me that now they know I won't try to change them, they would like to include me in their love affair and all three fuck each other. I am deliriously happy.

This is kind of nutty, because I'm not sure that Ed is even bisexual.

Other fantasies include being the mistress of a large harem of both men and women, all slaves; having the power to make anybody I want to fuck anybody else or me; walking around downtown naked; being with a black woman (I have a thing about Lola Falana and Diahann Carroll).

I would love being tied up and fucked very roughly by a man who swears and calls me names. Or do the same myself.

I should add that earthy language absolutely melts my drawers. That's why I've been so straightforward in this letter. My husband only rarely can be persuaded to talk this way and he hates it when I do. Oy!!

Bliss

I am a 23-year-old woman. I am currently in a computer school, but I eventually want to write and illustrate a book. I am very creative and rather strange in just about any way there is to be strange. My parents were not puritanical (though just behind the times). I masturbated freely as a child and even had a pet dog that would lick my genitals quite often.

It took me half a lifetime to achieve it, but I am very comfortable with my sexuality. (At one time I thought I was gay.) I don't hesitate in admitting that I am attracted to women and men. I just love sex. I've only had one fleeting lesbian encounter, but I would like to experiment with that more.

I have a very strong sex drive, and I have not run into very many men who can keep up with me. I am very good in bed and have blown quite a few minds (and dicks). I used to treat men as conquests, but in the last year or so I have tried to settle down some. I was married at one time, but it didn't work out. I realized after four years that I didn't even *like* the stupid oaf.

I'm willing to try anything (just about) once, and if I like it I'll keep doing it until I drop. I tend to deviate a little onto the kinky side (cucumbers, vibrators, leather, sunglasses, urination, and even blood sometimes), and I find it hard to find willing partners. Sometimes I just can't believe how inhibited men are. I don't like anything that really causes a lot of pain. The worst, I suppose, is that I like to be bitten a little briskly on the neck and breasts. I like to bite back, but they (men) usually aren't too fired up about that. And I've also found that some men will not bite me, no matter how hard I beg. (It makes me come.) Oh, by the way, when I mentioned blood earlier what I meant was I like to give blood and plasma. The whole process of the needle and everything is a turn-on. (I know, strange, huh?)

I am now deeply embroiled in a *great* relationship with a 30-year-old man. I love him very deeply. He's good in bed, likes to bite, and is also very horny. I'm in heaven to say the least. Now, if only I could get him to screw me while he wears a full-length leather coat and black sunglasses!!! He's been married once before, and his wife was quite a prude. (She thought it was kinky to fuck with her underwear on.) I was his first serious relationship after his marriage. I blew his mind to say the least.

I love sex and I'm good at it, but I also still consider sex to be a sacred and wonderful thing. I know from personal experience that the best sex is with someone you *really* love.

I have a nice little file of fantasies in my head, and here are the ones I use the most:

I am a man of about 25–30 years old who is married, owns a house and is exceedingly bored where sex is concerned. My wife and I have recently hired a 16-year-old girl to help around the house. I would come home from work in the evenings and notice that the girl kept wearing very short skirts and *no* underwear. She would bend over in front of me a lot so that I could get a good look at her juicy, hairy pussy. (I like hair.) But I never touched her. My dick just stayed hard all the time. Then one day I spied her loading the dishwasher in that skimpy dress she wore all the time. She bent over to put a plate in, and I got a wonderful, full view of her sweet cunt. I sat and watched her from my comfortable recliner in the living room. My cock throbbed wildly as I tried to maintain my composure.

All of a sudden she walked to the fridge and got out a nice long cucumber. I was quite befuddled. I rattled my newspaper in expectation. She then leaned forward onto the counter and slid the cucumber up her hot, waiting pussy. (By now I'm pumping on my cock.) She stopped for a second and glanced at me with a naughty smile, then went back to her beloved veggie. Finally, I just couldn't take it any longer. I got up and snuck up behind her. She knew I was there, and as I approached her round, soft ass, she turned around and let out a low, lustful moan. I wanted to fuck her so bad I thought I would simply explode.

She put the cucumber down and wiggled her ass at me. I grabbed her ass with both hands and savored it like a hungry animal. I growled. She giggled and shoved her ass out even further. At last, I plunged my rock-hard dick deep inside her. God, it was absolute heaven! Her pussy was like a vise! I'm afraid to say I did not last very long inside her. As I pumped her like an angry bull, I heard my wife's car come up the driveway. The girl gasped and clamped down even harder on my cock. I came deep inside of her as I heard the car door shut. I knew my wife was about to catch me fucking this girl, but I just didn't give a shit! . . .

At this point I have already come to orgasm. (God, I'm so horny!!) But I must go on. My second fantasy goes like this:

Again, I am a man, but a little older this time. I'm sitting in a recliner again and reading my paper. With me is my niece, a girl of about 12 to 16 or so. (It changes.) She's on the floor in front of me coloring or reading, she keeps bending over in front of me, and the flash of her little rear end in those white panties is making it harder and harder for me to read my paper.

After a few minutes of this, I tell the little girl to come and sit on my lap. At this point my fantasy takes one of two directions. The shortcut is her getting on my lap, and I tell her to wiggle her butt, and I just come right in my pants. The long version is this: I begin to caress her inner thigh while I explain to her that I am a doctor and her mummy told me it was time for me to examine her. She agrees, and I tell her to take her panties off. Gently, I continue to caress her thighs, slowly moving up to her pussy. I tell her to tell me how she feels as I am doing these things. I notice that her breathing is quickening, I begin to finger her sweet little pussy and sometimes I lay her on the floor and eat her. She finds these new feelings strange, but wonderful. Finally I unzip my pants and let my cock flop stiffly behind her. I caress her breasts and continue fingering her. She starts wiggling and gasping in my lap. I can feel her pussy having spasms around my fingers. She's really wet. I tell her that now I'm going to put something else inside her, but it will feel sort of like my fingers did. She nods her head in silence, and I maneuver her so that I can slip my dick into her. She's very tight, but once I get the head in she takes the rest with ease. I can tell by the way she instinctively starts pumping on me that she likes it, and I often ejaculate within a minute or so. Sometimes I take my dick out and come on her ass, and there are other slight variations—too many to write out.

Oh, the mind is a wondrous thing!

I fantasize a lot about my boyfriend. My favorite one is of

me giving him a knockout head job. I also have fantasies about group sex, sex in public, sex in graveyards (which I have done on many occasions), and sex with a *long* string of men, one after another (they are sometimes monks or construction workers). I give a head job to the one that performs the best.

I'm definitely not gay. I love dicks, pricks, cocks, whatever you want to call them! I like to make my boyfriend's dick hard just to admire it and play with it. I like to investigate all the dark, hot, hidden spots of the body—sucking, licking, nibbling all along.

Oh, I could go on all day!

Well, it's been a real *Ball!*

AN INVITATION TO WOMEN FROM NANCY FRIDAY

My research on the interaction between women's real lives and their sexual fantasies continues. If you would like to contribute, please write to me at the address below. Include biographical information that you feel is relevant to your sexual development, such as relationships with your mother and father, history of masturbation, loss of virginity, earliest sexual fantasies. I am also interested in your contraceptive history, meaning if and when you began to use contraceptives, and why you did or didn't. Also indicate whether or not you have had an abortion. Any musings on why you think your sexual fantasies have developed as they have would be useful.

An Invitation to Men

If you would like to contribute to my continuing research, you should include your sexual fantasies along with whatever biographical information you feel has influenced your sexual development and the nature and story line of your fantasies. This might include parental attitude toward your early sexuality, age of first masturbation along with current practice, plus any memory of how adolescence affected your life physically and emotionally. Ideas or opinions on how the current economic changes in men's and women's lives have influenced how we relate to one another today would also be of interest.

Send to:

Nancy Friday
P.O. Box 1371
Key West, Florida 33041
Online: www.nancyfriday.com
ANONYMITY GUARANTEED

Not sure what to read next?

Visit Pocket Books online at
www.simonsays.com

Reading suggestions for
you and your reading group
New release news
Author appearances
Online chats with your favorite writers
Special offers
Order books online
And much, much more!

POCKET BOOKS
A Division of Simon & Schuster
A CBS COMPANY

POCKET STAR BOOKS
A Division of Simon & Schuster
A CBS COMPANY

13456

3 1901 05381 0224